murach's
JavaScript
and DOM Scripting

Ray Harris

MIKE MURACH & ASSOCIATES, INC.

1-800-221-5528 • (559) 440-9071 • Fax: (559) 440-0963
murachbooks@murach.com • www.murach.com

Author:	Ray Harris
Editors:	Mike Murach
	Joel Murach
Cover Design:	Zylka Design
Production:	Tom Murach
	Cynthia Vasquez

Books for web developers

Murach's HTML, XHTML, and CSS

Murach's PHP and MySQL

Murach's ASP.NET 3.5 Web Programming with VB 2008

Murach's ASP.NET 3.5 Web Programming with C# 2008

Murach's Java Servlets and JSP (Second Edition)

Books for database programmers

Murach's ADO.NET 3.5, LINQ, and the Entity Framework with VB 2008

Murach's ADO.NET 3.5, LINQ, and the Entity Framework with C# 2008

Murach's SQL Server 2008 for Developers

Murach's Oracle SQL and PL/SQL

Books on Visual Basic, C#, and Java

Murach's Visual Basic 2010

Murach's C# 2010

Murach's Java SE 6

Books for IBM mainframe programmers

Murach's OS/390 and z/OS JCL

Murach's Mainframe COBOL

Murach's CICS for the COBOL Programmer

For more on Murach books, please visit us at www.murach.com

10 9 8 7 6 5 4 3 2
ISBN: 978-1-890774-55-4

Contents

Introduction   xiv

Section 1   Introduction to JavaScript programming

Chapter 1   Introduction to web development and JavaScript   3
Chapter 2   How to code a JavaScript application   43
Chapter 3   How to test and debug a JavaScript application   89
Chapter 4   A crash course in XHTML   121
Chapter 5   A crash course in CSS   169

Section 2   JavaScript essentials

Chapter 6   How to get input and display output   223
Chapter 7   How to work with numbers, strings, and dates   249
Chapter 8   How to code control statements   275
Chapter 9   How to create and use arrays   301
Chapter 10   How to create and use functions   327
Chapter 11   How to create and use objects   355
Chapter 12   How to use regular expressions, handle exceptions, and validate data 385

Section 3   DOM scripting

Chapter 13   Basic DOM scripting   421
Chapter 14   Advanced event handling   469
Chapter 15   Advanced DOM manipulation   523
Chapter 16   How to script CSS   555
Chapter 17   How to script tables and forms   591
Chapter 18   Animation with DOM scripting   633

Section 4   Other JavaScript skills

Chapter 19   How to control the web browser   663
Chapter 20   How to use JavaScript libraries   701

Reference Aids

Appendix A   How to set up your computer for this book   745
Index   753

Expanded contents

Section 1 Introduction to JavaScript programming

Chapter 1 Introduction to web development and JavaScript

The architecture of a web application **4**
How a client-server architecture works 4
How static web pages are processed 6
How dynamic web pages are processed 8
A survey of browsers, servers, and server-side scripting languages 10
How JavaScript fits into this architecture 12

The core web technologies **14**
An introduction to XHTML 14
An introduction to CSS 16
An introduction to the DOM 18
An introduction to JavaScript 20
The XHTML, CSS, DOM, and JavaScript standards 22

DOM scripting and AJAX **26**
How DOM scripting works 26
How AJAX works 28

The Sales Tax application **30**
The XHTML file 30
The CSS file 30
The JavaScript file 32

Two critical web development issues **34**
Cross-browser compatibility 34
User accessibility 34
How to access a web page 36
How to view the source code for a web page 38

Perspective **40**

Chapter 2 How to code a JavaScript application

How to edit and test your web pages **44**
How to edit a web page with Notepad++ 44
How to test a web page 46
How to display error messages in Firefox 48

Basic JavaScript skills **50**
How to include JavaScript with the script tag 50
How to code JavaScript statements 52
How to create identifiers 54
The primitive data types of JavaScript 56
How to code numeric and string expressions 58
How to declare variables and assign values to them 60

How to use objects in JavaScript **62**
An introduction to objects, properties, and methods 62
How to use the window and document objects 64
How to use the Number, String, and Date objects 66
How to get and display data with a Textbox object 68

How to code control statements **70**
How to code conditional expressions 70
How to code if statements 72
How to code while and for statements 74

How to create and use functions **76**
How to create and call a function 76
How to code an event handler 78

The Future Value application **80**
The XHTML code 80
The JavaScript code 82

Perspective **84**

Chapter 3   How to test and debug a JavaScript application

An introduction to testing and debugging **90**
Typical test phases for a JavaScript application 90
The three types of errors that can occur 90
Common JavaScript errors 92
How to get error messages with Firefox 94
A simple way to trace the execution of your JavaScript code 96

How to debug with the Firebug extension of Firefox **98**
How to install and enable the Firebug extension 98
How to get information in the Console tab 100
How to review your code in the Script tab 102
How to use breakpoints and step through code 104

How to use the Firebug console object **106**
The methods of the console object 106
How to trace an application with Firebug's console.log method 108

How to test and debug with other browsers **110**
How to get error messages with Internet Explorer 110
How to get error messages with Safari 112
How to get error messages with Opera 114
How to get error messages with Chrome 116

Perspective **118**

Chapter 4   A crash course in XHTML

An introduction to XHTML **122**
A web page and its XHTML 122
Basic XHTML syntax 126
How to validate an XHTML document 128

How to code web pages **130**
How to code the head section 130
How to code the core attributes 132
How to code blocks of text 134
How to format text with inline tags 136
How to code lists 138
How to code character entities 140
How to code links 142
How to include images 144

How to code tables **146**
How to code a simple table 146
How to code a table with spanned columns and rows 148

How to code forms **150**
How to create a form 150
How to code buttons 152
How to code labels and text fields 154
How to code radio buttons and check boxes 156
How to code select lists 158
How to code text areas 160
How to group controls 162
How to set the tab order for controls 164

Perspective **166**

Chapter 5   **A crash course in CSS**

A web page and its CSS **170**
The web page 170
The XHTML for the web page 172
The CSS for the web page 174

Basic skills for using CSS **178**
Basic CSS syntax 178
How to include CSS in a web page 180
How to specify measurements and colors 182

How to code selectors **184**
How to code selectors for tags, ids, and classes 184
How to code other types of XHTML selectors 186
How to code pseudo-class selectors 188
How the cascade rules work 190

How to work with text and lists **192**
How to style fonts 192
How to format text 194
How to format lists 196

How to work with the box model **198**
An introduction to the box model 198
A web page that illustrates the box model 200
How to set height, width, margins, and padding 202
How to set borders 204
How to set background colors and images 206

How to position elements **208**
How to change the display type of an element 208
How to float elements 210
How to use absolute positioning 212
How to use relative positioning 214
How to float controls on a form 216

Perspective **218**

Section 2 JavaScript essentials

Chapter 6   **How to get input and display output**

How to get input **224**
How to get data from the prompt method 224
How to get a response from the confirm method 226
How to get the state of a radio button 228
How to get the state of a check box 230
How to get the selected option in a select list 232
How to get data from a text area 234
How to use the methods and events for controls 236

How to display output **238**
How to display data in a span tag 238
How to set the state of a radio button 240
How to set the state of a check box 242
How to display data in a text area 244

Perspective **246**

Chapter 7   **How to work with numbers, strings, and dates**

How to work with numbers **250**
How represent special numerical values 250
The methods of the Number object 252
How to use the conditional operator 254

How to use the Math object **256**
How to use the methods of the Math object 256
How to use a random number generator 258

How to work with strings **260**
How to use escape sequences in strings 260
How to use the methods of the String object 262
Examples of working with strings 264

How to work with dates and times **266**
How to create Date objects 266
The methods of the Date object 268
Example of working with dates 270

Perspective **272**

Chapter 8   **How to code control statements**

How to use the equality and identity operators 276
How to use the relational operators 278
How to use the logical operators 280

How to code the selection structures **282**
How to code if statements with else clauses 282
How to code if statements with else if clauses 284
How to code switch statements 286
How to use a flag to simplify your selection structures 288

How to code the iteration structures **290**
How to code while loops 290
How to code do-while loops 292
How to code for loops 294
How to use the break and continue statements 296

Perspective **298**

Chapter 9   How to create and use arrays

How to create and use an array **302**
How to create an array 302
How to add and delete array elements 304
How to use for loops to work with arrays 306
How to use for-in loops to work with arrays 308
The methods of an Array object 310
How to use the Array methods 312

Other skills for working with arrays **314**
How to use a String method to create an array 314
How to create and use an associative array 316
How to create and use an array of arrays 318

The Task List Manager application **320**
The user interface and XHTML 320
The JavaScript code 320

Perspective **324**

Chapter 10   How to create and use functions

Basic skills for working with functions **328**
How to create and call a function 328
How values are passed to functions 330
How lexical scope works 332

Object-oriented skills for working with functions **334**
How to use the arguments property of a function 334
How to use the call and apply methods of a function 336

Advanced skills for working with functions **338**
How closures work with functions 338
How to write recursive functions 340

The Invoice application **342**
The user interface 342
The XHTML file 344
The library file 346
The invoice.js file 350

Perspective **352**

Chapter 11   How to create and use objects

Basic skills for working with objects **356**
How to create and use the native object types 356
How to create objects of the Object type 358
How to extend, modify, or delete an object 360
How to create and use your own object types 362

Advanced skills for working with objects **364**
How to inherit properties and methods from another object type 364
How to add methods to the JavaScript object types 366
How to create cascading methods 368
How to use the for-in statement with objects 370
How to use the in, instanceof, and typeof operators 372

The Invoice application **374**
The user interface 374
The XHTML file 376
The library file 378
The invoice.js file 382

Perspective **384**

Chapter 12 How to use regular expressions, handle exceptions, and validate data

How to use regular expressions **386**
How to create and use regular expressions 386
How to create regular expression patterns 388
How to use the global and multiline flags 392
String methods that use regular expressions 394
Regular expressions for data validation 396

How to handle exceptions **398**
How to create and throw Error objects 398
How to use the try-catch statement to handle exceptions 400

The Register application **402**
The user interface, XHTML, and CSS 402
The JavaScript code for the register_library.js file 406
The JavaScript code for the register.js file 414

Perspective **416**

Section 3 DOM scripting

Chapter 13 Basic DOM scripting

How to work with DOM nodes **422**
An introduction to DOM nodes 422
Types of DOM nodes 424
The Node interface 426
The Document interface 428
The Element interface 430
The Attr interface 432

How to work with DOM HTML nodes **434**
Types of HTMLElement nodes 434
The HTMLElement interface 436
The HTMLAnchorElement interface 436
The HTMLImageElement interface 436
The HTMLButtonElement interface 438
The HTMLInputElement interface 438

Other DOM scripting skills **440**
How to cancel the default action of an event 440
How to create image rollovers 442
How to preload images 444

The Image Gallery application **446**
The XHTML file 446
The JavaScript files 448

How to use timers **452**
How to call a function once 452
How to call a function repeatedly 454

The Slide Show application **456**
The XHTML file 456
The CSS file 456
The JavaScript files 458

Perspective **466**

Chapter 14   **Advanced event handling**

An introduction to event handling **470**
An overview of event handling 470
An overview of XHTML event types 472
An overview of mouse event types 474
An overview of keyboard event types 474

How to use our JavaScript libraries **476**
How to attach and remove event handlers 476
How to use the standardized Event object 478

The Slide Show application **480**
The XHTML file 480
The slide_show_library.js file 482
The slide_show.js file 484

The core event models **486**
How to access the Event object 486
The properties and methods of the Event object 488
The methods for attaching and detaching event handlers 490
Browser-compatible code for attaching and detaching event handlers 492
The jslib_event.js file 494

The mouse event models **500**
The properties of the Event object 500
The sequence of events for a mouse click 502
The jslib_event_mouse.js file 504

The keyboard event models **506**
The DOM Level 3 properties and methods for the Event object 506
The properties of the Event object that are implemented by the
major browsers 508
The key codes for keyboard events 510
The jslib_event_keyboard.js file 514

Perspective **520**

Chapter 15   **Advanced DOM manipulation**

How to detect when the DOM is ready **524**
A problem with the load event 524
The code that illustrates this problem 526
How to use a ready method to detect when the DOM is ready 528
The JavaScript library that contains the ready method 530

How to search the DOM **534**
How to use a walk method to walk the DOM tree 534
How to use a getElementsByClassname method to search the DOM 538
A JavaScript library for walking and searching the DOM 540

How to modify the DOM **542**
How to create new DOM nodes 542
How to add and remove DOM nodes 544
How to use a document fragment 546

The Headlines application **548**
The user interface 548
The XHTML file 548
The headlines_library.js file 550
The headlines.js file 552

Perspective **554**

Chapter 16   How to script CSS

How to work with style sheets **556**
Three types of external style sheets 556
How to enable and disable style sheets 558
How to add and remove style sheets 560

The Style Selector application **562**
The XHTML file 562
The JavaScript files 562

How to modify the style of an element **564**
How to set the style of an element 564
How to get the computed style of an element 566
How to change the appearance of an element 568
How to change the position of an element 570
How to get the current position of an element 572
A JavaScript library for working with styles 574

The Menu Bar application **576**
The XHTML file 576
The menubar.css file 578
The menubar_library.js file 580
The menubar.js file 586

Perspective **588**

Chapter 17   How to script tables and forms

How to script tables **592**
How to add rows and cells 592
How to remove rows and cells 594
How to reorder rows 596

The Table Sort application **598**
The XHTML file 598
The tablesort_library.js file 600
The product_list.js file 606

How to script forms **608**
How to handle form events 608
How to script radio buttons 610
How to script select lists 612
A JavaScript library for working with text selections 614
How to use the JavaScript library to work with text selections 616

The Product Configuration application **618**
The XHTML file 618
The config_library.js file 622
The config.js file 628

Perspective **630**

Chapter 18   Animation with DOM scripting

How to animate elements **634**
A review of the math used in animation 634
How to change the position of an element over time 636
How to detect boundaries 640
How to simulate depth 642

The Carousel application **644**
The image path in the carousel 644
The XHTML file 646
The CSS file 646
The carousel_library.js file 648
The carousel.js file 656

Perspective **658**

Section 4   Other JavaScript skills

Chapter 19   How to control the web browser

How to script browser windows **664**
How to open and close windows 664
How to move and resize windows 666
How to scroll a window 668
How to print a window 670
How to use window events 672

How to script browser objects **674**
How to use the navigator object 674
How to use the location object 676
How to use the history object 678
How to use the screen object 680

How to use cookies **682**
An introduction to cookies 682
How to create cookies 684
How to read cookies 686
How to delete cookies 688

The Task List application **690**
The user interface 690
The XHTML file 690
The jslib_cookies.js file 692
The tasklist_library.js file 694
The tasklist.js file 694

Perspective **698**

Chapter 20 **How to use JavaScript libraries**

How to use jQuery **702**
How to get started with jQuery 702
How to select elements with jQuery 704
How to use jQuery effects 706
How to handle events with jQuery 708
How to use jQuery to work with XHTML elements 710
How to use jQuery to work with the DOM 712

How to use Dojo **714**
How to get started with Dojo 714
How to select elements with Dojo 716
How to handle events with Dojo 718
How to use Dojo effects 720

How to use Dijits **722**
How to get started with Dijits 722
How to use the Form Dijit 724
How to use the Button Dijit 724
How to use the CheckBox Dijit 726
How to use the RadioButton Dijit 726
How to use the ValidationTextBox Dijit 728
How to validate a credit card with ValidationTextBox Dijits 730
How to use the FilteringSelect Dijit 732

The Register application **734**
The XHTML 734
The JavaScript 738

Perspective **742**

Reference Aids

Appendix A **How to set up your computer for this book**

How to install a text editor for JavaScript programming **746**
How to install Notepad++ 746
How to install TextWrangler 746

How to install Firefox and Firebug **748**
How to install Firefox 748
How to install Firebug 748
How to install the Rainbow extension for Firebug 748

How to install the source code for this book **750**

Introduction

Today, web users expect web sites to provide dynamic user interfaces, fast response times, and advanced features. To deliver that, you need to use JavaScript and DOM scripting. And that's why JavaScript has become such an important programming language for web developers.

Now, this new book helps you learn JavaScript and DOM scripting faster and better than ever. In fact, by the end of chapter 3, you'll be able to develop and debug significant JavaScript applications. And by the time you finish this book, you will have raised your JavaScript and DOM scripting skills to an expert level.

Who this book is for

This book is for anyone who needs to do client-side programming with JavaScript. Today, that includes just about anyone who is involved with web development. But to generalize, that includes these two groups:

- Server-side programmers who use languages like ASP, JSP, or PHP and would like to add JavaScript programming to their skill sets.

- Web designers who use XHTML and CSS and would like to build rich Internet applications (RIAs) with JavaScript and DOM scripting.

What this book does

To present the JavaScript skills that you need in a manageable progression, this book is divided into four sections.

- Section 1 is designed to get you off to a fast start whether or not you have any programming experience. So chapter 2 presents a complete subset of JavaScript, and chapter 3 shows you how to use Firefox and its free Firebug extension to debug your applications. Then, in case you need them, chapters 4 and 5 present crash courses on the XHTML and CSS (Cascading Style Sheets) skills that you'll need for developing JavaScript applications. When you complete this section, you'll have the background and perspective that you need for rapid learning in the next 3 sections.

- In section 2, you'll learn the rest of the JavaScript essentials, including how to use arrays, functions, regular expressions, exception handling, libraries, and your own object types. Along the way, you'll also learn advanced skills like how to use closures, recursion, and prototype-based inheritance, and how to extend built-in JavaScript objects. The last application in this section illustrates an object-oriented approach to data validation that you can use as a model for your own applications…and you just won't find anything like this in other books.

- To get the most from JavaScript, though, you need to know how to use it to manipulate the Document Object Model, or DOM. This is called DOM scripting, and section 3 shows you how to do that at an expert level. Here, you'll learn how to manipulate both the XHTML and CSS for a web page as you build applications that run slide shows, do image rollovers, use drop-down menus, rotate headlines, sort the data in tables, and provide animation. The last application in this section is a rotating, three-dimensional carousel of images that the user can control with the mouse or keystroke combinations. And here again, you won't find anything like this in other books.

- The last section in this book rounds out your professional skills by showing you how to use the objects, methods, and properties of a web browser and how to use third-party libraries like jQuery and Dojo. Then, the last application in this section shows you another approach to data validation that uses Dojo and Dijits. This demonstrates how valuable third-party libraries can be.

Why you'll learn faster and better with this book

Like all our books, this one has features that you won't find in competing books. That's why we believe you'll learn faster and better with our book than with any other. Here are just a few of those features.

- To show you how all of the pieces of a JavaScript application work together, this book presents 20 complete applications ranging from the simple to the complex that include the XHTML, CSS, and JavaScript code. As we see it, the only way to master JavaScript programming and DOM scripting is to study the code in applications like these. And yet, you won't find anything like this in other books.

- As part of the DOM scripting section, you'll learn how to create event handling libraries that standardize the differences in the way browsers handle the DOM events. These libraries are critical for browser compatibility because Microsoft's Internet Explorer frequently handles DOM events differently than other browsers. These libraries also include keyboard events, which most developers avoid because there are no standards for them. In fact, the three event libraries that come with this book are so valuable that we think they pay for this book by themselves.

- If you page through this book, you'll see that all of the information is presented in "paired pages," with the essential syntax, guidelines, and examples on the right page and the perspective and extra explanation on the left page. This helps you learn faster by reading less...and this is the ideal reference format when you need to refresh your memory about how to do something.

What software you need

To develop JavaScript applications, you can use any text editor that you like. However, a text editor that includes syntax coloring and auto-formatting will help you develop applications more quickly and with fewer errors. That's why we recommend Notepad++ for Windows users and TextWrangler for Mac OS users. Both are available for free, and both can be used for entering XHTML, CSS, and JavaScript.

To test and debug a JavaScript application, you need a web browser with debugging capabilities. For that, we recommend Mozilla Firefox and its Firebug extension. Both of these are free, and Firebug is an excellent tool for solving serious debugging problems.

To help you install these products, Appendix A provides the web site addresses and procedures that you'll need. In addition, the first figure in chapter 2 provides a quick guide to using Notepad++, and chapter 3 provides a tutorial on using Firebug.

Because Internet Explorer is the most widely-used browser and the one that deviates the most from the standards, you should always test your applications on it too. That way, you can be sure that your applications are compatible with both Internet Explorer and DOM-compliant browsers like Firefox. However, for the purposes of this book, that isn't essential.

How our downloadable files can help you learn

If you go to our web site at www.murach.com, you can download all the files that you need for getting the most from this book. These files include:

- all of the applications presented in this book, including three event-handling libraries and four other libraries for browser compatibility

- the starting points for all of the exercises

The code for the book applications is especially valuable because it lets you run the applications on your own PC, view all of the source code, experiment with the code, and copy and paste any of the source code into your own applications. Here again, appendix A shows you how to download and install these files.

Support materials for trainers and instructors

If you're a corporate trainer or a college instructor who would like to use this book for a course, we offer an Instructor's CD that includes: (1) a complete set of PowerPoint slides that you can use to review and reinforce the content of the book; (2) instructional objectives that describe the skills a student should have upon completion of each chapter; (3) test banks that measure mastery of those skills; and (4) the solutions to the exercises in this book.

To learn more about this Instructor's CD and to find out how to get it, please go to our web site at www.murach.com and click on the Trainers link or the Instructors link. Or, if you prefer, you can call Kelly at 1-800-221-5528 or send an email to kelly@murach.com.

Related books

If you want to learn server-side web programming when you finish this book, we offer three books that will help you master ASP.NET and JSP:

ASP.NET 3.5 Web Programming with Visual Basic 2008
ASP.NET 3.5 Web Programming with C# 2008
Java Servlets and JSP

The first two show you how to develop web applications on the Microsoft .NET platform using either Visual Basic or C#. The third book shows you how to develop web applications using Java and the Tomcat web server.

With either ASP.NET or JSP, you'll be glad that you already know how to use JavaScript. That way, you'll realize that JavaScript code is automatically generated for many of the .NET controls. You'll also know when it's best to use server-side programming and when client-side programming would be more efficient.

Please let us know how this book works for you

From the start of this project, I had two goals for this book. First, I wanted to make it easier than ever for you to learn the basics of JavaScript and DOM scripting. Second, I wanted to build on that foundation to raise your skills to an expert level. I hope that I've succeeded.

If you have any comments about this book, I would appreciate hearing from you. Thank you for buying this book. I hope you enjoy reading it. And I wish you all the best with your JavaScript programming and DOM scripting.

Ray Harris

Ray Harris, Author
ray@harris.net

Section 1

Introduction to JavaScript programming

The first three chapters in this section are designed to get you off to a fast start with JavaScript programming. In chapter 1, you'll learn how JavaScript works with XHTML, CSS (Cascading Style Sheets), and DOM scripting in a client-side application. In chapter 2, you'll learn the basics of JavaScript so you can write significant JavaScript applications of your own. And in chapter 3, you'll learn how to test and debug your JavaScript applications.

Then, since JavaScript is closely tied to the XHTML and CSS for a web page, chapters 4 and 5 present crash courses in those subjects. If you already know how to use XHTML and CSS, you can skip these chapters and refer back to them whenever necessary. Otherwise, these chapters present all of the XHTML and CSS skills that you need for using this book and for developing professional JavaScript applications.

1

Introduction to web development and JavaScript

This chapter introduces you to the concepts and terms that you need to work with JavaScript. Here, you'll learn how web browsers and web servers interact to display web pages. You'll learn how the core web technologies work together as you develop JavaScript applications. And you'll see where DOM scripting and AJAX fit into this architecture. When you're finished with this chapter, you'll be ready to learn how to develop your own JavaScript applications.

The architecture of a web application **4**
How a client-server architecture works 4
How static web pages are processed 6
How dynamic web pages are processed 8
A survey of browsers, servers, and server-side scripting languages 10
How JavaScript fits into this architecture 12

The core web technologies **14**
An introduction to XHTML 14
An introduction to CSS 16
An introduction to the DOM 18
An introduction to JavaScript 20
The XHTML, CSS, DOM, and JavaScript standards 22

DOM scripting and AJAX **26**
How DOM scripting works 26
How AJAX works 28

The Sales Tax application **30**
The XHTML file 30
The CSS file 30
The JavaScript file 32

Two critical web development issues **34**
Cross-browser compatibility 34
User accessibility 34
How to access a web page 36
How to view the source code for a web page 38

Perspective **40**

The architecture of a web application

The *World Wide Web*, or web, consists of many components that work together to bring a web page to your desktop over the *Internet*. Before you start JavaScript programming, you need to have a basic understanding of how these components interact and where JavaScript fits into this architecture.

How a client-server architecture works

The web uses a *client-server architecture*. This architecture consists of *servers* that share resources with *clients* over a *network*. Figure 1-1 shows the components of a simple client-server architecture.

A *server* can share resources such as files, printers, web sites, databases, and e-mail. A *web server* is a server that shares web sites, and a *web browser* is the client software used to access the web server.

A *network* is a communication system that allows clients and servers to communicate. A *network interface card* (*NIC*) connects the computer to the network. This connection can either be wired or wireless. Ethernet is a common type of wired network. Wi-Fi is a common type of wireless network.

The network is responsible for getting information from one computer to another. This process is called routing. A *router* is a device that is connected to two or more networks. When information comes in from one network, the router determines which network is closest to the destination and sends the information out on that network.

Networks can be categorized by size. A *local area network* (*LAN*) is a small network of computers that are near each other and can communicate with each other over short distances. Computers on a LAN are typically in the same building or in adjacent buildings. This type of network is often called an *intranet*, and it can be used to run web applications for use by employees only.

A *wide area network* (*WAN*) consists of multiple LANs that have been connected together over long distances using routers. A WAN can be owned privately by one company or it can be shared by multiple companies.

An *Internet service provider* (*ISP*) is a company that owns a WAN that is connected to the Internet. An ISP leases access to its network to other companies that need to be connected to the Internet.

The Internet is a global network consisting of multiple WANs that have been connected together. ISPs connect their WANs together at large routers called *Internet exchange points* (*IXP*). This allows anyone connected to the Internet to exchange information with anyone else.

This figure shows an example of data crossing the Internet. In the diagram, data is being sent from the client in the top left to the server in the bottom right. Here, the data leaves the client's LAN and enters the WAN owned by the client's ISP. Next, the data is routed through an IXP to the WAN owned by the server's ISP. Then, it enters the server's LAN and finally reaches the server. All of this can happen in less than 1/10th of a second.

The architecture of a web application

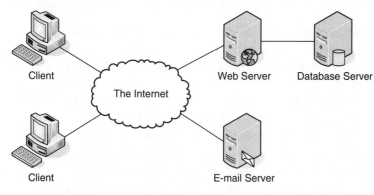

The architecture of the Internet

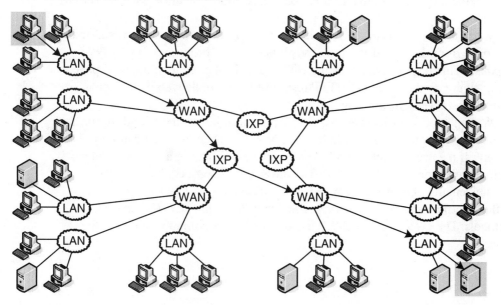

Description

- A *server* makes resources available to other computers called *clients* over a network. A server can share files, printers, web sites, databases, or e-mail.
- A *network* uses *routers* to get information from the sender to its destination.
- A *local area network* (LAN) directly connects computers that are near each other.
- A *wide area network* (WAN) uses routers to connect computers that are far from each other.
- The *Internet* consists of many WANs that have been connected together at *Internet exchange points* (IXP). There are several dozen IXPs located throughout the world. A list of major IXPs can be found at http://en.wikipedia.org/wiki/IXP.
- An *Internet service provider* (ISP) owns a WAN and leases access to this network. It connects its WAN to the rest of the Internet at one or more IXPs.

Figure 1-1   How a client-server architecture works

How static web pages are processed

A *static web page* is a web page that only changes when the web developer changes it. It is a plain text file that contains all the content to be displayed in the web browser. This web page is sent directly from the web server to the web browser when the browser requests it.

Figure 1-2 shows how a web server processes a request for a static web page. The process begins when a user requests a web page in a web browser. The user can either type in the address of the page into the browser's address bar or click a link in the current page that specifies the next page to load.

In either case, the web browser builds a request for the web page and sends it to the web server. This request, known as an *HTTP request*, is formatted using the *hypertext transport protocol* (HTTP), which lets the web server know which file is being requested. In this figure, you can see the content of a simple HTTP request.

When the web server receives the HTTP request, it retrieves the requested web page from the hard drive and sends it back to the browser as an *HTTP response*. This response includes the HTML for displaying the requested page. In this figure, you can see the HTTP response for a simple web page, which includes the HTML for the page.

When the browser receives the HTTP response, it uses the HTML to format the page and displays the page in the web browser. Then, the user can view the content. If the user requests another page, either by clicking a link or typing another web address in the browser's address bar, the process begins again.

Incidentally, this process depends not only on the HTTP protocol but also on the *Transmission Control Protocol/Internet Protocol* (*TCP/IP*) suite of protocols. The protocols in TCP/IP let two computers communicate over the network.

How a web server processes a static web page

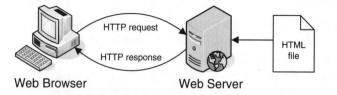

A simple HTTP request

```
GET / HTTP/1.1
Host: www.example.com
```

A simple HTTP response

```
HTTP/1.1 200 OK
Content-Type: text/html
Content-Length: 136
Server: Apache/2.2.3

<html>
<head>
    <title>Example Web Page</title>
</head>
<body>
    <p>This is a sample web page</p>
</body>
</html>
```

Two protocols that web applications depend upon

- *Hypertext Transfer Protocol* (*HTTP*) is the protocol that web browsers and web servers use to communicate. It sets the specifications for HTTP requests and responses.

- *Transmission Control Protocol/Internet Protocol*, or *TCP/IP*, is a suite of protocols that let two computers communicate over a network.

Description

- *Hypertext Markup Language* (*HTML*) is the language used to design the web pages of an application.

- A *static web page* is an HTML document that's stored on the web server and doesn't change in response to user input. Static web pages have a filename with an extension of .htm or .html.

- When the user requests a static web page, the browser sends an *HTTP request* to the web server that includes the name of the file that's being requested.

- When the web server receives the request, it retrieves the web page and sends it back to the browser in an *HTTP response*. This response includes the HTML document that's stored in the file that was requested.

Figure 1-2   How static web pages are processed

How dynamic web pages are processed

A *dynamic web page* is a page that's created by a web server program or script each time it is requested. This program or script is executed by an *application server*. This often means that the page is changed each time it is viewed.

The changes in the contents of the page can come from processing the form data that the user submits or by displaying data that's retrieved from a *database server*. A database server stores information that's organized in tables, and this information can be quickly retrieved by a database query.

Dynamic web pages enable web developers to create interactive *web applications*. As a result, users can purchase goods and services, search the web for information, and communicate with other users through forums, blogs, and social networking sites. Sites like these would be difficult or impossible to create without database-driven, dynamic web pages.

Figure 1-3 shows how a web server processes a dynamic web page. The process begins when the user requests a page in a web browser. The user can either type the URL of the page in the browser's address bar, click a link that specifies the dynamic page to load, or click a button that submits a form that contains the data that the dynamic page should process.

In each case, the web browser builds an HTTP request and sends it to the web server. If the user submits form data, that data will be included in the HTTP request.

When the web server receives the HTTP request, the server examines the file extension of the requested web page to identify the application server that should process the request. To do that, it uses *application mapping* to link the file extension of the requested script to the correct application server. The web server then forwards the request to the application server.

The application server retrieves the appropriate script from the hard drive. It also loads any form data that the user submitted. Then, it executes the script. As the script executes, it generates a web page as its output. The script may also request data from a database server and use this data as part of the web page it is generating.

When the script is finished, the application server sends the dynamically generated web page back to the web server. Then, the web server sends the page back to the browser in an HTTP response that includes the HTML for the page.

When the web browser receives the HTTP response, it formats and displays the web page. Note, however, that the web browser has no way to tell whether the HTML in the HTTP response was for a static page or a dynamic page.

When the page is displayed, the user can view the content. Then, when the user requests another page, the process begins again. The process that begins with the user requesting a web page and ends with the server sending a response back to the client is called a *round trip*.

How a web server processes a dynamic web page

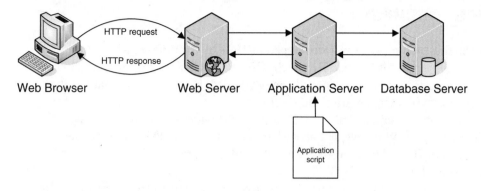

Description

- A *dynamic web page* is a web page that's generated by a server-side program or script. Often, the web page changes according to the information that is submitted by the web browser to the server.

- When a web server receives a request for a dynamic web page, it looks up the extension of the requested file in a list of *application mappings* to find out which *application server* should process the request.

- When the application server receives a request, it runs the specified application to process the data that's submitted by the web browser.

- The server-side application can use the data that it gets from the web browser to access the appropriate data in a *database server*. The application can also store the data that it gets from the web browser in the database server.

- When the server finishes processing the data, it generates a web page and returns it to the web server. The web server then returns the web page to the web browser.

- The browser can't tell whether the web page was retrieved from a static web page or generated dynamically by a server application. Either way, the browser simply displays the web page that was returned as a result of the request.

- The process that begins with the user requesting a web page and ends with the server sending a response back to the client is called a *round trip*.

Figure 1-3   How dynamic web pages are processed

A survey of browsers, servers, and server-side scripting languages

The first web browser was developed in 1991 by Tim Berners-Lee at the European Council for Nuclear Research (CERN) in Geneva, Switzerland. Since then, dozens of web browsers have been developed. Figure 1-4 summarizes the five web browsers that are used the most today.

Microsoft's Internet Explorer (IE) is the most widely used. It is currently available only for Windows, but an earlier version for Mac OS was available until January 2006. Although IE 8 was released in September 2008, IE 7 is still in widespread use.

Firefox is the second most used web browser. The most recent version is Firefox 3.1, which was released in August 2008. It is available for Windows, Mac OS, Linux, and other operating systems. Firefox was built using source code from the original Netscape Navigator web browser.

Safari and Opera are used by only a small percentage of users. Safari is the default web browser on Mac OS, but it is also available for Windows. Opera is available for Windows, Mac OS, Linux, and other operating systems.

Google's Chrome is a recent addition to the most popular web browsers, and its popularity is growing fast. Chrome is based on the WebKit rendering engine, which is the same one that Safari uses.

This figure also summarizes the two web servers that are used the most. The *Apache* web server, which was developed by the Apache Software Foundation, is the most widely used. It is an open-source software project that's available for free. Although there are Apache versions for most operating systems, it is typically used on a Linux server.

The other widely used web server is Microsoft's *Internet Information Services (IIS)*. It is included as part of the Windows Server operating system, and it supports the ASP.NET scripting language. This web server isn't open source, and new features other than scripting languages must be released by Microsoft.

Last, this figure summarizes the most common *scripting languages* for web servers. All of these languages except ASP.NET and JSP can be installed directly on either IIS or Apache. To use ASP.NET with Apache, you can use the module from the Mono project. Mono supports the most common ASP.NET features, but it isn't 100% complete. To learn more about ASP.NET, we recommend *Murach's ASP.NET 3.5 with VB 2008* or *Murach's ASP.NET 3.5 with C# 2008*.

To use JSP, you need the Tomcat web server to execute the JSP scripts. You can run your web site with IIS or Apache and use a connector module to forward JSP requests to the Tomcat web server. To learn more about JSP, we recommend *Murach's Java Servlets and JSP*.

ColdFusion is a commercial server-side scripting language released by Adobe that integrates well with Adobe Flash and Flex. In contrast, PHP, Ruby, Perl, and Python are open-source projects that are available for free.

Web browsers

Browser	Description
Internet Explorer	Published by Microsoft, the latest version is IE 8 released in September 2008. It is only available on the Windows platform.
Firefox	Published by the Mozilla Corporation, the latest version is 3.1 released in August 2008. It is available for all major operating systems.
Safari	Published by Apple, the latest version is 3.0 released in June 2008. It is available for OS X and Windows.
Opera	Published by Opera Software, the latest version is 9.5 released in June 2008. It is available for all major operating systems.
Chrome	Published by Google in December 2008 for Windows XP, Vista, and later versions.

Web servers

Server	Description
Apache	This is a modular, open-source web server that can run on any major operating system. It supports many server-side scripting languages and can interact with many different database servers. The most common configuration is known as LAMP, which consists of Linux, Apache, MySQL, and PHP.
IIS	This is the Microsoft Windows Server. It primarily supports the ASP.NET web server scripting language and the MS SQL Server database server, but it can be used with other web server scripting languages and database servers.

Server-side scripting languages

Language	Description
ASP.NET	Included with the Microsoft IIS web server, it uses the .aspx file extension.
JSP	Based on the Java programming language, it is used by the Apache Tomcat web server, but other web servers can be configured to run JSP scripts. It uses the .jsp file extension.
ColdFusion	Resembles HTML tags to make it easier to learn, it is available for both IIS and Apache. It uses the .cfml file extension. Learn more at http://www.adobe.com/products/coldfusion.
PHP	Typically used with the Apache web server, but it is also available for IIS. It uses the .php file extension. Learn more at http://www.php.net.
Ruby	Typically used with the Apache web server, it is combined with the Rails web application framework to simplify development. It uses the .rb file extension. Learn more at http://www.rubyonrails.org.
Perl	Originally developed for use at the UNIX command line to manipulate text, it was later used to build web applications. It uses the .pl file extension. Learn more at http://www.perl.org.
Python	Used to develop many types of applications in addition to web applications. It is typically used with the Apache web server. It uses the .py file extension. Learn more at http://www.python.org.

Figure 1-4   A survey of browsers, servers, and server-side scripting languages

How JavaScript fits into this architecture

As you have just seen, the application server processes dynamic requests for web pages. This can be referred to as *server-side processing*. That means that the processing is done by the server. All the browser does is format the HTML that's returned to it and display the page.

In contrast, JavaScript code is executed in the web browser by the browser's *JavaScript engine*. This is referred to as *client-side processing*. This takes some of the processing burden off the server and makes the application run faster. This is illustrated by the diagram in figure 1-5.

Each web browser uses its own JavaScript engine and they all implement JavaScript differently. This leads to the problem of *cross-browser incompatibility*. This means that your JavaScript application may run correctly in one web browser, but not in another. In chapter 3, you'll learn how to test and debug your JavaScript applications in the major web browsers.

As this figure shows, there are many uses for JavaScript. Some common ones are validating data on a client before it is sent to the server for processing; presenting slide shows; creating dynamic menus; sorting the data in tables; and animating the elements on a page. In this book, you'll learn how to use JavaScript for most of these applications.

How JavaScript fits into this architecture

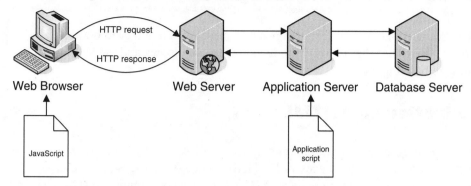

Common uses of JavaScript

- Validate the data for a form in a web page before it is sent to the server for processing.
- Respond to user actions such as mouse clicks and key presses.
- Create dynamic menus.
- Create slide shows.
- Animate elements in a web page.
- Create timers, clocks, and calendars.
- Change the style sheet that a web page uses.
- Sort the data that's in a table.
- Control the web browser window.
- Detect web browser plug-ins.
- Open new web browser windows.
- Load new content from a server and display it in the current web page.
- Change images when the user rolls the mouse over an image.
- Apply special effects to elements in a web page.

Description

- *JavaScript* is a scripting language that is run by the *JavaScript engine* of a browser. As a result, the work is done on the client, not the server, which takes some of the processing burden off the server.
- One of the issues in using JavaScript is to make sure that your web pages will work no matter what browser is being used.

Figure 1-5   How JavaScript fits into this architecture

The core web technologies

JavaScript is one of four technologies that must work together to build a web page. The topics that follow introduce these technologies and the standards that they're based upon.

An introduction to XHTML

Extensible hypertext markup language (*XHTML*) is used to structure and format a web page. It is the successor to HTML. Since XHTML is plain text, you can use any text editor to create an XHTML document. Figure 1-6 shows a simple XHTML document and how it is displayed in the Firefox web browser.

An XHTML document begins with a *DOCTYPE declaration*. This declaration indicates which version of XHTML is used to format the document. The DOCTYPE declarations are fixed for each version and cannot be changed. In this case, the DOCTYPE declaration indicates that this document follows the XHTML 1.0 Transitional standard. This is the version of XHTML that will be used throughout this book.

Although you're probably familiar with XHTML, what follows is a brief description. In chapter 4, though, you can learn what every JavaScript programmer needs to know about XHTML.

An *XHTML element* consists of an opening and closing tag that surrounds the text that is part of the element. The *opening tag* consists of the element name surrounded by angle brackets, and the *closing tag* consists of a left angle bracket, a forward slash, the element name, and the right angle bracket.. For example, <h1> is the opening tag for the level-1 header, and </h1> is the closing tag.

An opening tag can also have *attributes* that modify the way the content in the tag is displayed. These attributes are placed inside the angle brackets after the element name, and every attribute must have a value assigned to it. This value is placed inside quotation marks and is separated from the attribute by an equal sign. In the third line of the code in this figure, the html element has an xmlns attribute.

An *XHTML document* is completely contained inside of an <html> tag. The html section contains a head section followed by a body section. The head section contains elements that provide information about the XHTML document. The body section contains the text and tags that will be displayed in the web browser.

As this figure shows, the <title> tag is the only element that's required in the head section. It provides a description that is displayed in the web browser's title bar.

The code for a web page

```
<!DOCTYPE html PUBLIC "-//W3C//DTD XHTML 1.0 Transitional//EN"
    "http://www.w3.org/TR/xhtml1/DTD/xhtml1-transitional.dtd">
<html xmlns="http://www.w3.org/1999/xhtml">
<head>
<title>Mike's Bait and Tackle Shop</title>
</head>
<body>
    <h1>Mike's Bait and Tackle Shop</h1>
    <p>Welcome to Mike's Bait and Tackle Shop. We have all the gear you'll
    need to make your next fishing trip a great success!</p>
    <h2>New Products</h2>
    <ul>
        <li>Ultima 3000 Two-handed fly rod</li>
        <li>Phil's Faux Shrimp Fly - Size 6</li>
        <li>Titanium Open Back Fly Reel - Black</li>
    </ul>
    <p>Contact us by phone at 559-555-6624 to place your order today.</p>
</body>
</html>
```

The web page in a web browser

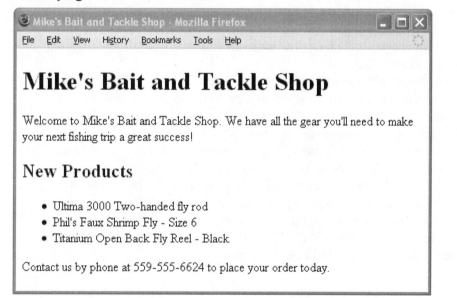

Description

- *Extensible hypertext markup language* (XHTML) is used to design the web pages of an application. It is based on HTML.

- Since *XHTML elements* are plain text, you can use any text editor to create and edit an XHTML document.

- XHTML elements consist of an *opening tag*, the content of the element, and a *closing tag*. *Attributes* in the opening tag are used to modify how an XHTML element works.

Figure 1-6   An introduction to XHTML

An introduction to CSS

In the early days of web development, HTML included elements that controlled both the structure and formatting of the document. However, this mix of structural and formatting elements made it hard to edit and maintain the web pages. Often, there would be more formatting tags than text.

Cascading style sheets (*CSS*) were developed to separate the formatting instructions from the body of the web page so all that would be left were structural tags and the content of the page. As a result, most of the formatting tags that were once in XHTML, such as the <font> tag, have now been deprecated and should not be used to build new web pages.

To apply a style sheet to an XHTML document, you can load the sheet from a separate file called an *external style sheet*, or you can use an *embedded style sheet* that is coded in the <style> tag of the document. Because external style sheets separate the CSS from the XHTML, that is the preferred method.

Figure 1-7 shows the start of an XHTML web page with a style sheet that's embedded in the <style> tag. This style sheet is used to format the XHTML in the last figure. If you compare the web page in this figure with the one in the last figure, you can see how the style sheet changes its appearance.

Although you're probably familiar with CSS, what follows is a brief description. In chapter 5, though, you can learn what every JavaScript programmer needs to know about CSS.

A CSS *rule set* consists of a *selector* and *declaration block*. The selector identifies an XHTML element or group of elements, and the declaration block specifies the formatting for those elements. In the CSS in this figure, there are three rule sets. The first one applies to the <body> tag, the second one applies to <h1> elements, and the last one applies to <ul> elements (unordered lists).

A declaration block consists of one or more *declarations* (or *rules*) surrounded by braces. A declaration consists of a property and a value separated by a colon with a semicolon at the end of the declaration. The properties control fonts, margins, borders, backgrounds, and colors. In the style sheet in this figure, the rules apply color to body elements, color and a bottom border style to h1 elements, and a square bullet style to unordered lists.

The code for a web page that's styled with CSS

```
<!DOCTYPE html PUBLIC "-//W3C//DTD XHTML 1.0 Transitional//EN"
    "http://www.w3.org/TR/xhtml1/DTD/xhtml1-transitional.dtd">
<html xmlns="http://www.w3.org/1999/xhtml">
<head>
<title>Mike's Bait and Tackle Shop</title>
<style type='text/css'>
body {
    background-color: #333366;
    color: #FFFFFF;
}
h1 {
    color: #FFCC33;
    border-bottom: 3px solid #FF3333;
}
ul {
    list-style-type: square;
}
</style>
</head>
<!-- The rest of this document is the same as in figure 1-6. -->
```

The web page in a web browser

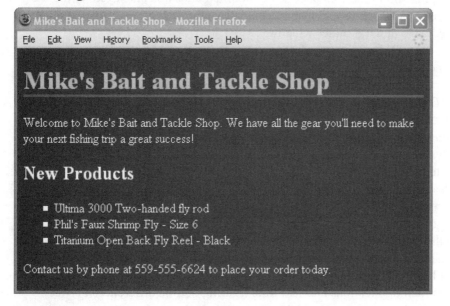

Description

- *Cascading style sheets* (CSS) are used to control how web pages are displayed by specifying the fonts, colors, borders, spacing, and layout of the pages.

- An *external style sheet* is loaded from a separate file. An *embedded style sheet* is coded in the <style> tag in the head section of an XHTML document.

- A CSS *rule set* consists of a *selector* that identifies one or more XHTML elements and a *declaration block* that describes the styles that should be applied to those elements.

Figure 1-7   An introduction to CSS

An introduction to the DOM

The *document object model* (*DOM*) is an internal representation of the XHTML elements in a web page. As an XHTML page is loaded by the web browser, the DOM for that page is created in the browser's memory. Figure 1-8 shows a simple XHTML document and the structure of the DOM for that document.

Each element of the web page is represented by a *node* in the DOM. The nodes in the DOM have a hierarchical structure based on how the XHTML elements are nested inside each other. The DOM starts with the <html> tag at the top and follows the nesting of the elements down to the text that is in each element.

There are several types of nodes used to represent the contents of the web page. XHTML elements are stored in *element nodes* and text is stored in *text nodes*. In this figure, element nodes are shown as ovals and text nodes are shown as rectangles. Other common node types are *attribute nodes* and *comment nodes*.

The nodes that make up the DOM can be modified by a script within the web page. This allows the web page to be modified after it is displayed by the web browser. When a change is made to the DOM, the web browser displays the updated page in the browser window.

Before the DOM was standardized, each web browser had its own interface that allowed a scripting language to manipulate the contents of the web page. These scripts that modified a web page using browser-specific techniques were known as *Dynamic HTML* (*DHTML*) scripts.

The first task a DHTML script had to do was determine which web browser was running the script. It then executed code specific to that web browser. Essentially, this meant you had to write a different script for each web browser you expected your visitors to use. DHTML scripts were also difficult to maintain and had to be updated when a new version of a web browser was released. For these reasons, DHTML was often ignored by professional web developers except for a few tasks such as image rollovers and form data validation.

With the DOM, however, scripts have a consistent interface to the web page. As a result, these scripts are easier to write and easier to maintain, and they don't have to be updated as often. This lets developers spend more time working on their applications and less time figuring out the differences between web browsers.

The code for a web page

```
<!DOCTYPE html PUBLIC "-//W3C//DTD XHTML 1.0 Transitional//EN"
    "http://www.w3.org/TR/xhtml1/DTD/xhtml1-transitional.dtd">
<html xmlns="http://www.w3.org/1999/xhtml">
<head>
<title>Mike's Bait and Tackle Shop</title>
</head>
<body>
    <h1>Mike's Bait and Tackle Shop</h1>
    <p>Welcome to Mike's Bait and Tackle Shop. We have all the gear you'll
    need to make your next fishing trip a great success!</p>
    <h2>New Products</h2>
    <ul>
        <li>Ultima 3000 Two-handed fly rod</li>
        <li>Phil's Faux Shrimp Fly - Size 6</li>
        <li>Titanium Open Back Fly Reel - Black</li>
    </ul>
    <p>Contact us by phone at 559-555-6624 to place your order today.</p>
</body>
</html>
```

The DOM for the web page

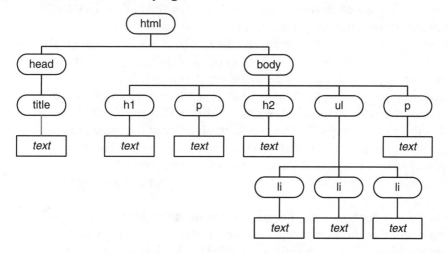

Description

- The *document object model* (DOM) is a collection of *nodes* in the web browser's memory that represent the current web page. These nodes are organized as a hierarchy.
- The DOM for a web page is built as the page is loaded by the web browser.
- JavaScript can modify the web page in the browser by modifying the DOM.
- When the DOM is changed, the web browser immediately displays the results of the change.
- Many JavaScript applications manipulate the DOM based on user actions.

Figure 1-8   An introduction to the DOM

An introduction to JavaScript

JavaScript is a programming language embedded in a web browser. It was developed by Brendan Eich at Netscape to allow web developers to build interactive web pages that run on the browser, instead of the server. JavaScript does this by manipulating the DOM to update the content on the page.

JavaScript is added to a web page by using the <script> tag. This tag can be in the head or body section of the web page. You can also have multiple script tags. The code in the script tags are executed from top to bottom.

When a script tag appears in the head section, it is usually used to set up parts of the application for later use. When a script tag appears in the body section, it is typically used to display information in the page at the point where the script is. Any output from the script will be used in the web page in place of the script. It will be as if the output had been typed in the web page instead of the script.

In figure 1-9, the shaded code is a simple JavaScript application. Here, the first line and last lines start and end the JavaScript code. Within those tags are two JavaScript statements. The first statement sets a variable named today to the current date. The second statement uses the writeln method of the DOM's document object to write the year of the date to the web page.

This figure also shows what this web page looks like in a web browser that has JavaScript enabled. Because the JavaScript code is within a <p> tag, the year that is returned by the JavaScript code follows the copyright mark (©) and precedes the text that's in this tag. If JavaScript were disabled in the web browser, the page would display just "© Mike's Bait and Tackle Shop".

As you will learn in section 2 of this book, the JavaScript language provides many capabilities that are typical of all programming languages. It can store and manipulate numbers, text, and dates. It has control structures that let you control the flow of the program. And it has facilities to detect and work around errors.

What JavaScript does not have, however, is the ability to get input and display output. For that, JavaScript relies on the web browser and the DOM. As you will see, JavaScript can use functions provided by the browser to display messages and get input directly from the user. JavaScript can use the DOM to get input from form fields and other elements in the web page and to update elements that display information directly in the web page. And JavaScript can update the structure of the DOM by adding or removing XHTML elements.

JavaScript that's embedded in an XHTML document

```
<!-- The code before this is the same as in figure 1-6. -->
<p>Contact us by phone at 559-555-6624 to place your order today.</p>
<p>&copy;
<script type="text/javascript">
    var today = new Date();
    document.writeln( today.getFullYear() );
</script>
Mike's Bait and Tackle Shop</p>
</body>
</html>
```

The JavaScript application in a web browser

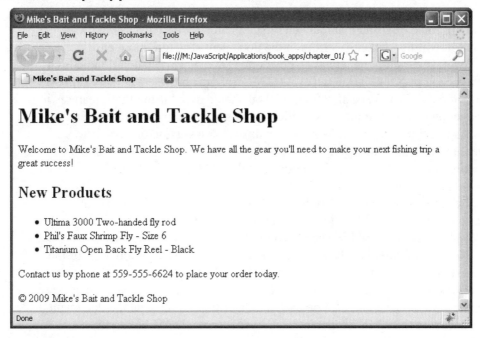

Description

- *JavaScript* lets web developers build interactive web pages.
- JavaScript can modify the contents of a web page when the code first executes or in response to a user action.
- In the web page above, the year 2009 was generated by the JavaScript code that's within a <script> tag inside a <p> tag in the body of the XHTML document.

Figure 1-9   An introduction to JavaScript

The XHTML, CSS, DOM, and JavaScript standards

As figure 1-10 shows, the standards for XHTML, CSS, the DOM, and JavaScript continue to change. As a web developer, you need to keep track of these changes for two reasons. First, you want to make sure that your current web pages will continue to work with new browsers. Second, you want take advantage of new features as they become widely available.

As this figure shows, HTML has been around since the early 1990's. The last version of HTML was HTML 4.01, which was released in December 1999. Then, XHTML 1.0 was introduced in January 2000.

XHTML is a modified version of HTML that supports the same tags as HTML 4.1, but uses the syntax of XML. This is a stricter syntax that allows XHTML to be read and manipulated by automated tools. This also allows XHTML editors to identify errors in the document structure more easily.

Work is currently underway to develop HTML 5. This standard includes a new version of XHTML known as XHTML 5. Some browsers already support parts of the HTML 5 specification, but you should avoid using these features in production web sites until the specification is supported by most browsers.

As this figure shows, CSS 2.1 is the most stable version of CSS. It was released as a candidate standard in February 2004, but it was returned to a working draft for further modification. In July 2007, it was released again as a candidate standard.

Because of the revisions to the standards, CSS has been inconsistently supported. However, the major web browsers support most of CSS 2.1. Once CSS 3 is stable, it should be supported by the major web browsers as well.

Next, this figure lists the major versions of the DOM standard. One of the interesting features of the DOM 3 standard is the ability to convert the internal representation of the DOM into an XML text document. This XML representation of the document can then be used at a later time to recreate the document by converting the XML document back to an internal DOM hierarchy.

Today, the DOM standard isn't under active development and modern web browsers support DOM 3. However, the HTML 5 standard includes updates to the DOM called DOM5 HTML. This version of the DOM will be used by future web browsers that support HTML 5 and XHTML 5.

Highlights in the history of the HTML and XHTML standards

Version	Description
HTML 1.0	A draft specification released in January 1993 that was never adopted as a standard.
HTML 2.0	Adopted in November 1995.
HTML 3.2	Adopted in January 1997. It formalized new features that were used by web browsers.
HTML 4.0	Adopted in December 1997. It formalized new features that were used by web browsers and deprecated older features. It had three versions: Strict, Transitional, and Frameset.
HTML 4.01	Adopted in December 1999 and updated through May 2001. It maintained the Strict, Transitional, and Frameset versions.
XHTML 1.0	Adopted in January 2000 and revised in August 2002. It reformulates HTML 4 using the syntax of XML, which makes it easier to parse the web page. This allows automated tools to find errors in a web page. It maintained the Strict, Transitional, and Frameset versions.
XHTML 1.1	Adopted in May 2001. The control of the presentation of content is now done through CSS.
XHTML 2	Released as a working draft in July 2006. It is intended to be a new version of XHTML, but it may be replaced by XHTML 5 before becoming a standard.
HTML 5	Released as a working draft in January 2008. It is a new version of HTML 4 and XHTML 1 that defines an HTML version called HTML 5, an XHTML version called XHTML 5, and a new version of the DOM called DOM5 HTML.

The CSS standards

Version	Description
1.0	Adopted in December 1996.
2.0	Adopted in May 1998.
2.1	First released as a candidate standard in February 2004, it was returned to working draft status in June 2005. It became a candidate standard again in July 2007.
3.0	A modularized version of CSS with the earliest drafts in June 1999. Only a few modules have been released as candidate standards, some were reverted back to working drafts.

The DOM standards

Version	Description
1.0	Adopted in October 1998. It describes the objects and interfaces that represent an HTML or XHTML document so it can be manipulated by a script.
2.0	Adopted in November 2000. It modularized the specification, updated the existing features of DOM, and added views, events, and a CSS interface.
3.0	Adopted in April 2004. It updated the core DOM module and added the ability to convert the DOM to and from an XML document. It also added guidance on ensuring document validity during dynamic updates.

Figure 1-10   The XHTML, CSS, DOM, and JavaScript standards (part 1 of 2)

Finally, this figure gives you a brief summary of the JavaScript versions. However, JavaScript has a muddled history that can be hard to unravel. In fact, there are actually three languages that are referred to collectively as JavaScript: JavaScript, JScript, and ECMAScript.

While in development at Netscape, JavaScript was known by the codename Mocha. Originally, it was going to be called LiveScript. However, as part of a licensing deal with Sun Microsystems, Netscape agreed to include the Java environment with Netscape Navigator in exchange for permission to rename LiveScript to JavaScript. The only relationship between Java and JavaScript is that both languages are based on the syntax of the C programming language.

After Netscape released JavaScript, Microsoft wanted to include it in Internet Explorer. Instead of licensing JavaScript, though, Microsoft developed an alternative language known as JScript that is mostly compatible with JavaScript. Nevertheless, small differences between JavaScript and JScript made it difficult to develop applications that would run on both browsers.

Later, Netscape submitted JavaScript to the European Computer Manufacturer's Association (ECMA) for standardization. The name of the resulting language was ECMAScript, which was first released in June 1997. JavaScript 1.5 in Netscape 6 and JScript 5.6 in Internet Explorer 6.0 are roughly equivalent to version 3 of ECMAScript, which was released in December 1999 and is still current.

In 2004, version 1.0 of the Firefox web browser was released. This browser, which is based on Netscape Navigator, later added new features to JavaScript and is now up to JavaScript 1.8. Although these enhancements aren't part of the current ECMAScript standard, they are expected to be part of the next version of ECMAScript.

Today, ECMAScript 4 is under development. It is a major update to the language and will add lots of new features to JavaScript while retaining backwards compatibility with ECMAScript 3. When it is released as a standard, it is expected to be adopted by all of the major web browsers.

JavaScript versions

Version	Date	Browser Support
1.0	March 1996	Netscape Navigator 2.0
1.1	August 1996	Netscape Navigator 3.0
1.2	June 1997	Netscape Communicator 4.0
1.3	June 1998	Netscape Communicator 4.06
1.5	November 2000	Netscape 6
	November 2004	Mozilla Firefox 1.0
1.6	November 2005	Mozilla Firefox 1.5
1.7	October 2006	Mozilla Firefox 2.0
1.8	June 2008	Mozilla Firefox 3.0

JScript versions

Version	Date	Browser Support	Equivalent to
1.0	August 1996	Internet Explorer 3.0	JavaScript 1.0
2.0	March 1997	Internet Explorer 3.02	JavaScript 1.1
3.0	October 1997	Internet Explorer 4.0	JavaScript 1.3
5.0	March 1999	Internet Explorer 5.0	JavaScript 1.3
5.5	July 2000	Internet Explorer 5.5	JavaScript 1.5
5.6	October 2001	Internet Explorer 6.0	JavaScript 1.5
5.7	November 2006	Internet Explorer 7.0	JavaScript 1.5
5.8	December 2008	Internet Explorer 8.0	JavaScript 1.5

ECMAScript editions

Edition	Date	Equivalent to
1	June 1997	JavaScript 1.3
2	June 1998	JavaScript 1.3
3	December 1999	JavaScript 1.5

Target releases for current web development projects

- XHTML 1.0
- CSS 2.1
- DOM 2
- JavaScript 1.5

Description

- As a web developer, you want to use the latest releases of XHTML, CSS, DOM, and JavaScript that are supported by the most popular web browsers.

Figure 1-10   The XHTML, CSS, DOM, and JavaScript standards (part 2 of 2)

DOM scripting and AJAX

Besides the core web technologies that you've just learned about, two other techniques have led to a surge in the use of JavaScript. The first is *DOM scripting*. This uses JavaScript to manipulate the DOM in order to build a web application that responds to user actions.

The second technique is *Asynchronous JavaScript and XML (AJAX)*. This allows JavaScript applications to communicate with a server to get updates to the web page that's being displayed. Specifically, AJAX uses DOM scripting to update part of a page with content from a web server without having to update the entire page.

How DOM scripting works

DOM scripting lets you use JavaScript to update a web page in response to user actions by changing the DOM. In figure 1-11, you can see the relationships between JavaScript, the DOM, XHTML, and CSS.

DOM scripting is a type of *event-driven programming*. This means that the code runs primarily in response to events in the web browser. An *event* is typically an action the user performs with the mouse or keyboard. The code that is executed in response to an event is called an *event handler*.

This figure describes the event cycle that drives DOM scripts. To start, event handlers are attached to the events on the page when the page is loaded. The browser then waits for an event to occur before executing the event handler for that event.

When you use event-driven programming, the code that's executed depends on the events that take place. As a result, an event-driven application needs to ensure that an event handler has all the information it needs when an event occurs. If an event is triggered too early, the event handler needs to be able to detect this and either inform the user of the problem or ignore the event.

In the next chapter and in section 2, you'll learn some basic DOM scripting because it is essential to the use of JavaScript. Then, in section 3, you'll get an advanced course in DOM scripting that shows you how to get the most from it. Along the way, you'll learn how to use DOM scripting for some advanced JavaScript applications.

How the web technologies interact in the web browser

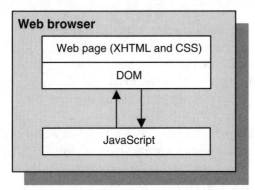

The DOM event cycle

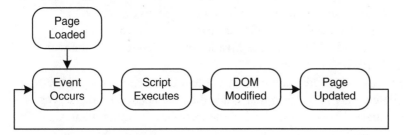

Description

- *DOM scripting* is the process of building a web application by using JavaScript to manipulate the DOM.

- DOM scripting uses *event-driven programming*. An *event* is an action the user performs such as clicking a mouse button or typing on the keyboard.

- Once the event occurs, JavaScript code is executed to process the event. This code is called an *event handler*.

- As the event handler executes, it has full access to the DOM. It can read the properties of the elements on the page through the DOM, and it can change the properties of those elements.

- When the DOM is modified, the web browser detects the changes to the DOM and updates the web page that's in the browser window.

- When the event handler is finished, the web browser waits for another event to occur and the cycle starts over again until another page is loaded.

- DOM scripting should be done only to enhance a web page. This is known as *progressive enhancement*. Then, if JavaScript is disabled, the page will continue to function.

Figure 1-11   How DOM scripting works

How AJAX works

A *rich Internet application* (*RIA*) is a web application that provides users with an enhanced user interface, advanced functionality, and a quick response time. Although there are many frameworks that you can use to build an RIA, most require the user to install a plug-in into the web browser. Only AJAX allows you to build a RIA using just the features that are built into all modern web browsers.

As figure 1-12 shows, *AJAX* (asynchronous JavaScript and XML) lets a web page communicate with a web server and update part of a web page without having to reload the entire page. However, AJAX isn't a single technology. Instead, it is comprised of DOM scripting, the *XMLHttpRequest object*, a server-side scripting language, *extensible markup language* (XML), and *JavaScript object notation* (JSON).

The XMLHttpRequest object allows JavaScript to exchange data with a script running on the server. XML and JSON are two common ways to format the data that will be exchanged between the JavaScript application and the web server with the XMLHttpRequest object.

When a page needs to be updated with new content from the server, AJAX can be used to initiate an HTTP request that sends the data needed by the server to respond to the request. This request can include information about what caused the request, as well as the relevant content of the web page. After the script has processed the request, the server sends an HTTP response back to the web browser. Then, the JavaScript application can use the data in the response to update the web page without having to reload the entire page.

AJAX HTTP requests can be initiated in two ways. The first way is by a user event that occurs in the web browser. The second way is by a timer that can be set to trigger an AJAX request after a specified delay or at set intervals. This allows part of the web page to be updated automatically.

AJAX-initiated HTTP requests can be repeated as many times as necessary to update a page. A normal HTTP request will be initiated when a new page needs to be loaded or when a part of the current page that isn't controlled by AJAX needs to be updated.

Although this book doesn't show you how to use AJAX, keep in mind that you need to know how to use both JavaScript and DOM scripting before you can use AJAX. That's why this book is a prerequisite for using AJAX.

AJAX-enabled request and response cycle

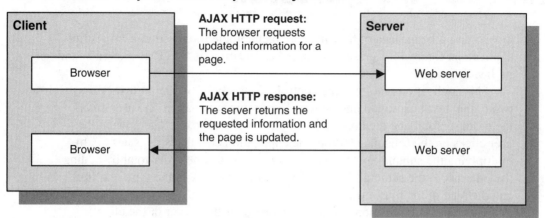

Description

- A *rich Internet application* (RIA) is an application that is displayed in a web browser but has the look and feel of a desktop application such as an enhanced user interface and quick response time.

- AJAX (a*synchronous JavaScript and XML*) lets you to build an RIA using just the features built into modern web browsers. AJAX also lets you update part of a web page without having to reload the entire page, which reduces the load on the web server.

- When you use AJAX, a web page is first loaded normally by the browser. Then, when an event happens on the page, such as the user clicking a button, the browser sends an HTTP request from the web page to the server.

- A special JavaScript object called the *XMLHttpRequest object* is used to manage this HTTP request from within a web page. It sends the data to the web server and identifies the code to run.

- The server processes the request and sends an HTTP response back to the web browser. Then, DOM scripting is used to process this response and to update the contents of the web page without having to reload the entire page.

- *Extensible markup language* (*XML*) and *JavaScript object notation* (*JSON*) are common ways of formatting the data that's exchanged between an AJAX application and a web server.

Figure 1-12   How AJAX works

The Sales Tax application

To give a better idea of how the core technologies are used in a JavaScript application, figure 1-13 presents a simple application, its XHTML, its CSS, and its JavaScript code.

This application requires nine controls: four labels, two input text boxes, two output text boxes, and one button. To run this application, the user enters the order subtotal and the tax rate in the first two text boxes. Then, when the user clicks on the Calculate button, the application calculates the sales tax by multiplying the subtotal by the tax rate and calculates the order total by adding the sales tax to the subtotal. It then displays the sales tax in the third text box and the total in the fourth text box.

This type of application could be run on either the server or the client. When you use JavaScript, of course, the processing is done by the browser on the client. That not only reduces the load on the server, but also returns the result faster.

The XHTML file

If you're familiar with XHTML, you should be able to understand most of the code for this application. If there are any lines that you don't understand, you can learn how they work in chapter 4.

One noteworthy point, though, is what the two shaded lines in the head section do. The first line says that the CSS for this application should be loaded from a file named sales_tax.css. The second line says that the JavaScript for this application should be loaded from a file named sales_tax.js. This assumes that both files are in the same folder as the XHTML file.

This is a common way to keep the XHTML, CSS, and JavaScript code separate from each other. That way, the three sets of code are easier to follow, and you can modify one of the files without modifying the others. As a result, this technique is commonly used in professional web applications.

The other noteworthy point is that id attributes have been coded for many of the XHTML elements. As you will see, the values of these attributes are used in both the CSS and the JavaScript code for this application.

The CSS file

In the CSS for this file in part 2 of this figure, you can see that six rule sets are applied to HTML elements. The first applies to the body element. The second applies to the element that has an id with a value of "content". The third applies to the elements that have "salesTax" and "total" as their ids. And the last three apply to three types of elements within the element that has "taxCalc" as its id: labels, input boxes, and br elements.

In chapter 5, you'll learn how to code the selectors and declarations for rule sets like these. For now, just realize that if there were no style sheet for this

The Sales Tax application in a web browser

The XHTML file

```
<!DOCTYPE html PUBLIC "-//W3C//DTD XHTML 1.0 Transitional//EN"
    "http://www.w3.org/TR/xhtml1/DTD/xhtml1-transitional.dtd">
<html xmlns="http://www.w3.org/1999/xhtml">
<head>
    <title>Sales Tax Calculator</title>
    <link rel="stylesheet" type="text/css" href="sales_tax.css" />
    <script type="text/javascript" src="sales_tax.js"></script>
</head>
<body>
<div id="content">
    <h1>Sales Tax Calculator</h1>
    <p>Enter the values below and click "Calculate".</p>
    <div id="taxCalc">
        <label for="subtotal">Subtotal:</label>
        <input type="text" id="subtotal" /><br />

        <label for="taxRate">Tax Rate:</label>
        <input type="text" id="taxRate" />%<br />

        <label for="salesTax">Sales Tax:</label>
        <input type="text" id="salesTax" disabled="disabled" /><br />

        <label for="total">Total:</label>
        <input type="text" id="total" disabled="disabled" /><br />

        <label> </label>
        <input type="button" id="calculate" value="Calculate" /><br />
    </div>
</div>
</body>
</html>
```

Figure 1-13   The Sales Tax application (part 1 of 2)

application, the controls in the application wouldn't be aligned properly, the text in the labels wouldn't be right aligned, and so on.

The JavaScript file

In the next chapter, you're going to learn how to write the JavaScript code for an application like this. But if you have some programming experience, the explanation that follows should help you understand what's happening right now. Here, the ids that refer to XHTML elements are highlighted, and the JavaScript code consists of three functions.

The first function is named $ (a common name for this type of function). This function uses the getElementById method of the document object (part of the DOM) to get the control that's specified by the parameter named id. If, for example, the $ function is sent an id of "subtotal", the function returns the object for the first input box in the XHTML code. Then, the code can use the value property of that object to get the data that the user entered into that text box. This is a type of DOM scripting.

The second function is named calculate_click. This function is executed when the user clicks on the Calculate button. It starts by using the $ function and the value property to get the values that have been entered into the subtotal and tax rate text boxes. It also uses the parseFloat method to convert those values into numbers. The third and fourth lines of this function use the $ function to set the value property of the third and fourth text boxes, named salesTax and total in the XHTML code, to empty strings.

This is followed by an if/else statement that checks to see whether the user entered valid numbers into the text boxes. If either entry is not a number (isNaN) or is less than zero, the alert method is used to display an error message.

If both entries are valid, the else clause calculates sales tax and rounds it to two decimal places using the toFixed and parseFloat methods. Then, it calculates the total. Finally, it uses the $ function to display these values in the text boxes named salesTax and total.

The third function is executed when the window.onload event occurs. This event occurs when the web page is sent to the browser and is fully loaded into the browser window. The first statement in this function uses the $ function to attach the function named calculate_click to the onclick event of the Calculate button. Once that's done, the calculate_click function will be executed whenever the onclick event occurs. The second statement in this function uses the focus method of the DOM element to move the focus to the subtotal box so the application is ready for the first user entry.

This simple application illustrates that JavaScript has many of the features of other programming languages, especially when you use it with the DOM. This application should also give you some idea of how data validation can be done on the client before the data is sent to a web server for processing. In the next chapter, you'll learn how to code all of the statements in an application like this.

The CSS file

```css
body {
    font-family: Arial, Helvetica, sans-serif;
    background: #333366; }
#content {
    width: 450px;
    margin: 10px auto;
    padding: 5px 20px;
    background: white;
    border: thin solid black; }
#salesTax, #total {
    color: black; }
#taxCalc label {
    display: block;
    width: 6em;
    text-align: right;
    padding-right: 1em;
    float: left; }
#taxCalc input {
    display: block;
    float: left; }
#taxCalc br {
    clear: left; }
```

The JavaScript file

```javascript
var $ = function (id) {
    return document.getElementById(id);
}

var calculate_click = function () {
    var subtotal = parseFloat( $("subtotal").value );
    var taxRate  = parseFloat( $("taxRate").value );

    $("salesTax").value = "";
    $("total").value = "";

    if ( isNaN(subtotal) || subtotal < 0 ) {
        alert("Subtotal must be a number that is zero or more!");
    } else if ( isNaN(taxRate) || taxRate < 0 ) {
        alert("Tax Rate must be a number that is zero or more!");
    } else {
        var salesTax = subtotal * (taxRate / 100);
        salesTax = parseFloat( salesTax.toFixed(2) );
        var total = subtotal + salesTax;
        $("salesTax").value = salesTax;
        $("total").value = total.toFixed(2);
    }
}

window.onload = function () {
    $("calculate").onclick = calculate_click;
    $("subtotal").focus;
}
```

Figure 1-13   The Sales Tax application (part 2 of 2)

Two critical web development issues

Whenever you develop a web application, you should be aware of the two issues that are presented in figure 1-14. Throughout this book, you will learn techniques that will help you write applications that are cross-browser compatible and accessibile to as many users as possible.

Cross-browser compatibility

If you want your web site to be used by as many visitors as possible, you need to make sure that your web pages are compatible with as many browsers as possible. That's known as *cross-browser compatibility*. Today, that means you should be using XHTML 1.0, CSS 2.1, DOM 2, and JavaScript 1.5. That also means you should test your applications on as many browsers and operating systems as possible.

User accessibility

The other major issue is *user accessibility*. That means that you should develop your applications so the content of your web site is still usable if images, CSS, and JavaScript are disabled. That will make your site accessible to people with disabilities. A side benefit of doing that is that your site will also be more accessible to search engines, which rely primarily on the text portions of your pages.

If you do make a web site that is inaccessible, you should also have a text-only version of your site. This is illustrated by the J. K. Rowling site shown in this figure. That way, search engines and users with disabilities can still access the information in your site.

Because users with disabilities typically can't use the JavaScript functions of your site, you need to make sure that DOM scripting is used only to enhance the functionality of a web page rather than provide the main functionality. Then, when you test an application like this, you should disable JavaScript to see if the most important aspects of the application still work. If they don't, you should consider rewriting your application to rely less on JavaScript or to provide an alternative version of your application that works without JavaScript.

In the Sales Tax application, for example, you could provide an alternate form that submits the data to a server-side script to perform the calculation when JavaScript is disabled. You could also provide a table of typical subtotals and tax rates with the sales tax and totals already calculated.

The text-only version of the J. K. Rowling web site

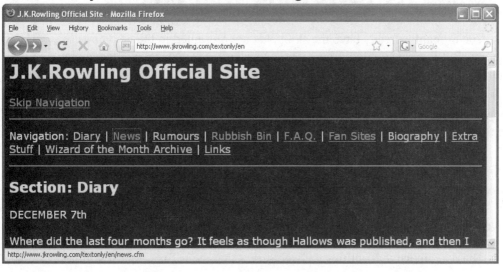

Guidelines for cross-browser compatibility

- Don't use browser-specific features in your web pages.
- Test your web pages on as many browsers as possible.

Guidelines for user accessibility

- Design your pages so the most important content will still be available if a visitor can't use images, CSS, or JavaScript. To learn more, go to http://www.w3.org/WAI.
- If you work for a government agency, you have to follow the guidelines in *Section 508* that are required by federal law. To learn more, go to http://www.section508.gov.
- For a commercial web site, you may need to follow the guidelines in the *Americans with Disabilities Act* (ADA). To follow the court case that will determine if this law applies to you, go to http://www.dralegal.org/cases/private_business/nfb_v_target.php.
- If you build a site that isn't accessible, you should also have a text-only version available. This version can be simple as long as it provides the same basic information. For an example, go to http://www.jkrowling.com for the full site and then to http://www.jkrowling.com/textonly/en for the text-only site.

Description

- As a web developer, you want your web pages to work on as many different web browsers as possible. This can be called *cross-browser compatibility*, but this concept is often described in the negative as *cross-browser incompatibility*.
- As a web developer, you also want to make your web pages accessible to as many users as possible, including the disabled. This can be referred to as *user accessibility*.
- Because search engines tend to index only the text content that is in your web pages, web sites that are accessible to disabled users are also accessible to search engines. This can make your site easier to find in search engines.

Figure 1-14   Cross-browser compatibility and user accessibility

Two skills for reviewing web pages

You probably already have the skills that are presented in the next two figures. But in case you don't, here's how to access a web page and display its source code.

How to access a web page

One way to access a web page on the Internet is to enter a *uniform resource locator* (*URL*) into the address bar of your browser. The other is to click on a link on a web page that requests another page.

In figure 1-15, you can see the four components of a URL for an Internet page. In most cases, the protocol is HTTP. If you omit the protocol, the browser uses HTTP as the default.

The domain name identifies the web server that the HTTP request will be sent to. The web browser uses this name to look up the address of the web server for the domain. Although you can't omit the domain name, most web sites let you omit "www." from the domain name.

The third component is the path where the file resides on the server. The path lists the folders that contain the file. A forward slash is used to separate names in the path and to represent the server's top-level folder at the beginning of the path. In the example in this figure, the path is "/books/". If you omit the path, you must also omit the file name. Then, the web server will return the web site's home page.

The last component is the name of the file. In this figure, the file is named index.htm. If you omit the file name, the web server will search for a default document in the path you specify. Depending on the web server, this file will be named Default.htm, index.html, or some other variation.

File and folder names should only contain lowercase letters, numbers, the period, and the underscore character. Lowercase letters are recommended because on some web servers, the names in the path may be case sensitive. If a URL contains a folder named "Images", but the folder on the server is actually named "images", the web server will report that it cannot find the file.

To access a web page on an intranet or your own computer, you can enter just the path and file name in the address bar of your browser. If, for example, you want to access the application that's illustrated in figure 1-11 from your own computer on a Windows system, you can enter this path:

```
C:\murach\javascript\book_apps\chapter_01\sales_tax\sales_tax.html
```

If the file is stored on an intranet server, you can enter a similar path with the appropriate letter for the disk drive.

In most cases, though, it's easier to use the File→Open command of your browser to open a web page. Or, if you're using Windows, you can find the file in the Windows Explorer and double-click on its file name.

A web page with links to other web pages

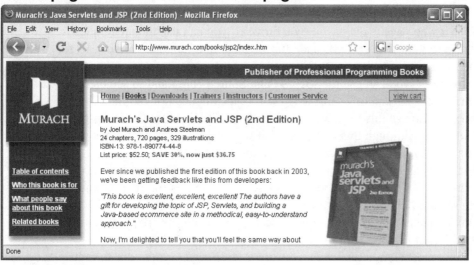

The components of an HTTP URL

What happens if you omit parts of a URL

- If you omit the protocol, the default of http:// will be used.
- If you omit the filename, the default document name for the web server will be used. This is typically either index.html or Default.htm.
- If you omit the path, you must also omit the filename. Then, the home page for the site will be requested.

Two ways to access a web page on the Internet

- Type the URL of a web page into the browser's address bar.
- Click on a link in the current web page to load the next web page.

Three ways to access a web page on an intranet or on your own computer

- Type the complete path and filename into the browser's address bar.
- Use the File→Open command.
- If you're using Windows, find the file in the Windows Explorer and double-click on it.

Description

- A *uniform resource locator* (URL) contains the protocol to be used, the domain name of the web site, the path to the web page, and the file name of the web page.

Figure 1-15   How to access a web page

How to view the source code for a web page

When a web page is displayed by a browser, you can use the techniques in figure 1-16 to view the XHTML code for the page in a separate window. If, for example, you open a web page that's stored on your own computer in the Firefox browser, you can use the View→Page Source command to see the XHTML code. This can be useful when you're testing an application.

You can also use this technique to view the XHTML source code for pages on the Internet. Although this can be a good way to learn how other sites work, there are two limitations that you should be aware of.

First, you can only see the JavaScript code for a page if the code is embedded in the XHTML when you view the source code. In this figure, for example, you can see the XHTML, but the JavaScript is in an external file named sales_tax.js. Then, to view the source code for the JavaScript file, you have to type the URL of the JavaScript file into the web browser's address bar.

Second, most commercial web sites use a JavaScript compressor to reduce file size and make downloads faster. This also makes the JavaScript code nearly impossible for you to read and understand.

If you compress your own JavaScript code, you should test the compressed code in as many browsers as possible. You should also keep a separate uncompressed copy of the source code so you can update your application as you add features and fix errors.

The source code for the Sales Tax application in Mozilla Firefox

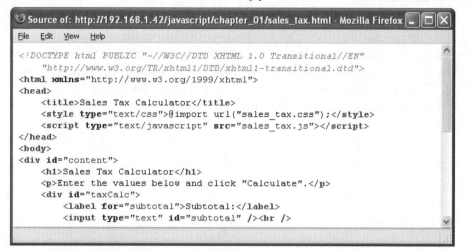

How to view the source code for a page in Mozilla Firefox

- Use the View→Page Source command.

How to view the source code for a page in Internet Explorer

- Use the View→Source command.

Two web sites that you can use to compress JavaScript code

- http://javascriptcompressor.com
- http://creativyst.com/Prod/3

Description

- When you view the source code for a web page in a web browser, the XHTML code is opened in a separate window.
- If the JavaScript code is embedded in the XHTML code, you can also see the JavaScript code. But if the JavaScript code is stored in a separate file, you have to open the file by typing its URL into the web browser.
- Many web sites use a JavaScript compressor to reduce the size of the JavaScript file. This also makes it more difficult to read and understand the code. If you use a compressor, be sure to test the compressed code in several browsers and to keep an uncompressed copy for yourself.

Figure 1-16   How to view the source code for a web page

Perspective

Now that you understand how web applications make use of the core web technologies, you're ready to learn how to develop JavaScript applications. In the next chapter, you're going to learn how to code a simple JavaScript application like the Sales Tax application. Then, in chapter 3, you'll learn how to use the features of a web browser to test and debug an application.

Terms

World Wide Web
Internet
client-server architecture
client
server
web server
web browser
network
network interface card (NIC)
router
local area network (LAN)
intranet
wide area network (WAN)
Internet service provider (ISP)
Internet exchange point (IXP)
static web page
HTTP request
hypertext transport protocol (HTTP)
HTTP response
TCP/IP
dynamic web page
application server
database server
web application
application mapping
round trip
server-side processing
client-side processing
JavaScript
JavaScript engine
extensible hypertext markup language
 (XHTML)
DOCTYPE declaration

XHTML element
opening tag
closing tag
attribute
XHTML document
cascading style sheets (CSS)
external style sheet
embedded style sheet
rule set
selector
declarative block
declaration
rule
document object model (DOM)
node
element node
text node
Dynamic HTML (DHTML)
DOM scripting
event-driven programming
event
event handler
progressive enhancement
rich Internet application (RIA)
asynchronous JavaScript and XML
 (AJAX)
XMLHttpRequest object
extensible markup language (XML)
JavaScript object notation (JSON)
cross-browser compatibility
user accessibility
uniform resource locator (URL)

Before you do the exercises for this book...

Before you do the exercises for this book, you should download and install the Mozilla Firefox browser because it is the best browser for testing and debugging JavaScript applications. You should also download and install the applications for this book. The procedures for installing the software and applications for this book are described in appendix A.

Exercise 1-1   Run the Sales Tax application

In this exercise, you'll run the Sales Tax application that's described in this chapter. You'll also use your browser to view its source code.

1. Start the Firefox browser.
2. Use the File→Open command to open the file named sales_tax.html in the chapter_01/sales_tax folder. This is the HTML file for the Sales Tax application. If you installed the book applications as described in appendix A, the path to that file on a Windows system is:

   `C:\murach\javascript\book_apps\chapter_01\sales_tax\sales_tax.html`
3. When the page is loaded, notice the path that's stored in the address bar.
4. Enter valid numeric values in the two input boxes and click the Calculate button. That should display valid results in the third and fourth text boxes.
5. Enter invalid values like xx and yy in the two input boxes and click the Calculate button. Then, respond to the first message box by entering valid data and clicking the Calculate button again. Do the same for the next message box that's displayed so valid results are displayed.
6. Use the View→Page Source command to view the source code for this application. Note that the JavaScript code is stored in a separate file.
7. Change the URL in the address bar so it points to the JavaScript file instead of the HTML file. Then, view the source code.
8. Click the Back button to return to the application interface, and click the Forward button to return to the JavaScript code.

Exercise 1-2   Review other book applications

In this exercise, you'll review some of the book applications that you'll learn how to write as you progress through this book.

1. Use Firefox to open the file named application_examples.html in the chapter_01 folder. This web page provides links to some of the applications that are presented in the other chapters in this book. The text for each link gives the chapter number, the name of the application, and the JavaScript features that it uses in parentheses. If you review these applications, you'll get an idea of how much you'll be able to do when you complete this book. After you review each application, click on the Back button to return to the links.

2. Click on the first link and run the application to see how it works. That's the application that you'll learn how to write in the next chapter.

3. Click the link for the chapter 12 application. This application provides complete, client-side data validation for a variety of entries.

4. Click the link for the chapter 13 application. This application uses basic DOM scripting to present a slide show.

5. Click the link for the chapter 18 application. This application presents a carousel of slides that you can slow down or reverse by using the mouse.

6. If you want to review any of the other applications, do that now. When you're through, close the applications.

Exercise 1-3   Visit some Internet web sites

In this exercise, you'll visit some Internet web sites and view the source code for those sites.

Visit the Mozilla web site

1. Use Firefox to go to the Mozilla home page: www.mozilla.com. Then, view the source code for the home page.

2. Scroll down the source code and note that this page uses several external JavaScript files in the head section as well as several embedded scripts in the body section.

Visit other web sites

3. Experiment with other sites to see what you find. At each site, view the source code to see whether JavaScript code is used.

Exercise 1-4   Visit a text-only web site

In this exercise, you'll visit the text-only web site for J. K. Rowling to see how accessible a site like this is for the visually impaired.

1. Use Google to search for and access the text-only web site for J. K. Rowling. Or, enter the URL shown in figure 1-14 to access the site.

2. Navigate the site by clicking on links.

3. View the source code for this site.

2

How to code a JavaScript application

In this chapter, you'll learn how to code simple JavaScript applications like the Sales Tax application in the last chapter. That will get you off to a fast start and give you the perspective you need for learning rapidly in subsequent chapters.

If you haven't done much programming, this chapter will move quickly for you. But if you take it slow and do the exercises, you should master all of the skills. When you're finished, you'll be able to write significant JavaScript applications of your own.

How to edit and test your web pages **44**
How to edit a web page with Notepad++ 44
How to test a web page 46
How to display error messages in Firefox 48

Basic JavaScript skills **50**
How to include JavaScript with the script tag 50
How to code JavaScript statements 52
How to create identifiers 54
The primitive data types of JavaScript 56
How to code numeric and string expressions 58
How to declare variables and assign values to them 60

How to use objects in JavaScript **62**
An introduction to objects, properties and methods 62
How to use the window and document objects 64
How to use the Number, String, and Date objects 66
How to get and display data with a Textbox object 68

How to code control statements **70**
How to code conditional expressions 70
How to code if statements 72
How to code while and for statements 74

How to create and use functions **76**
How to create and call a function 76
How to code an event handler 78

The Future Value application **80**
The XHTML code 80
The JavaScript code 82

Perspective **84**

How to edit and test your web pages

Before you can create a JavaScript application, you need to know how to edit and test a web page. To get you started, this topic provides the basic skills that you'll need. Then, in chapter 3, you'll learn more about testing and debugging.

How to edit a web page with Notepad++

Although you can use any text editor to enter and edit XHTML, CSS, and JavaScript files, using a better editor can speed development time and help reduce coding errors. Some features to look for in a text editor are syntax highlighting, auto-completion, and FTP access.

If you're using Windows, we recommend that you use Notepad++ as your editor because it provides all of these features. In addition to Notepad++, though, there are many other free and commercial text editors. For instance, Adobe Dreamweaver and Microsoft Expression Web Designer are two popular commercial editors. For the purposes of this book, however, Notepad++ provides all of the features that you'll need.

If you're a Mac OS user, we recommend that you use TextWrangler as your editor. This is a free editor that provides syntax highlighting and FTP access, although it doesn't provide auto-completion. Here again, though, you have other choices like commercial editors that do provide auto-completion. Three that do are BBEdit (the commercial version of TextWrangler), TextMate, and Dreamweaver.

To illustrate the use of a text editor for web pages, figure 2-1 shows Notepad++ as it's being used to edit a JavaScript file. As you can see, this editor provides tabs so you can edit more than one file at the same time. It color codes the syntax of the statements to reflect different coding elements. And its auto-completion feature helps you complete HTML, CSS, or JavaScript entries. If you experiment with Notepad++, you'll find that it has many other capabilities that this brief summary doesn't present.

Before you start using Notepad++, you should take the time to turn on the auto-completion feature. You will also want to change the style for comments because the default style is too small. These skills are summarized in this figure.

Then, when you start a new file, you should let Notepad++ know what language you're working with. To do that, you can either save the file with the .html, .css, or .js extension, or you can use the Language menu to select the language. Once you do that, this editor uses the appropriate color coding and auto-completion lists.

One feature not shown in this figure is how to access the files on an FTP server with Notepad++. To find out how to do that, you can search the Internet for "Notepad++ FTP".

Notepad++ with six tabs open and an auto-completion list displayed

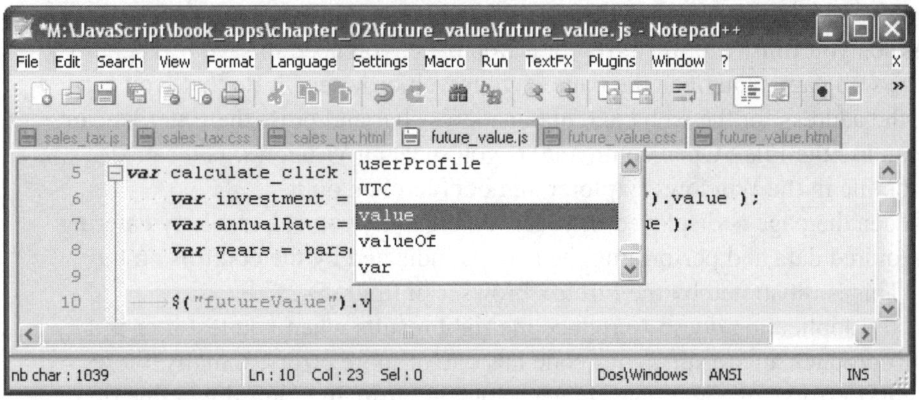

How to open, save, close, and start files

- To open a file, use the File→Open command. Or, right-click on the file in the Windows Explorer and select the Edit with Notepad++ command. The file is opened in a new tab.

- To save or close a file, select the tab that it's in and use the File→Save or File→Close command. Or right-click on the tab, and select the appropriate command.

- To start a new file in a new tab, use the File→New command.

How to change the style for comments

- Start the Settings→Styler Configurator command, and select JavaScript in the language list and COMMENT in the style list. Then, change the font name and font size in the drop-down lists to the blank entries at the top of the lists.

- Repeat this for COMMENTLINE and COMMENTDOC for the JavaScript language, for COMMENT for the HTML language, and for COMMENT for the CSS language.

How to use the auto-completion feature

- To enable auto completion, use the Settings→Preferences command, click the Backup/Auto-completion tab, and check the "Enable Auto-completion on each input" box.

- The auto-completion feature displays a list of terms that start with what you've typed. To insert one of those terms, double-click on it or use the arrows keys to highlight it and press the Tab key. To show the auto-completion list at any time, press Ctrl+Space.

How to let Notepad++ know which language you're working with

- Notepad++ provides color coding for each of the languages that you'll be using: HTML, CSS, and JavaScript. For a new file, you can use the Language menu to select the language that you're using. Or, you can save the file with the appropriate extension.

Figure 2-1   How to edit a web page with Notepad++

How to test a web page

When you finish editing a file for a web page, you need to save it. Then, to test the web page, you open the page in your web browser. To do that, you can enter the address for the web page in the address bar and press the Enter key, or you can use the File→Open command. If you're using Windows, you can also find the file in the Windows Explorer and double-click on it.

When the page is displayed in your web browser, you can test it by entering any required data and performing the actions indicated by the controls on the page. This is illustrated by the Firefox browser in figure 2-2.

If the application doesn't produce the right results when you test it or if it doesn't produce any results, your code has one or more errors. Usually, these are syntax errors but sometimes they are logical errors like omitting a line of required code. Either way, you need to find the errors.

When you find the errors, you need to edit the file to fix the errors and save the file. Then, to test the application again, you can return to the web browser and click the Reload or Refresh button. This reloads the edited file. At that point, you can test the application to see whether the problems have been fixed.

For some applications, though, clicking the Reload or Refresh button won't clear the browser memory completely so your changes won't work. In that case, you may need to close the browser window and open the application again.

To help you find the errors in simple applications, you can use the Error Console of Mozilla Firefox as shown in the next figure. Then, in the next chapter, you'll learn how your browser can help you find errors in more complex applications.

The Sales Tax application in the Firefox browser

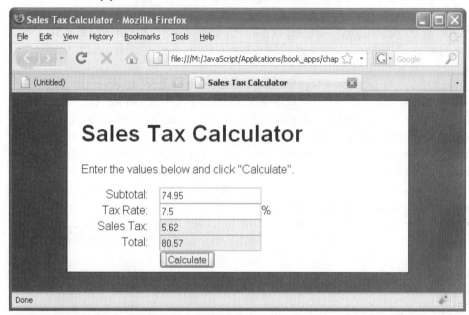

How to test a web page for the first time

- Open the web page in your browser using any of the techniques in figure 1-15 of the last chapter. Then, enter the required input data, and run the application.

How to retest a web page after you change the source code

- To reload the edited file for the page, click the Reload or Refresh button. Then, run the application.
- Sometimes, clicking the Reload or Refresh button won't clear the browser memory completely so your changes won't work correctly. In that case, you may need to close the browser window and reopen the application.

What to do if the application doesn't do anything when you test it

- If the application doesn't do anything when you test it, it either has syntax errors or other types of coding errors.
- In the next figure, you'll learn how to use Firefox to display error messages for syntax errors. That should be all you need for fixing simple programs like the ones you'll be able to write when you complete this chapter.

Description

- This chapter shows how to write JavaScript applications, and the next chapter shows you how to test and debug them.

Figure 2-2   How to test a web page

How to display error messages in Firefox

When you open a JavaScript application that has errors, the interface will still be displayed. When you try to use the application, however, it won't do anything because of the errors.

To see the error messages that Firefox produces, you have to open the Error Console window as described in figure 2-3. Here, the console shows the first error that's detected when the Sales Tax application is run with an error in it. In this case, the arrow under the message points to the character in the line that caused the error. In this case, the mistake is that a leading double quotation mark is matched by a single quotation mark, which is invalid.

To display the source code for the JavaScript file, you can click on the link in the error message. That opens the source code in a separate window with the error highlighted. You can't use that window to fix the code, though. Instead, you need to use your editor to fix and save the code and then reload the application in Firefox.

Often, the error messages are not as clear as in this example. Instead, an error in one line will be reported as an error somewhere else. Then, you start by looking for the error in the line indicated in the error message, but work your way to related portions of code until you find the error.

The buttons at the top of the Error Console let you select which types of messages you want displayed. If you have several pages open in tabs, all of their messages, warnings, and errors will be displayed in the same Error Console window. Then, you can show just the errors by clicking the Errors tab. You can also remove all messages from the Error Console by clicking the Clear button. Often, you will clear the Error Console after you've made changes to your code but before you reload your application.

The Firefox Error Console with an error displayed

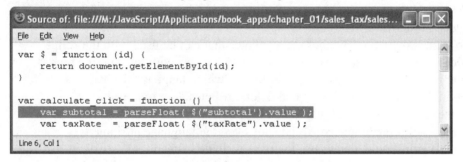

The source code that's displayed when you click on the link

How to display the Error Console and source code

- To display the Error Console, use the Tools→Error Console command or press Ctrl+Shift+J.

- To display the source code with the error highlighted, click on the link in the Error Console.

Description

- The Error Console in Firefox is used to display errors, warnings, and messages generated by web pages. That includes messages caused by errors in JavaScript code.

- The buttons at the top of the Error Console let you display all errors, just fatal errors, just warnings, or just messages. The Clear button removes all errors from the console.

- If you click the link to the file in the Error Console, Firefox will display the code and highlight the line at which the error occurred. You will not, however, be able to edit the file.

Figure 2-3   How to display error messages in Firefox

Basic JavaScript skills

Now that you know how to edit and test an application, you're ready to learn how to write the JavaScript code. You'll start with the basics.

How to include JavaScript with the script tag

In the last chapter, you saw JavaScript that was embedded in an XHTML file. You also saw an application that used one file for the XHTML, one for the CSS, and one for the JavaScript code. Now, figure 2-4 shows you how to use the XHTML <script> tag to include JavaScript code that's in an external file or embedded in the XHTML.

To start, this figure describes the attributes that can be used with the script tag. Since it is possible to use other scripting languages with this tag, the type attribute is required so the web browser knows which language the script is written in. In contrast, the charset and defer attributes are rarely used.

In the code for older web pages, the language attribute was often used to identify the scripting language. Today, however, the language attribute is obsolete so you should always use the type attribute instead.

In the examples in this figure, you can see how the script tag is used for external files and embedded scripts. In the first example, the src attribute is used to specify an external file named sales_tax.js. This assumes that the external file is in the same folder as the XHTML page. If it isn't, you can code the path to the file along with the file name.

In the second example, a script tag with JavaScript code is embedded in the head of an XHTML document. JavaScript code here is typically used to define functions and event handlers and to initialize any global variables.

In the third example, a script is embedded in the body of an HTML document. When the script is in the body, the script tag is replaced by the output of the JavaScript code when the application is loaded.

You can also load an external JavaScript file from a web server other than yours. This is illustrated by the fourth example. In this case, you provide the name of the web server including the http:// prefix. If you omit the http:// prefix, the browser will treat the server name as a folder name on your server.

In the last example, you can see how the <noscript> tag is used. It can be coded anywhere, but it is usually used after a script tag in the body of a document. Then, if JavaScript is disabled, the content of the noscript tag will be shown. But if JavaScript is enabled for the browser, the script tag is replaced by the output of the JavaScript code and the noscript tag is ignored. This way some output will be displayed whether JavaScript is enabled or not.

Attributes of the script tag

Attribute	Description
type	A required attribute that identifies the scripting language. For JavaScript, use type="text/javascript".
src	Specifies the location of an external file. This file will run as if it were typed into the script tag at this point in the web document.
charset	Specifies the character encoding of the script. If omitted, the character encoding of the script will be the same as the character encoding of the document.
defer	Specifies that the script doesn't generate any document content. Then, the web browser processes the script after the rest of the page has been loaded. Coded as defer="defer".

How to load JavaScript from an external file

```
<script type="text/javascript" src="sales_tax.js"></script>
```

How to embed JavaScript in the head of an HTML document

```
<head>
    ...
    <script type="text/javascript">
        var $ = function (id) { return document.getElementById(id); }
    </script>
    ...
</head>
```

How to embed JavaScript in the body of an HTML document

```
<p>&copy;
    <script type="text/javascript">
        var today = new Date();
        document.writeln( today.getFullYear() ); </script>
Mike's Bait and Tackle Shop</p>
```

How to load a script from a different web server

```
<script type="text/javascript"
    src="http://www.google-analytics.com/urchin.js">
</script>
```

How to use the noscript tag in the body of an HTML document

```
<script type="text/javascript">
    var today = new Date();
    document.writeln( today.getFullYear() );
</script>
<noscript>2009</noscript>
```

Description

- You can have multiple <script> tags in a web page. They are executed in the order that they appear in the document, unless the defer attribute has been used.

- In the body of a document, the <script> tag is replaced by the output of the code. The <noscript> tag is used to display content when JavaScript is disabled or not available.

- The XHTML document must be valid before and after all scripts have been executed.

Figure 2-4   How to include JavaScript with the script tag

How to code JavaScript statements

The *syntax* of JavaScript refers to the rules that you must follow as you code JavaScript *statements*. If you don't adhere to one or more of these rules, your web browser won't be able to interpret and execute your statements. These rules are summarized in figure 2-5.

The first syntax rule is that JavaScript is case-sensitive. This means that uppercase and lowercase letters are treated as different letters. For example, the names salestax and salesTax are treated as different words.

The second syntax rule is that JavaScript statements must end with a semicolon. If you don't end each statement with a semicolon, JavaScript won't be able to tell where one statement ends and the next one begins.

The third syntax rule is that JavaScript ignores extra whitespace in statements. Whitespace includes spaces, tabs, and new line characters. This lets you break long statements into multiple lines so they're easier to read. As far as JavaScript is concerned, your entire program could be written on one line and it would still work. However, that would result in code that would be extremely difficult for humans to read.

The last two syntax rules are that single-line comments can be added with two forward slashes and multi-line comments can be added between the /* and */ characters. *Comments* let you add descriptive notes to your code that are ignored by the JavaScript engine. Later on, these comments can help you or someone else understand the code if it needs to be updated.

Although semicolons are required at the end of a statement, JavaScript will try to help you out if you forget one. For instance, JavaScript will automatically add a semicolon at the end of a line if doing so will create a valid statement. Unfortunately, this usually causes more problems than it solves.

The problem usually occurs when you split a long statement over two lines in the wrong location. The result is that one statement is treated as two shorter statements that produce the wrong results. However, you can avoid this type of problem by following the guidelines in this figure for splitting a long statement.

This problem is illustrated by the two examples in this figure. In the first one, JavaScript will add a semicolon after the word *return*, which will cause an error. In the second one, because the statement is split after an assignment operator, JavaScript won't add a semicolon so the statement will work correctly.

The basic syntax rules for JavaScript

- JavaScript is case-sensitive.
- JavaScript statements end with a semicolon.
- JavaScript ignores extra whitespace in statements.
- Single-line comments begin with two forward slashes and continue until the end of the line.
- Multi-line comments begin with /* and end with */.

A single-line comment

```
nextYear = thisYear + 1; // Determine what the next year is
```

A multi-line comment

```
/* The following line determines what the
   next year is by adding 1 to the current year
*/
nextYear = thisYear + 1;
```

How to split a statement across multiple lines

- Split a statement after an arithmetic or relational operator such as +, -, *, /, =, ==, >, or <.
- Split a statement after an opening brace ({), bracket ([ ), or parenthesis.
- Split a statement after a closing brace (}).
- Do not split a statement after an identifier, a value, or the *return* keyword.
- Do not split a statement after a closing bracket ( ]) or parenthesis.

A split statement that results in an error

```
return
"Hello";
```

A split statement that works correctly

```
nextYear =
    thisYear + 1;
```

Description

- JavaScript has a syntax that's similar to the syntax of Java.
- JavaScript provides two forms of *comments*, which are ignored when the JavaScript is executed.
- In some cases, JavaScript will try to correct a missing semicolon by adding one at the end of a split line. This can cause errors. To prevent this, put a semicolon at the end of each statement, and follow the guidelines above for splitting a statement.

Figure 2-5   How to code JavaScript statements

How to create identifiers

Variables, functions, objects, properties, methods, and events must all have names so you can refer to them in your JavaScript code. An *identifier* is the name given to one of these components.

Figure 2-6 shows the rules for creating identifiers in JavaScript. Besides the first four rules, you can't use any of the JavaScript *reserved words* (also known as *keywords*) as an identifier. These are words that are reserved for use within the JavaScript language. You should also avoid using any of the JavaScript global properties or methods as identifiers. Although you can sometimes get away with this, it will lead to problems in some applications.

Besides the rules, you should give your identifiers meaningful names. That means that it should be easy to tell what an identifier refers to and easy to remember how to spell the name. To create names like that, you should avoid abbreviations. If, for example, you abbreviate the name for monthly investment as mon_inv, it will be hard to tell what it refers to and hard to remember how you spelled it. But if you spell it out as monthly_investment, both problems are solved.

Similarly, you should avoid abbreviations that are specific to one industry or field of study unless you are sure the abbreviation will be widely understood. For example, mpg is a common abbreviation for miles per gallon, but cpm could stand for any number of things and should be spelled out.

To create an identifier that has more than one word in it, most JavaScript programmers use a convention called *camel casing*. With this convention, the first letter of each word is uppercase except for the first word. For example, monthlyInvestment and taxRate are identifiers that use camel casing.

The alternative is to use underscore characters to separate the words in an identifier. For example, monthly_investment and tax_rate use this convention. If the standards in your shop specify one of these conventions, by all means use it. Otherwise, you can use either convention. In either case, though, be consistent.

Rules for creating identifiers in JavaScript

- Identifiers can only contain letters, numbers, the underscore, and the dollar sign.
- Identifiers can't start with a number.
- Identifiers are case-sensitive.
- Identifiers can be any length.
- Identifiers can't be the same as reserved words.
- Avoid using global properties and methods as identifiers. If you use one of them, you won't be able to use the global property or method that the identifier refers to.
- Avoid using names that are similar to reserved words, global properties, or global methods. For example, avoid using "Switch" since it is similar to "switch".

Reserved words in JavaScript (words for future use are italicized)

abstract	else	instanceof	switch
boolean	*enum*	*int*	*synchronized*
break	*export*	*interface*	this
byte	*extends*	*long*	throw
case	false	*native*	*throws*
catch	*final*	new	*transient*
char	finally	null	true
class	*float*	*package*	try
const	for	*private*	typeof
continue	function	*protected*	var
debugger	*goto*	*public*	void
default	if	return	*volatile*
delete	*implements*	*short*	while
do	*import*	*static*	with
double	in	*super*	

Global properties and methods in JavaScript

alert	focus	prompt
blur	getComputedStyle	resizeBy
clearInterval	Infinity	resizeTo
clearTimeout	isFinite	scroll
close	isNaN	scrollBy
confirm	moveBy	scrollTo
decodeURI	moveTo	setInterval
decodeURIComponents	NaN	setTimeout
encodeURI	open	undefined
encodeURIComponents	parseFloat	unescape
escape	parseInt	
eval	print	

Valid identifiers in JavaScript

subtotal	index_1	$
taxRate	calculate_click	$log

Description

- *Identifiers* are the names given to variables, functions, objects, properties, and methods.

Figure 2-6   How to create identifiers

The primitive data types of JavaScript

JavaScript provides for three *primitive data types*. The *number data type* is used to represent numerical data. The *string data type* is used to store character data. And the *Boolean data type* is used to store true and false values. This is summarized in figure 2-7.

The number data type can be used to represent either integers or decimal values. *Integers* are whole numbers, and *decimal values* are numbers that can have one or more decimal digits. The value of either data type can be coded with a preceding plus or minus sign. If the sign is omitted, the value is treated as a positive value. A decimal value can also include a decimal point and one or more digits to the right of the decimal point.

The value of a number data type can also include an *exponent*. If you're familiar with scientific notation, you know that this exponent indicates how many zeros should be included to the right or left of the decimal. Numbers that use this notation are called *floating-point numbers*. If you aren't familiar with this notation, you probably won't need to use it because you won't be coding applications that require it.

The number type can hold extremely large and small numbers so that is rarely an issue when you develop an application. For instance, the exponent of a number can indicate that the number should have 308 zeros to the left of the decimal point or 324 zeros to the right of the decimal point. However, if you try to store a number that is larger or smaller than the maximum and minimum values, which can happen if you divide a number by zero, the result will be stored as Infinity or -Infinity.

To represent string data, you code the *string* within single or double quotation marks (quotes). Note, however, that you must close the string with the same type of quotation mark that you used to start it. If you code two quotation marks in a row without even a space between them, the result is called an *empty string*, which can be used to represent a string with no data in it.

If you want to code a string that continues on a second line when it is displayed, you can use the \n *escape sequence*. As the example in this figure shows, this is equivalent to pressing the Enter key in the middle of a string. In chapter 7, you'll learn how to use some of the other escape sequences, but for now \n is the only one you need to know.

To represent Boolean data, you code either the word *true* or *false* with no quotation marks. As you will see, this data type can be used to represent data that is in one of two states such as yes/no, on/off, done/not done, or initialized/not initialized.

Examples of number values

```
15          // an integer
-21         // a negative integer
21.5        // a floating-point value
-124.82     // a negative floating-point value
-3.7e-9     // a floating-point value equivalent to -0.0000000037
```

The number data type

- The *number data type* is used to represent an integer or a decimal value.
- An *integer* is a whole number that can start with a positive or negative sign.
- A *floating-point value* consists of a positive or negative sign at the beginning, digits, an optional decimal point, optional decimal digits, and an optional exponent.
- An *exponent* consists of an upper or lowercase e, followed by a positive or negative sign and a whole number. The whole number must be between -324 and +308.
- If a result is stored in the number data type that is larger or smaller than the data type can store, it will be stored as the value Infinity or –Infinity.

Examples of string values

```
"JavaScript"    // a string with double quotes
'String Data'   // a string with single quotes
""              // an empty string
```

How the \n escape sequence can be used to start a new line in a string

```
"A valid variable name\ncannot start with a number."
// represents the string: A valid variable name
//                        cannot start with a number.
```

The string data type

- The *string data type* represents character (*string*) data. A string is surrounded by double quotes or single quotes. The string must start and end with the same type of quote mark.
- An *empty string* is a string that contains no characters. It is entered by typing two quotation marks with nothing between them.
- JavaScript provides for several *escape sequences* that can be used within strings. All escape sequences start with the backslash, and the \n escape sequence starts a new line.

The two Boolean values

```
true    // equivalent to true, yes, or on
false   // equivalent to false, no, or off
```

The Boolean data type

- The *Boolean data type* is used to represent a *Boolean value*. A Boolean value can be used to represent data that is in either of two states.

Description

- JavaScript provides for just three *primitive data types*. These data types are used for storing numbers, strings, and Boolean values.

Figure 2-7   The primitive data types of JavaScript

How to code numeric and string expressions

An *expression* can be as simple as a single value or it can be a series of operations that result in a single value. In figure 2-8, you can see the operators for coding both numeric and string expressions. If you've programmed in another language, these are probably similar to what you've been using. In particular, the first four *arithmetic operators* are common to most programming languages.

Most modern languages also have a modulus, or mod, operator that calculates the remainder when the left value is divided by the right value. In the example for this operator, 13 % 4 means the remainder of 13 / 4. Then, since 13 / 4 is 3 with a remainder of 1, 1 is the result of the expression.

One of the common uses of the mod operator is determining if a number is even or odd. For instance, any number % 2 will return 0 if the number is even and 1 if the number is odd. Another use is determining if a year is a leap year. If, for example, year % 4 returns 0, then year is divisible by 4.

In contrast to the first five operators in this figure, the increment and decrement operators add or subtract one from a variable. If you aren't already familiar with these operators, you'll see them illustrated later in this book.

When an expression includes two or more operators, the *order of precedence* determines which operators are applied first. This order is summarized in the table in this figure. For instance, all multiplication and division operations are done from left to right before any addition and subtraction operations are done.

To override this order, though, you can use parentheses. Then, the expressions in the innermost sets of parentheses are done first, followed by the expressions in the next sets of parentheses, and so on. This is typical of all programming languages, and the examples in this figure show how this works.

The one operator that you can use with strings is the *concatenation* operator. This operator joins two strings with no additional characters between them.

Since the plus sign is used for both addition and concatenation, JavaScript has to look at the data type of the values to determine whether it should add or concatenate the values. If both values are numbers, JavaScript adds them together. If both values are strings, JavaScript concatenates them. And if one value is a string and the other is a number, JavaScript converts the number to a string and then concatenates the two values.

Common arithmetic operators

Operator	Description	Example	Result
+	Addition	5 + 7	12
-	Subtraction	5 - 12	-7
*	Multiplication	6 * 7	42
/	Division	13 / 4	3.25
%	Modulus	13 % 4	1
++	Increment	counter++	adds 1 to counter
—	Decrement	counter--	subtracts 1 from counter

The order of precedence for arithmetic expressions

Order	Operators	Direction	Description
1	++	Left to right	Increment operator
2	--	Left to right	Decrement operator
3	* / %	Left to right	Multiplication, division, modulus
4	+ -	Left to right	Addition, subtraction

Examples of precedence and the use of parentheses

```
3 + 4 * 5      // Result is 23 since the multiplication is done first
(3 + 4) * 5    // Result is 35 since the addition is done first

13 % 4 + 9     // Result is 10 since the modulus is done first
13 % (4 + 9)   // Result is 0  since the addition is done first
```

The concatenation operator for strings

Operator	Description	Example	Result
+	Concatenation	"Ray " + "Harris"	"Ray Harris"
		"Months: " + 120	"Months: 120"

Description

- To code an *arithmetic expression*, you can use the *arithmetic operators* to operate on two or more values.
- An arithmetic expression is evaluated based on the *order of precedence* of the operators.
- To override the order of precedence, you can use parentheses.
- To *concatenate* two or more strings, you can use the + operator.
- Since the plus sign can be used for both numeric and string expressions, JavaScript looks at the data types to determine which operation to perform. If both values are numbers, JavaScript adds. If both values are strings, JavaScript concatenates. If one value is a number and one is a string, JavaScript converts the number to a string and concatenates.

Figure 2-8   How to code numeric and string expressions

How to declare variables and assign values to them

A *variable* stores a value that can change as the program executes. When you code a JavaScript application, you frequently declare variables and assign values to them. Figure 2-9 shows how to do both of these tasks.

To *declare* a variable in JavaScript, code the *var* (for variable) keyword followed by the identifier (or name) that you want to use for the variable. To declare more than one variable in a single statement, you code *var* followed by the variable names separated by commas. This is illustrated by the first group of examples in this figure.

To assign a value to a variable, you code an *assignment statement*. This type of statement consists of a variable name, an *assignment operator*, and an expression. Here, the expression can be a *numeric literal* like 74.95, a variable name like subtotal, an arithmetic expression, a *string literal* like "Harris", or a string expression.

The first assignment operator in the table in this figure assigns the value of the expression on the right of the equals sign to the variable on the left. The other five operators are called *compound assignment operators*. They modify the variable on the left by the value of the expression on the right. When you use these operators, the variable must already exist and have a value assigned to it.

To declare a variable and assign a numeric value to it, you code the keyword *var* followed by the assignment statement. This is illustrated by the second group of examples in this figure. The first one declares a variable named subtotal and assigns the literal value 74.95 to it. The second one declares a variable named salesTax and assigns the value of the subtotal variable to it after it has been multipled by .1. The third statement assigns the value false to a Boolean variable named isValid. And the fourth statement shows that you can declare and assign values to two or more variables with a single statement. Note here, though, that the *var* keyword is only coded once.

The last two statements in this group show how you can declare and assign values to string variables. Here, the fifth statement declares and assigns values to two variables named firstName and lastName. Then, the sixth statement concatenates lastName, a literal that consists of a comma and a space, and firstName, and places the result in a new variable named fullName.

The next group of examples illustrates the use of compound assignment statements. Here, the first statement assigns a value of 24.50 to a variable named subtotal, and the second statement uses the += operator to add a value of 75.50 to the value already in subtotal. This means that subtotal contains 100.00. Then, the third statement uses the *= operator to multiply the value in subtotal by .9. As a result, subtotal has a value of 90.

The rest of the statements in this group work with string variables and string expressions. If you study them, you can see that they're similar to numeric assignment statements. However, the += operator is the only compound assignment operator that you can use with strings. The last two statements in this group show that if an expression contains both string and numeric values, the numeric values are converted to strings before the expression is evaluated.

How to declare variables without assigning values to them

```
var subtotal;                    // declares a variable named subtotal
var lastName, state, zipCode;    // declares three variables
```

The assignment operators

Operator	Description
`=`	Assigns the result of the expression to the variable.
`+=`	Adds the result of the expression to the variable.
`-=`	Subtracts the result of the expression from the variable.
`*=`	Multiplies the variable by the result of the expression.
`/=`	Divides the variable by the result of the expression.
`%=`	Stores the modulus of the variable and the result of the expression in the variable.

How to declare variables and assign values to them

```
var subtotal = 74.95;                   // subtotal is 74.95
var salesTax = subtotal * .1;           // salesTax is 7.495
var isValid = false;                    // Boolean value is false
var zipCode = "93711", state = "CA";    // one statement with two assignments
var firstName = "Ray", lastName = "Harris"; // assigns two string values
var fullName = lastName + ", " + firstName; // fullName is "Harris, Ray"
```

How to code compound assignment statements

```
var subtotal = 24.50;
subtotal += 75.50;              // subtotal is 100
subtotal *= .9;                 // subtotal is 90 (100 * .9)
var firstName = "Ray", lastName = "Harris";
var fullName = lastName;        // fullName is "Harris"
fullName += ", ";               // fullName is "Harris, "
fullName += firstName;          // fullName is "Harris, Ray"
var months = 120, message = "Months: ";
message += months;              // message is "Months: 120"
```

Description

- A *variable* stores a value that can change as the program executes.

- To *declare* a variable, code the keyword *var* and a variable name. To declare more than one variable in a single statement, code *var* and the variable names separated by commas.

- To assign a value to a variable, you use an *assignment statement* that consists of the variable name, an *assignment operator*, and an expression. When appropriate, you can declare a variable and assign a value to it in a single statement.

- Within an expression, a *string literal* is enclosed in quotation marks. A *numeric literal* is a valid integer or number that isn't enclosed in quotation marks.

- When the expression in an assignment statement contains both strings and numbers, the numbers are converted to strings before the expression is evaluated.

Figure 2-9   How to declare variables and assign values to them

How to use objects in JavaScript

To use JavaScript effectively, you need to know how to use the objects that are provided by JavaScript and the web browser. So that's what you'll be introduced to next.

An introduction to objects, properties, and methods

An *object* is a collection of related variables and functions. A variable stored in an object is known as a *property*, and a function stored in an object is known as a *method*. In figure 2-10, you can learn the basic syntax for working with objects, properties, and methods. Then, the next three figures show you how to work with specific objects, properties, and methods.

The syntax at the top of this figure summarizes the code for creating an instance of an object. Here, the italicized words are the ones that vary. The words and characters that aren't italicized are the ones that are always the same. This notation is used in the syntax summaries throughout this book.

To create an object, then, you code the keyword *new*, the name of the object type, and a set of parentheses. This calls the object's *constructor function*, which creates the object and initializes its properties. The resulting object is called an *instance* of the object type. You can then use the object's properties and methods.

The two examples after the syntax show how this syntax is applied. The first one creates a Date object and stores it in a variable named today. The second one creates an Array object and stores it in a variable named states. Here, Date and Array are specific types of objects that are supported by JavaScript.

To access a property of an object, you code the name of the object followed by the *dot operator* (period) and the name of the property. This is illustrated by the second syntax summary and set of examples. Here, the first statement gets the screenX property of the window object, and the second statement assigns a URL to the location property of the window object. Since a property is a variable, you can usually use it in an expression or assign a value to it. However, some properties of JavaScript and browser objects are read-only so you can't assign values to them.

To *call* a method of an object, you code the name of the object, the dot operator, the name of the method, and a set of parentheses that contains any required *parameters* (which are also referred to as *arguments*). This is illustrated by the third set of examples. Here, the first statement calls the getElementById method of the document object and passes one parameter to it. Similarly, the second statement calls the writeln method of the document object and passes one parameter to it. In this case, though, the parameter is the value returned by the getFullYear method of the today object.

Often, when you use JavaScript, it's best to nest the use of one object within another. This is called *object chaining*, and this is illustrated by the fourth set of examples. Here, the first statement uses the getElementById method of the document object to get the object for an XHTML element with "rate" at its id,

The syntax for creating a new object

```
new ObjectType()
```

Examples that create new objects and store them in variables

```
var today = new Date();     // creates a Date object named today
var states = new Array();   // creates an Array object named states
```

The syntax for accessing a property of an object

```
objectName.propertyName
```

Examples that access a property of an object

```
alert(window.screenX); // Displays the width of the user's screen
window.location = "http://www.murach.com"; // Loads the murach.com home page
```

The syntax for calling a method of an object

```
objectName.methodName(parameters)
```

Examples that call a method of an object

```
// Stores a reference to the XHTML element with the id "rate"
var rateTextbox = document.getElementById("rate");
// Gets the full year and writes it to the web page
document.writeln( today.getFullYear() );
```

Examples of object chaining

```
// Uses the alert method to display the value property
// of the DOM object that is returned by the getElementById method.
alert( document.getElementById("rate").value );
// Uses the alert method to display the location property
// of the current page after it has been converted to lowercase letters
// by the toLowerCase method.
alert( window.location.toLowerCase() );
```

Description

- An *object* has *properties* that represent attributes like the width of a window or the value that's in an XHTML element.

- An object also has *methods* that do functions that are related to the object.

- When you *call* a method, you may need to pass one or more *parameters* (or *arguments*) to it by coding them within the parentheses after the method name. If the method requires more than one parameter, you must separate them with commas.

- *Object chaining* lets you access the properties or methods of objects that are nested inside other objects.

- Often, an object is stored in the property of another object or returned by a method of another object.

Figure 2-10   An introduction to objects, properties, and methods

and then it gets the value property of that object. The second statement gets the location property of the window object, which is a string, and then uses the toLowerCase method of the string object to convert the location property to lowercase letters.

If this is confusing right now, you're going to see many more examples of the use of objects and object chaining in the rest of this chapter. So by the end of this chapter, you should become comfortable with the use of object chaining.

How to use the window and document objects

When you use JavaScript, the *global object* provides access to predefined properties and methods that are useful in JavaScript applications. In a web browser, the global object is the *window object*, and all named methods and properties that are not a part of another object are part of this global object.

In figure 2-11, you can learn how to use one property and four methods of the window object. Note that you can omit the object name and dot operator when referring to the properties and methods of the window object because it is the global object. In other words, window.alert and alert are both calls to the alert method of the window object.

As the table in this figure describes, you can use the alert method to display a dialog box that displays the value of the one parameter that's passed to it. Similarly, you can use the prompt method to display an input dialog box, but this method also returns the value that the user enters into the dialog box. In the examples, the first statement uses the alert method to display a string literal. The second statement uses the prompt method to get a value from the user and save it in a variable named userEntry.

In contrast, the parseInt and parseFloat methods are used to convert strings to numbers. The parseInt method converts a string to an integer, and the parseFloat method converts a string to a decimal value. Note in the examples that the parseInt method doesn't round the value. It just removes, or truncates, any decimal portion of the string value. Also, if the string can't be converted to a number, these two methods will return the value NaN.

In contrast to the window object, the *document object* is the highest object in the DOM structure. It represents the XHTML document, and you do need to code the object name (document) and the dot when you use one of its methods. The document object is also a property of the window object. As a result, each of the references to the document object could be coded as window.document instead of just document.

This figure shows how to use three of the document object methods. The first is the getElementById method. It requires one parameter that is the id for an element in the XHTML document. When it is executed, it returns an object that represents that XHTML element.

In contrast, the write and writeln methods can be used to write a string into the XHTML document, and these methods are typically used in the body of an XHTML document. Note, however, that if you call either of these methods *after* the XHTML document has been loaded into the browser, the web page will be completely replaced by the value passed to the method.

One property of the window object

Property	Description
`location`	The URL of the current web page. If you set this property, the browser will load the new page.

Common methods of the window object

Method	Description
`alert(message)`	Displays a dialog box with the string that's passed to it.
`prompt(message, default)`	Displays a dialog box with the string in the first parameter and a text box that contains the default value from the second parameter. When the user enters a value and clicks OK, the value is returned.
`parseInt(string)`	Converts the string that's passed to it to an integer data type. Returns NaN if the string can't be converted to a valid integer.
`parseFloat(string)`	Converts the string parameter to a numeric data type. Returns NaN if the string can't be converted to a valid number.

Examples that use the properties and methods of the window object

```
alert("Invalid entry.");                    // displays "Invalid entry."
var userEntry = prompt(errorMessage,100); // accepts user entry

parseInt("12345.67");       // returns the integer 12345
parseFloat("12345.67");     // returns the floating point value 12345.67
parseFloat("Ray Harris");   // returns NaN
```

Common methods of the document object

Method	Description
`getElementById(id)`	Gets the XHTML element that has the id that's passed to it and returns the element to the script.
`write(text)`	Writes the string that's passed to it to the document.
`writeln(text)`	Writes the string that's passed to it to the document and advances to a new line.

Examples that use methods of the document object

```
// gets the DOM object that represents the XHTML element with "rate"
// as its id and stores it in a variable named rateTextbox
var rateTextbox = document.getElementById("rate");

// writes the string in the message variable to the document
document.writeln(message);
```

Description

- The *window object* is the *global object* when JavaScript is used in a web browser. It provides the global and browser properties and methods.
- JavaScript lets you omit the object name and period when referring to the window object.
- The *document object* is the object that allows you to work with the DOM.

Figure 2-11   How to use the window and document objects

How to use the Number, String, and Date objects

When you store a numeric or string value in a variable, it is automatically converted to the corresponding object type by JavaScript. This lets you use the properties and methods of the object without having to explicitly create the object. In figure 2-12, you can learn how to use some of the common methods of the Number, String, and Date objects.

For the Number object, only the toFixed method is listed. It rounds the numeric value of the object to the number of decimal places passed to it by the parameter and then converts the value to a string. As the first two statements in the examples show, using this method doesn't change the value of the variable. It just returns a rounded value as a string.

The third statement in this group of examples shows how you can chain the toFixed method and the parseFloat method to round a value to a fixed value and then convert it back to a numeric value. This numeric value is then assigned to the variable so it replaces the original value.

For the String object, just three methods are listed. The first lets you extract a substring from a string. The second and third methods let you convert a string to all lowercase or all uppercase. Here again, none of these methods modify the original value in the variable. If you want to change the original value, you need to assign the modified value to the variable as illustrated by the fourth statement in the examples.

Because there isn't a primitive data type for dates, you need to create a Date object before you can use its methods. When you create a new Date object, it is initialized with the date and time it was created. This is the date and time on the user's computer, not on the web server. If the date and time on the user's computer is wrong, the Date object will be initialized incorrectly.

Once a Date object has been created, you can use the methods in this figure to work with it. Here, the toDateString method converts the date to a string. And the getFullYear method extracts just the four-digit year from the date. In the last example, the getMonth method returns the month number. Note, however, that the month numbers start with 0, not 1.

In chapter 7, you'll learn that there are many other methods that you can use with Number, String, and Date objects. However, the methods in this figure should be all that you'll need for your first JavaScript applications.

One method of the Number object

Method	Description
toFixed(*digits*)	Returns a string that contains the value of the object rounded to the number of decimal places in the parameter.

Examples

```
var balance = 2384.55678;        // creates a number object named balance
alert ( balance.toFixed(2) );    // displays 2384.56
                                 // balance is still 2384.55678
balance = parseFloat( balance.toFixed(2) );    // balance is now 2384.56
```

Methods of the String object

Method	Description
substr(*start, length*)	Returns a new string that contains part of the original string. This substring starts at the position in the first parameter and contains the number of characters in the second parameter. The positions in a string start with zero.
toLowerCase()	Returns a new string with the letters converted to lowercase.
toUpperCase()	Returns a new string with the letters converted to uppercase.

Examples

```
var guest = "Ray Harris";        // creates a string object named guest
alert ( guest.toUpperCase() );   // displays "RAY HARRIS"
alert ( guest.substr(0,3) );     // displays "Ray"
guest = guest.substr(4,6);       // guest is now "Harris"
```

Methods of the Date object

Method	Description
toDateString()	Returns a string with the formatted date.
getMonth()	Returns the month number from the date. The months are numbered starting with zero. January is 0 and December is 11.
getDate()	Returns the day of the month from the date.
getFullYear()	Returns the four-digit year from the date.

Examples

```
var today = new Date();          // creates a Date object named today
                                 // assume the current date is 09/20/2008
alert ( today.toDateString() );  // displays Sat Sep 20 2008
alert ( today.getFullYear() );   // displays 2008
alert ( today.getMonth() );      // displays 8, not 9, for September
```

Description

- When you declare a number or string variable, a Number or String object is created. Then, you can use the Number or String methods with the variable.

- To create a Date object, assign new Date() to a variable. Then, you can use the Date methods with the variable.

Figure 2-12   How to use the Number, String, and Date objects

How to get and display data with a Textbox object

The Textbox object is one of the DOM objects. It represents a text box in the web page that can be used to get input from the user or display output to the user. In figure 2-13, the first set of examples shows the XHTML for two text boxes that have "rate" and "salesTax" as the ids. As you can see, the disabled attribute for the salesTax text box is turned on. That prevents the user from typing in the text box.

The next examples show how to use the value property of a Textbox object to get the value from a text box and store it in a variable. First, the examples show how to do that in two statements. Then, the examples show how to do that in a single statement.

When you use two statements, the first statement uses the getElementById method of the document object to get a Textbox object. Here, this object is assigned to a variable named rateTextbox. Then, the second statement uses the value property of the Textbox object to get the value that has been entered into the text box. In this case, the second statement also uses the parseFloat method to convert the string that's returned by the value property to a decimal value. This decimal value is then stored in a variable named rate.

Unless you're going to use the Textbox object again, though, you don't need to use two statements to do this. Instead, you can use object chaining as shown by the one-statement example. Here, the statement uses the getElementById method to get the Textbox object, the value property to get the value of that object, and the ParseFloat method to convert the string that's returned to a decimal value.

The next example shows how you can change the disabled attribute of a text box from your JavaScript code. To do that, you set the disabled property to true or false. In this example, object chaining is used to access the disabled property of the XHTML element with "salesTax" as its id, and the value false is assigned to that property.

The next examples show how to assign values to text boxes so they are displayed by the browser. Here, the first statement assigns an empty string to a text box so it won't display anything. The second statement assigns the value of a variable named salesTax.

The last example in this figure shows how to use the focus method of a Textbox object. This method moves the cursor into the text box so the user can start typing in that text box. When an application is loaded, the cursor is commonly moved into the first input box on the page as a convenience for the user.

Common properties of the Textbox object

Property	Type	Description
value	String	The contents of the text box.
disabled	Boolean	Controls whether the text box is disabled.

Two XHTML <input> tags that create text boxes

```
<input type="text" id="rate" />
<input type="text" id="salesTax" disabled="disabled" />
```

How to use the value property to get the value in a text box

In two statements

```
// Store a reference to the text box
var rateTextbox = document.getElementById("rate");
// Get the value and convert it to a number
var rate = parseFloat( rateTextbox.value );
```

In one statement with object chaining

```
var rate = parseFloat(document.getElementById("rate").value);
```

How to use the disabled property to enable a text box

```
document.getElementById("salesTax").disabled = false;
```

How to use the value property to display a value in a text box

```
// Assign an empty string to a text box
document.getElementById("salesTax").value = "";
// Assign the value of a variable named salesTax to a text box
document.getElementById("salesTax").value = salesTax.toFixed(2);
```

One method of the Textbox object

Method	Returns	Description
focus()	Nothing	Moves the cursor into the text box.

How to use the focus method to move the cursor to a text box

```
document.getElementById("investment").focus();
```

Description

- When you use a text box to get numeric data that you're going to use in calculations, you need to use either the parseInt or parseFloat method to convert the string data to numeric data.
- To place the cursor in a text box, you use the focus method of the Textbox object.

Figure 2-13   How to get and display data with a Textbox object

How to code control statements

Like all programming languages, JavaScript provides *control statements* that let you control how information is processed in an application. This topic will get you started with the use of these statements. But first, you'll learn how to code conditional expressions because all of the control statements use them.

How to code conditional expressions

Figure 2-14 shows you how to code *conditional expressions* that use the six *relational operators*. A conditional expression returns a value of true or false based on the result of a comparison between two expressions. If, for example, the value of lastName in the first expression in the first table is "Harrison", the expression will return false. Or, if the value of rate in the last expression is 10, the expression will return true (because 10 / 100 is .1 and .1 is greater than or equal to 0.1).

If you want to determine whether a string value is a valid numeric value, you can use the global isNaN method. This is illustrated by the next set of examples. To use this method, you pass a parameter that represents the string value that should be tested. Then, this method returns true if the value can't be converted to a number or false if it can be converted.

To code a *compound conditional expression*, you use the *logical operators* shown in the second table in this figure to combine two conditional expressions. If you use the AND operator, the compound expression returns true if both expressions are true. If you use the OR operator, the compound expression returns true if either expression is true. If you use the NOT operator, the value returned by the expression is reversed. For instance, !isNaN returns true if the parameter is a number, so isNaN(10) returns false, but !isNaN(10) returns true.

Note that the logical operators in this figure are shown in their order of precedence. That is the order in which the operators are evaluated if more than one logical operator is used in a compound expression. This means that NOT operators are evaluated before AND operators, which are evaluated before OR operators. Although this is normally what you want, you can override this order by using parentheses.

In most cases, the conditional expressions that you use are relatively simple so coding them isn't much of a problem. In the rest of this chapter, you'll see some of the types of conditional expressions that are commonly used.

The relational operators

Operator	Description	Example
==	Equal	`lastName == "Harris"` `testScore == 10`
!=	Not equal	`firstName != "Ray"` `months != 0`
<	Less than	`age < 18`
<=	Less than or equal	`investment <= 0`
>	Greater than	`testScore > 100`
>=	Greater than or equal	`rate / 100 >= 0.1`

The syntax of the global isNaN method

```
isNaN(expression)
```

Examples of the isNaN method

```
isNaN("Harris") // Returns true since "Harris" is not a number
isNaN("123.45") // Returns false since "123.45" can be converted to a number
```

The logical operators in order of precedence

Operator	Description	Example
!	NOT	`!isNaN(age)`
&&	AND	`age > 17 && score < 70`
||	OR	`isNaN(rate) || rate < 0`

How the logical operators work

- Both tests with the AND operator must be true for the overall test to be true.
- At least one test with the OR operator must be true for the overall test to be true.
- The NOT operator switches the result of the expression to the other Boolean value. For example, if an expression is true, the NOT operator converts it to false.
- To override the order of precedence when two or more logical operators are used in a conditional expression, you can use parentheses.

Description

- A *conditional expression* uses the *relational operators* to compare the results of two expressions.
- A *compound conditional expression* joins two or more conditional expressions using the *logical operators*.
- The isNaN method tests whether a string can be converted to a number. It returns true if the string is not a number and false if the string is a number.

Note

- Confusing the assignment operator (=) with the equality operator (==) is a common programming error.

Figure 2-14   How to code conditional expressions

How to code if statements

An *if statement* lets you control the execution of statements based on the results of conditional expressions. In the examples in figure 2-15, you can see that an if statement can include three types of clauses. This statement must begin with an *if clause*. Then, it can have one or more *else if clauses*, but it doesn't have to have any. Last, it can have an *else clause*, but that clause is also optional.

To code the if clause, you code the keyword *if* followed by a conditional expression in parentheses and a block of one or more statements inside braces. If the conditional expression is true, this block of code will be executed and any remaining clauses in the if statement will be skipped over. If the conditional expression is false, the if statement will continue with any clauses that follow.

To code an else if clause, you code the keywords *else if* followed by a conditional expression in parentheses and a block of one or more statements inside braces. If the conditional expression is true, its block of code will be executed and any remaining clauses in the if statement will be skipped over. This will continue until one of the else if expressions is true or they all are false.

To code an else clause, you code the keyword *else* followed by a block of one or more statements inside braces. This code will only be executed if all the conditional expressions in the if and else if clauses are false. If those expressions are false and there isn't an else clause, the if statement won't execute any code.

The first example in this figure shows an if statement with an else clause. If the value of the age variable is greater than or equal to 18, the first message will be displayed. Otherwise, the second message will be displayed.

The second example shows an if statement with an else if and an else clause. If the rate is not a number, the first message is displayed. If the rate is less than zero, the second message is displayed. Otherwise, the third message is displayed.

The third example shows an if statement with a compound conditional expression that tests whether the value of the userEntry variable is not a number or whether the value is less than or equal to zero. If either expression is true, a message is displayed. If both expressions are false, nothing will be displayed because this statement doesn't have else if clauses or an else clause.

The fourth example shows how you can test a Boolean variable to see whether it is true. Here, the conditional expression is just the name of the variable. This is a commonly-used shorthand that is equivalent to:

```
if ( invalidFlag == true )
```

The last example shows how to *nest* one if statement within another. Here, the second if statement is nested within the else clause of the first if statement. When these *nested if statements* are executed, an error message is displayed if totalMonths is not a number or totalMonths is a number less than or equal to zero. This ends the if statement and nothing else happens.

But if totalMonths is a number greater than zero, the else clause starts by calculating the values of the variables named years and months. Then, the if statement that's nested in the else clause composes the message that's displayed based on the values of the years and months variables.

An if statement with an else clause

```
if ( age >= 18 ) {
    alert ("You may vote.");
} else {
    alert ("You are not old enough to vote.");
}
```

An if statement with else if and else clauses

```
if ( isNaN(rate) ) {
    alert ("You did not provide a number for the rate.");
} else if ( rate < 0 ) {
    alert ("The rate may not be less than zero.");
} else {
    alert ("The rate is: " + rate + ".");
}
```

An if statement with a compound conditional expression

```
if ( isNaN(userEntry) || userEntry <= 0 ) {
    alert ("Please enter a valid number greater than zero.");
}
```

An if statement that tests whether a Boolean value is true

```
if ( invalidFlag ) {
    alert ("All entries must be numeric values greater than 0.");
}
```

A nested if statement

```
if ( isNaN(totalMonths) || totalMonths <= 0 ) {
    alert ("Please enter a number of months greater than zero.");
} else {
    var years = parseInt ( totalMonths / 12 );
    var months = totalMonths % 12;
    if ( years == 0 ) {
        alert ( "The investment time is " + months + " months.");
    } else if ( months == 0 ) {
        alert ( "The investment time is " + years + " years.");
    } else {
        var message = "The investment time is " + years + " years ";
        message += "and " + months + " months.";
        alert(message);
    }
}
```

Description

- An *if statement* can include multiple else if clauses and one else clause at the end. The if clause of the statement executes one or more statements if its condition is true.

- The else if clause is executed when the previous condition or conditions are false. The statement or statements within an else if clause are executed if its condition is true.

- The else clause is executed when all previous conditions are false.

- You can code one if statement within the block of statements of an if, else if, or else clause in another if statement. This is referred to as *nested if statements*.

Figure 2-15   How to code if statements

How to code while and for statements

The while and for statements let you code loops that repeat a block of statements one or more times. This is illustrated by the statements in figure 2-16.

To code a *while statement*, you code the keyword *while* followed by a conditional expression in parentheses and a block of code in braces. When the while statement is executed, the conditional expression is evaluated. If the expression is true, the block of code is executed and the *while loop* is tried again. As soon as the expression evaluates to false, the block of code is skipped and the while statement is done. If the expression evaluates to false the first time it is checked, the block of code won't be executed at all.

The first example in this figure shows a loop that adds the numbers 1 through 5. The variable named sumOfNumbers is used to store the sum, and it's initialized to 0. The variable named numberOfLoops is used to store the highest number to sum, and it's initialized to 5. The variable named counter stores the numbers to be added to sumOfNumbers, and it's initialized to 1.

The code in the while statement adds the value in the counter variable to the sumOfNumbers variable and uses the increment operator (++) to increment the value in the counter variable by 1. The loop ends when the value of counter is greater than the value of numberOfLoops. As a result, sumOfNumbers equals the sum of 1, 2, 3, 4, and 5 when it is displayed by the alert method.

To code a *for statement*, you code the keyword *for* followed by three statements in parentheses and a block of code in braces. The three statements are separated by semicolons. The first statement in parentheses initializes the counter. The second statement is a conditional expression that causes the block of code to be executed as long as it's true. The third statement modifies the counter. It's executed after the block of code in the *for loop* is executed.

The second example shows how to get the same result as the first example by using a for statement. Here, the variable counter is initialized to 1; the block of code is executed as long as counter is less than or equal to numberOfLoops; and the counter is incremented by 1 after the block of code is executed. For a loop like this, you can see that a for statement is easier to use than a while statement.

The third example uses another while statement. First, this code uses the prompt method to get a value from the user and store it in userEntry. Then, the while statement executes as long as the entry is not a number. Within the while statement, the user is notified of the error and prompted for a number again.

The fourth example uses another for statement. It calculates the future value of monthly investments at a fixed interest rate. The first three variables store the monthly investment, the monthly interest rate, and the number of months that the investments will be made. The futureValue variable will store how much you will have at the end of the number of months, and it's initialized to 0.

Within the for statement, the variable i is used to count the months, so it is incremented by 1 each time through the loop. Within the loop, the monthly investment is added to futureValue, that value is multiplied by 1 plus the monthly interest rate, and the result is stored back in futureValue. When the loop finishes, futureValue will hold the future value of the monthly investments.

A while loop that adds the numbers from 1 through 5

```
var sumOfNumbers = 0;
var numberOfLoops = 5;
var counter = 1;
while (counter <= numberOfLoops) {
    sumOfNumbers += counter;    // adds counter to sumOfNumbers
    counter++;                  // adds 1 to counter
}
alert(sumOfNumbers);            // displays 15
```

A for loop that adds the numbers from 1 through 5

```
var sumOfNumbers = 0;
var numberOfLoops = 5;
for (var counter = 1; counter <= numberOfLoops; counter++) {
    sumOfNumbers += counter;
}
alert(sumOfNumbers);            // displays 15
```

A while loop that gets a user entry

```
userEntry = prompt("Please enter a number:", 100);
while ( isNaN( userEntry ) ) {
    alert( "You did not enter a number.");
    userEntry = prompt("Please enter a number:", 100);
}
```

A for loop that calculates the future value of a monthly investment

```
var monthlyInvestment = 100;   // monthly investment is $100
var monthlyRate = .01;         // yearly interest rate is 12%
var months = 120;              // 120 months is 10 years
var futureValue = 0;           // futureValue starts at 0

for ( i = 1; i <= months; i++ ) {
    futureValue = ( futureValue + monthlyInvestment ) *
        (1 + monthlyRate);
}
```

Description

- The *while statement* is used to create a *while loop* that contains a block of code that is executed as long as a condition is true. This condition is tested at the beginning of the loop. When the condition becomes false, JavaScript skips to the code after the while loop.

- The *for statement* is used to create a *for loop* that contains a block of code that is executed a specific number of times.

- When you code one loop within another loop, you are coding *nested loops*.

- JavaScript also offers two other looping structures, which you'll learn about in chapter 8.

Figure 2-16   How to code while and for statements

How to create and use functions

When you develop JavaScript applications, you often need to create and call your own functions. This lets you handle events, get data from a field on a form, and display data in a field on a form. The next topics show how.

How to create and call a function

A *function* is a named block of statements that can receive parameters and return a value by using a *return statement*. Once you've defined a function, you can call it from other portions of your JavaScript code.

The benefit that you get from using functions is that you don't have to type the statements for the function each time you want to use them. This saves time and reduces the chance of introducing errors into your applications. Also, if you need to change the function, you only have to change it in one place.

Figure 2-17 shows one way to create and use functions. This lets you create a function value and store it in a variable. In chapter 10, though, you'll learn three other ways to create them.

To create a function this way, you code the keyword *var* followed by the name of the variable that will store the function. Then, you code an assignment operator, the keyword *function*, a list of parameters in parentheses, and a block of code in braces. The parentheses are required even if the function has no parameters.

To *call* a function, you code the function name followed by the function's parameters (or arguments) in parentheses. Then, the function uses the parameters as it executes its block of code. Here again, the parentheses are required even if the function has no parameters.

In the first example, you can see the code for a function named showYear that doesn't require any parameters and doesn't return a value. This function displays a dialog box that shows the current year.

The second example shows a function named $ that finds and returns the object for an XHTML element. This function's one parameter is the id for the element. In effect, this function is a shortcut for the document.getElementById method.

When you call a function that returns a value, you treat the function and its parameters as if it were the value it was returning. In this example, the XHTML object returned by the function will be stored in a variable named taxRate.

The third example shows a function named displayEmail. It takes two parameters, but doesn't return a value. The parameters are the username and domain name for an e-mail address. They are joined together with an @ sign and written into the document to prevent spammers from finding the e-mail address in your web page. A function like this can be defined in the head section of a page and used in the body section.

The fourth example shows a function named calculateTax. This function has two parameters separated by commas and returns a value. It calculates sales tax and rounds it to two decimal places.

A function with no parameters that doesn't return a value

```
var showYear = function () {
    var today = new Date();
    alert( today.getFullYear() );
}
```

How to call a function that doesn't return a value

```
showYear();      // displays the current year
```

A function with one parameter that returns a value

```
var $ = function ( id ) {
    return document.getElementById( id );
}
```

How to call a function that returns a value

```
var taxRate = $("taxRate");
```

A function with two parameters that doesn't return a value

```
var displayEmail = function ( username, domain ) {
    document.write( username + "@" + domain);
}
```

How to call a function with two parameters that doesn't return a value

```
displayEmail( "mike", "murach.com");
```

A function with two parameters that returns a value

```
var calculateTax = function ( subtotal, taxRate ) {
    var tax = subtotal * taxRate;
    tax = parseFloat( tax.toFixed(2) );
    return tax;
}
```

How to call a function with two parameters that returns a value

```
var subtotal = 74.95;
var taxRate = 0.07;
var salesTax = calculateTax( subtotal, taxRate ); // returns 5.25
```

Description

- A *function* is a block of code that you can use multiple times in an application. It can require one or more parameters.
- A function can return a value to the code that called it by using the *return statement*. When a return statement is executed, the function returns the specified value and ends.
- The code that *calls* a function may discard the returned value, store it in a variable, or use it in an expression.
- If a function ends without encountering a return statement, it returns a special value called *undefined*.

Figure 2-17   How to create and call a function

How to code an event handler

An *event handler* is a function that is executed when an *event* occurs. As figure 2-18 shows, some common events are the onclick event of a Button object and the onload event of the window object. These events are used by the application in this figure. This application uses the alert method to display a dialog box when the user clicks the Display Message button.

The first function in this application is the $ function, which is our shortcut for using the getElementById method to return an XHTML element. You'll use a function like this in most JavaScript applications.

The second function is the event handler, which is named display_click. This function just executes the alert method to display a message. At this point in the code, though, the display_click function is not an event handler. Its name is just a reminder of the purpose of the function. The name alone doesn't assign the function to an event.

It is the third function that assigns the display_click function to the onclick event of the XHTML element that has "btnDisplay" as its id. This function is executed when the onload event of the window object is fired. That happens after the XHTML document has been fully loaded into the web browser.

Note in this third function that display_click doesn't have a set of parentheses after it. That's because this code isn't calling the function. Instead, it is referring to the function as a whole and assigning that function to an event. As a result, that function will be called when the event is fired.

In contrast, if you were to put parentheses after display_click, the function would be called right away, the alert box would be displayed without the user clicking the button, and the return value of the function would be undefined. Then, when the user did click the button, nothing would happen since the function wouldn't be assigned to the event.

In summary, what the third function is doing is using one event handler to assign another event handler to an event. This delays the assignment of the display_click event handler until after the page is loaded. This is necessary because the code in the head section is executed before the DOM is built. By delaying this assignment until after the page is loaded, the application makes sure that the call to the $ function by the display_click event handler will be successful.

When you use this technique, a problem can arise if a page takes a few seconds to load. In that case, the user might start interacting with the elements on the page before the page is fully loaded and the event handlers are attached. In chapter 14, though, you'll learn how to add event handlers to a web page before the page is completely loaded.

Incidentally, the event handler for the window.onload event can do more than assign functions to events. In fact, it can do whatever needs to be done after the DOM is loaded. You'll see this illustrated in a moment.

Common events

Object	Event	Occurs when...
button	onclick	The button is clicked.
window	onload	The document has been loaded into the browser.

An application with an event handler for the onclick event

```
<head>
<title>JavaScript Event Handler</title>
<script type="text/javascript">
    // This function receives an id and gets the related XHTML object.
    var $ = function ( id ) {
        return document.getElementById( id );
    }

    // This is the event handler for the onclick event of the button.
    var display_click = function () {
        alert( "You clicked the button.");
    }

    // This is the event handler for the onload event of the page.
    // It is executed after the page is loaded and the DOM has been built.
    window.onload = function () {
        // This statement assigns the event handler named display_click
        // to the onclick event of the XHTML object named btnDisplay
        $("btnDisplay").onclick = display_click;
    }
</script>
</head>
<body>
    <p><input type="button" value="Display Message" id="btnDisplay" /></p>
</body>
</html>
```

The web browser after the Display Message button is clicked

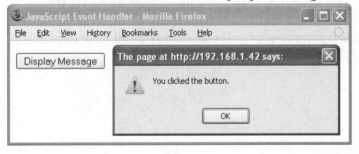

Description

- An *event handler* is executed when the *event* that triggers it occurs.
- The event handler for the onload event of the window object can be used to assign event handlers to other events after the DOM has been built.

Figure 2-18   How to code an event handler

The Future Value application

You have now learned enough about JavaScript to write simple applications of your own. To give you a better idea of how to do that, this chapter ends by presenting the Future Value application.

The Future Value application is shown in the web browser in figure 2-19. This application asks the user for three numbers that are needed for calculating the future value of a monthly investment. The user types these values into the first three text boxes and clicks the Calculate button. The application then parses the user entries into numbers, performs basic data validation, and either displays an error message in an alert box or the result of the calculation in the Future Value text box. In this figure, an error message is displayed because the user has entered an invalid investment amount ($100).

The XHTML and JavaScript for this application are described next. Although the CSS isn't shown, it is available in the downloadable applications for this book.

The XHTML code

The XHTML code for this application is an XHTML 1.0 Transitional document. The head section sets the title of the page, loads an external CSS file with the <link> tag, and loads an external JavaScript file with the <script> tag.

In the body of the page, there are four text boxes and one button. The text boxes have investment, rate, years, and futureValue as their ids. The button has calculate as its id. The fourth text box also has its disabled property set. As a result, the user can't type in the text box, but JavaScript can display a value in it.

Notice that by keeping the CSS and JavaScript code in separate files, the XHTML file is uncluttered. As a result, it is easy to see the content and structure of the page, and the three files will be easier to maintain. After the XHTML file for an application like this is complete, different developers could work on the CSS and JavaScript files to help speed development time.

The Future Value application in a web browser

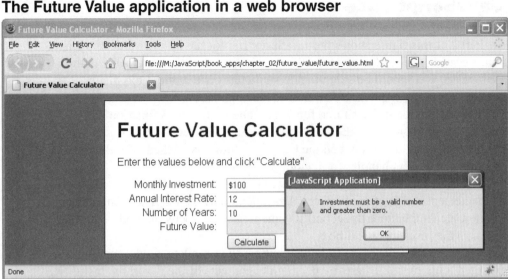

The XHTML file

```html
<!DOCTYPE html PUBLIC "-//W3C//DTD XHTML 1.0 Transitional//EN"
    "http://www.w3.org/TR/xhtml1/DTD/xhtml1-transitional.dtd">
<html xmlns="http://www.w3.org/1999/xhtml">
<head>
    <title>Future Value Calculator</title>
    <link rel="stylesheet" type="text/css" href="future_value.css" />
    <script type="text/javascript" src="future_value.js"></script>
</head>

<body>
    <div id="content">
        <h1>Future Value Calculator</h1>
        <p>Enter the values below and click "Calculate".</p>

        <label for="investment">Monthly Investment:</label>
        <input type="text" id="investment" /><br />

        <label for="rate">Annual Interest Rate:</label>
        <input type="text" id="rate" />%<br />

        <label for="years">Number of Years:</label>
        <input type="text" id="years" /><br />

        <label for="futureValue">Future Value:</label>
        <input type="text" id="futureValue" disabled="disabled" /><br />

        <label> </label>
        <input type="button" id="calculate" value="Calculate" /><br />
    </div>
</body>
</html>
```

Figure 2-19   The Future Value application (part 1 of 2)

The JavaScript code

Part 2 of this figure shows the JavaScript file for the Future Value application. Because you've already learned how to write all of the statements in this application, you should be able to understand this code without too much trouble. But here's a quick description of the application.

The application defines three functions. The first is the $ function that's used as a shortcut to the getElementById method. The second function is the event handler that will run when the Calculate button is clicked. The third function is the event handler for the onload event.

The third function runs after the page is loaded and the DOM is built. Its first statement assigns the calculate_click function as the onclick event handler for the Calculate button. Its second statement uses the focus method to put the cursor in the investment text box.

When the user clicks the Calculate button, the calculate_click function is executed. This function starts by parsing the contents of the first three text boxes and storing those values in appropriately named variables. Then, this function moves an empty string into the futureValue text box. That clears any value that was displayed by a previous calculation.

Next, this function uses an if statement to check each of the three user entries to see whether it is not numeric or it is less than or equal to zero. If one of these conditions is true, the alert method is used to display an appropriate error message and the if statement ends.

However, if all three user entries are valid, the else clause is executed. The code in this clause first converts the annual interest rate to a monthly rate and the years to months. Then, it uses those values in a for statement that calculates the future value. When the for statement ends, the future value is rounded to two decimal places and displayed in the futureValue text box.

If you understand all of this code, you're ready to write some significant applications. However, you should be aware that this application can be improved in several ways. For example, you could check to make sure that the user entries are not only valid but reasonable by making sure that the annual interest rate is less than 20 and the number of years is less than 50. You could also add a Clear button and an event handler that clears the first three text boxes when the user clicks the button. Improvements like these make an application easier to use, and you already have the skills for adding these improvements.

Another improvement could be made in the XHTML code. As it is now, if a browser has JavaScript disabled, the users will be able to enter values into the application, but nothing will happen when they click the Calculate button. To fix that, you could add a <noscript> tag that displays a message that says that the application won't work without JavaScript.

The JavaScript file

```javascript
var $ = function (id) {
    return document.getElementById(id);
}

var calculate_click = function () {

    // Get the user entries from the first three text boxes.
    var investment = parseFloat( $("investment").value );
    var annualRate = parseFloat( $("rate").value );
    var years = parseInt( $("years").value );

    // Set the value of the fourth text box to an empty string.
    $("futureValue").value = "";

    // Test the three input values for validity.
    if (isNaN(investment) || investment <= 0) {
        alert("Investment must be a valid number\nand greater than zero.");
    } else if(isNaN(annualRate) || annualRate <= 0) {
        alert("Annual rate must be a valid number\nand greater than zero.");
    } else if(isNaN(years) || years <= 0) {
        alert("Years must be a valid number\nand greater than zero.");

    // If all input values are valid, calculate the future value.
    } else {
        var monthlyRate = annualRate / 12 / 100;
        var months = years * 12;
        var futureValue = 0;

        for ( i = 1; i <= months; i++ ) {
            futureValue = ( futureValue + investment ) *
                (1 + monthlyRate);
        }

        // Set the value of the fourth text box to the future value
        // but round it to two decimal places.
        $("futureValue").value = futureValue.toFixed(2);
    }
}

window.onload = function () {
    $("calculate").onclick = calculate_click;
    $("investment").focus();
}
```

Figure 2-19   The Future Value application (part 2 of 2)

Perspective

The goal of this chapter has been to get you started with JavaScript and to get you started fast. Now, if you understand the Future Value application, you've come a long way. You should also be able to write basic JavaScript applications of your own. Keep in mind, though, that this chapter is just an introduction to the JavaScript essentials that will be expanded upon by the chapters in section 2.

Terms

syntax	property
statement	method
comment	instance
identifier	constructor function
reserved word	dot operator
keyword	call a method
camel casing	parameter
primitive data type	argument
number data type	object chaining
integer	global object
decimal value	window object
floating-point number	document object
exponent	control statement
string data type	conditional expression
string	relational operator
empty string	compound conditional expression
escape sequence	logical operator
Boolean data type	if statement
Boolean value	if clause
expression	else if clause
arithmetic operator	else clause
order of precedence	nested if statements
concatenate	while statement
variable	while loop
declare a variable	for statement
assignment statement	for loop
assignment operator	function
compound assignment operator	return statement
string literal	call a function
numeric literal	event
object	event handler

Before you do the exercises for this book...

If you haven't already done so, you should install the Mozilla Firefox browser and install the applications for this book as described in appendix A. Then, if you're new to programming, you should do exercise 2-1. But if you have some programming experience, you can start with exercise 2-2.

Exercise 2-1   Build the Sales Tax application

This exercise is for beginners. It steps you through the process of building the Sales Tax application of chapter 1. This exercise also gives you a chance to do some experimenting, which is a great way to learn JavaScript programming.

Open the files for the Sales Tax application

1. Start the Firefox browser. Then, use the File→Open command to open the file named sales_tax.html in the chapter 2 folder for the exercises. If you installed the downloadable applications as in appendix A, the path to that file on a Windows system is:

    ```
    C:\murach\javascript\exercises\chapter_02\sales_tax\sales_tax.html
    ```

2. Enter valid numeric values in the first two input boxes and click the Calculate button. Notice that nothing happens.

3. Use your text editor to open the sales_tax.js file for this application. It is in the same folder as the html file. Then, notice that this file only contains the $ function that's used to get the object for an XHTML element.

4. Use your text editor to open the sales_tax.html file for this application. Then, note the ids that are used for the text boxes for this application.

Start the event handlers for this application

5. Start the event handler for the window.onload event by entering this code:

    ```
    window.onload = function () {
        alert ("This is the window.onload event handler.");
    }
    ```

    Then, save the file, switch to Firefox, click the Reload button, and note the message that's displayed. Or, if nothing happens, check your code, fix it, and try this again. If necessary, you can access the Firefox Error Console as shown in figure 2-3. When you've got this working right, switch back to your editor.

6. Between the $ function and the window.onload event handler, start a function named calculate_click by entering this code:

    ```
    var calculate_click = function () {
            alert ("This is the calculate_click event handler.");
    }
    ```

    Then, save the code, switch to Firefox, click the Reload button, and note that this function isn't executed. That's because it hasn't been called. Now, switch to your editor.

7. Call the calculate_click function from the window.onload event handler by entering this statement after the alert statement:

```
calculate_click();
```

Then, save the file, switch to Firefox, and click the Reload button. This time, two message boxes should be displayed: one by the window.onload event handler and one by the calculate_click function. If this doesn't work, fix the code and try it again. Then, switch to your editor.

8. Assign the calculate_click function to the click event of the Calculate button by replacing the statement you entered in step 7 with this statement:

```
$("calculate").onclick = calculate_click;
```

Then, save the file, switch to Firefox, click the Reload button, and click on the Calculate button. If you did everything right, the two message boxes are again displayed. Otherwise, fix the code and try again. Then, switch to your editor.

Finish the calculate_click event handler

After you do each of the steps that follow, switch to Firefox, click the Reload button, and make sure your changes work. Otherwise, fix your code and try again.

9. Add these statements after the alert statement in the calculate_click function:

```
var subtotal = 200;
var taxRate = 7.5;
var salesTax = subtotal * (taxRate / 100);
var total = subtotal + salesTax;
alert ( "subtotal = " + subtotal + "\n" +
        "taxRate  = " + taxRate + "\n" +
        "salesTax = " + salesTax + "\n" +
        "total =    " + total);
```

10. If you have any questions about how variables and arithmetic statements work, review figures 2-7 through 2-9. Then, experiment with any statements that you don't understand in the calculate_click function. To display the results of your statements, you can use alert statements as in step 9.

11. Replace the statements that you entered in step 9 with these statements:

```
var subtotal = parseFloat( $("subtotal").value );
var taxRate  = parseFloat( $("taxRate").value );
// calculate results
var salesTax = subtotal * (taxRate / 100);
salesTax = parseFloat( salesTax.toFixed(2) );
var total = subtotal + salesTax;
// display results
$("salesTax").value = salesTax;
$("total").value = total.toFixed(2);
```

The first two statements will get the user entries; the last two statements will display the results. This is explained in figure 2-13. At this point, the application should work if the user enters valid numbers.

12. Comment out the two alert statements by entering slashes before them.

13. Check the user entries for validity by entering this code with the statements that do the calculations in the else clause:

```
if ( isNaN(subtotal) || isNaN(taxRate) ) {
    alert("Please check your entries for validity.");
} else {
    // the statements that do the calculations should be here
}
```

This just checks to make sure that both user entries are numeric before the calculations are done.

14. At this point, you have a working application, but one that can be improved. If you would like to improve it, review the code in figure 1-13 of the last chapter for ideas. For instance, you can check to make sure that each user entry is both numeric and greater than zero, and you can display a different error message for each text box. Or, you can add a statement to the window.onload function that moves the focus to the first text box. When you're through experimenting, close the files.

Exercise 2-2   Enhance the Future Value application

In this exercise, you'll enhance the Future Value application in several ways. That will give you a chance to use some of the skills that you've learned in this chapter.

Test the Future Value application

1. Start the Firefox browser. Then, open the file named future_value.html in the chapter 2 folder for the exercises. The path to that file on a Windows system is:

```
C:\murach\javascript\exercises\chapter_02\future_value\future_value.html
```

2. Enter valid numeric values in the three input boxes. For the first test run, keep these values simple like 100 for monthly investment, 12 for annual interest rate, and 1 for number of years. Then, click the Calculate button to display a valid result in the fourth text box.

3. Enter invalid values in the three input boxes and click the Calculate button. Then, respond to the first message box by entering valid data and clicking the Calculate button again. Do the same for the next two message boxes.

Enhance the validity checking

4. Use your text editor to open the future_value.js file for this application. This file should be in the same folder as the html file (see step 1).

5. Modify the validity testing for the annual interest rate so it has to be a valid number that's greater than zero and less than or equal to 20. Next, adjust the error message that's displayed to reflect this third validity test.

   To test this enhancement, save the JavaScript file, switch to Firefox, click on the Reload button, enter an interest rate that's greater than 20, and click the Calculate button.

6. Switch back to the JavaScript file in your text editor, modify the validity testing for the number of years so this value also has to be less than or equal to 50, and modify the error message to reflect this change. Then, save the file, switch to Firefox, and test this change.

Add a Clear button

7. Use your text editor to open the html file for this application and add a Clear button below the Calculate button. To do that, you can just copy the XHTML for the Calculate button and modify the id and value attributes. Then, save the file, switch to Firefox, and test this change.

8. Switch back to the JavaScript file in your text editor and add an event handler named clear_click that clears the text boxes when the Clear button is clicked. This handler should store empty strings in the four text boxes on the page. After you code the event handler, add a line to the window.onload handler that assigns the new event handler to the click event. Then, test this change.

Modify the calculation that's done

9. Change this application so it calculates the future value of a one-time investment instead of fixed monthly investments. To do that, modify the XHTML file so the first label reads "One-Time Investment". Next, modify the code in the calculate_click event handler so interest is calculated and added to future value just once each year for the number of years that were entered by the user. Then, test this change.

Disable and enable the text box for the annual interest rate

10. Modify the JavaScript code in the calculate_click event handler so it disables the text box for the annual interest rate after it finishes the for loop and displays the future value. Next, modify the code in the clear_click event handler so it enables this text box when the Clear button is clicked. Then, test these changes.

Add the date to the web page

11. Modify the XHTML file so it uses embedded JavaScript as shown in figure 2-4 to display the current date at the bottom of the web page like this:

   `Today is Thu Oct 23 2009`

   To do this, you need to use the toDateString method as shown in figure 2-12. Then, test this change.

Add a <noscript> tag to display a message when JavaScript is disabled

12. Add a <noscript> tag after the embedded <script> tag as shown in figure 2-4. The noscript tag should display "You must enable JavaScript for this application." To test this, use the Tools→Options command in the Firefox browser to disable JavaScript. When you're through testing, enable JavaScript again and close your files.

If you were able to do all of the steps in this exercise, congratulations! You're well on your way to learning JavaScript and DOM scripting.

3

How to test and debug a JavaScript application

As you build a JavaScript application, you need to test it to make sure that it performs as expected. Then, if there are any problems, you need to debug your application to correct any problems. This chapter shows you how to do both.

Since JavaScript runs in a web browser, you can only use the testing and debugging tools that are provided by the browser. But, as you will see, these tools are limited when compared to the tools that are provided by an integrated development environment like Visual Studio or NetBeans.

An introduction to testing and debugging **90**
Typical test phases for a JavaScript application 90
The three types of errors that can occur 90
Common JavaScript errors 92
How to get error messages with Firefox 94
A simple way to trace the execution of your JavaScript code 96

How to debug with the Firebug extension of Firefox **98**
How to install and enable the Firebug extension 98
How to get information in the Console tab 100
How to review your code in the Script tab 102
How to use breakpoints and step through code 104

How to use the Firebug console object **106**
The methods of the console object 106
How to trace an application with Firebug's console.log method 108

How to test and debug with other browsers **110**
How to get error messages with Internet Explorer 110
How to get error messages with Safari 112
How to get error messages with Opera 114
How to get error messages with Chrome 116

Perspective **118**

An introduction to testing and debugging

When you *test* an application, you run it to make sure that it works correctly. As you test the application, you try every possible combination of input data and user actions to be certain that the application works in every case. In other words, the goal of testing is to make an application fail.

When you *debug* an application, you fix the errors (bugs) that you discover during testing. Each time you fix a bug, you test again to make sure that the change that you made didn't affect any other aspect of the application.

Typical test phases for a JavaScript application

When you test an application, you typically do so in phases, like the three that are summarized in figure 3-1.

In the first phase, as you test the user interface, you should visually check the controls to make sure they're displayed properly with the correct text. Then, you should make sure that all the keys and controls work correctly. For instance, you should test the Tab key and Enter key as well as the operation of check boxes and drop-down lists.

In the second phase, you should test the application with valid data. To start, you can enter data that you would expect a user to enter. Before you're done, though, you should enter valid data that tests all of the limits of the application.

In the third phase, you go all out to make the application fail by testing every combination of invalid data and user action that you can think of. That should include random actions like pressing the Enter key or clicking the mouse at the wrong time.

The three types of errors that can occur

As you test an application, there are three types of errors that can occur: These errors are described in figure 3-1.

Because *syntax errors* prevent your application from running, they are the easiest to find and fix. As you will see, a typical web browser provides error messages that help you do that.

Although *runtime errors* don't violate the syntax rules, they do throw *exceptions* that stop the execution of an application. Unlike other languages, though, JavaScript doesn't throw many of the traditional exceptions. For instance, if you divide a number by zero, JavaScript returns "infinity" instead of throwing an exception. As a result, most JavaScript exceptions involve problems with the use of identifiers.

Logic errors can come from many places, and they are often the most difficult to find and correct. A mistake in a calculation, events not being triggered in the order you expect them to, and working with incorrect values are just a few of the ways that logic errors can creep into your applications. The Sales Tax application in this figure has a logic error. Can you tell what it is?

The Sales Tax application with a logic error

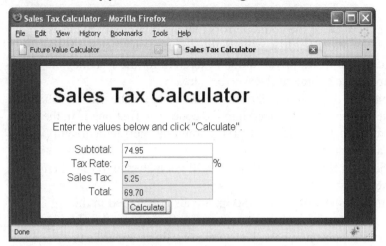

The goal of testing

- To find all errors before the application is put into production.

The goal of debugging

- To fix all errors before the application is put into production.

Three test phases

- Check the user interface to make sure that it works correctly.
- Test the application with valid input data to make sure the results are correct.
- Test the application with invalid data or unexpected user actions. Try everything you can think of to make the application fail.

The three types of errors that can occur

- *Syntax errors* violate the rules for how JavaScript statements must be written. These errors are caught by the web browser.
- *Runtime errors* don't violate the syntax rules, but they throw *exceptions* that stop the execution of the application.
- *Logic errors* are statements that don't cause syntax or runtime errors, but produce the wrong results.

Description

- To *test* a JavaScript application, you run it to make sure that it works properly no matter what combinations of valid or invalid data you enter or what sequence of controls you use.
- When you *debug* an application, you find and fix all of the errors (*bugs*) that you find when you test the application.

Figure 3-1   An introduction to testing and debugging

Common JavaScript errors

Figure 3-2 presents some of the coding errors that are commonly made as you write a JavaScript application. If you study this figure, you'll have a better idea of what to watch out for. And if you did the exercises for the last chapter, you've probably experienced some of these errors already.

The code at the top of this figure is the start of the code for the Future Value application but with four errors introduced into the code. The first one is in the second line. The error is that "getElementByID" should be "getElementById". Remember that JavaScript is case-sensitive.

Can you spot the other three errors? If not, you'll get a chance to find them when you do the exercises for this chapter.

Two problems that are peculiar to JavaScript are also discussed in this figure. The first involves floating-point arithmetic. JavaScript uses the IEEE 754 standard for floating-point numbers. Unfortunately, this standard can introduce strange results with even simple calculations. The figure suggests one way of dealing with this issue.

The other problem involves the way JavaScript converts values when performing comparisons. The general rule is that when JavaScript compares two values that are of different types, it converts them both to number values. It does this even if one is a string and the other is a Boolean value. So the expression "1" == true will return true because true is converted to 1, and the expression "0" == false will also return true because false will be converted to 0.

Testing for equality with the value NaN can also be troublesome because the expression NaN == NaN will return false. But you'll learn more about that in chapter 7.

JavaScript code that contains errors

```
var $ = function (id) {
    return document.getElementByID(id);
}

var calculate_click = function () {
    var investment = parseFloat( $("investment'").value );
    var annualRate = parseFloat( $("rat").value );
    var years = parseInt( $("years").value ;

    $("futureValue").value = "";
}
```

Common syntax errors

- Misspelling keywords.
- Forgetting an opening or closing parenthesis, bracket, brace, or comment character.
- Breaking a single line into two valid statements where JavaScript inserts a semicolon.
- Forgetting to use a semicolon that is essential to the logic of the code.
- Forgetting an opening or closing quote mark.
- Not using the same opening and closing quote mark.

Problems with identifiers

- Misspelling or incorrectly capitalizing an identifier.
- Using a reserved word, global property, or global method as an identifier.

Problems with values

- Not checking that a value is the right data type before processing it. For example, you expect the user to enter a date, but he enters a name instead.
- Forgetting to use the parseInt or parseFloat function to convert a user entry into a numeric value.
- Using one equal sign instead of two when testing for equality.

A problem with floating-point arithmetic

- The number data type in JavaScript uses floating-point numbers, and that can lead to arithmetic errors. For example, 0.2 + 0.7 in JavaScript is 0.8999999999999999.
- One way around this is to round the number to the desired decimal place with the toFixed method and then convert it back to a floating-point number with the parseFloat method.

A problem with comparing values of different data types

- When you compare two values that are of different data types, JavaScript will internally convert both values to numbers. In this conversion, an empty string is converted to 0; true is converted to 1; and false is converted to 0.
- This can lead to unexpected result when using the equality operator. For example, the expression 0 == "" will evaluate to true since an empty string is converted to 0.

Figure 3-2   Common JavaScript errors

How to get error messages with Firefox

When you run the Future Value application with the errors shown in figure 3-2, the interface will still be displayed. When you try to use the application, however, it won't do anything because of the errors.

To see the error messages that Firefox produces, open the Error Console as as in figure 3-3. Here, as you learned in chapter 2, the console shows the first error that's detected when the Future Value application is run with the errors of the previous figure. In this case, the arrow under the message points to the character in the line that caused the error. The mistake is that a leading double quotation mark is matched by a single quotation mark, which is invalid.

To display the source code for a JavaScript file, you can click on the link in the error message. That opens the source code in a separate window with the error highlighted. You can't use that window to fix the code, though. Instead, you need to use your editor to fix and save the code and then restart the application in Firefox by clicking on the Reload button.

Often, the error messages are not as clear as in this example. Instead, an error in one line will be reported as an error somewhere else. Then, you start by looking for the error in the line indicated in the error message, but work your way to related portions of code until you find the error.

The tabs at the top of the Error Console let you select which types of messages you want displayed. If you use many extensions or themes or if you have several pages open in tabs, all of their messages, warnings, and errors will be displayed in the same Error Console window. Then, you can show just the errors by clicking the Errors tab. You can also remove all messages from the Error Console by clicking the Clear button.

You can also use the Error Console to evaluate JavaScript expressions. To do that, you type the code you want to evaluate in the Code text box and click the Evaluate button. Then, the results will be displayed in the Error Console. Note, however, that you can't use functions or variables in an expression in the Error console. In this figure, the second message in the Error Console, which displays 101, is the result of the expression in the Code text box.

Incidentally, the error message in this figure is for the first error that's detected when the code in the previous figure is run, but that error isn't the first one in the code. That's because the JavaScript engine only detects syntax errors as the page is being loaded, but the first error in the code is a runtime error.

The JavaScript engine won't run the application until all of the syntax errors have been corrected. Then, the $ function will be called and its runtime error will be detected.

The Firefox Error Console with an error displayed

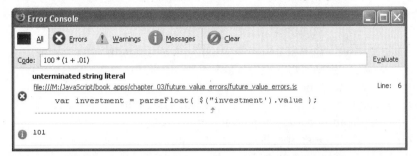

The source code that's displayed when you click on the link

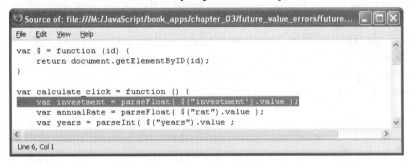

How to display the Error Console and source code

- To display the Error Console, use the Tools→Error Console command or press Ctrl+Shift+J.
- To display the source code with the error highlighted, click on the link in the Error Console.

How to evaluate expressions with the Error Console

- Enter the expression in the Code text box and click the Evaluate button. Note, however, that you can't use functions or variables in the expression.

Description

- The Error Console in Firefox is used to display errors, warnings, and messages generated by web pages. That includes messages caused by errors in JavaScript code.
- The buttons at the top of the Error Console let you display all errors, just fatal errors, just warnings, or just messages. The Clear button removes all errors from the console.
- If you click the link to the file in the Error Console, Firefox will display the code and highlight the line at which the error occurred. You will not, however, be able to edit the file.

Figure 3-3   How to get error messages with Firefox

A simple way to trace the execution of your JavaScript code

When you *trace* the execution of an application, you add statements to your code that display messages or variable values at key points in the code. This is typically done to help you find the cause of a logic error.

If, for example, you can't figure out why the future value that's calculated by the Future Value application is incorrect, you can insert three alert statements into the code for the application as shown in figure 3-4. These functions display dialog boxes that show the values for four of the variables as the code is executed. That should help you determine where the calculation is going wrong. Then, when you find and fix the problem, you can remove the alert statements.

When you use this technique, you usually start by adding just a few alert statements to the code. Then, if that doesn't help you solve the problem, you can add more. This works well for simple applications, but has its limitations. Later in this chapter, you'll learn other debugging techniques as well as a more sophisticated method of tracing the execution of an application.

JavaScript with alert statements that trace the execution of the code

```
var calculate_click = function () {
    var investment = parseFloat( $("investment").value );
    var annualRate = parseFloat( $("rate").value );
    var years = parseInt( $("years").value );
    $("futureValue").value = "";

    var monthlyRate = annualRate / 12 / 100;
    alert("Monthly Rate = " + monthlyRate);
    var months = years * 12;
    alert("Months = " + months);
    var futureValue = 0;
    for ( i = 1; i <= months; i++ ) {
        futureValue = ( futureValue + investment ) *
            (1 + monthlyRate);
        alert("Month = " + i + "\nFuture Value = " + futureValue);
    }
}
```

The alert dialog box the fifth time through the loop

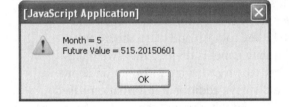

Description

- A simple way to *trace* the execution of a JavaScript application is to insert alert statements at key points in the code.

- The messages in the alert dialog boxes can display the values of variables or display messages that indicate what portion of the code is being executed.

- When you see an incorrect value displayed, there is a good chance that you have a logic error between the current alert statement and the previous one.

Figure 3-4   A simple way to trace the execution of your JavaScript code

How to debug with the Firebug extension of Firefox

Of the five major web browsers, Firefox and its Firebug extension provide the best environment for debugging JavaScript code. As a result, you should do most of your testing and debugging in Firefox. Once your code works in Firefox, you can test it in the other browsers to ensure that it still functions as expected.

How to install and enable the Firebug extension

The Firefox web browser lets you install extensions that add new functionality to the browser. Firebug is a free extension that enhances the JavaScript debugging capabilities of Firefox. You can learn how to install Firebug in appendix A.

When Firebug is installed, you will see the Firebug icon in the Firefox status bar, as shown in figure 3-5. Then, you can click this icon to open and close the panel. Or, you can press the F12 key to open and close this panel.

As you can see in this figure, the Firebug panel is divided into two panes. The left pane is the main pane and has six tabs for viewing information about the current web page, and the right pane displays additional information based on which tab is selected in the left pane. By default, three of the six tabs in the left pane are disabled, but you can enable them by using the techniques in this figure. To adjust the size of the panes, you can drag the divider between them. There is also an Options menu for each of the panes.

At the top left of the Firebug panel, there is a Firebug icon that drops down a menu, an Inspect button, and additional buttons that change based on the selected tab. At the top right of the Firebug panel, there is a search box, a button to open Firebug in a separate window, and a button to close the Firebug panel. You can drag the top edge of the Firebug panel to adjust its size.

The Console tab displays an enhanced error console. Here, you can view error messages, log messages from your application, execute code, and profile the performance of your application.

The HTML tab displays the XHTML code for your web page in an expandable tree view in the left pane. Here, you can browse to an XHTML tag and change its attributes to see the effect on your page. In the right pane, you can use the tabs to view the CSS style information, the layout information, and the DOM elements on the web page.

The CSS tab shows you the CSS code for your web page. If there is more than one file containing CSS, you can view a different file by using the drop-down list of file names at the top of the Firebug panel. You can also make changes to the CSS code to see the effect on the web page.

The Script tab shows you the JavaScript source code. If there is more than one file containing JavaScript, you can view a different file by using the drop-down list of file names at the top of the Firebug panel.

The DOM tab shows the objects in the DOM and their properties and

Firebug in Firefox

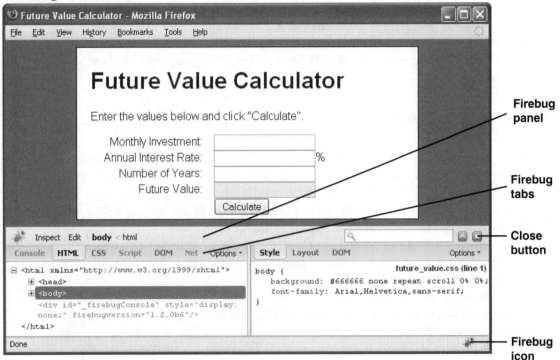

How to access the Firebug panel

- Click the Firebug icon, use the View➔Firebug command, or press F12.

How to enable or disable a tab

1. Click the tab to open it, and click the down arrow next to the tab name.

2. In the menu that appears, select Enabled or Disabled to enable or disable that tab for all websites. Or, select Enable for Local Files or Disable for Local Files to enable or disable that tab for the web site you are currently viewing.

Description

- Firebug is an extension for Firefox that adds debugging facilities to Firefox. To install the Firebug extension, see appendix A.

- Firebug has six tabs that are enabled by default that let you interact with a web page.

- The Console, Script, and Net tabs are disabled for all websites by default as a security precaution. You can enable these tabs for individual web sites or for all web sites.

- For more information about Firebug, you can go to http://www.getfirebug.com.

Figure 3-5   How to install and enable the Firebug extension

methods in an expandable tree view. It starts with the global object. You can edit the values of object properties to see the effect on the web page.

The Net tab displays information about each request sent to the web browser. It shows download times, the server used, the HTTP request headers, the HTTP response headers, the HTTP response entity body, and local caching information.

How to get information in the Console tab

The Firebug Console tab replaces and enhances the Firefox Error Console. Any messages that are displayed in the Firefox Error Console are also displayed in the Firebug Console tab. This is illustrated by the first example in figure 3-6. Then, if you click the line of code or file name in the Console tab, Firebug will switch to the Script tab and display the source code.

If you click the text of the error message in the Console tab or the plus sign that precedes the message, it will expand to display a *stack trace*. This is illustrated by the first example in this figure.

In programming, the *stack* is a list of all current function calls and their parameters. For example, in the Future Value application, when the user clicks the Calculate button, the calculate_click function is called, so it is placed on the stack. Inside this function, the $ function is called, so it is placed on the stack. Then, there are two items in the stack. When a function is finished, it is removed from the stack.

A *stack trace* is a display of the current state of the stack. This is useful for determining the state of your program when an error occurs. If, for example, an error occurs in the $ function, it sometimes helps to know whether this function was called from the onload event handler or the calculate_click function. That can speed up the debugging process.

Like the Firefox Error Console, the Firebug Console tab lets you execute JavaScript code. To do that, type statements in the command line or command pane as shown in this figure. Unlike the Error Console command line, the Console tab lets you use variables, call functions, and evaluate control structures such as if and while statements.

To make entering statements easier, the Console tab has an auto-complete feature. To use it, you type part of a JavaScript identifier, press the Tab key, and Firebug will try to find an identifier that starts with what you typed. If multiple identifiers are found, you can press the Tab key to cycle through them. You can also cycle through the properties of an object by typing the object's name and a period, and then pressing the Tab key.

The Firebug Console tab also provides an execution *profiler*. This keeps track of how many times each function is called and how much time each function call took to execute. To start the profiler, you click the Profile button at the top of the Firebug panel. Then, you run your application. When you're done, click the Profile button again. At that point, the profiler will stop and display its report, or *profile*, in the Console tab.

An error message with a stack trace and an expanded command line

```
  Inspect   Clear   Profile                                     [search]        [ ][ ]
 Console ▾  HTML  CSS  Script  DOM  Net          Options ▾   var year = 2009;
 ✗ ⊞ document.getElementByID is not a function   future_value.js (line 2)   alert(year + 1);
      return document.getElementByID(id);
 >>> var year = 2009; alert(year + 1);

                                                             Run   Clear   Copy      ▾
 Done                                                                      ✗ 1 Error
```

A profile of the functions that were called and a collapsed command line

```
  Inspect   Clear   Profile                                     [search]        [ ][ ]
 Console ▾  HTML  CSS  Script  DOM  Net                                       Options ▾
 ⊟ Profile (15.548ms, 18 calls)
   Function          ▼ Calls  Percent  Own Time  Time      Avg      Min     Max      File
   calculate_click()   3      97.49%   15.157ms  15.548ms  5.183ms  4.965ms  5.495ms  future_value.js (line 6)
   (?)()              15      2.51%    0.391ms   0.391ms   0.026ms  0.01ms   0.049ms  future_value.js (line 2)

 >>>                                                                                   ▣
 Done                                                                                  ▨
```

How to run code in the command line

- A collapsed command line is at the bottom of the Console indicated by >>>. To run code in this command line, type the code and press the Enter key. To expand the command line, click the red up arrow at the right side of the command line.

- The expanded command line is the pane on the right of the panel. To run code in this pane, enter the code and click Run to execute the code. To clear the code, click Clear. To collapse this pane, click the red down arrow at the bottom right of the command pane.

How to get a profile of the functions that were called

- To get a *profile* of the functions that were called, click the Profile button at the top of the Firebug panel to start the *profiler*. Then, after you've run the application a few times, click the Profile button again to display the profile report in the Console tab.

- *Note:* In the profile above, an error in Firebug causes the $ function to be displayed as (?). This indicates an unknown function name and should be corrected in later releases of this extension.

Description

- One of the uses of the Firebug Console tab is to display error messages like those that are displayed by the Error Console. If you click on the code link, the Script tab is opened and the line that caused the error is highlighted.

- A *stack trace* shows the functions that were called prior to the error with the most recent call at the top of the trace. To display a stack trace when an error message is displayed in the Console tab, click on the error message link or the plus sign before the link.

Figure 3-6   How to get information in the Console tab

How to review your code in the Script tab

The Script tab displays the JavaScript code for an application. This is illustrated by the Script tab in figure 3-7. This figure also shows you how to use this tab to review the JavaScript code for the current web page.

When you use this tab, you can review three types of scripts. A *static script* is a script in a file. An *eval script* is code that is dynamically executed by a call to the global eval method. And an *event script* is a script that is present in an event attribute of an XHTML tag such as the onclick attribute of the input tag. In this book, though, event scripts aren't used, and eval methods aren't presented because they expose your scripts to security vulnerabilities.

If you want the code in the Script tab highlighted with colors, you need to install the Rainbow extension for the Firebug extension. To do that, you must have Firebug version 1.2 or higher and Firefox version 3.0 or higher. If you add this extension to an earlier version of Firebug or Firefox, Firebug will no longer work so *please take this as a warning*. In that case, you will have to uninstall the Rainbow extension to get Firebug to work again.

The Script tab in Firebug

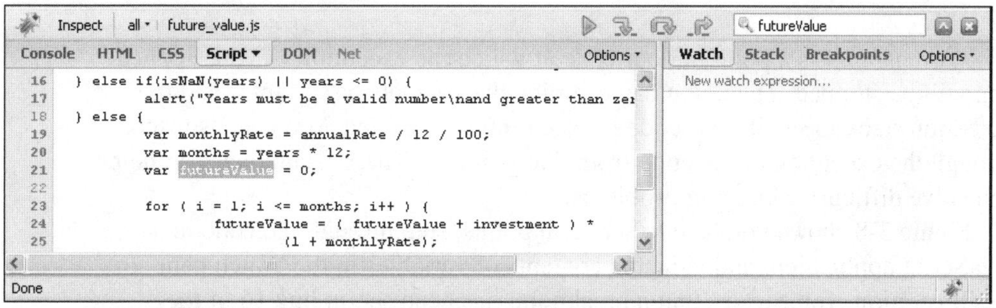

How to switch between JavaScript files

- If you have more than one JavaScript file for a web page, use the drop-down list that says "futureValue.js" in the screen above to switch from one file to another.

How to search through the code or jump to a line number

- Type your code in the search box in the upper right of the Firebug panel. Then, press Enter to find the next occurrence of your search term.

- Or, to jump to a line number in the code, type a pound sign (#) followed by a line number in the search box.

How to display the types of scripts that you want to see

- Use the drop-down list that shows "all" in the screen above. This lets you select combinations of static, eval, and event scripts. Because you probably won't be using eval or event scripts, though, you can leave this setting at "all."

Description

- In the Script tab, the code is displayed in black and white. If you want to enhance this so color is used to highlight specific coding elements, you can install the Rainbow extension for Firebug, as shown in appendix A.

- Although you can use the features of the Script tab to find errors, you can't change the code. You still need to use your text editor to make the changes.

Figure 3-7   How to review your JavaScript code in the Script tab

How to use breakpoints and step through code

A *breakpoint* is a point in your code at which the execution of your application will be stopped. Then, you can examine the contents of variables and the execution stack to see if your code is executing as expected. You can also step through the execution of the code from that point on. These techniques can help you solve difficult debugging problems.

Figure 3-8 shows you how to set breakpoints, step through the code in a JavaScript application, and view the contents of variables in the Watch pane. In the illustration, you can see that a breakpoint has been set on line 16 of the Future Value application.

When you run your application, it will stop at the first breakpoint that it encounters and display a yellow triangle on top of that breakpoint. While your code is stopped, you can hover your mouse over an object's name in the Script tab to display the current value of that object.

At a breakpoint, you can also view the current variables in the Watch pane on the right side of the panel. Those are the variables that are used by the function that is being executed. You can also see the value of other variables and expressions by clicking "New watch expression…" and typing the variable or expression you want to watch. (Note that the i variable in the for loop isn't listed in the Watch pane in this figure because it isn't created until the for statement is executed.)

To step through the execution of an application after a breakpoint is reached, you can use the Step Into, Step Over, and Step Out buttons. If you repeatedly click the Step Into button, you will execute the code one line at a time and the next line to be executed will be highlighted. After each line of code is executed, you can use the Watch tab to observe any changes in the variables. You can also click the Stack tab to view a stack trace that shows all of the executing functions and the value of their parameters.

As you step through an application, you can click the Step Over button if you want to execute any called functions without stepping through them. Or, you can use the Step Out button to step out of any functions that you don't want to step through. When you want to return to normal execution, you can click the Continue button. Then, the application will run until the next breakpoint is reached.

These are powerful debugging features that can help you find the causes of serious debugging problems. Stepping through an application is also a good way to understand how the code in an existing application works. If, for example, you step through the loop in the Future Value application, you'll get a better idea of how that loop works.

A breakpoint in the Firebug Script tab

Continue, Step Into, Step Over, and Step Out buttons

```
  Inspect    all ▾  futureValue.js   calculate_click()              ▷ 🔁 ➡ ➡  🔍                    ☐ ☒
 Console   HTML   CSS   Script ▾   DOM   Net           Options ▾   Watch   Stack   Breakpoints            Options ▾
   12         var monthlyRate = annualRate / 12 / 100;              New watch expression...
   13         var months = years * 12;                            ⊞ this              input#calculate Calculate
   14         var futureValue = 0;                                  annualRate    12
   15                                                               futureValue   0
 ◉ 16         for ( i = 1; i <= months; i++ ) {                     investment    100
   17             futureValue = ( futureValue + investment ) *      monthlyRate   0.01
   18                 (1 + monthlyRate);                            months        12
   19         }                                                     years         1
   20
 ◂                                              ▸
 Done                                                                                               ✦
```

How to set a breakpoint

- If necessary, use the drop-down list above the Script tab to select the right JavaScript file. Then, to set a breakpoint, click in the bar to the left of a statement. The breakpoint is marked by a red dot.

- To set a *conditional breakpoint*, right-click on a statement and enter a conditional expression in the resulting dialog box. Then, the application only stops at the breakpoint if the condition is true.

How to step through JavaScript code from a breakpoint

- Click the Step Into button to step through the code one line at a time. At each step, the Watch tab displays the values of the current variables. You can also hover the mouse cursor over a variable name to display its current value.

- Click the Step Over button to execute any called functions without stepping through them. Click the Step Out button to execute the rest of a function without stepping through it. Or, click the Continue button to resume normal execution.

How to set a watch expression

- Click "New watch expression…" in the Watch tab and type the variable name or the expression that you want to watch.

How to disable or remove breakpoints

- To remove a breakpoint, click on the red breakpoint marker in the Script tab, or click on the close button for the breakpoint in the Breakpoints tab.

- To disable a breakpoint, click on the check box for it in the Breakpoints tab.

Description

- You can set a *breakpoint* on any line except a blank line.

- When the JavaScript engine encounters a breakpoint, it stops before it executes the statement that contains the breakpoint.

- To see a stack trace when you're stepping through an application, click on the Stack tab.

Figure 3-8   How to set breakpoints and step through the execution of your code

How to use the Firebug console object

For most applications, you'll be able to test and debug your applications with the features that have been presented thus far. In some cases, though, you may need to use some of the methods of the Firebug console object to get information. In particular, you can use the console.log method to do an extensive trace of the execution of an application.

If you're new to programming, you can skip this topic and come back to it later because it uses some coding techniques that won't be presented until later in this book. If you're an experienced programmer, though, this is worth a quick read.

The methods of the console object

When the Firebug Console tab is enabled, it adds an object to the JavaScript environment called the console object. This object provides many methods for reporting information in the Console tab. The more common methods are summarized in figure 3-9. For instance, the log method can be used to display messages in the Console tab, the profile method turns on the profiler, and the profileEnd method turns off the profiler.

If the console object isn't available, though, the use of a console method causes a runtime error. This can happen if the Firebug extension isn't installed or the Firebug Console tab isn't enabled.

To prevent errors when the console object isn't available, you can *wrap* the console methods in if statements or functions that test for the existence of the console object before using one of its methods. This is illustrated by the code in this figure, which tests for the presence of the console object and its log method before using the console.log method.

You can also use a *debug flag* to control console logging even if the console object is available. A debug flag is just a global Boolean variable that indicates whether or not debugging should take place. For instance, the code that follows defines a debug flag and sets it to true:

```
var debug = true; // Set to false to skip debugging
```

This code should be near the start of the JavaScript code so it's easy to find.

Next, you modify any wrapper code so it checks the value of the debug flag before using any of the console methods. For instance, the code in this figure would be expanded to look like this:

```
if ( debug && typeof console == "object" && console.log ) {
    console.log ("Function complete.");
}
```

Now, if you set the debug flag to true and the console object is present, this code will call the console.log method. But if you set the debug variable to false, this code won't call the log method even if the console object is present.

Common methods of the Firebug console object

Method	Description
log()	Displays a message in the console. It takes one or more objects as parameters to display.
debug()	Displays a message in the console and includes a link to the source of the message. It takes one or more objects as parameters to display.
info()	Displays a message with an information icon in the console and includes a link to the source of the message. It takes one or more objects as parameters to display.
warn()	Displays a message with a warning icon in the console and includes a link to the source of the message. It takes one or more objects as parameters to display.
error()	Displays a message with an error icon in the console and includes a link to the source of the message. It takes one or more objects as parameters to display.
assert()	Displays an error message in the console and throws an exception if the boolean expression in its first parameter is false. It takes a Boolean expression as its first parameter and optional objects to display in the console if the assertion fails.
dir()	Displays an interactive list of the object's properties. It takes one object as a parameter.
profile()	Turns on the Firebug profiler which times every function call. It takes one optional parameter which is a string to display in the console.
profileEnd()	Turns off the Firebug profiler and displays the report in the console.

Examples of the console object methods

```
// Log the value of the months variable in the console.
console.log("Months", months);

// Display an error message in the console.
console.error("User entered an invalid value for months.");
```

How to test for the presence of the console object and the log method

```
if (typeof console == "object" && console.log) {
    console.log ("Function complete.");
}
```

Description

- The methods of the console object give you many ways to track and report what your program is doing.

- If the console object isn't available, you'll get a runtime error if you try to use it. To avoid that, you can use the code above, which tests to see whether the console object and the log method are available.

- Go to http://getfirebug.com/console.html for a complete list of the methods of the console object.

Figure 3-9   The methods of the Firebug console object

How to trace an application with Firebug's console.log method

One of the uses of the console.log method is to trace the execution of an application. This is illustrated by figure 3-10. In this case, the log method is used to display variable names and values at various points in the code. This data will be displayed in the Console tab as the application executes.

When the application is finished, you can review this data. This will help you determine where the bug is. Then, you'll have more information that will help you determine what the logic error is and how to fix it.

Note, however, that the log method isn't used directly in this figure. Instead, it's wrapped in the $log function. That will prevent runtime errors from occurring when the console object isn't available. In chapter 10, you'll learn how the apply method of a function works, but for now just know that the $log function accepts any number of parameters and uses the log function to display them in the Console tab. Statements that use the $log function are then inserted in strategic places in the code of the Future Value application to trace its execution.

The JavaScript file for the Future Value application with execution tracing

```javascript
var $log = function () {
    if (typeof console == "object" && console.log ) {
        console.log.apply(console, arguments);
    }
}

var $ = function (id) {
    return document.getElementById(id);
}

var calculate_click = function () {
    var investment = parseFloat( $("investment").value );
    var annualRate = parseFloat( $("rate").value );
    var years = parseInt( $("years").value );
    $log("investment", investment);
    $log("annualRate", annualRate);
    $log("years", years);

    $("futureValue").value = "";

    var monthlyRate = annualRate / 12 / 100;
    var months = years * 12;
    var futureValue = 0;
    $log("monthlyRate", monthlyRate);
    $log("months", months);

    for ( i = 1; i <= months; i++ ) {
        futureValue = ( futureValue + investment ) *
            (1 + monthlyRate);
        $log("month " + i + " futureValue", futureValue);
    }
}
```

The data that's written to the Console tab

```
Inspect  Clear  Profile                                    🔍            ⬆ ⬇

Console ▼  HTML   CSS   Script   DOM   Net        Options ▼
investment 100                                            ▲
annualRate 12
years 1
monthlyRate 0.01
months 12
month 1 futureValue 101
month 2 futureValue 203.01
month 3 futureValue 306.0401                             ▼    Run  Clear  Copy            ▼
```

Description

- The log method of Firebug's console object writes data to the Console tab.
- The $log function at the start of the code wraps the console.log method so calls to it won't cause a runtime error if Firebug isn't installed or enabled. The effect is that the $log function executes the console.log method.

Figure 3-10   How to trace an application with Firebug's console.log method

How to test and debug with other browsers

Although I recommend that you use Firebug in the Firefox browser to do your primary testing and debugging, you also need to know how to debug JavaScript in the other browsers. In some cases, for example, your code will work in Firefox, but fail in other browsers. Then, you need to know how get any help that those browsers offer. With that in mind, here's a quick tour of the features offered by Internet Explorer, Safari, Opera, and Chrome.

In these descriptions, the focus is on getting the error messages from the browser, not on using the debugging features. That will get you started with these browsers. Then, if you need to use their debugging features, you can experiment with them on your own.

Note too that these descriptions are for the current releases of these browsers at the time of this writing. But since these browsers are continually being upgraded, some of this information may change.

How to get error messages with Internet Explorer

When Internet Explorer encounters an error, it displays a yellow triangle with an exclamation mark in the lower left corner of the browser window. Then, to view the error message, you double-click this error icon. This is illustrated by figure 3-11.

When the message box is displayed for the first time, you may need to click the Show Details button to view the details of the message. Then, if you close the dialog box with the details still displayed, Internet Explorer will show the details the next time the message box is displayed.

Like Firefox, the details of the error message show the line number that caused the error, a description of the error, and the URL of the file where the error occurred. Note, however, that the error message in this figure is reported as line 3 of the XHTML file. This is where the script tag is used to load an external JavaScript file. However, the error actually occurs in line 2 of this JavaScript file. That means that when you use Internet Explorer you often have to search for the actual error.

Like the Firebug extension of Firefox, Internet Explorer 8 offers Developer Tools that support breakpoints, stack traces, and watch expressions. However, the tools are a separate download. Once you've downloaded and installed them, you can access them by pressing the F12 key.

Internet Explorer 6 with an error indicator in the lower left corner

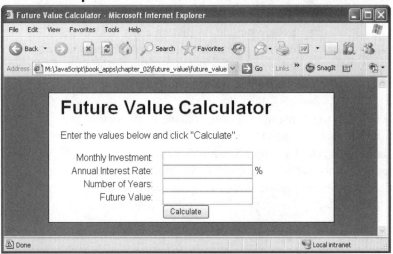

The Internet Explorer message box

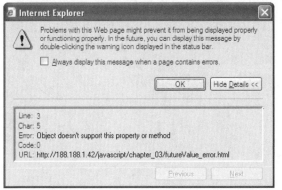

How to display an error message

- Double-click the error icon in the lower left corner to view the error message. Then, if necessary, click the Show Details button to view the entire message.

- If you always want the error message to be displayed, you can click the checkbox before closing the message box. Or, you can go to Tools→Internet Options, click on the Advanced tab, and check the "Display a notification about every script error" checkbox.

Description

- The error message feature of Internet Explorer doesn't let you jump to the statement that caused the error the way Firefox does.

- Internet Explorer 8 provides Developer Tools as a separate download. These tools support breakpoints, stack traces, and the display of variables while you're stepping through an application in a way that's similar to Firebug.

- To access the Developer Tools after you've downloaded and installed them, press F12.

Figure 3-11   How to get error messages with Internet Explorer

How to get error messages with Safari

Like Firefox, Safari doesn't display any indication that an error has occurred in the main web browser window, but it does have a console that displays error messages. To display this console, you can use the technique in figure 3-12. Unlike Firefox, you must open this console before you load the web page that you want to debug.

When an error occurs with the console open, the console displays the error message, the URL of the file that contains the error, and the line number where the error occurred. Like Firefox, the URL and line number identify the JavaScript file and the line number at which the error occurred. But unlike Firefox, Safari doesn't support breakpoints, stack traces, or watch expressions.

The Safari console with an error message displayed

```
Web Inspector — http://192.168.1.42/javascript/chapter_03/futureValue_error.html    [_][□][X]

◄  ►                    Clear              Q▾ Search

▼DOCUMENTS            ⊗ Value undefined (result of expression document.getElementByID) is not object.
                        http://192.168.1.42/javascript/chapter_03/futureValue_error.js (line 2) ⊙
    futureValue_error.html
    /javascript/chapter_03
```

The Safari console when you click on the URL in a message

```
Web Inspector — http://192.168.1.42/javascript/chapter_03/futureValue_error.html                   [_][□][X]

◄  ►                                                                    Q▾ Search

▼DOCUMENTS                 2      return document.getElementByID(id);
                           3  }
    futureValue_error.html 4
    /javascript/chapter_03 5  var calculate_click = function () {
                           6      var investment = parseFloat( $("investment").value );
▼STYLESHEETS              7      var annualRate = parseFloat( $("rate").value );
                           8      var years = parseInt( $("years").value );
    futureValue.css        9      $("futureValue").value = "";
    /javascript/chapter_03 10
                           11     var monthlyRate = annualRate / 12 / 100;
►IMAGES                   12     var months = years * 12;
                           13     var futureValue = 0;
▼SCRIPTS                  14     for ( i = 1; i <= months; i++ ) {
                           15         futureValue = ( futureValue + investment ) *
    futureValue_error.js ① 16             (1 + monthlyRate);
    /javascript/chapter_03 17     }
                           18     futureValue = Math.round( futureValue * 100) / 100;
    Console               19     if ( !isNaN(futureValue) ) {
    1 error               20         var fvDisplay = "$" + futureValue;
                           21         var cents = Math.round((futureValue - parseInt(futureValue)) * 100);
    Network               22         if (cents == 0) {
                           23             fvDisplay += ".00";
                           24         } else if ( cents % 10 == 0 ) {
```

How to display the Safari console

- First, display the Develop menu. To do that, use the Edit→Preferences command, click the Advanced tab, and check the "Show Develop menu in menu bar" checkbox.

- Then, to display the console, use the Develop→Show Error Console command.

Description

- To get messages in the Safari console, you must open the console *before* loading the web page you want to run.

- To see the JavaScript code for an error message, click on the URL in the message.

- To view your current web page in another browser, use the Develop→Open Page With command, and then select the browser you want to use.

- Safari doesn't support breakpoints, stack traces, or watch expressions.

Figure 3-12   How to get error messages with Safari

How to get error messages with Opera

Like Firefox, Opera doesn't display any indication that an error has occurred in the main web browser window, but it does have an Error Console for error messages. To display this console, you can use the technique in figure 3-13.

When an error occurs, the Error Console displays the URL of the web page that's being displayed, the error message, and a stack trace called a *backtrace*. The first entry in the backtrace is where the error occurred. This shows the line number, URL, and source code where the error occurred. Then, if you click the pencil icon to the right of the URL, Opera will display the source code for the file.

Like Firefox, Opera supports breakpoints, stack tracing, and watch expressions in a panel called the developer tools. In this panel, the Scripts tab displays information about the Scripts that are loaded. The DOM tab lets you view the document object model. The Error Console tab contains the same information as the Error Console window. And the Environment tab displays the version information for Opera and your operating system.

The Opera error console with an error message displayed

The Opera developer tools

How to open the error console and the developer tools

- To open the error console, use the Tools→Advanced→Error Console command.
- To open the developer tools, use the Tools→Advanced→Developer Tools command.

Description

- The error console shows all error messages, and the error messages are followed by a stack trace.
- To view the source code where an error occurred, click the pencil icon to the right of an error message.
- Opera provides developer tools that support breakpoints, stack traces, and the display of variables while you're stepping through an application in a way that's similar to Firefox.

Figure 3-13   How to get error messages with Opera

How to get error messages with Chrome

Like Firefox, Chrome doesn't display any indication that an error has occurred in the main web browser window, but it does have a JavaScript console for error messages. To display this console, you can use the menu that's shown in figure 3-14.

In the JavaScript console, you can click on the file link in the left pane of the Resources tab to display the source code for a file. Then, when you click on the link in an error message, an error indicator is displayed in the source code below the statement that caused the error.

The Chrome browser with the Developer menu displayed

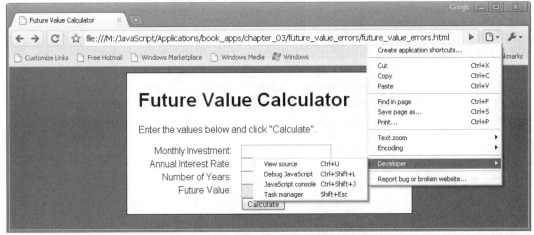

The JavaScript console with an error message displayed

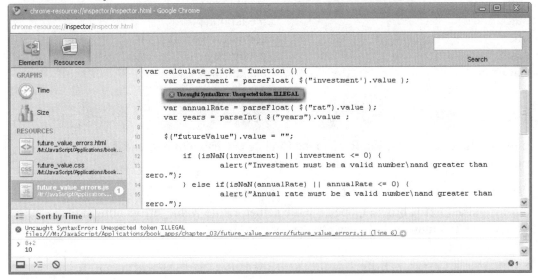

How to open the JavaScript console and the debugger

- To open the JavaScript console, select the Developer→JavaScript Console command from the menu that drops down from the page icon.
- To open the JavaScript debugger, select the Developer→Debug JavaScript command.

Description

- The JavaScript console lists the error messages. Then, you can click the link for an error message to highlight the error in the JavaScript code that's shown in the Resources tab.
- In the left pane of the Resources tab, you can click on any file that's listed to display its contents in the right pane.

Figure 3-14   How to get error messages with Chrome

Perspective

All too often, JavaScript applications are put into production before they have been thoroughly tested and debugged. In the early days of JavaScript programming, that was understandable because the tools for testing and debugging were limited. Today, however, Firefox and its Firebug extension give you the tools you need for finding all the bugs before an application is put into production. As a result, there's no longer a good excuse for inadequate testing and debugging.

Terms

test	profiler
debug	profile
syntax error	static script
runtime error	eval script
logic error	event script
bug	breakpoint
trace	conditional breakpoint
stack	debug flag
stack trace	backtrace

Exercise 3-1   Fix syntax errors

In this exercise, you'll use Firefox and the Firebug extension to find and fix four syntax errors in the Future Value application.

Use the Error Console to fix the first two errors

1. From the Firefox browser, open the file named future_value_errors.html in the chapter_03\future_value_errors folder for exercises. It contains the four errors shown in figure 3-2.

2. Enter valid values in the three input boxes and click the Calculate button. When nothing happens, open the Error Console as shown in figure 3-3. Then, click on the link for the code to display the JavaScript code with the error line highlighted.

3. Use your editor to open the JavaScript file and fix the first error. Next, return to Firefox, click the Reload button, and click the Calculate button to run the application again. Then, find and fix the second error.

Use the Firebug panel to fix the next two errors

4. If you haven't already done so, install the Firebug extension as shown in appendix A. Next, enable the Console and Script tabs. Then, run the Future Value application again, which still won't work.

5. Use the techniques in figure 3-6 to find and fix the next two bugs.

6. Once the application is working, get a profile of the functions that it uses. To do that, start the profiler, run the application twice with two sets of input values, stop the profiler, and review the profile in the Console tab.

Exercise 3-2   Trace with alert methods

In this exercise, you'll use alert methods to trace the execution of the Future Value application.

1. Open the html file in the chapter_03\future_value_alert folder for exercises. The related JavaScript file named future_value_alert.js includes the alert methods shown in figure 3-4.

2. Run the application to see how the alert methods work.

Exercise 3-3   Step through an application

In this exercise, you'll use Firefox and its Firebug extension to set a breakpoint and step through the Future Value application.

1. Open the html file in the chapter_03\future_value folder for exercises.

2. Use the drop-down list above the Script tab to display the code for the future_value.js file. Then, set a breakpoint on the return statement in the $ function (the second line of code in the file).

3. Enter valid values in the input boxes for the application, and click the Calculate button. The application should stop at the breakpoint.

4. Experiment with the Step Into, Step Over, and Step Out buttons as you step through the code of the application. At each step, notice the values that are displayed in the Watch tab. Also, hover the mouse over a variable in the Script tab to see what its value is.

5. When you're through experimenting, remove the breakpoint.

Exercise 3-4   Trace with console.log methods

In this exercise, you'll use Firefox, its Firebug extension, and the console.log method to trace the execution of the Future Value application.

1. Open the html file in the chapter_03\future_value_trace folder for exercises. The related JavaScript file named future_value_trace.js includes the tracing statements shown in figure 3-10.

2. Review the tracing statements that the JavaScript file contains. Next, run the application twice with two sets of input data. Then, review the tracing data in the Console tab of the Firebug panel.

4

A crash course in XHTML

Before you can learn how to build JavaScript applications, you need to know how to code XHTML documents. Although that's a large subject by itself, this chapter is a crash course in XHTML that presents the basic skills for coding most XHTML documents and all the skills you need for understanding the JavaScript applications in this book.

If you already know how to code web pages and forms with XHTML, you can skip this chapter. Then, if you encounter a tag or attribute that you aren't familiar with later in the book, you can come back to this chapter to learn how to use it.

An introduction to XHTML **122**
A web page and its XHTML 122
Basic XHTML syntax 126
How to validate an XHTML document 128
How to code web pages **130**
How to code the head section 130
How to code the core attributes 132
How to code blocks of text 134
How to format text with inline tags 136
How to code lists 138
How to code character entities 140
How to code links 142
How to include images 144
How to code tables **146**
How to code a simple table 146
How to code a table with spanned columns and rows 148
How to code forms **150**
How to create a form 150
How to code buttons 152
How to code labels and text fields 154
How to code radio buttons and check boxes 156
How to code select lists 158
How to code text areas 160
How to group controls 162
How to set the tab order for controls 164
Perspective **166**

An introduction to XHTML

This topic introduces you to some of the basic skills for coding a web page with XHTML and then validating it.

A web page and its XHTML

Figure 4-1 shows two versions of the same *XHTML web page* in a browser. The first version shows how the XHTML by itself is rendered in the browser. The second version shows how the page looks when CSS (Cascading Style Sheets) is used to format it.

In this chapter, you're going to learn how to code just the XHTML for a web page. As a result, the XHTML elements will be displayed using the browser's default settings. In this chapter, I used Firefox 3.0 for the examples, but the results may vary slightly if you use a different browser.

In the past, XHTML was commonly used to do most or all of the formatting for a web page. Today, however, the preferred way to do that formatting is to use CSS. You'll see why that's true in the next chapter.

If you look at the web page in this figure, you can see some of the XHTML effects that you'll learn how to code. In the title bar of the browser, for example, you can see the title for the document: "Mike's Bait & Tackle Shop". In the address bar and on the tab, you can see the fish icon that's used for this application. And in the body of the document, you can see a heading, a paragraph, a lower-level heading, an unordered list, and a link to another page ("Contact us").

An XHTML page that doesn't have a CSS file for formatting

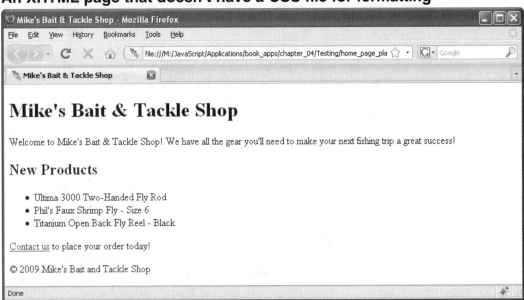

The same page with a CSS file for formatting

Description

- This chapter shows you how to code the XHTML for a web page. The next chapter shows you how to code the CSS that formats the web page.

Figure 4-1   A web page with and without CSS formatting

In figure 4-2, you can see the XHTML for the web page in the previous figure. This XHTML for a single page is commonly referred to as an *XHTML document*. Within this document are *tags* that define the elements of the page. Each of these tags has an opening bracket (<) and a closing bracket (>).

If you're already familiar with XHTML, you can probably follow most of this code right now. If not, you'll learn how to code all of these tags in this chapter. As you learn, you can refer back to this document to see how the tags are used within it. Before you go on, though, it's worth taking a look at the overall structure of this document.

To start, the <!DOCTYPE> declaration tells the web browser which markup language you're going to use for the web page. If you don't have a <!DOCTYPE> declaration or if you declare a standard but don't follow it, your browser might not format the elements as you intended.

After the <!DOCTYPE> declaration, this page uses an opening <html> tag to mark the beginning of the XHTML document, and a closing </html> tag to mark the end of the document. When working with XHTML, a *closing tag* has the same name as the *opening tag*, but is preceded by a forward slash (/).

Within the <html> tag, you can see a head section that's marked by the opening and closing <head> tags followed by a body section that's marked by the opening and closing <body> tags. In the head section, tags are used to provide information about the web page. For instance, the <title> tag provides the title that's shown in the browser's title bar. In the body section, tags are used to define the elements that are displayed in the web page.

Within the body section, you can use <div> tags to give more structure to the document. For instance, the first <div> tag has an *attribute* that gives it an id of "page". Then, three more <div> tags are used to divide the web page into three parts with "header", "main", and "footer" as the ids. Although the <div> tags don't affect the appearance of this web page, you can use CSS to provide formatting for the elements within each set of <div> tags. If, for example, you look back to the CSS version of this page in figure 4-1, you can see that CSS has been used to provide different formatting to the elements within each set of <div> tags.

Similarly, the class attribute that's applied to the last two <p> tags doesn't apply any formatting to these tags. But CSS can use those class names to provide different formatting to each paragraph. Here again, this is illustrated by the CSS version of the web page in figure 4-1.

Last, to make the code easier to read, you can use *comments* that start with <!-- and end with --> to provide clarifying notes that are ignored by the browser. And you can use blank lines to provide vertical space between different portions of code, and indentation to show that tags are nested within other tags. These extra carriage returns, tabs, and spaces are known as *whitespace*, and they have no effect on the XHTML.

The XHTML for the web page in figure 4-1

```
<!DOCTYPE html PUBLIC "-//W3C//DTD XHTML 1.0 Transitional//EN"
    "http://www.w3.org/TR/xhtml1/DTD/xhtml1-transitional.dtd">

<html xmlns="http://www.w3.org/1999/xhtml">

    <!-- the head section -->
    <head>
        <title>Mike's Bait &amp; Tackle Shop</title>
        <meta http-equiv="content-type" content="text/html; charset=utf-8" />
        <link rel="shortcut icon" href="site.ico" type="image/ico" />
    </head>

    <!-- the body section -->
    <body>
    <div id="page">
        <div id="header">
            <h1>Mike's Bait &amp; Tackle Shop</h1>
        </div>

        <div id="main">
            <p>Welcome to Mike's Bait &amp; Tackle Shop!
                We have all the gear you'll need to make your next
                fishing trip a great success!</p>
            <h2>New Products</h2>
            <ul>
                <li>Ultima 3000 Two-Handed Fly Rod</li>
                <li>Phil's Faux Shrimp Fly - Size 6</li>
                <li>Titanium Open Back Fly Reel - Black</li>
            </ul>
        </div>

        <div id="footer">
            <p class="contact"><a href="contact.html">Contact us</a> to place
                your order today!</p>
            <p class="copyright">&copy;
                <script type="text/javascript">
                    var today = new Date();
                    document.writeln( today.getFullYear() );
                </script>
                Mike's Bait and Tackle Shop</p>
        </div>
    </div>
    </body>
</html>
```

Description

- Every XHTML document requires one <head> and one <body> section. Within the body section, <div> tags can be used to give structure to the document.

- The id and class attributes that are applied to an element can be used by CSS to provide formatting for that element.

- *Whitespace* like carriage returns, tab characters, and spacing can be used to make the XHTML easier to read.

Figure 4-2   The XHTML for the web page in figure 4-1

Basic XHTML syntax

Figure 4-3 presents the basic structure of an XHTML document and some basic XHTML syntax rules that summarize what you've seen in the previous figure. Although XHTML isn't a programming language, it is highly structured.

To start, all XHTML documents must begin with a <!DOCTYPE> declaration that indicates which version of HTML or XHTML the document uses. In this book, we use a <!DOCTYPE> declaration that specifies XHTML 1.0 Transitional. However, we try to follow the XHTML 1.0 Strict guidelines. This works because 1.0 Strict is a subset of 1.0 Transitional. Then, if necessary, we can use an attribute or element from XHTML 1.0 Transitional.

After the <!DOCTYPE> declaration, you code the <html> tag. This tag requires an attribute named xmlns that specifies the XML namespace for the document. This is required and should always be set as shown here. This means you can start every XHTML document with the first three lines in this figure. To do that, you can copy these lines from an old document into each new document.

To provide notes that help make your document easier to read, you can code *comments*. You can also use comments to hide sections of a web page without deleting the content. However, users can still read your comments by viewing the source code for the page.

As you saw in the last figure, most XHTML tags have an *opening tag* and a *closing tag*. The opening tag contains the name of the tag and any attributes for the tag, and the closing tag contains a forward slash and the name of the tag. Within these tags, you can code other tags or text. For example, the <p> tag in this figure contains text that will be displayed by the browser.

In contrast, *self-closing tags* like the <br /> tag don't contain other tags or text. Instead, they are closed by a forward slash at the end of the opening tag. For maximum compatibility with older browsers, you should put a space just before the forward slash in these tags. Often, a self-closing tag will contain several attributes like the <img> tag in this figure.

Attributes are used to modify how a tag works. An attribute is added to an opening tag by coding the name of the attribute, an equal sign, and the value for the attribute in quotation marks. Although you can use double or single quotes for the value, you should be consistent. In this figure, the first <input> tag has type, name, and id attributes.

To code a Boolean attribute that's on, you code the name of the attribute followed by a value that is the same as the name. In this figure, for example, the checked attribute of the second <input> tag is a Boolean attribute that is on. To code a Boolean value that's off, you just omit the attribute.

When you code one XHTML tag within another, you must be sure that the tag is properly *nested*. That is, you can't close an outer tag before you close its inner tag. This is illustrated by the last set of examples in this figure.

When you use whitespace to make a document easier to read, the extra characters are ignored. In other words, whenever a browser encounters a sequence of one or more of these characters, it replaces them with a single space. That's why you often need to use the <br /> tag to start a new line.

The basic structure of an XHTML 1.0 Transitional document

```
<!DOCTYPE html PUBLIC "-//W3C//DTD XHTML 1.0 Transitional//EN"
    "http://www.w3.org/TR/xhtml1/DTD/xhtml1-transitional.dtd">
<html xmlns="http://www.w3.org/1999/xhtml">
    <head>
        <title>Mike's Bait and Tackle Shop</title>
    </head>
    <body>
        <!-- The body tags go here -->
    </body>
</html>
```

XHTML comments

```
<!-- This is a comment so it's ignored by the web browser. -->
```

Two types of tags

Tags that have both opening and closing tags

```
<p>This text is within the opening and closing paragraph tags.</p>
```

Self-closing tags

```
<br />
<img src="logo.gif" alt="Murach Logo" />
```

Tags with attributes

A tag with three attributes

```
<input type="text" name="firstName" id="firstName" />
```

A tag with four attributes including a Boolean attribute

```
<input type="checkbox" name="mailList" id="mailList" checked="checked" />
```

Correct and incorrect nesting of tags

A tag with correct nesting

```
<b>This text <i>demonstrates correct</i></b><i>nesting of tags.</i>
```

A tag with incorrect nesting

```
<b>This text <i>demonstrates incorrect</b> nesting of tags.</i>
```

The syntax rules for XHTML

- The document must begin with a <!DOCTYPE> declaration.
- The first tag must be the <html> tag.
- Tag names and attributes must be lowercase.
- All attributes must have values and those values must be in quotes.
- When you code one tag within another, you must close the inner tag before you close the outer tag. This is correct nesting.
- Extra whitespace is ignored.

Figure 4-3   Basic XHTML syntax

How to validate an XHTML document

When a browser opens an XHTML document that contains errors, it ignores the errors and does its best to render the page. Often, the errors are obvious so you can find and correct them. Other times, the errors aren't obvious, and they may cause problems with some browsers.

One solution to this problem is to use a validating program to *validate* your XHTML document. Some web development tools like Dreamweaver provide programs like that, and some web sites provide them. One of the most popular web sites is the one for the W3C Markup Validation Service that's shown in figure 4-4.

When you use this web site, you can provide the XHTML document that you want to validate in three ways. You can provide the URL for the page. You can upload the document. And you can copy and paste the document into their Validate by Direct Input tab. In this figure, the Validate by File Upload tab is shown.

If you embed JavaScript within an XHTML document, you should be aware that the validating program will assume that the JavaScript is XHTML. Then, if the JavaScript contains XHTML characters like the < and >, validation errors will be detected. One way to solve this problem is to enclose the JavaScript within the JavaScript comments that are shown in the example in this figure. Another solution is to move the JavaScript to a file so it isn't embedded in the XHTML, but that isn't always practical.

What's actually happening in this example is that the CDATA tag tells the validating program to ignore the JavaScript code that's within <![CDATA[and]]>. Although that by itself solves the validation problem, it causes JavaScript errors. Then, to get around that problem, you code // before the parts of this tag so JavaScript will treat them as comments and ignore them.

The web address of the W3C Markup Validation Service

```
http://validator.w3.org/
```

The home page for the W3C validator

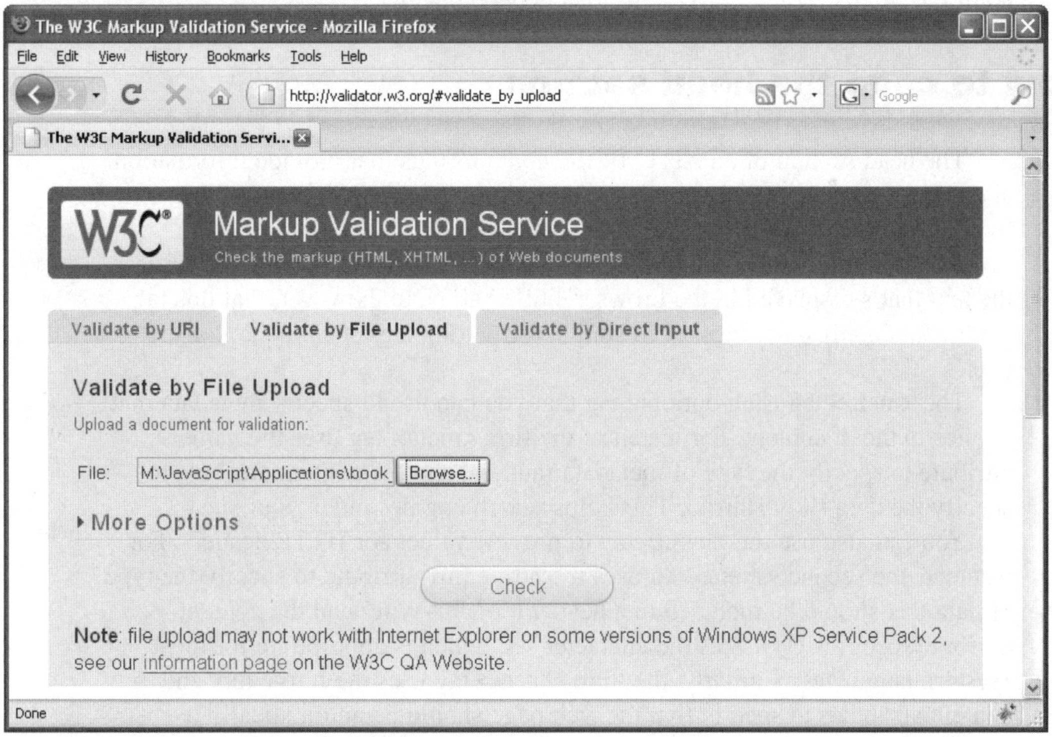

How to mark JavaScript as character data so it won't cause errors

```
<p class="copyright">&copy;
    <script type="text/javascript">
        //<![CDATA[
        var today = new Date();
        document.writeln( "<b>" + today.getFullYear() + "</b>");
        //]]>
    </script>
Mike's Bait and Tackle Shop</p>
```

Description

- When an XHTML document is opened in a browser, the browser ignores any errors and renders the web page as well as it can.

- To *validate* the XHTML for a page, you can use a program or web site for that purpose. One of the most popular is the web site for the W3C Markup Validation Service.

- If you embed JavaScript in an XHTML document that contains XHTML characters like < or >, it will cause validation errors. One solution is to mark the embedded JavaScript as character data as shown above. The other solution is to move the JavaScript to a separate file.

Figure 4-4   How to validate an XHTML document

How to code web pages

Now that you have a general idea of how XHTML works, you're ready to learn the details for using XHTML to code web pages.

How to code the head section

The head section of an XHTML file contains tags that provide information about the web page rather than the content of the page itself. This is illustrated by the head section in figure 4-5.

At a minimum, the <head> tag must contain a <title> tag, which specifies the text that's displayed in the browser's title bar. Note, however, that this tag can't contain any other tags, even simple formatting tags such as <b> or <i> tags.

The <meta> tag is an optional tag that you can use to specify metadata that applies to the document. For instance, the first <meta> tag uses the name attribute to specify the type of metadata (author) and the content attribute to specify the data (Ray Harris). This helps search engines index your site.

You can also use the <meta> tag to provide values for HTTP headers. For instance, the second <meta> tag uses the http-equiv attribute to specify the type of data that should be included in a header (content-type) and the content attribute specifies UTF-8 as the character set, which is appropriate for most Western languages. Similarly, the third <meta> tag uses the http-equiv and content attributes to specify that the web page should be automatically re-freshed every 30 seconds.

The <link> tag is another optional tag that you can use to specify a file that should be linked to the web page. For instance, the first <link> tag links an icon named site.ico to the web page. As a result, this icon will be shown in the browser's address bar, tabs, or bookmarks.

In this case, the example assumes that the icon file is in the same directory as the XHTML file. However, if the file was in a different directory, you could use the href attribute to specify an absolute or relative URL to navigate to that file. For example, to navigate back one directory and then up to the images directory, you could code a URL like this:

```
href="../images/site.ico"
```

You can also use the <link> tag to link to an external style sheet. For instance, the second <link> tag links to an external CSS file named main.css. Here again, this assumes that the CSS file is in the same directory as the XHTML file, but you can use the href attribute to specify an absolute or relative URL if that's necessary.

As you learned in chapter 2, you can use a <script> tag in the head section to link to an external JavaScript file. You can also use the <style> tag in the head section to load an external CSS file into an XHTML document or to embed CSS in the document. You'll learn more about that in the next chapter.

The XHTML for a head section

```
<head>
    <title>Mike's Bait and Tackle Shop</title>
    <meta name="author" content="Ray Harris" />
    <meta http-equiv="content-type" content="text/html; charset=utf-8" />
    <meta http-equiv="refresh" content="30" />
    <link rel="shortcut icon" href="site.ico" type="image/ico" />
    <link rel="stylesheet" href="main.css" type="text/css" />
    <script type="text/javascript" src="common.js"></script>
</head>
```

An icon file named site.ico

A browser that shows the title and the icon

File	Edit	View	History	Bookmarks	Tools	Help

file:///M:/JavaScript/Applications/book_a   G • Google

Mike's Bait and Tackle Shop

The attributes of the <meta> tag

Attribute	Description
name	Specifies the type of meta data being added to the document. Typical values are "author", "keywords", "description", "date", "revised", "generator", and "robots". Then, the content attribute provides the value.
http-equiv	Specifies the name of a metadata value in an HTTP header. Then, the content attribute provides the value.
content	Specifies the value to be used for the item specified by the name or http-equiv attribute.

The attributes of the <link> tag

Attribute	Description
href	Specifies the URL of the resource being linked to the web page.
rel	Specifies the relationship of the resource being linked to the web page. Typical values are "stylesheet", "shortcut icon", "index", "alternate", "next", and "prev".
type	Specifies the media type of the resource being linked. When the rel attribute is "stylesheet", the type should be "text/css". When the rel attribute is "shortcut icon", the type should be "image/ico".

Description

- The <title> tag specifies the text that's shown in the browser's title bar. It is required.
- The <meta> tag provides metadata that applies to the document or to HTTP headers.
- The <link> tag identifies files that are linked to the web page like a CSS or an icon file. As you will see in the next chapter, you can also use a <style> tag to identify a CSS file.
- The <script> tag identifies JavaScript files that are used by the web page.

Figure 4-5   How to code the head section

How to code the core attributes

Nearly all XHTML tags support several core attributes. The three that you'll use the most are summarized in figure 4-6.

As you've already seen, you use the id attribute to uniquely identify an XHTML element. That way, you can use CSS and JavaScript to work with the element. For instance, the example in this figure uses two <div> tags to divide the page into a main section and a footer section, and it uses the id attribute to uniquely identify each section. Then, you can use CSS to format these sections.

Similarly, the XHTML code includes an <input> tag that defines a text field, and it uses the id attribute to uniquely identify that field. Then, you can use JavaScript to work with that field. As you've seen in chapter 2, you can do that by passing the value of the id attribute to the document.getElementById method.

When you code the id attribute, remember that this attribute is designed to uniquely identify an XHTML element. As a result, you can't use the same id for more than one element. If you do, the getElementById method won't work correctly and the results of your code will be unpredictable.

In contrast to the id attribute, you can use the class attribute to mark one or more XHTML elements as members of a class. Typically, this attribute is used to apply CSS formatting to these elements. In the example in this figure, the <p> tag in the footer sets its class attribute to "copyright". As a result, you can use CSS to apply formatting to this paragraph.

The third core attribute in this figure can be used to provide a title for an XHTML element. For many XHTML elements, this title serves no purpose. However, for some XHTML elements, the browser will display the title in a tooltip when the mouse pointer hovers over the element. In the example in this figure, you can see the tooltip that's displayed for the email text box.

Besides these three core attributes, there are others that apply to most XHTML elements. For instance, the lang, xml:lang, and dir attributes can be used to change the default language by specifying the language that should be used for the content, the language that should be used for the XML content, and the direction that the text should be written on the page. If you ever need to use these attributes, you can get more information by searching the Internet.

Core XHTML attributes

Attribute	Description
id	Specifies a unique identifier for an element. This identifier is case sensitive and should be in the same format as a JavaScript identifier. This id can be used by JavaScript or referred to by a style sheet.
class	Specifies one or more classes that apply to an element. Multiple classes are separated with a space, and the same class names can be applied to more than one element. The classes can then be referred to by a style sheet.
title	Specifies additional information about the element. For some elements, this title appears in a tooltip when the user hovers the mouse over the element.

XHTML that uses these attributes

```
<div id="main">
    <h1>Mike's Bait and Tackle Shop</h1>
    <p class="first">Welcome to Mike's Bait &amp; Tackle Shop!</p>
    <form action="subscribe.php" method="post">
        <p>Please enter your e-mail address to subscribe to our
        newsletter.</p>
        <p>E-Mail: <input type="text" name="email" id="email"
            title="Enter e-mail here." /></p>
        <p><input type="submit" value="Subscribe"/></p>
    </form>
</div>
<div id="footer">
    <p class="copyright">Copyright 2009.</p>
</div>
```

The XHTML in a web browser

Mike's Bait and Tackle Shop

Welcome to Mike's Bait & Tackle Shop!

Please enter your e-mail address to subscribe to our newsletter.

E-Mail: [   ] I

[Subscribe]   Enter e-mail here.

Copyright 2009.

Description

- The id, class, and title attributes can be coded for most XHTML elements.
- Three other attributes that can be coded for most XHTML elements are lang, xml:lang, and dir. These attributes can be used to change the language that is used by default. If you need to do that, you can search the Internet for more information.

Figure 4-6   How to code the core attributes

How to code blocks of text

Block tags are used to organize the contents of a web page. These tags are used to contain other content. By default, a block tag is tall and wide enough to contain its content. However, you can use CSS to control the height and width of a block tag.

In contrast to block tags, *inline tags* are coded within block tags, and they are commonly used to format text. You'll learn more about them in the next figure.

Figure 4-7 shows how to code some of the common block tags. In the example in this figure, two <div> tags divide the page into a main section and a footer section. Here, the id attribute is used to uniquely identify each section so it can be formatted or modified by CSS or JavaScript.

Within block tags, you can code other block tags, inline tags, or text. For example, the <div> tag for the main section contains an <h1> tag, an <h2> tag, and two <p> tags. Then, the <div> tag for the <footer> section contains a single <p> tag.

Within the <h1> through <h6> tags, you code the text that's displayed in the headings for the page. Note, however, that you should use these headings to provide a logical structure for your document, not to format the text. As a result, you should use the <h1> tag to mark the most important headings on the page, the <h2> tag to mark the second most important headings, and so on. This helps search engines index your site properly, and it makes your page more accessible to devices like screen readers. Then, you can use CSS to size and format the text in these tags.

Within the <p> tag, you can code text and inline tags. In this figure, the <p> tags only contain text. However, these tags could contain inline tags such as the <i> tag that italicizes text.

Although the tags in this example are the most common block tags, you may occasionally come across other block tags such as the <pre> tag, the <blockquote> tag, and the <address> tag. If necessary, you can use these tags to identify preformatted blocks of text, block quotations, and addresses. Since the <pre> tag uses a monospaced font and preserves whitespace, you can use it to align text with spaces. As with all tags, though, you should only use these tags when they accurately reflect the structure of your XHTML document. Then, you can use CSS to format these elements so they look the way you want them to.

Common block tags

Tag	Description
<div>	Creates an unformatted block of text that can be styled and positioned with CSS. It can contain text, inline tags, and other block tags.
<h1>	Creates a level-1 heading displayed as 200%, bold text.
<h2>	Creates a level-2 heading displayed as 150%, bold text.
<h3>	Creates a level-3 heading displayed as 117%, bold text.
<h4>	Creates a level-4 heading displayed as 100%, bold text.
<h5>	Creates a level-5 heading displayed as 83%, bold text.
<h6>	Creates a level-6 heading displayed as 67%, bold text.
<p>	Creates a paragraph of text with a blank line after it.
<pre>	Creates a block of text that preserves whitespace and is displayed in a monospaced font.
<blockquote>	Creates a block of text that's indented. The contents of the <blockquote> tag must be enclosed in another block element such as the <p> tag.
<address>	Creates a block of text that's displayed in italics.

Examples of block tags

```
<div id="main">
    <h1>This is an h1 tag.</h1>
    <p>This is a p tag.</p>
    <h2>This is an h2 tag.</h2>
    <p>This is a p tag.</p>
</div>
<div id="footer">
    <p>This is a p tag in the footer.</p>
</div>
```

The block tags in a web browser

This is an h1 tag.

This is a p tag.

This is an h2 tag.

This is a p tag.

This is a p tag in the footer.

Description

- A *block tag* is used to organize the contents of a web page and begins on a new line.
- An *inline tag* is coded within a block tag and doesn't have to begin on a new line.

Figure 4-7   How to code blocks of text

How to format text with inline tags

Figure 4-8 shows how to use some of the most common inline tags. One tag that you'll use frequently is the <br /> tag. It starts a new line of text. In older versions of HMTL, the slash isn't required, so it's common to see this tag coded as <br>. However, XHTML requires that you include the slash.

In contrast to the <br /> tag, the other inline tags in this figure apply formatting to the text. Before CSS became widely used, it was common to use these tags for formatting. For example, it was common to use the <i> tag to apply italics to text. Note, however, that this tag doesn't give any meaning to the text. It just provides formatting information.

By contrast, the <em> tag means that the text should be emphasized. By default, most browsers emphasize text by applying italics to the text, but you can use CSS to change the way that text is emphasized. For example, you can emphasize text by applying boldfacing or by changing the color of the text. Since this tag lets you separate the meaning from the formatting, it is now considered a good practice to use this tag instead of the <i> tag, and then use CSS to do the formatting.

The same logic can be applied to the <b> and <strong> tags. Although the <b> tag was often used in the past to apply boldfacing, it doesn't provide any meaning. As a result, it's now considered a good practice to use the <strong> tag instead of the <b> tag.

If you want to display code such as XHTML or JavaScript on a web page, you can use the <code> tag. This tag provides meaning, and it uses a monospaced font by default, which is a typical font for displaying code.

To code subscripted or superscripted text, you can use the <sub> and <sup> tags. Although these tags don't provide meaning, it's still common to use these tags. Similarly, you can use the <big> and <small> tags to change the font size of the text.

Whenever necessary, you can use the <span> tag to create an inline tag that marks text within a block tag, and you can use the id or class attribute of this tag to identify the tag. In the examples, the <span> tag includes a class attribute with a value of "book". Then, you can use CSS to apply formatting to the tag.

In fact, you can always use the <span> tag and CSS to provide the formatting for text. This makes sense whenever the <span> tag allows you to more clearly identify the structure and meaning of your XHTML document. That way, you separate the structure of your content from the formatting of that content.

Common inline tags for formatting text

Tag	Description
 	Starts a new line of text.
<i>	Text displayed in italics.
<b>	Text displayed in bold.
<em>	Emphasized text displayed in italics.
<strong>	Strong text displayed in bold.
<code>	Programming code displayed in a monospaced font.
<sub>	Subscripted text.
<sup>	Superscripted text.
<big>	Text displayed larger than normal.
<small>	Text displayed smaller than normal.
<span>	Creates an unformatted group of text that can be styled by CSS.

Examples of inline tags that format text

```
<p>Text that breaks <br /> across two lines.</p>

<p>Text formatted in <i>italics</i> and <b>bold</b>.</p>

<p>Text that uses <em>the em tag</em> for italics and <strong>the strong
tag</strong> for boldfacing.</p>

<p>Text that uses <code>the code tag</code> to display a monospaced font.
</p>

<p>Text that uses the sub tag<sub>1</sub> and the sup tag<sup>3</sup>.</p>

<p>Text that uses <big>the big tag</big>,
and <small>the small tag</small>.</p>

<p>Text that uses the span tag to identify <span class="book">a book
title</span>.</p>
```

The inline tags in a web browser

Text that breaks
across two lines.

Text formatted in *italics* and **bold**.

Text that uses *the em tag* for italics and **the strong tag** for boldfacing.

Text that uses `the code tag` to display a monospaced font.

Text that uses the sub tag$_1$ and the sup tag^3.

Text that uses the big tag, and the small tag.

Text that uses the span tag to identify a book title.

Figure 4-8   How to format text with inline tags

How to code lists

Figure 4-9 shows how to code three types of lists. To create an *unordered list*, you use the <ul> tag. Then, within the <ul> tag, you code one or more <li> tags to identify the items in the list. Within each <li> tag, you code the text for the item in the list. By default, an unordered list places a bullet before each item, but you can change that with CSS.

To create an *ordered list*, you use the <ol> tag. This works like the <ul> tag, but by default it numbers the items in the list.

When you work with unordered and ordered lists, you can *nest* one list within another list. In other words, within a <ul> or <ol> tag, you can code another <ul> or <ol> tag where you would normally code a <li> tag. This indents the list one more level and changes the bullets or numbering used for the list.

When you work with the <li> tag, you should be aware that it can contain text, inline tags, or block tags. For example, an <li> tag can contain an <a> tag that identifies a link.

If you want to create a *definition list* that consists of terms and definitions, you can use the <dl>, <dt>, and <dd> tags. Then, the <dl> tag identifies the definition list, the <dt> tag identifies the term, and the <dd> tag identifies the definition for the term. When you code these tags, you must code the <dt> and <dd> tags in pairs, and you must code at least one pair for each list. In addition, the <dt> tag can only contain text and inline tags, but the <dd> tag can also contain block tags including nested lists.

Tags that create lists

Tag	Description
<ul>	Creates an unordered list.
<ol>	Creates an ordered list.
<li>	Creates a list item for an unordered or ordered list.
<dl>	Creates a definition list. It contains pairs of <dt> and <dd> tags.
<dt>	Creates a term in a definition list.
<dd>	Creates a definition in a definition list that's indented.

Examples of list tags

```
<ul>
    <li>Unordered List</li>
    <li>Ordered List</li>
    <li>Definition List</li>
</ul>

<ol>
    <li>XHTML</li>
    <li>CSS</li>
    <li>JavaScript</li>
</ol>

<dl>
    <dt>Local Area Network</dt>
    <dd>A network of computers directly connected to each other.</dd>
    <dt>Wide Area Network</dt>
    <dd>A network of LANs connected by routers.</dd>
</dl>
```

The lists in a web browser

- Unordered List
- Ordered List
- Definition List

1. XHTML
2. CSS
3. JavaScript

Local Area Network
>   A network of computers directly connected to each other.

Wide Area Network
>   A network of LANs connected by routers.

Figure 4-9   How to code lists

How to code character entities

Figure 4-10 shows how to display special characters in a web page by using *character entities*. A character entity starts with an ampersand (&) and ends with a semicolon (;). For example, "©" can be used to insert the copyright symbol (©) into an XHTML document.

When you work with character entities, you need to know that the name of the entity is case-sensitive. As a result, you must use the exact capitalization shown in this figure.

Since the ampersand character (&) is used to identify character entities, your browser won't interpret it correctly if you code it in a web page. As a result, you must use the & entity to insert it. Similarly, since the left bracket (<) and right bracket (>) characters are used for XHTML tags, your browser won't interpret these characters correctly if you code them directly in a web page. Instead, you must use the character entities.

Besides the entities for characters, you may sometimes need to insert a non-breaking space to force a browser to display a space. In this figure, for example, the third <p> tag contains the character entity for a non-breaking space. As a result, the browser will display an empty paragraph. In contrast, if the non-breaking space isn't coded within the <p> tag, the browser won't display the empty paragraph.

Common XHTML character entities

Entity	Character
&	&
<	<
>	>
©	©
®	®
™	™
¢	¢
°	°
±	±
	A non-breaking space. It will always be displayed.

Examples of character entities

```
<h1>Mike's Bait &amp; Tackle Shop</h1>
<p>Here is some sample HTML code:</p>
<p><code>&lt;h1&gt;Heading 1 Goes Here&lt;/h1&gt;</code></p>
<p> </p>
<p>&copy; 2008 Mike's Bait &amp; Tackle Shop</p>
```

The character entities in a web browser

Mike's Bait & Tackle Shop

Here is some sample HTML code:

```
<h1>Heading 1 Goes Here</h1>
```

© 2008 Mike's Bait & Tackle Shop

Description

- *Character entities* can be used to display special characters in an XHTML document.

Figure 4-10   How to code character entities

How to code links

Many web pages contain *links* to other web resources such as other web pages and files. Links can also be referred to as *hyperlinks*. To code a link, you use the <a> tag as shown in figure 4-11.

Since the <a> tag is an inline tag, it is usually coded within another tag such as a <p> tag. By default, links are underlined. As a result, most web users have been conditioned to associate underlined text with links.

The first example in this figure shows how to code an <a> tag that contains a relative link to another web page. Here, the href attribute uses a *relative URL* to navigate to an HTML file named products.html. To start, the two dots (..) navigate up one directory. Then, the slash (/) and filename specify the filename for the page.

If necessary, you can use a relative link to navigate up multiple levels and down several levels like this:

```
../../docs/catalog/products.html
```

This code navigates up two directories and then down to the docs and catalog directories.

The second example shows how to code an <a> tag that contains an absolute link to a file. Here, the href attribute contains an *absolute URL* that begins with a slash (/) that navigates to the root directory for the web site. Then, it specifies the name for an HTML file named services.html. As a result, this link loads the services.html file that's stored in the root directory for the web site. When you code an absolute URL, you always start at the root directory, but you can also navigate down one or more directories like this:

```
/docs/custserv/services.html
```

The third example shows how to code an <a> tag that provides an absolute link to a web page that's running on a different site. Here, the href attribute contains an absolute URL that starts with "http://". In addition, this example includes a target attribute with a value of "_blank". This causes the web page to be loaded in a new window. When a user clicks on this link, the home page for Amazon.com will be loaded into a new browser window.

The next set of examples shows how to create and use an *anchor*. An anchor acts like a bookmark within a page. For a long web page, anchors make it easier for the user to navigate through the page. For pages like these, it's common to include an anchor at the top of the page along with navigation links for each section of the page. Then, at the end of each section, it's common to include a link to return to the top of the page.

To create an anchor, you use the name attribute within an <a> tag at the spot where you want the anchor. Then, you code other <a> tags that provide links that jump to the anchor. In these tags, you identify the anchor by preceding its name with a pound sign (#). Although anchors are typically used for navigating within a single page, the last example in this figure shows how to code a link that jumps to an anchor on another page.

Attributes of the \<a> tag

Attribute	Description
href	Specifies the URL for a link.
target	Specifies where the destination document should be loaded. A value of "_blank" loads the document in a new window.
name	Creates an anchor within a web page. When you use the name attribute, you should use the same value in the id attribute.

Examples of \<a> tags

A relative link to another web page

```
<p>Go view our <a href="../products.html">product list</a>.</p>
```

An absolute link to another web page

```
<p>Read about the <a href="/services.html">services we provide</a>.</p>
```

A link to a web page on a different web site

```
<p>Search for our books on
    <a href="http://www.amazon.com" target="_blank">Amazon</a>.
</p>
```

The \<a> tags in a web browser

Go view our product list.

Read about the services we provide.

Search for our books on Amazon.

How to create and use an anchor within a page

How to create an anchor

```
<h3><a id="contact" name="contact">Contact Us</a></h3>
```

How to jump to an anchor on the same page

```
<p>For more information <a href="#contact">contact us</a>.</p>
```

How to jump to an anchor on a different page

```
<p>For more information <a href="info.html#contact">contact us</a>.</p>
```

Description

- You can use the name attribute of the \<a> tag to create an *anchor* that specifies a location within a web page.
- You can use the href attribute of the \<a> tag to create a *link* that jumps to an anchor or loads another web page or resource. When you code links, you can use a *relative URL* or an *absolute URL*.

Figure 4-11   How to code links

When you create a link, it's a good practice to code the text for the link so it indicates the function of the link. As a result, you shouldn't use text like "click here" because it doesn't indicate what the link does. Instead, you should use text like "contact us", "product list", or "customer service." In short, if you can't tell what a link does by reading its text, you should rewrite the text. This improves the accessibility of your site, and it helps search engines index your site.

How to include images

Images, of course, are an important part of most web pages. To display an image, you can use the <img> tag as shown in figure 4-12. This tag is a self-closing, inline tag that is used to embed images in a web page.

In the example in this figure, the <img> tag is used to display the image for our logo. This tag is coded within a <p> tag. Here, the src attribute for the <img> tag specifies a relative URL that navigates to an image file named logo.gif that's stored in a subdirectory named images.

This <img> tag also sets the alt attribute to a value of "Murach Logo". Although the alt attribute is a required attribute for XHTML, many web developers still leave it off. This isn't a good practice, though, becaue the alt attribute has several uses. First, web browsers display the text stored in the alt attribute if the user has images disabled or if the image is unavailable. Second, screen readers read the text stored in the alt attribute, which improves the accessibility of your page. Third, search engines use the alt attribute to help index your web page.

The images that you include in your web page need to be in one of the formats that modern web browsers support. Currently, most web browsers support the JPEG, GIF, and PNG formats. Typically, a web designer uses imaging software such as Adobe Photoshop to create and maintain these files for a web site and saves these files in a directory named images or graphics. Note that the JPEG format often uses a file extension of JPG.

As a good practice, you should only use the <img> tag to link to images that are on the current web site. However, it is possible to link to an image that's stored on another web site. This is known as *hot linking*, and it's highly discouraged.

Attributes of the \<img> tag

Attribute	Description
src	Specifies the URL of the image to display. It is a required attribute.
alt	Specifies alternate text to display in place of the image. This text is also read aloud by screen readers for users with disabilities. It is a required attribute.
longdesc	Specifies a long description of the image.
height	Specifies the height to use for the image in pixels or a percentage.
width	Specifies the width to use for the image in pixels or a percentage.

An \<image> tag

```
<p><img src="../images/logo.gif" alt="Murach Logo" /></p>
```

The image in a web browser

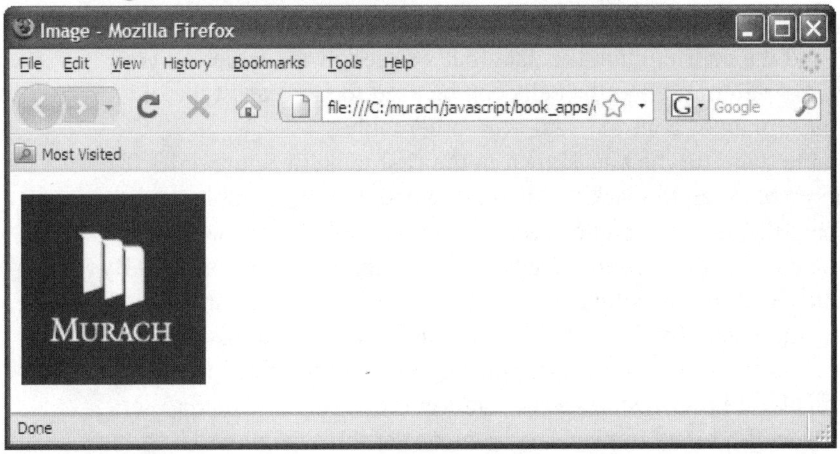

The image formats that are supported by most browsers

- GIF (Graphic Interchange Format)
- JPEG (Joint Photographic Experts Group)
- PNG (Portable Network Graphics)

Description

- JPEG files commonly use the JPG extension and are typically used for photographs and scans. This format doesn't support transparency.
- GIF files are typically used for small illustrations and logos. This format does support transparency.
- PNG files combine aspects of JPEG and GIF files. They can be used for photos or illustrations. This format supports a more complex type of transparency known as an alpha channel.

Figure 4-12   How to include images

How to code tables

In the past, web designers often used tables to organize the layout of the entire web page. However, this led to several problems. First, it resulted in layers of nested tables that were difficult to code and maintain. Second, the tables didn't accurately describe the structure of the web page. Third, the tables created accessibility problems, especially for people using screen readers.

So today, CSS should be used to control the layout of your web pages, and tables should only be used to present tabular data. In the next two figures, you'll learn how to code tables for that purpose.

How to code a simple table

Tables consist of *rows* and *columns*. The intersection of a row and column is known as a *cell*, and the cells contain the data that's stored in the table. As you work with tables, keep in mind that the cells can be used to store any type of data including links, images, controls, and even other tables.

To create a table, you use the tags shown in the first table in figure 4-13. To start, you use the <table> tag to mark the beginning and end of the table, and the <tr> tag to mark the start and end of each row in the table. Then, within each <tr> tag, you can use the <th> tag for headings or the <td> tag for data. By default, the text in a <th> tag is boldfaced, and the text in a <tr> tag isn't boldfaced. This is illustrated by the XHTML and rendered table in this figure.

In the <table> tag, you can use the attributes that are summarized in the second table in this figure. For instance, you can use the border attribute to set the thickness of the cell borders in pixels, or you can set this attribute to 0 to turn off the borders. You can use the cellspacing attribute to set the distance in pixels between the cells in a table. You can use the cellpadding attribute to set the distance between the edge of the cell and its content. And you can use the summary attribute to provide a text description of the table that isn't displayed by the browser.

Although it isn't shown in this figure, you can use the width attribute of the <table> tag to specify the width of the table in pixels. Then, the table will be stretched to the specified width. If the width attribute isn't set, the table will be set to the smallest size possible. In this figure, for example, the table is as small as it can be given the settings for the border, cellspacing, and cellpadding attributes.

In the <tr> tag, you can set the align and valign attributes that are summarized by the second table in this figure. These attributes indicate whether horizontal or vertical alignment should be used for a row. In the example in this figure, the first row is centered horizontally and the second and third rows are right aligned.

The tags for working with tables

Tag	Description
<table>	Marks the start and end of a table.
<tr>	Marks the start and end of each row.
<th>	Marks the start and end of each heading cell within a row.
<td>	Marks the start and end of each data cell within a row.

Common attributes of the <table> and <tr> tags

Tag	Attribute	Description
<table>	border	Specifies the thickness of the cell borders in pixels.
	cellspacing	Specifies the space between table cells in pixels.
	cellpadding	Specifies the padding between the cell borders and the contents of the cells.
	width	Specifies the width of the table in pixels or a percentage.
	summary	Specifies a text description of the contents of the table.
<tr>	align	Controls the horizontal alignment of the content in the row. Valid values include "left", "center", "right", and "justify". The default is "left".
	valign	Controls the vertical alignment of the content in the row. Valid values include "top", "middle", "bottom", and "baseline". The default is "middle".

The tags for a simple table

```
<table border="1" cellspacing="1" cellpadding="3"
    summary="First Quarter Sales By Region">
    <tr align="center">
        <th>Region</th>
        <th>Jan</th>
        <th>Feb</th>
    </tr>
    <tr align="right">
        <th>West</th>
        <td>$15,684.34</td>
        <td>$18,467.86</td>
    </tr>
    <tr align="right">
        <th>Central</th>
        <td>$22,497.14</td>
        <td>$13,371.34</td>
    </tr>
</table>
```

The table in a web browser

Region	Jan	Feb
West	$15,684.34	$18,467.86
Central	$22,497.14	$13,371.34

Figure 4-13   How to code a simple table

How to code a table with spanned columns and rows

Figure 4-14 presents the attributes that can be used for the <th> and <tr> tags. Here, the colspan and rowspan attributes can be used to merge cells so a cell in a row spans several columns or a cell in a column spans several rows. This is illustrated by the XHTML and the rendered table in this figure.

The other two attributes are the align and valign attributes, which can be applied to a row or a cell. As you saw in the last figure, if you apply these tags to a row, they apply to all the cells in the row. But if you apply these tags to a cell, they override any settings for the row.

In the example in this figure, you can see how the colspan and rowspan attributes work. If you study the table, you can see that it uses five columns and five rows. However, the first cell spans 2 rows and 2 columns. As a result, it is 2 rows tall and 2 rows wide. Similarly, the second cell spans 3 columns. As a result, it is 3 columns wide. This groups the Jan, Feb, and Mar headings under the First Quarter heading.

The second row only specifies <th> tags for 3 columns. However, the Sales cell from the first row takes up 2 columns of this row. As a result, the number of columns in this row still adds up to 5.

The third row begins with a cell that spans 3 rows. As a result, it is 3 rows tall. When cells are entered in the next two rows, the first column will be skipped to make room for this cell. This groups the West, Central, and East headings under the Regions heading.

Since this chapter is only a crash course in XHTML, it doesn't present all the tags for working with tables. That's why tags like the <caption>, <thead>, <tfoot>, or <tbody> tags aren't presented. For most tables, though, you won't need to use these tags.

Common attributes of the <th> and <td> tags

Attribute	Description
colspan	Causes a cell to span multiple columns. The default value is 1.
rowspan	Causes a cell to span multiple rows. The default value is 1.
align	Controls the horizontal alignment of the content of the cell. Valid values include "left", "center", "right", or "justify". The default value is "left".
valign	Controls the vertical alignment of the content of the cell. Valid values include "top", "middle", "bottom", or "baseline". The default value is "middle".

The tags for a table with spanned columns and rows

```
<table border="1" cellspacing="1" cellpadding="5"
    summary="First Quarter Sales By Region">
    <tr align="center">
        <th colspan="2" rowspan="2">Sales</th>
        <th colspan="3">First Quarter</th>
    </tr>
    <tr align="center">
        <th>Jan</th>
        <th>Feb</th>
        <th>Mar</th>
    </tr>
    <tr align="right">
        <th rowspan="3">Regions</th>
        <th>West</th>
        <td>$15,684.34</td>
        <td>$18,467.86</td>
        <td>$17,379.67</td>
    </tr>
    <tr align="right">
        <th>Central</th>
        <td>$22,497.14</td>
        <td>$13,371.34</td>
        <td>$25,693.80</td>
    </tr>
    <tr align="right">
        <th>East</th>
        <td>$25,741.06</td>
        <td>$31,633.25</td>
        <td>$26,712.55</td>
    </tr>
</table>
```

The table in a web browser

Sales		First Quarter		
		Jan	Feb	Mar
Regions	West	$15,684.34	$18,467.86	$17,379.67
	Central	$22,497.14	$13,371.34	$25,693.80
	East	$25,741.06	$31,633.25	$26,712.55

Figure 4-14 How to code a table with spanned columns and rows

How to code forms

Now that you know how to use XHTML to code web pages, you're ready to learn how to use XHMTL to code forms. A *form* contains one or more *controls* such as text boxes and buttons. Then, the data in the form can be submitted to a web server for processing, or it can be processed on the client with JavaScript. In many cases, the two approaches are combined so JavaScript is used to validate the form data on the client before it sends the valid data to the server.

How to create a form

Figure 4-15 shows how to code a form that contains three controls: a label, a text box, and a button. To start and end the form, you use the opening and closing <form> tags.

Within the <form> tag, you code an action attribute that specifies the file on the web server that should be used to process the data when the form is submitted. You also code a method attribute that specifies the HTTP method that should be used for sending the form. In this example, the action attribute runs the server-side code that's stored in the subscribe.php file, and the method attribute specifies the HTTP POST method

Since this book focuses on JavaScript, not on server-side code, that's all you need to know about the action and method attributes. In fact, if the data in the form is only going to be processed on the client with JavaScript, you can omit these attributes. Later on, if you learn how to do the server-side processing, you'll learn what the implications of these attributes are.

Within the opening and closing <form> tags, you code the controls for the form. In this example, the <label> tag provides a label for the text field that follows. The first <input> tag is for the text field that will receive the user's email address. And the second <input> tag displays a button. You'll learn how the tags for these controls are coded in the next two figures.

But first, this figure summarizes four attributes that are common to most of the control tags. To start, the name attribute specifies a name that can be used by the server-side code to get the data that's stored in the control. Since this works like the id attribute that you use with JavaScript, it usually makes sense to use the same name for both of these attributes.

In contrast, the value attribute provides the value that's stored in a control, but how this works depends on the control. For example, the value attribute of a text field stores the text that's in the field, while the value attribute for a button specifies the text that's displayed on the button.

Last, the disabled attribute disables a control, and the readonly attribute makes a control read-only, which prevents the user from modifying the value of the control. You'll see examples of how these attributes work as you progress through this book.

As you code controls, keep in mind that they don't have to be part of a form. Instead, they can be used anywhere inline tags are allowed. When controls aren't coded within a form, they are typically part of a JavaScript application.

Attributes of the <form> tag

Attribute	Description
action	Specifies the URL of the server-side script that will process the data in the form. The default is the current page.
method	Specifies the HTTP method to use to submit the form data. It's set to either "get" or "post". The default value is "get".

Attributes common to most control tags

Attribute	Description
name	Specifies the name for the field. Except for radio fields, the id attribute should be set to the same value. The specified value should be a valid JavaScript identifier. This is a required attribute for all controls except submit and reset buttons.
value	Sets the value stored in the control.
disabled	A Boolean attribute that disables and grays out the input so the user can't interact with it.
readonly	A Boolean attribute that prevents a user from changing the contents of the field. However, the user can still interact with the field and trigger events.

The tags for a simple form

```
<form action="subscribe.php" method="post">
    <p>Please enter your e-mail address to subscribe to our newsletter.</p>
    <p><label for="email">E-Mail:</label>
        <input type="text" name="email" id="email" />
    </p>
    <p><input type="submit" value="Subscribe" /></p>
</form>
```

The form in a web browser

Description

- A *form* contains one or more *fields* like text boxes, radio buttons, or check boxes that can receive data.
- When a form is submitted to the server for processing, the data in the fields is sent along with the HTTP request. When the get method is used, the data is sent as part of the URL for the next web page. When the post method is used, the data is hidden.

Figure 4-15   How to create a form

How to code buttons

Figure 4-16 shows three types of *buttons* and two ways to create each of them. The three types of buttons are "submit", "reset", and "button", and you can create them with the <button> tag or with the <input> tag. The primary difference between these tags is that the <input> tag only allows a button to contain plain text, while the <button> tag allows a button to contain formatted text as well as other XHTML elements such as images.

In this figure, the first four buttons are created by the <button> tag. Here, the first two buttons have a type attribute that is set to "submit". As a result, both of these buttons are "submit" buttons. In addition, both of these buttons have a name, id, and a value. When a user clicks on a submit button, its name/value pair is sent to the server. This lets the server perform different actions depending on which submit button is clicked. In this example, one button places an order, and the other saves a wish list.

The third button has a type attribute set to "button". As a result, it can be used to run JavaScript code. You were introduced to this type of button in chapter 2, and you'll learn more about it as you progress through this book. Since this button has an id attribute, it's easy to use JavaScript to work with it.

The fourth button has a type attribute set to "reset". When you click this type of button, the values in all of the controls on the form are reset to their default values.

In the examples, the first two buttons use the <b> tag to apply boldfacing to the text that's displayed on the buttons. Similarly, the third and fourth buttons use the <i> tag to apply italics to the text that's displayed on the buttons. This shows that the button tag can include formatting tags, although it's better to use CSS to do that formatting.

The other way to create buttons is to use the <input> tag. This is illustrated by the second group of examples. When you use this tag, the value attribute is displayed on the button as well as being submitted to the server. This is a self-closing tag that can't contain other tags.

If you don't specify a value attribute for an <input> tag, the web browser supplies some default text for each type of button. For example, the text for a submit button is usually "Submit", and the text for a reset button is usually "Reset". This is illustrated by the last example in this figure.

The advantage of the <input> tag is that it is shorter and easier to code than the button tag. In addition, the <input> tag has been widely used since the early days of the web. In contrast, the <button> tag provides more flexibility for creating buttons and is commonly used in modern web development.

Before you continue, you should know that you usually don't use submit buttons when you use JavaScript to validate the data in a form before the data is submitted to the server for processing. Instead, you use a regular button to initiate the JavaScript validation. Then, if the data is valid, you use the submit method of the form to submit the data to the server. You'll see how this works in chapter 12.

Attributes of the <button> tag and the <input> tag for buttons

Attribute	Description
type	Specifies the type of button. Valid values for buttons include "submit", "reset", or "button". The "submit" type submits the form to the server, the "reset" type resets all fields to their default values, and the "button" type is used to run JavaScript.
value	Specifies text to submit to the server when the button is clicked. For a <button> tag, this value is not displayed on the web page. For an <input> tag that displays a button, this value is displayed on the button.

Examples of the <button> tag

```
<p> <button type="submit" name="order" id="order" value="order">
        <b>Place Order</b>
    </button>
    <button type="submit" name="wish" id="wish" value="wish">
        <b>Save as Wish List</b>
    </button> </p>
<p> <button type="button" id="validate"><i>Validate</i></button>
    <button type="reset"><i>Reset</i></button> </p>
```

The <button> tags in a web browser

Examples of the <input> tag for buttons

```
<p> <input type="submit" name="order" id="order" value="Place Order" />
    <input type="submit" name="wish" id="wish" value="Save as Wish List" />
</p>
<p> <input type="button" id="validate" value="Validate" />
    <input type="reset" /> </p>
```

The <input> tag buttons in a web browser

Description

- When you click on a *submit button* for a form, the form data is sent to the server as part of an HTTP request. When you click on a *reset button*, the data in all of the fields are reset to their default values.
- When you use JavaScript to validate the data for a form, you usually use a button of the button type. Then, when the user clicks on the button, the JavaScript validates the data and if valid submits the data by calling the submit method of the form. You'll see how this works in chapter 12.

Figure 4-16   How to code buttons

How to code labels and text fields

Figure 4-17 shows how to use the <input> tag to create three types of *text fields*, which are also referred to as *text boxes*. This figure also shows how to use the <label> tag to provide *labels* that describe these text fields.

The first <input> tag in the example in this figure displays a text field that accepts input from a user. To do that, this tag sets the type attribute to "text". Then, it sets the name and id attributes to "quantity". Finally, it sets the value attribute to 1. As a result, when the browser displays this text box for the first time, it will contain a default value of 1.

The <label> tag that precedes the <input> tag displays "Quantity:" to the left of the text field. This <label> tag includes a single *for* attribute that specifies the text field that is associated with the label. For this attribute to work correctly, it must match the id attribute of the text field.

Most of the attributes for coding the first label and text field work the same for the other examples. For the second <input> tag, though, the disabled attribute is set to "disabled". As a result, the browser grays out the text field and prevents the user from interacting with it.

The third <input> tag creates a *password field* that works much like the first two text fields. However, the value in the text field is displayed as bullets or asterisks. This improves the security of an application by preventing others from reading a password when a user enters it.

In addition, this password field shows how to use the maxlength attribute. Here, this attribute is set to 6. As a result, the user can enter a maximum of six characters into this field. This is useful if you are working with a database that limits the number of characters that can be stored in a field.

The fourth <input> tag creates a *hidden field* that works much like the other three text fields. However, this field isn't displayed by the browser. Nevertheless, you can use JavaScript code or server-side code to work with the value that's stored in this field. In this example, the hidden field provides a product id of Q36 that can be read by JavaScript or server-side code.

If you want a text field to contain a default value, you code the value attribute. Although all of the text fields in this figure have value attributes, you often don't need to code this attribute for text fields. Then, the user can enter the values for these fields. In contrast, since a user can't enter text into a hidden field, you usually code a value for a hidden field.

In this figure, the text boxes are at their default width and they aren't aligned. In the next chapter, though, you'll learn how to use CSS to align labels and text fields like these and how to control their width and other formatting characteristics.

Attributes of the <label> tag

Attribute	Description
for	Specifies the id of the field that the label is associated with.

Attributes of the <input> tag for text fields

Attribute	Description
type	Specifies the type of text field. Valid values include "text", "password", or "hidden". The default value is "text".
value	Specifies the default value for the field, but the user can change this value. If a "reset" button is clicked, the field will revert to this value.
maxlength	Specifies the maximum number of characters that the user may enter in the field.
size	Specifies the width of the field in characters based on the average character width of the font. Instead of setting this attribute, though, you should use CSS to set the size of a field as described in chapter 5.

The XHTML for labels and text fields

```
<label for="quantity">Quantity:</label>
<input type="text" name="quantity" id="quantity" value="1" /><br />

<label for="futureValue">Future Value:</label>
<input type="text" name="futureValue" id="futureValue"
       value="$16,256.32" disabled="disabled" /><br />

<label for="pinCode">Pin Code:</label>
<input type="password" name="pinCode" id="pinCode" maxlength="6"
       value="sesame" /><br />

<input type="hidden" name="product_id" id="product_id" value="Q36" />
```

The text fields in a web browser

Quantity: `1`

Future Value: `$16,256.32`

Pin Code: `[          ]`

Description

- A *label* is commonly used to identify a related field, and a *text field* (or *text box*) is used to get data from the user.

- A *hidden field* has name and value attributes that are sent to the server when the form is submitted, but the field isn't displayed in the browser. However, if you view the source code for the web page, you can see the data for the hidden field.

- The data for a *password field* is obscured by bullets or asterisks, but the name and value attributes are passed to the server when the form is submitted.

Figure 4-17   How to code labels and text fields

How to code radio buttons and check boxes

Figure 4-18 shows how to use the <input> tag to code *checkbox fields* and *radio fields*. These fields are commonly referred to as *check boxes* and *radio buttons*. Although check boxes work independently of each other, radio buttons can be set up so the user can select only one radio button from a group of radio buttons. In the example in this figure, you can select only one of the three radio buttons. However, you can select or deselect any combination of check boxes.

To create a radio button, you set the type attribute of the <input> tag to "radio". Then, to create a group, you set the name attribute to the same name for all of the radio buttons in the group. In this figure, all three radio buttons have "crust" as their name attribute. That way, the user will only be able to select one of these radio buttons at a time.

Note, however, that each of these buttons has a different value attribute and a different id attribute. Later, when you write your JavaScript or server-side code, you can access the value that's coded for the radio button.

To create a check box, you set the type attribute of the <input> tag to "checkbox". Then, you can set the name and id attributes so you can access the value from your JavaScript and server-side code. When you submit a form to the server, a name/value pair for a check box is only submitted to the server if it is selected. If the checkbox isn't selected, its name/value pair isn't sent to the server.

If you want a check box or radio button to be selected by default, you can code a checked attribute with a value of "checked". In this figure, for example, the second radio button has been selected by default. You can also use this technique to select a check box.

Attributes of the <input> tag for radio and checkbox fields

Attribute	Description
type	Specifies the type of field. It's set to "radio" or "checkbox".
value	Specifies text to submit to the server when the field is checked.
checked	A Boolean attribute that causes the field to be checked when the page is loaded. If the Reset button is clicked, the field reverts to the checked state.

The XHTML for radio buttons and check boxes

```
<label>Crust: </label><br />
<input type="radio" name="crust" id="crust1" value="thin" />
Thin Crust<br />
<input type="radio" name="crust" id="crust2" value="deep"
       checked="checked" />
Deep Dish<br />
<input type="radio" name="crust" id="crust3" value="hand" />
Hand Tossed<br /><br />

<label>Toppings: </label><br />
<input type="checkbox" name="pepperoni" id="pepperoni" value="yes" />
Pepperoni<br />
<input type="checkbox" name="mushrooms" id="mushrooms" value="yes" />
Mushrooms<br />
<input type="checkbox" name="olives" id="olives" value="yes" />
Black Olives
```

The radio buttons and check boxes in a web browser

Crust:
- ○ Thin Crust
- ◉ Deep Dish
- ○ Hand Tossed

Toppings:
- ☐ Pepperoni
- ☐ Mushrooms
- ☐ Black Olives

Description

- Only one *radio button* in a group can be on at one time. The radio buttons in a group must have the same name attribute, but different ids and values.
- *Check boxes* are unrelated so more than one check box can be checked at the same time. The id and name attributes of a check box are set to the same value.

Figure 4-18   How to code radio buttons and check boxes

How to code select lists

Figure 4-19 shows how to code *select lists*. A select list can either be a *drop-down list* or a *list box*. With a drop-down list, the user can only select one option from a list of options. In this figure, for example, the drop-down list lets you select one type of crust for a pizza.

With a list box, the user can select more than one option from the list. To do that, the user can hold down the Ctrl key (or the Command key for Mac OS) and click multiple options. In this figure, for example, the list box lets you select one or more toppings for a pizza.

To code a drop-down list or list box, you use a <select> tag. Within the opening <select> tag, you code the name and id attributes. Then, between the opening and closing tags, you code two or more <option> tags that supply the options that are available for the list. Within each of the opening <option> tags, you code a value attribute. Between the opening and closing <option> tags, you supply the text that's displayed in the list. This text is often similar to the text of the value attribute.

If you want to group the options in a list, you can code one or more <optgroup> tags. In this figure, for example, two <optgroup> tags are used to divide the options that are available for the second select list into two groups: Free and Extra Charge. To do that, the label attribute specifies the label for each group.

The multiple attribute of the <select> tag determines whether you get a drop-down list or a list box. If you don't code this attribute, this tag displays a drop-down list that lets the user select just one option. If you do code this attribute, this tag displays a list box that lets the user select multiple options. For this to work correctly, the size attribute must be set to a value that's greater than 1.

In this figure, for example, the second list includes a multiple attribute with a value of "multiple". In addition, this list includes a size attribute with a value of 5. As a result, this <select> tag displays a list that shows 5 options. Since there are 6 options in this list (including option groups), the user must use the scroll bar on the right side of the list to scroll down to the sixth option.

If you want to set one or more default options for a list box, you code the selected attribute with a value of "selected" within the <option> tag. In the example in this figure, the "Pepperoni" option has been selected as the default option for the list box. Although you can also use this attribute with a drop-down list, the option that's shown is automatically selected so you don't need to use this attribute if you want the first option to be the default.

Attributes of the <select> tag

Attribute	Description
size	Specifies the number of items to display in the <select> field. If the value is 1, the field will be a drop-down list. The default value is 1.
multiple	A Boolean attribute that determines whether multiple items can be selected. It is only valid if size is greater than 1.

An attribute of the <option> tag

Attribute	Description
selected	A Boolean attribute that causes the option to be selected when the page is loaded.

An attribute of the <optgroup> tag

Attribute	Description
label	Specifies the text that's used to group the options.

The XHTML for select lists

```
<label>Crust: </label><br />
<select name="crust" id="crust">
  <option value="thin">Thin Crust</option>
  <option value="deep">Deep Dish</option>
  <option value="hand">Hand Tossed</option>
</select><br /><br />

<label>Toppings: </label><br />
<select name="toppings" id="toppings" size="5" multiple="multiple">
  <optgroup label="Free">
    <option value="pepperoni" selected="selected">Pepperoni</option>
    <option value="mushrooms">Mushrooms</option>
  </optgroup>
  <optgroup label="Extra Charge">
    <option value="chicken">Chicken</option>
    <option value="pineapple">Pineapple</option>
  </optgroup>
</select>
```

The selection lists in a web browser with "Pepperoni" selected

Figure 4-19   How to code select lists

How to code text areas

Figure 4-20 shows how to code a *textarea field*. This type of field can also be referred to as a *text area*. Although a text area is similar to a text field, a text area can display multiple lines of text. By default, a text area wraps each line of text to the next line and provides a vertical scroll bar that you can use to scroll up and down through the text.

To code a text area, you use a <textarea> tag. Within the opening tag, you code the name and id attributes so you can access the control through JavaScript and server-side code. You can also code the rows attribute to specify the approximate number of visible rows and the cols attribute to specify the width of the text area. If you need more precise control over the width or height of a text area or if you want to change formatting attributes like the font, you can use CSS as described in the next chapter.

Within the opening and closing <textarea> tags, you can code any default text that you want to appear in the text area. Within the default text, whitespace is preserved so spaces, tabs, and carriage returns are used. In this figure, for example, you can see that carriage returns have been used to start new paragraphs.

Attributes of the \<textarea\> tag

Attribute	Description
rows	Specifies the approximate number of rows in the text area. It is required.
cols	Specifies the approximate number of columns in the text area. It is required.

The XHTML for a text area with default text

```
<label>Comments:</label><br />
<textarea name="comments" id="comments" rows="4" cols="50">
If you have any comments, we would be delighted to hear from you.

Just delete this text and enter your own.
</textarea>
```

The text area in a web browser

Comments:

```
If you have any comments, we would be delighted to
hear from you.

Just delete this text and enter your own.
```

The text area after text has been entered into it

Comments:

```
This text area holds approximately 50 characters
per line, and it holds approximately 4 rows of
text.
By default, the text area wraps each line to the
next line, and it includes a vertical scroll bar
```

Description

- A *textarea field* (or just *text area*) can be used to get extensive text entries from the user.
- The values of the rows and cols attributes are approximate. In the example above, the rows attribute is set to 4, but the text box has five rows.

Figure 4-20   How to code text areas

How to group controls

Figure 4-21 shows how to use the <fieldset> tag to group related controls. To do that, you just code an opening and closing <fieldset> tag around the controls that you want to group. Then, by default, the browser places a thin border around all of the fields that are grouped. In this figure, for example, the crust options for a pizza are in one group, and the topping options are in a second group.

Within a <fieldset> tag, you can code a <legend> tag that specifies a legend for the group. In this figure, the code specifies a legend of "Crust" for the crust group and a legend of "Toppings" for the toppings group.

XHTML that uses the \<fieldset\> and \<legend\> tags

```
<fieldset>
<legend>Crust</legend>
    <input type="radio" name="crust" id="crust1" value="c1" />
    Thin Crust<br />
    <input type="radio" name="crust" id="crust2" value="c2"
        checked="checked" />
    Deep Dish<br />
    <input type="radio" name="crust" id="crust3" value="c3" />
    Hand Tossed
</fieldset>

<fieldset>
<legend>Toppings</legend>
    <input type="checkbox" value="yes" name="topping1" id="topping1" />
    Pepperoni<br />
    <input type="checkbox" value="yes" name="topping2" id="topping2" />
    Mushrooms<br />
    <input type="checkbox" value="yes" name="topping3" id="topping3" />
    Black Olives
</fieldset>
<p><input type="submit" value="Place Order" /></p>
```

The \<fieldset\> and \<legend\> tags in a web browser

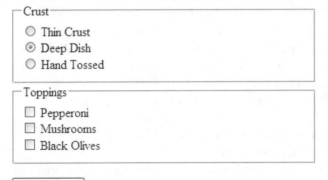

Description

- The \<fieldset\> tag is used to group controls like radio buttons or check boxes.
- The \<legend\> tag is coded within a \<fieldset\> tag. It is used to label the grouped controls.

Figure 4-21   How to group controls

How to set the tab order for controls

Figure 4-22 shows a web page that illustrates a form that contains many of the controls that you've just learned about including, text boxes, radio boxes, a check box, a drop-down list, and a button. When the user presses the Tab key on a page like this, the focus moves from one control to another, not including labels. This sequence is referred to as the *tab order* of the controls.

By default, when the user presses the Tab key, the focus moves from one field to another in the sequence that the fields appear in the XHTML. Often, this tab order is acceptable, so you don't need to change it.

However, if this default tab order isn't what you want, you can use the tabindex attribute to leave some fields out of the tab order or to change the tab order. To remove a field from the tab order, you assign a negative number to its tabindex attribute. This is illustrated by the example in this figure. Then, the rest of the controls retain the default tab order. Often, a change like this is all you'll want to do.

To change the default tab order, you use the tabindex attribute to assign zero or positive numbers to the fields that indicate the tab order that you want. If you use the same value for more than one field, the fields with that value will be accessed in the sequence of the XHTML. For instance, you can assign a value of 1 to all the controls in the first group that you want accessed and a value of 2 to all of the controls in the second group that you want accessed. Keep in mind, though, that if you don't assign a value to a field, it will be accessed after all the fields with values. As a result, you usually assign values to all of the fields.

When you work with the tab order, there is one browser variation that you should be aware of. That is, when you press the Tab key right after a page is loaded, the focus may move to a browser control like the address bar instead of the first field on the page. In fact, you may have to press the Tab key several times before the focus is moved to the first control.

To get around this problem, you can use JavaScript to move the focus to the first field that you want the user to enter. Then, if you set the tab order right, the users can move from one control to another without ever taking their hands off the keyboard.

Another consideration that you should be aware of is that most browsers include links in the tab order. So, if you include links on a web page that has one or more fields, you need to make sure that the tab order still works the way you want it to. In many cases, for example, you won't want to include the links in the tab order.

The attribute that's used to control the tab order

Attribute	Description
tabindex	To set the tab order for a field, use a value of 0 or more. To take a field out of the tab order, use a negative value.

An XHTML form for a survey

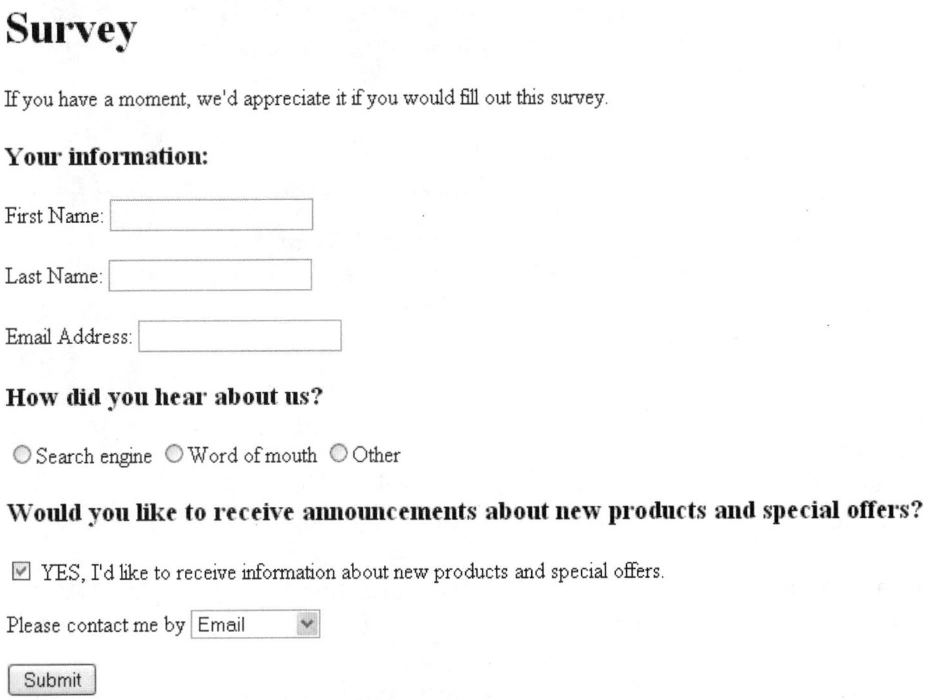

Survey

If you have a moment, we'd appreciate it if you would fill out this survey.

Your information:

First Name: [   ]

Last Name: [   ]

Email Address: [   ]

How did you hear about us?

○ Search engine ○ Word of mouth ○ Other

Would you like to receive announcements about new products and special offers?

☑ YES, I'd like to receive information about new products and special offers.

Please contact me by [Email   ▾]

[Submit]

Code that takes two controls out of the tab order

```
<input type=radio id="heardFrom2" name="heardFrom" value="Friend"
       tabindex="-1"/>Word of mouth
<input type=radio id="heardFrom3" name="heardFrom" value="Other"
       tabindex="-1" />Other
```

Description

- The *tab order* of a form is the sequence of the controls that receive the focus when the Tab key is pressed. By default, the tab order is the order of the controls in the XHTML, not including labels. But you can change that order by using the tabindex attribute.

- When you press the Tab key after a page is loaded, it may move the focus to browser controls before it reaches the fields on the form. To fix that, you can use JavaScript to set the focus to the first field when the page is loaded.

- Most browsers include links in the default tab order.

Figure 4-22   How to set the tab order for controls

Perspective

This has been a crash course on the tags that are commonly used with the XHTML 1.0 Strict standard. With these tags, you should be able to code most types of web pages and forms, and you have all of the XHTML skills you need for this book.

Remember, though, that the right way to format your XHTML tags is to use CSS. That's why the next chapter presents a crash course in CSS. There, you'll see that you can use CSS to control all aspects of formatting including the positioning of the elements on a page.

Terms

XHTML web page	Experts Group)
XHTML document	PNG (Portable Network Graphics)
tag	table
opening tag	row
closing tag	column
attribute	cell
comment	form
whitespace	control
self-closing tag	field
nested tag	button
XHTML validation	submit button
block tag	reset button
inline tag	label
unordered list	text field
ordered list	text box
nested list	password field
definition list	hidden field
character entity	radio field
link	radio button
hyperlink	checkbox field
relative URL	check box
absolute URL	select list
anchor	drop-down list
hot linking	list box
GIF (Graphic Interchange Format)	textarea field
	text area
JPEG (Joint Photographic	tab order

Exercise 4-1   Modify the survey page

In this exercise, you'll test, modify, and validate the survey.html page that's shown in figure 4-22.

Test and validate the survey page

1. From your Firefox browser, open the survey.html file that's in the chapter 4 folder for the exercises. Notice that the text boxes aren't aligned because this XHTML file doesn't have a CSS file that aligns them. You'll learn how to use CSS in the next chapter.

2. To test this form, enter data for all of its fields and click on the Submit button. This leads to an error page that shows the URL that the Submit button requested. After the question mark in this URL, you can see the data that is passed to the web server. This data consists of name/value pairs that are separated by ampersands. This is how the data gets passed to the web server when you use the GET method.

3. Click the Back button to return to the survey form. Then, press the Tab key to move from one field to another and notice the tab order that's used. Before the focus reaches the text box for the form, it may move through several items in the browser, but that depends on the browser.

4. Use your text editor to open the survey.html file. Then, review the XHTML code and note how it corresponds to the survey form in your web browser.

5. Go to web site for the W3C Markup Validation Service as shown in figure 4-4, and validate the survey page by using the File Upload tab. Since we put 2 errors in the starting XHTML file, 9 errors will be listed, even though the XHTML works. Once you fix the errors in lines 22 and 30, though, the rest of the errors will be fixed too. (An easy way to re-validate a page is to click on the Reload button in the browser and then on the Resend button in the dialog box that's displayed.)

Modify the survey page

After each step that follows, save the changes to the file, refresh the page in your browser, and make sure the changes are correct. If you think you've made the change correctly and the change doesn't show up, you may have to reopen the XHTML document rather than just refresh it.

6. Edit the survey.html page so it displays the image for the Murach logo at the top of the page. This image is in the exercises\chapter_04\images directory.

7. After the field that lets the user enter an email address, add another field that lets the user enter the date of birth.

8. Turn the Search Engine button on as the default button for the group of radio buttons. To get this to work, you may have to reopen the survey.html file.

9. Add an Advertising radio button before the Other radio button.

10. After the check box, add another check box that is checked by default and says, "YES, it's okay to send me email announcements."

11. Add a "Text messages" option after the "Postal mail" option in the drop-down list, and change the last option to "All methods".

12. Add a "reset" button to the form to the right of the Submit button. This button should reset all the fields on the form to their default values.

13. If necessary, modify the tab order so it includes the text box and reset button that you've added, but omits the radio button and check box that you added.

Change the way the page works

14. Change the method that's used to submit the form from GET to POST. Then, test this change by clicking on the button. Here again, to get this to work, you may have to reopen the survey.html file. When the URL appears, it shouldn't include the name/value pairs that are passed to the web server. However, those pairs are still available to the server.

15. Change the Submit button so it's a regular button, not a submit button. Then, test this change by clicking on the button. This time, nothing happens. When you use JavaScript, though, you can write an event handler for the click event of this button that validates the data in the controls. Then, if the data is valid, you can use the submit method of the form to submit the data for processing. (You'll see how this works in chapter 12.)

Validate the XHTML again

16. Validate the survey page again to see whether you've introduced any new errors.

5

A crash course in CSS

In chapter 1, you were introduced to CSS (Cascading Style Sheets). Now, you'll learn how to use CSS to format an XHTML document. Once you learn these skills, you'll be ready to create web pages for JavaScript applications. You'll also be ready to learn how to use JavaScript to control the CSS.

If you already know how to use CSS, you can skip this chapter. Then, if you encounter CSS code that you don't understand later in this book, you can return to this chapter to learn more about it.

A web page and its CSS **170**
The web page 170
The XHTML for the web page 172
The CSS for the web page 174

Basic skills for using CSS **178**
Basic CSS syntax 178
How to include CSS in a web page 180
How to specify measurements and colors 182

How to code selectors **184**
How to code selectors for tags, ids, and classes 184
How to code other types of XHTML selectors 186
How to code pseudo-class selectors 188
How the cascade rules work 190

How to work with text and lists **192**
How to style fonts 192
How to format text 194
How to format lists 196

How to work with the box model **198**
An introduction to the box model 198
A web page that illustrates the box model 200
How to set height, width, margins, and padding 202
How to set borders 204
How to set background colors and images 206

How to position elements **208**
How to change the display type of an element 208
How to float elements 210
How to use absolute positioning 212
How to use relative positioning 214
How to float controls on a form 216

Perspective **218**

A web page and its CSS

This chapter starts by showing you a web page, its XHTML, and the *CSS* (*Cascading Style Sheets*) code that's used to format the web page. As you read this chapter and learn how to use CSS, you can refer back to this web page, XHTML, and CSS to see how the CSS is applied.

The web page

Figure 5-1 shows a web page both before and after CSS has been applied to it. Here, you can see the dramatic effect that CSS can have on the XHTML. Note, for example, that the CSS has changed the fonts, changed the background color and some of the font colors (although that doesn't show in black and white), added horizontal rules, formatted the "Contact us" link with a dotted underline, and divided the middle portion of the page into two columns.

If you want to see how creatively CSS can be used, an interesting web site is http://www.csszengarden.com. On this site, many CSS designs can be applied to the same XHTML file. Each design uses a CSS file and custom images to achieve its look, and you can examine the CSS code for these designs to see how it works.

A web page before CSS has been applied

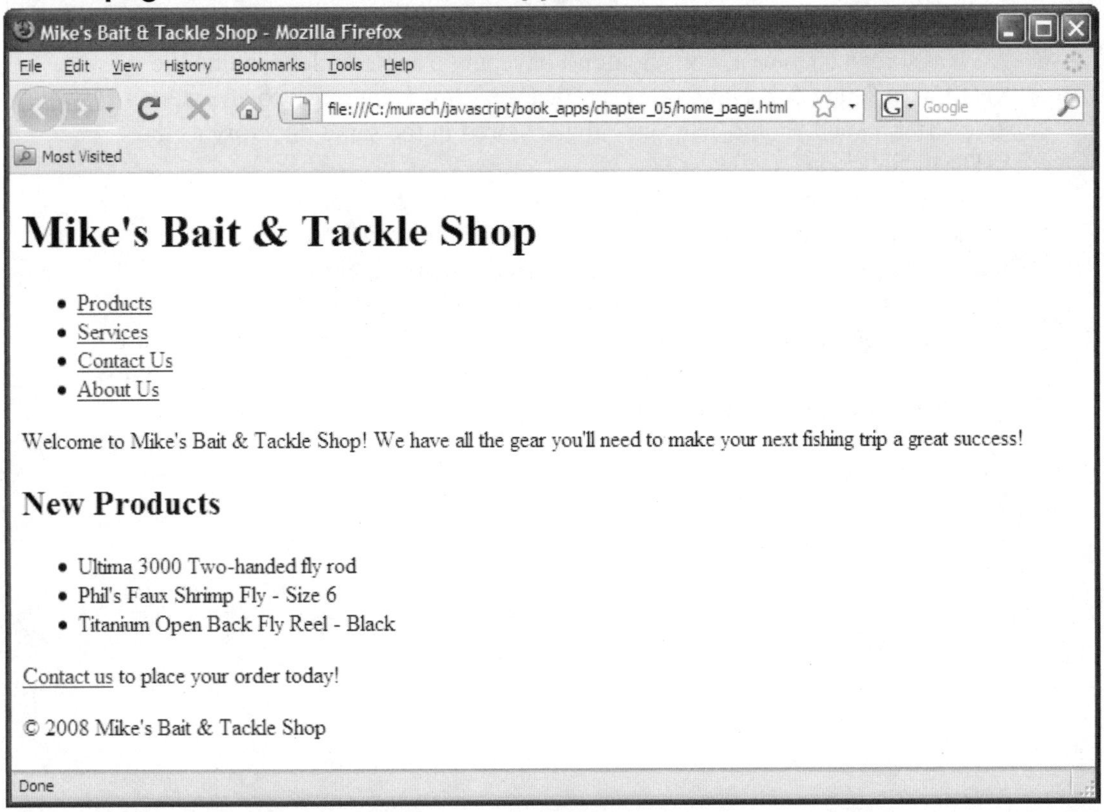

The same page after CSS has been applied

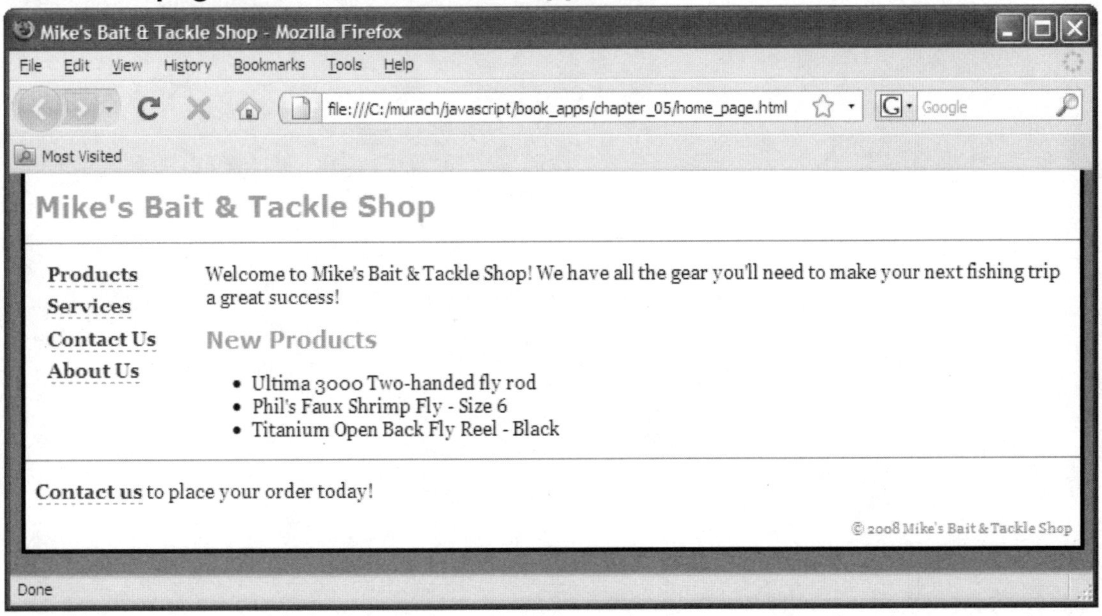

Figure 5-1   A web page with and without CSS

The XHTML for the web page

If you read chapter 4, you shouldn't have any trouble understanding the XHTML in figure 5-2. Note, however, that the <link> tag refers to an external style sheet named "home_page.css" that's stored in the same directory as the XHTML file.

As you review this XHTML, note how the <div> tags have been used to divide the body section into a "page" section that contains "header", "main", and "footer" sections. In addition, these tags divide the main section into "sidebar" and "content" sections. As you will see, the CSS uses the ids for these sections to format these sections. Note also that the class attribute has been used to identify two of the <p> tags and one of the <ul> tags, so CSS can be used to apply special formatting to each of them.

The XHTML for the home_page.html file

```
<!DOCTYPE html PUBLIC "-//W3C//DTD XHTML 1.0 Transitional//EN"
    "http://www.w3.org/TR/xhtml1/DTD/xhtml1-transitional.dtd">
<html xmlns="http://www.w3.org/1999/xhtml">

    <!-- the head section -->
    <head>
        <title>Mike's Bait &amp; Tackle Shop</title>
        <link rel="stylesheet" type="text/css" href="home_page.css" />
    </head>

    <!-- the body section -->
    <body>
    <div id="page">

        <div id="header">
            <h1>Mike's Bait &amp; Tackle Shop</h1>
        </div>

        <div id="main">
            <div id="sidebar">
                <ul class="nav">
                    <li><a href="products.html">Products</a></li>
                    <li><a href="services.html">Services</a></li>
                    <li><a href="contact.html">Contact Us</a></li>
                    <li><a href="about.html">About Us</a></li>
                </ul>
            </div>

            <div id="content">
                <p class="first">Welcome to Mike's Bait &amp; Tackle Shop!
                    We have all the gear you'll need to make your next
                    fishing trip a great success!</p>
                <h2>New Products</h2>
                <ul>
                    <li>Ultima 3000 Two-handed fly rod</li>
                    <li>Phil's Faux Shrimp Fly - Size 6</li>
                    <li>Titanium Open Back Fly Reel - Black</li>
                </ul>
            </div>
        </div>

        <div id="footer">
            <p><a href="contact.html">Contact us</a> to place your order
                today!</p>
            <p class="copyright">&copy; 2008 Mike's Bait &amp; Tackle
                Shop</p>
        </div>
    </div>
    </body>
</html>
```

Figure 5-2   The XHTML for the web page

The CSS for the web page

Figure 5-3 shows the *CSS style sheet* that applies the formatting to the XHTML file. For now, don't worry if you don't understand the details of this CSS code. You'll learn how CSS works as you progress through this chapter. Instead, focus on the overall structure of this code.

To start, the CSS specifies the formatting for the <body> tag. Here, the top margin is set to 0, the background color is set to a shade of blue, and the font family and size are changed. When you set the formatting for the <body> tag, those settings are *inherited* by most of the tags that are coded within the <body> tag. As a result, if you want to use the same font family or size for a tag that's in the body, you don't need to code those settings. But if you want to override one of those settings, you code the changed setting. For example, the <h1> tags on the next page override the font family and size that's set by the <body> tag.

After the CSS for the <body> tag, the CSS specifies the formatting for the <div> tags. To do that, it uses the pound character (#) to select the id attribute of each tag. Then, it applies formatting to each of the tags. Much of this formatting is used to set the background color, margins, padding, and borders for the different sections of the web page. For example, the background color of the page section is set to white. As a result, this section is displayed with a white background over the blue background for the body tag.

Note that the units of measurement change depending on the type of element that's being formatted. In this figure, for example, the font sizes are set in percentages (%). The width of the page is set in pixels (px), which is the number of dots that are used by the user's monitor. And the padding is set in ems.

An *em* is a unit of measurement that's equal to the current font size. For example, if the current font is 16 pixels tall, 1 em is equal to 16 pixels. As a result, if you increase the current font size, the amount of padding also increases. In other words, an em is a unit of measurement that's relative to the current font size.

The CSS for the home_page.css file   **Page 1**

```css
/* the styles for the body tag */
body {
    margin-top: 0;
    background-color: dodgerBlue;
    font-family: Georgia, "Times New Roman", Times, serif;
    font-size: 81.25%;
}

/* the styles for the div tags that divide the page into sections */
#page {
    width: 760px;
    margin: 0 auto;
    background-color: white;
    border: 3px solid black;
    border-top: none;
}

#header, #main, #footer {
    padding-left: 0.5em;
    padding-right: 0.5em;
}
#header {
    border-bottom: 1px solid gray;
}

#main {
    padding-top: 1em;
    padding-left: 0;
}
#sidebar {
    position: absolute;
    width: 10em;
}
#content {
    margin-left: 10em;
}

#footer {
    border-top: 1px solid gray;
    padding-bottom: 0.5em;
}
```

Figure 5-3   The CSS for the web page (part 1 of 2)

After the CSS for the <div> tags, the CSS specifies the formatting for the rest of the XHTML tags. For example, this code sets the color of the <h1> and <h2> tags to dark orange, and changes the font family for these tags. Then, this code increases the font size of the <h1> tag to 150% of the current font and sets the top margin and padding for this tag. Next, this code increases the font size of the <h2> tag to 120% of the current font.

After the CSS for the <h1> and <h2> tags, the CSS sets the margins and padding for the <ul> and <li> tags. When four values are specified like this, the values start at the top and rotate clockwise like this: top, right, bottom, left. In contrast, when only a single value is specified, that value is used for all four margin and padding values. As you progress through this chapter, you'll learn more about how this works.

After the CSS for the list tags, the CSS first specifies the formatting for an <a> tag when the mouse *isn't* hovering over the tag. This displays the link in a medium blue color, boldfaced, and with a bottom border that's 1 pixel wide, dashed, and dark orange.

Then, the CSS specifies the formatting for the <a> tag when the mouse *is* hovering over the tag. This changes the bottom border for the link from a dashed line to a solid line. As a result, the user can easily tell when the mouse is positioned over a link.

Finally, the CSS specifies the formatting for the classes that are used by the XHMTL code. To do that, it uses a dot operator (.) before the name of the class. For instance, the .copyright style applies to any tag that has a class attribute with a value of "copyright". If you look back to figure 5-2, though, you'll see that this only applies to the last paragraph in the XHTML document. The CSS formats this tag with the gray color, a smaller font, and alignment on the right side of the page.

The last three styles specify the formatting for classes too, but only for more specific circumstances. For example, the p.first style only applies to a <p> tag that has a class attribute with a value of "first". If you look back to figure 5-2, you'll see that this applies to the first <p> tag on the page. Similarly, the ul.nav declaration only applies to a <ul> tag that has a class attribute with a value of "nav". If you look back to figure 5-2, you'll see that this applies to the first <ul> tag, which contains the navigation links, not to the second <ul> tag. Similarly, the last style only applies to <li> tags that are coded within a <ul> tag that has a class attribute with a value of "nav".

Again, don't worry if you don't understand this code right now. As you progress through this chapter, you'll learn all the details that you need for creating professional style sheets. Then, when you refer back to this code, you'll be able to understand it.

The CSS for the home_page.css file   **Page 2**

```
/* the styles for the XHTML elements */
h1, h2 {
    color: darkOrange;
    font-family: Verdana, Arial, Helvetica, sans-serif;
}
h1 {
    font-size: 150%;
    margin-top: 0;
    padding-top: 0.5em;
}
h2 {
    font-size: 120%;
}

ul {
    margin: 0 0 1em 0;
    padding: 0 0 0 2.5em;
}
li {
    margin: 0;
    padding: 0;
}

a {
    color: mediumBlue;
    text-decoration: none;
    font-weight: bold;
    border-bottom: 1px dashed darkOrange;
}
a:hover {
    border-bottom: 1px solid darkOrange;
}

/* the styles for the XHTML classes */
.copyright {
    color: gray;
    font-size: 80%;
    text-align: right;
    margin-bottom: 0;
}
p.first {
    margin-top: 0;
}
ul.nav {
    margin: 0;
    padding-left: 1.25em;
    list-style-type: none;
}
ul.nav li {
    padding-bottom: 0.5em;
}
```

Figure 5-3   The CSS for the web page (part 2 of 2)

Basic skills for using CSS

With that as background, you're ready to learn how to use CSS. To start, here are some basic skills.

Basic CSS syntax

To format a web page with CSS, you code one or more *rule sets* as shown in figure 5-4. These rule sets are also referred to as *styles*.

As you can see in the diagram, each rule set starts with a *selector* that identifies the elements that the formatting should be applied to. This selector is followed by a *declaration block* that's coded within braces. Then, within the declaration block, you code the declarations that describe the formatting that should be applied to the selection.

Each *declaration* (or *rule*) consists of a *property*, a colon, a *value*, and a semicolon. Here, the semicolon for the last declaration in a declaration block is optional, but it's considered a best practice to code a semicolon after each declaration. That way, you can easily add other rules later on.

This is illustrated by the first rule set in this figure. Here, the selector is h1, and the declaration block contains two declarations. The first declaration has a property of color and a value of "blue". The second declaration has a property of font-size and a value of 14pt.

The selector for the second rule set in this figure is body, and it has a declaration block that contains four declarations. Here, the value for the third property, which is font-family, contains a list of values that are separated by commas. You'll learn more about coding multiple values for a single property as you progress through this chapter.

The selector for the third rule set in this figure uses commas to specify multiple elements for the same declaration block. As a result, the declarations in this block apply to the <h1> tag, to any tags with an id attribute of "footer", or to any tags with a class attribute of "gray". In this case, the declaration block consists of a single declaration that sets the color to gray.

If you want to include *CSS comments* in your CSS, you start them with the characters /* and end them with the characters */. These characters work like the multi-line comment that's available with JavaScript. As a result, you can use them to code single-line comments like the one in this figure. You can use them to code multi-line comments like this:

```
/*****************************************************
 * Description: Primary style sheet for murach.com
 * Author:     Ray Harris
 *****************************************************/
```

And you can use them to comment out blocks of CSS code. Note, however, that you can't use // to start a comment as you can with JavaScript.

The parts of a CSS rule set

```
selector

h1 {
    color: blue;
    font-size: 14pt;    ◀——— declaration
}
     ▲          ▲
  property    value
```

Another CSS rule set

```
body {
    margin-top: 0;
    background-color: dodgerBlue;
    font-family: Georgia, "Times New Roman", Times, serif;
    font-size: 10pt;
}
```

A CSS rule set with a complex selector

```
h1, #footer, .gray {
    color: gray;
}
```

A CSS comment

```
/* This is a CSS comment */
```

Description

- A *CSS rule set* consists of a selector and a declaration block.
- A *CSS selector* consists of the identifiers that are coded at the beginning of the rule.
- A *CSS declaration block* consists of an opening brace, zero or more declarations, and a closing brace.
- A *CSS declaration* consists of a *property*, a colon, a *value*, and a semicolon. Although the semicolon for the last declaration in a block is optional, it's a best practice to code it.
- *CSS comments* begin with the characters /* and end with the characters */. The JavaScript single-line comment // isn't valid in CSS.

Figure 5-4   Basic CSS syntax

How to include CSS in a web page

Figure 5-5 starts by showing two ways to include the CSS that's stored in an *external style sheet* in a web page. The first way is to use the <link> tag. This is currently considered a best practice because it's more efficient when you load more than one external style sheet for a page.

The second way is to use the <style> tag with the @import directive. This was considered a best practice until recently, so it's still widely used.

When you code a relative URL in a <link> or <style> tag, the URL is relative to the current file. For instance, the two dots (..) in the URL in the first example in this figure navigate up one directory from the current file. Then, this URL navigates down to the styles directory and selects a file named main.css.

Although it isn't recommended, you can also use *embedded style sheets* and *inline styles* within an XHTML document as shown by the second set of examples in this figure. When you embed a style sheet, the CSS declarations are coded in a <style> tag. For instance, the embedded style sheet in the first example in this group contains a single style for the <h1> tag.

When you use an inline style, you code a style attribute for the XHTML element with a value that contains all the CSS declarations that apply to the element. For instance, the inline style in the second example in this group applies two CSS declarations to the <span> tag.

If you do use embedded style sheets or inline styles, the styles in the embedded style sheets override the styles in the external style sheets, and the inline styles override the styles in the embedded style sheet. If, for example, you code the embedded style sheet in this figure after an @import directive, the declarations for the <h1> tag will override those in the external style sheet.

Remember, though, that using external style sheets is a best practice. When you use them, the CSS declarations are in a separate CSS file, which separates the formatting for a web page from its content. This also lets more than one web page share the same CSS file, which has several benefits. First, the XHTML files are smaller. Second, this lets you provide consistent formatting for an entire web site. Third, this means that you can modify the formatting for an entire site by modifying a single style sheet.

The last group of examples in this figure shows how you can use different style sheets for different types of media. To do that, you code the media attribute of a <link> or <style> tag. Here, the first example loads a style sheet that's used when the page is printed, and the second example loads a style sheet that's used when the page is rendered for a handheld device.

The trick of course is to code the style sheets so they're appropriate for the media. To do that, you may want to change font styles or sizes, add or remove borders, change colors, and so on. For printing, you may also want to hide controls like buttons so they aren't printed. You'll learn how to do that as you progress through this chapter.

Two ways to include an external style sheet

With the <link> tag (currently considered the best practice)

```
<link rel="stylesheet" type="text/css" href="../styles/main.css" />
```

With the <style> tag and the @import directive

```
<style type="text/css">
    @import "../styles/main.css";
</style>
```

How to embed styles in an XHTML document (not recommended)

Embedding a style sheet in a style tag in the head section

```
<style type="text/css">
    h1 {
        color: blue;
        font-size: 14pt;
    }
</style>
```

Using the style attribute of an inline tag

```
<span style="color: red; font-size: 14pt;">Warning!</span>
```

How to include external style sheets for specific media

Including a style sheet that's used when the page is printed

```
<link rel="stylesheet" type="text/css"
    href="../styles/main_print.css" media="print" />
```

Including a style sheet that's used for a handheld device

```
<link rel="stylesheet" type="text/css"
    href="../styles/main_handheld.css" media="handheld" />
```

Description

- It's a best practice to use *external style sheets* whenever possible. To do that, you can use either the <link> tag or the <style> tag with the @import directive.

- Currently, the best practice for including external style sheets is to use the <link> tag because it's more efficient when you use more then one style sheet for a web page. This is a recent change, though, so <style> tags are still commonly used.

- When you specify a relative URL for an external CSS file, the URL is relative to the current file.

- If you want to use different style sheets for different media, you can use the media attribute of the link tag to indicate the medium that the style sheet is for. Common media types are screen (the default), print, handheld (for devices like smart phones), speech (the content is read by a screen reader), braille (the content is displayed on a tactile device), and embossed (the content is printed in Braille).

Figure 5-5   How to include CSS in a web page

How to specify measurements and colors

Figure 5-6 shows the four units of measurement that are commonly used with CSS: pixels, points, ems, and percentages. Here, the first two are *absolute units of measurement*, and the second two are *relative units of measurements*. Other absolute units are inches and picas, but they aren't used as often.

When you use an absolute unit of measurement like pixels or points, the measurement won't change even if the user resizes the browser or uses the browser to change the font size. If, for example, you set the width of an element in pixels and the font size in points, the width and font size won't change.

In contrast, when you use a relative unit of measurement like ems or percentages, the measurement will change if the user resizes the browser or changes the font size. For example, if you set the width of an element to 80 percent, that element will change when the user resizes the browser.

After the table of measurements in this figure, you can see two groups of examples. Here, all four of the declarations in the first group specify the same font size. This works because the default font size for most modern browsers is 16 pixels, which is approximately 12 points. In the second group, you can see how pixels and a percent can be used to specify the width of an element.

Next, this figure shows three ways to specify colors. The easiest way is to specify a color name, and this figure lists the names for 16 colors that are supported by all browsers. In addition to these names, though, most browsers support many others. In the CSS in figure 5-3, for example, the style sheet uses dodgerBlue, darkOrange, and mediumBlue. To find a complete list of color names, you can go to the web site listed in this figure.

The second way to specify colors is to specify the percentages of red, green, and blue that make up a color in an *RGB value*. For instance, the example in this figure specifies 50% red, 25% green, and 25% blue. When you use this method, you can also use values from 0 through 255 instead of percentages. Then, 0 is equivalent to 0% and 255 is equivalent to 100%. This gives you more precision over the resulting colors.

The third way to specify colors is to use RGB values with *hexadecimal*, or *hex*, values that are preceded by the pound (#) sign. This is equivalent to using decimal values from 0 through 255. To get a complete list of the decimal or hex values for colors, you can go to the web site listed in this figure.

Common units of measurement

Symbol	Name	Type	Description
px	pixels	absolute	A pixel represents a single dot on the user's monitor.
pt	points	absolute	A point is 1/72 of an inch. One point is approximately 3/4 of a pixel.
em	ems	relative	One em is equal to the font size for the current font.
%	percentages	relative	A percentage specifies a value relative to the current value.

Four ways to specify font size

```
font-size: 12pt;
font-size: 16px;
font-size: 1em;
font-size: 100%;
```

Two ways to specify width

```
width: 760px;
width: 80%;
```

16 descriptive color names

black	silver	white	aqua	gray	fuchsia	olive	teal
red	lime	green	maroon	blue	navy	yellow	purple

Three ways to specify colors

With a color name

```
color: silver;
```

With an RGB (red-green-blue) value

```
color: rgb(50%, 25%, 25%);
```

With an RGB value that uses hexadecimal numbers

```
color: #cd5c5c;
```

Description

- To specify an *absolute unit of measurement*, you can use pixels or points. In most cases, an absolute unit of measurement doesn't change even if the user resizes the browser or uses the browser to change the font size.

- To specify a *relative unit of measurement*, you can use ems or percentages. This type of measurement is relative to the size of another element.

- The descriptive color names are easy to read and understand. All browsers support the 16 names shown above, and most browsers support many more.

- You can find a list of color names at http://en.wikipedia.org/wiki/Web_colors.

- Graphic designers often prefer to specify the relative amounts of red, green, and blue for a color in an *RGB value*, often by using *hexadecimal*, or *hex*, values.

Figure 5-6   How to specify measurements and colors

How to code selectors

Now that you have a general idea of how CSS works, you're ready to learn how to code selectors. Once you understand that, you should be able to apply CSS formatting to any part of a web page.

How to code selectors for tags, ids, and classes

Figure 5-7 shows how to code CSS selectors for XHTML elements. To start, it shows a snippet of XHTML that includes a <body> tag and two <div> tags. To allow the CSS to identify these tags, the first <div> tag has an id of "main", and the second <div> tag has an id of "footer".

Within the main section, the XHTML tags display a paragraph followed by a list of links. Here, the <ul> tag includes a class attribute of "nav". This allows CSS to apply formatting to this <ul> tag that's different from the formatting that's applied to <ul> tags that aren't members of the nav class.

Within the footer section, a single <p> tag displays a copyright notice. This tag includes a class attribute of "copyright inactive". This means that this tag belongs to two classes: the copyright class and the inactive class.

The first CSS rule set in this figure selects an XHTML element by its tag. To do that, the selector is simply the name of the tag. As a result, this rule set selects the <body> tag. Within this rule set, the declaration changes the font-family property to Arial or a generic sans-serif font if Arial isn't available. Since most tags inherit the <body> tag and since most tags inherit the font-family property, this causes all of the text in the XHTML to be displayed in the specified font.

The second CSS rule set selects an XHTML element by its id. To do that, the selector is a pound sign (#) followed by an id value that uniquely identifies the element. As a result, this rule set selects the <div> tag that has an id of "main". Then, the first rule adds a border around the main section, and the second rule adds .2 ems of padding between the border and the text.

The last three rule sets select XHTML elements by its class. To do that, the selector is a period (.) followed by a class name. As a result, the first rule set selects the <ul> list that has a class of "nav". Then, it changes the type of bullet that's used for the list from the default round bullet to a square bullet. In contrast, the last two rule sets both select the last <p> tag that has a class attribute of "copyright inactive".

When you use class selectors, you can apply the same rule set to many XHTML elements. In contrast, when you use id selectors, you apply one rule set to a single element. As a result, ids are used to apply formatting to elements that only occur once on each page, such as <div> elements that divide a page into sections. But classes are typically used to apply formatting to elements that occur multiple times on a single page, such as <p> tags.

XHTML elements that can be selected by tag, id, or class

```
<body>
    <div id="main">
        <p>Here is a list of links:</p>
        <ul class="nav">
            <li><a href="products.html">Products</a></li>
            <li><a href="services.html">Services</a></li>
        </ul>
    </div>
    <div id="footer">
        <p class="copyright inactive">Copyright 2009</p>
    </div>
</body>
```

CSS rule sets that select by tag, id, and class

Tag

```
body {
    font-family: Arial, sans-serif;
}
```

ID

```
#main {
    border: 2px solid black;
    padding: 0.2em;
}
```

Class

```
.nav {
    list-style-type: square;
}
.copyright {
    text-align: right;
}
.inactive {
    color: gray;
}
```

The elements displayed in a browser

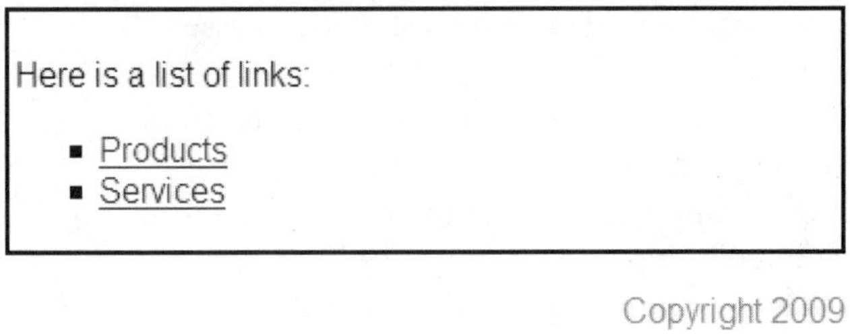

Here is a list of links:

- Products
- Services

Copyright 2009

Figure 5-7   How to code selectors for tags, ids, and classes

How to code other types of XHTML selectors

Figure 5-8 shows how to code other types of XHTML selectors. To start, you can select all XHTML elements by using the *universal selector*. To do that, you code an asterisk (*). In the first example, the universal selector selects all elements on the web page and changes their foreground color to black.

To code a selector that selects by tag and class, you code the tag name, followed by a period (.), followed by a class name. In the second example, the ul.nav selector only selects <ul> tags that have a class of "nav".

To code a *descendant selector* that selects elements only when they are descendants of the parent element, you code the selector for the parent element, a space, and the selector for the descendent element. In the third set of examples, the first descendant selector only selects <p> tags that are coded within a tag that has an id of "footer". The second descendant selector only selects <a> tags that are coded within <ul> tags. And the third descendant selector uses the universal selector to select all tags that are coded within a <ul> tag.

To code a *child selector* that selects elements only when they are direct child elements of the parent element, you use the greater than (>) sign. Unlike the descendant selector, the child selector doesn't select grandchildren or great grandchildren. In the fourth set of examples, the first child selector only selects <p> tags that are coded within a tag that has an id of "main". The second child selector only selects <li> tags that are coded within a <ul> tag that has a class of "nav".

To code an *attribute selector* that selects an element with the specified attribute value, you use brackets ([ ]) and an equals sign (=). In the fifth example, the attribute selector selects <input> tags that have a type attribute of "submit". In other words, this selector selects all "submit" buttons. Then, the three rules for this selector give the buttons a solid black border that's 1 pixel thick with white text on a blue background.

Although child selectors and attribute selectors are useful, they are relatively new additions to CSS. As a result, they aren't supported by some of the older browsers such as IE6. So, if you need to support older browsers, you should avoid using these types of selectors. Instead, you can use ids or classes to identify the elements that you want to format.

The last set of examples in this figure shows how to code multiple selectors for the same rule set. To do that, you separate the selectors with commas. Here, the first rule set uses multiple selectors to apply its rules to the <h1>, <h2>, and <h3> tags. Then, the second rule set uses multiple selectors to apply its rules to the <p> tag and also to li elements that are children of ul elements with "nav" as their class name.

Other ways to code selectors

The universal selector

```
* { color: black; }
```

Tag and class

```
ul.nav { list-style-type: square; }
```

Descendant elements

```
#footer p { font-size: 10pt; }
ul a { color: green; }
ul * { color: green; }
```

Child elements

```
#main > p { font-size: 12pt; }
ul.nav > li { margin-left: 20px; }
```

Attributes

```
input[type=submit] {
    border: 1px solid black;
    color: white;
    background-color: blue;
}
```

Multiple selectors

```
h1, h2, h3 { color: blue; }
p, ul.nav > li { font-family: "Times New Roman", serif; }
```

Description

- To select all elements, use the *universal selector* (*).
- To code a selector for a tag and class, code a tag name, the dot operator, and a class name.
- To select elements only when they are descendants of a parent element, use a *descendant selector* that consists of the parent element, a space, and the descendent element.
- To select elements only when they are direct child elements of the parent element, use a *child selector* that consists of the parent element, the greater than sign (>), and the child element.
- To select an element with a specific attribute value, use an *attribute selector* that consists of an element followed by the attribute name within brackets ([ ]).
- To code multiple selectors for the same rule set, use commas to separate the selectors.

Note

- Child selectors and attribute selectors aren't supported by some of the older browsers such as IE 6.

Figure 5-8   How to code other types of XHTML selectors

How to code pseudo-class selectors

Figure 5-9 shows how to code *pseudo-class selectors*. In the table of pseudo-class selectors, the first two can only be used with links, but the other three can be used with most XHTML elements. For example, the :hover selector can be used with an <a> tag or a <p> tag.

In the examples in this figure, the first pseudo-class selector displays all unvisited links in black. The second selector displays all visited links in gray. The third selector displays each link in bold when the mouse is hovering over it. The fourth selector displays the link in green after the user presses the mouse button but before the user releases the button. And the fifth selector indents the first line of the first <p> tag, but doesn't indent the second one.

After the CSS examples, you can see how the formatting looks in a web browser. Here, the first line of the first paragraph is indented, but not the first line of the second paragraph. Also, the mouse is hovering over the second link so it is displayed in bold.

When working with pseudo-class selectors, you may find that different browsers support them differently. For example, the :first-child selector isn't supported by Internet Explorer. However, the :visited and :hover selectors have been commonly used with links since the early days of the web. As a result, most browsers support these selectors when they're used with links.

Pseudo-class selectors

Name	Description
:link	A link that hasn't been visited.
:visited	A link that has been visited.
:hover	An element when the mouse is hovering over it.
:active	An element that's currently active. For example, a link is active after the user presses the mouse button but before the user releases the mouse button.
:first-child	An element that's the first child element.

XHTML that can be used by pseudo-class selectors

```
<div id="main">
    <p>Welcome to Mike's Bait and Tackle Shop. We have all the gear
        you'll need to make your next fishing trip a great success!</p>
    <ul class="nav">
        <li><a href="products.html">Products</a></li>
        <li><a href="services.html">Services</a></li>
    </ul>
    <p><a href="contact.html">Contact us</a> to place
        your order today!</p>
</div>
```

The CSS for pseudo-class selectors

```
a:link {
    color: black;
}
a:visited {
    color: gray;
}
a:hover {
    font-weight: bold;
}
a:active {
    color: green;
}
#main > p:first-child {
    text-indent: 1em;
}
```

The pseudo-class selectors in a web browser

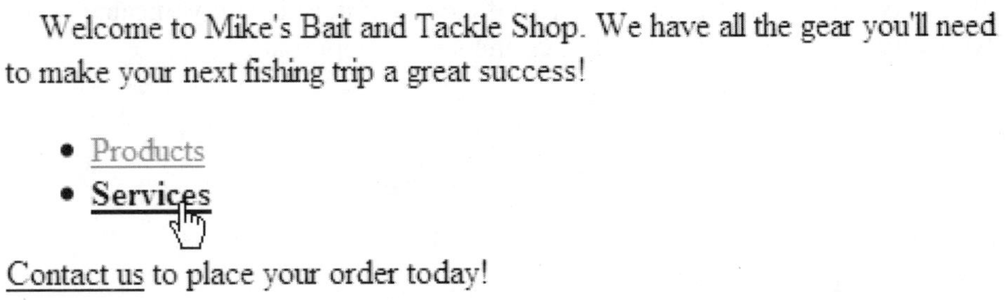

Welcome to Mike's Bait and Tackle Shop. We have all the gear you'll need to make your next fishing trip a great success!

- Products
- **Services**

Contact us to place your order today!

Figure 5-9   How to code pseudo-class selectors

How the cascade rules work

The term *Cascading Style Sheets* refers to the fact that more than one style sheet can be applied to a single web page. Then, if two or more rule sets are applied to the same element, the cascade order and rules determine which rule set takes precedence.

Before you can understand the cascade rules, though, you need to know that a user can create a *user style sheet* that provides default rule sets for web pages. Because most users don't create user style sheets, this usually isn't an issue. But some users do. For instance, users with poor vision often create user style sheets that provide for large font sizes. In that case, you need to consider how the user style sheets could affect your web pages.

You should also know how to identify one of your rules as important so it has precedence over other rules. To do that, you code "!important" as part of the rule. This is shown by the example in figure 5-10.

With that as background, this figure lists the five levels of the cascade order from strongest to weakest. As you can see, the important rules in a user style sheet override the important rules in a web page, but the normal rules in a web page override the normal rules in a user style sheet. Below these rules are the default rules in the web browser.

But what happens if an element has more than one rule applied to it at the same level? To start, the rule with the highest specificity takes precedence, and this figure shows you which parts of a selector are more specific. For instance, the #main selector is more specific than the .nav selector.

If a selector contains multiple parts, the additional parts add to that selector's specificity. This means that a selector with a class and a tag is more specific than a selector with just a class. For instance, the p.highlight selector is more specific than the .highlight selector. As a result, p.highlight takes precedence.

If that doesn't settle the conflict, the rule that's specified last is applied. For instance, inline styles are specified after an external style sheet or an embedded style sheet, so inline styles take precedence. This notion also applies if you accidentally code two rule sets for the same element in a style sheet. Then, the one that is last takes precedence.

If this sounds complicated, it usually isn't a problem if you organize your style sheets like the one in figure 5-3. Then, if a conflict does occur, you can usually resolve it by identifying one of the rule sets as important.

How to identify a rule as important

```
.highlight {
    font-weight: bold !important;
}
```

The cascade order for applying CSS rule sets

Search for the rule sets that apply to an element in the sequence that follows and apply the rule set from the first group in which it's found:

- !important rules in a user style sheet
- !important rules in a web page
- Normal rules in a web page
- Normal rules in a user style sheet
- Default rules in the web browser

If more than one rule set in a group is applied to an element...

- Use the rule set with the highest specificity. For example, the p.highlight selector is more specific than the .highlight selector.
- If the specificity is the same for two or more rule sets in a group, use the rule set that's specified last.

How to determine the specificity of a selector

- An id is the most specific.
- A class, attribute selector, or pseudo-class selector is less specific.
- An element or pseudo-element selector is least specific.

Description

- When two or more rule sets are applied to an XHTML element, CSS uses the cascade order and rules shown above to determine which rule set to apply.
- A user can create a *user style sheet* that provides a default set of rules for web pages. Users with poor vision often do this so the type for a page is displayed in a large font.
- Since most users don't create user style sheets, you usually can control the way the rules are applied for your web applications. But you should keep in mind how your web pages could be affected by user style sheets.
- If you want to create or remove a user style sheet, you can search the Internet for the procedures that your browser requires.

Figure 5-10   How the cascade rules work

How to work with text and lists

Now that you know how to select the elements that you want to format, you're ready to learn how to use CSS to apply that formatting. To start, you'll learn how to set fonts, format text, and format lists.

How to style fonts

Figure 5-11 presents the basic skills for styling fonts. To start, this figure summarizes three of the five generic font families (the other two are cursive and fantasy). Then, it shows an example of each. Here, Times New Roman is the serif font; Arial is the sans-serif font, and Courier New is the monospace font.

To set the font family, you code the font-family property followed by a list of fonts. Here, a font name that contains spaces must be enclosed in quotes. Then, when the browser tries to display the page, it searches for the fonts in the order in which they are listed. If a font isn't available, the browser tries to find the next one. As a result, you should specify the fonts in order of preference, and you should end with a generic font family. That way, if the browser can't find the other fonts in the list, it can use its default font for the generic font family.

To set the style, weight, or variant of a font, you can use the properties in the second group of examples in this figure. Here, the font-style property is used to display the font in italics. The font-weight property is used to display the font in boldface. And the font-variant property is used to display the font in small caps. To explicitly remove one of these properties, you set it to "normal".

By default, most browsers use 16 pixels as the font size for XHTML elements like the <p> tag. To change that, you can set the font-size property. One way to do that is to use an absolute unit of measurement such as pixels or points. However, some older browsers like IE6 won't let your users resize text that has been sized that way. As a result, it's usually better to set the font size in percentages or ems. Then, all modern browsers including IE6 will let your users resize the text. This is illustrated by the third group of examples in this figure.

After you've set the font-size property, you may want to set the line-height property, which increases or decreases the amount of vertical space for each line. Like the font-size property, you can specify a value for the line-height property in pixels or points, but it's usually better to set this property using percentages or ems. That way, all modern browsers will be able to adjust the line height relative to the current font size. This is also illustrated by the third group of examples.

To set all of six of these properties in one rule, you can use the *shorthand property* for fonts that's shown next. When you use this property, you code the six font properties separated by spaces without coding the property names. You combine the font-size and line-height properties separated by a slash, as in 90%/120%. You separate the list of fonts for the font-family property with commas. And you enclose a font name in quotes if it contains spaces.

Three of the five generic font families

Name	Description
serif	Fonts with tapered, flared, or slab stroke ends.
sans-serif	Fonts with plain stroke ends.
monospace	Fonts that use the same width for each character.

Examples of three common font families

- Times New Roman is a serif font. It is the default for most web browsers.
- Arial is a sans-serif font. It is widely used.
- `Courier New is a monospace font.`

How to specify a font family

```
font-family: "Times New Roman", Times, serif;
font-family: Arial, Helvetica, sans-serif;
font-family: "Courier New", Courier, monospace;
```

How to specify font styles, weights, and variants

```
font-style: italic;
font-weight: bold;
font-variant: small-caps;
```

How to specify font size and line height

```
font-size: 12pt;        /* in points */
font-size: 150%;        /* as a percentage of the current font */
font-size: 1.5em;       /* same as 150% for font-size */
line-height: 14pt;
line-height: 120%;
line-height: 1.2em;     /* same as 120% for line-height */
```

The syntax for the shorthand font property

```
font: [style] [weight] [variant] size[/line-height] family;
```

How to use the shorthand font property

```
font: italic bold 14px/16px Arial, sans-serif;
font: small-caps 150% "Times New Roman", Times, serif;
font: 90%/120% "Comic Sans MS", Impact, sans-serif;
```

Description

- For the font-family property, a font name that contains spaces must be enclosed in quotes.
- For the font-family property, the fonts are searched in the order listed. If a font isn't available, the next one is tried. If none of the fonts are available but a generic font has been specified, the web browser uses its default font for the specified generic font.
- If necessary, you can set the font-style, font-weight, or font-variant properties to a value of "normal" to remove any formatting that has been applied to these properties.
- You can use the *shorthand property* of a font to set all six font properties with a single rule. When you use this property, the font-size and font-family properties are required, but the other four properties are optional.

Figure 5-11   How to style fonts

When you use the shorthand font property, the font-size and font-family properties are required, but the other four properties are optional. For instance, the first example sets only five of the properties (no variant), and the second example sets only three of the properties.

How to format text

Figure 5-12 shows how to use other properties that let you format text. To start, you can use the text-transform property to display text in all uppercase letters, all lowercase letters, or with the first letter of each word capitalized.

To underline text or to apply other decorations to the text, you can use the text-decoration property. For example, you can use the overline value to draw a line over the text, the line-through value to draw a line through the text, or the blink value to make the text blink. In the early days of the web, blinking text was often used to attract attention, but today that practice is discouraged.

If you need to explicitly specify that you don't want to transform the text or add a decoration to it, you can specify a value of "none". For example, the text-decoration property of the <a> tag is set to "underline" by default. If you don't want that, you can set this property to "none".

To indent the first line of text in a paragraph, you can use the text-indent property. When you set this property, it usually makes sense to use a relative unit of measurement such as ems. That way, if the size of the current font changes, the indentation for the first line of the paragraph will also change.

To horizontally align text, you can use the text-align property. By default, most elements are left aligned, but you can use the "center", "right", or "justify" values to change that. When you justify text, the spacing between words is adjusted so the text is aligned on both the left and right sides.

The example in this figure shows how these properties work. Here, the <h3> tag is centered and its text is transformed into uppercase letters. Also, the text-decoration property is used to draw a line both under and over the text in this tag. Note that this formatting is done by using a space to separate the two decoration values.

The CSS also indents the first line of each <p> tag by 2 ems, but it explicitly doesn't indent the first line of the contact class. Since the second <p> tag is a member of this class, this paragraph isn't indented. Similarly, the CSS right aligns members of the copyright class. Since the third <p> tag is a member of this class, this paragraph is right aligned.

How to transform text

```
text-transform: uppercase;
```

Valid values

```
uppercase   lowercase   capitalize   none
```

How to add decorations to text

```
text-decoration: underline;
```

Valid values

```
underline   overline   line-through   blink   none
```

How to indent the first line of text

```
text-indent: 2em;
text-indent: 25px;
text-indent: 10%;
```

How to horizontally align text

```
text-align: left;
```

Valid values

```
left   center   right   justify
```

The XHTML for one heading and three paragraphs

```
<h3>Mike's Bait &amp; Tackle Shop</h3>
<p>We have all the gear you'll need to make your next
    fishing trip a great success!</p>
<p class="contact"><a href="contact.html">Contact us</a>
    to place your order today!</p>
<p class="copyright">&copy; 2008</p>
```

The CSS for the text

```
h3 {
    text-align: center;
    text-transform: uppercase;
    text-decoration: underline overline;
}
p { text-indent: 2em; }
.contact { text-indent: 0em; }
.copyright { text-align: right; }
```

The text in a browser

<u>MIKE'S BAIT & TACKLE SHOP</u>

We have all the gear you'll need to make your next fishing trip a great success!

<u>Contact us</u> to place your order today!

© 2008

Figure 5-12   How to format text

How to format lists

Figure 5-13 shows how to format ordered and unordered lists. To start, it shows how to use the list-style-type property to format the numbers or letters for an ordered list. By default, an ordered list uses standard decimal numbers, but you can change that by specifying another value for this property. In the example, you can see how uppercase letters are used for the first list in the XHTML.

Next, this figure shows how to use the list-style-type property to format the bullets for unordered lists. By default, a list displays a solid round bullet, but you can specify a value of "circle" to display a circle bullet or "square" to display a square bullet. In the example, you can see how circles are used.

If these predefined bullet types aren't adequate for your needs, you can display a custom image before each item in an unordered list. To do that, you start by getting or creating the image that you want to use. For instance, you can get many images that are appropriate for lists from the Internet. Often, these images are available for free or for a small charge. The other alternative is to use a graphics program to create your own image.

Once you have the image that you want to use, you use the list-style-image property to specify the URL for the image file. This is illustrated by the last example in this figure, which points to an image named star.gif that's stored in the same directory as the web page. If necessary, though, you can use a relative or absolute URL to navigate to the image, just as you use would in the href attribute of an <a> tag.

How to format the numbers for ordered lists

```
list-style-type: decimal;              /* default value, 1, 2, 3, ... */
list-style-type: decimal-leading-zero; /* 01, 02, 03, ... */
list-style-type: lower-alpha;          /* a, b, c, ... */
list-style-type: upper-alpha;          /* A, B, C, ... */
list-style-type: lower-roman;          /* i, ii, iii, iv, v, ... */
list-style-type: upper-roman;          /* I, II, III, IV, V, ... */
list-style-type: lower-greek;          /* α, β, γ, δ, ε, ... */
```

How to format the bullet for unordered lists

```
list-style-type: disc;     /* default value, solid circle */
list-style-type: circle;   /* hollow circle */
list-style-type: square;   /* square */
```

XHTML for a list example

```
<ol>
    <li>Windows</li>
    <li>Mac OS</li>
    <li>Linux</li>
</ol>
<ul>
    <li>Internet Explorer</li>
    <li>Firefox</li>
    <li>Safari</li>
</ul>
```

CSS for a list example

```
ol { list-style-type: upper-alpha; }
ul { list-style-type: circle; }
```

The list example displayed in a web browser

A. Windows
B. Mac OS
C. Linux

○ Internet Explorer
○ Firefox
○ Safari

How to use an image as a bullet

```
list-style-image: none;              /* default value */
list-style-image: url("star.gif");
```

An image as a bullet in the web browser

★ Internet Explorer
★ Firefox
★ Safari

Figure 5-13   How to format lists

How to work with the box model

When a browser displays a web page, it places each XHTML block element in a box. This is useful when you want to apply borders and other formatting to elements like <div>, <h1>, and <p> tags. However, you can also use this technique to format inline elements like <a>, <img>, and <span> tags. In CSS, this is known as working with the *box model*.

An introduction to the box model

Figure 5-14 presents a diagram that shows how the box model works. By default, the box for a block element is as wide as the block that contains it and as tall as it needs to be based on its contents. However, you can explicitly specify the size of the box for a block element by using the height and width properties. You can also use other properties to set the borders, margins, and padding for a block element.

If you look at the diagram in this figure, you can see that *padding* is the space between the box and a border. This is similar to the way that padding works for tables. Similarly, a *margin* is the space between the border and the side of the containing element.

If you need to calculate the overall height of a box, you can use the formula in this figure. Here, you start by adding the values for the margin, border width, and padding for the top of the box. Then, you add the height of the center box. Last, you add the values for the padding, border width, and margin for the bottom of the box. Similarly, you can use the other formula in this figure to calculate the overall width of a box.

When you set the height and width properties for a block element, you can use any of the units that you've learned about in this chapter, but you'll typically use pixels or percentages. In contrast, when you work with margins and padding, it's a good practice to use a relative unit of measurement such as ems. That way, the margins and padding are adjusted if the font size changes.

The CSS box model

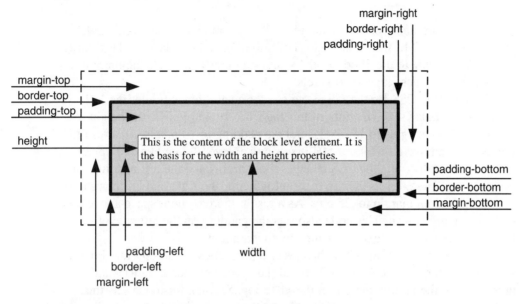

The formula for calculating the height of a box

```
top margin + top border + top padding +
height +
bottom padding + bottom border + bottom margin
```

The formula for calculating the width of a box

```
left margin + left border + left padding +
width +
right padding + right border + right margin.
```

Description

- By default, a block element is as wide as its containing block element and as tall as it needs to be based on its contents.
- You can use the height and width properties to specify the size of a box.
- You can use other properties to control the margins, border, and padding for a box.

Figure 5-14   An introduction to the box model

A web page that illustrates the box model

To make sure that you understand how the box model works, figure 5-15 presents the XHTML for a web page. Then, the CSS adds a dashed black border that's 1 pixel wide to the <body>, <h1>, and <p> tags and it sets the margin for all four sides of these tags to 10 pixels.

But then, the CSS for the <div> tag creates a solid black border that's 2 pixels wide. It also sets the width of this tag's box to 450 pixels, the height to 150 pixels, the margins to 15 pixels, and the padding to 10 pixels. As a result, this box has an overall width of 504 pixels and an overall height of 204 pixels.

After the <div> tag, the CSS changes the margins and the left padding for the <h1> tag. Here, it sets the top margin to .5 ems, the right and left margin to 0, and the bottom margin to .25 ems. As a result, there is more space above the <h1> tag than below it. This code also sets the padding on the left side of the box to 15 pixels so the text is indented by that amount

After the <h1> tag, the CSS changes two properties of the <p> tag. First, it sets the top margin to 0. As a result, all of the space between the <h1> and <p> tags is due to the bottom margin of the <h1> tag. Second, this code sets the padding on the left side of the box to 15 pixels. As a result, the browser displays 15 pixels of space between the border for the box and the text. This causes the text for the <h1> and <p> tags to align.

If you study the rendered code in the browser, you'll get a better idea of how the box model works. For instance, the box for the body of the document has margins of 10 pixels on the left, right, and top of the browser window, but not the bottom because that's determined by the size of the window. And within the body box, the box for the <div> tag has margins of 15 pixels on the left, top, and bottom, but not the right because the width of the box is set to 450 pixels.

Then, because the <div> box also has padding of 10 pixels, the <h1> and <p> boxes within it are set off from the left and right sides of the border by that much, even though their left and right margins are set to zero. Also, because the <h1> tag has its top and bottom margin set in ems, those margins are relative to the size of the <h1> text. Finally, within the <h1> and <p> boxes, the padding on the left is 15 pixels so the text is indented and aligned. In this case, if a relative unit of measurement was used for the padding, the text in those boxes wouldn't be indented by the same amount so the text wouldn't be aligned.

The XHTML for a box model

```
<body>
  <div id="main">
    <h1>Mike's Bait &amp; Tackle Shop</h1>
    <p>We have all the gear you'll need to make your next
        fishing trip a great success!</p>
  </div>
</body>
```

The CSS for a box model

```
body, h1, p {
    border: 1px dashed black;
    margin: 10px;
}
#main {
    border:  2px solid black;
    width:   450px;
    height:  150px;
    margin:  15px;    /* all four sides */
    padding: 10px;    /* all four sides */
}
h1 {
    margin:  .5em 0 .25em;  /* .5em top, 0 right and left, .25em bottom */
    padding-left: 15px;
}
p {
    margin: 0;        /* all four sides */
    padding-left: 15px;
}
```

The web page in a browser

Description

- The three dotted lines in this web page are the borders for the body, h1, and p tags. The solid line is the border for the "main" div tag.

Figure 5-15   A web page that illustrates the box model

How to set height, width, margins, and padding

Figure 5-16 shows how to set the height, width, margins, and padding for a block element. By default, the height and width properties are set to a value of "auto". As a result, the size of the box is automatically adjusted so it's as wide as the element that contains it and as tall as the content it contains. To change that, you can use the height and width properties, and you'll typically use pixels or percentages to set those properties.

To set the margins and padding for a block element, you can use individual properties like margin-top or padding-right. Or you can use the shorthand properties for margins and padding that let you set the margins and padding for all four sides.

When you use a shorthand property, you can specify one, two, three, or four values. If you specify all four values, they are applied to the sides of the box in a clockwise order: top, right, bottom, and left. To remember this order, you can think of the word *trouble*.

If you specify fewer than four values, this property still applies values to all four sides of the box. If, for example, you only specify one value, that value is applied to all four sides of the box. Similarly, for two values, the first value sets the top and bottom, and the second value sets the left and right. And for three values, the first value sets the top, the second value sets the left and right, and the third value sets the bottom.

When you work with margins and padding, it's generally considered a good practice to use a relative unit of measurement such as ems. That way, the margins and padding are adjusted if the font size changes.

How to set the width of a block

```
width: 450px;              /* an absolute width */
width: 75%;                /* a relative width */
width: auto;               /* default value */
```

How to set the height of a block

```
height: 125px;
height: 50%;
height: auto;              /* default value */
```

How to set the margins

With the margin properties

```
margin-top: .5em;
margin-right: 1em;
margin-bottom: 2em;
margin-left: 1em;
```

With the shorthand margin property

```
margin: 1em;               /* all four margins */
margin: 0 1em;             /* top and bottom 0, right and left 1em */
margin: .5em 1em 2em;      /* top .5em, right and left 1em, bottom 2em */
margin: .5em 1em 2em 1em;  /* top .5em, right 1em, bottom 2em, left 1em */
```

How to set the padding

With the padding properties

```
padding-top: 0;
padding-right: 1em;
padding-bottom: .5em;
padding-left: 1em;
```

With the shorthand padding property

```
padding: 1em;              /* all four sides */
padding: 0 1em;            /* top and bottom 0, right and left 1em */
padding: 0 1em .5em;       /* top 0em, right and left 1em, bottom .5em */
padding: 0 1em .5em 1em;   /* top 0em, right 1em, bottom .5em, left 1em */
```

Description

- When you use the shorthand properties for margins and padding, the values apply to the top, right, bottom, and left margins (as in the word *trouble*).

Figure 5-16   How to set height, width, margins, and padding

How to set borders

Figure 5-17 shows you how to set the borders for a box. To start, if you want the same border on all four sides of a box, you can use the shorthand border property, which lets you set the width, style, and color for a border. Otherwise, you can use the individual properties that are shown in this figure.

To specify the width of a border, you usually use pixels, but you can use other units of measurement too. In addition, you can use the width names shown in this figure: thin, medium, or thick.

To specify the style of a border, you specify one of the named values shown in this figure. For most borders, you'll probably use "solid". But if you're interested in the other styles, like double or ridge, it's worth taking the time to experiment with them. Or, if you want to turn a border off, you can set the style to hidden or none.

To specify the color of the border, you can use any of the techniques for specifying colors that you learned about in figure 5-6. However, if you don't specify a color for a border, the browser uses the color that's used for the block element that you're working with. That way, the color of the border changes if you change the color of the element.

If you want to work with all four borders, but you want to apply different values to the different sides, you can use the border-width, border-style, and border-color properties. These properties are shorthand properties that work like the margin and padding properties, so the sequential values are applied to the top, right, bottom, and left portions of the border.

Finally, if you want to work with the border for just one side of a box, you can use the border-top, border-right, border-bottom, and border-left properties. When you use these properties, you can set all of the properties for the border at once. If necessary, though, you can append the width, style, and color properties to any of these properties as shown at the bottom of this figure. Then, you end up with a specific property such as the border-top-width property.

The syntax for the shorthand border property

```
border: [width] [style] [color];
```

How to use the shorthand border property to set all four borders

```
border: thin solid green;
border: 2px dashed #808080;
border: 1px inset;              /* uses the element's color property */
```

How to set the width of all four borders

```
border-width: 1px;
border-width: 2px 4px;          /* top and bottom 2px, left and right 4px */
border-width: 2px 3px 4px;      /* top 2px, left and right 3px, bottom 4px */
border-width: 2px 3px 4px 5px; /* top 2px, right 3px,
                                        bottom 4px, left 5px */
```

Valid values for named widths

```
thin   medium   thick
```

How to set the style of all four borders

```
border-style: dashed;       /* a dashed line */
border-style: solid;        /* a solid line */
border-style: solid none;   /* solid top and bottom, left and right */
```

Valid values

```
dotted   dashed   solid   double   groove   ridge   inset   outset   none   hidden
```

How to set the color for all four borders

```
border-color: green;        /* a named color */
border-color: #808080;      /* a hexidecimal value for a color */
border-color: black gray;   /* black top and bottom, gray left and right */
```

How to work with individual borders

With the shorthand border property

```
border-top: 2px solid black;
```

With individual properties

```
border-top-width: 2px;
border-top-style: solid;
border-top-color: black
```

Other examples

```
border-right-style: dashed;
border-bottom-width: 4px;
border-left-color: gray;
```

Description

- You can use the shorthand property for borders to work with the borders for all four sides of a box.

Figure 5-17   How to set borders

How to set background colors and images

Figure 5-18 shows how to set the background for a box. In the browser, this background is displayed behind the content, padding, and border of the box, but not in the margins for the box.

When you specify the background for a box, you can set a background color, a background image, or both. If you set both, the browser displays the background color behind the image. As a result, you can only see the background color if the image has areas that are transparent or don't repeat.

As this figure shows, you can set all five properties of a background by using the shorthand background property. When you use this shorthand property, you don't have to specify the individual properties in a specific order, but it usually makes sense to use the order that's shown. If you omit one or more properties, the browser uses their default values.

By default, the background color for a box is set to "transparent". As a result, you can see through the box to the color that's behind it, and that's usually what you want. Otherwise, you need to set that color.

By default, a box doesn't display a background image. To set a background image, you specify a URL that points to the file for the image. As you would expect, you can use a relative or an absolute URL to do that. Or, if you want to hide the background image, you can set this property to a value of "none".

By default, a background image repeats horizontally and vertically to fill the box. This works well for small images that are intended to be tiled across a box. But if you want to change this behavior, you can set the background-repeat property to only repeat the image horizontally, to only repeat the image vertically, or to prevent the image from repeating at all.

For images that repeat horizontally and vertically, the image spans the entire box. As a result, you don't need to control how the background image responds to scrolling or where the background image is displayed in the box. Otherwise, you need to set the background-attachment and background-position properties. If, for example, you don't want the image to move off the screen when you scroll, you can set the background-attach property to fixed so the image maintains a fixed position relative to the browser window.

By default, an image is positioned in the top left corner of the box. However, you can use the background-position property to modify that position. If you use the keywords in this figure, the first value specifies the horizontal position (left, center, right), and the second value specifies the vertical position (top, center, bottom). For more control, though, you can use percentages instead of keywords.

To put these properties into context, this figure ends by showing the CSS for a web page and the web page in a browser. Here, the CSS for the <body> tag sets a background color and a background image that is repeated so it covers the entire browser window. Then, the CSS for the main section changes the background color to white. Last, the CSS for the class named nav changes the background color to gray, and the final CSS rule changes the color for the bullets and links that are coded within the nav class to white.

The syntax for the shorthand background property

```
background: [color] [image] [repeat] [attachment] [position];
```

How to use the background property

```
background: blue;
background: blue url("texture.gif");
background: #808080 url("header.jpg") repeat-y scroll center top;
```

How to set the background color and image

```
background-color: blue;
background-image: url("texture.gif");
```

How to control image repetition, scrolling, and position

```
background-repeat: repeat;          /* default value, repeats both directions */
background-repeat: repeat-x;        /* repeats horizontally */
background-repeat: repeat-y;        /* repeats vertically */
background-repeat: no-repeat;       /* doesn't repeat */
background-attachment: scroll;      /* image moves as you scroll */
background-attachment: fixed;       /* image does not move as you scroll */
background-position: left top;        /* default, 0% from left, 0% from top */
background-position: center top;      /* 50% from left, 0% from top */
background-position: 90% 90%;         /* 90% from left, 90% from top */
```

CSS for a web page

```
body {
    background: blue url("texture.gif");
}
#main {
    background-color: white;
    height: 200px;
    width: 460px;
    padding: 1em;
}
.nav {
    background-color: gray;
    width: 6em;
    padding: .5em 1em .5em 2em;
}
ul.nav, .nav a {
    color: white;
}
```

The web page in a browser

Figure 5-18   How to set background colors and images

How to position elements

One of the benefits of using CSS is that it lets you position the XHTML elements on a page. As a result, you don't have to use XHTML tables for that purpose. CSS also lets you change the positioning for different types of devices like computer screens and handhelds.

How to change the display type of an element

By default, a browser displays block tags like <h1>, <p>, or <div> tags on a new line, but it displays inline tags like <a> or <img> tags on the same line. To change this behavior, you can use the display property for an element as shown by the example in figure 5-19. Here, the CSS changes the display property of the <a> tags in the nav section from inline to block. As a result, each of these <a> tags is displayed on a new line.

Of course, you can get the same result by coding each <a> tag within an <li> tag as shown in some of the earlier examples. Then, you can easily apply bullets to the items or add text after them. But sometimes it makes sense to just change the display to block.

Another use of the display property is to hide an element by setting this property to none. For instance, it often makes sense to hide controls like buttons in the CSS for print media.

How to change the display type of an element

```
display: inline;    /* default value */
display: block;     /* treats the inline element as a block element */
display: none;      /* doesn't display the element */
```

The XHTML for a web page

```
<p>Welcome to Mike's Bait and Tackle Shop.</p>
<div id="nav">
    <a href="products.html">Products</a>
    <a href="services.html">Services</a>
    <a href="about.html">About Us</a>
</div>
<p><a href="contact.html">Contact us</a> to place
    your order today!</p>
```

The CSS for the web page

```
#nav > a {
    display: block;
    margin-left: 2em;
    padding-bottom: .1em;
}
```

The XHTML in a browser without the CSS

Welcome to Mike's Bait and Tackle Shop.

Products Services About Us

Contact us to place your order today!

The XHTML in a browser with the CSS

Welcome to Mike's Bait and Tackle Shop.

Products
Services
About Us

Contact us to place your order today!

Description

- By default, a browser displays a block element on a new line and an inline element on the same line. To change that, you can use the display property.
- If you set the display property for an element to "none", the element isn't displayed. This can be useful when you're printing a web page and want to hide controls like buttons.

Figure 5-19   How to change the display type of an element

How to float elements

Figure 5-20 shows how you can *float* an element on a web page, which is typically done with block elements. To do that, you use the float property and specify whether you want the element floated to the left or to the right of the other elements in the block. Then, the other block elements within the block flow into the space vacated by the floated element.

This is illustrated by the example in this figure. Here, the menu section has a width of 10 ems and is floated to the right. As a result, the content section fills in the space that's vacated by the floated menu section. Since the width for the content section hasn't been set, it expands to be as wide as possible.

To force the placement of an element that's after a floated element, you can use the clear property to specify whether or not the element will fill in to the left, right, or both sides of the floated element. This is illustrated by the footer section in the example. Here, its clear property is set to "both", which means it won't flow to the right or left of any floated elements. As a result, it begins on a new line.

How to float an element

```
float: none;    /* default value */
float: left;
float: right;
```

How to force the placement of an element that's after a floated element

```
clear: none;    /* default, element will fill in beside floated blocks */
clear: left;    /* element will not fill in beside left floated blocks   */
clear: right;   /* element will not fill in beside right floated blocks */
clear: both;    /* element will not fill in beside any floated blocks    */
```

The XHTML for a web page

```
<div id="header">
    <h2>Mike's Bait &amp; Tackle Shop</h2>
</div>
<div id="menu">
    <ul class="nav">
        <li><a href="products.html">Products</a></li>
        <li><a href="services.html">Services</a></li>
        <li><a href="contact.html">Contact Us</a></li>
    </ul>
</div>
<div id="content">
    <p>Welcome to Mike's Bait &amp; Tackle Shop! We have all the gear
        you'll need to make your next fishing trip a great success!</p>
</div>
<div id="footer">
    <p>&copy; 2008 Mike's Bait &amp; Tackle Shop</p>
</div>
```

CSS that floats the menu

```
div {
    border: 1px solid black;
    padding: 0px 10px;
}
#menu {
    width: 10em;
    float: right;
}
#footer {
    clear: both;
}
```

The web page in a browser

Figure 5-20   How to float elements

How to use absolute positioning

Figure 5-21 shows how to use *absolute positioning* to position a block element within a containing block. To do that, you set the position property to absolute, and then use the left, right, top, and bottom properties to specify the absolute position of the element with the block that contains it.

This is illustrated by the example in this figure, which uses absolute positioning to position the menu section of the XHTML in figure 5-20 within the body of the page. Here, the top edge of the menu section is set to 72 pixels from the top of the body tag, and the right edge is set to 10 pixels from the right side of the body tag. This causes the menu section to be positioned in the upper right corner of the content section.

To get this positioning right, the top property is set to a value that's equal to the sum of the vertical space settings for the <body> tag and the header section. To start, the <body> tag provides 5 pixels of top margin and 5 pixels of top padding. Then, the header section provides 1 pixel of top border, 60 pixels of height, and 1 pixel of bottom border. If you add all of this up (5 + 5 + 1 + 60 + 1), you get 72 pixels.

Similarly, the right property is set to a value that's equal to the sum of the right margin and padding of the <body> tag. If you add this up (5 + 5), you get a total of 10 pixels.

When you use absolute positioning, the browser takes the element out of the flow of elements on the web page. As a result, the element may overlap other elements that are displayed on the page. For instance, the menu section in this example overlaps the content section. However, the properties for the height, width, padding, and margins for these two sections have been set so the text in these sections doesn't overlap. In particular, the width of the menu section has been set to 10 ems, and the right padding for the content section has been set to 12 ems. That creates a gap between these two sections that's 2 ems wide.

When you use absolute positioning, the browser sets the size of the positioned element before it takes the element out of the normal flow of elements. Since this can yield unpredictable results, you usually need to set the height and width for elements that use absolute positioning. In the example in this figure, the width of the menu section has been set so you know how wide this element will be when it's displayed by a browser.

How to enable absolute positioning

```
position: absolute;
```

How to position the element horizontally

```
left: auto;      /* default value */
left: 5px;       /* left edge is 5px inside left edge of containing block */
left: -5px;      /* left edge is 5px outside left edge of containing block */
right: 5px;      /* right edge is 5px inside right edge of containing block */
right: -5px;     /* right edge is 5px outside right edge of containing block */
```

How to position the element vertically

```
top: auto;       /* default value */
top: 5px;        /* top edge is 5px inside top of containing block */
top: -5px;       /* top edge is 5px outside top of containing block */
bottom: 5px;     /* bottom edge is 5px inside bottom of containing block */
bottom: -5px;    /* bottom edge is 5px outside bottom of containing block */
```

CSS with absolute positioning for the XHTML in figure 5-20

```
body {
    margin: 5px;
    padding: 5px;
}
div {
    border: 1px solid black;
    padding: 0px 10px;
}
#header {
    height: 60px;
}
#menu {
    position: absolute;
    top: 72px;
    right: 10px;
    width: 10em;
}
#content {
    padding-right: 12em;
    height: 120px;
}
```

The web page in a browser

Figure 5-21   How to use absolute positioning

How to use relative positioning

Figure 5-22 shows how to use *relative positioning* to position an element. To do that, you set the position property to relative, and then use the left and top properties to specify the relative position of the element within the block that contains it.

This is illustrated by the example in this figure, which uses relative positioning to position the footer section of the XHTML in figure 5-20 within the body of the page. Here, the CSS sets the position property to "relative". Then, the CSS sets the top property for the footer section to a value of 10 pixels. As a result, the footer section is moved down 10 pixels from where it would have been positioned in the normal flow of elements.

When you use relative positioning to position an element, the remaining elements leave space for the moved element as if it were still there. In other words, no other elements will flow into the space vacated by the positioned element. In this example, this doesn't matter since there aren't any more elements, but you often need to provide for this.

How to enable relative positioning

```
position: relative;
```

How to move the element horizontally

```
left: auto;        /* default value */
left: 5px;         /* moves the element right 5px */
left: -5px;        /* moves the element left 5px */
```

How to move the element vertically

```
top: auto;         /* default value */
top: 5px;          /* moves the element down 5px */
top: -5px;         /* moves the element up 5px */
```

CSS with relative positioning for the XHTML in figure 5-20

```
div {
    border: 1px solid black;
    padding: 0px 10px;
}
#menu {
    width: 10em;
    float: right;
}
#footer {
    clear: both;
    position: relative;
    top: 10px;
}
```

The web page in a browser

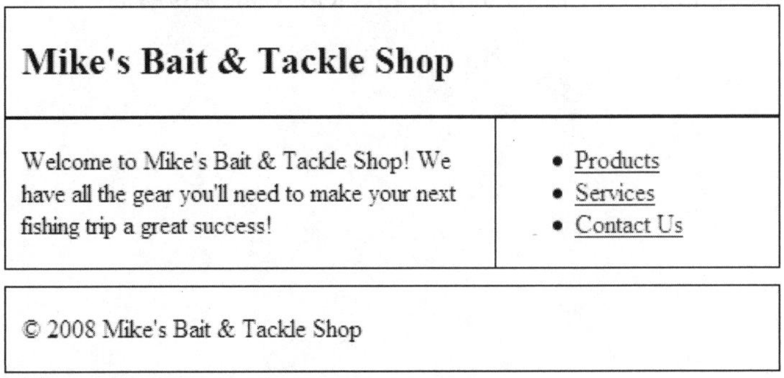

Mike's Bait & Tackle Shop

Welcome to Mike's Bait & Tackle Shop! We
have all the gear you'll need to make your next
fishing trip a great success!

- Products
- Services
- Contact Us

© 2008 Mike's Bait & Tackle Shop

Description

- When you use relative positioning to position an element, the remaining elements leave space for the moved element as if it were still there.

Figure 5-22   How to use relative positioning

How to float controls on a form

When you need to align controls on a form, you can use the float property as shown in figure 5-23. In general, this works the way it does with block elements, but it's worth taking the time to see how it works with inline tags like <label> and <input> tags.

When you float inline elements, the other inline elements within the block will flow into the space vacated by the floated element. For instance, the CSS in this figure floats the <label> and <input> tags to the left side of the form. As a result, the first <label> tag floats to the left side of the form and the <input> tag that follows flows to the right of that <label> tag. Then, the <br> tag that follows starts a new line and clears the left-floated elements. As a result, the second <label> tag floats to the left side of the form.

In this example, the CSS sets the width of each label so it's wide enough to contain the text. If it isn't wide enough, the browser won't align the controls correctly and you will get unexpected results. This CSS also sets the bottom margin for each label so it provides some vertical space between the rows in this form.

The third label in the XHTML doesn't contain any visible text. Instead, it contains a non-breaking space character ( ). Although this non-breaking space isn't required, it may help some browsers to display the blank label correctly, which allows the control that follows to align correctly.

One interesting feature of the technique in this figure is that it uses the <br> tag to specify the end of a line. As a result, you can display several controls on a line and then end the line by coding the <br> tag. If, for example, you want to code several label and text box controls on the same line, this technique lets you do that.

The XHTML for the form

```
<h3>Subscribe to our newsletter:</h3>
<form action="subscribe.php" method="post">

    <label for="name">Name:</label>
    <input type="text" name="name" id="name" /><br />

    <label for="email">Email:</label>
    <input type="text" name="email" id="email" /><br />

    <label for="subscribe"> </label>
    <input type="submit" name="subscribe" value="Subscribe" /><br />

</form>
```

The CSS for the form

```
form label {
    float: left;
    width: 4em;             /* Needs to be wide enough to contain all labels */
    margin-bottom: .5em;
}
form input {
    float: left;
}
form br {
    clear: left;
}
```

The form in the web browser

Description

- When you float inline elements, such as the label and input elements, other inline elements within the block will flow into the space vacated by the floated element.

Figure 5-23   How to float controls on a form

Perspective

This has been a crash course in the CSS that is supported by modern web browsers and that is commonly used for web applications. With this as background, you should be able to understand and modify the CSS for most web pages and forms, and you have all of the CSS skills that you need for this book.

Terms

CSS (Cascading Style Sheets)	absolute unit of measurement
style sheet	relative unit of measurement
inherited formatting	RGB value
em	hexadecimal (hex)
rule set	universal selector
style	descendant selector
selector	child selector
declaration block	attribute selector
declaration	pseudo-class selector
rule	user style sheet
property	shorthand property
value	box model
CSS comment	padding
external style sheet	floating an element
embedded style sheet	absolute positioning
inline style	relative positioning

Exercise 5-1   Work with CSS

In this exercise, you'll learn how to use CSS to work with a web page that's similar to the one in figure 5-1.

Review the web page, its XHTML, and its CSS

1. Use Firefox to open the index.html file in the chapter 5 folder for exercises. Then, note the formatting.

2. Use your text editor to open the index.html file for this application. Note that this code is similar to the code presented in figure 5-2, but it uses the primary.css file that is stored in the styles folder to format the page.

3. Use your text editor to open the primary.css file for this application. Note that this code is similar to the code presented in figure 5-3.

4. Click on one of the links in the web page and note that the color scheme has been carried over to the page that is displayed. If you open the html file for this page, you'll see that it also uses the primary.css file for formatting. Now, click on the back button to return to the main page.

View the box model for the page

5. Add a CSS rule set that displays a 1 pixel solid black border around each <div> tag element. Then, view the page in your browser and note that the boxes divide the page into four sections: header, sidebar, content, footer.

6. Turn the borders off by coding a comment around the rule set. Then, view the page in a web browser to make sure the extra borders are gone.

Modify the external style sheet for the page

After each step that follows, view the page to make sure the changes are correct.

7. Change the background color for the <body> element to yellow. Then, change the color for the <h1> and <h2> elements to blue.

8. Change the font size for the <body> element to 87.5 percent of the default font size. Note how this increases the font size for all elements on the page.

9. Change the line height for the <body> element so the line height is 1.4 ems as tall as the current font size.

10. Click on one of the links in the web page and note that the changes that you've made in the last three steps have been carried over to the page that is displayed. Now, click on the back button to return to the main page.

11. Change the bullet that's used for the list of products to the image that's stored in the star.gif file located in the exercises\chapter_05 directory. Make sure, however, that you don't add a bullet to the navigation links. To do that, add a new rule set that only selects the <ul> tag in the content section.

12. Add 2 ems of padding to the left and right sides of the content section.

Change the page layout

13. Modify the CSS so the sidebar is displayed on the right side of the content instead of the left and so the content text is indented or padded by 1 em on the left and 2 ems on the right.

14. If you have any doubts about how any of the CSS for this application works, continue to experiment. When you're through, close the files.

Section 2

JavaScript essentials

The first three chapters in this section expand upon what you learned in chapter 2. In chapter 6, you'll learn how to get input from the user and display output in XHTML elements. In chapter 7, you'll learn more about working with numbers, strings, and dates. And in chapter 8, you'll learn more about working with control structures like if and for statements. These chapters should answer any questions you might have had about the JavaScript basics that were presented in chapter 2.

Then, the next four chapters build upon those basics. In chapter 9, you'll learn how to work with arrays. In chapter 10, you'll learn how to create and use functions. In chapter 11, you'll learn how to create and use your own objects. And in chapter 12, you'll learn how to use regular expressions, handle exceptions, and do client-side data validation in a form before that data is submitted to the server.

When you finish this section, you'll know the JavaScript language. Then, section 3 will show you how to use JavaScript to script the DOM and raise your web pages to a new level of excellence.

6

How to get input and display output

There are three main stages to any application. They are gather information, process the information, and display the results.

In chapter 2, you learned simple techniques for getting data from a text box and displaying information in a text box. Now, this chapter shows you other techniques for getting an application to interact with a user.

How to get input **224**
How to get data from the prompt method 224
How to get a response from the confirm method 226
How to get the state of a radio button 228
How to get the state of a check box 230
How to get the selected option in a select list 232
How to get data from a text area 234
How to use the methods and events for controls 236
How to display output **238**
How to display data in a span tag 238
How to set the state of a radio button 240
How to set the state of a check box 242
How to display data in a text area 244
Perspective **246**

How to get input

This topic shows you six more ways to get information from the user. The first two use methods that are provided by the browser. The last four use form controls in the web page.

How to get data from the prompt method

The prompt method is a global method provided by the web browser. When called, it displays a dialog box like the one in figure 6-1. As you can see, this dialog box contains a message, a text box for the user to enter the requested data, and OK and Cancel buttons.

As the syntax in this figure shows, the prompt method has two parameters. The message parameter contains the message that should be displayed. The defaultValue parameter contains the default value that's displayed in the text box. If this parameter isn't included when the method is called, the text box will be empty.

If the user enters data in the text box and clicks the OK button, the entry is returned as a string. If the user clicks the Cancel button, a null value is returned by this method.

The first example in this figure shows you how to call the method when you expect string data to be entered by the user. The next two examples show you how to call the method when you expect numerical data to be entered. These examples use the parseInt and parseFloat methods to convert the string that's entered to a number. But recall that these methods return the value NaN if the text can't be converted to a number.

The last example shows how to determine if the user clicked the Cancel button in the dialog window. Here, the first if statement tests if the value of age is null. If it is, the user clicked Cancel. If it isn't, the age is converted to a number. Then, the nested if statement determines if the conversion was successful and, if so, whether the user is old enough to vote.

Syntax of the prompt method

```
prompt( message, defaultValue );
```

Parameters of the prompt method

Parameter	Description
message	The message to display in the prompt dialog box.
defaultValue	The value to display in the text box.

Return values of the prompt method

Value	Description
null	Returned when the user clicks the cancel button.
string	The value in the text box when the user clicks OK or presses the Enter key.

How to call the prompt method when expecting string data

```
var username = prompt("Please enter your name:");
```

How to call the prompt method when expecting numerical data

```
var age = parseInt( prompt("Please enter your age:", "18") );
var wage = parseFloat( prompt("Please enter the hourly wage", "5.35") );
```

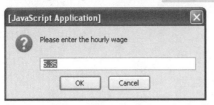

How to determine if the user clicked "Cancel"

```
var age = prompt("Please enter your age:");
if ( age == null ) {
    alert("You clicked cancel.");
} else {
    age = parseInt(age);
    if ( isNaN(age) ) {
        alert("You did not enter a number.");
    } else if ( age >= 18 ) {
        alert("You can vote.");
    } else {
        alert("You cannot vote.");
    }
}
```

Description

- The prompt method displays a text box in a dialog box, and it returns a String value.
- If you omit the defaultValue parameter, an empty string is displayed in the text box.
- If the user clicks on the Cancel button, the prompt method returns a null value.
- Because the prompt method returns a string when the user clicks on the OK button, you need to use the parseInt or parseFloat method to convert the string to a number.

Figure 6-1   How to get data from the prompt method

How to get a response from the confirm method

The confirm method is another global method provided by the web browser. When called, it displays a dialog box like the one in figure 6-2 with an OK button and a Cancel button. This method requires one parameter that consists of the message that should be displayed in the dialog box. Then, if the user clicks the OK button, this method returns true. If the user clicks the Cancel button, this method returns false.

The example in this figure uses the confirm method to ask whether the user agrees to the privacy policy before allowing him into the store. Then, it stores the user's response in the variable named response. If the value of this variable is true, the user clicked the OK button and is allowed into the store. If the value is false, the user clicked the Cancel button and is prevented from entering the store.

If you're new to programming, you might note that the condition in the if statement is just the name of the Boolean variable (response), which contains either a true or false value. This is equivalent to

```
(response == true)
```

You'll see this shorthand throughout this book.

Syntax of the confirm method

```
confirm( message );
```

Parameter of the confirm method

Parameter	Description
message	The message to display in the confirm dialog box.

Return values of the confirm method

Value	Description
true	Returned when the user clicks the OK button.
false	Returned when the user clicks the Cancel button or the Close button.

How to call the confirm method

```
var response = confirm("Do you agree to the web site privacy policy?");
if (response) {
    alert("Thank you. You may continue to the web store.");
} else {
    alert("You cannot use the web store at this time.");
}
```

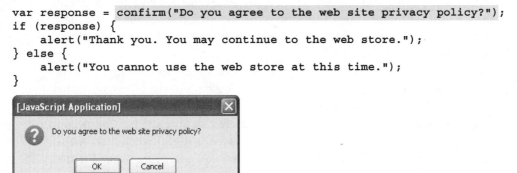

Description

- The confirm method displays a dialog box that contains a message, an OK button, and a Cancel button.
- If the user clicks the OK button, this method returns a value of true.
- If the user clicks the Cancel button, this method returns a value of false.

Figure 6-2   How to get a response from the confirm method

How to get the state of a radio button

A group of radio buttons in a web page lets a user select one of several options. When the user clicks one button in a group, the other buttons in the group are deselected. Then, you can use the two properties of the Radio object shown in figure 6-3 to determine which button is selected.

When you create a group of radio buttons, they must have the same name so the web browser knows they are in the same group. However, they must have different id values.

In the example in this figure, the XHTML code displays two radio buttons. Both of these buttons have the name *policy*, but one has an id of *policy_accept* and a value of *accept* while the other has an id of *policy_decline* and a value of *decline*. Neither button is initially checked.

When the JavaScript code executes, it creates a variable named status and initializes its value to unknown. Then, if the policy_accept button is checked, the status is set to the value of the accept button, which is accept. But if the policy_decline button is checked, the status is set to the value of the decline button, which is decline.

Then, the next if statement tests for the three values and displays an appropriate message for each. If the user didn't click a button, she is reminded that she needs to select one of the options. If the user clicked the accept button, she is allowed into the store. If she clicked the decline button, she isn't allowed in.

This technique for working with radio buttons is useful when there are a small number of predefined buttons. But if there are a large number of radio buttons or they are generated by a script running on the web server, you'll need more advanced techniques to work with radio buttons. You'll learn these techniques in section 3.

Two properties of a Radio object

Property	Description
checked	If set to true, the button is selected; if set to false, it isn't selected.
value	The contents of the value attribute for the button.

How to get the state of a radio button

XHTML code for two radio buttons

```
<p>Accept or decline the web site privacy policy:</p>
<p><input type="radio" name="policy"
    id="policy_accept" value="accept" />Accept</p>
<p><input type="radio" name="policy"
    id="policy_decline" value="decline" />Decline</p>
```

Accept or decline the web site privacy policy:

○ Accept

○ Decline

JavaScript code to process the radio buttons

```
var $ = function (id) { return document.getElementById(id); }

var status = "unknown";
if ( $("policy_accept").checked ) {
    status = $("policy_accept").value;
}
if ( $("policy_decline").checked ) {
    status = $("policy_decline").value;
}

if ( status == "unknown" ) {
    alert("You must accept or decline the privacy policy");
} else if ( status == "accept" ) {
    alert("Thank you. You may continue to the web store.");
} else {
    alert("You cannot use the web store at this time.");
}
```

Description

- All radio buttons in a group must have the same name, but different ids.
- Only one radio button in a group may be checked at a time, but none of the buttons has to be checked.

Figure 6-3   How to get the state of a radio button

How to get the state of a check box

A check box in a web page lets a user select an option by checking a box. Unlike radio buttons, each check box is independent. This is illustrated by the XHTML code in figure 6-4. Then, you can use the properties of the Checkbox object to determine whether a checkbox is checked.

When the JavaScript code is this figure executes, it creates a variable named accept and sets its value to the checked property of the accept check box, which is either true or false. Then, if the accept variable is true, the user is allowed into the store. But if the accept variable is false, the user isn't allowed in.

Two properties of a Checkbox object

Property	Description
checked	If set to true, the check box is selected; if set to false, it isn't selected.
value	The contents of the value attribute for the check box.

How to get the state of a check box

XHTML code for a check box

```
<p><input type="checkbox" name="accept" id="accept" value="accept" />
    I accept the web site privacy policy.</p>
```

☐ I accept the web site privacy policy.

JavaScript code to process the check box

```
var $ = function (id) { return document.getElementById(id); }

var accept = $("accept").checked;

if ( accept ) {
    alert("Thank you. You may continue to the web store.");
} else {
    alert("You cannot use the web store at this time.");
}
```

Description

- Each check box is independent of the other check boxes on the page. They aren't treated as a group.
- The name and id attributes of a check box should be set to the same value.

Figure 6-4   How to get the state of a check box

How to get the selected option in a select list

A select list lets the user select an option from a drop-down list or from a list box. When displayed in a list box, a user may be allowed to select more than one option. In this chapter, you'll learn how to get the selected option in lists that let the user choose just one option. Then, in section 3, you'll learn how to use select lists that let the user select more than one option.

To determine which option a user has selected, you need to use the value property of the Select object as shown in figure 6-5. The example in this figure shows you how to use this property to get the selected option in the drop-down list. Here, the XHTML code creates a drop-down list with three options. The id of the select list is contact. The three options have the values of phone, email, and txtmsg.

When the JavaScript code executes, it first finds the value of the selected option and stores it in a variable named contact. Then, the code uses an if statement to display a message based on the value in the contact variable.

Properties of a Select object

Property	Description
value	The content of the value attribute for the selected option.

How to get the selected option in a select list

XHTML code for a select list

```
<p>Select your preferred contact method:
    <select name="contact" id="contact">
        <optgroup label="Method">
            <option value="phone">Phone</option>
            <option value="email">E-Mail</option>
            <option value="txtmsg">Text Message</option>
        </optgroup>
    </select>
</p>
```

The select list

```
Phone                    ▼
Method
    Phone
    E-Mail
    Text Message
```

JavaScript code to process the list

```
var $ = function (id) { return document.getElementById(id); }

var contact = $("contact").value;

if ( contact == "phone" ) {
    alert("Preferred contact method: Phone");
} else if ( contact == "email" ) {
    alert("Preferred contact method: E-mail");
} else if ( contact == "txtmsg" ) {
    alert("Preferred contact method: Text Message");
} else {
    alert("Error selecting preferred contact method.");
}
```

Description

- The name and id attributes of a select list should be set to the same value.
- This technique only works with select lists that don't have the multiple attribute set. But in section 3, you'll learn how to process select elements with multiple values.

Figure 6-5   How to get the selected option in a select list

How to get data from a text area

A text area in a web page is essentially a multiline text box as shown in figure 6-6. This lets the user enter a larger amount of data than a text box allows. To get the data from a text area, you use the value property of a Textarea object.

In the example in this figure, the XHTML code creates a text area that has a name and id of comment. It also sets the area to 40 columns wide and 5 lines tall.

When the JavaScript code runs, it copies the content of the text area into a variable named comment. Then, it uses the length property of a String object to store the number of characters in the text area in a variable named charCount. The if statement that follows either displays a message asking the user to enter a comment, or it displays a message that shows the number of characters in the comment and the comment itself.

One property of a Textarea object

Property	Description
value	The text in the textarea.

How to get the content of a text area

XHTML code for a text area

```
<p>Please enter your comment in the text box below.</p>
<p><textarea name="comment" id="comment" rows="5" cols="40"></textarea></p>
```

Please enter your comment in the text box below.

```
Please note that I'm at extension 15, but
you can also contact Kelly at extension
18.
```

JavaScript code to process the text area

```
var $ = function (id) { return document.getElementById(id); }

var comment = $("comment").value;
var charCount = comment.length;

if ( comment == "" ) {
    alert("Please enter a comment.");
} else {
    alert("Your comment is " + charCount + " characters:\n\n" + comment);
}
```

[JavaScript Application]

Your comment is 85 characters:

Please note that I'm at extension 15, but you can also contact Kelly at extension 18.

[OK]

Description

- When the user presses the Enter key while typing in a text area, a *hard return* is entered into the text. Hard returns appear as characters in the value property.

- When the user types past the end of a line and a new line is automatically started, a *soft return* occurs. Soft returns do not appear as characters in the value property.

- After you use the value property of a Textarea object to get the text string, you can use the length property of the String object to get the number of characters in the string.

Figure 6-6   How to get data from a text area

How to use the methods and events for controls

Figure 6-7 presents some of the common methods and events that you are likely to use with controls. In chapter 2, you learned how to use the focus method to move the focus to a control. But as this figure shows, you can also use the blur method to remove the focus from a control.

Similarly, you learned how to use the onclick event of a button to start an event handler. But as this figure shows, you can also use other events to work with controls like text boxes, lists, and text areas. For instance, you can write an event handler for a list that handles its onchange event. Then, you can do special processing whenever the user selects one of the options in the list.

As the code in this figure shows, this is similar to using an event handler for the click event of a button. First, you write the event handler. Then, in the event handler for the window.onload event, you assign the new event handler to the event.

Two methods that are commonly used with controls

Method	Description
focus	Moves the focus to the control.
blur	Removes the focus from the control.

Common control events

Event	Description
onfocus	The control receives the focus.
onblur	The control loses the focus.
onclick	The user clicks the control.
ondblclick	The user double-clicks the control.
onchange	The value of the control changes.
onselect	The user selects text in a text box or text area.

The XHTML for a select list

```
<select name="investment" id="investment">
    <option value="1000">$1,000</option>
    <option value="5000">$5,000</option>
    <option value="10000">$10,000</option>
    <option value="25000">$25,000</option>
</select><br />
```

The event handler for the onchange event of a select list

```
var investmentChange = function () {
    calculateClick();        // Recalculate future value when changed
    $("investment").blur();  // Remove the focus from the select list
}
```

The event handler for the dblclick event of a text box

```
var yearsDblclick = function () {
    $("years").value = "";   // Clear textbox when double clicked
}
```

The code that assigns the event handlers to the events

```
window.onload = function () {
    $("calculate").onclick = calculateClick;
    $("investment").onchange = investmentChange;
    $("years").ondblclick = yearsDblclick;
    $("years").focus();
}
```

Description

- When you use XHTML controls, you can use the focus or blur method to move the focus to or remove the focus from a control.

- When you use XHTML controls, you sometimes need to provide event handlers for common control events.

Figure 6-7   How to use the methods and events for controls

How to display output

In chapter 2, you learned how to display output in a text box. This topic shows you four more ways to provide output in your application. The first lets you display output by modifying the contents of a span tag. The other three let you display output by changing a form element.

How to display data in a span tag

A span tag is typically used to control formatting in a web page. It lets you apply a CSS class to a section of text. In figure 6-8, though, you'll learn how to access and change the text that's inside a span tag.

In the DOM, a span element represents a span tag from the XHTML. This span element has a child node that points to a Text node object that stores the text that is in the span tag. So, to access the text inside a span tag, you use the firstChild property of the span element to access the Text node object for the span element. Then, you use the nodeValue property of the Text node object to access the text in the span tag.

In the example in this figure, the XHTML code creates a span tag with an id of date_output. Initially, the text for this span tag will be empty. However, to ensure that a Text node is created in all web browsers, a non-breaking space ( ) is placed inside the span tag. This is needed because some browsers won't create a Text node for a span element if the span tag is empty or if it only contains whitespace such as spaces and return characters.

When the JavaScript code in this example runs, it creates a new Date object and stores it in a variable named now. Then, it uses methods of the Date object to create a text string that represents today's date in a variable named dateText.

The JavaScript code then uses object chaining to store the date in the span element's Text node. To do that, the code gets a reference to the span element, a reference to its Text node object (the firstChild property), and access to the Text node object's content (the nodeValue property).

One property of a span element

Property	Description
firstChild	A pointer to the Text node object inside the span element.

One property of a Text node object

Property	Description
nodeValue	The text in the text node.

How to set the contents of a span element

XHTML code for a span element

```
<p>Today is <span id="date_output"> </span>.</p>
```

JavaScript code to use a span element

```
var $ = function (id) { return document.getElementById(id); }

var now = new Date();

var month = now.getMonth() + 1;
var day = now.getDate();
if (day < 10) day = "0" + day;
var year = now.getFullYear();

var dateText = month + "/" + day + "/" + year;

$("date_output").firstChild.nodeValue = dateText;
```

Today is 5/28/2009.

Description

- When you define an empty span tag, be sure to include an   in the tag to force the creation of a Text node for the span tag.

- See chapter 13 for more information on how DOM scripting uses the firstChild and nodeValue properties.

Figure 6-8   How to display data in a span tag

How to set the state of a radio button

When you have radio buttons on a web page, you can use JavaScript to check one of the radio buttons in a group. To do that, you set the checked property of the radio button as shown in figure 6-9.

The XHTML code in the example in this figure creates two radio buttons and a regular button with an id of toggle. Both radio buttons have the name policy and their disabled attribute is set so the user can't change them by clicking on them. The first radio button has the id of policy_accept and the value of accept. The second radio button has the id of policy_decline and the value of decline, and its checked property is set so it will be checked when the page first loads.

When the JavaScript code runs, it creates an event handler named toggleClick and attaches it to the onclick event of the toggle button. When the user clicks the toggle button, the event handler examines the state of the policy_accept radio button. If it is checked, it checks the policy_decline radio button instead, which also unchecks the policy_accept radio button.

If the policy_accept radio button isn't checked, that means the policy_decline radio button is checked. As a result, the code checks the policy_accept radio button, which also unchecks the policy_decline radio button.

How to set the state of a radio button

XHTML code for two radio buttons

```
<p>Click the button to toggle whether you accept or decline
the web site privacy policy.</p>
<p><input type="radio" name="policy" disabled="disabled"
    id="policy_accept" value="accept" />Accept</p>
<p><input type="radio" name="policy"
    disabled="disabled" checked="checked"
    id="policy_decline" value="decline" />Decline</p>
<p><input type="button" id="toggle" value="Toggle" /></p>
```

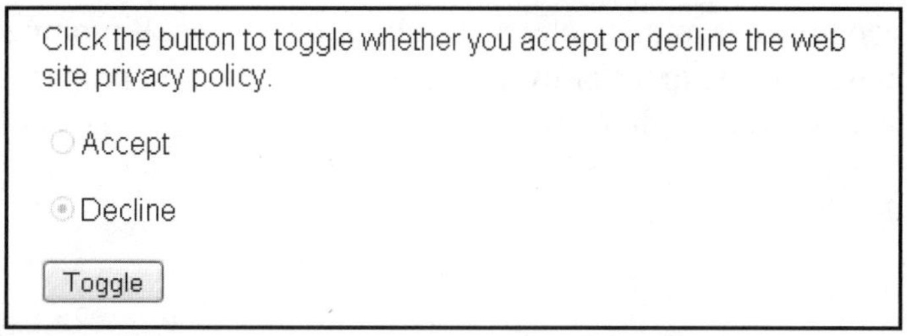

Click the button to toggle whether you accept or decline the web
site privacy policy.

○ Accept

◉ Decline

[Toggle]

JavaScript code to set the state of the radio button

```
var $ = function (id) { return document.getElementById(id); }

var toggleClick = function () {
    if ( $("policy_accept").checked ) {
        $("policy_decline").checked = true;
    } else {
        $("policy_accept").checked = true;
    }
}

window.onload = function () {
    $("toggle").onclick = toggleClick;
}
```

Description

- To clear a radio button, set its checked property to false. When you clear a radio button, no other button will become checked.

- To set a radio button, set its checked property to true. When you set a radio button, any other checked button in the same group will be cleared.

Figure 6-9   How to set the state of a radio button

How to set the state of a check box

When you have a check box on a web page, you can use JavaScript to check or uncheck the box. As figure 6-10 shows, to check a check box, you set its checked property to true. To uncheck a check box, you set its checked property to false.

The XHTML code in the example in this figure creates a check box with a name and id of vote_status. The disabled property of this check box is also set so the user can't check this check box by clicking on it. Instead, the state of the check box can only be changed by code.

When the JavaScript code runs, it initially clears the check box. Then, it prompts the user for his age. If a numerical age of 18 or over is entered, the checked property is set to true indicating the user is old enough to vote.

How to set the state of a check box

XHTML code for a check box

```
<p><input type="checkbox" disabled="disabled"
    name="voteStatus" id="vote_status" />
    You can vote when checked.</p>
```

```
☐ You can vote when checked.
```

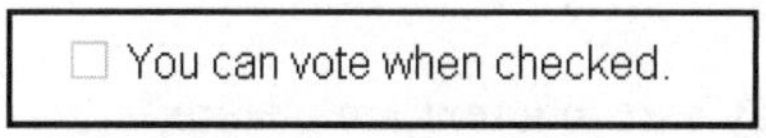

JavaScript code to set the state of the check box

```
var $ = function (id) { return document.getElementById(id); }

$("vote_status").checked = false;
var age = prompt("Please enter your age:");
if ( age == null ) {
    alert("You clicked cancel.");
} else {
    age = parseInt(age);
    if ( isNaN(age) ) {
        alert("You did not enter a number.");
    } else if ( age >= 18 ) {
        $("vote_status").checked = true;
    }
}
```

Description

- To clear a check box, set its checked property to false.
- To set a check box, set its checked property to true.

Figure 6-10   How to set the state of a check box

How to display data in a text area

When you have a text area in a web page, you can use JavaScript to display text in the area. To do this, you set the text area's value property to the text you want displayed. This text can contain return characters, and the text area will start a new line whenever it encounters one.

The example in figure 6-11 shows how to display text in a text area. Here, the text is generated based on the state of three check boxes. If no check boxes are checked, the text indicates that. But if one or more check boxes are checked, the text indicates which check boxes have been checked.

The XHTML code for this example creates three check boxes and one text area. The check boxes have ids and names of privacy, use, and license. The text area has a name and id of policies. Its size is set to 40 columns and 6 rows.

When the JavaScript code runs, the code for the onload event attaches the event handler named updatePolicies to the onclick event of each of the check boxes. This event handler updates the text in the text area whenever one of the check boxes is changed. After the onload event handler attaches the updatePolicies function to the events, it calls the updatePolicies function to initialize the content of the text area.

When the updatePolicies function runs, it stores the state of each of the check boxes in a variable. The names of these variables match the names of the check boxes. It also creates an empty variable named message that will store the message that will be displayed in the text area.

If at least one of the check boxes is checked, the if statement creates a header for the message and adds a line for each of the check boxes that is checked. If none of the check boxes are checked, the if statement creates a message indicating that.

Once the message is created, the event handler stores the message in the value property of the text area. This displays the message in the text area in the web page.

How to display data in a text area

XHTML code for three checkboxes and a text area

```
<p>Select the policies you agree with.</p>
<p><input type="checkbox" name="privacy" id="privacy" />
    Privacy Policy</p>
<p><input type="checkbox" name="use" id="use" />
    Acceptable Use Policy</p>
<p><input type="checkbox" name="license" id="license" />
    End User License Agreement</p>
<textarea name="policies" id="policies" rows="6" cols="40"></textarea>
```

JavaScript code to display output in a text area

```
var $ = function (id) { return document.getElementById(id); }

var updatePolicies = function () {
    var privacy = $("privacy").checked;
    var use = $("use").checked;
    var license = $("license").checked;

    var message;
    if ( privacy || use || license ) {
        message = "You agreed to these policies:\n\n";
        if ( privacy ) {
            message += "- Privacy Policy\n";
        }
        if ( use ) {
            message += "- Acceptable Use Policy\n";
        }
        if ( license ) {
            message += "- End User License Agreement\n";
        }
    } else {
        message = "You haven't agreed to any policies.";
    }
    $("policies").value = message;
}

window.onload = function () {
    $("privacy").onclick = updatePolicies;
    $("use").onclick = updatePolicies;
    $("license").onclick = updatePolicies;
    updatePolicies();
}
```

Description

- Setting the value property of a Textarea object replaces the contents in the text area.

Figure 6-11   How to display data in a text area

Perspective

In this chapter, you learned new ways to get input and display output. These are essential JavaScript skills that you'll use often, and some of these skills require the use of basic DOM objects. Keep in mind, though, that you're just getting started with the use of DOM. That's why section 3 of this book presents a complete course on DOM scripting.

Terms

hard return
soft return

Exercise 6-1   Enhance the Future Value application

In this exercise, you'll write the JavaScript code for enhancing the Future Value application of chapter 2. This time, the interface will include radio buttons, select lists, a check box, and a text area.

Open and test the application

1. From your Firefox browser, open the html file in the future_value folder that's in the chapter 6 folder for exercises. Notice that this application now includes radio buttons, drop-down lists, a check box, and a text area.

2. Use your text editor to review the JavaScript code for this application. Here, the only change to the code for the Future Value application of chapter 2 is that the calculation has been modified so it gets the future value of a one-time investment instead of a monthly investment.

3. Test the application by selecting values from the drop-down lists and entering a valid number of years. Note that application still works, even though the JavaScript code doesn't provide for the drop-down lists.

4. Test the application by using the option buttons and check box. Note that these controls don't work because the JavaScript code doesn't provide for them.

Add the code for the option buttons

5. Modify the JavaScript code so it provides for the option buttons. When the user clicks the Yearly Interest button, the application should compound the interest yearly. When the user clicks the Monthly Interest button, the application should compound the interest monthly.

Add the code to the check box and text area

6. Modify the JavaScript code so it displays a message in the text area when the check box is checked. If, for example, the user selects a value of $5000, the message in the text area should look like this:

```
Future Value of $5000

When compounded monthly: 5415.00
When compounded yearly:  5400.00
```

Use the prompt method to get other investment amounts

7. Modify the JavaScript code so it uses the prompt method to get the investment amount when the user selects "Other value" from the drop-down list. (Remember that the parseFloat method returns NaN if the parameter isn't a valid numeric value.)

Add two event handlers

8. Add an event handler that clears the years text box when the user double-clicks on it.

9. Add an event handler for the onchange event of the investment control. This event handler should call the calculate_click event handler, but only if the years text box contains a valid number.

7

How to work with numbers, strings, and dates

In chapter 2, you learned some basic skills for working with numbers, strings, and dates. Now, you'll learn the other essential skills that you'll need for working with data in your JavaScript applications.

How to work with numbers **250**
How represent special numerical values 250
The methods of the Number object 252
How to use the conditional operator 254

How to use the Math object **256**
How to use the methods of the Math object 256
How to use a random number generator 258

How to work with strings **260**
How to use escape sequences in strings 260
How to use the methods of the String object 262
Examples of working with strings 264

How to work with dates and times **266**
How to create Date objects 266
The methods of the Date object 268
Example of working with dates 270

Perspective **272**

How to work with numbers

In chapter 2, you learned how to enter numbers, perform common arithmetic operations, and convert a number to a fixed decimal value. In this topic, you'll build on those skills.

How represent special numerical values

In theory, numbers can be as large or as small as you like. In practice, however, you're limited to a particular range of values based on how a programming language internally represents numerical values.

Internally, JavaScript uses the IEEE 754 standard to represent numerical values. To illustrate, figure 7-1 shows a broken number line that indicates the range of values that can be represented by JavaScript numbers.

In the middle of the number line, zero stands by itself. Just to the right of zero is the smallest positive value, 5.0e-324. That is equivalent to a decimal point, 323 zeros, and the digit 5, which is an extremely small number. Any number that lies between 0 and 5.0e-324 will be rounded to one of these values.

The value Infinity is on the far right side of the number line. This special value is used to represent any number larger than the maximum positive value, which is approximately 1.798e+308. That is, 1798 followed by 305 zeros, which is an extremely large number.

The left half of the number line is a mirror image of the right half. Any number between -5.0e-324 and 0 will rounded to one of these values and any number less than -1.798e+308 will be converted to -Infinity.

Finally, there is the special value NaN. This value, which stands for "not a number", is used to indicate a non-numerical value. In the IEEE 754 specification, there are over 9 quadrillion separate NaN values. JavaScript, however, treats them all as a single NaN value. Because the JavaScript NaN value could potentially stand for any of the IEEE NaN values, the equality test NaN == NaN in JavaScript will always return false since it is unknown which specific IEEE values the two NaN values represent. To test for the presence of a NaN value, you must use the isNaN method.

The Number object has five properties that represent these special values. They are listed in this figure. There are also three global shortcuts for Infinity, -Infinity, and NaN. The first example in this figure shows how to test a result for Infinity, -Infinity, or NaN and display an appropriate message.

The second example shows how JavaScript treats division by zero. When you divide 0 by 0, the result is NaN. However, when you divide a non-zero number by zero, the result will be either Infinity or -Infinity, depending on the sign of the non-zero number. This is different than the way most languages handle this. In other languages, division by zero usually results in a runtime error because there is no way to represent Infinity.

The minimum and maximum values of the number data type

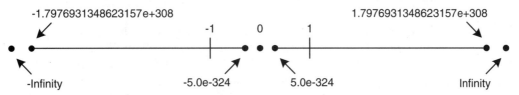

Properties of the Number object

Property	Description
Number.MAX_VALUE	The largest positive value that can be represented.
Number.MIN_VALUE	The smallest positive value that can be represented.
Number.POSITIVE_INFINITY	Represents positive infinity.
Number.NEGATIVE_INFINITY	Represents negative infinity.
Number.NaN	Represents a value that isn't a number.

Shortcut numerical values

Value	Description
Infinity	A shortcut for Number.POSITIVE_INFINITY
-Infinity	A shortcut for Number.NEGATIVE_INFINITY.
NaN	A shortcut for Number.NaN.

Example 1: Testing for Infinity, -Infinity, and NaN

```
if ( result == Infinity ) {
    alert( "The result exceeds " + Number.MAX_VALUE );
} else if ( result == -Infinity ) {
    alert( "The result is below -" + Number.MAX_VALUE );
} else if ( isNaN(result) ) {
    alert( "The result is not a number." );
} else {
    alert( "The result is " + result );
}
```

Example 2: Division by Zero

```
alert(  0 / 0 );      // Displays NaN
alert( 10 / 0 );      // Displays Infinity
```

Description

- Any numerical operation that results in a number greater than Number.MAX_VALUE will return the value Infinity, and any operation that results in a number less than Number.MIN_VALUE will return the value -Infinity.

- Any numerical operation with a non-numeric operand will return NaN.

- You cannot test for equality with the value NaN. You must use the global method isNaN() to test if a value is NaN.

- Division of zero by zero results in NaN, but division of a non-zero number by zero results in either Infinity or -Infinity.

Figure 7-1   How to represent special numerical values

The methods of the Number object

There are four methods of the Number object that allow you to format the display of the numerical value. These methods are described in figure 7-2.

The first example shows you how to use the toFixed method. It first stores a subtotal and a tax rate. Then, it calculates the amount of tax owed. For the values shown, this number is 1.49925 and must be rounded to two decimal places.

Next, the tax is converted to a two-digit value, 1.50 in this example. Because the toFixed method returns a string, the parseFloat method has to be used to convert the string "1.50" back to a number. After this statement is executed, the tax variable contains 1.5.

Finally, this example displays the tax using the toFixed method again to ensure that any number that was rounded to 0 in the hundreds place is correctly displayed with two digits. As a result, 1.5 is displayed as 1.50.

The second example shows how the toString method is used implicitly by JavaScript. Here, the integer value in age is automatically converted to a string by the toString method when age is concatenated with a string literal. This implicit conversion is done whenever a number is used in an expression that mixes string and number values. As a result, you only need to use the toString method explicitly when you need to convert a number to a base other than 10.

The third example shows how to explicitly use the toString method to convert a string to binary or hexadecimal values. If you're familiar with binary and hexadecimal values, you may find this useful, but otherwise you shouldn't need to do this.

The fourth example shows how to use the toExponential method. This method is useful for displaying scientific values, but if you aren't developing scientific applications, you probably won't need this method. This example gets a mass from the user in kilograms and then uses Einstein's mass-energy equivalency equation to convert the kilograms to Joules and displays the result in exponential format to 4 digits. Because a small amount of mass stores a large amount of energy, exponential format is more convenient in this case.

The fifth example shows how to use the toPrecision method, which specifies the number of significant digits (or *precision*) that should be used. When you use JavaScript, a number can have a maximum of about 16 significant digits, and the significant digits include those before and after the decimal point. For example, the number 124.599 has six significant digits.

For most applications, you want to include all of the significant digits, so you may never need this method. But this example shows you how to use it if you do need it. After the miles per gallon value is calculated, it is displayed with three significant digits. If, for example, the result is actually 22.85714, it will be displayed as 22.9. If the result is 5.86538, it will be displayed as 5.87.

Methods of the Number object

Method	Description
toFixed(*digits*)	Returns a string with the number rounded to the specified number of decimal places.
toString(*base*)	Returns a string with the number in the given base. The base can range from 2 to 36. If base isn't provided, 10 is used.
toExponential(*digits*)	Returns a numeric string with the number in exponential format with the specified number of digits after the decimal place. If digits isn't provided, it returns all digits.
toPrecision(*precision*)	Returns a numeric string with the specified number of significant digits. The result may be in exponential format. If precision isn't provided, it returns the same result as toString().

Example 1: Using the toFixed method

```
var subtotal = 19.99, rate = 0.075;
var tax = subtotal * rate;          // tax is 1.49925
tax = parseFloat( tax.toFixed(2) ); // tax is 1.5
alert ( tax.toFixed(2) );           // displays 1.50
```

Example 2: Implicit use of the toString method for base 10 conversions

```
var age = parseInt( prompt("Please enter your age.") );
alert( "Your age in decimal is " + age );
```

Example 3: Using the toString method with other bases

```
var age = parseInt( prompt("Please enter your age.") );
alert( "Your age in binary is " + age.toString(2) );
alert( "Your age in hexadecimal is " + age.toString(16) );
// If you enter 30, displays 11110 and 1e
```

Example 4: Using the toExponential method

```
var m = parseFloat( prompt("Please enter a mass in kg.") );
var c = 2.99792458e+8;
var e = m * c * c;
alert( "The amount of energy is " + e.toExponential(4) + " Joules.");
// If you enter 80, displays 7.1900e+18
```

Example 5: Using the toPrecision method

```
var miles = parseFloat( prompt("Please enter the miles.") );
var gallons = parseFloat( prompt("Please enter the gallons.") );
var mpg = miles / gallons;
alert( "Your mpg is " + mpg.toPrecision(3) );
// If you enter 320 and 14, displays 22.9
// If you enter 15.25 and 2.6, displays 5.87
```

Description

- For business applications, you usually only need to use the toFixed method.
- The toString method with no parameters is used implicitly whenever JavaScript needs to convert a number to a string.

Figure 7-2   The methods of the Number object

How to use the conditional operator

The conditional operator is JavaScript's only *ternary operator*. This means it has three operands. In contrast, a *unary operator*, such as ++, has one operand and a *binary operator*, such as *, has two operands.

Since the conditional operator has three operands, it needs two symbols to separate them. The question mark and colon are used as the operand separators. This is shown by the syntax in figure 7-3.

When executed, the conditional operator first evaluates the conditional expression to get a true or false result. If the conditional expression is true, the result of the expression in the middle operand is used as the result of the conditional operator. If the conditional expression is false, the result of the expression in the last operand is used as the result of the conditional operator.

The first example in this figure shows how to use the conditional operator to set a variable to one of two values based on the comparison. If the age is 18 or more, message will contain "Can vote". If the age is less than 18, message will contain "Cannot vote".

The second example shows how to use an expression in one of the operands. If hours is over 40, overtime will contain 1.5 times the pay rate for the hours over 40. If hours is not over 40, overtime will be zero.

The third example shows how to select between a singular or plural ending for use in a message to the user. If error_count is 1, the ending will be empty. Otherwise, "s" will be used for the ending.

The fourth example shows how to add one to a value or set it back to 1 depending on whether the value is at its maximum. For example, if max_value is 10 and value is 6, then the test will be false and value will become value + 1. However, when value reaches 10, it will be set to 1 rather than value.

If you need to perform this kind of rollover of a variable, but the starting value is 0 instead of 1, you don't have to use the conditional operator. Instead, you can use the % operator. For example, if you execute this statement repeatedly starting with a value of 9

```
value = (value + 1) % 10
```

value will range from 0 to 9 and then back to 0.

The fifth example shows how to combine the conditional operator with the return keyword so the result is returned by a function. Here, if number is greater than highest, highest is returned. Otherwise, the number is returned.

The last example shows how to keep a value within a fixed range. It uses a nested conditional operator to do this. If value is greater than max, value is set to max. If value is not greater than max, the second conditional operator is evaluated. Here, if value is less than min, value is set to min. If value is not less than min, value is set to value leaving it at its original value.

For clarity, it is usually better to use if statements than conditional operators. This is illustrated by the last two examples in this figure. Nevertheless, many JavaScript programmers like to use conditional operators because it means less coding.

Syntax of the conditional operator

```
( conditional_expression ) ? value_if_true : value_if_false
```

Examples of using the conditional operator

Example 1: Setting a string based on a comparison

```
var message = ( age >= 18 ) ? "Can vote" : "Cannot vote";
```

Example 2: Calculating overtime pay

```
var overtime = ( hours > 40 ) ? ( hours - 40 ) * rate * 1.5 : 0;
```

Example 3: Selecting a singular or plural ending based on a value

```
var ending = ( error_count == 1 ) ? "" : "s".
var message = "Found " + error_count + " error" + ending + ".";
```

Example 4: Setting a value to 1 if it's at a maximum value when adding 1

```
var value = ( value == max_value ) ? 1 : value + 1;
```

Example 5: Returning one of two values based on a comparison

```
return ( number > highest ) ? highest : number;
```

Example 6: Bounding a value within a fixed range

```
value = ( value > max ) ? max : ( ( value < min ) ? min : value );
```

How conditional operators can be rewritten with if statements

Example 1 rewritten with an if statement

```
var message;
if ( age >= 18 ) {
    message = "Can vote";
} else {
    message = "Cannot vote";
}
```

Example 6 rewritten with an if statement

```
if ( value > max ) {
    value = max;
} else if ( value < min ) {
    value = min;
}
```

Description

- The conditional operator first evaluates the conditional expression. Then, if the conditional expression is true, the value that results from the middle expression is returned. But if the conditional expression is false, the value that results from the last expression is returned.

- Although the use of the conditional operator can lead to cryptic code, JavaScript programmers commonly use this operator. For clarity, though, conditional operators can be written with if statements.

Figure 7-3   How to use the conditional operator

How to use the Math object

The Math object is a built-in object that provides many specialized mathematical methods and numerical values. This topic covers some of the more commonly used methods.

How to use the methods of the Math object

Figure 7-4 shows how to use some of the common methods of the Math object. When you use these methods, you always start by coding Math with a capital letter.

The first example shows you how to use the abs, or absolute value, method. When given a negative number, it returns that number as a positive value.

The second example show you how to use the round method. Note that in the third statement, -3.5 rounds up to -3. It does not round down to -4.

The third example shows you how to use the ceil (ceiling) and floor methods. The ceil method always rounds a fractional value towards positive infinity. The floor method always rounds a fractional value towards negative infinity. You can think of the floor method as truncating or removing the fractional portion.

The fourth example shows you how to use the pow and sqrt methods. The power parameter of the pow method can be a fractional value. In the second statement, 125 is raised to the 1/3rd power. This is the equivalent of taking the cube root of 125.

The fifth example shows you how to use the min and max methods. These methods are not limited to two parameters so you can supply as many parameters as needed. Then, these methods will find the minimum or maximum value in the list of parameters.

The Math object also provides many trigonometric and logarithmic methods. If you have the appropriate mathematical background, you should be able to use these methods with no problem. They are documented at the web page shown in this figure. If you find you need to use them, though, one point to remember is that the trigonometric methods use radians to measure angles, not degrees.

Common methods of the Math object

Method	Description
Math.abs(*x*)	Returns the absolute value of x.
Math.round(*x*)	Returns the value of x rounded to the closest integer value. If the decimal part is .5, x is rounded up to the next higher integer value.
Math.ceil(*x*)	Returns the value of x rounded to the next higher integer value.
Math.floor(*x*)	Returns the value of x rounded to the next lower integer value.
Math.pow(*x, power*)	Returns the value of x raised to the power specified. The power may be a decimal number.
Math.sqrt(*x*)	Returns the square root of x.
Math.max(*x1, x2, … *)	Returns the largest value from its parameters.
Math.min(*x1, x2, … *)	Returns the smallest value from its parameters.

Example 1: The abs method

```
var result_1a = Math.abs(-3.4);        // result_1a is 3.4
```

Example 2: The round method

```
var result_2a = Math.round(12.5);      // result_2a is 13
var result_2b = Math.round(-3.4);      // result_2b is -3
var result_2c = Math.round(-3.5);      // result_2c is -3
var result_2d = Math.round(-3.51);     // result_2d is -4
```

Example 3: The floor and ceil methods

```
var result_3a = Math.floor(12.5);      // result_3a is 12
var result_3b = Math.ceil(12.5);       // result_3b is 13
var result_3c = Math.floor(-3.4);      // result_3c is -4
var result_3d = Math.ceil(-3.4);       // result_3d is -3
```

Example 4: The pow and sqrt methods

```
var result_4a = Math.pow(2,3);         // result_4a is 8 (the cube of 2)
var result_4b = Math.pow(125, 1/3);    // result_4b is 5 (cube root of 125)
var result_4c = Math.sqrt(16);         // result_4c is 4
```

Example 5: The min and max methods

```
var x = 12.5, y = -3.4;
var max = Math.max(x, y);              // max is 12.5
var min = Math.min(x, y);              // min is -3.4
```

Description

- The max and min methods can take one or more parameters. If there are no parameters, the max method returns -Infinity and the min method returns Infinity.

- For a complete list of the methods and constants of the Math object, see this web page: https://developer.mozilla.org/en/Core_JavaScript_1.5_Reference/Global_Objects/Math

Figure 7-4   How to use the methods of the Math object

How to use a random number generator

The random method of the Math object generates a random number that is equal to or greater than zero but less than one. This is illustrated by the first example in figure 7-5. Often, though, you want a random number that is in a range other than from zero to one.

The second example shows you a function that will generate a random number in a specified range. It also lets you specify the number of digits after the decimal point that you want your random number to have.

The random_number function takes either two or three parameters. The first two parameters are the minimum and maximum values for the range of random numbers that the function should generate. They are required. The third function is the number of digits after the decimal point. It is optional and will default to zero if omitted.

This function first validates the digits parameter to ensure it is a number. If it fails the isNaN test, then digits is set to zero. Otherwise, digits is converted to a whole number using parseInt. This function then ensures that digits is in the range from 0 to 16. If it's above this range, it's set to 16. If it's below this range, it's set to zero.

This function then generates the random number. If digits is equal to zero, it computes a whole number between min and max. To do this, the equation takes a value from the random method and multiplies it by the number of values in the range from min to max (calculated by max - min + 1). It then takes the floor of this intermediate result to remove any fractional part. Finally, the function adds the min value to the result of the floor method.

For example, if min is 5 and max is 10, then max − min + 1 is 6, and 6 times a random number from 0 to just under 1 returns a value in the range of 0 to just less than 6. Next, using the floor method to truncate the fractional part returns a whole number in that range. Last, adding 5 to any number in this range returns a number in the range 5 to 10, which is the range requested.

If digits is a number other than zero, this function computes a decimal number between min and max with the specified number of digits. Here, the first statement takes a value from the random method and multiplies it by the difference between min and max. It then adds min to this result. Then, the second statement uses the toFixed method to convert the number to a string with the specified number of digits and the parseFloat method to convert it back to a number before returning the result.

For example, if min is 2.2, max is 5.7, and digits is 2, the difference between min and max is 3.5. When this is multiplied by a value from the random method, the result is in the range from 0 to just under 3.5. Then, when the minimum value of 2.2 is added to it, the result is in the range from 2.2 to just under 5.7. Last, when the second statement rounds the result to 2 decimal places, the result is a decimal number with two decimal places in the range from 2.2 to 5.7.

Although you won't need random numbers for most JavaScript applications, they can be used for testing as in exercise 7-2. And random numbers are often used in games or applications that provide animation as in chapter 18.

The random method of the Math object

Method	Description
Math.random()	Returns a random decimal number >= 0.0 but < 1.0.

Example 1: Generating a random number

```
var result_1a = Math.random();
```

Example 2: A function to generate random numbers in a range

```
var random_number = function ( min, max, digits ) {
    // If digits is not a number, set it to zero
    // Otherwise, make it a whole number
    digits = isNaN(digits) ? 0 : parseInt(digits);

    // Make sure digits is between 0 and 16
    if ( digits < 0 ) {
        digits = 0;
    } else if ( digits > 16 ) {
        digits = 16;
    }

    if ( digits == 0 ) {
        // Return an integer
        return Math.floor( Math.random() * ( max - min + 1 ) ) + min;
    } else {
        // Return a decimal with the specified number of digits
        var rand = Math.random() * ( max - min ) + min;
        return parseFloat( rand.toFixed(digits) );
    }
}

// Returns 1, 2, 3, 4, 5, or 6
var dice = random_number(1,6);

// Returns 0.0, 0.1, 0.2, ..., 99.9, 100.0
var percentage = random_number( 0, 100, 1 );

// Returns 0.050, 0.051, 0.052, ..., 0.099, 0.100
var interest_rate = random_number( 0.05, 0.10, 3);
```

Description

- You can use the random_number function that's shown above to generate a random number with the specified minimum and maximum values and with the specified number of digits after the decimal point.

- If digits is zero, the random_number function returns an integer value. Otherwise, it returns a decimal value with the specified number of digits.

- Random numbers can be used for testing and are often used in games or applications that provide animation.

Figure 7-5   How to use a random number generator

How to work with strings

In chapter 2, you learned how to create and work with basic strings. In this topic, you'll learn how to create more complex strings and how to manipulate those strings with the methods of the String object.

How to use escape sequences in strings

Figure 7-6 shows you how to use *escape sequences* in your strings. These sequences let you include special characters in a string. To start all escape sequences, you code the backslash. For instance, \n starts a new line when a string is displayed, and \t represents a tab character. Similarly, \" adds a double quotation mark to a string, and \\ adds a single backslash to a string.

You can also include any Unicode character in a JavaScript string by using the \u escape sequence. Unicode is a standard set of 16-bit codes that allows more than 65,000 characters to be identified in a text string. These 16-bit values are entered as four-digit hexadecimal (hex) values that aren't case sensitive. For example, \u00a2 is the escape sequence for the cents character, where 00a2 is the hex value.

As the third table in this figure shows, you can also include Unicode characters with hex values that start with 00 by using the \x escape sequence. In this case, you don't code the 00, so \u00a2 and \xa2 are equivalent.

For a complete list of Unicode characters, you can go to the web site specified in this figure. Be aware, however, that not all fonts provide representations for all Unicode characters. If you specify a Unicode character that isn't available in the font used in the web browser, a filler character (often just an empty box) will be used instead.

Basic escape sequences

Sequence	Description
\b	Backspace
\t	Tab
\n	New line
\r	Carriage return
\f	Form feed
\v	Vertical tab
\"	Double quote
\'	Single quote
\\	Backslash

Examples of strings using the basic escape sequences

```
var quote = "He said \"Goodbye.\"";
var message = "Error\t123\nText\tInvalid Operation";
var info = "The file is in C:\\murach";
```

Escape sequences for some of the Unicode characters

Sequence	Character	Sequence	Character	Sequence	Character
\u00a2	¢	\u00bd	½	\u03b2	β
\u00a9	©	\u00d7	×	\u03c0	π
\u00ae	®	\u00f7	÷	\u2026	…
\u00b0	°	\u0394	Δ	\u2122	™
\u00b1	±	\u03a3	Σ	\u221e	∞
\u00b5	µ	\u03a9	Ω	\u2248	≈
\u00bc	¼	\u03b1	α	\u2260	≠

Two ways to code Unicode escape sequences

Sequence	Description
\u*dddd*	Character whose Unicode value (UTF-16) is given by a four-digit hexadecimal number.
\x*dd*	Equivalent to \u00*dd*. This is in the Latin-1 range of the Unicode characters.

Examples of strings using the Unicode escape sequences

```
alert( "99\u00a2" ); // Displays 99¢
alert( "\xa9 2008" ); // Displays © 2008
```

Description

- *Escape sequences* let you insert characters that aren't on the keyboard.
- For a complete list of Unicode characters, go to http://www.unicode.org/charts/.
- Be aware that not all fonts provide all of the Unicode characters. If you use a Unicode character that isn't in the user's font, a filler character will be used instead.

Figure 7-6   How to use escape sequences in strings

How to use the methods of the String object

Figure 7-7 describes one property and several methods of String objects. The length property lets you find out how many characters are in a string. This is illustrated by the first example. Because the positions in a string are numbered from zero, not 1, the last character in a string is at the position identified by the length minus 1.

Example 2 in this figure shows you how to use the charAt method. Here, the J in JavaScript is the character at position 0, and the character at position 4 is S.

Example 3 shows you how to use the concat method. If you specify more than one parameter, the strings are concatenated in order. This is the same operation performed by the + operator when one of the two operands is a string. Although there was a performance difference between using + and the concat method in earlier implementations of JavaScript, there is little difference today. As a result, you can usually use whichever coding method you prefer.

Example 4 shows the use of the indexOf method. If you omit the position parameter, the search is performed from the start of the string. If the search string isn't found, the method returns -1.

Example 5 shows the use of the substring method. Note that the character specified in the end parameter is *not* included in the result. If start is greater than end, the two values are swapped. If either value is less than 0, it is replaced with 0. If either value is greater than the length of the string, it is replaced with the length of the string.

Example 6 shows you how to use the toUpperCase and toLowerCase methods. These methods have no parameters, but don't forget to include the empty set of parentheses after the method name.

If you're familiar with the string methods for other languages, you may be wondering whether there are useful methods that aren't shown in this figure. In particular, you may be looking for methods that make it easier to format numbers and dates. For instance, both Java and C# provide string methods that make it easy to insert commas into numbers and to format dates and times.

The answer is that this figure summarizes all of the useful string methods that JavaScript provides, except for the ones that use arrays and regular expressions, which you'll learn how to use in chapters 9 and 12. What this means is that JavaScript doesn't have as rich a set of string methods as some languages. Although this means more coding for some tasks, this isn't a serious limitation as you can see by the examples in the next figure.

One property of String objects

Property	Description
length	The number of characters in the string.

Example 1: Displaying the length of a string

```
var message_1 = "JavaScript";
var result_1 = message_1.length;      // result_1 is 10
```

Methods of String objects

Method	Description
charAt (*position*)	Returns the character at the specified position in the string.
concat(*string1*, *string2*, …)	Returns a new string that is the concatenation of this string with each of the strings specified in the parameter list.
indexOf(*search*, *position*)	Searches the string for the first occurrence of the search string starting at the position specified or at the beginning if the position is omitted. If the search string is found, it returns the position in the string, starting from 0. If not found, it returns -1.
substring(*start*)	Returns a new substring that contains part of the original string from the start position to the end of the string.
substring(*start*, *end*)	Returns a new substring that contains part of the original string from the start position to, but not including, the end position.
toLowerCase()	Returns a new string with all uppercase letters converted to lowercase.
toUpperCase()	Returns a new string with all lowercase letters converted to uppercase.

Example 2: The charAt method

```
var message_2 = "JavaScript";
var letter = message_2.charAt(4);         // letter is "S"
```

Example 3: The concat method

```
var message_3 = "Java";
var result_3 = message_3.concat("Script"); // result_3 is "JavaScript"
```

Example 4: The indexOf method

```
var result_4a = message_2.indexOf("a");    // result_4a is 1
var result_4b = message_2.indexOf("a", 2); // result_4b is 3
var result_4c = message_2.indexOf("s");    // result_4c is -1
```

Example 5: The substring method

```
var result_5a = message_2.substring(4);    // result_5a is "Script"
var result_5b = message_2.substring(0,4);  // result_5b is "Java"
```

Example 6: The toLowerCase and toUpperCase methods

```
var result_6a = message_2.toLowerCase();   // result_6a is "javascript"
var result_6b = message_2.toUpperCase();   // result_6b is "JAVASCRIPT"
```

Figure 7-7   How to use the methods of the String object

Examples of working with strings

In the previous figure, you saw simple examples that used the string methods. Now, figure 7-8 shows you how to perform more complex manipulations by using combinations of string methods and loops. This should give you some ideas for how you can apply these methods in your own applications.

Example 1 shows you how to count the number of times a letter occurs in a string by using a function named letter_count that takes three parameters. The haystack parameter is the string to be searched, the needle parameter is the letter to search for, and the ignore parameter is a Boolean value used to indicate whether the function should ignore case.

To start, the letter_count function checks to see if ignore is true. If it is, both needle and haystack are converted to lowercase letters. Then, the variables named position and count are initialized to 0. The position variable will store the starting position for each search, and it will be updated each time a letter is found. The count variable will store the count of the letters that are found.

Next, the while loop tests to see if the needle is in the haystack. If it is, count is incremented and position is set to the position that's one after the letter that was just found. When the indexOf method returns -1 indicating that no more letters were found, the loop ends and the function returns the value in count.

Example 2 shows how to trim the spaces off the beginning of a string by using a function named ltrim that takes the string to be trimmed as its only parameter. This function first initializes the start variable to 0. Then, its while loop tests the character at the start position. As long as it is a space, the start position is moved forward one character and the loop continues. The loop exits when it finds a non-space character, and the function returns the substring from the current value of the start position to the end.

Example 3 shows you how to use a function named rtrim to trim spaces off the end of a string. This is like the ltrim function, but the end variable is set to the last position in the string (length - 1). Then, the while loop tests the character at the end position. As long as it is a space, the end position is moved backward one character. The loop exits when it finds a non-space character, and the function then returns the substring from the beginning to the current value of the end position + 1. Here, end + 1 is used because the substring method doesn't return the character specified by the end position.

Example 4 shows you how to trim spaces off both ends of a string by combining the ltrim and rtrim functions of examples 2 and 3. This type of trimming is often done when working with user entries.

Example 5 shows you how to use a function named equal_ignore_case to perform a case insensitive test for equality between two strings. This is useful because the == operator is case sensitive when used with strings. To perform the case insensitive test, this function tests the equality of the two parameters that are passed to it after it converts them both to lowercase.

Example 1: Counting the number of occurrences of a letter in a string

```
var letter_count = function ( haystack, needle, ignore ) {
    if (ignore) {
        haystack = haystack.toLowerCase();
        needle = needle.toLowerCase();
    }
    var position = 0, count = 0;
    while ( haystack.indexOf(needle, position) != -1 ) {
        count++;
        position = haystack.indexOf(needle, position) + 1;
    }
    return count;
}
var count_1a = letter_count( "JavaScript", "a" );         // count_1a is 2
var count_1b = letter_count( "JavaScript", "s" );         // count_1b is 0
var count_1c = letter_count( "JavaScript", "s", true ); // count_1c is 1
```

Example 2: How to trim spaces off the beginning of a string

```
var ltrim = function ( text ) {
    var start = 0;
    while ( text.charAt(start) == " " ) {
        start++;
    }
    return text.substring(start);
}
var result_2 = ltrim( "  JavaScript");    // result_2 is "JavaScript"
```

Example 3: How to trim spaces off the end of a string

```
var rtrim = function ( text ) {
    var end = text.length - 1;
    while ( text.charAt(end) == " " ) {
        end--;
    }
    return text.substr(0, end + 1);
}
var result_3 = rtrim( "JavaScript   " );    // result_3 is "JavaScript"
```

Example 4: Combining ltrim and rtrim

```
var trim = function ( text ) { return ltrim( rtrim(text) ); }

var result_4 = trim( "  JavaScript   ");    // result_4 is "JavaScript"
```

Example 5: How to compare two strings ignoring case

```
var equal_ignore_case = function ( text1, text2 ) {
    return text1.toLowerCase() == text2.toLowerCase();
}

if ( equal_ignore_case("JavaScript", "javascript") ) {
    alert( "The strings are the same.");
}
```

Figure 7-8   Examples of working with strings

How to work with dates and times

In JavaScript, dates are represented by the number of milliseconds since Midnight, January 1, 1970. Positive values come after this date while negative values come before. Internally, the dates are stored in universal time, or Greenwich Mean Time (GMT). However, JavaScript has access to the time zone on the client's computer and adjusts the dates to the local time.

The Date object provides convenient ways to create dates based on more familiar representations. It also provides methods to read and work with dates after they're created. In chapter 2, you saw one way to create Date objects and four methods for working with them. In this topic, you'll learn more about working with Date objects.

How to create Date objects

There are four ways to create Date objects with JavaScript. These are illustrated in figure 7-9.

The first example shows how to create a Date object that represents the local time on the user's computer. This is done by specifying the Date constructor with no parameters. This is the method that you learned in chapter 2.

The second example shows how to create a Date object by specifying a date and time in a string parameter. In this case, the year must be four digits, and the hours must be specified in 24-hour (or military) time. For example, 3:15pm is 15:15 on a 24-hour clock. If you omit the time, midnight is used.

The third example shows how to create a Date object by specifying the parts of the date. Here, year and month are required. Then, if day is omitted, 1 is used. And if any of the remaining date parts are omitted, 0 is used.

When you use this method, remember that the months are numbered from 0 through 11 where 0 is January and 11 is December. As a result, 3 is April and 10 is November. This makes it easier to use the month numbers with arrays, which are also numbered starting with 0. In chapter 10, you'll learn how to use arrays with Date objects.

The last example shows you how to create a Date object by copying another Date object. This lets you manipulate the copy without affecting the original. You'll learn more about that in the next two figures.

How to create a Date object that represents the current date and time

```
var now = new Date();
```

How to create a Date object by specifying a date string

```
var election_day = new Date("11/8/2008");
var grand_opening = new Date("2/16/2009 8:00");
var departure_time = new Date("4/6/2009 18:30:00");
```

How to create a Date object by specifying date parts

Syntax of the constructor

```
new Date( year, month, day, hours, minutes, seconds, milliseconds)
```

Examples

```
var election_day = new Date(2008, 10, 4);       // 10 is November
var grand_opening = new Date(2009, 1, 16, 8);   // 1 is February
var depart_time = new Date(2009, 3, 6, 18, 30); // 3 is April
```

How to create a Date object by copying another date object

```
var check_out = new Date("11/8/2008");
var due_date = new Date( check_out );
// You can then add a number of days to due_date. See figure 7-11.
```

Description

- When you create a Date object, the date and times are specified as local time. Local time is in the time zone specified on the computer that is running the user's web browser.

- Month numbers start with 0, so January is 0 and December is 11. This allows these values to be used with arrays. You'll learn how to do this in chapter 11.

- If you call the Date constructor with no parameters, it creates a new Date object and sets it to the current date and time.

- If you call the Date constructor with a string as the parameter, the constructor parses the string as a date or a date and time and uses it to create a new date object.

- If you call the date constructor with two or more numbers as parameters, the numbers are used in the order shown above to create a new date object. In this case, year and month are required, but the remaining parameters are optional.

- If you call the Date constructor with another date object as the parameter, it creates a new Date object that is a copy of the other date object.

Figure 7-9   How to create Date objects

The methods of the Date object

Figure 7-10 describes several methods that are provided by the Date object. The first group of methods creates a formatted string from a date. However, as the examples show, you can't control the format used by these methods. In the next figure, though, you'll learn how to create your own formats for date and time strings.

The methods in the second group are used to extract the parts from a Date object. Here, all of the methods except the getTime method return the date part from the local time. In contrast, the getTime method uses universal time. There is also a getYear method that returns a two-digit year, but its use is not recommended.

The methods in the third group are used to set new values for the parts in a Date object. These methods let you use values that are outside the allowed range. Then, any value over or under the allowed range will cause the next most significant date part to roll over.

For example, if you set the hours of a date to 25, the time will be set to 1 and one day will be added to the day of the month. Or, if you set the date to -1, the month will be rolled back one and the day set to one day prior to the end of the new month. By letting you use values that are out of the normal range, JavaScript provides a mechanism to perform date math using any of the parts of the date or time. You'll see examples of this in the next figure.

The formatting methods of a Date object

Method	Description
toString()	Returns a string containing the date and time in local time using the client's time zone.
toDateString()	Returns a string representing just the date in local time.
toTimeString()	Returns a string representing just the time in local time.

Examples of the formatting methods

```
var birthday = new Date( 2005, 0, 4, 8, 25); // Jan 4, 2005 8:25am
alert( birthday.toString() );       // "Tue Jan 04 2005 08:25:00 GMT-0500"
alert( birthday.toDateString() );   // "Tue Jan 04 2005"
alert( birthday.toTimeString() );   // "08:25:00 GMT-0500"
```

The get methods of a Date object

Method	Description
getTime()	Returns the number of milliseconds since Midnight, January 1, 1970 in universal time (GMT).
getFullYear()	Returns the four-digit year in local time.
getMonth()	Returns the month in local time, starting with 0 for January.
getDate()	Returns the day of the month in local time.
getHours()	Returns the hour in 24-hour format in local time.
getMinutes()	Returns the minutes in local time.
getSeconds()	Returns the seconds in local time.
getMilliseconds()	Returns the milliseconds in local time.

The set methods of a Date object

Method	Description
setFullYear(*year*)	Sets the four-digit year in local time.
setMonth(*month*)	Sets the month in local time.
setDate(*day*)	Sets the day of the month in local time.
setHours(*hour*)	Sets the hour in 24-hour format in local time.
setMinutes(*minute*)	Sets the minutes in local time.
setSeconds(*second*)	Sets the seconds in local time.
setMilliseconds(*ms*)	Sets the milliseconds in local time.

Description

- Except for the getTime method, the get and set methods use the time zone specified on the user's computer to work with local time.
- There are complementary get and set methods that start with getUTC and setUTC that work with the Date object in universal time (GMT). For example, the getUTCHours method returns the hour in 24-hour format in universal time.

Figure 7-10 The methods of the Date object

Example of working with dates

Figure 7-11 shows how you can apply the methods of the last figure. The first two examples show you how to format dates and times. The last three examples show you how to perform calculations with dates. This should give you some ideas for how you can use Date objects in your own applications.

Example 1 shows you how to format a date. To do that, the JavaScript code first creates a new Date object that contains the current date and time. Next, it extracts the year, month, and date parts, and it adds 1 to the month number. Then, it builds a text string using these values. As the string is built, the month and date numbers are padded with a leading zero if they are less than ten.

Example 2 shows you how to format the time. It first creates a Date object and then extracts the hours, minutes, and seconds. Next, to build the formatted string for the time, the hours are converted from 24-hour to 12-hour time. Here, if hours % 12 is 0 (hours has a value of 0 or 12), then 12 is used in the hours place. Otherwise, hours % 12 is used. Then, the minutes and seconds are added to the string separated by colons. If either of these values is less than 10, it is padded with a leading zero. Finally, an am or pm is added to the string based on the value of hours.

Example 3 shows you how to calculate the number of days from the current date until the New Year. First, the current date is retrieved in a Date object and a copy of this object is made. Then, the month and day in the copy are set to January 1st, and 1 is added to the year. At this point, the now variable contains the current date and the new_year variable contains the January 1st date.

Next, the number of milliseconds between the two dates is calculated by subtracting the dates that are extracted by the getTime method. Then, the number of days is calculated by dividing the number of milliseconds by the number of milliseconds in one day (86,400,000) and rounding that value up using the ceil method. Last, a message is displayed that indicates the number of days remaining. To do that, a conditional operator is used to alter the message when there is only one day left.

Example 4 shows you how to calculate a due date. Here, the check_out variable contains a Date object with the current date. Then, a due_date variable is created that contains a copy of the check_out Date object. Last, 21 is added to the date in the due_date object so the due date is 21 days after the check_out date.

Example 5 shows you how to determine the last day of the current month. Here, the last_day variable starts at today's date. Then, 1 is added to the month, and the date is set to zero. This rolls the date back one day, which causes 1 to be subtracted from the month and the day of the month to be set to the last day of the month. If, for example, the current date is December 2, adding 1 to the month number rolls it over to month 0, or January. Then, when the date is set to zero, the date and month roll back to December 31.

Example 1: Display the date in your own format

```
var depart_time = new Date(2009, 3, 6, 18, 30); // Apr. 6, 2009 6:30pm
var year = depart_time.getFullYear();
var month = depart_time.getMonth() + 1;  // Add 1 since months start at 0
var date = depart_time.getDate();

var dateText = year + "-";
dateText += ((month < 10) ? "0" + month : month) + "-";  // Pad month
dateText += (date < 10) ? "0" + date : date;             // Pad date
// Final dateText is "2009-04-06"
```

Example 2: Display the time in your own format

```
var depart_time = new Date(2009, 3, 6, 18, 30); // Apr. 6, 2009 6:30pm
var hours = depart_time.getHours();
var minutes = depart_time.getMinutes();
var seconds = depart_time.getSeconds();

var timeText = (hours % 12 == 0) ? 12 : hours % 12;    // Convert to 12-hour
timeText += ":";
timeText += ( minutes < 10 ) ? "0" + minutes : minutes;   // Pad minutes
timeText += ":";
timeText += ( seconds < 10 ) ? "0" + seconds : seconds;   // Pad seconds
timeText += ( hours < 12 ) ? " am" : " pm";               // Add am or pm
// Final timeText is "6:30:00 pm"
```

Example 3: Calculate the days until the New Year

```
var now = new Date();              // Get the current time
var new_year = new Date(now);      // Copy the current time
new_year.setMonth(0);              // Set the month to January
new_year.setDate(1);               // Set the day to the 1st
new_year.setFullYear( new_year.getFullYear() + 1 );  // Add 1 to the year

var time_left = new_year.getTime() - now.getTime(); // Time in milliseconds
var days_left = Math.ceil( time_left / 86400000);   // Convert ms to days

var message = "There ";
message += ( days_left == 1 ) ? "is one day" : "are " + days_left + " days";
message += " left until the New Year.";
// If today is April 6, 2009, message is
// "There are 271 days left until the New Year."
```

Example 4: How to calculate a due date

```
var check_out = new Date()
var due_date = new Date( check_out );
due_date.setDate( due_date.getDate() + 21 ); // Due date is 3 weeks later
```

Example 5: How to find the end of the month

```
var end_of_month = new Date();
// Set the month to next month
end_of_month.setMonth( end_of_month.getMonth() + 1 );
// Set the date to one day before the start of the month
end_of_month.setDate( 0 );
```

Figure 7-11   Examples of working with dates

Perspective

In this chapter, you've learned new ways to work with numbers, strings, and dates. When you combine these skills with those that you learned in chapter 2, you have the essential skills for working with data that you need for most JavaScript applications. Then, in chapters 9 and 12, you'll learn how to use the string methods for working with arrays and regular expressions.

Unlike some other languages, though, JavaScript doesn't provide methods that make it easy to format numbers and dates. As a result, you need to write your own code for that type of formatting. If you do the exercises that follow, you'll get a chance to do that.

Terms

precision
ternary operator
binary operator
unary operator
escape sequence

Exercise 7-1   Validate string and date entries

In this exercise, you'll use string methods to validate two types of entries: an email address and a date. That will give you a chance to use the string methods. Note, however, that a better way to do this type of validation is to use regular expressions as shown in chapter 12.

Open and test the application

1. From your Firefox browser, open the html file in the strings_and_dates folder that's in the chapter 7 folder for exercises. Then, test the application by entering values in the input boxes and clicking the Process buttons. All this application does is display what you've entered in the boxes.

2. Use your text editor to open the Javascript file for this application. There you can see the code that you'll start with.

Validate the email address

3. Modify the JavaScript code so it validates the email address that has been entered when the user clicks the first Process button. To keep this simple, assume that a valid email address is one that contains an @ sign and a dot (period) with the dot after the @ sign. If the address is invalid, the application should display messages like these, depending on what the problem is:

   ```
   A valid email address must include an @ sign.
   A valid email address must include a period after the @ sign.
   ```

4. Enhance this code so it displays the domain name (everything after the @ sign) if the email address is valid in a message like this:

    `The domain name is murach.com.`

Validate the date and display the number of the day of the year

5. Modify the JavaScript code so it validates the date that has been entered when the user clicks the second Process button. To keep this simple, assume that a valid date is in this form: mm/dd/yyyy. If the date is invalid, the application should display a message like this:

    `A valid date must be in this format: mm/dd/yyyy.`

6. Enhance the JavaScript code so a message like this is displayed when the date is valid:

    `This is day 356 in the year 2009.`

Exercise 7-2   Enhance the Future Value application

In this exercise, you'll write the JavaScript code for enhancing a Future Value application like the one in chapter 2. Along the way, you'll work with large numbers, use a random number generator, work with dates, and work with strings.

Open, review, and test the application

1. From your Firefox browser, open the html file in the future_value folder that's in the chapter 7 folder for exercises. Notice that this application now calculates the future value of a one-time investment, not a monthly investment. It also displays the current date.

2. Use your text editor to review the XHTML for this application. There you can see the code for displaying the date.

3. Use your text editor to review the JavaScript code for this application. There you can see that these changes have been made to the code for the Future Value application of chapter 2: (1) the calculation has been modified so it gets the future value of a one-time investment; and (2) the random-number function of figure 7-5 has been copied into the file so you can use it later on.

4. Test the application with valid values to see how it works. Then, test it with these values: 10000 for investment amount; 12.5 for interest rate; and 1000 for number of years. Notice that this returns the future value with e notation and as many significant digits as JavaScript provides for.

5. Now, change the number of years to 10000 and test the application again. This time, it returns Infinity for the future value amount. Runaway loops like this are a common way that applications produce values of Infinity and -Infinity.

Work with large numbers

6. Modify the JavaScript code by adding an if statement to the for loop that calculates the future value. This if statement should test whether future value is equal to infinity. If it is, the if statement should use the alert method to display a message like this, where i is the counter for the loop:

```
Future value = Infinity
i = 5342
```

The if statement should also set the value of i to the value of years so the loop will end.

7. After the if statement and still within the for loop, add an alert statement that displays the maximum value of a JavaScript number with its precision set to 3.

Use a random number generator

8. Comment out the three statements that get investment, rate, and years from the text boxes. Then, use the random_number function to get random values for investment, rate, and years. Investment should range from 1000 to 50000; rate should range from 3.5 to 12 with 2 decimal places; and years should range from 1 to 50. The application should get these random values each time the user clicks the Calculate button; these values should be displayed in the three input boxes; and future value should be calculated.

9. Test this application by clicking on the Calculate button several times to see how the values are varied. This illustrates how a random number generator can be used to quickly test an application with a wide range of values.

Format the future value with a dollar sign and commas

10. Modify the JavaScript code so the future value that's calculated is formatted with a dollar sign and commas as in these examples:

```
$1,234.56
$1,234,456.78
```

To do that, you need to use the indexOf method to get the location of the decimal point and the substring methods to extract the cents, hundreds, thousands, and millions digits from the future value. Then, you can concatenate the parts with a dollar sign, commas, and decimal point. The trick is that some future values won't have millions digits so you need to provide for that with if statements.

Use your own formatting for the date

11. Modify the JavaScript code in the XHTML file so the date is displayed in this format:

```
Today is 12/04/2008 at 14:29.
```

To do that, you need to get a Date object that contains the current date. Then, you need to use the Date methods to extract the appropriate date and time parts so you can format them as shown above. Note that 24-hour format is used.

8

How to code control statements

In chapter 2, you were introduced to conditional expressions and if, while, and for statements. Now, you'll learn more about coding these expressions and statements. You'll also learn how to use switch, do-while, break, and continue statements.

How to code conditional expressions **276**
How to use the equality and identity operators 276
How to use the relational operators 278
How to use the logical operators 280

How to code the selection structures **282**
How to code if statements with else clauses 282
How to code if statements with else if clauses 284
How to code switch statements 286
How to use a flag to simplify your selection structures 288

How to code the iteration structures **290**
How to code while loops 290
How to code do-while loops 292
How to code for loops 294
How to use the break and continue statements 296

Perspective **298**

How to code conditional expressions

In chapter 2, you learned the basics of writing conditional expressions. In this topic, you'll learn more about using the equality, relational, and logical operators.

How to use the equality and identity operators

Figure 8-1 summarizes the use of the equality and identity operators in conditional expressions. For simple comparisons, the two *equality operators* are sufficient. If, for example, you want to test whether a numeric variable contains a certain number, the equal operator (==) works just fine.

When the tests are more complex, however, unexpected results may occur when you use the equality operators. To illustrate, this figure lists several equality expressions that don't produce the results you might expect.

The problems that you get when you use the equality operators come from two sources. The first is that the equality operators perform *type coercion*. This means that if different types of data are being compared, the values will be converted to the same data type before the comparison takes place. For example, in the test 3 == "3", the string "3" is converted to the number 3 and then the comparison is done so the result is true. Although the rules for doing the type coercion are complex, they tend to convert values of different data types into numerical values before performing the comparison.

The other problem with the use of equality operators is that the type conversion that's done for type coercion is different than the type conversion that's done by the parseInt and ParseFloat methods. For instance, an empty string is converted to 0 during type coercion, but the parseFloat method converts an empty string to NaN.

These problems can be avoided by using the *identity operators*, because the identity operators don't perform type conversion. Then, if two values of different types are compared, the result will always be false. In fact, if you were to replace all of the equality operators in the table of unusual results with identity operators, all of the results would be false.

When you use the identity operators, it's usually best to use the parseInt or parseFloat methods to do your own data conversions before you do the comparisons. That way, you're sure that you're comparing values of the same type.

The equality operators

Operator	Description	Example
==	Equal	lastName == "Harris"
!=	Not equal	months != 0

Unusual results with the equality operator

Expression	Result	Description
null == undefined	true	Null and undefined are treated as equivalent.
3.5 == " \t3.5\n "	true	Whitespace around a number is ignored.
"" == 0	true	The empty string is converted to 0.
" \t\n " == 0	true	A string of all whitespace is converted to 0.
false == 0	true	False is converted to 0.
false == "0"	true	False and "0" are converted to 0.
false == "false"	false	False is converted to 0 but "false" is converted to NaN.
true == 1	true	True is converted to 1.
true == "1"	true	True and "1" are converted to 1.
true == "true"	false	True is converted to 1 but "true" is converted to NaN.
Infinity == "Infinity"	true	The string "Infinity" is converted to the value Infinity.
NaN == NaN	false	You must use the isNaN method to test for NaN.
NaN == "NaN"	false	The string "NaN" is converted to NaN, but two NaNs still return false.

The identity operators

Operator	Description	Example
===	Equal	lastName === "Harris"
!==	Not equal	months !== 0

Description

- The *equality operators* perform *type coercion*. Type coercion converts data from one type to another. For example, it often converts strings to numbers.

- The type conversion that's done by the equality operators is different from that done by the parseInt or parseFloat methods.

- The *identity operators* do not perform type coercion. If the two operands are of different types, the result will always be false. As a result, all of the expressions listed above for the equality operator would return false for the identity operator.

- When comparing different data types, it is often best to use parseInt or parseFloat to perform your own type conversion and then use the identity operator to perform the comparison.

Figure 8-1   How to use the equality and identity operators

How to use the relational operators

In chapter 2, you learned how to use the four relational operators with examples that showed two values of the same type being compared. Those operators are summarized in the first table in figure 8-2.

Like the equality operators, the relational operators perform type coercion when the two values are of different types. For instance, when you compare strings and numbers, the string value is converted to a numerical value before the comparison takes place. This is illustrated by the second table in this figure. As a result, you often need to make sure that you're comparing two values of the same type before you use these operators.

When you use these operators to compare two strings, the strings are compared character by character from the start of the strings based on the Unicode value of each character. However, the Unicode values of all of upper-case letters are less than (come before) the Unicode values of all of the lower-case letters. This is illustrated by the examples in the third table in this figure.

In many cases, this isn't the way you would like the comparison of two strings to be evaluated. To get around that, though, you can use the toLowerCase method that you learned about in the last chapter (figure 7-7) to convert the strings to lowercase characters before they are compared:

```
string_1.toLowerCase() < string_2.toLowerCase()
```

Here, if string_1 is "Orange" and string_2 is "apple", the result of the expression is false.

Finally, this figure shows some unusual results that you get when you use the relational operators. Here again, the results are unusual because the type conversions that are done by type coercion are different from those that are done by the parseInt and parseFloat methods.

The last example is probably the most unusual. Given that null == undefined is true, as shown in the previous figure, you would think that null <= undefined would also be true. However, although the equality test explicitly says that null is equal to undefined, the relational test ignores this and lets null and undefined be converted to numbers before being compared. Then, since they are both converted to NaN and any comparison involving NaN is false, the result is false. Fortunately, the value null is rarely used in JavaScript applications.

The relational operators

Operator	Description	Example
<	Less than	age < 18
<=	Less than or equal	investment <= 0
>	Greater than	testScore > 100
>=	Greater than or equal	rate / 100 >= 0.1

Comparing strings to numbers with the relational operators

Expression	Result	Description
1 < "3"	true	The string "3" is converted to the number 3.
"10" < 3	false	The string "10" is converted to the number 10.

Comparing strings with the relational operators

Expression	Result	Description
"apple" < "orange"	true	An earlier letter is less than a later letter.
"apple" < "appletree"	true	Shorter strings are less than longer strings.
"Orange" < "apple"	true	Any capital letter is less than any lowercase letter.
"@" < "$"	false	Characters are compared using their Unicode values.

Unusual results with the relational operators

Expression	Result	Description
0 < NaN	false	A value of NaN as an operand will always return false.
0 < "test"	false	The string "test" is converted to NaN and the result is false.
"" < 5	true	The empty string is converted to 0.
"2000" < "3"	true	Two strings are not converted to numbers.
false < true	true	False is converted to 0 and true is converted to 1.
null <= undefined	false	Given that null == undefined is true, this should be true. However, null and undefined are both converted to NaN and the result is false.

Description

- When you use the relational operators, the operands are converted to numbers, except when both operands are strings.
- Whenever one of the operators is NaN or converted to NaN, the result will be false.
- When both operands are strings, they are compared character by character from the start of the strings based on the Unicode value of each character.
- If one string is shorter than the other but contains the same characters as the start of the longer string, the shorter string is the lesser of the two.

Figure 8-2   How to use the relational operators

How to use the logical operators

The first table in figure 8-3 lists the three logical operators that you learned about in chapter 2. This is followed by four examples that use these operators in *compound conditional expressions*. Since these expressions use just one of the logical operators, this type of expression is relatively easy to evaluate.

In the first example, the NOT operator is used to reverse the Boolean value that's returned by the isNaN method so this expression is true when the value of the variable named number is a number. In the second example, the AND operator is used to return true only when age is 18 or higher and credit score is 680 or higher.

In the third example, the OR operator is used to return true if the state variable is either CA or NC. A common mistake when using the OR operator is to write an expression like this:

```
state == "CA" || "NC"
```

But you need to repeat the entire equality test on both sides of the OR.

The second table in this figure shows the order of precedence for conditional expressions. For instance, this table shows that relational operations are done before equality and identity operations, and AND operations are done before OR operations. This table is followed by three examples that use these operators in *complex conditional expressions*. These expressions mix two or more of the logical operators. That makes these expressions more difficult to evaluate.

In example 4, the AND and OR operators are used in the conditional expression. Because the AND operator is evaluated first, this expression will return true if the age is 18 or more *and* the score is 680 or more. This expression will also return true if the state is NC.

In example 5, the AND, OR, and NOT operators are used in one expression. This expression will return true if oldCustomer is false. It will also return true if the loan amount is greater than or equal to 10000 *and* the score is less than the minimum score plus 200. Note that this expression uses an arithmetic operator, which is evaluated before the relational operators.

In example 6, you can see how parentheses affect the evaluation of the code that's in example 5. This time, the OR operation is inside a set of parentheses. As a result, this expression will return true if oldCustomer is false *and* the score is less than the minimum score plus 200. It will also return true if the loan amount is greater than or equal to 10000 *and* the score is less than the minimum score plus 200.

As I think these examples illustrate, complex conditional expressions are hard to evaluate. That's why you should use parentheses to clarify the order of evaluation. But even then, you need to carefully test these expressions with all of the possible combinations of data to make sure they work correctly.

The logical operators

Operator	Name	Description
!	NOT	Returns the opposite Boolean value of its expression.
&&	AND	Returns true only when the expressions on both sides are true.
||	OR	Returns true when the expression on either side or both sides is true. The logical operators in compound conditional expressions

Example 1: The NOT operator

```
!isNaN(number)
```

Example 2: The AND operator

```
age >= 18 && score >= 680
```

Example 3: The OR operator

```
state == "CA" || state == "NC"
```

The order of precedence for conditional expressions

Order	Operators	Direction	Description
1	!	Left to right	The NOT operator
2	<, <=, >, >=	Left to right	Relational operators
3	==, !=, ===, !==	Left to right	Equality and identity operators
4	&&	Left to right	The AND operator
5	||	Left to right	The OR operator

The logical operators in complex conditional expressions

Example 4: AND and OR operators

```
age >= 18 && score >= 680 || state == "NC"
```

Example 5: AND, OR, and NOT operators

```
!oldCustomer || loanAmount >= 10000 && score < minScore + 200
```

Example 6: How parentheses can change the evaluation

```
(!oldCustomer || loanAmount >= 10000) && score < minScore + 200
```

Description

- You can use arithmetic expressions within a conditional expression. In the order of precedence, the arithmetic operators come between the NOT operator and the relational operators.
- Parentheses have the highest order of precedence so the operations within parentheses are done first, working from the innermost sets of parentheses to the outermost sets.
- To clarify the way an expression will be evaluated, you should use parentheses.

Figure 8-3   How to use the logical operators

How to code the selection structures

In chapter 2, you were introduced to the if statement. Now, this topic will expand upon what you learned. It will also present the switch statement. These statements implement structures that are often referred to as the *selection structures*.

How to code if statements with else clauses

Figure 8-4 presents some new information about the if and else clauses of an if statement. To start, you don't have to use braces to enclose the statements in these clauses if each clause consists of just one statement. This is illustrated by the first example. When you omit the braces, it's best to place the entire if statement on one line to make it clear that the if clause executes only one statement.

The second example is like the first example, but braces are used even though they're not required. If you write your code this way, it's easy to see which statements are part of the if clause. This will also make it easier to add more statements to the if clause if you need to do that as you develop your application.

The third example shows an if statement that has just one statement in both the if and the else clauses and no braces are used. Here, although the braces aren't required for either clause, it's best to use braces for the else clause. The reason for this is shown in the fourth example.

In the fourth example, a statement is added after the statement in the else clause of the third example. The intent is to have it be executed as part of the else clause. But when you don't use braces for the else clause, only the first statement is part of that clause, no matter how it's indented. As a result, the last statement in this example will always be executed.

The fifth example is similar to example 3, but braces are used around the if and else clauses even though they consist of only one line. Here the extent of the if statement is well defined and you will be less likely to introduce errors if you enhance this code later.

Last, the sixth example illustrates an if statement that's nested three layers deep. Here, the use of braces and indentation help make the code easier to read. To understand this code, though, you need to know that a leap year isn't just a year that is divisible by 4. If a year is divisible by 100, it must also be divisible by 400 to be a leap year. That's why 2000 was a leap year but 2100 won't be.

Example 1: An if clause with one statement and no braces

```
if ( rate === undefined ) rate = 0.075;
```

Example 2: An if clause with one statement and braces

```
if ( qualified ) {      // This expression is equivalent to qualified == true.
    alert("You qualify for enrollment.");
}
```

Example 3: If and else clauses with one statement each and no braces

```
if ( age >= 18 )
    alert("You may vote.");
else
    alert("You may not vote.");
```

Example 4: Why you should always use braces with else clauses

```
if ( age >= 18 )
    alert("You may vote.");
else
    alert("You may not vote.");
    may_vote = false;    // This statement isn't a part of the else clause.
```

Example 5: Braces make your code easier to modify or enhance

```
if ( score >= 680 ) {
    alert("Your loan is approved.");
}
else {
    alert("Your loan is not approved.");
}
```

Example 6: A nested if statement to determine if a year is a leap year

```
var isLeapYear;
if ( year % 4 == 0 ) {
    if ( year % 100 == 0 ) {
        if ( year % 400 == 0) {
            isLeapYear = true;      // divisible by 4, 100, and 400
        } else {
            isLeapYear = false;     // divisible by 4 and 100, but not 400
        }
    } else {
        isLeapYear = true;          // divisible by 4, but not 100
    }
} else {
    isLeapYear = false;             // not divisible by 4
}
```

Description

- If you only have one statement after an if statement or an else clause, you don't have to put braces around that statement.

- Using braces around single statements in if or else clauses makes your code easier to read, modify, and enhance.

- Combining braces with indentation makes your code easier to read and debug.

Figure 8-4   How to code if statements with else clauses

How to code if statements with else if clauses

In figure 8-5, there are four more examples of if statements. This time, the statements use else if clauses. This will give you more ideas for coding if statements.

When you code else if clauses, you should always use braces to enclose the blocks of statements. This is illustrated by all of these examples. That will make your code easier to read, modify, and enhance.

The third example shows how to use else if clauses to validate the value in the variable named rate. Before the if statement starts, a Boolean value named rateIsValid is set to false. Then, the if statement uses a series of tests to determine the validity of the rate variable, starting with the worst case first (is not a number). If any of the tests fails, an appropriate message is displayed. But if the variable passes all of the tests, the rateIsValid variable is set to true.

The fourth example also shows the use of multiple else if clauses. This code is testing the value of the variable named average in order to set the value of the variable named grade. Note here that the values must be tested from the high end of the range to the low. If, for example, the first test was >= 69.5, the code wouldn't work for the A and B ranges.

Of course, the first test could be average >= 69.5 && average < 79.5, but that would mean extra code. Also, testing the ranges out of order would make the code harder to read and maintain. In general, then, it's best to test for a range of values in sequence.

Incidentally, the fourth example illustrates a coding style that I often use. Here, I code the keywords else if or else on the same line that contains the closing brace for the previous clause. This is especially useful for the book examples because it saves vertical space.

Example 1: An if statement with one else if clause

```
if ( age < 18 ) {
    alert("You're too young for a loan.");
}
else if ( score < 680 ) {
    alert("Your credit score is too low for a loan.");
}
```

Example 2: An if statement with an else if and an else clause

```
if ( age < 18 ) {
    alert("You're too young for a loan.");
}
else if ( score < 680 ) {
    alert("Your credit score is too low for a loan.");
}
else {
    alert("You're approved for your loan.");
}
```

Example 3: An if statement with two else if clauses and an else clause

```
rateIsValid = false;
if ( isNaN(rate) ) {
    alert("Rate is not a number.");
}
else if (rate < 0) {
    alert("Rate cannot be less than zero.");
}
else if (rate > 0.2) {
    alert("Rate cannot be greater than 20%.");
}
else {
    rateIsValid = true;
}
```

Example 4: An if statement to determine a student's letter grade

```
if ( average >= 89.5 ) {
    grade = "A";
} else if ( average >= 79.5 ) {
    grade = "B";
} else if ( average >= 69.5 ) {
    grade = "C";
} else if ( average >= 64.5 ) {
    grade = "D";
} else {
    grade = "F";
}
```

Description

- Using braces around single statements in else if clauses makes your code easier to read, modify, and enhance.

- Combining braces with indentation makes your code easier to read and debug.

- You can *nest* an if statement within the if, else if, or else clause of another if statement. This nesting can continue many layers deep.

Figure 8-5   How to code if statements with else if clauses

How to code switch statements

A *switch statement* is a convenient way to express a certain form of if statement. Specifically, it can be used in place of an if statement with multiple else if clauses in which one expression is tested for equality with several values. This is illustrated by the statements in figure 8-6. The switch statement implements a control structure that is often referred to as the *case structure*.

The switch statement starts with the word switch followed by a *switch expression* inside of parentheses. This expression is *not* a conditional expression. It is an expression that returns a single value that will be used to determine which *case* to execute. The expression is often as simple as a single variable as shown in the first example in this figure.

Once the value for the expression is found, the switch statement checks each of the values in the *case labels*. Then, it begins executing the code that follows the first case label that is equal to the result of the expression. It continues executing until it reaches either a break statement or the end of the switch statement.

If no case labels match the value in the switch expression, the switch statement starts executing the code that follows the default label. But this default case is optional. If it is omitted and no case labels match the expression, the switch statement won't execute any code.

In the first example in this figure, the expression is just a variable named letterGrade that should contain a letter. Then, each case label is checked against the value of this variable. If, for example, letterGrade is "B", the switch statement starts executing the code after the label for that case and sets the message variable to "above average". It then encounters a break statement and no further code is executed by the switch statement. If letterGrade had been "Z", however, the code after the default label would have been executed and the message would have been set to "invalid grade".

In the second example, the case labels are coded in a way that provides *fall through*. This occurs when code starts executing at one case label but doesn't encounter a break statement, so it passes another case label and keeps executing. Although this is often discouraged because it can be confusing, this example shows one case where fall through is useful.

In this instance, the same code should be executed when letterGrade is "A" or "B". Instead of repeating the code, two case labels are placed before the code. Then, if letterGrade is "A", the switch statement will fall through and execute the code after the case for "B". Likewise, if letterGrade is "D", the switch statement will fall through and execute the code after the case for "F". Except for cases like this, though, you should avoid using fall through in your switch statements because that can lead to unexpected errors and be hard to debug.

When you use a switch statement, you can nest if statements within the cases. You can also nest switch statements within the cases of another switch statement.

A switch statement with a default case

```
switch ( letterGrade ) {
    case "A":
        message = "well above average";
        break;
    case "B":
        message = "above average";
        break;
    case "C":
        message = "average";
        break;
    case "D":
        message = "below average";
        break;
    case "F":
        message = "failing";
        break;
    default:
        message = "invalid grade";
        break;
}
```

A switch statement with fall through

```
switch ( letterGrade ) {
    case "A":
    case "B":
        message = "Scholarship approved.";
        break;
    case "C":
        message = "Application requires review.";
        break;
    case "D":
    case "F":
        message = "Scholarship not approved.";
        break;
}
```

Description

- The *switch statement* starts by evaluating the *switch expression* in the parentheses.
- After evaluating the expression, the switch statement transfers control to the *case label* that has the value that matches the value of the expression. Then, it executes the statements for that *case*. It stops executing when it reaches a break statement or the end of the switch statement.
- The default case is optional and may be omitted. If included, you can only have one default case. It is usually the last case in the switch statement, but it can be anywhere.
- The values in the case label may be literal values or they may be expressions.
- If a case doesn't contain a break statement, execution will *fall through* to the next label.
- You can nest if statements or other switch statements within the cases of a switch statement.

Figure 8-6   How to code switch statements

How to use a flag to simplify your selection structures

When you code complex conditional expressions and when you nest if and switch statements, your selection structures often become hard to follow and difficult to debug. Then, you should do whatever you can to simplify them. One way to do that is to break an if statement down into two or more if statements by using a Boolean variable. This is illustrated by the two examples in figure 8-7.

In the first example, which has been taken from the Future Value application, all of the processing is done in a single if statement. In the if clause and the two else if clauses, the three input values are tested for validity. Then, if they're valid, all of the processing is done in the else clause.

In the second example, this processing is broken down into two if statements. These statements use a Boolean variable named valid that indicates whether the three input values are valid. Programmers often refer to a Boolean variable that's used like this as a *flag*, or *switch*. Then, if the flag is set one way, one type of processing is done. But if the flag is set the other way, another type of processing or no processing is done.

In this second example, the first if statement just determines whether the three input values are valid. Before this if statement is executed, the flag variable named valid is set to true. Then, if one of the clauses in the first if statement determines that one of the variables isn't valid, it sets the value of this flag to false.

Once this flag is set, the second if statement uses it to determine whether or not it should do the processing for valid data. To do that, it uses this condition:

```
if ( valid )
```

Here, the condition is just the name of the flag, which is shorthand for

```
valid == true
```

As you progress through this chapter and book, you'll see other examples of using flags. You'll also see that this technique is especially useful when you need to test a flag in more than one portion of your code.

The single if statement in the Future Value application of chapter 2

```
// Test the three input values for validity.
if (isNaN(investment) || investment <= 0) {
    alert("Investment must be a valid number\nand greater than zero.");
} else if(isNaN(annualRate) || annualRate <= 0) {
    alert("Annual rate must be a valid number\nand greater than zero.");
} else if(isNaN(years) || years <= 0) {
    alert("Years must be a valid number\nand greater than zero.");

// If all input values are valid, calculate the future value.
} else {
    var monthlyRate = annualRate / 12 / 100;
    var months = years * 12;
    var futureValue = 0;
    for ( i = 1; i <= months; i++ ) {
        futureValue = ( futureValue + investment ) *
            (1 + monthlyRate);
    }
    $("futureValue").value = futureValue.toFixed(2);
}
```

Code that uses a flag named valid to get the same results

```
// Test the three input values for validity.
var valid = true;
if (isNaN(investment) || investment <= 0) {
    alert("Investment must be a valid number\nand greater than zero.");
    valid = false;
} else if(isNaN(annualRate) || annualRate <= 0) {
    alert("Annual rate must be a valid number\nand greater than zero.");
    valid = false;
} else if(isNaN(years) || years <= 0) {
    alert("Years must be a valid number\nand greater than zero.");
    valid = false;
}

// If all input values are valid, calculate the future value.
if ( valid ){
    var monthlyRate = annualRate / 12 / 100;
    var months = years * 12;
    var futureValue = 0;
    for ( i = 1; i <= months; i++ ) {
        futureValue = ( futureValue + investment ) *
            (1 + monthlyRate);
    }
    $("futureValue").value = futureValue.toFixed(2);
}
```

Description

- A *flag* is a Boolean value that gets set to true or false based on some processing that's done. Then, that value can be used to determine what other processing gets done.

- Using a flag often simplifies your code. This is especially true if the flag needs to be tested in more than one place in your code.

Figure 8-7   How to use a flag to simplify your selection structures

How to code the iteration structures

In chapter 2, you learned how to use while statements and for statements. Now, you'll learn more about coding those statements, and you'll learn how to code the do-while, break, and continue statements. These statements implement structures that are often referred to as the *iteration structures*.

How to code while loops

As you saw in chapter 2, a *while loop* executes a block of code as long as its conditional expression is true. If the conditional expression starts off as false, the code isn't executed at all. If the conditional expression never becomes false, the while loop becomes an infinite loop. Figure 8-8 shows four examples that will give you some ideas for what you can do with while loops.

In the first example, the while loop is used to validate user input. Here, the user is prompted for a number from 1 to 10. If the user enters a valid number, the conditional expression in the while loop will be false and the loop will be skipped. If the user enters an invalid number, the expression will be true and the user will be informed of the error and prompted for another number. The while loop will then check the value again and the loop will continue as long as the value that the user enters is invalid.

In the second example, the while loop is used to collect the numbers to average. To get out of this loop, the user enters a non-numeric value. Inside the loop, the value that the user enters is added to the total, the count is incremented by one, and the user is prompted for another number.

After the user enters a non-numeric value to end the loop, the average is calculated. But if the first value the user enters is non-numeric, both total and count will be 0, and average will be undefined because 0 / 0 in JavaScript returns "undefined" rather than an error. So after the average calculation, the if statement tests the average to see if it's numeric. If it isn't, an error message is displayed. Otherwise, the average is displayed.

In the third example, one dice (or die) is rolled until a 6 appears and the loop counts the number of times the die needed to be rolled to get that 6. This code assumes that the random_number function from figure 7-5 has been included at the beginning of the code. Since the first roll of the die takes place in the while loop's expression, the increment statement in the loop won't be executed if the first roll is a 6. That's why the value for rolls is initially set to 1.

In the fourth example, the loop from example 3 is nested inside another loop that is executed 10,000 times. Each time the inner loop rolls a 6, the number of rolls to get that 6 is added to the variable named total. In addition, the value of the variable named max is changed if the number of rolls is greater than the current value of max. Since the value of max starts at –Infinity, any number of rolls the first time through the inner loop will be greater than that and the starting value of max will be changed. Then, when the outer loop finishes, the average number of tries to get a 6 is calculated and the average and maximum values are displayed.

Example 1: A while loop to validate user input

```
var value = parseInt( prompt("Please enter a number from 1 to 10") );
while ( isNaN(value) || value < 1 || value > 10 ) {
    alert("You did not enter a number between 1 and 10.");
    value = parseInt( prompt("Please enter a number from 1 to 10") );
}
```

Example 2: A while loop that finds the average of a series of numbers

```
var total = 0, count = 0, number;
alert("Enter the numbers to average. Enter any non-number to stop.");

number = parseFloat( prompt("Enter a number") );
while ( !isNaN(number) ) {
    total += number;
    count++;
    number = parseFloat( prompt("Enter another number") );
}
var average = total / count;
if ( isNaN(average) ) {
    alert("You didn't enter any numbers.");
} else {
    alert("The average is: " + average);
}
```

Example 3: A while loop that counts dice rolls until a six is rolled

```
// See figure 7-5 for the random_number function
var rolls = 1;
while ( random_number(1,6) != 6 ) {
    rolls++;
}
alert("Number of times to roll a six: " + rolls);
```

Example 4: Nested while loops that find the average and max to roll a six

```
// See figure 7-5 for the random_number function
var total = 0, count = 0, max = -Infinity;
var rolls;

while ( count < 10000 ) {
    rolls = 1;
    while ( random_number(1, 6) != 6 ) {
        rolls++;
    }
    total += rolls;
    count++;
    if ( rolls > max ) max = rolls;
}
var average = total / count;
alert ("Average rolls: " + average);
alert ("Max rolls: " + max);
```

Description

- The *while statement* executes the block of statements within its braces as long as its conditional expression is true.

- When you use a while statement, the condition is tested before the *while loop* is executed.

Figure 8-8   How to code while loops

How to code do-while loops

The *do-while loop* is similar to the while loop except that the conditional expression is tested at the end of the loop. The result is that the code inside the loop will always be executed at least once.

The first example in figure 8-9 shows how to validate user input. This is similar to the first example in figure 8-8, but the user is only prompted for a value from within the loop. To start, this code declares two variables named value and valid without initializing them. Then, within the loop, the value that the user enters is tested and a flag is set to indicate whether the value is valid. This loop continues as long as the flag indicates that the value isn't valid.

The second example counts the number of rolls that it takes to get a 6. This is similar to the third example in figure 8-8. But here, the variable named rolls is initialized to zero since it will be incremented at least once inside the loop.

The third example uses a do-while loop to prompt the user for a series of numbers. It then displays the minimum and maximum values that the user entered. There are two flags used in this code. The first is value_entered, which is used to indicate that at least one number was entered. The second is stop, which is used to indicate that a non-numeric value was entered so the do-while loop should stop.

The do-while loop in this example starts by prompting for a number. If the user enters a number, value_entered is set to true and the value is compared to the min and max variables. If the user enters a non-numeric value, stop is set to true. This loop continues as long as stop is false.

After the do-while loop, the code checks the value_entered flag. If it is true, the maximum and minimum values are displayed. If it is false, the user entered a non-numeric value at the first prompt and an appropriate message is displayed.

Example 1: A do-while loop to validate user input

```
var value, valid;
do {
    value = parseInt( prompt("Please enter a number between 1 and 10") );
    if (isNaN(value) || value < 1 || value > 10) {
        alert("You did not enter a number between 1 and 10.");
        valid = false;
    } else {
        valid = true;
    }
} while ( !valid );
```

Example 2: A do-while loop that counts dice rolls until a six is rolled

```
// See figure 7-5 for the random_number function
var rolls = 0;
do {
    rolls ++;
} while ( random_number(1,6) != 6 );

alert("Number of times to roll a six: " + rolls);
```

Example 3: A do-while loop that finds the maximum and minimum values

```
var max = -Infinity, min = Infinity, number;
var value_entered = false, stop = false;
alert("Enter values to find the max and min. " +
    "Enter any non-number to stop.");

do {
    number = parseFloat( prompt("Enter a number") );
    if ( isNaN(number) ) {
        stop = true;
    } else {
        value_entered = true;
        if ( number > max ) max = number;
        if ( number < min ) min = number;
    }
} while ( !stop );

if (value_entered) {
    alert("Max: " + max + ", Min: " + min);
} else {
    alert("No numbers entered.");
}
```

Description

- The *do-while statement* executes the block of statements within its braces as long as its conditional expression is true.

- When you use a do-while statement, the condition is tested at the end of the *do-while loop*. This means the code will always execute at least once.

Figure 8-9   How to code do-while loops

How to code for loops

A *for loop* is convenient notation for a while loop that requires a counting variable. This is illustrated by the for and while loops at the start of figure 8-10. Here, the first line of the for statement declares the counter variable, provides the condition that will end the loop, and provides the code for incrementing the counter variable. In the while loop, these tasks are done separately.

The first example in this figure shows that you can start and increment the counter variable with values other than 1. Here, the statement initializes the counter to 2 and increments the counter by 2. As a result, the loop displays the numbers from 2 through 10.

The second example shows that you can increment the counter by negative values (which in effect decrements the value). Here, the counter named position is initialized to one less than the length of a string. Then, the counter is decremented by 1 after each iteration of the loop, and the loop executes as long as position is greater than or equal to zero. Inside the loop, the character from the current position in the original string is added to the end of the variable named reverse. Since this loop runs backwards, the characters from the message variable are added to the reverse variable in reverse order.

The third example displays all the factors of a number. A *factor* is any number that can be divided into the number with a remainder of zero, so 1, 2, 3, 6, and 9 are factors of 18. This time, the counter starts at 1 and is incremented by 1, and the loop continues as long as the counter is less than the original number. Inside the loop, a message is displayed if the original number divided by the current value of the counter has a remainder of zero.

The fourth example determines whether a number is prime. A *prime number* has no factors other than one and itself. This code starts by assuming that the number is prime so it sets the flag named prime to true. Then, the number is tested against each of the possible factors that is less than the value of the number starting with 2. If any factor is found, the flag named prime is set to false. After the for loop, a message is displayed based on the value in the prime flag.

Incidentally, the third and fourth examples use i as the variable name for the counter. This is a common practice. And when one loop is nested within another loop, j is often used as the counter name for the inner loop.

The for statement compared to the while statement

The for statement

```
for ( var count = 1; count <= 10; count++ ) {
    alert ( count );
}
```

The while statement

```
var count = 1;
while ( count <= 10 ) {
    alert ( count );
    count++;
}
```

Example 1: A for loop to display even numbers from 2 to 10

```
for ( var number = 2; number <= 10; number += 2 ) {
    alert( number );
}
```

Example 2: A for loop to reverse a string

```
var message = "JavaScript", reverse = "";
for (var position = message.length - 1; position >= 0; position-- ) {
    reverse += message.charAt(position);
}
alert(reverse);   // Displays "tpircSavaJ"
```

Example 3: A for loop to display all the factors of a number

```
var number = 18;
for ( var i = 1; i < number; i++ ) {
    if ( number % i == 0 ) {
        alert( i + " is a factor of " + number );
    }
}
```

Example 4: A for loop to determine if a number is prime

```
var number = 31, prime = true;
for ( var i = 2; i < number; i++ ) {
    if ( number % i == 0 ) prime = false;
}
if (prime) {
    alert( number + " is prime.");
} else {
    alert( number + " is not prime.");
}
```

Description

- The *for statement* is useful when you need to increment or decrement a counter that determines how many times the *for loop* is executed.

- Within the parentheses of a for statement, you code an expression that declares a counter variable and assigns a starting value to it, a conditional expression that determines when the loop ends, and an increment expression that indicates how the counter should be incremented or decremented each time through the loop.

Figure 8-10   How to code for loops

How to use the break and continue statements

The break and continue statements give you additional control over loops. The *break statement* causes the loop to end immediately. The *continue statement* causes the loop to skip to the start of the loop.

The first example in figure 8-11 shows the break statement inside a while loop. Here, the while loop is intentionally coded as an infinite loop. However, if the conditional expression in the if statement is false, the break statement will execute and that will end the while loop. This will occur when the number that the user enters is valid.

The second example shows the break statement used inside a for loop. Here, the loop determines whether the value in the number variable is prime. Once one factor is found, though, the number isn't prime so the code sets the value of the prime variable to false and issues the break statement. If, for example, the value of number is 42, the loop will end as soon as 2 is found to be a factor so the loop won't check the values from 3 to 41.

The third example shows the continue statement used in a for loop. Here, when the number to be displayed is a multiple of 3, the continue statement skips the remainder of the loop and starts the loop again after the counter is incremented. As a result, only numbers that are not multiples of 3 will be displayed by the loop.

The fourth example shows the use of the continue statement in a while loop. Here, the while loop is based on the for loop from the previous example so the number++ statement had to be added as part of the if statement and before the continue statement. Had this increment statement not been added to the if statement, the loop would have become an infinite loop as soon as the number variable became 3. After that, the continue statement would repeat the loop but the number variable would never be incremented so the loop would never end. This would continue until the browser stopped the script because it was taking too long to execute or the user closed the browser.

When you use break and continue statements within nested loops, you need to know that the break or continue statement applies only to the loop that it's in. If, for example, you code the break statement within an inner loop, it skips to the end of that loop, not the end of the outer loop. Although you can get around this limitation by using statement labels, that isn't illustrated in this book.

Example 1: The break statement in a while loop

```
var number;
while (true) {
    number = parseInt( prompt("Enter a number from 1 to 10.") );
    if ( isNaN(number) || number < 1 || number > 10 ) {
        alert("Invalid entry. Try again.");
    } else {
        break;
    }
}
```

Example 2: The break statement in a for loop

```
var number = 31, prime = true;
for ( var i = 2; i < number; i++ ) {
    if ( number % i == 0 ) {
        prime = false;
        break;
    }
}

if (prime) {
    alert( number + " is prime.");
} else {
    alert( number + " is not prime.");
}
```

Example 3: The continue statement in a for loop

```
for ( var number = 1; number <= 10; number++ ) {
    if ( number % 3 == 0 ) continue;
    alert(number);
}
// Only displays 1, 2, 4, 5, 7, 8, and 10
```

Example 4: The continue statement in a while loop

```
var number = 1;
while ( number <= 10 ) {
    if ( number % 3 == 0 ) {
        number++;
        continue;
    }
    alert(number);
    number++;
}
// Only displays 1, 2, 4, 5, 7, 8, and 10
```

Description

- The *break statement* ends a loop. In other words, it jumps out of the loop.
- The *continue statement* ends the current iteration of a for or while loop, but allows the next iteration to proceed. In other words, it jumps to the start of the loop.
- When you're working with nested loops, the break and continue statements apply only to the loop that they're in.

Figure 8-11   How to use the break and continue statements

Perspective

Now that you've finished this chapter, you should know how to code if statements, switch statements, while statements, do-while statements, and for statements. These are the JavaScript statements that implement the selection, case, and iteration structures, and they provide the logic of an application. As you progress through this book, you'll see many examples of the use of these statements that will help you use them effectively.

Terms

equality operator	switch
type coercion	iteration structure
identity operator	while statement
compound conditional expression	while loop
complex conditional expression	do-while statement
selection structure	do-while loop
switch statement	for statement
case structure	for loop
switch expression	factor
case	prime number
casel label	break statement
fall through	continue statement
flag	

Exercise 8-1   Use if and switch statements

This exercise will give you a chance to experiment with nested if and switch statements.

Open and test the application

1. From your Firefox browser, open the html file in the invoice_total folder that's in the chapter 8 folder for exercises. Then, test this application by entering either "R" or "C" in the Customer Type box and a value from zero to 500 in the Invoice Subtotal box. When you click on the Calculate button, you can see that the discount percent is based on both the customer type and subtotal amount.

2. Use your text editor to open the JavaScript file for this application. There you can see the nested if statement that determines the discount percent.

Change the code that determines the discount percent

3. Change the if statement so customers of type R with a subtotal that's greater than or equal to $250 but less than $500 get a 25% discount and those with a subtotal of $500 or more get a 30% discount. Next, change the if statement so customers of type C always get a 20% discount. Then, test these changes.

4. Add another type to the if statement so customers of type T get a 40% discount for subtotals of less than $500, and a 50% discount for subtotals of $500 or more. Also, make sure that customer types that aren't R, C, or T get a 10% discount. Then, test these changes.

5. Test the application again, but use lowercase letters for the customer types. Note that these letters aren't evaluated as capital letters.

6. Modify the code so the users can enter either capital or lowercase letters for the customer types. To do that, you can use either the toUpperCase string method or a compound conditional expression. Then, test this change.

Use a switch statement with nested if statements to get the same results

7. Code a switch statement right before the if statement. This statement should provide the structure for handling the three cases for customer types: R, C, and T. Then, within each of these cases, you can copy the related code from the if statement below to provide for the discounts that are based on subtotal variations. In other words, the if statements will be nested within the switch cases.

8. Comment out the entire if statement that's above the switch statement. Then, test to make sure the switch statement works correctly.

9. If you haven't done so already, modify the switch statement so it works for both lowercase and uppercase entries of the three customer types. Then, test that change.

Exercise 8-2   Use loops

This exercise will give you some practice using loops.

Open the application

1. From your Firefox browser, open the html file in the using_loops folder that's in the chapter 8 folder for exercises. This application starts by running the code for example 2 in figure 8-8. To see how this example works, enter two numbers and then click on the OK button with the entry blank. The average of the numbers is displayed. After that, the web page for another part of this exercise is displayed.

2. Use your text editor to open the JavaScript file for this application. There you can see a function named finding_average that contains the code for example 2 in figure 8-8. That's the function that you tested in step 1. You can also see functions named rolling_six and finding_primes that implement two of the other examples in chapter 8, followed by the start of a function named process_test_scores. Last, you can see the function for the onload event that calls the other functions, but note that the last three calls are commented out.

Modify two of the functions that implement the book examples

Now, you'll modify two of the functions that implement examples from the book. This will help you understand when each type of loop is appropriate.

3. Modify the finding_average function so it uses a do-while loop instead of a while loop. After you've tested the modifications, comment out the call to this function in the onload event handler.

4. Remove the comments from the call to the rolling_six function in the onload event handler and run the application so see how this function works. Then, modify the code for this function so it uses a for loop as the outer loop instead of a while loop. After you've tested the modifications, comment out the call to this function in the onload event handler.

Modify the function for finding prime numbers

5. Remove the comments from the call to the finding_primes function in the onload event handler. Then, run this application. This displays a message that says that 31 is a prime number.

6. Modify the code for this function so it finds and lists all of the prime numbers between 1 and 100 in an alert box like this:

```
The prime numbers from 1 through 100 are:
1   2   3   5   etc.
```

   To do this, you need to add an outer loop to the code that presents the numbers 1 through 100 so they can be tested to see whether they're prime. Then, test this code until you've got it working.

7. If you haven't already done so, modify the code so it uses a break statement to exit from the inner loop as soon as the loop determines that a number isn't prime. This will make this function run more efficiently. When you've got this working right, comment out the call to this function in the onload event handler.

Implement the process_test_scores function

8. Remove the comments from the call to the process_test_scores function in the onload event handler. Then, run this application. It displays a message that asks the user to enter a number between 0 and 100 or to enter 999 to end the function. Now, enter 999 to end this function and display the web page.

9. For each number that the user enters, the text boxes on the web page should display: the last score that was entered, the number of scores that have been entered, the total of these scores, the average score, the best score, and the worst score. When you write the code for this function, you should enclose the prompt method within a loop, but you decide which type of loop is best for this application. Now, write and test the code.

10. When you've got this function working right, remove the comments from all of the calls in the unload event handler. Than, run the application one last time.

9

How to create and use arrays

In this chapter, you'll learn how to work with arrays, which are important in a variety of JavaScript applications. For example, you can use an array to hold a list of tasks to complete. Then, you can update and display the tasks in the list.

How to create and use an array **302**
How to create an array 302
How to add and delete array elements 304
How to use for loops to work with arrays 306
How to use for-in loops to work with arrays 308
The methods of an Array object 310
How to use the Array methods 312

Other skills for working with arrays **314**
How to use a String method to create an array 314
How to create and use an associative array 316
How to create and use an array of arrays 318

The Task List Manager application **320**
The user interface and XHTML 320
The JavaScript code 320

Perspective **324**

How to create and use an array

In the topics that follow, you'll learn the basic skills for creating and using arrays. You'll also learn how to use the built-in methods that JavaScript provides for working with arrays.

How to create an array

An *array* is an object that contains one or more items called *elements*. Each of these elements can be a primitive data type or an object. For instance, you can store numbers, strings, and Date objects in the same array.

The *length* of an array indicates the number of elements that it contains. Because JavaScript arrays are dynamic, you can change the length of an array by adding or removing elements from the array.

Figure 9-1 shows two ways to create an array. When you use the first method, you use the new keyword with the Array constructor to create an array with the number of elements that is indicated by the length parameter. This length must be a whole number that is greater than or equal to zero. If you don't specify the length, the array will be empty.

When you use the second method, you just code a set of brackets. This gives you the same result that you get with the first method and no parameter, an empty array.

Next, this figure shows you how to create a new array and assign values to its elements in a single statement. In this case, you code the values in a list that's separated by commas. For instance, the first group of examples shows a statement that creates an array named rates that contains four numeric values and a statement that creates an array named names that contains three strings.

Note, however, that when you create an array with the new keyword, the array list must not be a single number. Otherwise, it will be treated as the length of the array, not a value in the array.

To refer to the elements in an array, you use an *index* that ranges from zero to one less than the number of elements in an array. In an array with 12 elements, for example, the index values range from 0 to 11. This is the reason the getMonth method of a Date object numbers the months from 0 to 11 instead of 1 to 12. Then, the return value of the getMonth method can be used as an index for an array of month names.

To use an index, you code it within brackets after the name of the array. In this figure, all of the examples use literal values for the indexes, but an index can also be a variable that contains an index value. If you try to access an element that hasn't been assigned a value, the value of undefined will be returned.

The last group of examples in this figure, shows how to assign values to an empty array. To do that, you refer to the elements by using indexes, and you assign values to those elements.

The syntax for creating an array

Using the new keyword with the Array object name

```
var arrayName = new Array(length);
```

Using the brackets literal

```
var arrayName = [];
```

The syntax for creating an array and assigning values in one statement

Using the new keyword with the Array object name

```
var arrayName = new Array(arrayList);
```

Using the brackets literal

```
var arrayName = [arrayList];
```

How to create an array and assign values in one statement

```
var rates = new Array(14.95, 12.95, 11.95, 9.95);
var names = ["Ted Lewis", "Sue Jones", "Ray Thomas"];
```

The syntax for referring to an element of an array

```
arrayName[index]
```

Code that refers to the elements in an array

```
rates[2]        // Refers to the third element in the rates array
names[1]        // Refers to the second element in the names array
```

How to assign values to an array by accessing each element

How to assign rates to an array that starts with four undefined elements

```
var rates = new Array(4);
rates[0] = 14.95;
rates[1] = 12.95;
rates[2] = 11.95;
rates[3] = 9.95;
```

How to assign strings to an array that starts with no elements

```
var names = [];
names[0] = "Ted Lewis";
names[1] = "Sue Jones";
names[2] = "Ray Thomas";
```

Description

- An *array* can store one or more *elements*. The *length* of an array is the number of elements in the array.

- If you create an array without specifying the length, the array doesn't contain any elements.

- When you create an array of one or more elements without assigning values to them, each element is set to undefined.

- To refer to the elements in an array, you use an *index* where 0 is the first element, 1 is the second element, and so on.

Figure 9-1   How to create an array

How to add and delete array elements

There is one property and one operator that can help you modify arrays. They are described in figure 9-2.

To add an element to the end of an array, you can use the length property of the array as the index of the new element. Since this property will always be 1 more than the highest index used in the array, this adds the new element at the end of the array.

To add an element at a specific index, you use its index to refer to the element and assign a value to it. If you use an index that's greater than the length of the array, the elements that you skipped over will be created and assigned the value of undefined.

To delete an element from an array, you can use the delete operator. This is illustrated by the third example. When you do this, the deleted element is left in the array with an undefined value. In other words, the elements that are above the element that you deleted are not shifted down to fill in this gap. In figures 9-5 and 9-6, though, you'll learn how to use the splice method of an array to delete elements without leaving a gap in the array.

In JavaScript, a *sparse array* is an array with a large number of elements but few assigned elements. This is illustrated by the fourth example in this figure. Here, the array has 1001 elements, but only two of these elements have assigned values. With some programming languages, space would be reserved for all 1001 elements in the computer's memory. With JavaScript, though, space is only reserved for the elements that have assigned values.

One property and one operator for an array

Property	Description
`length`	The number of elements in an array.

Operator	Description
`delete`	Deletes the contents of an element and sets the element to undefined, but doesn't remove the element from the array.

How to add an element to the end of an array

```
var numbers = [1, 2, 3, 4];      // array is 1, 2, 3, 4
numbers[numbers.length] = 5;     // array is 1, 2, 3, 4, 5
```

How to add an element at a specific index

```
var numbers = [1, 2, 3, 4];   // array is 1, 2, 3, 4
numbers[6] = 7;               // array is 1, 2, 3, 4, undefined, undefined, 7
```

How to delete a number at a specific index

```
var numbers = [1, 2, 3, 4];   // array is 1, 2, 3, 4
delete numbers[2];            // array is 1, 2, undefined, 4
```

A sparse array that contains 999 undefined elements

```
var numbers = [1];        // array is 1
numbers[1000] = 1001;     // array contains 1 and 1001 with 999
                          // undefined elements in between
```

Description

- One way to add an element to the end of an array is to use the length property as the index.

- If you add an element at a specific index that isn't the next one in sequence, undefined elements are added to the array between the new element and the end of the original array.

- A *sparse array* is a large array with few defined elements. For efficiency, though, JavaScript only reserves space for the elements that are assigned values.

- You can also add items to an array by using the methods of an Array object as shown in figures 9-5 and 9-6.

Figure 9-2   How to add and delete array elements

How to use for loops to work with arrays

For loops are commonly used to process one array element at a time by incrementing an index variable. Figure 9-3 shows how this works.

The first example in this figure shows how to create an array and fill it with the numbers 1 thorough 10. First, the code creates an empty array named numbers. Then, an index variable named i is used to loop through the first ten elements of the array by using values that range from 0 to 9. In the body of this loop, one is added to the value in i and the result is stored in the element. As a result, the element at index 0 stores a 1, the element at index 1 stores a 2, and so on.

Next, this example displays the values in the array. First, it creates an empty string named numbersString. Then, it uses a for loop to access the elements in the array. In the for loop, the length property of the array is used to control how many times the loop executes. This allows the same code to work with arrays of different lengths. Inside the for loop, the value in the element and a space are concatenated to the end of numbersString. Finally, numbersString is displayed, which shows the ten numbers that were stored in the array.

The second example in this figure shows how you can calculate the sum and average of an array of totals. First, the code creates an array named totals that stores four total values. Then, it creates a variable named sum that is initialized to zero. Next, it uses a for loop to access each of the elements in the totals array and add it to the sum. Finally, it calculates the average by dividing the sum by the length of the array.

Next, this example displays the totals, the sum, and the average. First, it creates an empty string named totalsString. Then, it uses a for loop to concatenate the value of each element and a new line character to totalsString. Finally, it displays a message containing totalsString, the sum, and the average.

Code that puts the numbers 1 through 10 into an array

```
var numbers = [];
for (var i = 0; i < 10; i++) {
    numbers[i] = i + 1;
}
```

Code that displays the numbers array

```
var numbersString = "";
for (var i = 0; i < numbers.length; i++) {
    numbersString += numbers[i] + " ";
}
alert (numbersString);
```

The message that's displayed

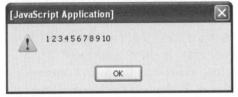

Code that computes the sum and average of an array of totals

```
var totals = [141.95, 212.95, 411, 10.95];
var sum = 0;
for (var i = 0; i < totals.length; i++) {
    sum += totals[i];
}
var average = sum / totals.length;
```

Code that displays the totals array, the sum, and the average

```
var totalsString = "";
for (var i = 0; i < totals.length; i++) {
    totalsString += totals[i] + "\n";
}
alert ("The totals are:\n" + totalsString + "\n" +
        "Sum: " + sum.toFixed(2) + "\n" + "Average: " + average.toFixed(2)
);
```

The message that's displayed

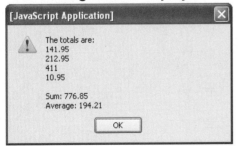

Description

- When you use a *for loop* to work with an array, you can use the counter for the loop as the index for the array.

Figure 9-3   How to use for loops to work with arrays

How to use for-in loops to work with arrays

In contrast to a for loop, a *for-in loop* makes it easier to work with an array. Figure 9-4 shows how this type of loop works.

As the syntax at the top of this figure shows, the for-in loop doesn't require separate expressions that initialize, test, and increment an index counter like a for loop does. Instead, you declare a variable that will be used to refer to the index of each element in the array. Then, within the loop, you can use this variable to access each element in the array.

The first example in this figure stores the numbers 1 through 10 in an array and creates an empty string named numbersString. Then, it uses a for-in loop to concatenate each of the numbers in the array and a space to the string. Last, it displays the numbers in a message box.

The second example shows the differences in the ways that for loops and for-in loops handle the undefined elements in an array. In short, a for loop processes the undefined elements, but a for-in loop skips over them. You can see these differences in the messages that are displayed for each of the loops in this example.

Occasionally, it's worth knowing that two types of undefined elements can be in an array. The first type is an element that doesn't have a value assigned to it so it is undefined. The second type is an element that has a value of "undefined" assigned to it. Although the for-in loop skips the first type of undefined element, it processes the second type of undefined element.

To illustrate, the fourth line in the second example in this figure

```
delete names[2]
```

creates the first type of undefined element. But if this line of code had been coded as

```
names[2] = undefined
```

the element would be the second type of undefined element. Then, the for-in loop would process this undefined value and the message would have one "undefined" between Anne and Joel. Note, however, that the message for the for loop would still show both undefined values.

The syntax of a for-in loop

```
for (var elementIndex in arrayName) {
    // statements that access the elements
}
```

A for-in loop that displays the numbers array in a message box

```
var numbers = [1, 2, 3, 4, 5, 6, 7, 8, 9, 10];
var numbersString = "";
for (var index in numbers) {          // The start of the for-in loop
    numbersString += numbers[index] + " ";
}
alert(numbersString);
```

The message that's displayed

Code that shows the difference between for and for-in loops

```
var names = ["Mike", "Anne", "Ray"];
names[4] = "Joel";               // Array is Mike, Anne, Ray, undefined, Joel
names[names.length] = "Pren";    // Pren is added to the array
delete names[2];                 // Ray is deleted from the array

var namesString1 = "The elements displayed by the for loop:\n\n";
for (var i = 0; i < names.length; i++) {  // The start of the for loop
    namesString1 += names[i] + "\n"; }    // Includes undefined elements

var namesString2 = "The elements displayed by the for-in loop:\n\n";
for (var i in names) {                     // The start of the for-in loop
    namesString2 += names[i] + "\n"; }    // Omits undefined elements

alert (namesString1);
alert (namesString2);
```

The messages that are created by the for and the for-in loops

Description

- You can use a *for-in statement* to create a *for-in loop* that accesses only those elements in an array that are defined.

Figure 9-4   How to use for-in loops to work with arrays

The methods of an Array object

To make it easier to work with arrays, JavaScript provides many methods. The most useful of these are summarized in figure 9-5. All of these methods, except for the last five, modify the original array.

The first two methods, push and pop, are used to add elements to and remove elements from the end of an array. This lets you use an array as a stack in which the last element added to it is the first element removed (last-in, first-out). In this case, the oldest element is at the start of the array.

The next two methods, unshift and shift, are used to add elements to and remove elements from the start of an array. These methods also let you use an array as a stack in which the last element added to it is the first element removed. In this case, though, the oldest element is at the end of the array.

If you combine the unshift and pop methods, you can use an array as a queue in which the first element added is the first element removed (first-in, first out). In this case, the oldest element is at the end of the array. You can also use push and shift to use an array as a first-in, first-out queue. In this case, though, the oldest element is at the start of the array.

The reverse and sort methods of an Array object let you change the order of the elements in an array. By default, the sort method treats all of the elements as strings. This means that the numbers 5, 10, 101, and 250 are sorted as 10, 101, 250, and 5. If you need to sort the array in numeric order, though, you can pass a function to the sort method that compares two values at a time. You'll see how this works in the next figure.

The splice method lets you remove, replace, and add elements anywhere in an array. To remove elements, you call the splice method with the index of the first element to remove and the number of elements to remove. To replace elements, you call the splice method with the index of the first element to replace, the number of elements to be replaced, and a list of the replacement values. To add elements, you call the splice method with the index of the element just after the insertion point in the array, a zero, and a list of the values to add to the array.

The slice and concat methods let you create a new array from part or all of an array. In either case, the original array isn't modified. If you want the original array to be replaced by the new array, you can set the old array equal to the new array.

The join, toString, and toLocaleString methods let you create a single string that contains the elements in the array. They differ mainly in how they handle the separator string. These methods will use an empty string for any undefined elements, both those that aren't defined and those that were set equal to undefined.

The methods of an Array object

Methods	Description
`push(elements_list)`	Adds one or more elements to the end of the array, and returns the new length of the array.
`pop()`	Removes the last element in the array, decrements the length, and returns the element that it removed.
`unshift(elements_list)`	Adds one or more elements to the beginning of the array, and returns the new length of the array.
`shift()`	Removes the first element in the array, decrements the array length, and returns the element that it removed.
`reverse()`	Reverses the order of the elements in the array.
`sort()`	When no parameter is passed, this method sorts the elements in an array into ascending alphanumeric sequence. If necessary, it converts numeric elements to strings for this sort.
`sort(comparison_function)`	To change the default order of the sort method, you can pass the name of a comparison function to the method. This function should receive two parameters and return a positive value if the first parameter is greater than the second, zero if the two parameters are equal, and a negative value if the first parameter is less than the second parameter.
`splice(start, number)`	Removes the number of elements given by the second parameter starting with the index given by the first parameter. It returns the elements that were removed.
`splice(start, number, elements_list)`	Removes the number of elements given by the second parameter starting with the index given by the first parameter, and replaces those elements with the ones given by the third parameter. It returns the elements that were removed.
`slice(start, number)`	Returns a new array that starts with the index given by the first parameter and continuing for the number of elements given by the second parameter.
`concat(array_list)`	Returns a new array that consists of the original array concatenated with the arrays in the array list.
`join(separator)`	When no parameter is passed, this method converts all the elements of the array to strings and concatenates them separated by commas. To change the separator, you can pass this method a string literal.
`toString()`	Same as the join method without any parameter passed to it.
`toLocaleString()`	Same as the toString method but using a locale-specific separator.

Description

- The push and pop methods are commonly used to add elements to and remove elements from the end of an array.

Figure 9-5   The methods of an Array object

How to use the Array methods

Figure 9-6 shows you how to use the methods that are summarized in the last figure. If you study the summary, the examples, and the comments in the code, you shouldn't have much trouble understanding how these methods work.

For instance, the first example uses the push and pop methods to add and remove elements. The second example uses the unshift and shift methods to do the same. And the third example uses the splice method to delete, replace, and add an element.

In the fourth example, the slice method is used to create a new array that consists of two elements taken from an array named names. Then, the concat method is used to combine the two arrays in another new array. When all of the statements are finished, there are three arrays named names, namesSlice, and namesConcat, and the names array hasn't changed.

The fifth example shows how to use the sort method without and with a parameter. Without a parameter, the elements are sorted as strings. This means that alphabetic elements are sorted in alphabetic order, but numbers aren't sorted in numeric order.

If you want to sort the elements in an array numerically, though, you can pass a function to the sort method. As the summary in the last figure states, this function should receive two parameters, and it should return a positive, zero, or negative value based on a comparison of the two parameter values. The returned value should be positive if the first parameter is greater than the second, zero if they're equal, and negative if the first parameter is less than the second.

In this example, this function is named comparison, and it returns x – y. As a result, it returns the proper positive, zero, or negative value. Then, when this function is used as the parameter for the sort method, the entire function (not the result of calling the function) is passed to the method.

The sixth example shows how to use the reverse method to reverse the order of the elements in an array. This method can be used after you use the sort method if you want the elements in descending order.

The last example shows how to use the join and toString methods. The difference is that the join method lets you supply a parameter that is used as the separator for the list of elements. Otherwise, the comma is used.

How to use the push and pop methods to add and remove elements

```
var names = ["Mike", "Anne", "Joel"];
names.push("Ray", "Pren");      // names is Mike, Anne, Joel, Ray, Pren
var removedName = names.pop(); // removedName is Pren
alert (names.join());           // displays Mike,Anne,Joel,Ray
```

How to use the unshift and shift methods to add and remove elements

```
var names = ["Mike", "Anne", "Joel"];
names.unshift("Ray", "Pren");  // names is Ray, Pren, Mike, Anne, Joel
removedName = names.shift();    // removedName is Ray
alert (names.join());           // displays Pren,Mike,Anne,Joel
```

How to use the splice method

```
var names = ["Mike", "Anne", "Joel", "Pren"];
names.splice(2, 1);             // names is Mike, Anne, Pren
names.splice(2, 1, "Judy");     // names is Mike, Anne, Judy
names.splice(2, 0, "Ray");      // names is Mike, Anne, Ray, Judy
```

How to use the slice and concat methods

```
var names = ["Mike", "Anne", "Joel", "Ray"];
var namesSlice = names.slice(0, 2);   // namesSlice is Mike, Anne
alert (names.join());                  // displays Mike,Anne,Joel,Ray

var namesConcat = names.concat(namesSlice);
alert (namesConcat.join()); // displays Mike,Anne,Joel,Ray,Mike,Anne
```

How to use the sort method

For alphanumeric sorting

```
var names = ["Mike", "Anne", "Joel", "Ray", "Pren"];
names.sort();                    // names is Anne, Joel, Mike, Pren, Ray

var numbers = [520, 33, 9, 199];
numbers.sort();                  // numbers is 199, 33, 520, 9
```

For numeric sorting

```
// The function used for the parameter of the sort method
var comparison = function(x, y) {
    return x - y;
}

var numbers = [520, 33, 9, 199];
numbers.sort(comparison);       // numbers is 9, 33, 199, 520
```

How to use the reverse method

```
var names = ["Mike", "Anne", "Joel", "Ray", "Pren"];
names.reverse();                // names is Pren, Ray, Joel, Anne, Mike
```

How to use the join and toString methods

```
var names = ["Mike", "Anne", "Joel", "Ray"];
alert (names.join());           // displays Mike,Anne,Joel,Ray
alert (names.join(", ")).       // displays Mike, Anne, Joel, Ray
alert (names.toString());       // displays Mike,Anne,Joel,Ray
```

Figure 9-6   How to use the Array methods

Other skills for working with arrays

Now that you've learned the basic skills for creating and working with arrays, you're ready to learn some other skills for working with arrays.

How to use a String method to create an array

Figure 9-7 presents the split method of a String object. This method can be used to divide a string into multiple substrings based on a separator character that's coded as the first parameter. It then creates a new array with each of the substrings as elements. If you code a second parameter, it is used to limit the number of elements that can be included in the new array.

The first example in this figure shows how to split a string that's separated by spaces into an array named nameParts. Next, it displays the length of the new array and the elements in the array. Then, it moves the element at the last index in the array (length – 1) into a variable named lastName and displays the contents of that variable.

Similarly, the second example shows how to split a string that's separated by hyphens into an array. Then, the third example shows how to split a string into individual characters. This happens when you call the split method with an empty string as its parameter.

The fourth example shows what happens if the separator character isn't in the string. Here, a date string is created that has hyphens, but the split method is called with a slash as the separator. In this case, the resulting array only has one element and it is a copy of the original date string.

The fifth example shows how to limit the number of substrings copied into the new array. Here, the split method uses a space as the separator, but it limits the number of substrings to one. The result is an array that contains just the first name in one element.

Note in this example that the last statement uses the alert method to display this one-element array. Since the alert method expects a string, it automatically calls the toString method for any parameter that isn't a string. Then, since there is only one element in the array, the toString method of the array returns that element without using a separator.

A String method that creates an array

Method	Description
split(*separator*, *limit*)	Splits a string into an array based on the value of the separator parameter and returns the array. The optional limit parameter specifies the maximum number of elements in the new array.

How to split a string that's separated by spaces into an array

```
var fullName = "Ray L Harris";
var nameParts = fullName.split(" ");      // creates an array
alert (nameParts.length);                 // displays 3
alert (nameParts.join());                 // displays Ray,L,Harris
var lastName = nameParts[nameParts.length - 1];
alert (lastName);                         // displays Harris
```

How to split a string that's separated by hyphens into an array

```
var date = "1-2-2009";
var dateParts = date.split("-");          // creates an array
alert (dateParts.length);                 // displays 3
alert (dateParts.join("/"));              // displays 1/2/2009
```

How to split a string into an array of characters

```
var fullName = "Ray Harris";
var nameCharacters = fullName.split("");
alert (nameCharacters.length);            // displays 10
alert (nameCharacters.join());            // displays R,a,y, ,H,a,r,r,i,s
```

What happens if the string doesn't contain the separator

```
var date = "1-2-2009";
var dateParts2 = date.split("/");
alert (dateParts2.length);                // displays 1
alert (dateParts2.join());                // displays 1-2-2009
```

How to get just one element from a string

```
var fullName = "Ray L Harris";
var firstName = fullName.split(" ", 1);
alert (firstName.length);                 // displays 1
alert (firstName);                        // displays Ray
```

Description

- The split method of a String object is used to convert the components of a string into the elements of an array.

- If a string doesn't include the separator that's specified in the parameter of the split method, the entire string is returned as the first element in a one-element array.

- If the separator that's specified by the parameter is an empty string, each character in the string becomes an element in the array that's returned by the method.

Figure 9-7   How to use a String method to create an array

How to create and use an associative array

So far, the arrays you've worked with have used whole numbers as the indexes. In contrast, an *associative array* is an array that uses strings as the indexes. In figure 9-8, you can learn how to create and work with associative arrays.

The first example in this figure creates an associate array with four elements. First, it creates an empty array. Then, it stores four values in the array using strings for the indexes. Finally, it displays the length of the associative array. However, because the length property of an array only counts elements with numeric indexes, the length is zero.

The second example adds an element to the array with another string index. The new value is the result of a calculation that uses two existing elements of the array, and the toFixed method is used to round the result.

The third example displays a formatted string that's built from the elements in the array. Here, you can see that the array now contains five elements.

The fourth example shows how to use the for-in loop with an associative array. This for-in loop builds a formatted string that contains the element indexes and values. Then, this string is displayed.

Although you can mix numeric and string indexes within a single array, you usually should avoid doing that because mixed arrays present some unnecessary complications. If you do mix them, the length property indicates only the number of elements with numeric indexes. If you process a mixed array with a for loop, the associative elements aren't included in the processing. And if you process a mixed array with a for-in loop, all of the elements are processed.

How to create an associative array with four elements

```
var item = [];
item["itemCode"] = 123;
item["itemName"] = "Visual Basic 2008";
item["itemCost"] = 52.5;
item["itemQuantity"] = 5;
alert( item.length );                    // Displays 0
```

How to add an element to the associative array

```
item["lineCost"] = (item["itemCost"] * item["itemQuantity"]).toFixed(2);
```

How to retrieve and display the elements in the associative array

```
alert ("Item elements:\n\nCode = " + item["itemCode"] +
       "\nName = " + item["itemName"] +
       "\nCost = " + item["itemCost"] +
       "\nQuantity = " + item["itemQuantity"] +
       "\nLine Cost = " + item["lineCost"]);
```

The message that's displayed

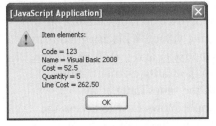

How to use a for-in loop with the associative array

```
var result = "Item elements:\n\n";
for ( var i in item ) {
    result += i + " = " + item[i] + "\n";
}
alert(result);
```

The message that's displayed

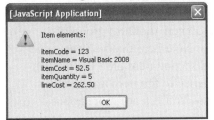

Description

- When you create an *associative array*, you use strings as the indexes. Then, the length of the array is 0, and you refer to the elements by using the strings as the index values.

- If you mix numeric and string indexes in an array, the length will indicate only the number of elements with numeric indexes, a for loop will only process the elements with numeric indexes, and a for-in loop will process all the elements.

Figure 9-8 How to create and use an associative array

How to create and use an array of arrays

Although JavaScript doesn't let you create multi-dimensional arrays, you can get the same effect by creating an *array of arrays*. To do that, you store arrays in each element of another array. These arrays don't have to be the same length, and you will often see an associative array nested inside a numerically indexed array. In figure 9-9, you can learn how to create and use an array of arrays.

The first example in this figure shows how to create and use an array of arrays. In the first group of statements, the first statement creates an empty array named timesTable. Then, a for loop is used to store empty arrays in the first five elements of the timesTable array. This is the equivalent of coding

```
var timesTable = [ [], [], [], [], [] ]
```

but of course the for loop can be used to create any number of nested arrays.

The second group of statements in the first example fills this array of arrays. To do that, it uses nested for loops. Here, the outer loop uses an index named i that is varied from 0 to 4, and the inner loop uses an index named j that is varied from 0 through 4. Within the inner loop, the value i * j is assigned to the element that's addressed by the values of the indexes i and j. If, for example, i equals 2 and j equals 3, the value 6 is assigned to the fourth element (index 3) in the array that's in the third element (index 2) of the timesTable array.

The third group of statements in the first example shows how to access the elements in this array. Here, the first statement displays the value in the element at index 1 of the array that's in the element at index 1 of the timesTable array. The second statement displays the value in the element at index 3 of the array that's in the element at index 4 of the timesTable array.

The second example in this figure shows how to nest associative arrays in a numerically indexed array. Here, the first group of statements creates an array named invoice that will be numerically indexed. It also creates two empty arrays that will hold item information. They will be associative arrays.

The second group of statements in this example initializes the first associative item array and pushes it onto the invoice array. Then, the third group of statements does the same thing for a different item. Note here that you can't use the first associative array to push both the first and second item onto the invoice array. That's because the push method puts a reference to the item array, rather than a copy of it, in the element of the invoice array. You'll learn more about references in the next chapter.

The fourth group of statements accesses the elements of the nested arrays. Here, the first statement uses the alert method to display the value of the itemCode element that's in the first element (index 0) of the invoice array. This displays 123. Then, the second statement uses the alert method to display the value of the itemName element that's in the second element (index 1) of the invoice array. This displays C++ 2008.

How to create and use an array of arrays

Code that creates an array of arrays

```
var timesTable = [];            // create an empty array
for (var i = 0; i < 5; i++) {   // add 5 elements to the array
    timesTable[i] = [];         // that contain empty arrays
}
```

Code that adds values to the array of arrays

```
for (var i = 0; i < 5; i++) {
    for (var j = 0; j < 5; j++) {
        timesTable[i][j] = i * j;
    }
}
```

Code that refers to elements in the array of arrays

```
alert (timesTable[1][1]);        // displays 1
alert (timesTable[4][3]);        // displays 12
```

How to create and use an array of associative arrays

Code that creates an array

```
var invoice = [];               // create an empty invoice array
var item1 = [], item2 = [];     // create an empty item array
```

Code that creates an associative array and adds it to the invoice array

```
item1["itemCode"] = 123;
item1["itemName"] = "Visual Basic 2008";
item1["itemCost"] = 52.5;
item1["itemQuantity"] = 5;
invoice.push(item1);            // add the item array to the invoice array
```

Code that creates and adds another associative array to the invoice array

```
item2["itemCode"] = 456;
item2["itemName"] = "C++ 2008";
item2["itemCost"] = 52.5;
item2["itemQuantity"] = 2;
invoice.push(item2);  // add the item array to the end of the invoice array
```

Code that refers to the elements in the array of associative arrays

```
alert (invoice[0]["itemCode"]);    // displays 123
alert (invoice[1]["itemName"]);    // displays C++ 2008
```

Description

- Although JavaScript doesn't provide for multi-dimensional arrays, you can get the same effect by creating an *array of arrays*. In an array of arrays, each element in the first array is another array.

- The arrays within an array can be regular arrays or associative arrays.

- To refer to the elements in an array of arrays, you use two index values for each element. The first value is for an element in the primary array. The second value is for an element in the array that's in the element of the primary array.

- If necessary, you can nest arrays beyond the two dimensions that are illustrated here. In other words, you can create an array of arrays of arrays.

Figure 9-9   How to create and use an array of arrays

The Task List Manager application

To show you how some of the skills you've just learned can be used in an application, this chapter concludes by presenting a Task List Manager application.

The user interface and XHTML

Figure 9-10 presents the user interface for the Task List Manager application. Here, the three buttons let the user add a task to the task list, sort the tasks in the task list, and delete a task from the task list. The task list itself is displayed in a text area this is floated to the right side of the web page.

Although the XHTML and CSS code aren't included in this figure, you shouldn't need to refer to it because all you need to know are the ids for the four controls. These are summarized in this figure. You can also review the XTHML and CSS code when you do the exercise for this chapter.

The JavaScript code

To start, the JavaScript code for this application creates an empty array named task_list. This is the array that will be used for the tasks in the task list with one task in each element. Note here that this array is given the same name as the id for the XHTML text area. This shows that it's okay to use the same identifier for an XHTML element and a JavaScript variable.

Next, this code defines the $ function. This is the same function that you've been using throughout this book.

The $ function is followed by a function named update_task_list. This function is called by each of the four event handlers that follow. This function updates the text area to reflect the latest changes to the task_list array. To start, this function tests to see if there are any tasks in the array. If there is none, the text area is set to an empty string.

If there are tasks in the array, this function uses a for-in loop to build a string of numbered tasks that is displayed in the text area. Since users expect lists to start with one instead of zero, the for-in loop adds one to the index number to get the number for each task. Since the index in a for-in loop is always a string, even when numeric indexes are used, the parseInt method must be used to convert the index value to a number before one is added to it. When the loop finishes, the list is displayed in the text area.

The user interface for the Task List Manager application

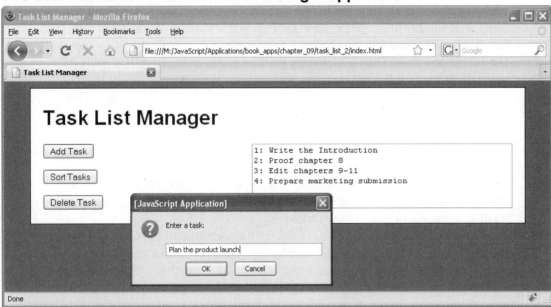

The XHTML ids for the three buttons and the task area

```
add_task                          task_list
sort_tasks
delete_task
```

The JavaScript code for the application

```javascript
var task_list = [];

var $ = function (id) { return document.getElementById(id); }

var update_task_list = function () {
    if ( task_list.length == 0 ) {
        $("task_list").value = "";
    } else {
        var list = "";
        for ( var i in task_list ) {
            list += (parseInt(i)+1) + ": " + task_list[i] + "\n";
        }
        $("task_list").value = list;
    }
}
```

Figure 9-10   The Task List Manager application (part 1 of 2)

The update_task_list function is followed by three event handlers for the click events of the buttons. Each of these event handlers modifies the task_list array and then calls the update_task_list function to display the updated task list. For instance, the add_task_click function uses the prompt method to get the entry for a new task. Then, if the entry isn't an empty string or null, it adds the new task to the task list and calls the update_task_list function. Recall that the result will be null if the user clicks the Cancel button in the prompt dialog box.

Similarly, the sort_tasks_click function uses the sort method to sort the task list. Then, it calls the update_task_list function.

The next event handler is the delete_task_click function. This function starts by checking to see if there are any tasks in the task list. If there is none, this function displays an error message and terminates the event handler with the return statement. But if there are tasks, this function uses the prompt method to get the number of the task to delete.

Then, if the task number is null because the user clicked the Cancel button, the function is terminated without displaying a message. Otherwise, the user entry is converted to an integer and checked to make sure that it is a valid integer that isn't less than 1 and isn't greater than the length of the task_list array. If the entry is invalid, an appropriate message is displayed and the function ends. But if the entry is valid, the entered number is decreased by one so it's a valid index for the array, and the splice method is used to delete the element at that index. Last, the update_task_list function is called to display the updated task list.

In all three of these event handlers, the first statement blurs the button that was clicked to start the event. That removes the focus from the button, which gained the focus when the user clicked on it. If the blur method wasn't issued, the focus would remain on the button, and that button would be activated if the user pressed the Enter key. This is a minor point, but one that can make the application easier to use.

The last function in this program is the event handler for the onload event. First, this function assigns the three event handlers to the click events of the three buttons. Then, it calls the update_task_list function to update the task list display. By doing that, the text area will be reset to an empty string if the user reloads the web page by clicking on the Reload or Refresh button. Otherwise, the task_list array will be set to an empty array when the page is reloaded, but the text area may not be cleared out.

The JavaScript code for the application (continued)

```
var add_task_click = function () {
    $("add_task").blur();
    var task = prompt("Enter a task:", "");
    if ( task != "" && task != null) {
        task_list[task_list.length] = task;
        update_task_list();
    }
}

var sort_tasks_click = function () {
    $("sort_tasks").blur();
    task_list.sort();
    update_task_list();
}

var delete_task_click = function () {
    $("delete_task").blur();
    if ( task_list.length == 0 ) {
        alert("No task to delete.");
        return;
    }

    var to_delete = prompt("Enter the task number to delete:", "");
    if (to_delete == null) { return; }

    to_delete = parseInt(to_delete);
    if ( isNaN(to_delete) ) {
        alert("You did not enter a number.");
        return;
    }
    if ( to_delete < 1 ) {
        alert("The task number is too low.");
        return;
    }
    if ( to_delete > task_list.length ) {
        alert("The task number is too high.");
        return;
    }
    to_delete--;
    task_list.splice(to_delete, 1);
    update_task_list();
}

window.onload = function() {
    $("add_task").onclick = add_task_click;
    $("sort_tasks").onclick = sort_tasks_click;
    $("delete_task").onclick = delete_task_click;
    update_task_list();
}
```

Figure 9-10   The Task List Manager application (part 2 of 2)

Perspective

Arrays are an important part of many JavaScript applications, and JavaScript provides some excellent methods for working with arrays. In the chapters that follow, you'll see other uses of arrays and other ways to work with them. In the next chapter, for example, you'll study an application that uses an array of associate arrays.

Terms

array
element
length
index
sparse array
for loop
for-in statement
for-in loop
associative array
array of arrays

Exercise 9-1 Work with the arrays of the Task List Manager application

This exercise will give you a chance to experiment with arrays and array methods in the context of the Task List Manager application.

Open and test the Task List Manager application

1. From your Firefox browser, open the index.html file in the task_list folder that's in the chapter 9 folder for exercises. This is a modified version of the Task List Manager application with the Sort Tasks button changed to Modify Task and a new button called Promote Task.

2. Test this application by using the Add Task button to enter three tasks and the Delete Task button to delete one of the tasks. These buttons should work as described in the text, but the other two buttons aren't implemented.

3. If you're interested in the XHTML and CSS code, use your text editor to open these files and review the code. Then, use your text editor to open the JavaScript file for this application.

Modify the code so it uses Array methods to add and delete tasks

4. Modify the add_task_click function so it uses the push method to add a new task to the end of the task_list array. Then, test this change.

5. Modify the delete_task_click function so it uses the shift method to remove the task at the start of the list. Then, test this change.

Add event handlers for the modify and promote buttons

6. Add an event handler for the Modify Task button. This event handler should use the prompt method to get the number of the task to be modified. Then, it should use the prompt method to present the text for the selected task and let the user modify that text. Last, this handler should update the task_list array with the modified text and call the update_task_list function to update the text area. Now, test this change.

7. Add an event handler for the Promote Task button. This event handler should use the prompt method to get the number of the task to be promoted. Then, that task should be moved to the start of the task_list array. Last, this handler should call the update_task_list function to update the text area. Now, test this change.

10

How to create and use functions

In chapter 2, you learned how to write simple functions and you've been using functions ever since. Now, this chapter reviews some of the skills you already know and presents the advanced skills that you need to know. As you will see, JavaScript treats all functions as objects, and you're going to learn how to use one of the properties and two of the methods of a function object.

As you read this chapter, keep in mind that there are two reasons for using functions. First, functions provide a way to divide the code of an application into manageable blocks. Second, some functions can be used by more than one application.

Basic skills for working with functions **328**
How to create and call a function 328
How values are passed to functions 330
How lexical scope works 332

Object-oriented skills for working with functions **334**
How to use the arguments property of a function 334
How to use the call and apply methods of a function 336

Advanced skills for working with functions **338**
How closures work with functions 338
How to write recursive functions 340

The Invoice application **342**
The user interface 342
The XHTML file 344
The library file 346
The invoice.js file 350

Perspective **352**

Basic skills for working with functions

This topic reviews the basic skills that you've already learned for working with functions. Then, it adds some new perspective and skills to those basics.

How to create and call a function

Figure 10-1 shows two ways to create a function. The first method is the one that you've been using. It creates an *anonymous function* because it doesn't provide a function name in the function declaration. In this case, you have to decide where to store it. In this example, the function is stored in a variable named display_error and that name is used to call the function.

When you declare an anonymous function, you can pass the declaration as a parameter to another function without having to store it. As you will learn in the next chapter, you can also store an anonymous function as a property of an object so it is treated as a method. The one restriction on the use of anonymous functions is that you must declare them in your code before you can call them, as illustrated in figure 10-3.

The second method in figure 10-1 creates a *named function* by providing a function name in the declaration. This creates the function and stores it in a variable with the name that's provided. The one advantage of this method is that you can place your function declaration anywhere in the code. For instance, you can call the function at the start of the code, but place the declaration at the end of the code. Otherwise, this method works the same as storing an anonymous function in a variable.

The *parameter* list in a function declaration lets you specify variable names for the arguments that will be passed to the function. In this figure, the coin_toss function expects no parameters, so its list is empty, but the avg_of_3 function expects three parameters named x, y, and z.

When you *call* a function, you code the name of the function and a set of parentheses that contains a list of the parameters that you're passing to the function. If no parameters are required, you code an empty set of parentheses.

If a function returns a value, you can use the function call as if it were the value it returns. But if the function doesn't return a value or your code is going to ignore the return value, you can place the function call on a line by itself.

Please note that when you call a function, the parameters are commonly referred to as *arguments* instead of parameters. In other words, you code a parameter list when you declare a function, but you code an argument list when you call a function. From this point forward, then, you'll see these terms used in this way. In practice, though, *parameter* and *argument* are commonly treated as synonyms.

Two ways to create a function

How to create an anonymous function

```
var display_error = function ( message ) {
    alert("Error: " + message);
}
```

How to create a named function

```
function isEven (value) {
    return value % 2 == 0;
}
```

How to specify parameters in a function

A function with no parameters

```
var coin_toss = function() {
    return ( Math.random() > 0.5 ) ? "Heads" : "Tails";
}
```

A function with three parameters

```
var avg_of_3 = function( x, y, z ) {
    return ( x + y + z ) / 3;
}
```

How to call a function

Calling a function that returns a value

```
var average = avg_of_3( 5, 2, 8 );      // average is equal to 5
alert( coin_toss() );                   // displays "Heads" or "Tails"
```

Calling a function that doesn't explicitly return a value

```
display_error("Value out of range");
```

Description

- An *anonymous function* is a function that isn't given a name in its function declaration.
- A *named function* is a function that is given a name in its function declaration.
- If a function requires that one or more values be passed to it, a list of *parameters* is coded within the parentheses for the function declaration.
- When you *call* a function, you code a list of the parameters that will be passed to the function. When they're passed, parameters are commonly referred to as *arguments*.
- All functions return a value. If a function isn't ended by a return statement, the function returns a value of undefined.
- A function call may be used anywhere its return value could be used. Typically, it will be stored in a variable, used in an expression, or passed as a parameter to another function.

Figure 10-1   How to create and call a function

How values are passed to functions

When you pass a number, string, or Boolean value to a function, it is *passed by value*. This means that a copy of the value is sent to the function, not the value itself. As a result, the function can't change the original value.

This is illustrated by the first example in figure 10-2. Here, a string named message is passed by value to the add_timestamp function. Then, this function concatenates a date and time to the string and displays the entire string, which shows that the argument has been changed. However, as the last statement in this example shows, the original message string was never changed because a copy of the string was passed to the function.

In constrast to the primitive types, when you pass an object to a function it is *passed by reference*. This means that a reference to the object is sent to the function instead of a copy of the object. Then, the function changes the object that the reference identifies. As a result, those changes will persist after the function has finished.

This is illustrated by the second example in this figure. Here, an array is passed by reference to the uppercase_first function. Then, this function converts the letters in the first element of the array to uppercase by using the toUpperCase function of a string. In this example, the last statement displays the first element of the original array, which shows that the original array has been changed.

A primitive type is passed to a function by value

A function that receives a string, adds a timestamp to it, and displays it

```
var add_timestamp = function ( text ) {
    var now = new Date();
    text = text + " " + now.toString();
    alert(text);
}
```

Code that calls the function and passes a string argument

```
var message = "Error: Value out of range.";
add_timestamp(message);   // displays message and timestamp
```

Code that displays the value that was passed to the function

```
alert(message);           // message hasn't been changed
```

An object passed is passed to a function by reference

A function that receives an array and changes its first element

```
var uppercase_first = function ( x ) {
    x[0] = x[0].toUpperCase();
}
```

Code that calls the function and passes an array argument

```
var fruits = [ "apple", "orange" ];
uppercase_first(fruits);
```

Code that displays the first element in the array that's passed to the function

```
alert( fruits[0] );       // displays "APPLE" so the array has been changed
```

Description

- The *primitive types* are numbers, strings, and Booleans.

- When a primitive type is passed to a function, it is *passed by value*. This means that a copy of the value is sent to the function. As a result, the function changes the copy, not the original value.

- When an object is passed to a function, it is *passed by reference*. This means that a reference to the object, not the object itself, is sent to the function. As a result, when the function changes the object, it is actually changing the original object.

Figure 10-2   How values are passed to functions

How lexical scope works

Scope in a programming language refers to the visibility of variables and functions. That is, it tells you where in your program you are allowed to use the variables and functions that you've defined. Unlike many programming languages, JavaScript uses *lexical scoping* to determine where you can access variables and functions.

With lexical scope, *global variables* are variables that are defined outside of functions. These variables have *global scope* so they can be used by a function without passing them to the function. In contrast, *local variables* are variables that are defined within functions. They have *local scope*, which means that they can only be used within the functions that define them.

The first example in figure 10-3 illustrates the use of global and local variables. Here, the display_message function displays the contents of a global variable named message. But if that variable hasn't been defined, it creates a local variable named message1 and then displays that variable.

The code that follows first calls the display_message function. But since the message variable hasn't been defined, the function creates the local variable named message1 and displays that. Next, the code creates a global variable named message and calls the display_message function to display it. This shows that a function has access to all global variables. Last, the code tries to display the message1 variable from outside the function. This, however, causes a runtime error, which shows that local variables aren't available outside of the function that defines them.

Another result of lexical scope, is that named functions can be called before they are defined. That's because the JavaScript engine scans your code before it starts executing it and creates the named functions first. Then, it goes back and starts executing your code from the beginning. This is illustrated by the second example in this figure.

In contrast, anonymous functions can't be called before they are defined. This is illustrated by the third example in this figure. In this case, the code will cause a runtime error because the function hasn't been created yet.

If you've programmed in other languages, you may be familiar with *block scope*. In block scope, variables that are created within blocks of code aren't available outside the blocks. With JavaScript, though, this isn't true, as shown by the fourth example in this figure. Here, the can_vote variable that's defined within the block of code in the if clause is available outside of the block.

Global and local scope

A function that creates a local variable and displays a global variable

```
var display_message = function() {
    if ( message == undefined ) {
        var message1 = "Unknown message.";   // message1 has local scope
        alert ( message1 ); }
    else { alert(message); }                 // displays a global variable
}
```

All functions have access to global variables

```
display_message();          // Displays "Unknown message."
var message = "Index out of range.";         // message has global scope
display_message();          // Displays "Index out of range."
```

Local variables are only available to the function that defines them

```
alert ( message1 );         // Runtime error: message1 isn't defined
```

Named functions are created before any code is executed

```
alert( coin_toss() );       // Displays Heads or Tails
function coin_toss() {
    return (Math.random() > 0.5) ? "Heads" : "Tails";
}
```

Anonymous functions are created in sequence when the code is executed

```
alert( coin_toss() );       // Runtime error: coin_toss is not a function
var coin_toss = function () {
    return (Math.random() > 0.5) ? "Heads" : "Tails";
}
```

Variables created inside a block of code can be used outside the block

```
if ( age >= 18 ) {
    var can_vote = "Yes";
    alert ( can_vote );
}
alert( "Voting status: " + can_vote );   // can_vote is available
```

Discussion

- The *scope* of a variable or function determines what code has access to it. Since JavaScript uses *lexical scope*, you can determine the scope of a variable or function by analyzing the code.

- Any variable created outside of a function has *global scope*, and the code in a function has access to these *global variables*.

- Any variable created inside a function has *local scope*, and the code outside a function doesn't have access to these *local variables*.

- Because all named functions are created before any code runs, you can call a named function before it is defined.

- Because anonymous functions are created when the code is executed, a runtime error occurs if the call to an anonymous function comes before the function declaration.

- Variables that are created within blocks of code are available outside the blocks.

Figure 10-3   How lexical scope works

Object-oriented skills for working with functions

In JavaScript, all functions are objects. This means that functions have properties and methods, just like other objects. In this topic, you'll learn how to use one property and two methods of a function object.

How to use the arguments property of a function

When you call a function in JavaScript, the arguments are stored in the parameters of the function declaration. This is similar to other programming languages. What sets JavaScript apart, however, is that the parameters are also stored in the arguments property of the function object.

This arguments property is similar to an array. Within this property, each of the arguments that was passed to the function is stored in an element starting with index 0. Then, you can access these elements by using indexes. Note, however, that this property isn't a true array object, so you can't use the properties and methods of an array that you learned about in chapter 9.

The first example in figure 10-4 shows how to use the arguments property to access an argument that's passed to a function. Here, the element at index 0 in the arguments property is used in an expression that returns true if the argument is divisible by 2 with no remainder.

The second example shows how to use the length property of the arguments property to determine the number of arguments passed to a function. Here, the count_args function just displays the number of arguments that are passed to it.

One of the benefits that you get from using the arguments property is that you can create functions that can receive fewer arguments than the parameter list calls for. This lets you create functions with optional parameters.

This is illustrated by the third example in this figure. Here, the pad_left function lists three parameters, but the last parameter is optional. To provide for that, the function first checks to make sure that at least two arguments are passed to it. If not, an empty string is returned. Next, if the function received only two arguments, the third parameter (pad) is set to a space character. Last, the function uses a while loop to add the pad character to the text argument while the length of that string is less than the width argument. Then, the function returns the padded text.

By using the arguments property, a function can also process more arguments than the parameter list calls for. This is illustrated by the fourth example in this figure. Here, the function has no parameters in its list, but it will calculate the average of all of the arguments that are passed to it.

A function that uses the arguments property to get an argument

```
var isEven = function (value) {
    return arguments[0] % 2 == 0;
}
```

How to determine the number of arguments that have been passed

```
var count_args = function () {
    alert("Number of arguments: " + arguments.length );
}

count_args( 1, "Text", true );        // Displays "Number of arguments: 3"
```

Calling a function with fewer arguments than the named parameters

```
var pad_left = function(text, width, pad) {
    if ( arguments.length <  2 ) return "";
    if ( arguments.length == 2 ) pad = " ";
    while( text.length < width ) {
        text = pad + text;
    }
    return text;
}

alert( "Welcome to " + pad_left("JavaScript", 15) );
// Displays "Welcome to      JavaScript"
```

Calling a function with more arguments than the named parameters

```
var average = function () {
    if ( arguments.length == 0 ) return 0;
    var sum = 0;
    for ( var i = 0; i < arguments.length; i++) {
        sum += arguments[i];
    }
    return sum / arguments.length;
}

alert ( average(8, 15, 5, 10) ); // Displays 9.5
```

Discussion

- In JavaScript, all functions are objects, and all of the arguments passed to a function are stored in the arguments property of the function object.

- The arguments property is similar to an array, so you can use an index to access its elements. However, the arguments property isn't a true array, so you can't use the array methods of chapter 9 with it.

- If a function uses the arguments property to get the arguments that are passed to it, the calling statement can pass more or fewer arguments than the parameter list specifies.

Figure 10-4   How to use the arguments property of a function

How to use the call and apply methods of a function

When a function is called, it has an internal parameter that can be referred to by the *this* keyword. The value that the this keyword represents depends on how the function is called. When you call a function normally, the this keyword is set to the global variable, which is the window object. But when you call a function by using either the call or apply method of the function, you can use the first argument to set the object that you want to use for the this keyword.

The first example in figure 10-5 presents a function called this_test that illustrates the use of the this keyword. Here, the if statement uses the strict identity operator to check whether the this keyword and window are equivalent. If so, the function displays a message that indicates that. Otherwise, the else clause displays the value of the this keyword.

The second example shows three calls to the this_test function. The first one is a normal call so the this keyword is equivalent to the window object and a message to that effect is displayed. But the second call uses the call method of the function to call the function, and it uses the first parameter of that method to change the this parameter to a string. As a result, the alert statement in the else clause of the function displays the this parameter, which is "Test String". Similarly, the third call in this group uses the apply method of the function to call the function, and it uses the first parameter to change the this parameter to a number. As a result, the function displays 456.72.

With both the call and the apply methods, you use the first argument to set the object for the this keyword. But with the call method, you pass any other arguments to the function in the arguments list. And with the apply method, you pass any other arguments in an array that's used as the second argument.

The third and fourth examples in this figure show how to use the call and apply methods to call the log method of Firebug's console object, which you learned about figures 3-9 and 3-10 in chapter 3. In the third example, console is used as the first argument and the variable named message is used as the second argument. In the fourth example, console is used as the first argument and an array named arguments is used as the second argument. In both cases, since log is a method of the console object, it needs to have the this keyword be the console object, rather than the window object.

Both of these calls are made within a wrapper function named $log, which uses the typeof operator to check that Firebug's console and its log method are available before the calls to the method are made. In the fourth example, if the log method isn't available, the arguments in the array are concatenated into a string and that string is displayed. Remember here that the arguments property isn't a true array, so you can't use the join method of an array to join the elements together. Instead, you have to use a for loop to join them.

When you learn how functions are used as object methods in the next chapter, keep in mind that JavaScript uses the call method internally when you call a method of an object. Also, JavaScript passes the object as the first argument of the call method so the this keyword in the method refers to that object rather than the global object.

A function that uses the this keyword

```
var this_test = function () {
    if (this === window) {
        alert("This is the window object.");
    } else {
        alert( this );
    }
}
```

How call a function using the call and apply methods

```
this_test();                          // Displays "This is the window object."
this_test.call("Test String"); // Displays "Test String"
this_test.apply(456.72);        // Displays 456.72
```

A $log function that uses the call method to call the console.log function

```
var $log = function (message) {
    if (typeof console == "object" && typeof console.log == "function") {
        console.log.call(console, message);    // sets this to console
    } else {
        alert(message);
    }
}
```

A $log function that uses the apply method to call the console.log function

```
var $log = function () {
    if (typeof console == "object" && typeof console.log == "function") {
        console.log.apply(console, arguments); // sets this to console
    } else {
        var message = "";
        for ( var i = 0; i < arguments.length; i++ ) {
            message += arguments[i] + " ";
        }
        alert(message);
    }
}
```

Description

- When a function is called, it has an internal parameter that can be referred to by the *this* keyword. The value of the this parameter depends on how the function is called.

- When a function is called normally, the value of the this parameter is the global object, which is the window object.

- The call and apply methods of a function let you call the function and also set the object that will be used as the function's this parameter by sending it as the first argument.

- When you use the apply method to call a function, you pass the other arguments in an array as the second argument instead of listing them individually.

Note

- The typeof operator lets you determine the type of a variable. It evaluates to "number", "string", or "boolean" for the primitive values; to "object" for objects and nulls; to "function" for functions; and to "undefined" if the operand is undefined.

Figure 10-5   How to use the call and apply methods of a function

Advanced skills for working with functions

Next, this chapter presents two advanced skills for working with functions. If you're new to programming, you can skip them now and come back to them when you need them.

How closures work with functions

In JavaScript, when one function is nested inside another function, the inner function has access to the outer function's variables. This is called *closure*. As long as the inner function exists, the outer function's variables also exist, even if the outer function has finished running. Later, when the external reference to the inner function is deleted, the outer function and its variables are also removed.

There are two common ways to ensure that an inner function exists after the outer function is done. One way is to return a reference to the inner function as the result of the outer function. The other way is to store a reference to the inner function somewhere outside the outer function. This can be a global variable, a property of another object, or as an element's event handler.

In section 3, you'll see that closures are commonly used to ensure that event handlers can correctly access the properties of an object that controls an application. You'll also see that closures are used to limit access to variables. This is useful in creating counters and controlling animation.

For now, figure 10-6 shows an example of how closure is used with two counters. In the XHTML code, you can see the tags for two buttons for updating the counters and two span tags named counter_a and counter_b that display the counter values.

The JavaScript code starts with the usual $ function and a function named make_counter. To start, the make_counter function defines an internal variable named count that is initialized to zero and a nested function named increment that adds one to count and returns the new value. Then, the make_counter function returns a reference to the internal increment function. As long as this reference to the internal increment function exists, the count variable will exist and its value will be retained.

Next, two counter variables are created by calling the make_counter function and storing the results in the variables. Since the call to make_counter returns a function, counter_a_increment and counter_b_increment now store functions that refer to different increment functions and count variables.

Then, the code creates event handlers for the click events of the two buttons. These event handlers call the appropriate increment functions and display the results in the appropriate span tags. Last, the handler for the onload event assigns the event handlers for the buttons to their click events.

When the code runs, the counters are initially set to zero. Then, when the user clicks a button, the increment function is executed, one is added to the appropriate counter variable, and the counter value is displayed. These counter variables are maintained as long as there is a reference to the internal increment function.

XHTML for two counters

```
<p><span id="counter_a">0</span></p>
<p><input type="button" value="Increment" id="button_a" /></p>
<p><span id="counter_b">0</span></p>
<p><input type="button" value="Increment" id="button_b" /></p>
```

The JavaScript code

```
var $ = function (id) { return document.getElementById(id); }

var make_counter = function () {
    var count = 0;
    var increment = function () {
        count++;
        return count;
    }
    return increment;
}

var counter_a_increment = make_counter();
var counter_b_increment = make_counter();

var button_a_click = function() {
    $("counter_a").firstChild.nodeValue = counter_a_increment();
}

var button_b_click = function() {
    $("counter_b").firstChild.nodeValue = counter_b_increment();
}

window.onload = function () {
    $("button_a").onclick = button_a_click;
    $("button_b").onclick = button_b_click;
}
```

The code running in a web browser

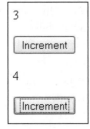

Description

- In JavaScript, a nested function has access to the outer function's variables. This is called *closure*.

- The outer function's variables are available as long as there is a reference to the inner function.

Figure 10-6   How closures work with functions

How to write recursive functions

A *recursive function* is a function that calls itself, perhaps multiple times, to solve a problem. To illustrate, figure 10-7 presents a recursive function that searches an array of numbers for a specific value by using a *binary search*.

To put that in perspective, a sequential search starts with the first element in an array and continues sequentially until the value is found. So on average, the search goes through half the elements before it finds the value. If, for example, an array contains 256 elements, the search takes an average of 128 comparisons. And if the size of the array doubles, the average search time doubles.

In contrast, a binary search starts at the midpoint of the array. Then, if the searched for value is higher than the value at the midpoint, the search continues at the midpoint of the upper half of the array. Or, if the value is lower, the search continues at the midpoint of the lower half of the array. The search continues by halving the number of elements until the value is found.

In this type of search, half of the array is discarded with each comparison. As a result, searching an array of 256 items takes at most 9 comparisons. And if the size of the array doubles, the search takes just one more comparison.

In this figure, you can see how a recursive function does a binary search. To start, this code uses the random_number function that was presented in chapter 7 to create an array of 256 random numbers that range from 1 through 1000. Then, this code uses the sort method of an array to sort the numbers into numeric order. This sorting is required for a binary search.

Next, this figure presents the code for the search function. Here, the needle parameter stores the value to search for; the haystack parameter stores the array to be searched; the lo parameter stores the index of the lowest position that should be searched; and the hi parameter hi stores the index of the highest position that should be searched.

In the body of this function, the code first checks the number of arguments passed to the function. If only two arguments are passed, it initializes lo and hi to the first and last elements of the array. Next, it calculates the midpoint of the array. Then, if hi is less than lo it returns -1. This means that all the elements have been discarded and the value hasn't been found. Next, it checks to see if hi and lo are the same. If they are, there is only one element to check and it is tested to see if it is the right value. Then, either the position or -1 is returned.

Finally, the middle value is compared to the value being searched for. If they are the same, the position is returned. Otherwise, if the needle is less than the middle element, the search function is called again with a changed hi argument so the search is repeated on the lower half of the remaining part of the array. Or, if the needle is greater than the middle element, the search function is called with a changed lo argument so the search is repeated on the upper half of the array. This is where the function becomes recursive.

The last part of this figure shows the code for using the search function. Here, the prompt method is used to get a number from the user. Then, the search function is called with that number and the numbers array as arguments. This is repeated until the user clicks the Cancel button.

Code that creates a sorted array of 256 numbers

```
var numbers = [];
for ( var i = 0; i < 256; i++) {
    numbers[i] = random_number(1,1000);
}

var numeric_order = function (a,b) {
    if ( a < b ) return -1;
    if ( a > b ) return 1;
    return 0;
}
numbers.sort(numeric_order);
```

A recursive function that uses a binary search to search the array

```
var search = function(needle, haystack, lo, hi) {
    if ( arguments.length == 2 ) {
        lo = 0;
        hi = haystack.length - 1;
    }

    var middle = Math.ceil( (hi + lo) / 2 );

    if ( hi < lo ) return -1;
    if ( hi == lo ) {
        if ( needle == haystack[middle] ) {
            return middle;
        } else {
            return -1;
        }
    }

    if ( needle == haystack[middle] ) {
        return middle;
    } else if ( needle < haystack[middle] ) {
        return search( needle, haystack, lo, middle - 1);
    } else if ( needle > haystack[middle] ) {
        return search( needle, haystack, middle + 1, hi);
    }
}
```

A loop that searches for the numbers entered by the user

```
var number, position;
do {
    number = prompt("Number to find (click cancel to quit):");
    if ( number == null ) break;
    number = parseInt(number);
    if ( isNaN(number) ) continue;
    position = search(number, numbers);
    if ( position == -1 ) {
        alert(number + " is not in the list.");
    } else {
        alert(number + " was found at position " + position + ".");
    }
} while ( true );
```

Figure 10-7   How to write recursive functions

The Invoice application

Figures 10-8 though 10-11 present an Invoice application that illustrates the use of functions. This application also illustrates the use of two JavaScript files for a single application. The first file is a library file that holds helper or utility functions. The second file contains the JavaScript code that interacts with the user. This file uses the functions in the library file. As you will see, dividing the functions of an application into two or more files can help keep the functions organized.

The user interface

Figure 10-8 presents the user interface for the Invoice application. This application lets the user enter the item code, item name, item cost, and quantity for each line item of an invoice. As each line item is added to the invoice, the application calculates the line cost (quantity times item cost), the subtotal of all the line items, the sales tax, and the invoice total. In this example, the user has entered three line items and the first two fields for a fourth line item.

Because this application doesn't get each item name and cost from a database and doesn't save the invoice data to a database, this isn't really an invoicing application. To do that, you would need to use a server–side application. Instead, you can think of this as a scratch pad application that lets you create a dummy invoice that you could use to give a customer a cost estimate.

The Invoice application in the web browser

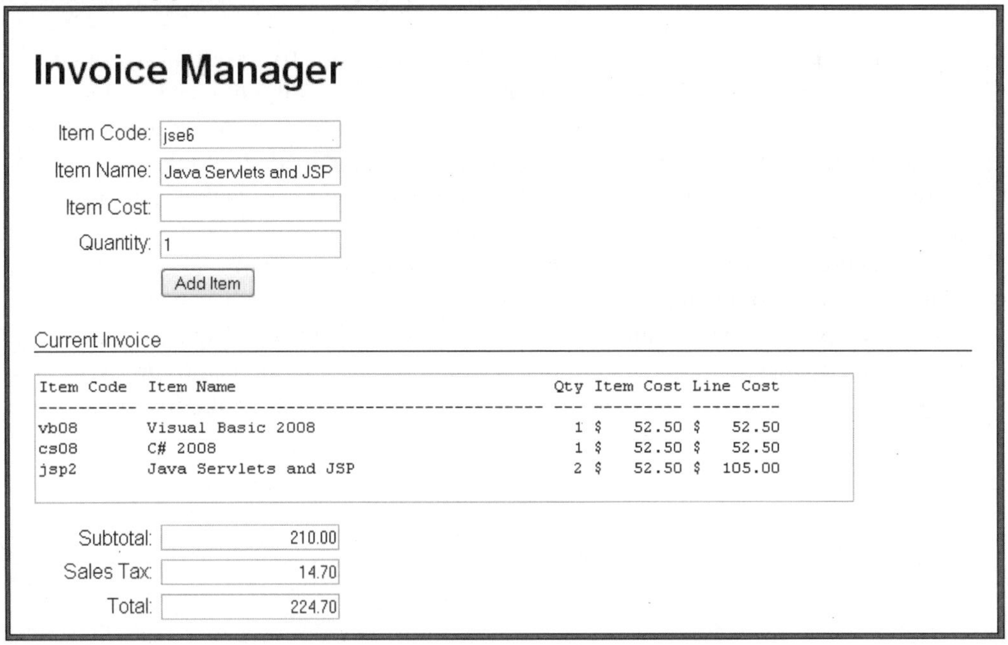

Invoice Manager

Item Code: `jse6`

Item Name: `Java Servlets and JSP`

Item Cost: ` `

Quantity: `1`

[Add Item]

Current Invoice

```
Item Code   Item Name                           Qty Item Cost Line Cost
----------  ----------------------------------- --- --------- ---------
vb08        Visual Basic 2008                     1 $   52.50 $    52.50
cs08        C# 2008                               1 $   52.50 $    52.50
jsp2        Java Servlets and JSP                 2 $   52.50 $   105.00
```

Subtotal: `210.00`

Sales Tax: `14.70`

Total: `224.70`

Description

- This application lets you enter the items for an invoice so you can see what the cost for each line item will be as well as the subtotal, sales tax, and total cost for all of the line items.

- To enter each line item, you enter the appropriate data into the four text boxes and click the Add Item button. The line item is then added to the invoice and the line cost, subtotal, sales tax, and total are calculated.

Figure 10-8   The user interface of the Invoice application

The XHTML file

Figure 10-9 presents the XHTML for this application. To start, please notice that the script tags identify two JavaScript files. The first is the library file; the second is the main file that uses the functions in the library file. When the page is loaded into the browser, the JavaScript in these files is loaded into the browser in the sequence in which the files are listed. The result is the same as if all of the JavaScript was stored in a single file.

In the body of the XHTML, the code is divided into two parts. The first part contains the form fields for adding an item to the invoice. It consists of four text fields and a button. The second part contains the form fields for displaying the invoice: a text area and three text fields. If you refer back to the last figure, you can see that two heading lines and the line items are displayed in the text area.

The XHTML file

```
<!DOCTYPE html PUBLIC "-//W3C//DTD XHTML 1.0 Transitional//EN"
    "http://www.w3.org/TR/xhtml1/DTD/xhtml1-transitional.dtd">
<html xmlns="http://www.w3.org/1999/xhtml">
<head>
<title>Invoice Manager</title>
<link rel="stylesheet" type="text/css" href="invoice.css" />
<script type="text/javascript" src="invoice_library.js"></script>
<script type="text/javascript" src="invoice.js"></script>
</head>

<body>
<div id="content">

    <h1>Invoice Manager</h1>
    <div class="formLayout">
        <label for="item_code">Item Code:</label>
            <input type="text" name="item_code" id="item_code" /><br />
        <label for="item_name">Item Name:</label>
            <input type="text" name="item_name" id="item_name" /><br />
        <label for="item_cost">Item Cost:</label>
            <input type="text" name="item_cost" id="item_cost" /><br />
        <label for="item_qty">Quantity:</label>
            <input type="text" name="item_qty" id="item_qty"
                    value="1" /><br />
        <label> </label>
            <input type="button" id="item_add"
                value="Add Item" /><br />
    </div>

    <p class="startInvoice">Current Invoice</p>
    <p><textarea id="item_list" rows="5" cols="80"></textarea></p>
    <div class="formLayout">
        <label for="subtotal">Subtotal:</label>
            <input type="text" name="subtotal" id="subtotal"
                    class="disabled" disabled="disabled" /><br />
        <label for="sales_tax">Sales Tax:</label>
            <input type="text" name="sales_tax" id="sales_tax"
                    class="disabled" disabled="disabled" /><br />
        <label for="total">Total:</label>
            <input type="text" name="total" id="total"
                    class="disabled" disabled="disabled" /><br />
    </div>
</body>
</html>
```

Figure 10-9   The XHTML for the Invoice application

The library file

A *library file* can be used to store the helper or utility functions that an application requires. Often, these functions can be used by more than one application. For instance, the first two functions in the library file of figure 10-10 are general-purpose functions that let you pad a string with spaces or other characters on the left or right.

If you study the pad_left function, you'll see that it has text, width, and pad parameters. The first parameter is the string to be padded. The second parameter is the width that the string should be padded to. And the third parameter, which is optional, is the character to be used for the padding. If this parameter is omitted, a space is used.

In the body of this function, the arguments property of the function is used to make sure that the right number of arguments are passed to the function. If less than two or more than three are passed, this function returns an empty string. If two are passed, the pad parameter is set to a space.

Once that checking is done, the text parameter is converted to a string (in case it isn't one already), and it's assigned to a variable named result. Next, a while loop pads out the result variable, and then it is returned to the calling statement.

The pad_right function is like the pad_left function. The only difference is in the while loop where the pad character is added to the end of the result rather than the start.

The invoice_library.js file   **Page 1**

```javascript
var pad_left = function(text, width, pad) {
    if ( arguments.length < 2 || arguments.length > 3 ) {
        return "";
    }
    if ( arguments.length == 2 ) {
        pad = " ";
    }
    var result = text.toString();
    while ( result.length < width ) {
        result = pad + result;
    }
    return result;
}

var pad_right = function(text, width, pad) {
    if ( arguments.length < 2 || arguments.length > 3 ) {
        return "";
    }
    if ( arguments.length == 2 ) {
        pad = " ";
    }

    var result = text.toString();
    while ( result.length < width ) {
        result = result + pad;
    }
    return result;
}
```

Figure 10-10   The library file for the Invoice application (part 1 of 2)

The third function in the library file is the get_item_list function. This function has one parameter that receives an array that contains the line items of an invoice. It returns a formatted string that contains the line item data for the invoice. This string can then be displayed in the text area of the application.

In the body of this function, you can see that the pad_left and pad_right functions are used to align the data. First, this function builds a heading for the line items that consists of field names in the first line and a series of dashes in the second line. Then, this function uses a for-in loop to format each of the line items for the invoice.

The next three functions also receive the array that contains the line items for the invoice. Then, they calculate and return the subtotal, sales tax, and total for the invoice.

Unlike the first three functions in this library file, the last four functions probably couldn't be used by other applications. That's because these functions have details that are specific to this application. With just a few modifications, though, these functions could be used by any application that uses an array of associative arrays that represent line items.

The invoice_library.js file

```javascript
var get_item_list = function(item_list) {
    if ( item_list.length == 0 ) {
        return "";
    }

    var list, line_cost, item_cost, item_count = 0;
    list  = pad_right("Item Code", 10) + " ";
    list += pad_right("Item Name", 40) + " ";
    list += "Qty ";
    list += "Item Cost ";
    list += "Line Cost\n";
    list += pad_right("", 10, "-") + " ";
    list += pad_right("", 40, "-") + " ";
    list += "- ";
    list += pad_right("", 9, "-") + " ";
    list += pad_right("", 9, "-") + "\n";

    for ( var i in item_list ) {
        item_cost = parseFloat(item_list[i]["item_cost"]);
        line_cost = item_list[i]["item_qty"] * item_list[i]["item_cost"];
        list += pad_right(item_list[i]["item_code"], 10) + " ";
        list += pad_right(item_list[i]["item_name"], 40) + " ";
        list += pad_left (item_list[i]["item_qty"],   3) + " ";
        list += "$" + pad_left(item_cost.toFixed(2),  8) + " ";
        list += "$" + pad_left(line_cost.toFixed(2),  8) + "\n";
    }
    return list;
}

var get_subtotal = function (item_list) {
    var subtotal = 0, line_cost;
    for ( var i in item_list ) {
        line_cost = item_list[i]["item_qty"] * item_list[i]["item_cost"];
        subtotal += parseFloat( line_cost.toFixed(2) );
    }
    return subtotal;
}

var get_sales_tax = function (item_list) {
    var subtotal = get_subtotal(item_list);
    var sales_tax = subtotal * 0.07;
    return parseFloat( sales_tax.toFixed(2) );
}

var get_total = function (item_list) {
    var total = get_subtotal(item_list) + get_sales_tax(item_list);
    return parseFloat( total.toFixed(2) );
}
```

Figure 10-10   The library file for the Invoice application (part 2 of 2)

The invoice.js file

The invoice.js file contains the code that interacts with the user. To start, it defines a global array named invoice and the standard $ function. This code is followed by an update_display function and event-handler functions for the click event of the Add Item button and the onload event of the window.

The update_display function has no parameters. It displays the invoice data and gets the item form ready for the next line item. To display the data, it calls the four "get" functions that are defined in the library file. Note here that these functions are available just as if they were coded in the same file. Then, this function resets the fields in the form and moves the focus to the first field.

The item_add_click function is the event handler for the Add Item button. It creates an empty item array and copies the values from the form fields into associative elements in this array. Next, it checks to make sure that the item code and name aren't empty and that the cost and quantity are numbers. Then, it pushes the item array onto the invoice array. Last, it calls the update_display function to update the display.

The last function in this file is the one for the window's onload event. Like other onload event handlers, it assigns a function to the click event of the one button on the form and moves the focus to the first entry field on the form.

Unlike the functions in the library files, the last three functions in this file are specific to this application. In particular, they use the ids of the XHTML elements. As a result, these functions can't be used by other applications without significant changes. That's why these functions are separated from the functions in the library file.

The invoice.js file

```javascript
var invoice = [];

var $ = function(id) { return document.getElementById(id); }

var update_display = function () {
    $("item_list").value = get_item_list(invoice);
    $("subtotal").value = get_subtotal(invoice).toFixed(2);
    $("sales_tax").value = get_sales_tax(invoice).toFixed(2);
    $("total").value = get_total(invoice).toFixed(2);

    $("item_code").value = "";
    $("item_name").value = "";
    $("item_cost").value = "";
    $("item_qty").value = "1";

    $("item_code").focus();
}

var item_add_click = function() {
    var item = [];
    item["item_code"] = $("item_code").value;
    item["item_name"] = $("item_name").value;
    item["item_cost"] = parseFloat($("item_cost").value);
    item["item_qty"]  = parseInt($("item_qty").value);

    if ( item["item_code"] == "" ) return;
    if ( item["item_name"] == "" ) return;
    if ( isNaN(item["item_cost"]) ) return;
    if ( isNaN(item["item_qty"] ) ) return;

    invoice.push(item);
    update_display();
}

window.onload = function () {
    $("item_add").onclick = item_add_click;
    $("item_code").focus();
}
```

Figure 10-11   The invoice.js file for the Invoice application

Perspective

Now that you have completed this chapter, you should have all the skills that you need for using functions. In particular, you should be able to use the arguments property of a function object to handle optional arguments. You should understand how primitive variables and objects are passed to a function and how lexical scope works. And you should understand how a library file can be used to separate reusable functions from the code that interacts with the user.

In the next chapter, you'll see that functions play a central role in JavaScript's object-oriented architecture. In fact, it is through functions that JavaScript creates new types of objects.

Terms

anonymous function	global scope
named function	global variable
parameter	local scope
calling a function	local variable
argument	block scope
primitive type	closure
passed by value	recursive function
passed by reference	binary search
scope	library file
lexical scope	

Exercise 10-1   Work with the Invoice application

This exercise will give you a chance to experiment with functions and function calls in the Invoice application that was presented in this chapter.

Open, test, and enhance the Invoice application

1. From your Firefox browser, open the index.html file in the invoice folder that's in the chapter 10 folder for exercises. Then, test this application by adding two line items to the form. To do that, you can enter whatever data you want for the item code and description, but you must enter a valid item cost and quantity.

2. Click the Reload button in the Firefox browser to start a new invoice. Note that this doesn't clear the data from the last invoice.

3. Use your text editor to open the two JavaScript files for this application. Then, modify the event handler for the onload event so it clears the invoice data when the Reload button is clicked. To do that, you just need to call one of the functions that has already been defined from the onload event handler.

Use the arguments property and call method of a function

4. Modify the pad_left function so it uses its arguments property to get the first two arguments that are passed to it.

5. Modify the last statement in the item_add_click function so it calls the update_display function by using the call method of that function (see figure 10-5). In this case, you don't need to pass any arguments because you don't need to change the object that's used for the this parameter.

6. When you're through experimenting, close the files.

Exercise 10-2   Experiment with the binary search application

This exercise will give you a chance to experiment with global and local variables in the context of the binary search application, which uses a recursive function.

1. From your Firefox browser, open the index.html file in the recursive_search folder that's in the chapter 10 folder for exercises. Then, test this application by entering search values that can range from 1 through 512. To end the application, click the Cancel button.

2. Use your text editor to open the index.html file for this application, which contains the JavaScript code for this application.

3. Modify this application so it uses a global variable to count the number of times the search function is executed for each number that it searches for. Then, use the alert method to display the value of the counter after the number is found or not found in a message like this:

    `The search function was called 8 times.`

    To do this right, the counter needs to be reset to zero at the start of each search and incremented each time the search function is called.

4. Add statements to the search function that use the alert method to display the last values of lo and hi when the number is found.

5. If you want to prove to yourself that the parameters of a function have local scope, try to display the last values of lo and hi from outside the search function.

6. When you're through experimenting, close the files.

11

How to create and use objects

In earlier chapters, you learned how to use native JavaScript object types such as the String, Number, Date, and Array object types. Now, you'll learn how to create and use your own objects and object types. Along the way, you'll see how the use of your own objects can help you improve the code within a JavaScript application.

Basic skills for working with objects **356**
How to create and use the native object types 356
How to create objects of the Object type 358
How to extend, modify, or delete an object 360
How to create and use your own object types 362

Advanced skills for working with objects **364**
How to inherit properties and methods from another object type 364
How to add methods to the JavaScript object types 366
How to create cascading methods 368
How to use the for-in statement with objects 370
How to use the in, instanceof, and typeof operators 372

The Invoice application **374**
The user interface 374
The XHTML file 376
The library file 378
The invoice.js file 382

Perspective **384**

Basic skills for working with objects

This topic will show you how to create and use objects in JavaScript. That will include objects of the Object type as well as objects of your own object types.

How to create and use the native object types

In contrast to other languages, JavaScript has the flat hierarchy of native *object types* that's shown by the chart in figure 11-1. At the top level is the Object object type. At the next level are the other native object types like the String, Number, Boolean, Date, Array, and Function object types that you've already learned about.

This hierarchy means that all of the object types at the second level *inherit* the properties and methods of the Object type. This means that every object type can use the properties and methods of the Object type. For instance, the Object type has a toString method that converts an object to a string. However, because this toString method is so general, most of the other object types override this toString method with a specific method that converts the object type to a string.

In fact, the Object type in JavaScript doesn't offer any properties or methods that are commonly used in typical applications. Later in this chapter, though, you'll see how one of the methods of the Object type can be used.

After the hierarchy chart, this figure shows how to create a new object from one of the native object types by using the *new* keyword. Then, this figure shows how to create new objects for the primitive object types: String, Number, and Boolean. When you create a string, number, or Boolean value and store it in a variable, JavaScript automatically converts these values to native objects. Note, however, that you can also use the new keyword to create these objects.

Last, this figure shows the two ways that you can use to access properties and methods. First, you can code the object name, the dot operator, and the property or method name. Second, you can code the object name followed by the property or method name within parentheses. Note, however, that when you use brackets, the property or method name must be in quotes. Otherwise, JavaScript will interpret the identifier as a variable name rather than a property name.

Note too that if you're accessing a method, you must follow it with a set of parentheses that lists the arguments. This is required whether you use the dot operator or brackets to identify the method, even if the method doesn't require any arguments. If you omit the parentheses, you'll get a reference to the method rather than a call for the method.

The JavaScript hierarchy of some of the native object types

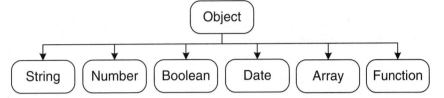

The syntax for creating a new object of a native type

```
var variable_name = new Object_Type(arguments);
```

How to create a new object of the Date type

```
var today = new Date();
```

How to create a new object of the Object type

```
var invoice = new Object();
```

How to create new String, Number, and Boolean objects

How to create a new object of the String type

```
var lastName = "Harris";      // Same as = new String("Harris");
```

How to create a new object of the Number type

```
var taxRate = .0875;          // Same as = new Number(.0875);
```

How to create a new object of the Boolean type

```
var validFlag = true;         // Same as = new Boolean(true);
```

How to use the properties and methods of the native object types

How to use the length property of a String object

```
length = lastName.length;               // Same as lastName["length"]
```

How to use the toFixed method of a Number object

```
formattedRate = taxRate.toFixed(4);   // Same as taxRate["toFixed"](4)
```

Description

- JavaScript provides a two-level hierarchy of *object types*. The top-level consists of the Object object type. The next level consists of types like String, Number, Date, and Array.

- All object types at the second level *inherit* the properties and methods of the Object object type. One of these is the toString method, which converts the object to a string.

- All native object types at the second level also provide properties and methods for working with those objects. Most of these object types have a toString method that overrides the toString method that's inherited from the Object type.

- When you create variables for string, number, or Boolean values, JavaScript converts them to the native object types.

- To access a property or method, you can use the dot operator or brackets.

Figure 11-1   How to create and use the native object types

How to create objects of the Object type

One way to create your own objects is to create objects of the Object type. Figure 11-2 shows that you can do that by using the new keyword with the Object type or by coding a set of braces. Both methods create a new object of the Object type that can be stored in a variable.

When you use braces to create an object of the Object type, you can also initialize properties or methods of that object. In example 1, the invoice object is initialized with one property named taxRate that has a value of 0.0875. As you can see, the property name and value must be separated by a colon.

In example 2, the invoice object is initialized with one method named getSalesTax. Here, the method name is followed by a colon and an anonymous function that does the task of the method. What's happening here is that a function is stored as a property of the object, which turns it into a method of the object.

In example 3, the invoice object is initialized with two methods and two properties. Here, the property and value pairs must be separated by commas.

After you create the properties and methods for an object, you can use them just as you use the properties and methods of native objects. That means you can use either the dot operator or brackets to refer to the properties and methods.

The last set of examples in this figures shows that you can also *nest* one object within another. In this case, a terms object is nested within an invoice object. To do that, the invoice object is initialized with one property named terms, and the terms property is itself an object that is initialized with two properties named taxRate and dueDays.

To access the properties and methods of a nested object, you chain the property names with dot operators or square brackets. You can also can mix dot operators and square brackets when accessing nested objects. In practice, though, the dot operator is commonly used because it's easier to code and easier to understand.

Two ways to create an empty object of the Object type

Using the new keyword

```
var invoice = new Object();
```

Using braces

```
var invoice = {};
```

How to initialize a new object with properties and methods

Example 1: How to initialize a new object with one property

```
var invoice = { taxRate: 0.0875 };
```

Example 2: How to initialize a new object with one method

```
var invoice = {
    getSalesTax: function( subtotal ) {
        return ( subtotal * invoice.taxRate );
    }
}
```

Example 3: How to initialize a new object with properties and methods

```
var invoice = {
    getSalesTax: function( subtotal ) {
        return ( subtotal * invoice.taxRate );
    },
    getTotal: function ( subtotal, salesTax ) {
        return subtotal + salesTax;
    },
    taxRate: 0.0875,
    dueDays: 30
}
```

How to nest objects and refer to the nested properties and methods

How to nest one object within another

```
var invoice = {
    terms: {
        taxRate: 0.0875,
        dueDays: 30
    }
}
```

How to refer to the properties and methods of a nested object

```
alert( invoice.terms.taxRate );          // Displays 0.0875
alert( invoice["terms"]["dueDays"] );    // Displays 30
```

Description

- To create a new object of the Object type, you can use the *new Object* keywords or code a set of braces.

- When you use a set of braces to create a new Object object, you can add properties and methods to the object by coding pairs of property names and values that are separated by colons. When a property name is paired with a function, the function becomes a method.

- If necessary, you can *nest* one object inside another.

Figure 11-2   How to create objects of the Object type

How to extend, modify, or delete an object

After you create an object, you can extend the object by adding new properties and methods to it. This is illustrated by the first set of examples in figure 11-3. To add a property, you just assign a new property to an object and give it a value. To add a method, you just assign a new property and code an anonymous function as its value. Here again, you can use the dot operator or brackets to refer to a property.

Once a property or method has been created, you can modify it by assigning a new value to it. This is illustrated by the second example in this figure. You can also change a method by assigning a new function declaration to it.

To remove a property from an object, you can use the delete operator as shown in the third example. Here, this operator is used to remove the taxRate property from the invoice object. Once deleted, the property has a value of undefined, just as though it had never been created.

When you create an object and store it in a variable, you need to realize that JavaScript actually stores a reference to the object in the variable. This is illustrated by the diagram in this figure. In this case, both the today and now variables refer to the same Date object.

This means that if you change the Date object that the today variable refers to, the change will also be seen through the now variable. If, for example, you use the setFullYear method of the today variable to set the year to 2010, the getFullYear method of the now variable will get 2010. This is the same mechanism that is used with you pass an argument by reference.

After you're through with an object in your code, you can free up the memory it used by deleting the object. To do that, you use the delete operator followed by the object name. For instance, the next example in this figure shows how to delete the object named today.

If more than one variable refers to the object, though, the object isn't deleted until all of the other references to it have been deleted. This is illustrated by the last example in this figure. Here, the today and now variables both refer to the same Date object. As a result, when the delete operator is used with the today variable, only the today reference is deleted. The now variable still refers to the Date object.

How to add properties and methods to an object

Using the dot operator

```
invoice.taxRate = 0.0875;                    // Adds the taxRate property
invoice.getSalesTax = function(subtotal) {   // Adds the getSalesTax method
    return ( subtotal * invoice.taxRate );
};
```

Using brackets

```
invoice["taxRate"] = 0.0875;                 // Adds the taxRate property
```

How to modify the properties of an object

```
invoice.taxRate = 0.095;
```

How to remove a property from an object

```
delete invoice.taxRate;
alert( invoice.taxRate );     // Displays undefined
```

Two variables that refer to the same object

```
var today = new Date();
var now = today;
```

A diagram that illustrates these references

How to delete an object

```
var today = new Date();
delete today;
alert(today);                 // Displays undefined
```

How to delete a reference to an object

```
var today = new Date();
var now = today;
delete today;
alert( today );               // Displays undefined
alert( now.getFullYear() );   // Displays the year
```

Description

- Once an object is created, you can add new properties and methods to it. You can also change the value of an existing property by assigning it a new value.
- To remove a property or method from an object, you can use the delete operator.
- A variable holds a reference to an object, not the object itself. When you pass an object to a function as an argument, you are passing a reference to the object.
- You can also use the delete operator to delete an object or a reference to an object. If two or more variables refer to an object, the delete operator deletes the reference to the object. But if there are no references to the object, the object is deleted.

Figure 11-3   How to extend, modify, or delete an object

How to create and use your own object types

When you use JavaScript, you can also create your own object types. For instance, you can create an object type named Invoice that contains the properties and methods related to an Invoice.

The first set of examples in figure 11-4 shows how to create your own object types. To do that, you code a *constructor function* (or just *constructor*) that creates and initializes a new object, and you give this function a name that will become the object type. By convention, these names start with a capital letter. In these examples, the two object types are InvestmentTerms and Invoice.

Within the body of the constructor, you can use the *this* keyword to refer to the new object that the function will create. In these examples, the InvestmentTerms constructor takes two parameters and uses the this keyword to store these parameters in the rate and years properties of the new object. In contrast, the Invoice constructor doesn't take any parameters, but it creates a property named items that is an array and a property named tax_rate that is initialized to 0.07.

Because these are constructor functions, they don't have to return values. Instead, these functions will be called with the new keyword, and they will automatically return new objects, just as though their last statements were "return this".

To add a method to an object type, you add the method to the object type's *prototype object*. This is illustrated by the second set of examples in this figure. Here, the getMonths method is added to the prototype object of the InvestmentTerms object type, and the delete_item method is added to the prototype object of the Invoice object. These prototype objects are stored in the prototype properties of the constructor functions. Within the functions that become the methods, you can use the this keyword to refer to the object that is created from the constructor.

To create a new object of an object type, you use the new keyword with the name of the constructor function. This is illustrated by the next set of examples. Here, a new InvestmentRate object named terms is created with a rate property that has a value of 0.04 and term property that has value of 10. Then, a new Invoice object named invoice is created.

After the objects have been created, you can refer to their properties and methods just as you refer to the properties and methods of any other object. This is illustrated by the next two sets of examples. Here, the fourth set of examples displays the value of the rate property of the terms object and the tax_rate property of the invoice object. Then, the first statement in the fifth set of examples displays the result of the getMonths method of the terms object, and the second statement calls the delete_item method of the invoice object to delete an item in the items array.

How to code constructor functions

```
// A constructor that creates an InvestmentTerms object
var InvestmentTerms = function (init_rate, init_years) {
    // Define properties of the object
    this.rate = init_rate;
    this.years = init_years;
}

// A constructor that creates an Invoice object
var Invoice = function () {
    this.items = [];
    this.tax_rate = 0.07;
}
```

How to add methods to object types

```
// The getMonths method is added to the InvestmentTerms object type
InvestmentTerms.prototype.getMonths = function () {
    return this.years * 12;
}

// The delete_item method is added to the Invoice object type
Invoice.prototype.delete_item = function(item_code) {
    if ( item_code in this.items ) {
        delete this.items[item_code];
    }
    return this;
}
```

How to create a new instance of an object type

```
var terms = new InvestmentTerms(0.04, 10);
var invoice = new Invoice();
```

How to access a new object's properties

```
alert (terms.rate);              // Displays 0.04
alert (invoice.tax_rate);        // Displays 0.07
```

How to use a new object's methods

```
var months = terms.getMonths();      // Sets months to 120
invoice.delete_item(item_code);      // Deletes an item
```

Description

- To create your own object type, you code a *constructor function* (or just *constructor*) with the name of the object type. By convention, this name should start with a capital letter. Then, the constructor creates an object of that type.

- Within a constructor, the *this* keyword refers to the object that is created by the constructor.

- In JavaScript, every object type has a *prototype object* that contains the properties and methods of that object type. So to add a method to an object type, you add the method to this prototype object. Within this method, you can use the this keyword to refer to the properties and methods of the object.

Figure 11-4   How to create and use your own object types

Advanced skills for working with objects

This topic presents some advanced skills for working with objects. Although you won't use these skills in every application, you should at least be aware of them so you can use them when they're appropriate.

How to inherit properties and methods from another object type

After you've created an object type, that object type can inherit properties and methods from another object type. This lets you create a base object type with common methods and then extend that object type with more specialized methods. This is illustrated by the examples in figure 11-5.

To start this figure shows how to create a base object type called Vehicle and add methods to it by using the techniques of the last figure. This object type has properties and methods that are common to all vehicle types. Here, the constructor gets two parameters and stores them as properties of the object. This constructor also initializes two other properties. Then, three methods are added to the object type.

Next, the code in this figure creates a new object type called Car that will inherit the methods of the Vehicle type. Here, the constructor function gets four parameters and stores them as properties of the object, including the two parameters of the Vehicle type. The Car constructor also initializes the other two properties of the Vehicle object type.

Initially, as with all new object types, this object type inherits the properties and methods of the Object object type. Then, the next statement in this figure sets the prototype object of the Car object type to a new Vehicle object. This causes the Car object type to inherit the methods of the Vehicle object type. After doing this, you can add other methods to the Car object type by adding them to the Car.prototype object.

The last example in this figure shows how to create a new Car object named myCar and how to call the methods that this object inherited from the Vehicle object type. Here, the second statement chains the use of the drive, change_oil, and drive methods. As a result, the need_oil_change method returns a value of true.

If you're familiar with languages that inherit properties and methods from classes, you must realize by now that JavaScript doesn't do that. Instead, JavaScript uses *prototype inheritance*. With prototype inheritance, each object type has a prototype object that contains the properties and methods of that object type, and those properties and methods can be inherited.

An object type that represents a vehicle

The Vehicle constructor function

```
var Vehicle = function (make, model) {
    this.make = make;
    this.model = model;
    this.miles = 0;
    this.last_oil_change = 0;
}
```

Methods of the Vehicle object type

```
Vehicle.prototype.drive = function ( miles ) {
    this.miles += miles;
    return this;
}
Vehicle.prototype.change_oil = function () {
    this.last_oil_change = this.miles;
    return this;
}
Vehicle.prototype.need_oil_change = function () {
    return ( this.miles - this.last_oil_change > 3000 );
}
```

An object type that inherits from the Vehicle object type

The Car constructor must initialize the parameters of the Vehicle type

```
var Car = function ( make, model, door_count, hatch_back ) {
    this.make = make;
    this.model = model;
    this.door_count = door_count;
    if ( arguments.length == 4 ) {
        this.hatch_back = hatch_back;
    } else {
        this.hatch_back = false;
    }
    this.miles = 0;
    this.last_oil_change = 0;
}
```

The Car object type inherits the properties and methods of the Vehicle type

```
Car.prototype = new Vehicle();
```

A Car object can use the methods that it inherits

```
var myCar = new Car("Univeral Imports", "Q", 2);
myCar.drive(2000).change_oil().drive(4000);
alert( myCar.need_oil_change() );              // Displays true
```

Description

- The constructor for an object type that is going to inherit from another object type must initialize all of the properties of the parent object type.

- To inherit the properties and methods from another object, you set the prototype object for the child object equal to a new instance of the parent object.

Figure 11-5   How to inherit properties and methods from another object type

How to add methods to the JavaScript object types

Because JavaScript object types are based on prototype inheritance, you can extend the functionality of any object type at any time. This includes the native JavaScript objects, the DOM objects, and the browser objects.

To extend any JavaScript object, you simply add a new method to the prototype object of that object type. In fact, many JavaScript libraries start by extending the functionality of the existing object types.

To illustrate, figure 11-6 shows how to add new methods to the Date and String functions. In the first example, the isLeapYear method is added to the Date.prototype object. This method first retrieves the full year from the Date object by using the this keyword to call the getFullYear method of the object. The method then uses a nested if statement to return true or false depending on whether the year is a leap year. If a year is divisible by 4, it is a leap year if it isn't divisible by 100 or if it is divisible by 400.

In the second example, the reverse method is added to the String.prototype object. This method returns a new string with the characters in the reverse order of the original string. Because the object that is referred to by the this keyword is never modified, this method doesn't change the original string.

The third example in this figure shows how to add a function to the Math object. Note, however, that the Math object isn't an object type so it doesn't have a prototype object. Instead, you add new methods directly to the Math object. In this case, an add method is added to the Math object. This method converts the two parameters that are passed to it to numbers and returns their sum.

How to add a method to the Date object type

```
Date.prototype.isLeapYear = function () {
    var year = this.getFullYear();
    if ( year % 4 == 0 ) {
        if ( year % 100 == 0 ) {
            if ( year % 400 == 0) {
                return true;
            } else {
                return false;
            }
        } else {
            return true;
        }
    } else {
        return false;
    }
}

var opening = new Date( 2009, 1, 1 );     // Feb 1, 2009
alert( opening.isLeapYear() );            // Displays false
```

How to add a method to the String object type

```
String.prototype.reverse = function () {
    var reverse = "";
    for (var position = this.length - 1; position >= 0; position-- ) {
        reverse += this.charAt(position);
    }
    return reverse;
}

var message = "JavaScript";
alert( message.reverse() );          // Displays "tpircSavaJ"
```

How to add a method to the Math object

```
Math.add = function( x, y ) {
    return parseFloat(x) + parseFloat(y);
}

alert( "3" + "5" );               // Displays 35
alert( Math.add("3", "5") );      // Displays 8
```

Description

- To add a method to a JavaScript object type, you add the method to the prototype object of the object type. Then, all objects of that type, including existing objects, will inherit the new method.

- Within a new method, you can use the this keyword to refer to the object that's created by the object type.

- Because the Math object isn't an object type, it doesn't have a prototype object. As a result, you add new methods directly to the Math object.

Figure 11-6   How to add methods to the JavaScript object types

How to create cascading methods

A *cascading method* is a method of an object type that can be chained with other methods. To do that, the method must return a reference to the original object by using the this keyword. This is illustrated by figure 11-7.

In the first example, a method named add_value is added to the Array object type. However, this method doesn't return a reference to the object so it can't be chained with other Array methods. If you do try to chain the methods, a runtime error will occur.

In the second example, the add_value method ends with a "return this" statement. This returns a reference to the original object so this method can be chained. Then, a delete_value method is added to the Array object type. Since it too ends with a "return this" statement, it can also be chained.

This example then shows two add_value calls that are chained, followed by an add_value and a delete_value call that are chained. Since chaining is commonly used with method calls, it is a good practice to provide for chaining by ending all your methods with a return this statement.

A method that modifies an object but doesn't return the object

An add method that's added to the Array object type

```
Array.prototype.add_value = function (key, value) {
    this[key] = value;
}
```

Chaining the add method calls won't work

```
var pin_codes = [];
pin_codes.add_value("Mike", "1234").add_value("Ray", "9876");
```

The add methods must be called one at a time

```
var pin_codes = [];
pin_codes.add_value("Mike", "1234");
pin_codes.add_value("Ray", "9876");
```

Methods that modify an object and return the object

An add method that's added to the Array object type

```
Array.prototype.add_value = function (key, value) {
    this[key] = value;
    return this;
}
```

A delete method that's added to the Array object type

```
Array.prototype.delete_value = function (key) {
    delete this[key];
    return this;
}
```

Chaining the method calls does work

```
var pin_codes = [];
pin_codes.add_value("Mike", "1234").add_value("Ray", "9876");

pin_codes.add_value("Kelly", "4567").delete_value("Ray");
```

Description

- A *cascading method* is a method of an object type that can be chained with other methods.
- A method must return the object represented by the this keyword if it is going to be chained with other methods.

Figure 11-7   How to create cascading methods

How to use the for-in statement with objects

In JavaScript, you can use a for-in statement to loop through the properties of an object. This is illustrated by the examples in figure 11-8. In example 1, the alert statement in the for-in loop displays the property name and property value of the two properties in the application object.

In example 2, the statement in the loop builds a string of property names and values. Then, when the loop finishes, the alert statement displays the string. In this case, the first two properties contain functions (which makes them methods). As a result, the alert statement will display four properties and values, but the first two values will be the code in the functions.

Note, however, that a for-in statement may not process all of the properties of an object. First, like a for-in statement for an array, it will ignore properties that are undefined because they haven't been assigned values (although it will process properties that have been assigned the value of undefined).

Second, a for-in statement will only process properties that are *enumerable*. Although all of the properties that are added by your code are enumerable, most built-in properties aren't enumerable. For example, the length property of an Array object isn't enumerable.

Although you can't change whether a property is enumerable, you can determine if it is enumerable. To do that, you can use the propertyIsEnumerable method of an object with the property name as the argument. This is illustrated by the last set of examples in this figure.

Here, the rate property of the application object is enumerable, but the propertyIsEnumerable property of the object isn't enumerable. In this case, the propertyIsEnumerable property is inherited from the Object object, and it contains the propertyIsEnumerable method.

The syntax of the for-in statement

```
for ( var property_name in object ) {
    // code to execute
}
```

The objects used by the for-in loops that follow

```
var application = {
    rate: 0.04,
    years: 10
};

var invoice = {
    getSalesTax: function( subtotal ) {
        return ( subtotal * invoice.taxRate );
    },
    getTotal: function ( subtotal, salesTax ) {
        return subtotal + salesTax;
    },
    taxRate: 0.0875,
    dueDays: 30
}
```

How to use the for-in statement with an object

Example 1: With the application object

```
for ( var property in application ) {
  alert( property + ": " + application[property] );
}
```

Example 2: With the invoice object

```
var propList = "";
for ( var property in invoice ) {
    propList += property + ": " + invoice[property] + "\n";
}
alert ( propList );
```

The propertyIsEnumerable method tells if a property is enumerable

```
// Displays true
alert( application.propertyIsEnumerable("rate") );

// Displays false
alert( application.propertyIsEnumerable("propertyIsEnumerable") );
```

Description

- A for-in statement loops through all the defined properties of an object that are *enumerable*. Each time through the loop, it saves the next property name in the loop variable.
- Most built-in properties aren't enumerable, but the properties you add to an object are always enumerable. You can't change whether or not a property is enumerable.
- You can use the propertyIsEnumerable method of the Object object to determine whether a property is enumerable.

Figure 11-8   How to use the for-in statement with objects

How to use the in, instanceof, and typeof operators

To help you get information about an object or variable, JavaScript provides the in, instanceof, and typeof operators. These operators can be used within a method to ensure that the right type of object or variable has been passed as an argument. The use of these operators is illustrated in figure 11-9.

The *in operator* is used to determine if an object has a specific property. It returns true if the property has been assigned a value. In the examples, the rate property of the application object has been defined so the operator returns true. But the month property hasn't been defined so the operator returns false. Similarly, both the items and tax_rate properties of the invoice object have been defined by the constructor so the in operator returns true.

The *instanceof operator* is used to determine the type of an object. If an object is an instance of the specified object type, the instanceof operator returns true. That includes instances of inherited object types. If an object isn't an instance of the specified object type, the instanceof operator returns false.

In the examples, the today object is obviously an instance of the Date object type. But it is also an instance of the Object object type because Date inherits from that type. Similarly, the application object is an instance of the Object object type because all objects inherit from that type. Clearly, though, the application object isn't an instance of the Date object type. Last, the invoice object, which was built by the Invoice constructor, is an instance of both the Object and the Invoice type.

The *typeof operator* lets you determine whether a variable is a number, string, Boolean, object, or function. This is illustrated by the third set of examples. Notice here that the type of the Invoice constructor is "function".

The objects and variables used by the operators that follow

```
var application = {
    rate: 0.04,
    years: 10
};

function Invoice() {
    this.items = [];
    this.tax_rate = 0.07;
}
var invoice = new Invoice();

var today = new Date();
var testArray = [];
var testString = "123";
var testNumber = 123;
```

How to use the in operator

```
alert( "rate" in application );          // Displays true
alert( "month" in application );         // Displays false
alert( "items" in invoice );             // Displays true
alert( "tax_rate" in invoice );          // Displays true
```

How to use the instanceof operator

```
alert( today instanceof Object );        // Displays true
alert( today instanceof Date );          // Displays true
alert( application instanceof Object );  // Displays true
alert( application instanceof Date );    // Displays false
alert( invoice instanceof Object );      // Displays true
alert( invoice instanceof Invoice );     // Displays true
```

How to use the typeof operator

```
alert( typeof application );             // Displays object
alert( typeof testArray );               // Displays object
alert( typeof testString );              // Displays string
alert( typeof testNumber );              // Displays number
alert( typeof application.rate );        // Displays number
alert( typeof Invoice );                 // Displays function
```

Description

- The *in operator* returns true if an object has the named property.

- The *instanceof operator* returns true if an object is an instance of the specified object type. That includes the object type of the object as well as an inherited object type.

- The *typeof operator* lets you determine the type of a variable. It evaluates to "number", "string", or "boolean" for the primitive values; to "object" for objects and nulls; to "function" for functions; and to "undefined" if the operand is undefined.

Figure 11-9   How to use the in, instanceof, and typeof operators with objects

The Invoice application

The Invoice application in this chapter illustrates the effective use of objects, methods, and properties. This is an enhanced version of the Invoice application of the last chapter, which used functions instead of objects to implement the application. As you study this application, you'll see how object-oriented programming can help organize the code for an application.

The user interface

Figure 11-10 presents the user interface for the Invoice application. This works like the Invoice application of the last chapter, but with three enhancements. First, you can modify a line item by entering the item code and clicking the Add/Update Item button. Second, you can delete a line item by entering the item code and clicking the Delete Item button. Third, the line items are displayed in item-code sequence.

The user interface for the Invoice application

Invoice Manager

Item Code: `jse6`

Item Name: `Java SE 6`

Item Cost:

Quantity: `1`

[Add/Update Item]

- -

Item Code:

[Delete Item]

Current Invoice

```
Item Code  Item Name                               Qty Item Cost Line Cost
---------- --------------------------------------  --- --------- ---------
CS08       C# 2008                                   1 $   52.50 $    52.50
JSP2       Java Servlets and JSP                     2 $   52.50 $   105.00
VB08       Visual Basic 2008                         1 $   52.50 $    52.50
```

Subtotal: `210.00`

Sales Tax: `14.70`

Total: `224.70`

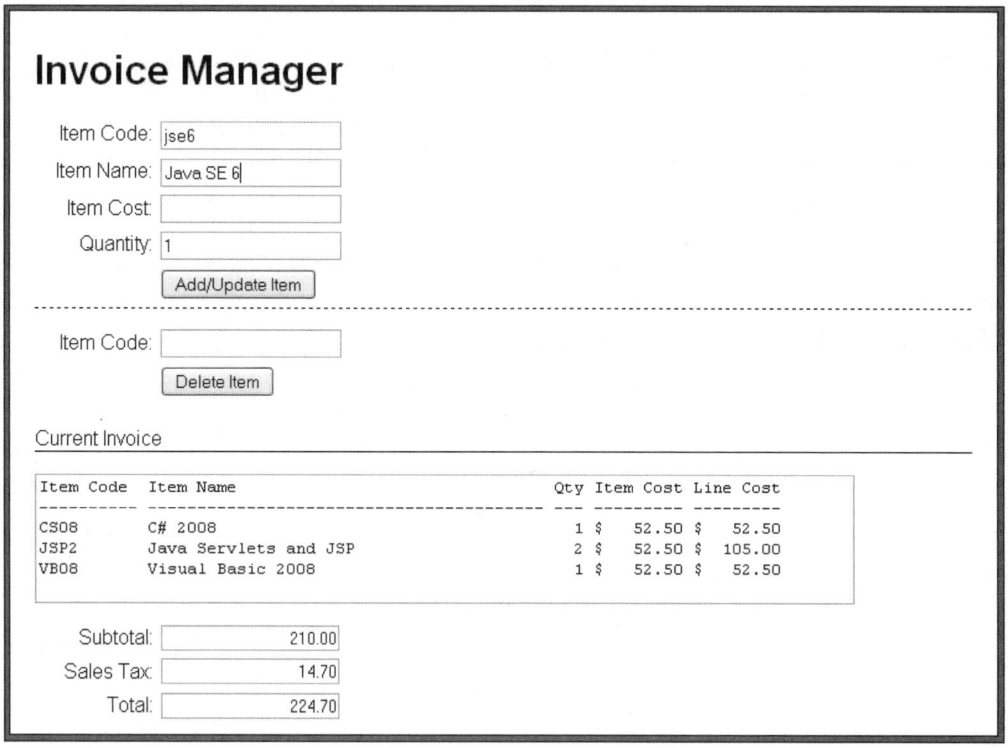

Description

- This application is an enhanced version of the application in chapter 10 that uses objects, properties, and methods instead of functions.

- This application lets you enter the items for an invoice so you can see what the cost for each line item will be as well as the subtotal, sales tax, and total cost for all of the line items.

- To enter each line item, you enter the appropriate data into the four text boxes and click the Add/Update Item button. The line item is then added to the invoice and the line cost, subtotal, sales tax, and total are calculated.

- To update a line item, you enter the item code and the updated data. Then, click the Add/ Update Item button.

- To delete a line item, you enter the item code and click the Delete Item button.

Figure 11-10   The user interface for the Invoice application

The XHTML file

Figure 11-11 presents the XHTML for this application. Here again, the script tags identify a library file and a file that contains the event handlers that interact with the user. This time, the library file contains the objects, methods, and properties that are used by the application.

In the body of the XHTML, the code is divided into three parts. The first part contains the elements for adding an item to the invoice. It consists of four text fields and a button called item_add. The second part contains the elements for deleting an item. It contains the field for getting the item code and a button called item_delete. And the third part contains the fields for displaying the invoice: a text area and three text fields.

The XHTML file

```
<!DOCTYPE html PUBLIC "-//W3C//DTD XHTML 1.0 Transitional//EN"
    "http://www.w3.org/TR/xhtml1/DTD/xhtml1-transitional.dtd">
<html xmlns="http://www.w3.org/1999/xhtml">
<head>
<title>Invoice Manager</title>
<link rel="stylesheet" type="text/css" href="invoice.css" />
<script type="text/javascript" src="invoice_library.js"></script>
<script type="text/javascript" src="invoice.js"></script>
</head>

<body>
<div id="content">
    <h1>Invoice Manager</h1>
    <div class="formLayout">
        <label for="item_code">Item Code:</label>
            <input type="text" name="item_code" id="item_code" /><br />
        <label for="item_name">Item Name:</label>
            <input type="text" name="item_name" id="item_name" /><br />
        <label for="item_cost">Item Cost:</label>
            <input type="text" name="item_cost" id="item_cost" /><br />
        <label for="item_qty">Quantity:</label>
            <input type="text" name="item_qty" id="item_qty"
                   value="1" /><br />
        <label> </label>
            <input type="button" id="item_add"
                value="Add/Update Item" /><br />
    </div>

    <div class="formLayout deleteForm">
        <label for="item_delete_code">Item Code:</label>
            <input type="text"
                name="item_delete_code" id="item_delete_code" /><br />
        <label> </label>
            <input type="button" id="item_delete"
                value="Delete Item" /><br />
    </div>

    <p class="startInvoice">Current Invoice</p>
    <p><textarea id="item_list" rows="5" cols="80"></textarea></p>
    <div class="formLayout">
        <label for="subtotal">Subtotal:</label>
            <input type="text" name="subtotal" id="subtotal"
                   class="disabled" disabled="disabled" /><br />
        <label for="sales_tax">Sales Tax:</label>
            <input type="text" name="sales_tax" id="sales_tax"
                   class="disabled" disabled="disabled" /><br />
        <label for="total">Total:</label>
            <input type="text" name="total" id="total"
                   class="disabled" disabled="disabled" /><br />
    </div>
</body>
</html>
```

Figure 11-11   The XTHML for the Invoice application

The library file

The library file in figure 11-12 reflects the object-oriented structure of this application. To start, it adds pad_left and pad_right methods to the String object. These methods operate like the pad_left and pad_right functions from the Invoice application in the last chapter, but they only take width and pad arguments now since they get the text from the String object. If the number of arguments isn't one or two, the original string is returned.

Next, the library file defines a constructor function for an Item_Info object. This object type will store the data for a line item in the invoice. It takes three parameters, converts two of them to numeric types, and stores the data in properties of the new object.

Then, the library file defines a constructor function for an Invoice object. This object type will store the line items for an invoice in an array. Its constructor takes no parameters, initializes an items array, and initializes the tax_rate property to 7%. After an invoice object is created, you can modify the tax rate by setting the tax_rate property to a different value.

After the constructor for the Invoice object, the library file defines seven methods for that object type. These methods work with the data in an instance of the Invoice object. For instance, the first of these methods adds an item to an instance of the Invoice object. It takes two parameters. The first is the item code for the item. The second is an Item_Info object that contains the data for the item.

In the body of this method, the code does some basic data validation on the parameters and returns the invoice object if any problems are found. Next, it converts the item_code parameter to uppercase. Then, if the item code is already in the items array, that array element is deleted. Last, this method adds the item_info object to the invoice array, calls the sort_by_code method to sort the invoice array, and returns the invoice object.

In the code for this method, note that the this keyword is used to refer to the invoice object. Note also that this method uses the this keyword in the last statement to return the invoice object. That way, this method can be chained.

The invoice_library.js file

```javascript
String.prototype.pad_left = function() {
    if ( arguments.length < 1 || arguments.length > 2 ) {
        return this;
    }
    var width = parseInt(arguments[0]);
    var pad = " ";
    if ( arguments.length == 2 ) pad = arguments[1];
    var result = this;
    while ( result.length < width ) {
        result = pad + result;
    }
    return result;
}

String.prototype.pad_right = function() {
    if ( arguments.length < 1 || arguments.length > 2 ) {
        return this;
    }
    var width = parseInt(arguments[0]);
    var pad = " ";
    if ( arguments.length == 2 ) pad = arguments[1];
    var result = this;
    while ( result.length < width ) {
        result = result + pad;
    }
    return result;
}
var Item_Info = function ( item_name, item_cost, item_qty ) {
    this.item_name = item_name;
    this.item_cost = parseFloat(item_cost);
    this.item_qty  = parseInt(item_qty);
}

var Invoice = function () {
    this.items = [];
    this.tax_rate = 0.07;
}

Invoice.prototype.add_item = function(item_code, item_info) {
    if ( ! item_info instanceof Item_Info ) return this;
    if ( isNaN(item_info.item_cost) ) return this;
    if ( isNaN(item_info.item_qty)  ) return this;
    if ( item_info.item_name == ""  ) return this;
    if ( item_code == "" ) return this;

    item_code = item_code.toUpperCase();
    if ( item_code in this.items ) {
        delete this.items[item_code];
    }

    this.items[item_code] = item_info;
    this.sort_by_code();

    return this;
}
```

Figure 11-12   The JavaScript code for the Invoice application (part 1 of 3)

If you understand how the add_item method works, you should also understand the five methods on page 2 of the library file so I won't take the time to describe them. You might notice, though, how the get_item_list method calls the pad_left and pad_right methods from string literals. JavaScript implements this notation by converting the string literals to temporary String objects and then calling the methods on those objects. Once the method calls are finished, the temporary objects are deleted.

The invoice_library.js file   **Page 2**

```javascript
Invoice.prototype.delete_item = function(item_code) {
    item_code = item_code.toUpperCase();
    if ( item_code in this.items ) {
        delete this.items[item_code];
    }
    return this;
}

Invoice.prototype.get_item_list = function() {
    var item_list, line_cost, item_count = 0;
    item_list  = "Item Code".pad_right(10) + " ";
    item_list += "Item Name".pad_right(40) + " ";
    item_list += "Qty ";
    item_list += "Item Cost ";
    item_list += "Line Cost\n";
    item_list += "".pad_right(10,"-") + " ";
    item_list += "".pad_right(40,"-") + " ";
    item_list += "---";
    item_list += "".pad_right(9,"-") + " ";
    item_list += "".pad_right(9,"-") + "\n";
    for ( var code in this.items ) {
        line_cost = this.items[code].item_qty * this.items[code].item_cost;
        item_list += code.pad_right(10) + " ";
        item_list += this.items[code].item_name.pad_right(40) + " ";
        item_list +=
            this.items[code].item_qty.toString().pad_left(3) + " ";
        item_list +=
            "$" + this.items[code].item_cost.toFixed(2).pad_left(8) + " ";
        item_list += "$" + line_cost.toFixed(2).pad_left(8) + "\n";
        item_count++;
    }
    return (item_count == 0) ? "" : item_list;
}

Invoice.prototype.get_subtotal = function () {
    var subtotal = 0, line_cost;
    for ( var code in this.items ) {
        line_cost =
            this.items[code].item_qty * this.items[code].item_cost;
        subtotal += parseFloat( line_cost.toFixed(2) );
    }
    return subtotal;
}

Invoice.prototype.get_sales_tax = function () {
    var subtotal = this.get_subtotal();
    var sales_tax = subtotal * this.tax_rate;
    return parseFloat( sales_tax.toFixed(2) );
}

Invoice.prototype.get_total = function () {
    var total = this.get_subtotal() + this.get_sales_tax();
    return parseFloat( total.toFixed(2) );
}
```

Figure 11-12   The JavaScript code for the Invoice application (part 2 of 3)

The last method in the library file is the sort_by_code method that was called by the add_item method on page 1. This method sorts the items array in the invoice object by item code. In this case, the items array is an associative array so the sort method of an Array object can't be used with it. That's why this sort_by_code method is necessary.

To start, this method uses a for-in loop to copy the item codes from the items array into a separate array named codes. Then, it uses the sort method of an Array object to sort those codes. Next, it uses a for-in loop to copy the item_info objects from the original items array into a new array named sorted_list. These items are inserted into the new item list in the order in which they appear in the array of sorted codes so the resulting array is sorted. Finally, the original items property is replaced by the sorted list, and the invoice object is returned.

The invoice.js file

The invoice.js file provides the functions and event handlers that control the user interface for the Invoice application. To start, this file creates a new Invoice object named invoice and defines the standard $ function. Then, it defines an update_invoice function that displays the invoice data in the web page along with event handlers for the click events of the buttons and the upload event.

If you study the code for these functions, you can see how they use the constructors, methods, and properties that are defined by the library file. For instance, the update_invoice function calls four methods of the Invoice object to display the invoice data in the XHTML elements. The item_add_click function calls the Item_Info constructor with three arguments to create a new Item_Info object that contains the user's entries. And the item_delete_click function calls the delete_item method of the Invoice object to delete an item.

If you compare the code in the two JavaScript files for this application with the code for the Invoice application of the last chapter, I think you'll see the benefits that you get from using your own objects. In particular, the code for this application is organized around the Invoice object, so it's easy to tell what the properties and methods relate to.

The invoice_library.js file

```javascript
Invoice.prototype.sort_by_code = function () {
    var code, codes = [], sorted_list = [];
    for ( code in this.items ) codes.push(code);
    codes.sort();
    for ( code in codes ) {
        sorted_list[ codes[code] ] = this.items[ codes[code] ];
    }
    this.items = sorted_list;
    return this;
}
```

The invoice.js file

```javascript
var invoice = new Invoice();

var $ = function(id) { return document.getElementById(id); }

var update_invoice = function () {
    $("item_list").value = invoice.get_item_list();
    $("subtotal").value = invoice.get_subtotal().toFixed(2);
    $("sales_tax").value = invoice.get_sales_tax().toFixed(2);
    $("total").value = invoice.get_total().toFixed(2);

    $("item_code").value = "";
    $("item_name").value = "";
    $("item_cost").value = "";
    $("item_qty").value = "1";
    $("item_delete_code").value = "";

    $("item_code").focus();
}

var item_add_click = function() {
    var item_code = $("item_code").value;
    var item_name = $("item_name").value;
    var item_cost = $("item_cost").value;
    var item_qty  = $("item_qty").value;
    var item_info = new Item_Info(item_name, item_cost, item_qty);

    invoice.add_item(item_code, item_info);
    update_invoice();
}

var item_delete_click = function() {
    var item_code = $("item_delete_code").value;
    invoice.delete_item(item_code);
    update_invoice();
}

window.onload = function () {
    $("item_add").onclick = item_add_click;
    $("item_delete").onclick = item_delete_click;
    $("item_code").focus();
}
```

Figure 11-12   The JavaScript code for the Invoice application (part 3 of 3)

Perspective

Now that you've finished this chapter, you should be able to develop applications that are built around your own objects, methods, and properties. That in turn should help make your applications easier to code, test, and debug. That's especially true for applications that are large or complex, and that's why object-oriented techniques are used in all of the applications that are presented in the rest of this book.

Terms

object type	prototype inheritance
inheritance	cascading method
nested object	enumerable property
constructor function	in operator
constructor	instanceof operator
prototype object	typeof operator

Exercise 11-1   Enhance the Invoice application

In this exercise, you'll enhance the Invoice application that was presented in this chapter. This will give you a chance to work with an object-oriented application.

Open and test the Invoice application

1. From your Firefox browser, open the index.html file in the invoice folder that's in the chapter 11 folder for exercises. Notice that this web page now provides a field for each line item that can be used for entering notes, although that field hasn't yet been implemented by the JavaScript code.

2. Test this application, but ignore the Notes field as you do that because it hasn't been implemented. Note that the line items are sorted by item code in the text area display.

Enhance the Invoice application

3. Use your text editor to open the two JavaScript files for this application.

4. Enhance this application so it implements the Notes field as an optional entry for each line item and displays it in a 25-character column to the right of the line cost column. The data in this Notes column should be right-justified. To make room for the Notes column in the text area, you can shorten the Item Name column to 25 characters. To make these changes efficiently, first modify the library file, then the invoice.js file.

5. Test this application until you get it working right. Has the object-oriented code made it relatively easy to make these enhancements?

12

How to use regular expressions, handle exceptions, and validate data

In this chapter, you'll learn how to use regular expressions and how to handle any exceptions that might be thrown by an application. Then, you'll study a Register application that uses regular expressions and exception handling to do a thorough job of data validation. When you complete this chapter, you'll be able to develop bulletproof JavaScript applications.

How to use regular expressions **386**
How to create and use regular expressions 386
How to create regular expression patterns 388
How to use the global and multiline flags 392
String methods that use regular expressions 394
Regular expressions for data validation 396

How to handle exceptions **398**
How to create and throw Error objects 398
How to use the try-catch statement to handle exceptions 400

The Register application **402**
The user interface, XHTML, and CSS 402
The JavaScript code for the register_library.js file 406
The JavaScript code for the register.js file 414

Perspective **416**

How to use regular expressions

Regular expressions are coded patterns that can be used to search for matching patterns in strings. These expressions are commonly used to validate the data that is entered by users.

How to create and use regular expressions

Figure 12-1 shows how regular expressions work. To start, you create a *regular expression object* that contains the *pattern* that will be used. To do that, you can use either of the techniques that are shown in this figure. With the first technique, you code the pattern in quotation marks as the parameter of the RegExp constructor. With the second technique, you code a *regular expression literal*, which consists of the pattern between slashes. In either case, you create a new RegExp object that contains the pattern. In the first two examples, that pattern is simply "Harris".

Once you've created a regular expression object, you can use it to find pattern matches in a string. To do that, you can use the test method of the regular expression object. This is illustrated by the two examples. In the first one, the test method searches for the pattern "Harris" in the variable named author. Since that variable contains "Ray Harris", the pattern is found and the method returns true. In the second example, the variable contains "Mike Murach" so the pattern isn't found, and the method returns false.

By default, the search that's done is case-sensitive. However, you can change that to case-insensitive as shown in the next set of examples. What you're actually doing is changing the ignoreCase property of the regular expression object to true. Then, the last example shows that a pattern of "murach" will match "Murach" when this property is set to true.

Two ways to create a regular expression object that will find "Harris"

By using the RegExp constructor function

```
var pattern = new RegExp("Harris");   // Creates a regular expression object
```

By coding a regular expression literal

```
var pattern = /Harris/;               // This creates the same object
```

One method of a regular expression

Method	Description
test(*string*)	Searches for the regular expression in the string. It returns true if the pattern is found and false if it's not found.

How to use the test method of a regular expression

Two strings to test

```
var author = "Ray Harris";
var editor = "Mike Murach";
```

How to use the test method to search for the pattern

```
alert ( pattern.test(author) );    // Displays true
alert ( pattern.test(editor) );    // Displays false
```

How to create a case-insensitive regular expression

When using the RegExp constructor function

```
var pattern = new RegExp("murach", "i");
```

When coding a regular expression literal

```
var pattern = /murach/i;
```

By setting the ignoreCase property of the regular expression

```
var pattern = /murach/;      // Initially case sensitive
pattern.ignoreCase = true;   // Now it's case-insensitive
```

How to use a case-insensitive regular expression

```
alert ( pattern.test(editor) );     // Displays true
```

Description

- A *regular expression* defines a *pattern* that can be searched for in a string. This pattern is stored in a *regular expression object*.

- To create a regular expression object, you can use the RegExp constructor function. Then, the pattern is coded within quotation marks as the only parameter.

- Another way to create a regular expression object is to code a *regular expression literal*. To do that, you code a pattern within two forward slashes.

- You can use the test method of a regular expression object to search for the pattern in the string parameter.

- By default, a regular expression pattern is case-sensitive, but you can change that by setting the ignoreCase property of the regular expression object to true.

Figure 12-1   How to create and use regular expressions

How to create regular expression patterns

The trick to using regular expressions is coding the patterns, and that can get complicated. That's why figure 12-2 moves from the simple to the complex as it shows you how to create patterns. To start, though, remember that all letters and numbers represent themselves in a pattern.

The first table in this figure shows you how to include special characters in a pattern. To do that, you start with the *escape character*, which is the backslash. For instance, \\ is equivalent to one backslash; \/ is equivalent to one forward slash; and \xA9 is equivalent to \u00A9, which is equivalent to the copyright symbol.

Note, however, that this table doesn't include all of the special characters that you need to precede with backslashes. For instance, the second table points out that you need to use \. to represent a period, and the third table points out that you need to use \$ to match a dollar sign.

The examples after the first table show how these special characters can be used in regular expression patterns. Here, the second and third statements use a regular expression literal followed by .test to call the test method for that expression object. The second statement looks for one slash in the variable named string and finds it. The third statement looks for the copyright symbol and finds it.

Then, the fourth statement uses the first technique in figure 12-1 to create a RegExp object. But when you use the RegExp constructor to create a regular expression object, you have to code two backslashes in the pattern for every one that you use in a regular expression literal. That's because the RegExp constructor takes a string parameter, and the backslash is also the escape character for strings. For this reason, it's easier to use regular expression literals. In this example, the pattern is equivalent to one backslash, but the fifth statement doesn't find it because the string variable contains the escape sequence for a new line (\n), not a backslash.

The second table shows how to match types of characters instead of specific characters. If, for example, the literal is /MB\d/, the pattern will match the letters MB followed by any digit. Or, if the literal is /MB.../, the pattern will match MB followed by any three characters.

The examples after this table show how this works. Here, the second statement looks for MB followed by any character and finds it. The third statement looks for MB followed by either T or F and finds it. And the fourth statement looks for MBT- followed by any character that's not a letter, number or the underscore. It doesn't find a match, though, because the string contains MBT-3.

How to match special characters

Pattern	Matches
\\	Backslash character
\/	Forward slash
\t	Tab
\n	Newline
\r	Carriage return
\f	Form feed
\v	Vertical tab
[\b]	Backspace (the only special character that must be inside brackets)
\u*dddd*	The Unicode character whose value is the four hexadecimal digits.
\x*dd*	The Latin-1 character whose value is the two hexadecimal digits. Equivalent to \u00*dd*.

Examples

```
var string = "©2009 Mike's Bait and Tackle\nAll rights reserved (5/2009).";
alert( /\//.test(string) );        // Matches / and displays true
alert( /\xA9/.test(string) );      // Matches © and displays true
var pattern = new RegExp("\\\\");  // Same as /\\/
alert( pattern.test(string) );     // Displays false since there's no \
```

How to match types of characters

Pattern	Matches
.	Any character except a newline (use \. to match a period)
[ ]	Any character in the brackets (use \[or \] to match a bracket)
[^]	Any character not in the brackets
[a-z]	Any character in the range of characters when used inside brackets
\w	Any letter, number, or the underscore
\W	Any character that's not a letter, number, or the underscore
\d	Any digit
\D	Any character that's not a digit
\s	Any whitespace character (space, tab, newline, carriage return, form feed, or vertical tab)
\S	Any character that's not whitespace

Examples

```
var string = "The product code is MBT-3461.";
alert( /MB./.test(string) );       // Displays true
alert( /MB[TF]/.test(string) );    // Displays true
alert( /MBT-\W/.test(string) );    // Displays false
```

Description

- The backslash is used as the *escape character* in regular expressions. It gives special meaning to some characters and removes the special meaning from others.

- When you use the RegExp constructor, any backslash in your pattern must be preceded by another backslash. That's because the backslash is also the escape character in strings.

Figure 12-2   How to create regular expression patterns (part 1 of 2)

The first table in part 2 of this figure shows how to match characters at specific positions in a string. For instance, the pattern /^com/ will find the letters "com" at the start of a string. And the pattern /com$/ will find the letters "com" at the end of a string. This is illustrated by the examples after this table. Here, the last example displays false because "Ann" is found at the beginning of a word but isn't found at the end of a word (the first word in the string is "Anne"). As a result, the \b pattern allows you to easily find whole words.

The second table shows how to group and match a *subpattern* that is coded in parentheses. This is illustrated by the examples after this table. Here, the second statement will match a subpattern of either "Rob" or "Bob".

If you code more than one subpattern in a pattern, the patterns are numbered from left to right. Then, if you want to repeat the subpattern in the pattern, you can specify the number of the pattern that you want to repeat. This is illustrated by the third statement after the table. Here, the \1 indicates that the first pattern, which matches any three letters, numbers, or underscores, should be used again. This returns true because that pattern is repeated. It would also return true if the pattern were /(Rob) \1/ because "Rob" is repeated.

The third table shows how to use a *quantifier* that's coded in braces to match a repeating pattern. For instance, /\d{3}/ will match any three digits in succession, and /\${1,3}/ will match from one to three occurrences of a dollar sign. Here again, this is illustrated by the examples that follow the table. The third statement matches three digits at the start of a string, a hyphen, three more digits, another hyphen, and four digits at the end of the string. And the fourth statement matches a left parenthesis at the start of the string, three digits, a right parenthesis, zero or one space (as indicated by the question mark quantifier after the space), and four digits at the end of the string.

Then, the pattern in the fifth statement combines the patterns of the third and fourth statements so a phone number can start with either three digits in parentheses or three digits followed by a hyphen. Here again, the question mark after the space means that zero or one space can be used after an area code in parentheses, so this pattern will find telephone numbers like 559-555-1234, (559)555-1234, and (559) 555-1234.

These tables and examples should get you started coding patterns of your own. And you'll get more proficient with them as you study the examples in the rest of this chapter.

How to match string positions

Pattern	Matches
^	The beginning of the string (use \^ to match a caret)
$	The end of the string (use \$ to match a dollar sign)
\b	The beginning or end of a word (must not be inside brackets)
\B	A position other than the beginning or end of a word

Examples

```
var author = "Ray Harris";
alert( /^Ray/.test(author) );          // Displays true
alert( /Harris$/.test(author) );       // Displays true
alert( /^Harris/.test(author) );       // Displays false
var editor = "Anne Boehm";
alert( /Ann/.test(editor) );           // Displays true
alert( /Ann\b/.test(editor) );         // Displays false
```

How to group and match subpatterns

Pattern	Matches
(*subpattern*)	Creates a numbered subpattern group (use \(and \) to match a parenthesis)
(?:*subpattern*)	Creates an unnumbered subpattern group
|	Matches either the left or right subpattern (use \\| to match a vertical bar)
\n	Matches a numbered subpattern group

Examples

```
var name = "Rob Robertson";
alert( /^(Rob)|(Bob)\b/.test(name) );  // Displays true
alert( /^(\w\w\w) \1/.test(name) );    // Displays true
```

How to match a repeating pattern

Pattern	Matches
{*n*}	Pattern must repeat exactly *n* times (use \{ and \} to match a brace)
{*n*,}	Pattern must repeat *n* or more times
{*n,m*}	Subpattern must repeat from *n* to *m* times
?	Zero or one of the previous subpattern (same as {0,1})
+	One or more of the previous subpattern (same as {1,})
*	Zero or more of the previous subpattern (same as {0,})

Examples

```
var phone = "559-555-6627";
var fax   = "(559) 555-6635";
alert( /^\d{3}-\d{3}-\d{4}$/.test(phone) );      // Displays true
alert( /^\(\d{3}\) ?\d{3}-\d{4}$/.test(fax) );   // Displays true
var phonePattern = /^(\d{3}-)|(\(\d{3}\) ?)\d{3}-\d{4}$/;
alert( phonePattern.test(phone) );               // Displays true
alert( phonePattern.test(fax) );                 // Displays true
```

Figure 12-2   How to create regular expression patterns (part 2 of 2)

How to use the global and multiline flags

In figure 12-1, you saw how you could set the ignoreCase property of a regular expression object to true to make a match case-insensitive. Now, figure 12-3 shows you how to use the global and multiline properties of a regular expression object.

To turn these properties on, you can use one of the three techniques in this figure. If, for example, you use the RegExp constructor, you code "g" or "m" as the second parameter. If you use a regular expression literal, you code "g" or "m" after the literal. And if you've already created the regular expression object, you set the global or multiline property to true. This works the same as it does for the ignoreCase property.

When you use "g" or "m" to turn the property on, the "g" or "m" is commonly called a *flag*. So you can refer to the g flag, the m flag, or the i flag (for the case-insensitive flag). When you use these flags, they cause the corresponding property to be set to true.

When the global property is on, you can use the test method to find more than one match in a string. To do that, the test method uses the lastIndex property of the regular expression object to determine where the next search should start. This property starts with a value of zero, but is reset to the starting position for the next search after each match.

This is illustrated by the global example in this figure. Here, the test method is used four times in a row with the same string. The first time, it finds a match for the pattern "MBT" in the first three characters of the string so it returns true and sets the lastIndex property to 3. The second time, it finds another match so it returns true and sets the lastIndex property to 12. The third time, it doesn't find a match so it returns false and sets the lastIndex property back to zero. And the fourth time, the results are the same as the first time.

When the multiline property is off, the ^ and $ characters look for matches at the start and end of the string. But when this property is on, those characters look for matches at the start and end of each line in the string. This is illustrated by the multiline example. Here, the string contains two lines with "Ray Harris" on the first line and "Author" on the second line. As a result, the pattern /Harris$/ returns false if the multiline flag isn't on, but true if the flag is on.

How to create a global regular expression

By using the RegExp constructor function

```
var pattern = new RegExp("Harris", "g");
```

By coding a regular expression literal

```
var pattern = /Harris/g;
```

By setting the global property of the regular expression

```
var pattern = /Harris/;        // Initially not global
pattern.global = true;         // Now it's global
```

One property of a regular expression

Property	Description
lastIndex	The position in the string at which the search is started. This property is initially set to zero. But if a match is found, this property is reset to one more than the position of the last character matched by the pattern, even if this position is past the end of the string. If a match isn't found, this property is reset to zero.

How to use a global regular expression

```
var pattern = /MBT/g;
var string  = "MBT-6745 MBT-5712";
alert( pattern.test(string) + ", " + pattern.lastIndex );   // true, 3
alert( pattern.test(string) + ", " + pattern.lastIndex );   // true, 12
alert( pattern.test(string) + ", " + pattern.lastIndex );   // false, 0
alert( pattern.test(string) + ", " + pattern.lastIndex );   // true, 3
```

How to create a multiline regular expression

By using the RegExp constructor function

```
var pattern = new RegExp("Harris$", "m");
```

By coding a regular expression literal

```
var pattern = /Harris$/m;
```

By setting the multiline property of the regular expression

```
var pattern = /Harris$/;           // Initially not multiline
pattern.multiline = true;          // Now it's multiline
```

How to use a multiline regular expression

```
var pattern1 = /Harris$/;          // A non-multiline regular expression
var pattern2 = /Harris$/m;         // A multiline regular expression
var string   = "Ray Harris\nAuthor";  // A multiline string
alert( pattern1.test(string) );    // Displays false
alert( pattern2.test(string) );    // Displays true
```

Description

- If the global property is set to true, you can use the test method to look for more than one match in a string.

- If the multiline property is set to true, the ^ pattern looks for matches at the beginning of each line and the $ pattern looks for matches at the end of each line.

Figure 12-3   How to use the global and multiline flags

String methods that use regular expressions

Besides the test method of a regular expression object, you can use three string methods to work with regular expressions. These expressions are summarized in figure 12-4. Note that all three take the regular expression object as the first parameter.

The search method of a string searches for a match in the string. If it finds one, it returns the index of the first character of the match within the string. Otherwise, it returns -1. The first set of examples in this figure shows how this works.

The match method of a string is often used with the global flag turned on. Then, it returns an array of all the matches. This is illustrated by the second set of examples. If no matches are found, this method returns null.

If you use the match method without the global flag turned on, it returns an array with the first match in element 0 and any subpatterns in the pattern in the subsequent elements. This is illustrated by the third set of examples in which "MBT-6745" is the first match, and "6745" is the only subpattern that was used in the pattern. Here again, if a match isn't found, this method returns null.

The replace method is like the search method, but it replaces a match with the value of the second parameter. If the global flag is set, it replaces all matches with the value. If the global flag isn't set, it replaces just the first match. This is illustrated by the last two sets of examples.

All three of these methods are often used in combination with the string methods that you learned about in chapter 7. Together, they give you all of the capabilities that you'll need for working with the characters within a string.

Three string methods that you can use with regular expressions

Method	Description
search(*reg_exp*)	Searches for the regular expression in the string. If not found, it returns -1. If found, it returns the index of the first character in the match within the string.
match(*reg_exp*)	Searches for the regular expression in the string. If the global flag is set, it returns an array of all matching substrings. If the global flag isn't set, it returns an array with the matched characters in element 0, numbered substrings in subsequent elements, and the index property set to the index of the first character in the match. If a match isn't found, this method always returns null.
replace(*reg_exp*, *value*)	Searches for the regular expression in the string. When found, the matched string is replaced by the string in the value parameter. If the global flag is set, all matches are replaced. If the global flag isn't set, only the first match is replaced.

How to use the search and match methods with a regular expression

How to use the search method

```
var email = "mike@murach.com";
alert ( email.search( /\.com$/ ) );      // displays 11
alert ( email.search( /\.net$/ ) );      // displays -1
if ( email.search( /\.edu$/ ) == -1 ) {
    alert ("Not a .edu address");        // displays the message
}
```

How to use the match method with a global regular expression

```
var items = "Items: MBT-6745 MBT-572";
var result = items.match( /MBT-(\d{1,4})/g );
// result is the array [ "MBT-6745", "MBT-572" ]
```

How to use the match method with a non-global regular expression

```
var items = "Items: MBT-6745 MBT-572";
var result = items.match( /MBT-(\d{1,4})/ );
// result is the array [ "MBT-6745", "6745" ]
// result.index is 7, the offset of the first match
```

How to use the replace method with a regular expression

How to replace text

```
var items = "MBT-6745 MBT-572";
alert( items.replace(/MBT/,  "ITEM") );   // Displays ITEM-6745 MBT-572
alert( items.replace(/MBT/g, "ITEM") );   // Displays ITEM-6745 ITEM-572
```

How to trim whitespace from a string

```
var message = "    JavaScript    ";
string = message.replace(/^\s+/,"");      // Trim start of string
string = message.replace(/\s+$/,"");      // Trim end of string
alert( "(" + message + ")" );             // Displays (JavaScript)
```

Description

- Be careful when using these methods in conditional expressions. You must build the conditional so that it works correctly with the values returned by the methods.

Figure 12-4   String methods that use regular expressions

Regular expressions for data validation

Figure 12-5 starts with some patterns that are commonly used for data validation. For instance, the first pattern is for phone numbers so it matches 3 digits at the start of the string, a hyphen, 3 more digits, another hyphen, and 4 digits at the end of the string. Similarly, the second one is for credit card numbers so it matches four groups of 4 digits separated by hyphens.

The third pattern is for 5- or 9-digit zip codes. It requires 5 digits at the start of the string. Then, it uses the ? quantifier with a subpattern that contains a hyphen followed by four digits. As a result, this subpattern is optional.

The fourth pattern is for dates in the mm/dd/yy format, but it also accepts a date in the m/yy/dd format. To start, this pattern uses the ? quantifier to show that the string can start with zero or one occurrences of 0 or 1. This means that the month in the date can be coded like 03/19/1940 or 3/19/1940. But if two digits are used for the month, the first digit has to be either 0 or 1.

Then, the pattern calls for one digit, a slash, either 0, 1, 2, or 3, another digit, another slash, and four more digits. As a result, this pattern doesn't match a string if its first month digit is greater than 1 or if its first day digit is greater than 3. But this will still match invalid dates like 19/21/2009 or 9/39/2010 so additional data validation is required.

The examples that follow these patterns show how they can be used in your code. The first example uses the phone number pattern with the match method and displays an error message if a match isn't found. Here, the if statement works because the match method returns a null if a match isn't found.

The second example works the same, but it uses the date pattern. However, this pattern will match some invalid date formats so other validation is needed.

The last example shows a function named isEmail that is based on the SMTP specification for how an email address may be formed. This specification calls the part before the @ symbol the local part, and the part after the @ symbol the domain part. Then, it gives the requirements for each part.

In brief, this isEmail function splits the address into the parts before and after the @ symbol and returns false if there aren't two parts. Next, this function builds a regular expression pattern named localPart by combining two subpatterns with the | character, which means that the string can match either subpattern. Then, it looks for a match in the part of the address before the @ symbol. If it doesn't find one, it returns false.

Similarly, the last part of this function builds a regular expression pattern named domainPart by combining two subpatterns. Then, it looks for a match in the part of the address after the @ symbol. If it doesn't find one, it returns false. Otherwise, this function returns true because the email address is valid.

Of course, it is the patterns in this function that are the most difficult to understand. For instance, [^\\\\\\\\\\"] matches any character that isn't a backslash or a quotation mark. If you're interested in how these patterns work, you can learn more when you read about this function in the description of the JavaScript code for the Register application at the end of this chapter. Otherwise, you can copy and use this function without understanding it.

Regular expressions for testing validity

A pattern for testing phone numbers in this format: 999-999-9999

```
/^\d{3}-\d{3}-\d{4}$/
```

A pattern for testing credit card numbers in this format: 9999-9999-9999-9999

```
/^\d{4}-\d{4}-\d{4}-\d{4}$/
```

A pattern for testing zip codes in either of these formats: 99999 or 99999-9999

```
/^\d{5}(-\d{4})?$/
```

A pattern for testing dates in this format: mm/dd/yyyy

```
/^[01]?\d\/[0-3]\d\/\d{4}$/
```

Examples that use these expressions

Testing a phone number for validity

```
var phone = "559-555-6624";                 // Valid phone number
var phonePattern = /^\d{3}-\d{3}-\d{4}$/;
if ( !phone.match(phonePattern) ) {
    alert("Invalid phone number");          // Not displayed
}
```

Testing a date for a valid format, but not for a valid month, day, and year

```
var startDate = "8/10/209";                 // Invalid date
var datePattern = /^[01]?\d\/[0-3]\d\/\d{4}$/;
// This pattern will match dates like 19/21/2009 and 9/39/2010
if ( !startDate.match(datePattern) ) {
    alert("Invalid start date");            // Displays error message
}
```

A function that does complete validation of an email address

```
var isEmail = function (email) {
    if (email.length == 0) return false;
    var parts = email.split("@");
    if (parts.length != 2 ) return false;
    if (parts[0].length > 64) return false;
    if (parts[1].length > 255) return false;

    var address =
        "(^[\\w!#$%&'*+/=?^`{|}~-]+(\\.[\\w!#$%&'*+/=?^`{|}~-]+)*$)";
    var quotedText = "(^\"(([^\\\\\"])|(\\\\[\\\\\"]))+\"$)";
    var localPart = new RegExp( address + "|" + quotedText );
    if ( !parts[0].match(localPart) ) return false;

    var hostnames =
        "(([a-zA-Z0-9]\\.)|([a-zA-Z0-9][-a-zA-Z0-9]{0,62}[a-zA-Z0-9]\\.))+";
    var tld = "[a-zA-Z0-9]{2,6}";
    var domainPart = new RegExp("^" + hostnames + tld + "$");
    if ( !parts[1].match(domainPart) ) return false;

    return true;
}
```

Figure 12-5   Regular expressions for data validation

How to handle exceptions

To prevent your applications from crashing due to runtime errors, you can write code that handles any *exceptions*. These are runtime errors that occur due to unexpected error conditions. You can also "throw" your own exceptions and then write code that handles them.

How to create and throw Error objects

In some applications, like the one that's illustrated at the end of this chapter, you will want to *throw* your own exceptions. To do that, you can create a new Error object and use the *throw statement* to throw it. This is illustrated by figure 12-6.

To create a new Error object, you call the Error constructor and pass one parameter to it that contains a message. This message is then stored in the Error object's message property.

After you create an Error object, you can throw it. This is illustrated by the first example in this figure. Here, a function that calculates future value throws an exception if one of the values that is passed to it is invalid. When the exception is thrown, the function ends and control is passed to the function that called it. Then, that function can catch the exception and display its message property as shown in the next figure.

Besides Error objects, JavaScript throws other types of error objects that inherit from the Error object. These are summarized in the second table in this figure. For instance, a RangeError object is thrown when a numeric value has exceeded an allowable range. In the examples after this table, the first statement throws this type of error because the parameter of the toFixed method is out of range. Similarly, a SyntaxError object is thrown when the syntax of a statement is invalid. In the third statement in the examples, this occurs because "x" is an invalid second parameter for the RegExp constructor.

You can also create and throw objects of these other Error types in your applications. This is illustrated by the fourth statement in the examples. Here, the throw statement is used to throw a RangeError object with a message that says a user entry is invalid.

To determine what type of error has been thrown, you can use the name property of the error object. If, for example, an Error object has been thrown, this property is set to "Error". But if a RangeError object has been thrown, this property is set to "RangeError".

The syntax for creating a new Error object

```
new Error(message)
```

The syntax for the throw statement

```
throw errorObject;
```

A calculate_future_value method that throws a new Error object

```
var calculate_future_value = function( investment, annualRate, years ) {
    if ( investment <= 0 || annualRate <= 0 || years <= 0 ) {
        throw new Error("Please check your entries for validity.");
    }

    var monthlyRate = annualRate / 12 / 100;
    var months = years * 12;
    var futureValue = 0;

    for ( i = 1; i <= months; i++ ) {
        futureValue = ( futureValue + investment ) * (1 + monthlyRate);
    }
    return futureValue.toFixed(2);
}
```

Two properties of Error objects

Property	Description
message	The message used when the Error object was created
name	The type of error ("Error" for Error objects)

Other types of error objects that inherit from the Error type

Type	Thrown when
RangeError	A numeric value has exceeded the allowable range
ReferenceError	A variable is read that hasn't been defined
SyntaxError	A runtime syntax error is encountered
TypeError	The type of a value is different from what was expected
URIError	A URI handling function was used incorrectly

Example of statements that generate these errors

```
alert( (3.275).toFixed(101) );               // Throws RangeError
alert( firstName );                          // Throws ReferenceError
var pattern = new RegExp("Harris", "x");     // Throws SyntaxError
throw new RangeError("Annual rate is invalid."); // Throws RangeError
```

Description

- To create a new Error object, use the syntax above. If the message parameter isn't a string, it is converted to one.

- You use the *throw statement* to trigger a runtime error. It can throw a new or existing Error object.

Figure 12-6   How to create and throw Error objects

How to use the try-catch statement to handle exceptions

When Error objects are thrown, your application needs to "catch" and handle them. Otherwise, your application will end with a runtime error.

To catch errors, you use a *try-catch statement* as shown in figure 12-7. First, you code a *try block* around the statement or statements that may throw an exception. Then, you code a *catch block* that contains the statements that will be executed if an exception is thrown by any statement in the try block. This is known as *exception handling*.

The first example in this figure shows how you can use a try-catch statement to catch any exceptions that are thrown by the four statements in the try block. Here, the fourth statement calls the calculate_future_value function in the previous figure. Then, if that function throws an exception, control immediately jumps to the first statement in the catch block. In addition, the Error object is passed to the catch block.

In the parentheses after the catch keyword, you code a name that you can use to refer to this Error object. Then, you can use the message property of this object to access the message that's associated with the object. You can also use the name property to find out what type of Error object has been thrown. In this example, the catch block uses the alert method to display the value of the message property.

If an exception is thrown within a try block, the exception is caught by the catch block. Otherwise, the exception is passed to the calling function. This passing of the exception continues until the exception is caught or the application ends with a runtime error.

In some cases, you may want use a catch block to rethrow an error to the calling function. This is illustrated by the second example in this figure. Here, the throw statement throws the variable that the Error object was stored in. Then, this error can be handled by the next function in the call stack.

In general, you only code the try and catch blocks for a try-catch statements. But as the syntax at the top of this figure shows, you can also code a *finally block*. Then, the code in the finally block is executed after the statements in the try block if no exception occurs or after the statements in the catch block if an exception occurs. In most cases, though, you won't need to use a finally block.

The syntax for a try-catch statement

```
try { statements }
catch(errorName) { statements }
finally { statements }        // The finally block is optional
```

A try-catch statement that contains a throw statement

```
var calculate_click = function () {
    try {
        var investment = parseFloat( $("investment").value );
        var annualRate = parseFloat( $("rate").value );
        var years = parseInt( $("years").value );

        $("futureValue").value =
            calculate_future_value(investment, annualRate, years);
    } catch(error) {
        alert (error.message);
    }
}
```

The dialog box that displays the message property of the error object

A try-catch statement that rethrows an Error object to its calling function

```
try {
    $("futureValue").value =
        calculate_future_value(investment, annualRate, years);
} catch(error) {
    // If needed, do something before rethrowing error
    throw error;
}
```

Description

- You can use a *try-catch statement* to process any errors that are thrown by an application. These errors are often referred to as *exceptions*.

- In a try-catch statement, you code a *try block* that contains the statements that may throw exceptions. Then, you code a *catch block* that contains the statements that are executed when an exception is thrown in the try block.

- In the catch block, the Error object is available for use in the *errorName* variable. When execution leaves this block, the Error object is no longer available.

- JavaScript syntax requires that you have either a catch block, a *finally block*, or both. In most cases, however, you will just have a catch block. The finally block is executed whether or not the statements in the catch block are executed.

Figure 12-7   How to use the try-catch statement to handle exceptions

The Register application

Now, to show you how exception handling and data validation are used in a real-world JavaScript application, this chapter presents a Register application. This application validates the data that the user enters into the form before submitting it to the server for processing.

The user interface, XHTML, and CSS

Figure 12-8 presents the user interface for this application. After the user enters the required data and clicks the Register button, the JavaScript code checks the data for validity. Then, if the data is valid, it submits the data to the server for processing. Otherwise, it displays error messages to mark the invalid entries so the user can correct them. In this figure, you can see error messages to the right of seven fields, and these messages are displayed in red.

Figure 12-9 presents the XHTML for the body of this application. Near the start of this code, you can see that a form tag is used to post the fields within the form to the server. Near the bottom of this code, you can see that the Register button is defined as an input button of the button type, not the submit type. Then, to submit the form, the JavaScript code uses the submit method of the form.

After the Register button, you can see the code for the Reset button. It too is defined as an input button of the button type, not the reset type. Then, to reset all the fields in the form, the JavaScript code uses the reset method of the form.

For each of the fields in the form, you can see an id attribute and a span tag that has an id that consists of the id of the field followed by _error. For instance, the field for the email address has an id of email, and the span tag that follows has an id of email_error. Within each span tag is a message that describes how the data should be entered, like "Must be a valid email address." Later, you'll see how the JavaScript code changes this message when an error is found or the form is reset.

Within each fieldset tag, you can see a div tag that assigns a class of "formLayout". You can also see that a class named "notice" has been assigned to the paragraph at the bottom of the form. These class names are used by the CSS to format those elements.

After the first fieldset tag, you can see a comment that indicates that this figure doesn't show all of the fieldset tags for this application. If you're interested, though, you can see all of them in the downloadable code for this application.

In figure, 12-10, you can see the CSS for this application. There you can see five rule sets that apply to the formLayout class. You can also see a rule set that applies the color red to the notice class. Last, you can see a rule set that applies the color red to the error class. However, if you look through the XHTML, you won't find an error class. Instead, as you will see in a moment, this class name is assigned to the span tags for the fields that contain invalid data. As a result, the error message that gets assigned to the span tag is displayed in red.

The user interface

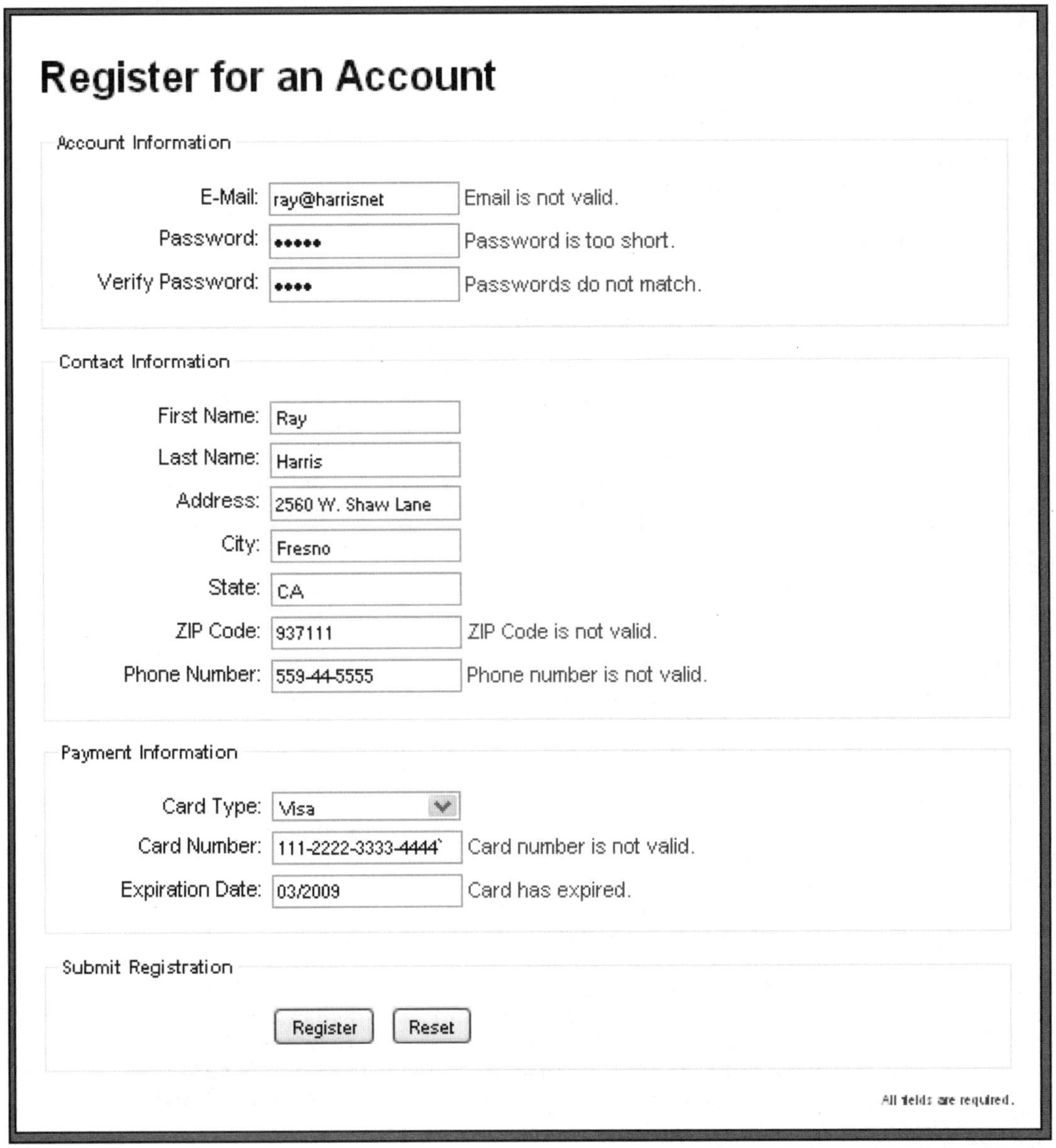

Register for an Account

Account Information

E-Mail:	ray@harrisnet Email is not valid.
Password:	●●●●● Password is too short.
Verify Password:	●●●● Passwords do not match.

Contact Information

First Name:	Ray
Last Name:	Harris
Address:	2560 W. Shaw Lane
City:	Fresno
State:	CA
ZIP Code:	937111 ZIP Code is not valid.
Phone Number:	559-44-5555 Phone number is not valid.

Payment Information

Card Type:	Visa
Card Number:	111-2222-3333-4444` Card number is not valid.
Expiration Date:	03/2009 Card has expired.

Submit Registration

[Register] [Reset]

All fields are required.

Description

- This application validates the data in a form before the data is submitted to the server for processing. If the data isn't valid, the form isn't submitted to the server.
- The JavaScript for this application does a thorough job of validating the data for every field on the form. You can use this code as a model for validating the data in any form.

Figure 12-8   The user interface for the Register application

Some of the XHTML for the body of the document

```
<body>
<div id="content">
    <h1>Register for an Account</h1>
    <form action="register_account.html" method="get"
        name="registration_form" id="registration_form">
    <fieldset>
        <legend>Account Information</legend>
        <div class="formLayout">
            <label for="email">E-Mail:</label>
                <input type="text" name="email" id="email" />
                <span id="email_error">Must be a valid
                    email address.</span><br />
            <label for="password">Password:</label>
                <input type="password" name="password" id="password" />
                <span id="password_error">Must be at least 6 characters.
                    </span><br />
            <label for="verify">Verify Password:</label>
                <input type="password" name="verify" id="verify" />
                <span id="verify_error"> </span><br />
        </div>
    </fieldset>

    /* Missing fieldset elements */

    <fieldset>
        <legend>Payment Information</legend>
        <div class="formLayout">
            <label for="card_type">Card Type:</label>
                <select name="card_type" id="card_type">
                    <option value="">Select One:</option>
                    <option value="m">MasterCard</option>
                    <option value="v">Visa</option>
                </select>
                <span id="card_type_error"> </span><br />
            <label for="card_number">Card Number:</label>
                <input type="text" name="card_number" id="card_number" />
                <span id="card_number_error">
                    Use 1111-2222-3333-4444 format.</span><br />
            <label for="exp_date">Expiration Date:</label>
                <input type="text" name="exp_date" id="exp_date" />
                <span id="exp_date_error">Use mm/yyyy format.</span><br />
        </div>
    </fieldset>
    <fieldset>
        <legend>Submit Registration</legend>
        <div class="formLayout">
            <label> </label>
                <input type="button" id="register" value="Register" />
                <input type="button" id="reset_form" value="Reset" /><br />
        </div>
    </fieldset>
    </form>
    <p class="notice">All fields are required.</p>
</body>
</html>
```

Figure 12-9   The XHTML for the Register application

The CSS for the Register application

```css
body {
    font-family: Arial, Helvetica, sans-serif;
    background: #666666;
}

#content {
    width: 760px;
    margin: 10px auto;
    padding: 5px 20px;
    background: #FFFFFF;
    border: 1px solid #000000;
}

.center { text-align: center; }

fieldset {
    margin-top: 1em;
    margin-bottom: 1em;
}

legend {
    color: black;
    font-weight: bold;
    font-size: 85%;
}

.formLayout { padding-top: 1em; }

.formLayout label {
    float: left;
    width: 10em;
    text-align: right;
}

.formLayout input, .formLayout select {
    margin-left: 0.5em;
    margin-bottom: 0.5em;
}

.formLayout select { width: 11em; }

.formLayout br {
    clear: both;
}

.error {
    color: red;
}

.notice {
    color: red;
    font-size: 67%;
    text-align: right;
}
```

Figure 12-10   The CSS for the Register application

The JavaScript code for the register_library.js file

The JavaScript code for this application is divided into two files. The register_library.js file is shown in the four parts of figure 12-11. At the start of this code, you can see the standard $ function. The rest of the code on this page is the constructor for a RegisterForm object that will contain all the properties and methods for validating the data that the user enters.

The first statement in this constructor declares an array named fields. This constructor creates one object for each of the fields on the form and stores these objects in this array.

The rest of this constructor is divided into two parts that are identified by comments. First, the starting message that will be displayed in the span tag of each field is assigned to the message property of each field object. Second, the error messages that will be used for each field are assigned to other properties of each field object.

For instance, the message property of the email object is assigned a value of "Must be a valid email address." Then, its required property is assigned a value of "Email is required." And its isEmail property is assigned a value of "Email is not valid." As you will see in a moment, the properties for the error messages are also used to determine what validation tests should be done for each field.

Note, however, that there are two exceptions to the way the properties are coded in the error messages. First, the tooShort property of the password object is an array with the error message in element 0 and the required length in element 1. Second, the noMatch property of the verify object is an array with the error message in element 0 and "password" (the name of the related password field) in element 1. You'll see how these array elements are used in the tooShort and noMatch methods that are defined on the next page.

This is the start of a highly structured approach to form validation. At this point, all of the field objects, field properties, starting messages, and error messages have been defined.

The register_library.js file   **Page 1**

```javascript
var $ = function (id) { return document.getElementById(id); }

var RegisterForm = function () {
    // The array of field objects
    this.fields = [];
    this.fields["email"] = {};
    this.fields["password"] = {};
    this.fields["verify"] = {};
    this.fields["first_name"] = {};
    this.fields["last_name"] = {};
    this.fields["address"] = {};
    this.fields["city"] = {};
    this.fields["state"] = {};
    this.fields["zip"] = {};
    this.fields["phone"] = {};
    this.fields["card_type"] = {};
    this.fields["card_number"] = {};
    this.fields["exp_date"] = {};

    // Starting field messages
    this.fields["email"].message = "Must be a valid email address.";
    this.fields["password"].message = "Must be at least 6 characters.";
    this.fields["state"].message = "Use 2 letter abbreviation.";
    this.fields["zip"].message = "Use 5 or 9 digit ZIP code.";
    this.fields["phone"].message = "Use 999-999-9999 format.";
    this.fields["card_number"].message = "Use 1111-2222-3333-4444 format.";
    this.fields["exp_date"].message = "Use mm/yyyy format.";

    // Field error messages
    this.fields["email"].required = "Email is required.";
    this.fields["email"].isEmail = "Email is not valid.";
    this.fields["password"].required = "Password is required.";
    this.fields["password"].tooShort = ["Password is too short.", 6];
    this.fields["verify"].required = "Please retype your password.";
    this.fields["verify"].noMatch = ["Passwords do not match.", "password"];
    this.fields["first_name"].required = "First name is required.";
    this.fields["last_name"].required = "Last name is required.";
    this.fields["address"].required = "Address is required.";
    this.fields["city"].required = "City is required.";
    this.fields["state"].required = "State is required.";
    this.fields["state"].isState = "State is not valid.";
    this.fields["zip"].required = "ZIP Code is required.";
    this.fields["zip"].isZip = "ZIP Code is not valid.";
    this.fields["phone"].required = "Phone number is required.";
    this.fields["phone"].isPhone = "Phone number is not valid.";
    this.fields["card_type"].required = "Please select a card type.";
    this.fields["card_number"].required = "Card number is required.";
    this.fields["card_number"].isCC = "Card number is not valid.";
    this.fields["exp_date"].required = "Expiration date is required.";
    this.fields["exp_date"].isDate = "Expiration date is not valid.";
    this.fields["exp_date"].expired = "Card has expired.";
}
```

Figure 12-11   The JavaScript code for the register_library.js file (part 1 of 4)

In parts 2 through 4 of this figure, you can see the code for the methods that are added to the RegisterForm object. This code starts with two helper methods named tooShort and matches that can be used by the methods that follow. Both of these methods require two parameters. The second parameter of the tooShort method is the minimum length for a field, and the second parameter of the matches method is the text for the field that the first field should match.

In contrast, the methods that follow validate specific fields, and each of these methods has just one parameter named text. For instance, the isEmail method validates an email entry, and the isState method validates a state entry.

In the isState method, a for loop is used to loop through all of the state codes in the states array to see if the text that is passed to it is equal to one of those codes. Then, if a match is found, true is returned. Otherwise, false is returned.

Please note that all of the other methods also return true if the text that is passed to it is valid, and false if it isn't. Note too that each of these method names is the same as one of the property names that are assigned in part 1.

Although you were introduced to the isEmail function in figure 12-5, the text that follows describes it in more detail. If you're interested, read on. Otherwise, you can skip to the next page.

To start, the isEmail function splits the email address into its local and domain parts. Then, if there aren't two parts or one part is too long, it returns false. Otherwise, it uses regular expressions to test each part for validity.

As you study these expressions, remember that a backslash or double quote must be preceded by a backslash when it is stored in a string. For example, the pattern (^\\") in a regular expression literal, which matches any character except a backslash or quote, needs three more backslashes when it's in a string (^\\\\\\").

The local part of an email address can be in one of two formats: an address format or a quoted text format. According to the SMTP specification, the address format can contain letters, numbers, and 19 symbols (_!#$%&'*+/ =?^`{|}~-) called *atoms*. Also, atoms can be joined together with dots. For instance, "ray.harris" consists of two atoms joined by a dot. In this method, the pattern in the address variable tests for a local part in this format.

In the quoted text format, the string begins and ends with a double quote and can contain any character. As a result, "Ray Harris" is valid in the quoted text format. As in JavaScript strings, though, a backslash or double quote inside the quotes must be preceded by a backslash. In this method, the pattern in the quotedText variable tests for a local part in this format. Then, the regular expression in the localPart variable combines the address and quotedText patterns in a single regular expression.

The domain part of an email address consists of one or more hostnames separated by dots followed by a top-level domain such as com or net. A hostname can contain up to 64 letters, numbers or dashes, but cannot begin or end with a dash. As a result, the pattern in the hostnames variable tests for either a single character hostname or a hostname that begins and ends with a letter or number and contains up to 62 letters, numbers, and dashes for a maximum of 64 characters. Then, the pattern in the tld variable tests for top-level domains of 2 to 6 characters. Last, the regular expression in the domainPart variable combines the hostnames and tld patterns.

The register_library.js file   **Page 2**

```javascript
// Validation methods
RegisterForm.prototype.tooShort = function (text, length) {
    return (text.length < length);
}


RegisterForm.prototype.matches = function (text1, text2) {
    return (text1 == text2);
}


RegisterForm.prototype.isEmail = function (text) {
    if (text.length == 0) return false;
    var parts = text.split("@");
    if (parts.length != 2 ) return false;
    if (parts[0].length > 64) return false;
    if (parts[1].length > 255) return false;
    var address =
        "(^[\\w!#$%&'*+/=?^`{|}~-]+(\\.[\\w!#$%&'*+/=?^`{|}~-]+)*$)";
    var quotedText = "(^\"(([^\\\\\\"])|(\\\\[\\\\\\"]))+\"$)";
    var localPart = new RegExp( address + "|" + quotedText );
    if ( !parts[0].match(localPart) ) return false;
    var hostnames =
        "(([a-zA-Z0-9]\\.)|([a-zA-Z0-9][-a-zA-Z0-9]{0,62}[a-zA-Z0-9]\\.))+";
    var tld = "[a-zA-Z0-9]{2,6}";
    var domainPart = new RegExp("^" + hostnames + tld + "$");
    if ( !parts[1].match(domainPart) ) return false;
    return true;
}


RegisterForm.prototype.isState = function (text) {
    var states = new Array(
        "AL", "AK", "AZ", "AR", "CA", "CO", "CT", "DE", "DC", "FL",
        "GA", "HI", "ID", "IL", "IN", "IA", "KS", "KY", "LA", "ME",
        "MD", "MA", "MI", "MN", "MS", "MO", "MT", "NE", "NV", "NH",
        "NJ", "NM", "NY", "NC", "ND", "OH", "OK", "OR", "PA", "RI",
        "SC", "SD", "TN", "TX", "UT", "VT", "VA", "WA", "WV", "WI", "WY");
    for( var i in states ) {
        if ( text == states[i] ) {
            return true;
        }
    }
    return false;
}


RegisterForm.prototype.isZip = function (text) {
    return /^\d{5}(-\d{4})?$/.test(text);
}


RegisterForm.prototype.isPhone = function (text) {
    return /^\d{3}-\d{3}-\d{4}$/.test(text);
}


RegisterForm.prototype.isCC = function (text) {    // Checks credit card number
    return /^\d{4}-\d{4}-\d{4}-\d{4}$/.test(text);
}
```

Figure 12-11   The JavaScript code for the register_library.js file (part 2 of 4)

In part 3, you can see two more validation methods. Here, the isDate method tests whether the date that is passed is valid. The hasExpired method tests whether the date has already expired. Here again, both of these methods return true if the date is valid, false if it isn't.

If you look at the isDate method, you can see that it uses a regular expression to check the format of the date. But it also checks to see whether the month is less than 1 or greater than 12. Then, the hasExpired method checks to see whether the current date is greater than the date that's passed to it. In this case, the isDate method must be called before the hasExpired method. Otherwise, the hasExpired method would have to duplicate the work of the isDate method.

Instead, the hasExpired method tests the expiration date in an interesting way. Typically, you would subtract one from the expiration month before using it in JavaScript. But here, because credit cards are valid until the end of the month, you can test the current date against the month after the card expires so you don't have to subtract one from the expiration month.

These methods are followed by the validateField method. This is the top-level method that is used to validate all of the fields on the form after the user clicks on the Register button. It receives two parameters. The first one is the name of the field. The second one is the text that the user enters.

To start, this method stores the field object that has the field name that's passed to it in a variable named field. Then, the if statements that follow use the field's properties to determine what methods should be called to validate the text that's passed to it.

For instance, if the field has a required property, the nested if statement calls the tooShort method to determine whether the text has a length of at least 1. If not, it throws an Error object with the message that's in the field's required property. If, for example, the fieldName is "email", the error message is "Email is required."

The rest of the nested if statements in this validateField function also work this way. First, they test whether the field requires a specific test. Then, they call the method for that test and throw an Error object with the related error message if the method returns false.

To take another example, if the field has an isPhone property, the last if statement on this page calls the isPhone method. Then, if that method returns false, it throws a new Error object that contains the message in the isPhone property.

Please note that only two of the methods that are called to do the data validation require two parameters. They are the tooShort and matches methods, and they are called by the first three nested if statements. In the first nested if statement, for example, the tooShort method is called with the text of the field as the first parameter and 1 as the second parameter. This determines whether an entry has been made in a required field.

In the second nested if statement, the tooShort method is called with the text as the first parameter and element 1 of the array in the tooShort property as the second parameter. If you refer back to page 1, you can see that this element contains the minimum length for the field. Then, if the tooShort method returns

The register_library.js file

```javascript
RegisterForm.prototype.isDate = function (text) {
    if ( ! /^[01]?\d\/\d{4}$/.test(text) ) return false;
    var dateParts = text.split("/");
    var month = parseInt(dateParts[0]);
    var year = parseInt(dateParts[1]);
    if ( month < 1 || month > 12 ) return false;
    return true;
}

RegisterForm.prototype.hasExpired = function (text) {
    var dateParts = text.split("/");
    var month = parseInt(dateParts[0]);
    var year = parseInt(dateParts[1]);
    var now = new Date();
    var exp = new Date( year, month);
    return ( now > exp );
}

RegisterForm.prototype.validateField = function (fieldName, text) {
    var field = this.fields[fieldName];
    if (field.required) {
        if ( this.tooShort(text,1) ) {
            throw new Error(field.required);
        }
    }
    if (field.tooShort) {
        if ( this.tooShort(text, field.tooShort[1]) ) {
            throw new Error(field.tooShort[0]);
        }
    }
    if (field.noMatch) {
        if ( ! this.matches(text, $(field.noMatch[1]).value ) ) {
            throw new Error(field.noMatch[0]);
        }
    }
    if (field.isEmail) {
        if ( ! this.isEmail(text) ) {
            throw new Error(field.isEmail);
        }
    }
    if (field.isState) {
        if ( ! this.isState(text) ) {
            throw new Error(field.isState);
        }
    }
    if (field.isZip) {
        if ( ! this.isZip(text) ) {
            throw new Error(field.isZip);
        }
    }
    if (field.isPhone) {
        if ( ! this.isPhone(text) ) {
            throw new Error(field.isPhone);
        }
    }
```

Figure 12-11   The JavaScript code for the register_library.js file (part 3 of 4)

a false value, the message property of the Error object is set to element 0 in the array for the tooShort property of the field.

The third nested if statement works similarly. When it calls the matches method, the second parameter is the value property of the field that's named by element 0 in the field's noMatch property. And it throws an Error object with a message property that contains element 0.

Up to this point all of the methods are called by other methods in the register_library.js file. But two of the last three methods are called by event handlers in the register.js file. The resetErrors method is called when the user clicks the Reset button. The validateForm method is called when the user clicks the Register button.

To start, look at the resetErrors method. It starts by declaring a variable named message. Then, it loops through each field in the fields array. Within the loop, the first statement sets the class name for each XHTML span tag that has an id that consists of the field name followed by "_error" to an empty string. Then, it sets the message variable to the value of the field's message property, which contains the starting message for the field. Last, it sets the value within the span tag to the value of the message variable if it isn't null or to an empty string if it is null.

Now, look at the validateForm method. It first declares a variable named hasErrors and sets it to false. Then, it loops through each field in the fields array. For each field, it calls the clearError method to set the class name for its span tag to an empty string and to clear the message in the span tag.

Next, within a try block within the loop, this method calls the validateField method to validate the field. As you have seen, this method will call all of the validation methods that are appropriate for the field. If one of these methods determines that the field is invalid, the validateField method will throw an error that will be caught by the catch block. So within the catch block, the hasErrors variable is set to true, the class name for the related span tag is set to "error", and the message property in the Error object is displayed in the span tag.

When this loop ends and all of the fields have been processed, this method returns the hasErrors variable. As you will see on the next page, this variable is used to determine whether the form should be submitted for processing by the server.

At this point, the RegisterForm constructor has all of the properties and methods that are required for validating all of the fields on the form. That means that the requirements of the register.js file are limited. In general, all it has to do is use the constructor to create a RegisterForm object, and then call its validateForm method to validate all the fields on the form or call its resetError method to clear the messages on the form.

The register_library.js file

```javascript
            if (field.isCC) {
                if ( ! this.isCC(text) ) {
                    throw new Error(field.isCC);
                }
            }
            if (field.isDate) {
                if ( ! this.isDate(text) ) {
                    throw new Error(field.isDate);
                }
            }
            if (field.expired) {
                if ( this.hasExpired(text) ) {
                    throw new Error(field.expired);
                }
            }
        }
}

// The method that's called when the user clicks the Reset button
RegisterForm.prototype.resetErrors = function () {
    var message;
    for ( var fieldName in this.fields ) {
        $(fieldName + "_error").className = "";
        message = this.fields[fieldName].message;
        $(fieldName + "_error").firstChild.nodeValue =
            ( message ) ? message : "";
    }
}

// A method that's used by the validateForm method
RegisterForm.prototype.clearError = function ( fieldName ) {
    $(fieldName + "_error").className = "";
    $(fieldName + "_error").firstChild.nodeValue = "";
}

// The method that's called when the user clicks the Register button
RegisterForm.prototype.validateForm = function () {
    var hasErrors = false;
    for ( var fieldName in this.fields ) {
        this.clearError(fieldName);
        try {
            this.validateField(fieldName, $(fieldName).value );
        } catch (error) {
            hasErrors = true;
            $(fieldName + "_error").className = "error";
            $(fieldName + "_error").firstChild.nodeValue = error.message;

        }
    }
    return hasErrors;
}
```

Figure 12-11   The JavaScript code for the register_library.js file (part 4 of 4)

The JavaScript code for the register.js file

Figure 12-12 presents the JavaScript code in the register.js file that uses the RegisterForm object. To start, this file declares a variable that will be used for the RegisterForm object. Then, it defines two event handlers for the Register and Reset buttons. Last, it defines the onload event handler.

In the event handler for the Register button, the button is first blurred. Then, an if statement is used to call the validateForm method of the RegisterForm object. If this method returns true, which means the form has errors, an error message is displayed. If this message returns false, the submit method of the form is issued, which submits the form to the server for processing.

In the event handler for the Reset button, the button is first blurred. Then, the reset method of the form is used to reset all of the fields on the form. But that doesn't clear all of the error messages. To do that, this event handler calls the resetErrors method of the RegisterForm object.

In the onload event handler, the function calls the constructor to generate a RegisterForm object and stores it in the registerForm variable. Then, it attaches the event handlers to the click events of the Register and Reset buttons.

The register.js file

```
var registerForm;

// The event handler for the click event of the Register button
var registerClick = function () {
    $("register").blur();
    if ( registerForm.validateForm() ) {
        alert("Please correct the errors on the page.");
    } else {
        $("registration_form").submit();
    }
}

// The event handler for the click event of the Reset button
var resetClick = function () {
    $("reset_form").blur();
    $("registration_form").reset();
    registerForm.resetErrors();
}

// The event handler for the onload event
window.onload = function () {
    registerForm = new RegisterForm();
    $("register").onclick = registerClick;
    $("reset_form").onclick = resetClick;
}
```

Figure 12-12   The JavaScript code for the register.js file

Perspective

Although you can code a data validation application in many different ways, the Register application in this chapter is worth studying because it presents a highly structured approach to data validation. If at first it seems complicated, this structure actually makes it easier to test, debug, and enhance an application like this.

Another benefit to using an approach like this is that it can be easily modified so it can be used for the data on any form. To customize the approach, you just change the field objects, starting messages, error messages, and validation methods so they're appropriate for the form that you're developing.

Now, if you understand the code in the Register application, that's a good indication that you've got a solid grounding in the use of objects, methods, and properties, and that you've mastered the skills in section 2 of this book. That also means that you're ready to learn more about DOM scripting, which is the subject of the next six chapters.

Terms

regular expression	exception
regular expression object	throw an exception
pattern	throw statement
regular expression literal	try-catch statement
escape character	try block
subpattern	catch block
quantifier	exception handling
flag	finally block

Exercise 12-1   Add exception handling to the Future Value application

This exercise will give you a chance to use try-catch and throw statements.

1. From your Firefox browser, open the html file in the future_value folder that's in the chapter 12 folder for exercises. Then, use your text editor to open the Javascript file for this application.

2. Enclose all of the statements for the calculate_click function in a try block, and code a catch block that displays the message property of the error object that's thrown. Then, run the application, and note that the application doesn't throw an exception, no matter what combinations of invalid data you use.

3. Add a throw statement after the first three statements in the try block of the calculate_click function that throws a new error with the message: "Please check your entries for validity." Then, run the application, and note that the error message is displayed.

4. Move the throw statement from the calculate_click function to the if statement in the calculate_future_value function. Then, run the application with a negative entry value. This time the calculate_future_value function throws an exception that is handled by the calculate_click function.

5. Code a throw statement before the alert statement in the catch clause of the calculate_click function. This throw statement should rethrow the error object. Then, run the application with a negative entry value. Since the calculate_click function doesn't have a calling function, this exception is never caught and the application ends with a runtime error.

Exercise 12-2   Modify the Register application

This exercise will give you a chance to use regular expressions. It will also demonstrate how easy it is to modify the data validation functions when you use a coding model like this.

Open and test the application

1. From your Firefox browser, open the index.html file in the register folder that's in the chapter 12 folder for exercises. Then, run the application to see how it works. If you enter all valid data, you'll see that an XHTML page is displayed that indicates that your registration has been submitted.

2. Use your text editor to open the register_library.js and register.js files for this application. Then, review the code.

Use the test method of a regular expression

3. Change the isPhone validation method so it uses the search method of a string instead of the test method of a regular expression object. Then, test this change.

4. Change the isEmail validation method so the address is invalid if it ends with .gov. To do that, use a simple pattern of your own early in the function that tests just for that condition. Then, test this change.

Change the validation rules for the password

5. Delete the tooShort property of the password object. Next, add an isPassword property that contains this value: "Start with 4 or more letters; end with 2 or more digits." Then, add a method named isPassword that uses a regular expression to validate the password entry as described in the error message. Last, add a nested if statement to the validateField method that uses the method to make sure the password entry is valid. Now, test this change.

6. Change the message property of the password object so it reads: "Start with 4 or more letters; end with 2 or more digits." Then, test this change. (In a real application, you would also change this message in the index.html file, but that isn't necessary for this exercise.)

Section 3

DOM scripting

To get the most from JavaScript, you need to know how to use it to manipulate the Document Object Model, or DOM. So that's what this section shows you how to do.

In chapter 13, you'll learn how to work with common DOM objects and timers. In chapter 14, you'll learn how to build libraries that let you handle DOM events in a way that is compatible across browsers. In chapters 15 and 16, you'll learn advanced techniques for DOM scripting and controlling the CSS for an application. In chapter 17, you'll learn how to script tables and forms. And in chapter 18, you'll learn how to use DOM scripting to provide animation within an application.

As you learn these DOM scripting skills, you'll study complete applications that show you how to run slide shows, rotate headlines, use drop-down menus, sort the data in tables, provide animation, and more. And when you complete this section, you'll have taken your JavaScript skills to an expert level.

13

Basic DOM scripting

In previous chapters, you've done some elementary DOM scripting as part of your JavaScript applications. But now, you'll begin to focus more on DOM scripting as you learn to build more complex applications. To get you started, this chapter teaches you how to work with the common DOM objects, how to use cross-browser techniques for working with the event object, and how to use timers in your applications.

How to work with DOM nodes 422
An introduction to DOM nodes 422
Types of DOM nodes 424
The Node interface 426
The Document interface 428
The Element interface 430
The Attr interface 432
How to work with DOM HTML nodes 434
Types of HTMLElement nodes 434
The HTMLElement interface 436
The HTMLAnchorElement interface 436
The HTMLImageElement interface 436
The HTMLButtonElement interface 438
The HTMLInputElement interface 438
Other DOM scripting skills 440
How to cancel the default action of an event 440
How to create image rollovers 442
How to preload images 444
The Image Gallery application 446
The XHTML file 446
The JavaScript files 448
How to use timers 452
How to call a function once 452
How to call a function repeatedly 454
The Slide Show application 456
The XHTML file 456
The CSS file 456
The JavaScript files 458
Perspective 466

How to work with DOM nodes

As you learned in chapter 1, the DOM is a hierarchical set of nodes that represents the web page that's displayed in the browser. To effectively use JavaScript to work with the DOM, you need to understand how the DOM is structured, what the types of DOM nodes are, and how to work with each type of node.

When you work with the DOM, you should be aware that two different DOM specifications deal with DOM nodes: the *DOM Core specification* and the *DOM HTML specification*. In this topic, you'll learn how to work with the basic properties and methods of the most common DOM nodes in the Core specification. In the next topic, you'll learn how to work with the most common DOM HTML nodes in the HTML specification. These are the objects, properties, and methods that modern browsers support.

An introduction to DOM nodes

Figure 13-1 shows the XHTML for a web page, and it shows a diagram for the DOM that's built by the browser to represent this web page. As you can see, the DOM starts at the global window object, and that object stores all other elements in the DOM.

In this diagram, italics are used to identify each type of DOM node, and most of these DOM nodes are Element nodes. For example, the <body> tag is an Element node, the <div> tag is an Element node, and the <li> tags are Element nodes. Note, however, that some of these Element nodes contain Text nodes. For example, the <h1> tag is an Element node that has a Text node. Here, the Text node provides access to the text that's displayed by the <h1> tag ("Fishing Image Gallery").

Although this diagram shows the most important parts of the DOM, it doesn't show them all. For example, it doesn't show the attributes for the various elements in the XHTML page. However, this level of detail is all you need for this chapter. As you progress through this chapter, you can refer back to this diagram if you need help visualizing the DOM.

The XHTML for a web page

```
<!DOCTYPE html PUBLIC "-//W3C//DTD XHTML 1.0 Transitional//EN"
    "http://www.w3.org/TR/xhtml1/DTD/xhtml1-transitional.dtd">
<html xmlns="http://www.w3.org/1999/xhtml">
<head>
    <title>Image Gallery</title>
    <link rel="stylesheet" type="text/css" href="image_gallery.css"/>
</head>

<body>
<div id="content">
    <h1 class="center">Fishing Image Gallery</h1>
    <p class="center">Click one of the links below to view the image.</p>
    <ul class="center" id="imageList">
        <li><a href="casting1.jpg" title="Casting 1">Casting 1</a></li>
        <li><a href="casting2.jpg" title="Casting 2">Casting 2</a></li>
        <li><a href="catchrelease.jpg" title="Catch and Release">
            Catch and Release</a></li>
        <li><a href="fish.jpg" title="Fish">Fish</a></li>
        <li><a href="lures.jpg" title="Lures">Lures</a></li>
    </ul>
    <p class="center">
        <img src="casting1.jpg" alt="Fishing Images" id="image" />
    </p>
    <p class="center"><span id="caption">Casting 1</span></p>
</div>
</body>
</html>
```

The DOM for the web page

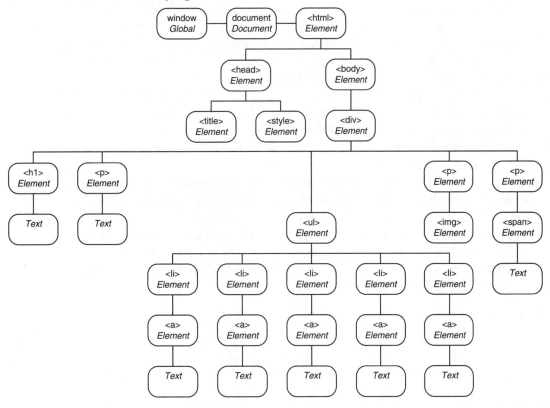

Figure 13-1   An introduction to DOM nodes

Types of DOM nodes

Figure 13-2 describes seven of the most common types of DOM nodes. To start, it shows the inheritance hierarchy for these nodes. Here, the Node type is at the top of the hierarchy. In other words, all nodes in the DOM hierarchy inherit the Node type. As a result, all nodes can use the properties and methods of the Node type.

Similarly, the CharacterData type is the base type for the Text and Comment types. As a result, the Text and Comment types can use the properties and methods of the CharacterData and Node types.

This figure also lists the numerical values that are assigned to the most common node types. But note that the Node and CharacterData types don't have numerical values. That's because these types of nodes are base types that exist only to provide methods for other nodes. As a result, you can't create an object from these types, and you won't need to check the type for these nodes.

As this figure shows, the DOM Core specification has rules that indicate which nodes can have children and what types of children they can have. First, a Document node can have only one Element node as a child. In figure 13-1, for example, the Document node has only one child, the Element node for the <html> tag.

Second, an Element node may have multiple Element, Text, and Comment nodes as child nodes. In figure 13-1, for example, the Element node for the <ul> tag contains multiple Element nodes, one for each <li> tag.

Third, an Attr node may be attached to an Element node. Technically, though, an Attr node isn't considered a child node. As a result, when you write JavaScript code, you must use a different technique for working with attributes than you use for working with child elements.

Fourth, an Attr node can have a Text node as a child node. In figure 13-1, the Attr nodes aren't shown in the diagram. However, the XHTML code does attach Attr nodes to some Element nodes. For example, this XHTML code attaches two attributes to the Element node for the <ul> tag: the class attribute and the id attribute.

Fifth, the Text and Comment nodes cannot have child nodes. In figure 13-1, for example, the Text node for the <h1> tag contains the text value that's displayed by the <h1> tag, but it doesn't have a child node.

For now, you don't need to remember these rules. But it's important to know that the DOM Core specification provides rules for constructing the DOM. Later in this book, when you learn how to add and remove nodes with JavaScript, you must follow these rules.

The inheritance hierarchy for DOM nodes

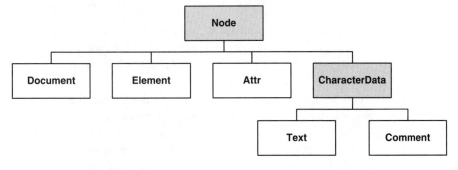

Types of DOM nodes

Type	Description
Node	Base type for all DOM nodes
Document	Root node of the DOM
Element	An element in the web page
Attr	An attribute of an element
CharacterData	Base type for nodes that contain character data
Text	Text displayed on the web page
Comment	A comment in the web page

Numerical values used to indicate the node type

Type	Value
Element	1
Attr	2
Text	3
Comment	8
Document	9

Rules for child nodes in the DOM

- A Document node may have only one Element node as a child node.
- An Element node may have Element, Text, and Comment nodes as child nodes.
- Attr nodes can be attached to Element nodes, but they are not considered child nodes.
- An Attr node may have a Text node as a child node.
- Text and Comment nodes may not have child nodes.

Description

- The Node and CharacterData types are base types that provide properties and methods for other types of nodes. All types of DOM nodes inherit the properties and methods of the Node object. The Text and Comment nodes inherit the properties and methods of the CharacterData type.

Figure 13-2   Types of DOM nodes

The Node interface

An *interface* defines the properties and methods for an object type. For instance, figure 13-3 describes eight properties and two methods of the Node interface. In other words, this figure describes the properties and methods of the Node object type.

In the previous figure, you learned that all types of DOM nodes inherit the Node type. As a result, when you write JavaScript, you can use the properties and methods in this figure to work with any type of DOM node.

The first example uses the nodeType property to check if the node is an Element node. If it is, this code displays a dialog box that indicates that the element with the id of imageList is an Element node. Here, the integer 1 corresponds with the Element node.

The second example uses the childNodes property to loop through an array of child nodes for the current node. Within the loop, the first statement gets the node from the array of child nodes. Then, the second statement uses the nodeName and nodeValue properties to add the values returned by these properties to a string.

When you work with the nodeName and nodeValue properties, you'll find that they work differently depending on the node type. For example, a Text node doesn't contain a name. As a result, its nodeName property returns a value of "#text". However, an Element node does contain a name. As a result, its nodeName property returns the name of the XHTML tag for the element.

Conversely, a Text node does contain a value. As a result, its nodeValue property returns its text value. However, an Element node doesn't contain a value. As a result, its nodeValue property returns a null value.

Similarly, the parentNode property returns the parent node of the current node if one exists. Since most nodes have a parent node, this property usually returns a value. However, some nodes such as the Document node return a null value. This makes sense because the window object in the diagram in figure 13-1 isn't a part of the DOM hierarchy. As a result, the Document node is at the top of the DOM hierarchy and doesn't have a parent node.

The third and fourth examples show how to use two methods of the Node object. Here, the third example displays a message if the current node has any child nodes. Then, the fourth example displays a message if the current node has any attributes.

Common properties of the Node interface

Property	Description
nodeType	An integer value that represents the type of node.
nodeName	The name of the node. This name varies depending on the node type. For an Element or Attr node, this property returns the name of the tag or attribute. For a Document, Text, or Comment element, this property returns a value of "#document", "#text", or "#comment".
nodeValue	The value of the node. For a Text, Comment, or Attr node, this property returns the text value that's stored in the node. Otherwise, this property returns a null value.
attributes	An array of Attr objects representing the attributes of the current node.
parentNode	The parent node of the current node if one exists. Otherwise, this property returns a null value.
childNodes	An array of Node objects representing the child nodes of the current node.
firstChild	A Node object for the first child node. If this node doesn't have child nodes, this property returns a null value.
lastChild	A Node object for the last child node. If this node doesn't have child nodes, this property returns a null value.

How to determine if a node is an Element node

```
var element = document.getElementById("imageList");
if (element.nodeType == 1) {
    alert( "imageList is an Element node!" );
}
```

How to perform an action on each child node

```
var element = document.getElementById("imageList");
var node, displayString;
for (var i = 0; i < element.childNodes.length; i++) {
    node = element.childNodes[i];
    displayString += node.nodeName + ": " + node.nodeValue + "\n";
}
```

Two methods of the Node object

Method	Description
hasChildNodes()	Returns a true value if this node has child nodes.
hasAttributes()	Returns a true value if this node has attributes.

How to determine if a node has child nodes

```
var element = document.getElementById("imageList");
if ( element.hasChildNodes() ) {
    alert( "imageList has child nodes!" );
}
```

How to determine if a node has attributes

```
var element = document.getElementById("imageList");
if ( element.hasAttributes() ) {
    alert( "imageList has attributes!" );
}
```

Figure 13-3   The Node interface

The Document interface

Figure 13-4 shows how to use the documentElement property of the Document object. In an XHTML document, this is the Element node for the <html> tag.

Without this property, you can find the root Element node by looping through all the child nodes of the Document node and testing each one to see if it is an Element node. The documentElement property just provides an easy way to do that. As you progress through this chapter, you'll see that many of the properties and methods make it easier to work with certain types of nodes.

This figure also describes three methods of the Document object. First, you can use the getElementsByTagName method to return an array that contains all the Element nodes in the document that match the specified tag name. Then, you can loop through the array and perform an action on each Element node. For instance, the second example finds all of the <a> tags for the document. Then, it loops through these tags and stores the nodeType property for each tag in a string variable named displayString. If you want to return an array that contains all Element nodes in the document, you can specify an asterisk (*) instead of a tag name.

Second, you can use the getElementsByName method to return an array of all the Element nodes in the document that have a name attribute that matches the specified value. Since a group of radio buttons share the same name, this method is commonly used with radio buttons. For instance, the third example gets all Element nodes that have a name attribute of card_type. Then, this code performs an action on each of them.

Third, you can use the getElementById method to return a reference to the Element node with the specified id. This is the method that you've been using since chapter 2.

One property of the Document interface

Property	Description
documentElement	The root Element node for the document. In other words, this property returns the Element node for the html tag.

How to use the documentElement property

```
var htmlElement = document.documentElement;
```

Three methods of the Document interface

Method	Description
getElementsByTagName(tagname)	Returns an array of all Element objects in the DOM that have a nodeName that matches the specified value. This method returns all Element objects if a value of * is specified.
getElementsByName(name)	Returns an array of all Element objects in the DOM that have a name attribute that matches the specified value.
getElementById(elementId)	Returns the Element object from the DOM whose ID matches the specified. Returns null if no element matches.

How to find all the <a> tags and perform an action on them

```
var links = document.getElementsByTagName("a");
var displayString = "";
for ( var i = 0; i < links.length; i++ ) {
    displayString += links[i].nodeType + "\n";
}
```

How find all the buttons in a radio button group

```
var cardTypeButtons = document.getElementsByName("card_type");
for ( var i = 0; i < cardTypeButtons.length; i++ ) {
    alert( cardTypeButtons[i].nodeName );
}
```

How to determine if an element exists with a specified id

```
var element = document.getElementById("imageList");
if ( element ) {
    // not null is treated as true
    alert( "imageList found" );
}
else {
    // null is treated as false
    alert( "imageList not found" );
}
```

Figure 13-4   The Document interface

The Element interface

Figure 13-5 starts by showing how to use the tagName property of an Element object to get the name of the XHTML tag. Here, the example starts by using the getElementById method of the Document object to get an Element object for an unordered list of images. Then, it displays the tag name for that Element object in a dialog box. To do that, it uses the tagName property of the Element object.

By default, the tagName property displays the tag name in uppercase letters. In this example, the Element object is an unordered list, so the tagName property returns a value of UL. If necessary, however, you can use the toLowerCase method to convert the tag name to lowercase letters.

This figure also describes six methods of the Element object. Of these methods, the first four work with an element's attributes, and the last two work with the descendants of the current element.

The first example for these methods uses the hasAttributes method to check if that element has an attribute named class. If so, it uses the getAttribute method to display the value of the class attribute.

The second example starts by getting an Element object for an element that displays an image. Then, it uses the setAttribute method to set the border attribute for this element to a value of 1. As a result, this code displays a border around the element that's 1 pixel wide.

The third example shows how to remove an attribute from an element. Like the first two examples, it begins by retrieving an Element object. Then, it removes the attribute named class from the Element object. By default, the class attribute for this element is set to a value of "center", which causes the element to be centered. As a result, removing this attribute removes the centering from this element.

The fourth example shows how to search the descendants of an element. To start, this code gets an Element object for an unordered list of images. Then, it uses the getElementsByTagName method to retrieve an array of all Element objects that are <li> tags.

Here, you can see that the getElementsByTagName method of the Element object works like the getElementsByTagName method of the Document object. However, it lets you get elements from the specified Element object rather than from the entire Document object. Similarly, the getElementsByName method of the Element object works like the getElementsByName method of the Document object.

One property of the Element interface

Property	Description
tagName	Name of the tag for this element. It will be in uppercase.

How to get the tag name of an element

```
var element = document.getElementById("imageList");
alert("Tag name: " + element.tagName);
```

Common methods of the Element interface

Method	Description
hasAttribute(name)	Returns true if the Element has the attribute specified in name.
getAttribute(name)	Returns the value of the attribute specified in name or the empty string if an attribute of that name isn't set.
setAttribute(name, value)	Sets the attribute specified in name to the specified value.
removeAttribute(name)	Removes the attribute specified in name.
getElementsByTagName(tagname)	Returns an array of all Element objects descended from this element that have a nodeName that matches the specified tag. If * is specified, this method returns all Element objects.
getElementsByName(name)	Returns an array of all Element objects descended from this element that have a name attribute that matches the specified name.

How to test for and retrieve an attribute

```
var list = document.getElementById("imageList");
if ( list.hasAttribute("class") ) {
    alert ("class: " + list.getAttribute("class") );
}
```

How to change an attribute

```
var image = document.getElementById("image");
image.setAttribute("border", "1");
```

How to remove an attribute

```
var list = document.getElementById("imageList");
list.removeAttribute("class");
```

How to search for descendent elements

```
var list = document.getElementById("imageList");
var items = list.getElementsByTagName("li");
```

Figure 13-5   The Element interface

The Attr interface

Figure 13-6 describes four properties of the Attr object. Typically, you can use the methods of the Element object to work with the attributes of an element. However, when you need to treat the attributes property of an element as an array, you can use the properties of the individual Attr objects rather than the methods of the Element object.

In this figure, the example displays the name and value for all attributes of the specified element. To start, this code retrieves the Element object for the unordered list of images. Then, it declares a variable named result and sets it equal to an empty string. Next, this code loops through the Attr objects that are stored in the attributes array of the Element object. To do that, it uses the attributes property to retrieve the array of attributes. Within the loop, the code appends the name, an equals sign, and the value for each attribute to the variable named result. Finally, the last statement displays the result string.

The dialog box displayed in this figure shows that the specified element contained two attributes: id and class. Here, the id attribute has a value of "imageList", and the class attribute has a value of "center". If you compare these attributes to the XHTML in figure 13-1, you'll see that they are correct.

Four properties of the Attr interface

Property	Description
name	The name of the attribute.
value	The value of the attribute.
ownerElement	The Element node that this Attr object is attached to or null if the object isn't attached to an element.
specified	Returns true if the attribute was set in the XHTML file or by JavaScript. Returns false if the attribute value is a default value of the element.

How to use the name and value properties

```
var list = document.getElementById("imageList");
var result = "";
for (var i = 0; i < list.attributes.length; i++) {
    result += list.attributes[i].name + " = " +
            list.attributes[i].value + "\n";
}
alert(result);
```

The dialog box that's displayed

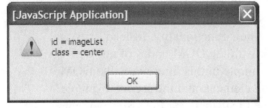

Description

- The properties of the Attr interface are useful when you loop through the Attribute nodes in the attributes property of an Element node.

Figure 13-6   The Attr interface

How to work with DOM HTML nodes

Now that you understand how to work with the DOM Core specification, you're ready to learn how to use the DOM HTML specification. This specification adds properties and methods to the Element nodes that make it easier to work with XHTML elements.

Types of HTMLElement nodes

The DOM HTML specification provides over 50 node types for working with nearly every type of XHTML tag. Figure 13-7 introduces five of the most commonly used types in the DOM HTML specification.

To start, this figure presents an inheritance hierarchy that shows that the HTMLElement type inherits properties and methods from the Element and Node types of the DOM Core specification. In turn, the HTMLElement type is the base type for several more elements such as the HTMLAnchorElement type and the HTMLImageElement type. As a result, these types inherit all properties and methods that are available to the HTMLElement type.

When you work with the DOM HTML specification, you should remember that its properties and methods don't provide new functionality. Instead, they provide shortcuts that make it easier to work with the DOM nodes of an XHTML document. For instance, the first example in this figure uses the DOM Core specification to get the id attribute of an element, and the second example uses the DOM HTML specification to get the id attribute for the same element. As you can see, the second example is significantly shorter and easier to read. However, both code examples accomplish the same task.

Once you understand how to work with the node types in this figure, you have the skills that you need to use the other types of nodes that are available from the DOM HTML specification. To learn more about these types, you can visit the URL shown in this figure, or you can search the Internet for more information about working with specific node types.

The inheritance hierarchy for the HTMLElement nodes

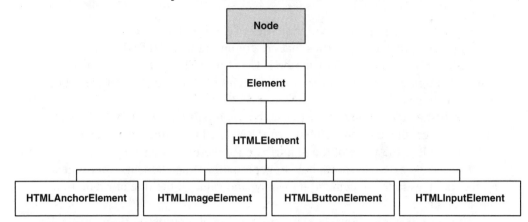

How to get the id attribute using the DOM Core specification

```
list.getAttribute("id")
```

How to get the id attribute using the DOM HTML specification

```
list.id
```

A URL that includes a complete list of HTMLElement types

```
www.w3.org/TR/DOM-Level-2-HTML/html.html
```

Description

- The properties of the HTMLElement nodes don't provide new functionality, but they do provide shortcuts that make it easier to work with the DOM nodes.

- The HTMLElement type inherits the DOM Element type. As a result, it provides access to all the properties and methods of the Node and Element types.

- The HTMLElement type is the base type for other element types that correspond with HTML tags. For example, the HTMLAnchorElement type corresponds with the <a> tag, the HTMLImageElement type corresponds with the <img> tag, and so on.

Figure 13-7   Types of DOM HTML nodes

The HTMLElement interface

Figure 13-8 summarizes two properties of the HTMLElement interface. This interface provides properties that are common to all XHTML elements such as the HTMLAnchorElement, the HTMLImageElement, and so on. The rest of this figure summarizes the properties and methods for four of the subordinate interfaces.

The first example shows how to use the id property of the HTMLElement interface to get the id of an element. After it gets all the <img> tags in a document, it displays the value of the id attribute for the first <img> tag.

The second example shows how to get the title of an element. After it gets all the <a> tags in the document, it displays the value of the title attribute for the second tag.

The third example shows how to set the value of a property. Here, it sets the title property of the second <a> tag to a new string value.

The HTMLAnchorElement interface

The HTMLAnchorElement interface provides an href property that makes it easier to work with links. For example, you can use the href property to get the URL for the link. Or, you can set the href property to a string that specifies a URL.

The HTMLImageElement interface

The HTMLImageElement interface provides a src property that makes it easier to work with images. Here, the first example shows how to get the value of the src property. First, it gets a reference to the element with an id of "image". Then, it displays its src property.

The second example shows how to set the value of the src property. First, it gets a reference to the element with the id of "image". Then, it set its src property to "lures.jpg".

When the src property of an image is changed, the web browser immediately downloads the new image and displays it. If the new image is a different size than the previous image, the web page layout is adjusted so it accommodates the new image size.

Two properties of the HTMLElement interface

Property	Description
id	The id attribute of the XHTML element.
title	The title attribute of the XHTML element.

How to get the id of an element

```
var images = document.getElementsByTagName("img");
alert("first image id: " + images[0].id);
```

How to get the title attribute of an element

```
var links = document.getElementsByTagName("a");
alert("second link title: " + links[1].title);
```

How to set the title attribute of an element

```
var links = document.getElementsByTagName("a");
links[1].title = "New Title";
```

One property of the HTMLAnchorElement interface

Property	Description
href	The href attribute of the XHTML <a> element.

How to get the href attribute of an anchor element

```
var links = document.getElementsByTagName("a");
alert("second link href: " + links[1].href);
```

One property of the HTMLImageElement interface

Property	Description
src	The src attribute of the XHTML <img> element.

How to get the src attribute of an image element

```
var imageElement = document.getElementById("image");
alert("image element src: " + imageElement.src);
```

How to set the src attribute of an image element

```
var imageElement = document.getElementById("image");
imageElement.src = "lures.jpg";
```

Figure 13-8   The DOM HTML interfaces (part 1 of 2)

The HTMLButtonElement interface

The HTMLButtonElement interface provides one property and two methods that make it easier to work with buttons. Here, the first example shows how to disable a button by setting its disabled property to true. Conversely, the second example shows how to enable a button by setting its disabled property to false. Then, the third example shows how to toggle the state of a button. It uses the NOT operator (!) to set the disabled property to the opposite of its original value.

As you have learned in chapters 2 and 6, you can use the focus method to move the focus to an XHTML element. Conversely, you can use the blur method to remove the focus from an element.

If you don't use the blur method to remove the focus after a button has been clicked, the button is highlighted by the browser to indicate that it has the focus. Then, if the user presses the Enter key, the click event of the button is triggered. If you don't want that, you can use the blur method to remove the focus from the button. Or, you can use the focus method of another control to move the focus somewhere else.

The HTMLInputElement interface

The properties and methods in this figure work the same for an HTMLInputElement object as they do for an HTMLButtonElement object. As a result, you can use the same skills to work with an HTMLInputElement object.

For example, when a web page contains a form, it's common to use the focus method to move the focus to the first text field on the form. To do that, you can use code like this:

```
var txtFirstName = document.getElementById("txtFirstName");
txtFirstName.focus();
```

After this code is executed, the user can enter text into the field.

One property of the HTMLInputElement and HTMLButtonElement interface

Property	Description
disabled	The disabled attribute of the XHTML <input> or <button> element.

How to disable an element

```
var btnPlay = document.getElementById("btnPlay");
btnPlay.disabled = true;
```

How to enable an element

```
var btnPlay = document.getElementById("btnPlay");
btnPlay.disabled = false;
```

How to toggle an element's disabled property

```
var btnPlay = document.getElementById("btnPlay");
btnPlay.disabled = ! btnPlay.disabled;
```

Two methods of the HTMLInputElement and HTMLButtonElement interface

Method	Description
focus()	Moves the focus to this XHTML <input> or <button> element.
blur()	Removes the focus from this XHTML <input> or <button> element.

How to set focus on an element

```
var btnPlay = document.getElementById("btnPlay");
btnPlay.focus();
```

How to blur an element

```
var btnPlay = document.getElementById("btnPlay");
btnPlay.blur();
```

Figure 13-8   The DOM HTML interfaces (part 2 of 2)

Other DOM scripting skills

This topic describes other DOM scripting skills that are commonly used in JavaScript applications.

How to cancel the default action of an event

When a user clicks on a button of the button type, the button doesn't perform any action unless a JavaScript event handler has been attached to the button. In other words, there is no default action for a button of the button type. However, when a user clicks on some other elements of a web page, the browser performs a default action.

Figure 13-9 lists the default action for several elements. If, for example, a user clicks on a link, the browser loads the URL specified by the link. Similarly, if a user clicks on a button of the submit type, the browser submits the form to the server.

Although these default actions usually work the way you want, you may occasionally need to cancel a default action. If, for example, the user clicks on a link that loads an image, the browser by default loads the specified URL, which causes the user to exit the application. But if the application is running a slide show, you don't want that. As a result, you need to cancel the default action for this event. You'll see that illustrated in the two applications for this chapter.

When an event occurs, an event object is created. This object contains information about the event that occurred and provides methods that let you control the behavior of the event. To cancel the default action of an event, for example, you need to code an event handler that accesses the event object and uses one of its methods to cancel the default action.

As the first example in this figure shows, most web browsers are DOM-compliant so they pass the event object as the first parameter to the event handler. In addition, this event object has a method named preventDefault that you can use to prevent the default action from occurring.

Unfortunately, Internet Explorer isn't completely DOM-compliant. So, as the second example shows, you get the event object by using the global window.event property. In addition, you set the returnValue property of this event object to false to prevent the default action from occurring.

To make your applications compatible with both types of browsers, you can use the code in the third example. Here, the first if statement tests the evt parameter to see if it's undefined. If so, the browser is IE, so this code assigns the event object in the window.event property to the evt parameter. Otherwise, the browser is DOM-compliant, so the evt parameter already contains the event object.

Then, the second if statement tests the evt parameter to see if it provides a preventDefault method. If so, this code calls the preventDefault method. If not, this code sets the returnValue property to false.

Common XHTML tags that have default actions for the click event

Tag	Default action for the click event
<a>	Load the page in the href attribute.
<input>	Submit the form if the type attribute is set to submit.
<input>	Reset the form if the type attribute is set to reset.
<button>	Submit a form if the type attribute is set to submit.
<button>	Reset a form if the type attribute is set to reset.

DOM-compliant code that cancels the default action

```
var event_handler = function (evt) {
    evt.preventDefault();
}
```

IE code that cancels the default action

```
var event_handler = function () {
    var evt = window.event;
    evt.returnValue = false;
}
```

Browser-compatible code that cancels the default action

```
var event_handler = function (evt) {
    // If the event object is not sent, get it
    if (!evt) evt = window.event;  // for IE

    // Cancel the default action
    if (evt.preventDefault) {
        evt.preventDefault();      // for most browsers
    }
    else {
        evt.returnValue = false;   // for IE
    }
}
```

Description

- All browsers except IE send an event object as the first parameter of the event handler.
- IE stores the event object in the global window.event property.
- All browsers except IE provide a DOM-compliant preventDefault method for the event object. When called, this method prevents the default action of the event from occurring.
- IE provides a property named returnValue in the event object. When set to false, this property prevents the default action of the event from occurring.

Figure 13-9   How to cancel the default action of an event

How to create image rollovers

An *image rollover* occurs when the user positions the mouse over an image and the image changes to another image. Then, when the user moves the mouse out of the image, the image changes back to the first image. To achieve this effect, you can use a Rollover object type like the one in figure 13-10.

The constructor for this Rollover object takes two parameters. The first parameter (imageId) specifies the id of the <img> tag that's used for the rollover. The second parameter (newImageURL) specifies the URL of the image that should be displayed when the user positions the mouse over the image. Note here that you don't need to specify the URL of the image that's displayed when the mouse isn't over the image since this URL is specified in the XHTML code.

This constructor begins by copying the object that the this keyword refers to into a variable named that. Since the this keyword refers to the Rollover object that's created by the constructor, the that variable also refers to the Rollover object. You'll see why the that variable is necessary in a moment.

Next, this constructor creates a new property named newImageURL and copies the newImageURL parameter into this property. Then, it creates another new property named image that refers to the DOM node identified by the imageId parameter.

After the constructor sets up these three variables, it validates the image node. First, it checks whether the node specified by the imageId parameter exists. Then, it checks whether the node is an image element. To do that, this code checks to make sure the nodeType is equal to 1 (an Element node) and that the nodeName is equal to "IMG".

After the image node is validated, this constructor copies the original image URL from the image's src property into a new property named oldImageURL. This makes the original image URL available after the mouse is moved out of the image.

At this point, the constructor creates the two event handlers for the image rollover. It's within these event handlers that the variable named that has to be used to refer to the Rollover object. That's because the this keyword within the event handlers refers to the image object, not the Rollover object.

The first event handler runs when the user triggers the onmouseover event, and it copies the newImageURL property to the src property of the image. This displays the new image. The second event handler runs when the user triggers the onmouseout event, and it copies the oldImageURL property to the src property of the image. This displays the original image.

After the code for the Rollover constructor, this figure shows how to use the Rollover object type to create an image rollover. To start, the XHTML creates an <img> tag with a src attribute that points to the first image. Then, when the window.onload event occurs, the JavaScript code creates a new Rollover object and stores it in a variable named rollover.

Later, when the user positions the mouse over the original image, the onmouseover event will occur, its event handler will be executed, and the old

Two mouse events

Event	Occurs when...
onmouseover	The mouse is moved inside an element.
onmouseout	The mouse is moved outside an element.

The JavaScript code for a Rollover object type

```
var Rollover = function ( imageId, newImageURL ) {
    var that = this;        // both that and this refer to the Rollover object
    this.newImageURL = newImageURL;
    this.image = document.getElementById(imageId);

    // Validate node
    if ( ! this.image ) {
        throw new Error("Rollover: Image ID not found.");
    }
    if ( this.image.nodeType !== 1 || this.image.nodeName !== "IMG" ) {
        throw new Error("Rollover: Image ID is not an img tag.");
    }

    // Copy original image URL
    this.oldImageURL = this.image.src;

    // Attach event handlers
    this.image.onmouseover = function () {
        that.image.src = that.newImageURL;
    }
    this.image.onmouseout = function () {
        that.image.src = that.oldImageURL;
    }
}
```

How to create an image rollover

The XHTML code for the image

```
<img src="image1.jpg" id="image" />
```

The JavaScript code to create the rollover

```
var rollover;
window.onload = function () {
    rollover = new Rollover("image", "image2.jpg");
}
```

Description

- An *image rollover* is an image that changes when the user positions the mouse over the image. To create an image rollover, you can change the src attribute of an <img> tag in response to the onmouseover and onmouseout events.

- The Rollover object defined above makes it easy to create multiple rollovers in a web application.

- Rollovers work best when the two images are the same size. Otherwise, the layout of the page changes in response to the rollover.

Figure 13-10   How to create image rollovers

image will be replaced with the new image. And when the user moves the mouse out of the new image, the onmouseout event will occur, its event handler will be executed, and the old image will be restored.

How to preload images

In JavaScript applications that load an image in response to a user event, the image isn't downloaded until the JavaScript code changes the src attribute of the <img> tag. For large images or slow connections, this can cause a delay of a few seconds before the browser is able to display the image.

To solve this problem, your application can download the images before the user event occurs. This is known as *preloading images*. Then, the browser can display the images without noticeable delays. Although this may result in a longer delay when the page is initially loaded, the user won't encounter any delays when using the application.

Figure 13-11 shows how to preload images. To start, the first line of code creates a new Image object and stores it in a variable named image. This creates a new image node that's empty. Then, the second line of code sets the src property to the URL of the image. This causes the web browser to preload the image.

The second example shows two lines of code for preloading the second image that you can add to the Rollover object type of the last figure. Note here that you don't need to preload the original image. Since the src attribute of the <img> tag specifies that image, the browser downloads it and displays it when it loads the page.

The third example shows how to preload the images for all the links on a page. First, the code defines five variables. The links variable stores an array of all the links in the page. The images variable stores an array of the new Image objects that will be used to preload the images. And the last three variables are used by the loop to process each link. Here, the code loops through every link that's stored in the array of links.

Within the loop, the first statement copies the current link into the link variable. Then, an if statement uses a regular expression to test whether the href property of the link ends with ".jpg". If so, the code creates a new Image object and stores it in the image variable. Next, the code sets the src property of the Image object to the href property of the link. This preloads the image. Finally, this code stores the Image object in the images array for future reference.

At this point, an application can work with the array of preloaded images. For example, it could count the number of preloaded images, or it could refer to the src attribute for each of the preloaded images.

How to preload an image with the Image object

How to create an Image object

```
var image = new Image();
```

How to load an image in an Image object

```
image.src = "image_name.jpg";
```

How to preload the second image in the Rollover object type

```
var Rollover = function ( imageId, newImageURL ) {
    // Validate node - same as previous figure
    // Copy original image url - same as previous figure

    // Preload the new image
    this.newImage = new Image();
    this.newImage.src = this.newImageURL;

    // Attach event handlers - same as previous figure
}
```

How to preload all the images in the links of a page

```
var links = document.getElementsByTagName("a");
var images = [];
var i, link, image;
for ( i = 0; i < links.length; i++ ) {
    link = links[i];
    if ( /\.jpg$/i.test( link.href ) ) {
        image = new Image();
        image.src = link.href;
        images.push( image );
    }
}
```

Description

- When an application *preloads images*, it loads all of the images that it's going to need when the page loads, and it stores these images in the web browser's cache for future use.

- When the images are preloaded, the browser can display them without any noticeable delay.

- The Image object creates a new, empty image node. Setting the src attribute of this image node causes the web browser to preload the image.

Figure 13-11   How to preload images

The Image Gallery application

Figure 13-12 shows the Image Gallery application in a web browser after the user clicks on the second image name in the list. When the user clicks an image name, the browser displays that image on the page, and it displays the title attribute of the <a> tag in the <span> tag under the image as a caption. In this figure, for example, the browser displays the Casting 2 image and caption.

The XHTML file

Figure 13-12 presents the XHTML code for the Image Gallery application. This XHTML is similar to the XHTML presented in figure 13-1, but it includes the two shaded <script> tags that load the JavaScript files.

The unordered list with the id of imageList provides the links to the images that make up the gallery. To add or remove images from the gallery, you can modify the XHTML code to add or remove entries from this list. That way, a web designer without JavaScript experience can manage the image list without having to modify the JavaScript code. Although it's also possible to use a server-side language to build this list from images that are stored in a database, the approach used by the Image Gallery application is a simple approach that's adequate for many situations.

When the page initially loads, the <img> and <span> tags in the last two paragraphs display the first image and caption in the list. Then, when the user clicks on one of the links in the image list, the Image Gallery application displays the image and caption for that link. This is done by the JavaScript for this application.

The Image Gallery in the browser

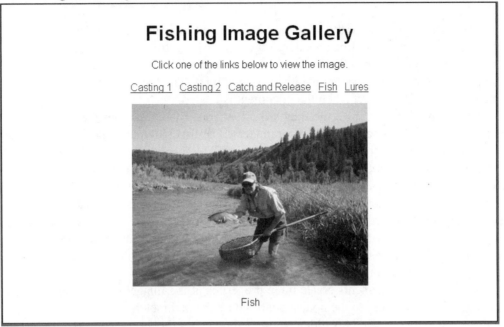

The XHTML file

```
<!DOCTYPE html PUBLIC "-//W3C//DTD XHTML 1.0 Transitional//EN"
    "http://www.w3.org/TR/xhtml1/DTD/xhtml1-transitional.dtd">
<html xmlns="http://www.w3.org/1999/xhtml">
<head>
    <title>Image Gallery</title>
    <link rel="stylesheet" type="text/css" href="image_gallery.css"/>
    <script type="text/javascript" src="image_gallery_library.js"></script>
    <script type="text/javascript" src="image_gallery.js"></script>
</head>
<body>
<div id="content">
    <h1 class="center">Fishing Image Gallery</h1>
    <p class="center">Click one of the links below to view the image.</p>
    <ul class="center" id="imageList">
        <li><a href="casting1.jpg" title="Casting 1">Casting 1</a></li>
        <li><a href="casting2.jpg" title="Casting 2">Casting 2</a></li>
        <li><a href="catchrelease.jpg" title="Catch and Release">
            Catch and Release</a></li>
        <li><a href="fish.jpg" title="Fish">Fish</a></li>
        <li><a href="lures.jpg" title="Lures">Lures</a></li>
    </ul>
    <p class="center">
        <img src="casting1.jpg" alt="Fishing Images" id="image" />
    </p>
    <p class="center"><span id="caption">Casting 1</span></p>
</div>
</body>
</html>
```

Figure 13-12   The Image Gallery application (part 1 of 3)

The JavaScript files

The JavaScript code for this application is in two files. The first file is a library file that defines an ImageGallery object type that retrieves the image links, attaches an event handler to each link that displays the image on the page, and preloads the images that are identified by the links. The second file creates a new ImageGallery object when the document is loaded.

The library file starts with the standard $ function. Then, it defines the ImageGallery constructor with three parameters. The first parameter specifies the id for the <ul> tag that contains the image list. The second parameter specifies the id for the <img> tag that displays the images. And the third parameter specifies the id for the <span> tag that displays the caption.

Within the constructor, the first statement creates a variable named that and assigns the this keyword to it. Since the this keyword refers to the ImageGallery object that's created by the constructor, this means that both this and that refer to the ImageGallery object. Later on, the that variable is needed in the event handler for the links to refer back to the ImageGallery object.

The next three statements create three properties of the ImageGallery object that will store references to the nodes identified by the parameters. Then, the next three statements call the validateNode method that's shown on the next page to validate these properties. Here, the list node can be any element, the image node can only be an <img> element, and the caption node can only be a <span> element. If the nodes don't exist or aren't the correct type, the validateNode method throws an error and displays an error message.

After validating the nodes, the constructor gets all the <a> tags from the list node and stores them in an array in the imageLinks property. If there aren't any <a> tags, an error is thrown.

Next, this constructor creates three local variables and one new property named imageCache that will store an array of the images. Then, this constructor loops through each of the links that are stored in the imageLinks property.

Within the loop, the first statement copies each link element into a variable named node. This is followed by an event handler for the onclick event of the node. Within this event handler, the this keyword refers to the node, and it's copied into a local variable named link. Then, this code gets the window's event object if it wasn't passed as a parameter to the event function, which is necessary for the IE browser. Last, this code uses the that variable, not the this keyword, to call the linkClick method of the ImageGallery object with the event object and the link node as parameters.

To finish the loop, the constructor function preloads the images. To do that, it creates a new Image object and assigns the href attribute of the link node to the src property of the Image object. Then, the Image object is stored in the imageCache array.

At this point, the constructor for the ImageGallery object has defined an imageLinks property that is an array of all the objects for the link nodes in the unordered list. It has assigned an event handler to the click event for each of these links. It has preloaded all of the images for the links. And it has defined an

The image_gallery_library.js file

```javascript
var $ = function (id) { return document.getElementById(id); }

var ImageGallery = function ( listId, imageId, captionId ) {
    var that = this;      // both that and this refer to the ImageGallery object
    this.listNode = $(listId);
    this.imageNode = $(imageId);
    this.captionNode = $(captionId);

    // Validate nodes
    this.validateNode( this.listNode, "*", "List ID");
    this.validateNode( this.imageNode, "img", "Image ID");
    this.validateNode( this.captionNode, "span", "Caption ID");

    // Retrieve image links
    this.imageLinks = this.listNode.getElementsByTagName("a");
    if ( this.imageLinks.length == 0 ) {
        throw new Error("Image Gallery: List ID contains no image links.");
    }

    // Process image links
    var i, node, image;
    this.imageCache = [];
    for ( i = 0; i < this.imageLinks.length; i++ ) {
        node = this.imageLinks[i];

        // Attach event handler
        node.onclick = function (evt) {
            var link = this;           // this refers to the Anchor node object
            if (!evt) evt = window.event;
            that.linkClick(evt, link); // that refers to the ImageGallery object
        }

        // Preload image
        image = new Image();
        image.src = node.href;
        this.imageCache.push( image );
    }
}
```

Figure 13-12   The Image Gallery application (part 2 of 3)

imageCache property that is an array of all the image objects that are defined by the links.

After the constructor, the library file defines the validateNode and linkClick methods of the ImageGallery object type. You have already seen these methods called from the ImageGallery constructor.

The validateNode method is used to validate the nodes that are passed to the constructor, and it takes three parameters. The first parameter refers to the node to be validated. The second parameter specifies the name of the XHTML tag that the node should represent. And the third parameter stores a description that will be used in the error message if an exception is thrown.

The validateNode method checks each node that's passed to it for three conditions. First, it checks that the node is defined. Second, it checks that the node is an Element node. To do that, it tests the nodeType property. Third, it checks to make sure the node is of the specified type. To do that, it checks whether the tagName parameter is an asterisk (*) or whether the nodeName property of the element matches the tagName parameter. If a node doesn't pass all three conditions, this method throws an appropriate error message.

The linkClick method is called by the event handler for the click event of each link. Its first parameter refers to the event object for the event. Its second parameter refers to the Anchor node that was clicked to trigger the event.

Within the linkClick method, the first statement copies the href attribute of the link that was clicked into the src property of the image node. That displays the image. The second statement copies the title attribute of the link into the <span> tag referenced by the captionNode property. That displays the caption for the image. Then, the third statement calls the blur method of the link parameter to remove the focus from the link that was clicked. And the fourth statement is an if statement that cancels the default action for the link.

At this point, the library file consists of an ImageGallery constructor that has all the objects and methods that are needed for running the Image Gallery application. As a result, the image_gallery.js file just needs to call the ImageGallery constructor from the event handler for the window.onload event and pass the right parameters to it.

In the one statement for this event handler, you can see that the ids for the <ul> tag, the <img> tag, and the <span> tag are passed to the ImageGallery constructor. They refer to the image list, the image, and the caption that are used by the application. Then, when the application is loaded, the ImageGallery object is created, and that includes the event handlers for the click events of all of the links.

Incidentally, this application could be coded in a simpler way by using functions instead of an ImageGallery object. However, the ImageGallery object provides code that can be reused without any changes whenever you need to include image galleries in other applications.

The image_gallery_library.js file (continued)

```
ImageGallery.prototype.validateNode = function ( node, tagName, nodeDesc ) {
    if ( ! node ) {
        throw new Error("Image Gallery: " + nodeDesc + " not found.");
    }
    if ( node.nodeType !== 1 ) {
        throw new Error("Image Gallery: " + nodeDesc +
            " is not an element node.");
    }
    if ( tagName !== "*" && node.nodeName !== tagName.toUpperCase() ) {
        throw new Error("Image Gallery: " + nodeDesc +
            " is not a " + tagName.toLowerCase() + " tag.");
    }
}

ImageGallery.prototype.linkClick = function (evt, link) {
    this.imageNode.src = link.href;
    this.captionNode.firstChild.nodeValue = link.title;
    link.blur();

    // Cancel the default action of the event
    if ( evt.preventDefault ) {
        evt.preventDefault();
    }
    else {
        evt.returnValue = false;
    }
}
```

The image_gallery.js file

```
var gallery;

window.onload = function () {
    gallery = new ImageGallery("imageList", "image", "caption");
}
```

Figure 13-12   The Image Gallery application (part 3 of 3)

How to use timers

Timers let you execute a function after specified periods of time. However, timers aren't a part of the DOM or ECMAScript standards. Instead, they're provided by the web browser. As you will soon see, timers are often useful in DOM scripting applications, and you'll learn about the two types of timers in this topic.

How to call a function once

The first type of timer only calls its function once. To create this type of timer, you use the global setTimeout method as described in figure 13-13. Its first parameter is the function that the timer calls. Its second parameter is the number of milliseconds to wait before calling the function.

When you use the setTimeout method to create a timer, this method returns a reference to the timer that's created. Then, if necessary, you can use this reference to cancel the timer. To do that, you pass this reference to the global clearTimeout method.

The example in this figure begins by declaring a variable for the timer. Then, it defines an event handler for the onload event of the window. Within this event handler, the first statement creates a timer that calls the displayDate function after a delay of 5 seconds (5000 milliseconds). This statement also stores a reference to the new timer in the variable named timer. When the displayDate function is called, an alert statement is used to display the current date.

The second statement in this onload event handler attaches an event handler to a Cancel button that the user can click to cancel the timer. This event handler passes the time variable to the clearTimeout method. As a result, if the user clicks on the Cancel button before the 5 seconds have elapsed, the current date isn't displayed. Instead, a dialog box that indicates that the timer has been cancelled is displayed.

Two methods for working with a timer that calls a function once

```
setTimeout ( function, delayTime )      // creates a timer
clearTimeout ( timer )                  // cancels a timer
```

How to work with a timer that calls a function once

```
var timer;

window.onload = function () {
    // Create a time that calls the displayDate function after 5 seconds
    timer = setTimeout ( displayDate, 5000 );

    // Attach the event handler for the Cancel button
    document.getElementById ("btnCancel").onclick = cancel_click;
}

// Define the function that displays the date
var displayDate = function () {
    var now = new Date ();
    alert (now);
}

// Define the event handler for the Cancel button
var cancel_click = function () {
    clearTimeout (timer);
    alert ("The timer has been cancelled.");
}
```

Description

- The setTimeout method creates a timer that calls the specified function once after the specified delay in milliseconds. This method returns a reference to the new timer that can be used to cancel the timer.
- The clearTimeout method cancels the timer that was created with the setTimeout method.

Figure 13-13   How to work with a timer that calls a function once

How to call a function repeatedly

The second type of timer calls its function repeatedly. To create this type of timer, you use the global setInterval method. Its first parameter is the function to be called. Its second parameter is the time interval between function calls. To cancel this type of timer, you pass the timer to the global clearInterval method.

The example in this figure shows how to use the setInterval method to create a counter that is incremented every second. To start, this code creates two variables. The first variable stores the value of the counter. The second variable stores a reference to the timer.

After declaring the variables, the onload event handler uses the setInterval method to create a timer that calls the updateCounter method every second (1000 milliseconds). This updateCounter method updates the counter variable and displays the updated variable on the web page.

After it creates the timer, the onload event handler attaches an event handler for the Cancel button that the user can click on to cancel the timer. The code for this event handler passes the timer variable to the clearInterval method.

When you use the setInterval method to create a timer, the timer waits for the specified interval to pass before calling the function. As a result, if you want the function to be called immediately, you need to call the function before you create the timer.

On a related note, once you create a timer, you can't modify the timer. As a result, if you want to change the way a timer works, you must cancel the old timer and create a new one that works the way you want.

Two methods for working with a timer that calls a function repeatedly

```
setInterval( function, intervalTime )        // creates a timer
clearInterval ( timer )                      // cancels a timer
```

How to work with a timer that calls a function repeatedly

```
var counter = 0;
var timer;

window.onload = function () {
    // Create a timer that calls the updateCounter function every second
    timer = setInterval( updateCounter, 1000 );

    // Attach the event handler for the Cancel button
    document.getElementById("btnCancel").onclick = cancel_click;
}

// The function for the timer
var updateCounter = function () {
    counter++;
    document.getElementById("counter").firstChild.nodeValue = counter;
}

// The event handler for the Cancel button
var cancel_click = function () {
    clearInterval(timer);
}
```

Description

- The setInterval method creates a timer that calls the specified function at the specified interval in milliseconds. This method returns a reference to the new timer that can be used to cancel the timer.

- The clearInterval method cancels the specified timer that was created with the setInterval method.

Figure 13-14   How to work with a timer that calls a function repeatedly

The Slide Show application

Now that you know how to use timers, you're ready to learn how to convert the Image Gallery application into a Slide Show application like the one in figure 13-15. When the user starts this application, it displays the images and captions, one at a time, using the time interval that's set for the timer. Then, the user can click the Fast button to change the speed of the slide show or the Pause button to pause it. If the user clicks the Pause button, the user can click the Next and Previous buttons to move forwards or backwards through the images.

The XHTML file

For the XHTML file, the main difference between the Image Gallery and Slide Show applications is the addition of the four buttons that control the slide show. Three of these buttons are created using the <button> tag so they can contain images. For example, the button with the id of btnPrevious displays an image that's stored in the prev.gif file, and the button with the id of btnNext displays an image that's stored in the next.gif file.

Similarly, the button with the id of btnPlay button starts with the image that's stored in the pause.gif file. But when the user clicks on this button, the application changes this image to reflect the appropriate action. For instance, the first time this button is clicked, the JavaScript code changes its image to the one that's stored in the play.gif file.

The fourth button is created with an <input> tag. This makes it easy to toggle the value that's displayed on this button from "Fast" to "Slow" when the user clicks this button. Alternately, this page could have used a <button> tag with a <span> tag inside of it.

When the slide show is playing, the Previous and Next buttons are disabled. As a result, the user can't use them to move to the previous or next image. However, if the user pauses the slide show, the Previous and Next buttons are enabled, and the user can use them to move to the previous or next image.

The CSS file

Although the CSS file isn't shown in this figure, it's important because it hides the image list. To do that, the CSS file sets the display property of the image list to none. Note, however, that the DOM still contains the elements that represent the image list and its contents, even though the images aren't displayed. As a result, the Slide Show application can still use the DOM to work with these elements.

The Slide Show in the browser

The XHTML file

```
<!DOCTYPE html PUBLIC "-//W3C//DTD XHTML 1.0 Transitional//EN"
    "http://www.w3.org/TR/xhtml1/DTD/xhtml1-transitional.dtd">
<html xmlns="http://www.w3.org/1999/xhtml">
<head>
<title>Slide Show</title>
<link rel="stylesheet" type="text/css" href="slide_show.css"/>
<script type="text/javascript" src="slide_show_library.js"></script>
<script type="text/javascript" src="slide_show.js"></script>
</head>

<body>
<div id="content">
    <h1 class="center">Fishing Slide Show</h1>
    <ul class="center" id="imageList">
        <li><a href="casting1.jpg" title="Casting 1">Casting 1</a></li>
        <li><a href="casting2.jpg" title="Casting 2">Casting 2</a></li>
        <li><a href="catchrelease.jpg" title="Catch and Release">
            Catch and Release</a></li>
        <li><a href="fish.jpg" title="Fish">Fish</a></li>
        <li><a href="lures.jpg" title="Lures">Lures</a></li>
    </ul>
```

Figure 13-15   The Slide Show application (part 1 of 5)

The JavaScript files

Like the Image Gallery application, the library file for the Slide Show application contains one constructor and the methods that are added to it. This constructor creates a SlideShow object type that retrieves the image links, attaches an event handler to each of the control buttons, and preloads the images. Then, the slide_show.js file just calls that constructor and passes the right parameters to it.

The constructor function for the SlideShow object type takes just one parameter named params. However, this parameter is an object that has one property for each of the eight id parameters that are required by the constructor. When a function requires a large number of parameters, this technique for passing them reduces the chance of introducing an error by coding the parameters in the wrong sequence.

Within the constructor, the first statement copies the contents of the this keyword into a local variable named that. Later, that variable is used in the event handlers to refer to the SlideShow object because the this variable within those event handlers doesn't refer to the SlideShow object.

After setting up the that variable, the constructor stores references to the element nodes needed by the application. To do that, this code starts by checking whether the params object exists. If not, the code sets the params object equal to an empty object. That way, the next few lines won't throw an error. Then, the ids stored as properties of the params object are used to retrieve references to the element nodes, and these references are stored in properties of the SlideShow object. After storing the references to the element nodes in properties, the constructor calls the validateNode method to validate each of these eight nodes.

Next, this constructor defines some other properties that this application requires. Here, the imageCounter property identifies the image to display. The play property controls whether the slide show is in play mode or pause mode. The fast property specifies the number of milliseconds for the timer interval when the slide show is in fast mode. The slow property specifies the number of milliseconds for the timer interval when the slide show is in slow mode. And the speed property specifies the current speed of the slide show. By default, the slide show begins on the first image, in play mode, and in fast mode. This causes a new image to be displayed every 3 seconds.

The XHTML file continued

```
<p class="center">
    <button id="btnPrevious" disabled="disabled">
        <img src="prev.gif" alt="Previous Image" />
    </button>
    <button id="btnPlay">
        <img src="pause.gif" alt="Play or Pause" id="imgPlayPause" />
    </button>
    <input type="button" id="btnSpeed" value="Fast" />
    <button id="btnNext" disabled="disabled">
        <img src="next.gif" alt="Next Image" />
    </button>
</p>
<p class="center"><span id="caption">Casting 1</span></p>
<p class="center">
    <img src="casting1.jpg" alt="Casting 1" id="image" />
</p>
</div>
</body>
</html>
```

The slide_show_library.js file

```
var $ = function (id) { return document.getElementById(id); }

var SlideShow = function ( params ) {
    var that = this;

    // Store references to the element nodes as properties
    if ( !params ) params = {};
    this.listNode = $(params.listId);
    this.imageNode = $(params.imageId);
    this.captionNode = $(params.captionId);
    this.previousNode = $(params.previousId);
    this.playNode = $(params.playId);
    this.playPauseNode = $(params.playPauseId);
    this.nextNode = $(params.nextId);
    this.speedNode = $(params.speedId);

    // Validate nodes
    this.validateNode( this.listNode, "*", "List ID");
    this.validateNode( this.imageNode, "img", "Image ID");
    this.validateNode( this.captionNode, "span", "Caption ID");
    this.validateNode( this.previousNode, "button", "Previous Button ID");
    this.validateNode( this.playNode, "button", "Play Button ID");
    this.validateNode( this.playPauseNode, "img", "PlayPause Image ID");
    this.validateNode( this.nextNode, "button", "Next Button ID");
    this.validateNode( this.speedNode, "input", "Speed Button ID");

    // Define application parameters
    this.imageCounter = 0;
    this.play = true;
    this.fast = 3000;
    this.slow = 8000;
    this.speed = this.fast;
```

Figure 13-15   The Slide Show application (part 2 of 5)

The next block of code in the constructor retrieves all the <a> tags from within the list node and stores them in the imageLinks property. If there aren't any <a> tags, the if statement throws an error.

After retrieving the links, this constructor processes these links. To do that, it creates three local variables, and it creates one array and stores it in a property named imageCache. Then, this code loops through each of the links in the imageLinks array.

Within the loop, the first statement copies the image link element into the node variable that was declared before the loop. Then, the next two statements preload the images. To do that, they create an Image object and assign the href property of the link node to the src property of the Image object. Next, the code copies the title property of the link node to the title property of the new Image object. The last statement in the loop pushes the Image object onto the imageCache array.

After the loop, the constructor defines the four event handlers for the four buttons. Here, each event handler contains two statements. The first statement calls a method of the SlideShow object to perform the task of the event handler. These methods are defined later in the code for this object. Then, the second statement in the event handler calls the blur method on the appropriate node. This causes the button that was clicked to be displayed without any highlighting.

After defining the event handlers, the constructor attaches the event handlers to the four buttons. This code calls the event handlers indirectly from within anonymous functions. To do that, the calls to the function use the that variable to refer to the SlideShow object.

After attaching the event handlers, the constructor disables the Previous and Next buttons by setting the disabled property of the previous and next nodes to true. Although the XHTML file also disables these buttons, the JavaScript code repeats this to make sure that the buttons are disabled even if the XHTML file is changed.

Finally, the constructor uses the setInterval method to create a timer to start the slide show, and stores a reference to this timer in the timer property. The first parameter for the setInterval method is an anonymous function that calls the displayNextImage method using the variable named that. The second parameter is the interval that's specified by the speed property of the SlideShow object. As a result, this timer executes the displayNextImage method repeatedly.

The slide_show_library.js file continued

```
    // Retrieve image links
    this.imageLinks = this.listNode.getElementsByTagName("a");
    if ( this.imageLinks.length == 0 ) {
        throw new Error("Slide Show: List ID contains no image links.");
    }

    // Process image links
    var i, node, image;
    this.imageCache = [];
    for ( i = 0; i < this.imageLinks.length; i++ ) {
        node = this.imageLinks[i];

        // Preload image and copy title properties
        image = new Image();
        image.src = node.href;
        image.title = node.title;
        this.imageCache.push( image );
    }

    // Create event handlers
    this.playClick = function () {
        that.togglePlay();
        that.playNode.blur();
    }
    this.previousClick = function () {
        that.displayPrevImage();
        that.previousNode.blur();
    }
    this.nextClick = function () {
        that.displayNextImage();
        that.nextNode.blur();
    }
    this.speedClick = function () {
        that.toggleSpeed();
        that.speedNode.blur();
    }

    // Attach event handlers
    this.playNode.onclick = this.playClick;
    this.previousNode.onclick = this.previousClick;
    this.nextNode.onclick = this.nextClick;
    this.speedNode.onclick = this.speedClick;

    // Set button states
    this.previousNode.disabled = true;
    this.nextNode.disabled = true;

    // Start slide show
    this.timer = setInterval(
        function () { that.displayNextImage(); },
        this.speed
    );
}
```

Figure 13-15   The Slide Show application (part 3 of 5)

The validateNode method for the SlideShow object type works like the validateNode method of the ImageGallery object type. As a result, you shouldn't have any trouble understanding how it works.

The displayImage method of the SlideShow object type displays the current image. Here, the first statement uses the imageCounter property to retrieve a reference to the Image object in the imageCache array and stores this object in the image variable. Then, the second statement copies the src property of the Image object into the src property of the image node. This causes the application to display the image. Finally, this method stores the title property of the Image object in the <span> tag for the caption node. This causes the application to display the caption for the image.

The displayNextImage method of the SlideShow object type displays the next image in the array of images. To do that, this method adds one to the imageCounter property. Then, it uses the modulus operator (%) to get the remainder when the imageCounter property is divided by the length of the imageCache array. This ensures that the imageCounter property loops through the bounds of the array. If, for example, the imageCache array contains 5 images, the counter values will range from 0 through 4. Then, the second statement in this method calls the displayImage method to display the image.

The displayPrevImage method of the SlideShow object type displays the previous image in the array of images. To do that, this method adds one less than the length of the imageCache array to the imageCounter property. Then, it uses the modulus operator to divide this number by the length of the imageCache array. This ensures that the imageCounter property stays within the bounds of the array. The second statement in this method calls the displayImage method to display the image.

The togglePlay method of the SlideShow object toggles the Play/Pause button. The first statement in this method copies the contents of the this keyword into a local variable named that. Later in this method, the that variable is used by the timer function to refer back to the SlideShow object.

Next, the togglePlay method uses an if statement to check whether the slide show is playing. If so, this method cancels the timer, sets the image in the Play/Pause button to the play.gif image, and enables the Previous and Next buttons. If the slide show is not playing, this method starts the timer to play the slide show, sets the image in the Play/Pause button to the pause.gif image, and disables the Previous and Next buttons. Finally, the togglePlay method toggles the value in the play property.

The slide_show_library.js file continued

```javascript
SlideShow.prototype.validateNode = function ( node, nodeName, nodeDesc ) {
    if ( ! node ) {
        throw new Error("Slide Show: " + nodeDesc + " not found.");
    }
    if ( node.nodeType !== 1 ) {
        throw new Error("Slide Show: " + nodeDesc +
            " is not an element node.");
    }
    if ( nodeName != "*" && node.nodeName !== nodeName.toUpperCase() ) {
        throw new Error("Slide Show: " + nodeDesc +
            " is not a " + nodeName.toLowerCase() + " tag.");
    }
}

SlideShow.prototype.displayImage = function () {
    var image = this.imageCache[this.imageCounter];
    this.imageNode.src = image.src;
    this.captionNode.firstChild.nodeValue = image.title;
}

SlideShow.prototype.displayNextImage = function () {
    this.imageCounter = ++this.imageCounter % this.imageCache.length;
    this.displayImage();
}

SlideShow.prototype.displayPrevImage = function () {
    this.imageCounter =
        (this.imageCounter + this.imageCache.length - 1) %
        this.imageCache.length;
    this.displayImage();
}

SlideShow.prototype.togglePlay = function () {
    var that = this;
    if ( this.play ) {
        clearInterval( this.timer );
        this.playPauseNode.src = "play.gif";
        this.previousNode.disabled = false;
        this.nextNode.disabled = false;
    }
    else {
        this.timer = setInterval(
            function () { that.displayNextImage(); },
            this.speed
        );
        this.playPauseNode.src = "pause.gif";
        this.previousNode.disabled = true;
        this.nextNode.disabled = true;
    }
    this.play = ! this.play;
}
```

Figure 13-15   The Slide Show application (part 4 of 5)

The toggleSpeed method of the SlideShow object type is the event handler for the Speed button. Like the togglePlay method, this method begins by copying the contents of the this keyword into a local variable named that so it can be used later in the method. Then, if the current speed is "Fast", the toggleSpeed method changes the label on the Speed button to "Slow" and sets the speed property of the application to the slow value. Otherwise, this method changes the label on the speed button to "Fast" and sets the speed property of the application to the fast value.

Next, the toggleSpeed method checks to see whether the slide show is currently playing. If so, this method cancels the current timer and creates a new timer to play the slide show at the new speed.

At this point, the SlideShow constructor is ready to create an object that will run the slide show. So all the slide_show.js file has to do is create a SlideShow object in the event handler for the window.onload event.

Within the onload event handler, the code first creates an object named params with eight properties that store the ids of the eight elements needed by the SlideShow constructor. Then, the event handler creates a new SlideShow object by passing the params object to the constructor, and it stores this object in the variable named slideShow.

Like the Image Gallery application, you could simplify the code for the Slide Show application by using functions instead of a SlideShow object. But by using the object, you create tested code that you can reuse without any changes whenever you want to add a slide show to an application.

The slide_show_library.js file continued

```javascript
SlideShow.prototype.toggleSpeed = function () {
    var that = this;
    if ( this.speedNode.value == "Fast" ) {
        this.speedNode.value = "Slow";
        this.speed = this.slow;
    }
    else {
        this.speedNode.value = "Fast";
        this.speed = this.fast;
    }

    if ( this.play ) {
        clearInterval( this.timer );
        this.timer = setInterval(
            function () { that.displayNextImage(); },
            this.speed
        );
    }
}
```

The slide_show.js file

```javascript
var slideShow;

window.onload = function () {
    var params = {
        listId     : "imageList",
        imageId    : "image",
        captionId  : "caption",
        previousId : "btnPrevious",
        playId     : "btnPlay",
        playPauseId: "imgPlayPause",
        nextId     : "btnNext",
        speedId    : "btnSpeed"
    }
    slideShow = new SlideShow( params );
}
```

Figure 13-15   The Slide Show application (part 5 of 5)

Perspective

Now that you're done with this chapter, you should have a solid grasp on the basics of DOM scripting. If so, you're ready to tackle the more advanced DOM scripting topics in the next few chapters. As you progress, you'll see that DOM scripting lets you take JavaScript to a new level.

Terms

DOM Core specification
DOM HTML specification
interface
image rollover
preloaded image

Exercise 13-1   Use the Rollover object

In this exercise, you'll use the Rollover object that's presented in figure 13-10.

1. Use the Firefox browser to view the index.html file in the rollover folder that's in the chapter 13 folder for exercises. Note that two images are displayed.

2. Move the mouse over the top image to see that a new image replaces it. Then, move the mouse over the bottom image and note that the rollover feature isn't implemented for this image.

3. Use your text editor to open the html and JavaScript files for this application. Then, modify the code so the bottom image is replaced by the catchrelease.jpg file when the mouse is held over it. To do that, you just need to create another instance of the Rollover object and pass the right parameters to it.

Exercise 13-2   Enhance the Slide Show application

This exercise will give you a chance to use the SlideShow object and to see how easy it is to enhance that object.

Open and test the application

1. Use the Firefox browser to view the index.html file in the slide_show folder that's in the chapter 13 folder for exercises. Then, experiment with this application until you understand how the Play/Pause, Previous, Next, and Speed buttons work. Note that the Fast Speed selection list doesn't work.

2. Use your text editor to open the JavaScript files for this application. Then, review the code. Note that the end of the slide_show_library.js file includes an event handler named changeFastSpeed that contains some comments but no code.

Modify the application so the Fast Speed selection list works

3. Modify the slide_show.js file so it includes a parameter for the Fast Speed selection list. Be sure to get the right id for this control from the index.html file.

4. Modify the SlideShow constructor in the slide_show_library.js file so it stores a reference to the Fast Speed element node as a property, validates this node, and attaches the existing event handler named fastSpeedChange to the onchange event of this node.

5. Test the application to make sure the event handler has been attached correctly. To do that, you can add an alert statement to the event handler. Then, when you select an item from the selection list, the alert dialog box should be displayed.

6. Modify the event handler named fastSpeedChange so it changes the speed for the Fast mode to the value selected by the user from the Fast Speed selection list. This event handler should also put the application into Play mode and Fast mode. Then, test the application to make sure it works correctly.

7. Enhance the SlideShow constructor so the Fast Speed selection list displays a default value of 3 when the user clicks the Reload button to reload the web page. Then, test this change.

Advanced event handling

Throughout this book, you have been using basic techniques to handle simple events like the click event of a button. Now, in this chapter, you'll learn how to handle a wide range of mouse and keyboard events. First, you'll learn to use the three JavaScript libraries for event handling that come with this book. These libraries provide browser-compatible code that makes it easy to handle both mouse and keyboard events. Then, after you learn how to use these libraries, you'll learn how to write and modify libraries like these.

An introduction to event handling **470**
An overview of event handling 470
An overview of XHTML event types 472
An overview of mouse event types 474
An overview of keyboard event types 474

How to use our JavaScript libraries **476**
How to attach and remove event handlers 476
How to use the standardized Event object 478

The Slide Show application **480**
The XHTML file 480
The slide_show_library.js file 482
The slide_show.js file 484

The core event models **486**
How to access the Event object 486
The properties and methods of the Event object 488
The methods for attaching and detaching event handlers 490
Browser-compatible code for attaching and detaching event handlers 492
The jslib_event.js file 494

The mouse event models **500**
The properties of the Event object 500
The sequence of events for a mouse click 502
The jslib_event_mouse.js file 504

The keyboard event models **506**
The DOM Level 3 properties and methods for the Event object 506
The properties of the Event object that are implemented
by the major browsers 508
The key codes for keyboard events 510
The jslib_event_keyboard.js file 514

Perspective **520**

An introduction to event handling

Before you can learn how to use our libraries, you need to learn some general concepts about how events work. That's why this topic describes how an event is dispatched and gives you an overview of the types of events that are available.

An overview of event handling

When an event occurs, the event is dispatched to the target element. This dispatch occurs in the three phases described in figure 14-1.

The event dispatch starts at the document object and travels down the DOM tree to the target element. This is the *capturing phase*. Then, the event is processed by the target. This is the *target phase*. After the target phase, some events bubble back up to the document object. This is the *bubbling phase*, and some events have a bubbling phase and some don't.

In DOM-compliant browsers, you can attach event handlers to either the capturing phase, the targeting phase, or the bubbling phase. However, Internet Explorer doesn't support the capturing phase. As a result, until Internet Explorer supports the capturing phase, you should limit your event handlers to the target and bubbling phases.

For now, you can think of all events as being one of three types. First, HTML events are triggered by a change to the HTML or XHTML page. For example, when the browser loads an XHTML page, it triggers the load event of the XHTML page.

Second, mouse events are triggered by the user's mouse. For example, when a user clicks on an element, a click event is triggered.

Third, keyboard events are triggered by the user's keyboard. For example, when a user presses a key, a keypress event is triggered. In this chapter, you'll learn how to work with all three of these types of events.

Three phases of event dispatch

Phase	Description
Capturing	The event travels downward from the document object to the target element.
Target	The event triggers on the target element.
Bubbling	The event travels upward from the target element to the document object.

Event dispatch in the DOM tree

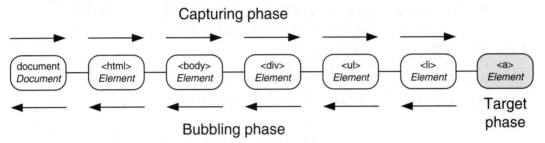

Common types of events

Event type	Description
HTML event	An event that's triggered by the HTML or XHTML page.
Mouse event	An event that's triggered by the user's mouse.
Keyboard event	An event that's triggered by the user's keyboard.

Description

- The bubbling phase of event dispatch is optional depending on the event type.
- Internet Explorer doesn't support the capturing phase of event dispatch.

Figure 14-1   An overview of event handling

An overview of XHTML event types

Figure 14-2 describes the XHTML events types that are defined in the XHTML standard and referenced by the DOM standard. Some of these events may be defined in future versions of the DOM standard.

Next, the figure provides three details about each event. The Bubbles column indicates whether the event bubbles up to elements higher in the DOM tree. Note that the load and unload events are the only ones that don't bubble.

The Cancelable column indicates whether the event can be canceled. If an event is canceled, the default action isn't taken, but the event still completes the dispatch process.

The Valid For column indicates the types of XHTML elements that can act as a target for the event. Other elements in the DOM tree can be triggered on the event, but only during the capturing or bubbling phases.

XHTML events

Event	Description
load	Triggers when the browser loads all content in a document. This works the same as the window.onload event.
unload	Triggers when the browser removes a document from the window.
submit	Triggers when a form is submitted.
reset	Triggers when a form is reset.
select	Triggers when the user selects text in a field.
change	Triggers when the content of an element has changed.
focus	Triggers when an element gains focus.
blur	Triggers when an element loses focus.

XHTML event details

Event	Bubbles	Cancelable	Valid For
load	No	No	body
unload	No	No	body
submit	Yes	Yes	form
reset	Yes	Yes	form
select	Yes	No	input, textarea
change	Yes	No	input, select, textarea
focus	Yes	No	a, area, label, input, select, textarea, button
blur	Yes	No	a, area, label, input, select, textarea, button

Description

- The XHTML specification defines the XHTML events and the DOM Level 2 specification refers to them.
- The Bubbles column indicates whether the event has a bubbling phase that can be captured by elements higher in the DOM tree.
- The Cancelable column indicates whether the default action of the event can be canceled.
- The Valid For column indicates which XHTML elements can act as the target for the event.

Figure 14-2   An overview of XHTML event types

An overview of mouse event types

Figure 14-3 gives an overview of mouse events. Most of these events were originally defined in the HTML and XHTML standards. In addition, most of these events were defined again in more detail in the DOM standard.

Although most of these events are defined by both the XHTML and DOM standards, there are two methods that aren't. First, the dblclick event is defined in the XHTML standard but not in the DOM standard. However, since this event is supported by all major browsers, you can use it as if it was defined by both standards.

Second, the contextclick event, which occurs when you right-click on an element, isn't defined by any standard. By default, this event causes a context menu to be displayed. As a result, if you want your application to handle this event, you typically want to cancel the default action for this event. Unfortunately, since Opera doesn't support this event, you can't cancel the default action for this event for Opera.

Unlike XHTML events, which are only valid for certain XHTML elements, mouse events are valid for all XHTML elements. For example, you can handle the click event for an <h1> element.

When two or more elements could be the target of a mouse event, the element that is deepest in the DOM tree will be the target. For example, if you click an image that's inside a link that's inside a paragraph, the image will be the target of the mouse event. Since all mouse events bubble, though, you can trigger a mouse event on a parent element during the bubbling phase.

An overview of keyboard event types

Figure 14-3 also gives an overview of keyboard events. These events were originally defined in the XHTML standard. However, these events weren't defined by the DOM standard until DOM Level 3.

In the DOM Level 3 standard, the textInput event replaces the keypress event. However, most browsers have yet to implement support for this event and only provide support for the older keypress event.

Although keyboard events are cancelable in general, they aren't cancelable on all browsers for all keys. In addition, canceling the default action may or may not stop the events from occurring. For example, if you want to prevent a user from entering text into a text field, you might try canceling the default action for the keydown event of the field. This works for all browsers except Opera. As a result, to prevent the user from typing in the text field in all browsers, you need to cancel the default action for the keypress event.

In general, it's even more difficult to cancel the events for key combinations that work with the browser's user interface. For example, for most browsers, you can press the F5 key to reload the current page. As a result, each browser may handle the canceling of events for these types of keys differently. That's why it's a good practice to design your application so it avoids using key combinations that are used by the browser.

Mouse events

Event	Description
mousedown	Triggers when a mouse button is pressed down.
mouseup	Triggers when a mouse button is released.
click	Triggers when a mouse button is pressed and released over the same spot.
dblclick	Triggers when a mouse button is pressed and released twice over the same spot. This event is defined by the XHTML specification, but not by the DOM specification.
contextclick	Triggers when the right mouse button is pressed and released over the same spot. This event isn't defined in any specification, but it's supported by all browsers except Opera.
mouseover	Triggers when the mouse moves into an element.
mouseout	Triggers when the mouse moves out of an element.
mousemove	Triggers when the mouse moves over an element without leaving it.

Mouse event details

Event	Bubbles	Cancelable
mousedown	Yes	Yes
mouseup	Yes	Yes
click	Yes	Yes
dblclick	Yes	Yes
contextclick	Yes	Yes, except for Opera
mouseover	Yes	Yes
mouseout	Yes	Yes
mousemove	Yes	No

Keyboard events

Event	Description
keydown	A key has been pressed down.
keypress	A key has generated text input. This event is defined in the DOM Level 2 standard.
textInput	A key has generated text input. This event is defined in the DOM Level 3 standard.
keyup	A key has been released.

Keyboard event details

Event	Bubbles	Cancelable
keydown	Yes	Yes
keypress	Yes	Yes
keyup	Yes	Yes

Description

- Most mouse events are defined by the DOM Level 2 standard.
- Most keyboard events are defined by the DOM Level 3 standard.

Figure 14-3   An overview of mouse and keyboard event types

How to use our JavaScript libraries

When you start to work with mouse and keyboard events, you discover that there are many differences between the DOM and IE event models. Then, to provide for these differences, you need to write a lot of extra code. That's why it's common to use JavaScript libraries like the three downloadable libraries in this chapter to handle mouse and keyboard events. Since the DOM standard has been widely accepted by all browsers except Internet Explorer, these libraries standardize on the DOM event model, not the IE event model.

How to attach and remove event handlers

Figure 14-4 starts by summarizing the three JavaScript libraries that are presented in this chapter. Like all JavaScript libraries, you must import these libraries before you can use them. To do that, you add <script> tags like the ones in this figure to the XHTML page. After you import these libraries, you can use the add method of the jsLib.event object to attach an event handler to an event, and you can use the remove method to detach an event handler from an event.

When you use the add method in the jslib_event library, you get several benefits. First, this add method lets you attach more than one event handler to the same event of the same element. This is often necessary in applications that load two or more JavaScript files. Second, if you use the add method to attach an event handler, you can use the remove method to detach the event handler. Third, when you use this add method, it standardizes the Event object for the event handler. As a result, you can use the properties and methods in the next figure to work with the Event object.

The examples in this figure show how to use the add method in the event library to attach event handlers for the click event of a button, the keydown event of the document, and the load event of the document. Here, the event handler for the load event of the document contains the code that attaches the other two event handlers.

Although it isn't shown in this figure, you can also use the add method to attach an anonymous function to an event. However, if you do that, you won't be able to use the remove method to detach the event handler from the event.

The three JavaScript libraries presented in this chapter

Filename	Description
jslib_event.js	This library defines the jsLib.event object that has methods that you can use to attach and detach events. When you use this library to attach an event handler to an event, it standardizes some core properties and methods of the Event object.
jslib_event_mouse.js	This library standardizes some properties and methods of the Event object for working with mouse events.
jslib_event_keyboard.js	This library standardizes some properties and methods of the Event object for working with keyboard events.

The methods available from the jsLib.event object

Method	Description
add(element, event, handler)	This method attaches the specified event handler to the specified event of the specified element.
remove(element, event, handler)	This method detaches the specified event handler from the specified event of the specified element.

XHTML code that imports these libraries

```
<script type="text/javascript" src="jslib_event.js"></script>
<script type="text/javascript" src="jslib_event_mouse.js"></script>
<script type="text/javascript" src="jslib_event_keyboard.js"></script>
```

An event handler for the click event of a button

```
var submitClick = function (evt) {
    alert("The Submit button was clicked!");
}
```

An event handler for the keydown event of the document

```
var documentKeydown = function (evt) {
    alert("A key was pressed down!");
}
```

An event handler for the load event of the document

```
var documentLoad = function () {
    var btnSubmit = document.getElementById("btnSubmit");
    jsLib.event.add ( btnSubmit, "click", submitClick );
    jsLib.event.add ( document, "keydown", documentKeydown);
}
```

Code that attaches an event handler to the load event

```
jsLib.event.add( window, "load", documentLoad );
```

Description

- The jslib_event.js library lets you attach more than one event handler to the same event of the same element. It lets you detach event handlers. And it standardizes the Event object for the event handlers that it attaches.

Figure 14-4   How to use the event library to attach and detach event handlers

How to use the standardized Event object

When you use the add method in the event library to attach event handlers, the Event object is standardized. As a result, you can use the properties and methods in figure 14-5 to work with the Event object. These properties and methods reflect the most current property or method in the DOM Level 2 or DOM Level 3 standard.

The two event handlers in this figure show how the standardized Event object makes it easier to handle events. Here, the first event handler doesn't use the standardized object. As a result, this event handler contains seven lines of code. This code is needed to account for the differences between the DOM and IE event models.

In contrast, the second event handler uses the standardized Event object. As a result, it needs just a single line of code to accomplish the same task as the first event handler. Later in this chapter, when you study the code for the event library, you'll see exactly how this works.

Properties of the standardized Event object

Property	Description
type	The type of event.
target	The node that is the target of the event.
timeStamp	The time the event occurred expressed as the number of milliseconds after midnight, January 1, 1970 UTC.
clientX	The distance from the left side of the document window to where the event occurred.
clientY	The distance from the top of the document window to where the event occurred.
screenX	The distance from the left side of the screen to where the event occurred.
screenY	The distance from the top of the screen to where the event occurred.
button	A value that indicates which mouse button was pressed or released where 0 is the left button, 1 is the middle button, and 2 is the right button.
relatedTarget	For a mouseout event, the element the mouse is moving to. For a mouseover event, the element the mouse is moving from.
keyIdentifier	For a keyup or keydown event, the name of the key. For a complete list of keys, see figure 14-17.
data	For a keypress or textInput event, the text generated by the key.
keyLocation	For a keyup or keydown event, the location of the key being pressed. Set to 0 for "Standard", 1 for "Left", 2 for "Right", or 3 for "Number Pad".

Methods of the standardized Event object

Method	Description
stopPropagation()	Stops the event from being dispatched any further up or down the DOM tree.
preventDefault()	Prevents the default action of the event from occurring.
getModifierState(key)	Returns true if the specified modifier key is pressed. Valid parameter values include "Shift", "Ctrl", "Alt", and "Meta" (the Command key on a Mac).

An event handler that doesn't use the event library

```
var submitClick = function (evt) {
    // get the Event object for the IE event model
    if (!evt) evt = window.event;

    // use the appropriate event model
    if ( evt.preventDefault ) {
        evt.preventDefault();      // DOM
    }
    else {
        evt.returnValue = false;   // IE
    }
}
```

The same event handler when the event library is used

```
var submitClick = function (evt) {
    evt.preventDefault();
}
```

Figure 14-5   How to use the standardized Event object

The Slide Show application

To show you how the three libraries can be used in a JavaScript application, figure 14-6 presents an enhanced version of the Slide Show application that you studied in the previous chapter. This version uses our event libraries to attach the event handlers and to work with mouse and keyboard events.

If you look at the user interface, you can see that this application now lets the user adjust the slide show with either keyboard events or mouse events. Specifically, the summary to the right of the slide show presents the keystroke combinations and mouse actions that you can use with the application.

If, for example, you press the space key, the slide show toggles between pausing and playing. Then, when the slide show is paused, you can press the left or right arrow key to move through the slides. Similarly, if you hold down the Shift key and click on the image, the slide show toggles between pausing and playing. And when the slide show is paused, you can left click or right click to move through the images.

The XHTML file

The XHTML file for the Slide Show application includes the JavaScript files for the three libraries described in this chapter. In addition, this file includes some new tags that aren't shown in this figure. These tags display the instructions for using the keyboard and mouse to work with the application.

The Slide Show application in the browser

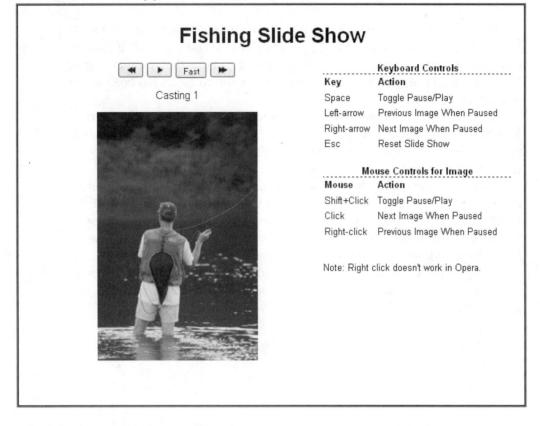

An excerpt from the XHTML file

```
<!DOCTYPE html PUBLIC "-//W3C//DTD XHTML 1.0 Transitional//EN"
    "http://www.w3.org/TR/xhtml1/DTD/xhtml1-transitional.dtd">
<html xmlns="http://www.w3.org/1999/xhtml">
<head>
    <title>Slide Show</title>
    <link rel="stylesheet" type="text/css" href="slide_show.css"/>
    <script type="text/javascript" src="jslib_event.js"></script>
    <script type="text/javascript" src="jslib_event_mouse.js"></script>
    <script type="text/javascript" src="jslib_event_keyboard.js"></script>
    <script type="text/javascript" src="slide_show_library.js"></script>
    <script type="text/javascript" src="slide_show.js"></script>
</head>

<!-- Except for the XHTML that describes how to use the keyboard and mouse
controls, the rest of the XHTML file is the same as the XHTML for the Slide
Show application show in chapter 13 -->
```

Figure 14-6   The Slide Show application (part 1 of 3)

The slide_show_library.js file

Because most of the code in the slide_show_library.js file is the same as it was in chapter 13, this figure doesn't present all of the code. Instead, it uses comments to indicate portions of code that are the same as they were in chapter 13. That should make it easier for you to focus on the code that has been added or changed.

To start, this code defines the event handlers inside the constructor for the SlideShow object. Here, the first four functions are event handlers for the click events of the four buttons on the page. Each of these event handlers calls its method and then blurs the button that was clicked.

In contrast, the docKeydown function handles the keyboard events for the application. To start, this event handler checks the keyIdentifier property of the Event object to see which button was pressed. For the spacebar, this function toggles the Play mode. For the left arrow, this function displays the previous image if the slide show is paused. For the right arrow, this function displays the next image if the slide show is paused. For the Escape key, this function resets the slide show by displaying the first image, setting the speed to fast, and playing the show.

An excerpt from the slide_show_library.js file

```javascript
var $ = function (id) { return document.getElementById(id); }

var SlideShow = function ( params ) {
    var that = this;

    // Store element ids as node references - same as chapter 13
    // Validate nodes - same as chapter 13
    // Define application parameters - same as chapter 13
    // Retrieve image links - same as chapter 13
    // Process image links - same as chapter 13

    // Create event handlers
    this.playClick = function () {
        that.togglePlay();
        that.playNode.blur();
    }
    this.previousClick = function () {
        that.displayPrevImage();
        that.previousNode.blur();
    }
    this.nextClick = function () {
        that.displayNextImage();
        that.nextNode.blur();
    }
    this.speedClick = function () {
        that.toggleSpeed();
        that.speedNode.blur();
    }
    this.docKeydown = function (evt) {
        switch ( evt.keyIdentifier ) {
            case "U+0020":  // Space bar
                that.togglePlay();
                break;
            case "Left":     // Left arrow
                if ( ! that.play ) that.displayPrevImage();
                break;
            case "Right":    // Right arrow
                if ( ! that.play ) that.displayNextImage();
                break;
            case "U+001B":   // Escape key
                that.imageCounter = 0;
                that.displayImage();
                if ( that.speed == that.slow ) that.toggleSpeed();
                if ( ! that.play ) that.togglePlay();
                break;
        }
    }
}
```

Figure 14-6   The Slide Show application (part 2 of 3)

The imageMousedown function handles the mouse event that occurs when the user clicks on the image. To start, this event handler checks the button property of the Event object to see if the left button was pressed. If it was and the Shift key was pressed, this function toggles the Play mode. If the Shift key wasn't pressed and the slide show is paused, this function displays the next image.

The imageContextmenu function handles the mouse event that occurs when user right clicks on the image. If the slide show is paused, this displays the previous image and prevents the context menu from displaying by calling the preventDefault method. Since Opera doesn't support the contextmenu event, the right-click function of the application won't work correctly if you're using Opera.

After defining these event handlers, this code uses the jsLib.event.add method to attach them to events. Here, the first four statements attach the event handlers for the buttons to the click events of the buttons. Then, the fifth statement attaches the event handler for the keyboard events to the keydown event of the document. And the last two statements attach the event handlers for the mouse events to the mousedown and contextmenu events of the image that's displayed on the web page.

As you review this code, note that the code for the event handlers of the keyboard and mouse events is simple and elegant. This is possible because the JavaScript libraries that are presented in this chapter make sure the Event object works as defined by the DOM standards. That's why there's no need to begin these event handlers with code that checks whether the Event object exists. That's why the docKeydown event handler can use the keyIdentifier property to get the key that was pressed down. That's why the imageMousedown event handler can use the button property to check if the left mouse button was pressed. And that's why the imageMousedown event handler can use the getModifierState method to check if the Shift key is down. If the Event object wasn't fixed by the libraries, the code for these event handlers wouldn't be nearly as simple and elegant.

The slide_show.js file

The slide_show.js file uses the jsLib.event.add method to add the slideShowSetup event handler to the load event of the window. As a result, when the page loads, the slideShowSetup event handler runs and creates the SlideShow object.

An excerpt from the slide_show_library.js file (continued)

```javascript
        this.imageMousedown = function (evt) {
            if (evt.button == 0 ) {
                if ( evt.getModifierState("Shift") ) {
                    that.togglePlay();
                } else if ( ! that.play ) {
                    that.displayNextImage();
                }
            }
        }
        this.imageContextmenu = function (evt) {
            if ( ! that.play ) {
                that.displayPrevImage();
                evt.preventDefault();
            }
        }

        // Attach event handlers
        jsLib.event.add ( this.playNode, "click", this.playClick );
        jsLib.event.add ( this.previousNode, "click", this.previousClick );
        jsLib.event.add ( this.nextNode, "click", this.nextClick );
        jsLib.event.add ( this.speedNode, "click", this.speedClick );
        jsLib.event.add ( document, "keydown", this.docKeydown );
        jsLib.event.add ( this.imageNode, "mousedown", this.imageMousedown );
        jsLib.event.add ( this.imageNode, "contextmenu", this.imageContextmenu );

        // Set button states - same as chapter 13
        // Start slide show - same as chapter 13
    }

    // the following methods are the same as chapter 13:
    // validateNode()
    // displayImage()
    // displayNextImage()
    // displayPrevImage()
    // togglePlay()
    // toggleSpeed()
```

The slide_show.js file

```javascript
var slideShow;

var slideShowSetup = function () {
    var params = {
        listId      : "imageList",
        imageId     : "image",
        captionId   : "caption",
        previousId  : "btnPrevious",
        playId      : "btnPlay",
        playPauseId : "imgPlayPause",
        nextId      : "btnNext",
        speedId     : "btnSpeed"
    }
    slideShow = new SlideShow( params );
}

jsLib.event.add( window, "load", slideShowSetup );
```

Figure 14-6   The Slide Show application (part 3 of 3)

The core event models

Now that you know how to use our JavaScript libraries, you're ready to learn how they're coded. As you do that, you'll deepen your knowledge of how the event models work. You'll also learn how to modify these libraries if that becomes necessary. If, for example, a library doesn't work correctly with a new version of a browser, you'll be able to modify it so it does work correctly.

To start, this topic shows the differences between the core event models for the DOM standard and the Internet Explorer. Then, this topic shows how to code a library that provides a standard way to work with the core event model.

How to access the Event object

When you code an event handler, you can use the Event object to get more information about the event. Unfortunately, although most browsers use the DOM event model to work with the Event object, Internet Explorer uses its own event model. As a result, if you want to work with the Event object, you need to write code that works with both event models.

This is illustrated by the code in figure 14-7. As you can see, most browsers pass the Event object as the first parameter of the event handler, but Internet Explorer doesn't. Instead, Internet Explorer stores the Event object in the window.event property.

To resolve this difference, the third example checks whether the evt parameter is undefined. If so, this code uses the window.event property of the Internet Explorer event model to get the Event object. After that, the evt parameter contains the Event object no matter which model was used.

The DOM standard way of accessing the Event object

```
var eventHandler = function ( evt ) {
    // The Event object is in the evt parameter
    alert( evt.type );    // Displays the type property of the Event object
}
```

The IE way of accessing the Event object

```
var eventHandler = function () {
    // The event object is in the global window.event property
    var evt = window.event;
    alert( evt.type );    // Displays the type property of the Event object
}
```

A cross-browser way to access the Event object

```
var eventHandler = function (evt) {
    // If the evt parameter is undefined, copy the
    // global window.event property into it
    if (!evt) evt = window.event;

    // Now the Event object is in the evt parameter in all browsers
    alert( evt.type );    // Displays the type property of the Event object

}
```

Description

- Most browsers implement the DOM Level 2 event model. In this model, the browser passes the Event object as the first parameter to the event handler function.

- Internet Explorer implements its own event model. In this model, the browser makes the Event object available through the global window.event property.

Figure 14-7   How to access the Event object

The properties and methods of the Event object

Figure 14-8 describes some of the properties and methods of the Event object that are used by the DOM and IE event models. Here, the type property is the only one that's common to both models. Most of the other properties and methods aren't the same for both models, but they do provide the same functionality.

If, for example, you want to stop an event from bubbling up the DOM tree, you can set the cancelBubble property of the IE Event object to true, and you can call the stopPropagation method of the DOM Event object. Similarly, if you want to cancel the default action of an event, you can set the returnValue property of the IE Event object to false, and you can call the preventDefault method of the DOM Event object. Finally, if you want to get the node that's the target of the event, you can use the srcElement property of the IE Event object or the target property of the DOM Event object.

Although the IE Event object doesn't have a property similar to the timeStamp property of the DOM Event object, you can simulate its use. To do that, you can create a new Date object and store it in a timeStamp property.

The key modifier properties in this figure work the same for both the DOM and IE event models. These properties let you determine if any of the four modifier keys were held down when the event occurred, and they are useful for working with keyboard events and also with mouse events. For example, you can use these properties to determine if the user was holding down the Shift key when she clicked on a button.

Because a Mac keyboard uses the Command key in a manner similar to the Control key on a PC keyboard, you may want to check both the ctrlKey and the metaKey properties in your application. If, for example, if you want to use the sequence Ctrl-1 in your application, you should perform the action if either the ctrlKey or metaKey property is true.

One property of the DOM and IE Event object

Property	Description
type	The type of event.

Two properties of the DOM Event object

Property	Description
target	The node that is the target of the event.
timeStamp	The time the event occurred expressed as the number of milliseconds after midnight, January 1, 1970 UTC.

Two methods of the DOM Event object

Method	Description
stopPropagation()	Stops the event from being dispatched any further up or down the DOM tree.
preventDefault()	Prevents the default action of the event from occurring.

Three properties of the IE Event object

Property	Description
cancelBubble	Set to true to stop the event from being dispatched any further up the DOM tree.
returnValue	Set to false to prevent the default action of the event from occurring.
srcElement	The node that is the target of the event.

Key modifier properties in both the DOM standard and IE Event objects

Property	Description
shiftKey	Returns a true value if the Shift key is being pressed.
altKey	Returns a true value if the Alt key (or Option key on a Mac) is being pressed.
ctrlKey	Returns a true value if the Ctrl key is being pressed.
metaKey	Returns a true value if the Meta key (Command key on a Mac) is being pressed.

Description

- The three properties of the IE Event object have functionality that corresponds with the properties and methods of the DOM Event object in this figure.

- Although the IE Event object doesn't provide a timeStamp property, you can simulate this property by creating a new Date object.

- The DOM Level 3 standard drops the key modifier properties in favor of a method named getModifierState. For more information about this method, see figure 14-15.

Figure 14-8   The properties and methods of the Event object

The methods for attaching and detaching event handlers

Figure 14-9 describes the methods used to attach an event handler to an event in the DOM and IE event models. It also describes the methods used to detach an event handler from an event.

First, this figure describes the addEventListener and removeEventListener methods that the DOM model provides for attaching and detaching event handlers. Since the IE model doesn't support event handlers during the capturing phase, you can get these methods to work like the corresponding IE methods by setting the useCapturing property to false.

Next, this figure describes the attachEvent and detachEvent methods that the IE event model provides for attaching and detaching event handlers. Note here that when you specify the eventType parameter for the attachEvent method, you must prefix the name with "on". For example, to specify a click event, you use a value of "onclick". However, when you use the DOM model's addEventListener method, you don't prefix the name of the event. As a result, you use a value of "click".

When you use the removeEventListener method of the DOM model, you must use the same values for the eventType and useCapturing parameters that you used when you registered the event handler. This makes it possible to use the same event handler for different events and phases.

Note that you can use the addEventListener and attachEvent methods to attach an anonymous function to an event. That way, the anonymous function acts as the event handler. However, if you attach an anonymous function to an event, you can't use the removeEventListener or detachEvent methods to detach the function from the event. As a result, if you need to detach an event handler, you need to use a named function, not an anonymous function.

The syntax of the DOM addEventListener method

```
element.addEventListener( eventType, handler, useCapturing );
```

The syntax of the DOM removeEventListener method

```
element.removeEventListener( eventType, handler, useCapturing );
```

The parameters for these DOM methods

Parameter	Description
eventType	A string containing the event type. For this parameter, you don't specify the "on" before the name of the event. To specify the click event, for example, you specify "click".
handler	The function that defines the event handler.
useCapturing	An optional Boolean parameter. When it is false or omitted, the handler triggers during the Target and Bubbling phases of event dispatch. When it is true, the handler also triggers during the Capturing phase of event dispatch. Since Internet Explorer doesn't support the capturing phase, it's a common practice to set the useCapturing parameter to false for cross-browser compatibility.

The syntax of the IE attachEvent method

```
element.attachEvent( eventType, handler );
```

The syntax of the IE detachEvent method

```
element.detachEvent( eventType, handler );
```

The parameters for these IE methods

Parameter	Description
eventType	A string containing the event type. For this parameter, you specify "on" before the name of the event. To specify the click event, for example, you specify "onclick".
handler	The function that defines the event handler.

Description

- You can use these methods to attach event handlers to events and to detach event handlers from events.

Figure 14-9   The methods for attaching and detaching event handlers

Browser-compatible code for attaching and detaching event handlers

Figure 14-10 shows three ways to attach an event handler. First, you can use an XHTML attribute to attach an event handler to an XHTML element, but that isn't recommended since it mixes JavaScript code with XHTML code. That also makes it difficult to track down and fix errors with event handlers.

Second, you can use JavaScript properties, as you've been doing so far in this book. This doesn't mix JavaScript with your XHTML code, and this is adequate for many types of web pages. However, it only lets you add one event handler to each event. Although that may not seem like much of a limitation at first, it becomes a serious limitation for any web page that hosts two or more JavaScript applications. In that case, both applications need to register an event handler for the onload event of the window, and you can't do that with this technique.

Third, you can use the addEventListener and attachEvent methods to attach event handlers as shown in the fourth example in this figure. This browser-compatible code starts by declaring a variable for a button element. Then, it defines an event handler named windowReady that's run when the page is loaded. Within this event handler, the first statement gets a reference to the button element. Then, an if statement checks if the addListenerEvent method of the DOM model is available, and it calls this method if it is available. If it isn't, this if statement checks if the attachEvent method of the IE model is available, and it calls this method if it is available. The result is code that works with both the DOM and IE event models.

Last, this example attaches the event handler named windowReady to the load event of the window. Here again, this code checks for the appropriate methods in the DOM and IE models and uses the right method for each model.

To remove an event handler that was added with the addEventListener or attachEvent methods, you use the removeEventListener or detachEvent methods as shown in the last example in this figure. Note that this code works because the code declares the variable named btnPlay outside of the event handler named windowReady. As a result, this variable is available for use within the event handler named detachClick. The rest of this code works like the previous example, except that it uses the methods for detaching an event handler instead of the methods for attaching an event handler.

Please note in the last two examples that the useCapturing parameter of the addEventListener method is set to false. In addition, the eventType parameters of the IE methods are prefixed with "on", but the eventType parameters of the DOM methods aren't prefixed with "on".

As I mentioned earlier, you can attach an anonymous event handler when you use these techniques but that isn't recommended for two reasons. First, it increases the chances of bugs because you have to type the function twice (once for the addEventListener method and once for the attachEvent method). Second, you can't detach an anonymous event handler since you don't have a reference to the event handler to pass to the removeEventListener and detachEvent methods.

An event handler for a Play button

```
var playClick = function () {
    alert("The Play button was clicked!");
}
```

How to attach the event handler using XHTML attributes (bad)

```
<input type="button" value="Play" id="btnPlay" onclick="playClick()" />
```

How to attach the event handler using JavaScript properties (better)

```
window.onload = function () {
    document.getElementById("btnPlay").onclick = playClick;
}
```

How to attach the event handler using JavaScript methods (best)

```
// The variable for the Play  button
var btnPlay;

// The code that attaches the event handler for the Play button
var windowReady = function () {
    btnPlay = document.getElementById("btnPlay");

    if ( btnPlay.addEventListener ) {
        btnPlay.addEventListener( "click", playClick, false );
    } else if ( btnPlay.attachEvent ) {
        btnPlay.attachEvent( "onclick", playClick );
    }
}

// The code that attaches the event handler named windowReady
if ( window.addEventListener ) {
    window.addEventListener( "load", windowReady, false );
} else if ( window.attachEvent ) {
    window.attachEvent( "onload", windowReady );
}
```

How to detach an event handler

```
var detachClick = function () {
    if ( btnPlay.removeEventListener ) {
        btnPlay.removeEventListener( "click", playClick, false );
    } else if ( btnPlay.detachEvent ) {
        btnPlay.detachEvent( "onclick", playClick );
    }
    alert("The event handler has been detached from the Play button!");
}
```

Description

- It is generally considered a best practice to use the addEventListener and attachEvent methods to attach event handlers to events. This lets you attach more than one event handler per event type to an element, and it lets you detach event handlers.

- Although using JavaScript object properties to attach event handlers is okay for simple applications, you should avoid using XHTML attributes to attach event handlers.

Figure 14-10   Browser-compatible code for attaching and detaching event handlers

The jslib_event.js file

Figure 14-11 presents the JavaScript event library that you can use to standardize event handling in a mixed-browser environment. This library defines add and remove methods that you can use to attach and detach event handlers in both the DOM and IE models. This library also standardizes the properties and methods of the Event object so your event handler only has to use the properties and methods described in the DOM event model.

The jslib_event.js file begins by checking whether the jsLib object exists. If not, it creates this object. Then, it checks whether the event object exists in the jsLib object. If not, it creates the event object. This object stores the methods of the library that are related to event handling. Later in this chapter, you'll see how this object allows this library to be expanded.

After creating the required objects, this code defines a property named handlerId and sets its value to 1. The add method in this library uses this property to create a unique identifier for each event handler.

The add method takes three parameters. The first parameter specifies the element to add the event handler to. The second parameter specifies the event type. And the third parameter specifies a reference to the event handler function.

Within the add method, the first statement checks whether the handler parameter has a handlerId property. If not, it adds the handlerId property to this parameter and assigns a value to it. To get this value, this code increments the handlerId property of the jsLib.event object.

After setting up the handlerId property, the next two statements create two property names: one for the original event handler and one for the new event handler. To create these names, this code combines a prefix, the event name, and the handlerId property. If, for example, the type parameter that's passed to the add method is "click" and the handlerID is 2, the oldHandlerName variable is "jsLib_old_click_2 and the newHandlerName variable is "jsLib_new_click_2".

After creating the property names, this code fixes the Event object, and it attaches the event handler to the event. To do that, this code begins by checking whether the element supports the addEventListener method. If so, it stores a reference to the original handler in the property that's referred to by the oldHandlerName variable. Then, it adds a new event handler to the property that's referred to by the newHandlerName variable. This handler calls the old handler and uses the fixEvent method of the jsLib.event object to standardize the Event object for the new handler. Next, this code attaches the new handler using the addEventListener method. Finally, it returns a value of true that indicates that the event handler was successfully attached.

If the element doesn't support the addEventListener method, this code checks whether the element supports the attachEvent method. If so, this code fixes the Event object and uses the attachEvent method to attach the event handler. This code works like the DOM code.

The jslib_event.js file

```javascript
if ( ! jsLib ) {
    var jsLib = {};
}

if ( ! jsLib.event ) {
    jsLib.event = {};
}

jsLib.event.handlerId = 1;

jsLib.event.add = function (element, type, handler) {
    // Create a unique ID for each event handler
    if (!handler.handlerId) {
        handler.handlerId = jsLib.event.handlerId++;
    }

    // Create two property names for event handlers
    var oldHandlerName = "jsLib_old_" + type + "_" + handler.handlerId;
    var newHandlerName = "jsLib_new_" + type + "_" + handler.handlerId;

    //////// Fix the Event object and attach the event handler
    // DOM Standard
    if ( element.addEventListener ) {
        element[oldHandlerName] = handler;
        element[newHandlerName] = function(evt) {
            element[oldHandlerName](jsLib.event.fixEvent(evt));
        }
        element.addEventListener( type, element[newHandlerName], false);
        return true;
    // IE
    } else if ( element.attachEvent ) {
        element[oldHandlerName] = handler;
        element[newHandlerName] = function() {
            element[oldHandlerName](jsLib.event.fixEvent(window.event));
        }
        element.attachEvent("on"+type, element[newHandlerName]);
        return true;
    }
    return false;
}
```

Figure 14-11   The jslib_event.js file (part 1 of 3)

For both the IE and DOM code, the add method returns a value of true if it successfully attaches the event handler. However, if neither the addEventHandler or attachHandler method exists, the add method returns false to indicate that the event handler wasn't attached. Alternately, this method could throw an error to indicate that the event handler wasn't attached.

As you review this code, note that the oldHandlerName and newHandlerName properties of the element store references to the event handlers. In particular, the oldHandlerName property stores a reference to the original event handler that was passed to the add method, and the newHandlerName property stores a new event handler that fixes the properties of the Event object and passes this fixed Event object to the original event handler.

The remove method takes the same three parameters as the add method. Within this method, the first two statements create the same two property names for the event handlers that are used within the add method. Then, the remove method checks whether the element supports the removeEventListener method. If so, it uses this method to detach the event handler, and it deletes the original and new event handlers by setting their references to null. This avoids a memory leak issue in older versions of IE. Finally, this code returns a value of true to indicate that the event handler has been detached successfully.

After the DOM code, the IE code checks whether the element supports the detachEvent method. If so, this code uses this method to remove the handler. Then, the rest of this code works like the DOM code. Finally, if neither the removeEventListener or detachEvent method exists, the last statement in the remove method returns false to indicate that the event handler wasn't detached.

The fixEvent method takes an Event object parameter named oEvt (for original event) and returns a new Event object that has standardized properties and methods. To start, this method checks whether the Event object has already been fixed. If so, it returns the object and exits the fixEvent method.

But if the Event object hasn't been fixed, this code creates a new Event object named evt and sets the fixed property to true. Then, it stores a reference to the original Event object in the oEvt property of the new Event object, and it copies the type property from the oEvt object to the evt object. The rest of the code in this method fixes the properties and methods of the Event object so they're browser-compatible and use the DOM standards.

This fixEvent method fixes the target property by checking whether the target or srcElement properties exist in the old Event object. If so, this code copies these properties into the target property for the new Element object. Otherwise, this code copies the document element into the target property. This code also fixes a problem in an older version of Safari that occurs if you attach an event handler to a span tag. This problem causes the target of the Event object to be the text node inside the span tag instead of the span tag. As a result, this code checks if the nodeType of the target is 3 (a text node). If so, the target is reset to the parent of the target.

The jslib_event.js file (continued)

```javascript
jsLib.event.remove = function (element, type, handler) {
    var oldHandlerName = "jsLib_old_" + type + "_" + handler.handlerId;
    var newHandlerName = "jsLib_new_" + type + "_" + handler.handlerId;

    //////// Remove the event handler
    // DOM Standard
    if ( element.removeEventListener ) {
        element.removeEventListener(type, element[newHandlerName], false);
        element[newHandlerName] = null;
        element[oldHandlerName] = null;
        return true;
    // IE
    } else if ( element.detachEvent ) {
        element.detachEvent( "on"+type, element[newHandlerName] );
        element[newHandlerName] = null;
        element[oldHandlerName] = null;
        return true;
    }
    return false;
}

jsLib.event.fixEvent = function (oEvt) {
    // if the Event object has already been fixed, exit this method
    if ( oEvt.fixed === true ) return oEvt;

    // Create the new Event object
    var evt = {};
    evt.fixed = true;

    // Set the  properties that don't need to be fixed
    evt.oEvt = oEvt;
    evt.type = oEvt.type;

    // Fix the target property
    if ( "target" in oEvt ) {
        evt.target =  oEvt.target;
    } else if ( "srcElement" in oEvt ) {
        evt.target =  oEvt.srcElement;
    } else {
        evt.target = document;
    }
    if ( evt.target == null ) evt.target = document;
    if ( evt.target.nodeType == 3 ) {              // Fix Safari "span" problem
        evt.target = evt.target.parentNode;
    }
```

Figure 14-11   The jslib_event.js file (part 2 of 3)

This method fixes the timeStamp property by checking whether the timeStamp property exists. If so, it copies the timeStamp property from the old Event object to the new Event object. Otherwise, it creates a new Date object and copies the timestamp stored in this object into the timeStamp property of the new Event object.

This method fixes the key modifier properties by copying them from the old Event object to the new Event object. In addition, if the metaKey property doesn't exist in the old Event object, this code copies the ctrlKey property from the old Event object to the metaKey property in the new Event object. That way, the metaKey property works as you would expect for a Mac computer.

This method fixes the preventDefault method by defining the preventDefault method for the new Event object. This method begins by checking if the preventDefault method exists in the original Event object. If so, it calls this method. Otherwise, it sets the returnValue property of the old Event object to false.

This method uses a similar technique to fix the stopPropagation method. In short, the method in the new Event object checks what methods are available and uses the stopPropagation method or the cancelBubble property to stop the event from bubbling.

Last, this method checks whether the mouse and keyboard event libraries are available. If so, it calls the fixMouse and fixKeys methods in those libraries to fix the properties in the Event object for mouse and keyboard events. To do that, it passes references to the old and new event objects to these methods, and these methods fix the new event object. In the next two topics, you'll learn how these mouse and keyboard libraries work.

The jslib_event.js file (continued)

```javascript
        // Fix the timeStamp property
        evt.timeStamp = ( "timeStamp" in oEvt ) ?
            oEvt.timeStamp : (new Date()).valueOf();

        // Set and fix the control key properties
        evt.shiftKey = oEvt.shiftKey;
        evt.ctrlKey = oEvt.ctrlKey;
        evt.altKey = oEvt.altKey;
        evt.metaKey = ( "metaKey" in oEvt ) ? oEvt.metaKey : oEvt.ctrlKey;

        // Fix the preventDefault method
        evt.preventDefault = function () {
            if ( "preventDefault" in oEvt ) {      // DOM Standard
                oEvt.preventDefault();
            } else if ( "returnValue" in oEvt) { // IE
                oEvt.returnValue = false;
            }
        }

        // Fix the stopPropagation method
        evt.stopPropagation = function () {
            if ( "stopPropagation" in oEvt ) {       // DOM Standard
                oEvt.stopPropagation();
            } else if ( "cancelBubble" in oEvt ) { // IE
                oEvt.cancelBubble = true;
            }
        }

        // Fix the mouse event properties
        if ( jsLib.event.mouse && jsLib.event.mouse.fixMouse ) {
            jsLib.event.mouse.fixMouse( oEvt, evt );
        }

        // Fix the keyboard event properties
        if ( jsLib.event.keyboard && jsLib.event.keyboard.fixKeys ) {
            jsLib.event.keyboard.fixKeys( oEvt, evt );
        }

        return evt;
    }
```

Figure 14-11   The jslib_event.js file (part 3 of 3)

The mouse event models

This topic begins by describing the differences between the DOM and the Internet Explorer models for mouse events. Then, this topic describes the code for the JavaScript library that standardizes these mouse event models.

The properties of the Event object

Figure 14-12 describes the properties of the Event object for mouse events. The first table in this figure describes the properties that are the same for both the DOM and IE event models. Here, the first four properties return the same values for both the DOM and IE models. However, the button property returns different values depending on the event model.

The second table shows that the two event models return different values when the user presses mouse buttons. If, for example, the user presses the left mouse button, the DOM model returns a value of 0 in the button property and the IE model returns a value of 1.

Beyond that, the two models work differently when the user presses more than one mouse button at the same time. If, for example, the user presses the left button and then the right button before releasing the left one, two mousedown events occur. Then, in the DOM model, each mouse event returns a value for the button property that corresponds with the event. As a result, the first event returns a value of 0, and the second event returns a value of 2.

In contrast, the IE model returns the sum of the button values if the user presses more than one button at the same time. So, if the user presses the left button and then the right button, the first event returns a value of 1 indicating the left button, and the second event returns a value of 3 indicating the left button plus the right button.

The third and fourth tables show that the properties of the Event object that are used in the mouseover and mouseout events are different for the DOM and IE models. In the DOM model, the relatedTarget property identifies the element that the mouse went to in the mouseout event or came from in the mouseover event. In the IE model, the toElement property identifies the element the mouse went to in the mouseout event, and the fromElement property identifies the element the mouse came from in the mouseover event.

The example in this figure shows how to use the clientX and clientY properties to track the mouse by displaying its coordinates in XHTML text boxes. To start, the XHTML code defines two text boxes that will display the position of the mouse. Then, the JavaScript code defines an event handler named trackMouse that copies the clientX and clientY values into the two text boxes. Remember that these properties work the same in both the DOM and IE event models.

Next, the JavaScript code defines an event handler named ready for the window's load event. This event handler registers the trackMouse function as an event handler for the document object's mousemove event. Since the

Event object properties for the DOM and IE event models

Property	Description
clientX	The distance from the left side of the document window to where the mouse event occurred.
clientY	The distance from the top of the document window to where the mouse event occurred.
screenX	The distance from the left side of the screen to where the mouse event occurred.
screenY	The distance from the top of the screen to where the mouse event occurred.
button	A value that indicates which mouse button was pressed or released.

Values for the button property

Button	DOM Value	IE Value
Left	0	1
Middle	1	4
Right	2	2

Event object properties for the DOM event model

Property	Description
relatedTarget	For a mouseout event, the element the mouse is moving to. For a mouseover event, the element the mouse is moving from.

Event object properties for the IE event model

Property	Description
toElement	For a mouseout event, the element the mouse is moving to.
fromElement	For a mouseover event, the element the mouse is moving from.

How to track the mouse position

The XHTML code

```
<p>X: <input type="text" id="mouseX" />
   Y: <input type="text" id="mouseY" /></p>
```

The JavaScript code

```
var trackMouse = function (evt) {
    document.getElementById("mouseX").value = evt.clientX;
    document.getElementById("mouseY").value = evt.clientY;
}

var ready = function () {
    jsLib.event.add( document, "mousemove", trackMouse );
}

jsLib.event.add( window, "load", ready );
```

Figure 14-12   The properties of the Event object for mouse events

mousemove event bubbles, the document object triggers the event handler whenever the mouse moves over any element in the page. Finally, the JavaScript code registers the ready function as an event handler for the load event.

Note that this code uses the jsLib.event.add method of the jsLib event library to attach event handlers. As a result, the trackMouse event handler doesn't have to check for the presence of the Event object since this has already been done by the event library.

The sequence of events for a mouse click

Figure 14-13 describes the sequence of events that occur when a user clicks one of the mouse buttons. In all cases, the mousedown event occurs when the uses presses the mouse button. The remaining events start to occur when the user releases the mouse button. One important point to take away from these tables is that the mousedown and mouseup events are more consistent for cross-browser compatibility than the other mouse button events.

For the left mouse button, the default action depends on the element being clicked, but it is always cancelable. For the middle mouse button, the default action of scrolling the page with the mouse isn't cancelable in any browser. For the right mouse button, the default action of displaying the context menu is cancelable in all browsers except Opera.

Internet Explorer sets the button property to a non-zero value only for mousedown and mouseup events. For click and contextmenu events, IE sets the button property to a value of 0. However, the other browsers set the value of the button property consistently for mouse button events.

If scrollbars are present in the window when the user presses the middle mouse button, Internet Explorer and Firefox display a page scroll marker and stop the event sequence after the mousedown event. Chrome and Opera, however, always display a page scroll marker. In Chrome, only the mouseup event triggers for the middle mouse button, and in Opera, only the mousedown event triggers. Conversely, Safari never displays a page scroll marker.

Event sequence and button values in IE

Left Button Event	Value	Middle Button Event	Value	Right Button Event	Value
mousedown	1	mousedown	4	mousedown	2
click	0	click	0	contextmenu	0
mouseup	1	mouseup	4	mouseup	2

Event sequence and button values in Firefox

Left Button Event	Value	Middle Button Event	Value	Right Button Event	Value
mousedown	0	mousedown	1	mousedown	2
click	0	click	1	click	2
mouseup	0	mouseup	1	contextmenu	2
				mouseup	2

Event sequence and button values in Safari and Chrome

Left Button Event	Value	Middle Button Event	Value	Right Button Event	Value
mousedown	0	mousedown	1	mousedown	2
click	0	click	1	contextmenu	2
mouseup	0	mouseup	1	mouseup	2

Event sequence and button values in Opera

Left Button Event	Value	Middle Button Event	Value	Right Button Event	Value
mousedown	0	mousedown	1	mousedown	2
click	0			mouseup	2
mouseup	0				

Description

- In all four browsers, a context menu appears after the user clicks and releases the right button. This default action can't be canceled in Opera, but it can be canceled in the other browsers.

- In IE and Firefox, if the web page won't fit in the window, a page scroll marker appears after the user presses the middle button, and the event sequence always stops after the mousedown event. This default action can't be canceled.

- In Chrome, a page scroll marker always appears after the user presses the middle mouse button and only the mouseup event occurs. In Opera, a page scroll marker always appears and only the mousedown event occurs. In Safari, a page scroll marker never appears. This default action can't be canceled.

Figure 14-13   The sequence of events for a mouse click

The jslib_event_mouse.js file

Figure 14-14 shows the code for a JavaScript library that standardizes the properties of the Event object for mouse events. To start, this code checks whether the jsLib and jsLib.event objects exist. If not, it throws an appropriate error. Then, this code creates an empty object named mouse and adds it to the jsLib.event object.

The fixMouse method takes two parameters: oEvt and evt. The first parameter refers to the original Event object. The second one refers to the new Event object that's being fixed. Remember that this method is called by the jsLib.event.fixEvent method at the end of figure 14-11.

Within the fixMouse method, the first four statements copy the four mouse position properties from the original Event object to the new Event object. This works because these properties work the same for both the DOM standard and IE.

To fix the button property, the fixMouse method uses the preventDefault method to check whether the browser supports the DOM standard. This is necessary because both DOM and IE browsers support the button property. As a result, you need to use a different method to determine what type of browser you're working with. In other words, the code assumes that any browser that supports the DOM standard preventDefault method also uses the DOM standard values for the button property.

As a result, if the browser supports the preventDefault method, this code copies the button property of the original Event object to the new Event object. Otherwise, this code converts the values returned by the IE button property so they conform to the DOM values.

To convert the IE button values to DOM values, the fixMouse method uses the *bitwise AND operator* (&). This operator treats its operands as a sequence of 32 bits (zeros and ones), rather than as a decimal number. To understand this code completely, you need to learn more about how this operator works. For now, though, all you need to know is that you can use this operator as shown in this figure to determine which button was pressed in the IE event model. (This operator isn't treated in this book because this is one of the rare cases in which you'll need it.)

Last, to fix the relatedTarget property, the fixMouse method begins by checking if this property exists in the original Event object. If so, this code copies the property from the old Event object to the new Event object. Otherwise, this code checks the event type and copies the appropriate IE property from the old Event object into the relatedTarget property of the new Event object.

The jslib_event_mouse.js file

```
if ( ! jsLib ) {
    throw new Error("jsLib Mouse Events: jsLib not loaded");
} else if ( ! jsLib.event ) {
    throw new Error("jsLib Mouse Events: jsLib event not loaded");
}

jsLib.event.mouse = {};

jsLib.event.mouse.fixMouse = function (oEvt, evt) {
    // Copy the User Interface properties
    evt.screenX = oEvt.screenX;
    evt.screenY = oEvt.screenY;
    evt.clientX = oEvt.clientX;
    evt.clientY = oEvt.clientY;

    // Fix the button property
    if ( "preventDefault" in oEvt ) {
        evt.button = oEvt.button;
    } else {
        if ( oEvt.button & 1 ) {              // The left button was pressed
            evt.button = 0;
        } else if ( oEvt.button & 2 ) {  // The right button was pressed
            evt.button = 1;
        } else if ( oEvt.button & 4 ) {  // The middle button was pressed
            evt.button = 2;
        } else {
            evt.button = 0;
        }
    }

    // Fix the relatedTarget property
    if ( "relatedTarget" in oEvt ) {
        evt.relatedTarget = oEvt.relatedTarget;
    } else {
        if ( evt.type == "mouseout" ) {
            evt.relatedTarget = oEvt.toElement;
        } else if ( evt.type == "mouseover" ) {
            evt.relatedTarget = oEvt.fromElement;
        }
    }
}
```

Description

- In the IE event model, you can use the *bitwise AND operator* (&) to determine which button was clicked as shown above. Specifically, this operator lets you determine which bit is on in the button property.

Figure 14-14   The jslib_event_mouse.js file

The keyboard event models

The keyboard event models are the most difficult to standardize. That's mainly because the keyboard event model wasn't defined by the DOM standard until DOM Level 3. As a result, most browsers don't support this event model yet. Instead, they support older event models that were defined in the HTML and XHTML standards.

This topic, though, presents our library for standardizing keyboard events on the DOM Level 3 standard. That way, you can use the DOM Level 3 standard right now to work with keyboard events, and it will work with browsers that don't yet support this standard.

To start, this topic describes the keyboard event model described by the DOM Level 3 standard as well as the keyboard event models that are currently supported by most browsers. Then, it presents our JavaScript library that standardizes these mouse event models on the DOM Level 3 standard.

The DOM Level 3 properties and methods for the Event object

Figure 14-15 describes the properties and methods of the Event object for keyboard events in the DOM Level 3 standard. These properties are used with the keypress event, and they are also used with the textInput event that's defined by the DOM Level 3 standard. This textInput event is designed to replace the keypress event.

An important point to take away from this figure is that keys aren't the same as characters. For instance, a key may or may not generate a character, and a key may generate different characters depending on which modifier keys are pressed at the same time. In general, the keydown and keyup events deal primarily with keys, while the keypress and textInput events deal primarily with characters.

In the DOM Level 3 standard, the keyIdentifier property stores the name of the key during the keydown and keyup events, and the data property stores the character that was generated by the key during the textInput event. In addition, the getModifierState method replaces the older shiftKey, ctrlKey, altKey, and metaKey properties.

When you press a character key, a DOM Level 3 browser sets the keyIdentifier property to a value that consists of the characters "U+" followed by a Unicode value. For example, the "A" and "/" keys have the same keyIdentifier property regardless of whether the Shift key is pressed. However, the data property changes to reflect whether the Shift key is pressed.

When you press control keys, a DOM Level 3 browser sets the keyIdentifier property to a text value such as "PageUp" or "F8". In contrast, the keyIdentifier property for keys like the Backspace and Tab keys are set to Unicode values. For a complete list of keys and their keyIdentifier values, you can visit the URL shown in this figure.

Properties of the Event object for the DOM Level 3 standard

Property	Description
keyIdentifier	For a keyup or keydown event, the name of the key.
data	For a textInput event, the text generated by the key.
keyLocation	For a keyup or keydown event, the location of the key being pressed. Set to 0 for "Standard", 1 for "Left", 2 for "Right", or 3 for "Number Pad".

Methods of the Event object for the DOM Level 3 standard

Method	Description
getModifierState(key)	Returns true if the specified modifier key is pressed. Valid parameter values include "Shift", "Ctrl", "Alt", and "Meta".

Some typical property values

Key	Modifier keys	keyIdentifier	data
A	None	U+0041	a
A	Shift	U+0041	A
/	None	U+002F	/
/	Shift	U+002F	?
Page Up	None	PageUp	
F8	None	F8	
Enter	None	Enter	
Backspace	None	U+0008	
Tab	None	U+0009	
Escape	None	U+001B	

The URL for the full list of key names

```
http://www.w3.org/TR/2003/NOTE-DOM-Level-3-Events-20031107/keyset.html
```

Description

- Currently, most browsers don't support the DOM Level 3 standard. However, Safari and Chrome do support this standard.
- In the DOM Level 3 standard, the textInput event replaces the keypress event.

Figure 14-15   The DOM Level 3 properties and methods for the Event object

The properties of the Event object that are implemented by the major browsers

Figure 14-16 describes the properties of the Event object for keyboard events as they are currently implemented by the major browsers. The values for these properties vary from browser to browser and are listed in the next figure.

To start, Internet Explorer and Opera use the keyCode property to work with keyboard events. For the keydown and keyup events, these browsers use this property to store the keyboard scan code for the key. For the keypress event, they use this property to store the ASCII code for the character.

In contrast, Firefox only uses the keyCode property to work with keydown and keyup events. For these events, it uses the keyCode property to store the keyboard scan code. However, for a keypress event, Firefox uses the charCode property to store the ASCII code for the character. In addition, Firefox provides a property named "which" that acts like the keyCode property in Internet Explorer.

Finally, Safari and Chrome support the keyCode and charCode properties in a way that's compatible with IE and Firefox. In addition, they provide support for the three properties specified by the DOM Level 3 standard.

At first glance, it seems like it would be easy to write a library to standardize the properties described in this figure. To complicate the problem, though, different browsers use different values for some of these properties. As a result, before you can write a library to standardize these properties, you need to know what these values are. That's why the next figure lists all the values generated for these properties and describes the differences that occur in some browsers.

Properties of the Event object for Internet Explorer and Opera

Property	Description
keyCode	For a keydown or keyup event, the keyboard scan code for the key. For a keypress event, the ASCII code for the character.

Properties of the Event object for Firefox

Property	Description
keyCode	For a keydown or keyup event, the keyboard scan code for the key.
charCode	For a keypress event, the ASCII code for the character.
which	The same as the IE keyCode property.

Properties of the Event object for Safari and Chrome

Property	Description
keyCode	For a keydown or keyup event, the keyboard scan code for the key. For a keypress event, the ASCII code for the character.
charCode	For a keypress event, the ASCII code for the character.
keyIdentifier	For a keydown or keyup event, the name of the key.
data	For a textInput or keypress event, the text generated by the key.
keyLocation	For a keydown or keyup event, the location of the key. Set to 3 for "Number Pad" keys and 0 for all other keys.

Description

- In the DOM Level 2 standard, keyboard events aren't defined. In the XHTML standard, the keyboard events are defined, but the values for keyCode and charCode are not specified.
- The next figure shows the values for the keyIdentifier property, the data property, the key scan code, and the ASCII code.

Figure 14-16   The Event object properties for keyboard events in the major browsers

The key codes for keyboard events

Figure 14-17 lists all the keys and characters on a standard US 104-key keyboard and the values they generate in the major browsers during the keydown, keyup, and keypress events.

Here, the keyIdentifier column shows the values of the keyIdentifier property for each key. This value is the same for characters located on the same key such as the colon (:) and semicolon (;) characters.

The data column shows the value of the data property. This property only provides a value for character keys like those in part 1 of this figure, not for control keys like those in part 2.

The Scan column shows the most common keyboard scan code for each key. For a keydown or keyup event, these values are available from the keyCode property.

The ASCII column shows the ASCII code for each character. For a keypress event, these values are available from the keyCode or charCode properties, depending on the browser.

The Exceptions column lists exceptions to the keyboard scan codes and ASCII values. If you read through this column, you'll see that there are many differences between the major browsers.

The Exceptions column also identifies sections of the table that are omitted. In particular, there are three ranges where there are no exceptions and the values continue in sequence. These ranges occur between "0" and "9", "A" and "Z", and "a" and "z".

Codes for letters, numbers, and symbols

Key	keyIdentifier	data	Scan	ASCII	Exceptions
Space Bar	U+0020	a space	32	32	
!	U+0031	!	49	33	
"	U+0027	"	222	34	
#	U+0033	!	51	35	
$	U+0034	$	52	36	
%	U+0035	%	53	37	
&	U+0037	&	55	38	
'	U+0027	'	222	39	
(	U+0039	(	57	40	
)	U+0030	)	48	41	
*	U+0038	*	56	42	
+	U+002B	+	187	43	Scan is 107 in Firefox, 61 in Opera
,	U+002C	,	188	44	
-	U+002D	-	189	45	Scan is 109 in Firefox and Opera
.	U+002E	.	190	46	
/	U+002F	/	191	47	
0	U+0030	0	48	48	0 to 9 are in sequence
9	U+0039	9	57	57	
:	U+003B	:	186	58	Scan is 59 in Firefox and Opera
;	U+003B	;	186	59	Scan is 59 in Firefox and Opera
<	U+002C	<	188	60	
=	U+002B	=	107	61	Scan is 187 in IE, 61 in Opera
>	U+002E	>	190	62	
?	U+002F	?	191	63	
@	U+0032	@	50	64	
A	U+0041	A	65	65	A to Z are in sequence
Z	U+005A	Z	90	90	
[	U+005B	[	219	91	
\	U+005C	\	220	92	
]	U+005D	]	221	93	
^	U+0036	^	54	94	
_	U+002D	_	189	95	Scan is 109 in Firefox and Opera
`	U+0060	`	192	96	
a	U+0041	a	65	97	a to z are in sequence
z	U+005A	z	90	122	
{	U+005B	{	219	123	
|	U+005C	|	220	124	
}	U+005D	}	221	125	
~	U+0060	~	192	126	

Figure 14-17   The key codes used in Event object properties (part 1 of 3)

Key codes for control keys

Key	keyIdentifier	Scan	Exceptions
Backspace	U+0008	8	
Tab	U+0009	9	
Enter	Enter	13	
Shift	Shift	16	
Ctrl	Control	17	
Alt	Alt	18	
Break	Break	19	Pause in Safari and Chrome
Caps Lock	CapsLock	20	
Escape	U+001B	27	
Page Up	PageUp	33	
Page Down	PageDown	34	
End	End	35	
Home	Home	36	
Left Arrow	Left	37	
Up Arrow	Up	38	
Right Arrow	Right	39	
Down Arrow	Down	40	
Print Screen	PrintScreen	44	No keydown in any browser. No keyup in Opera.
Insert	Insert	45	
Delete	U+007F	46	
Left Windows	Win	91	Scan is 219 in Opera, conflicts with [
Right Windows	Win	92	Scan is 220 in Opera, conflicts with \
Select	Apps	93	Reported as "U+005D" in Safari, no events in Chrome
F1	F1	112	
F2	F2	113	
F3	F3	114	
F4	F4	115	
F5	F5	116	Not captured in Safari, only keyup in Chrome
F6	F6	117	
F7	F7	118	
F8	F8	119	
F9	F9	120	
F10	F10	121	Reported as "F11" in Safari and Chrome
F11	F11	122	Reported as "U+005A" in Safari
F12	F12	123	
Scroll Lock	Scroll	145	

Figure 14-17   The key codes used in Event object properties (part 2 of 3)

Key codes for number pad control keys not affected by Number Lock

Key	keyIdentifier	Scan	Exceptions
Number Lock	NumLock	144	Reported as U+0090 in Safari
Enter	Enter	13	

Key codes for number pad symbols not affected by Number Lock

Key	keyIdentifier	data	Scan	ASCII	Exceptions
+	U+002B	+	107	43	Scan 43 in Opera PC, 61 in Opera Mac
-	U+002D	-	109	45	Scan 45 in Opera PC, 109 in Opera Mac
*	U+002A	*	106	42	Scan 42 in Opera PC, 56 in Opera Mac
/	U+002F	/	111	47	Scan 47 in Opera PC, 191 in Opera Mac
=	U+003D	=	61	61	Only on Mac, conflicts with + in Opera Mac

Key codes for number pad keys with Number Lock on

Key	keyIdentifier	data	Scan	ASCII	Exceptions
.	U+002E	.	110	46	Scan 78 in Opera PC, 190 on Mac
0	U+0030	0	96	48	
1	U+0031	1	97	49	
2	U+0032	2	98	50	
3	U+0033	3	99	51	
4	U+0034	4	100	52	
5	U+0035	5	101	53	
6	U+0036	6	102	54	
7	U+0037	7	103	55	
8	U+0038	8	104	56	
9	U+0039	9	105	57	

Key codes for number pad keys with Number Lock off

Key	keyIdentifier	Scan	Exceptions
5	Clear	12	Same as "Clear" key on Mac number pad
PgUp	PageUp	33	
PgDn	PageDown	34	
End	End	35	
Home	Home	36	
Left Arrow	Left	37	
Up Arrow	Up	38	
Right Arrow	Right	39	
Down Arrow	Down	40	
Ins	Insert	45	
Del	U+007F	46	

Figure 14-17   The key codes used in Event object properties (part 3 of 3)

The jslib_event_keyboard.js file

Figure 14-18 shows the code for our JavaScript library that standardizes the properties and methods of the Event object for keyboard events so they follow the DOM Level 3 specification. This lets you use the DOM Level 3 standards with all major browsers.

This library begins by checking whether the jsLib and jsLib.event objects exist. If they don't, it throws an appropriate error. Then, it creates the keyboard object and adds it to the jsLib.event object.

The updownKeyID and pressData arrays store the keys for the keyboard events. In particular, the updownKeyID array stores the keys for the keydown and keyup events, and the pressData array stores the keys for the keypress event. Both of these arrays are populated by the init method that's defined later in this library and used by the fixKeys method.

The codeToUnicode method is used in the init method to convert ASCII codes to Unicode values in the format that's used by the keyIdentifier property. This method takes an ASCII code as a parameter, and it returns a Unicode value. Within this method, the first statement uses the toString method to convert the code to a hexadecimal value, and it uses the toUpperCase method to convert the code to uppercase. Then, if the hexadecimal value is a single digit, it adds a zero to the beginning of the string. Finally, it adds "U+00" to the beginning of the string. For example, this method converts an ASCII code of 32 to a hexadecimal value of 20, which results in a string of "U+0020".

The keydownTracker event handler sets the value of a property named lastKeydownWasControl to indicate whether the last key that was pressed was a control key. To understand this code, you need to know that the Escape key has a keyIdentifier property of "U+001B", and it is the only control key that starts with a value of "U+". In other words, this method sets this property to true if the Escape key was pressed. Next, this code uses a regular expression to check whether the value starts with "U+", which means a character key was pressed. If so, it sets the property to false. Since all other keys are control keys, this code sets this property to true for all other keys.

The init method initializes the keyboard library. It starts by attaching the keydownTracker event handler to the keydown event for the document object. Then, this method converts keyboard scan codes to keyIdentifier values and stores them in the updownKeyId array. To do that, it converts the letters, numbers, symbols, control keys, and number pad keys. Finally, this method converts the characters for codes 32 to 126 and stores them in the pressData array. After this init method is defined, it is called so the keydownTracker event handler is attached, and the updownKeyId and pressTable arrays are initialized.

In part 3 of this figure, you can see the start of the fixKeys method, which takes two parameters: oEvt and evt. The first one refers to the original Event object, and the second one refers to the Event object that's being fixed. Remember that this method is called by the jsLib.event.fixEvent method at the end of figure 14-11.

The jslib_event_keyboard.js file

```javascript
if ( ! jsLib ) {
    throw new Error("jsLib Keyboard Events: jsLib not loaded");
} else if ( ! jsLib.event ) {
    throw new Error("jsLib Keyboard Events: jsLib event not loaded");
}

// Create the keyboard object
jsLib.event.keyboard = {};

// Define an array of keys for the keydown and keyup events
jsLib.event.keyboard.updownKeyId = [];

// Define an array of keys for the keypress event
jsLib.event.keyboard.pressData = [];

// Define a method that converts key code values to Unicode
jsLib.event.keyboard.codeToUnicode = function(code) {
    var unicode = code.toString(16).toUpperCase();
    if ( unicode.length == 1 ) { unicode = "0" + unicode; }
    return "U+00" + unicode;
}

// Define a property that indicates if the last key down was a control key
jsLib.event.keyboard.lastKeydownWasControl = false;

// Define an event handler for the keydown event
jsLib.event.keyboard.keydownTracker = function (evt) {
    if ( evt.keyIdentifier == "U+001B" ) {
        jsLib.event.keyboard.lastKeydownWasControl = true;
    } else if ( /^U\+/.test( evt.keyIdentifier ) ) {
        jsLib.event.keyboard.lastKeydownWasControl = false;
    } else {
        jsLib.event.keyboard.lastKeydownWasControl = true;
    }
}

// Define a method that initializes the keyboard library
jsLib.event.keyboard.init = function () {
    // Attach the keydownTracker handler to the document object
    jsLib.event.add(document, "keydown", this.keydownTracker);

    //////// updownKeyId conversions
    // Letters
    var code;
    for ( code = 65; code <= 90; code++ ) {
        this.updownKeyId[code] = this.codeToUnicode(code);
    }

    // Numbers
    for ( code = 48; code <= 57; code++ ) {
        this.updownKeyId[code] = this.codeToUnicode(code);
    }
```

Figure 14-18   The jslib_event_keyboard.js file (part 1 of 4)

The fixKeys method starts by creating a variable named code that stores the scan code or ASCII code that was generated by the event. Then, it fixes the necessary properties and methods.

To fix the keyIdentifier property, the fixKeys method begins by checking for the keyIdentifier property in the original Event object. If it exists, this method copies the value for this property from the old Event object to the new one. In addition, this method uses a switch statement to check for and fix three misidentified keys in the Safari implementation of the keyIdentifier property.

On the other hand, if the keyIdentifier property doesn't exist, the code variable contains the keyboard scan code that was generated from the keydown or keyup event. In that case, the value of the code variable is used as the index of the updownKeyId array to assign the correct value to the keyIdentifier property. Or, if the code variable isn't in the array, a value of "Unidentified" is assigned to the keyIdentifier property.

To fix the data property, the fixKeys method checks whether the data property exists in the original Event object. If so, it copies the value to the fixed Event object. Otherwise, this method creates a data property value for keypress events. To do that, it checks whether the last key pressed wasn't a control key and whether the code variable is in the pressData array. If so, the value of the code variable is used as the index of the pressData array to assign the correct value for the data property. Otherwise, an empty string is assigned to the data property.

To fix the keyLocation property, this method checks whether the keyLocation property exists in the original Event object. If so, it copies the value to the new Event object. If not, it sets the value to zero. This doesn't implement the DOM Level 3 standard completely, but it is adequate for most purposes.

To fix the getModifierState method, this method checks whether the getModifierState method exists in the original Event object. If so, this code copies the method from the old Event object to the new Event object. If not, this code defines a new function that works like the getModifierState method of the DOM Level 3 standard, and it assigns this function to the getModifierState method of the new Event object.

The jslib_event_keyboard.js file (continued)

```
// Symbols
this.updownKeyId[32] = this.codeToUnicode(" ".charCodeAt(0));
this.updownKeyId[59] = this.codeToUnicode(";".charCodeAt(0));
this.updownKeyId[61] = this.codeToUnicode("=".charCodeAt(0));
this.updownKeyId[107] = this.codeToUnicode("=".charCodeAt(0));
this.updownKeyId[109] = this.codeToUnicode("-".charCodeAt(0));
this.updownKeyId[186] = this.codeToUnicode(";".charCodeAt(0));
this.updownKeyId[187] = this.codeToUnicode("=".charCodeAt(0));
this.updownKeyId[188] = this.codeToUnicode(",".charCodeAt(0));
this.updownKeyId[189] = this.codeToUnicode("-".charCodeAt(0));
this.updownKeyId[190] = this.codeToUnicode(".".charCodeAt(0));
this.updownKeyId[191] = this.codeToUnicode("/".charCodeAt(0));
this.updownKeyId[192] = this.codeToUnicode("`".charCodeAt(0));
this.updownKeyId[219] = this.codeToUnicode("[".charCodeAt(0));
this.updownKeyId[220] = this.codeToUnicode("\\".charCodeAt(0));
this.updownKeyId[221] = this.codeToUnicode("]".charCodeAt(0));
this.updownKeyId[222] = this.codeToUnicode("'".charCodeAt(0));

// Control Keys
this.updownKeyId[8] = this.codeToUnicode(8); // Backspace
this.updownKeyId[9] = this.codeToUnicode(9); // Tab
this.updownKeyId[13] = "Enter";
this.updownKeyId[16] = "Shift";
this.updownKeyId[17] = "Control";
this.updownKeyId[18] = "Alt";
this.updownKeyId[19] = "Break";
this.updownKeyId[20] = "CapsLock";
this.updownKeyId[27] = this.codeToUnicode(27); // Escape
this.updownKeyId[33] = "PageUp";
this.updownKeyId[34] = "PageDown";
this.updownKeyId[35] = "End";
this.updownKeyId[36] = "Home";
this.updownKeyId[37] = "Left";
this.updownKeyId[38] = "Up";
this.updownKeyId[39] = "Right";
this.updownKeyId[40] = "Down";
this.updownKeyId[44] = "PrintScreen";
this.updownKeyId[45] = "Insert";
this.updownKeyId[46] = this.codeToUnicode(127); // Delete
this.updownKeyId[91] = "Win";  // Left Windows Logo Key
this.updownKeyId[92] = "Win";  // Right Windows Logo Key
this.updownKeyId[93] = "Apps"; // The Application Key
this.updownKeyId[112] = "F1";
this.updownKeyId[113] = "F2";
this.updownKeyId[114] = "F3";
this.updownKeyId[115] = "F4";
this.updownKeyId[116] = "F5";
this.updownKeyId[117] = "F6";
this.updownKeyId[118] = "F7";
this.updownKeyId[119] = "F8";
this.updownKeyId[120] = "F9";
this.updownKeyId[121] = "F10";
this.updownKeyId[122] = "F11";
this.updownKeyId[123] = "F12";
this.updownKeyId[145] = "Scroll"; // Scroll Lock
```

Figure 14-18   The jslib_event_keyboard.js file (part 2 of 4)

The jslib_event_keyboard.js file (continued)

```
    // Numeric Keypad
    this.updownKeyId[144] = "NumLock";
    this.updownKeyId[42] = this.codeToUnicode("*".charCodeAt(0));
    this.updownKeyId[43] = this.codeToUnicode("+".charCodeAt(0));
    this.updownKeyId[47] = this.codeToUnicode("\/".charCodeAt(0));
    this.updownKeyId[106] = this.codeToUnicode("*".charCodeAt(0));
    this.updownKeyId[107] = this.codeToUnicode("+".charCodeAt(0));
    this.updownKeyId[109] = this.codeToUnicode("-".charCodeAt(0));
    this.updownKeyId[110] = this.codeToUnicode(".".charCodeAt(0));
    this.updownKeyId[111] = this.codeToUnicode("\/".charCodeAt(0));
    for ( code = 96; code <= 105; code++ ) {
        this.updownKeyId[code] = this.codeToUnicode(code - 48);
    }
    this.updownKeyId[12] = "Clear"; // NumPad5 with NumLock Off

    //////// pressData conversions
    for ( code = 32; code <= 126; code++ ) {
        this.pressData[code] = String.fromCharCode(code);
    }
}

// Call the method that initializes the keyboard library
jsLib.event.keyboard.init();

jsLib.event.keyboard.fixKeys = function (oEvt, evt) {

    var code = ( oEvt.keyCode || oEvt.charCode || 0 );

    // Fix the keyIdentifier property
    if ( "keyIdentifier" in oEvt ) {
        evt.keyIdentifier = oEvt.keyIdentifier;

        // Fix three Safari issues
        switch ( evt.keyIdentifier ) {
            case "U+0090": evt.keyIdentifier = "NumLock"; break;
            case "U+005D": evt.keyIdentifier = "Apps"   ; break;
            case "U+005A": evt.keyIdentifier = "F11"    ; break;
        }
    } else {
        if ( evt.type == "keydown" || evt.type == "keyup" ) {
            if ( jsLib.event.keyboard.updownKeyId[code] ) {
                evt.keyIdentifier = jsLib.event.keyboard.updownKeyId[code];
            } else {
                evt.keyIdentifier = "Unidentified";
            }
        }
    }
```

Figure 14-18   The jslib_event_keyboard.js file (part 3 of 4)

The jslib_event_keyboard.js file (continued)

```
// Fix the data property
if ( "data" in oEvt ) {
    evt.data = oEvt.data;
} else {
    if ( evt.type == "keypress" ) {
        if ( ! jsLib.event.keyboard.lastKeydownWasControl &&
            jsLib.event.keyboard.pressData[code]) {
            evt.data = jsLib.event.keyboard.pressData[code];
        } else {
            evt.data = "";
        }
    }
}


// Fix the keyLocation property
if ( "keyLocation" in oEvt ) {
    evt.keyLocation = oEvt.keyLocation;
} else {
    evt.keyLocation = 0;
}


// Fix the getModifierState method
if ( "getModifierState" in oEvt ) {
    evt.getModiferState = oEvt.getModifierState;
} else {
    evt.getModifierState = function ( modifier ) {
        switch ( modifier ) {
            case "Shift":
                return this.shiftKey;
            case "Ctrl":
                return this.ctrlKey;
            case "Alt":
                return this.altKey;
            case "Meta":
                return this.metaKey;
            default:
                return false;
        }
    }
}
}
```

Figure 14-18   The jslib_event_keyboard.js file (part 4 of 4)

Perspective

Now that you've completed this chapter, you should understand how libraries can be used to standardize event handling and Event objects. You should know how to use libraries like this with your own applications. And you should know how to write and modify these libraries.

To start, you can use the three libraries that are described in this chapter for all of your event handling. These libraries will make it easy for you to develop applications with cross-browser compatibility. And if you've downloaded the applications for this book from our web site, you already have these libraries on your system. Later, if you need to enhance one of these libraries, you should be able to do that too.

When you use our libraries, you should always use the basic event library (jslib_event.js) to attach and detach event handlers. That way, you'll be able to attach more than one event handler to the same event for the same element, and the Event object will be standardized. On the other hand, you only need to use the mouse library if your application is going to use mouse events other than the click event. And you only need to use the keyboard library if your application is going to use keyboard events.

Terms

capturing phase
target phase
bubbling phase
bitwise AND operator

Exercise 14-1   Use the event libraries with the Image Gallery application

This exercise gives you a chance to use one of the event libraries described in this chapter to attach events.

1. Use the Firefox browser to view the index.html file in the image_gallery folder that's in the chapter 14 folder for exercises.

2. Use your text editor to open the index.html file and the JavaScript files for this application. Note that the JavaScript files include the jslib_event.js file that's described in this chapter. Then, review the code in these files.

3. Modify the index.html file so it includes the jslib_event.js file.

4. Modify the image_gallery.js file so it uses the event library to attach the onload event of the window. Then, test this change.

5. Modify the image_gallery_library.js file so it uses the event library to attach the event handlers to the click events of the links. Then, test this change.

6. Modify the image_gallery_library.js file so it only uses the properties and methods defined by the DOM standard for working with the Event object. For example, to cancel the default action for an event, you only need to use the preventDefault method. Note how this makes the code shorter and simpler. Then, test your changes in both IE and Firefox browsers.

Exercise 14-2   Use the event libraries with the Register application

This exercise gives you a chance to use the event libraries described in this chapter to work with keyboard events.

1. Use the Firefox browser to view the index.html file in the register folder that's in the chapter 14 folder for exercises.

2. Use your text editor to open the index.html file and the JavaScript files for this application. Note that the JavaScript files include the jslib_event.js and jslib_event_keyboard.js files that are described in this chapter. Then, review this code.

3. Modify the index.html file so it includes the two event libraries.

4. Modify the register.js file so it uses the event library to attach the onload event of the window. Then, test this change.

5. Modify the register.js file so it uses the JavaScript event library to attach the event handlers to the click events of the buttons. Then, test this change.

6. Modify the register.js file so it resets the form if the user presses the Escape key. Then, test this change.

Exercise 14-3   Modify the Slide Show application

This exercise gives you a chance to use the libraries described in this chapter to work with mouse and keyboard events.

1. Use the Firefox browser to view the index.html file in the slide_show folder that's in the chapter 14 folder for exercises.

2. Modify the slide_show_library.js file so the slide show is reset if the user clicks the image while holding down the Ctrl key.

15

Advanced DOM manipulation

Many JavaScript applications need to manipulate the DOM tree. That's why this chapter shows you how to detect when the DOM is ready, how to search the DOM, and how to modify it. At the end of this chapter, you'll see a Headlines application that uses many of these skills.

How to detect when the DOM is ready **524**
A problem with the load event 524
The code that illustrates this problem 526
How to use a ready method to detect when the DOM is ready 528
The JavaScript library that contains the ready method 530

How to search the DOM **534**
How to use a walk method to walk the DOM tree 534
How to use a getElementsByClassname method to search the DOM 538
A JavaScript library for walking and searching the DOM 540

How to modify the DOM **542**
How to create new DOM nodes 542
How to add and remove DOM nodes 544
How to use a document fragment 546

The Headlines application **548**
The user interface 548
The XHTML file 548
The headlines_library.js file 550
The headlines.js file 552

Perspective **554**

How to detect when the DOM is ready

So far, the code in this book uses the load event of the window object to detect when the DOM tree is completely built and ready to be used. However, when a web page needs to load large files such as image files, this can delay the use of the page. This topic describes this problem in more detail and shows you how to solve it.

A problem with the load event

Figure 15-1 shows a web page that illustrates the problem that occurs when you use the load event of a window to detect when the DOM is ready. Here, the Test button looks like it's ready to use, but the load event hasn't occurred yet because the image hasn't been loaded. As a result, the event handler for the load event hasn't been run yet, and the event handler for the Test button hasn't been attached yet.

The problem is that the user may click on the Test button and then be confused when it doesn't work. This problem is compounded when a web page consists of several controls and has to load many images.

The XHTML page in a browser

Description

- The load event of a window doesn't occur until after the entire page is loaded, including large images. Often, though, the other elements in the DOM tree are displayed and appear to be ready for use before all of the images are loaded.
- If your application depends on the load event to attach event handlers, the elements on the page won't respond to the user until the entire page finishes loading.
- The image on this page is about 2MB and takes several seconds to download, even on a fast Internet connection.

Figure 15-1   A problem with the load event

The code that illustrates this problem

Figure 15-2 shows the code for the web page in figure 15-1. Here, the first highlighted line in the XHTML code defines a <span> tag that shows the DOM status. The second highlighted line uses a <button> tag to define the Test button.

After that, this page contains a <script> tag that uses JavaScript code to write an <img> tag into the document. This forces the browser to download the image from the server each time the page is loaded. Otherwise, the browser could get this image more quickly from the browser's local cache. This script is designed to make it easy for you to test the web page in this figure, but it shouldn't be used in production applications.

This type of script is known as a *cache busting script*, and it works by adding a unique query string to the end of the URL each time the browser loads the page. Although this query string is ignored by the web server, the web browser thinks the URL is new and downloads the entire file from the server each time the page is loaded, even though the image is in cache memory.

The ready_test.js file in this figure contains the JavaScript code for the page. To start, it defines an event handler for the Test button. This event handler displays a dialog box that indicates that the button is ready.

Then, this code defines an event handler for the load event of the window object. Within this event handler, the first statement attaches the event handler for the Test button, and the second statement changes the text in the status span tag from "Not Ready" to "Ready".

Unfortunately, the load event of the window won't occur until the browser finishes loading all of the files for the current page, including the image file. As a result, the Test button will look like it's ready, but its event handler won't be attached. Depending on the type application, this can result in a frustrating experience for the user.

In cases like this, though, the DOM is ready well before the browser finishes loading all of the files for the current page. That's why the next figure shows how to use a custom method to detect when the DOM is ready. Then, you can use that method to call a function that attaches the event handlers before the images are loaded so your users can start using the page.

The XHTML for the page

```
<!DOCTYPE html PUBLIC "-//W3C//DTD XHTML 1.0 Transitional//EN"
    "http://www.w3.org/TR/xhtml1/DTD/xhtml1-transitional.dtd">
<html xmlns="http://www.w3.org/1999/xhtml">
<head>
<title>DOM Ready Test</title>
<link rel="stylesheet" type="text/css" href="ready_test.css"/>
<script type="text/javascript" src="ready_test.js"></script>
</head>

<body>
<div id="content">
    <h1 class="center">DOM Ready Test</h1>
    <p>DOM Status: <span id="status">Not Ready</span></p>
    <p><button id="btnTest">Test</button></p>
    <p>
        <!-- this script prevents the browser from caching the image -->
        <script type="text/javascript">
            var ms = (new Date()).getTime();
            var site = "http://solarsystem.nasa.gov";
            var path = "/multimedia/gallery/GPN-2001-000009.jpg";
            var url = site + path + "?ms=" + ms;
            document.write( '<img src="' + url + '" width="600" />' );
        </script>
    </p>
</div>
</body>
</html>
```

The ready_test.js file

```
var $ = function (id) { return document.getElementById(id); }

// The event handler for the Test button
var testClick = function () {
    alert("This button is ready!");
}

window.onload = function () {
    $("btnTest").onclick = testClick;                // Attach event handler
    $("status").firstChild.nodeValue = "READY";  // Update status
}
```

Description

- The load event doesn't occur until the image finishes downloading. But the event handler isn't attached and the DOM status isn't updated until the load event occurs.

- To make it easy to test this application, the <img> tag is written into the document using a script that prevents the browser from caching the image. As a result, the browser must download the image every time the user loads the page.

Figure 15-2   The code that illustrates the problem with the load event

How to use a ready method to detect when the DOM is ready

Figure 15-3 shows how to use ready method to detect when the DOM is ready. This method is stored in the JavaScript library that's presented in the next figure. This library is loaded by the <script> tag in this figure.

Then, within your JavaScript code, you can define a function that contains the code that you want to run when the DOM is ready. For instance, the code in this figure defines a function named domReady. Note that this function contains the same statements as the event handler for the load event that was presented in the previous figure.

To call this domReady function, you use the ready method of the jsLib.dom object. This method calls the specified function almost immediately when the page starts to load, and well before the image is loaded. As a result, your users can get to work faster.

In the browser, for example, you can see that the DOM status has changed to "Ready" even though the image hasn't finished downloading. Similarly, the Test button has already responded to a click event.

The XHTML page in a browser

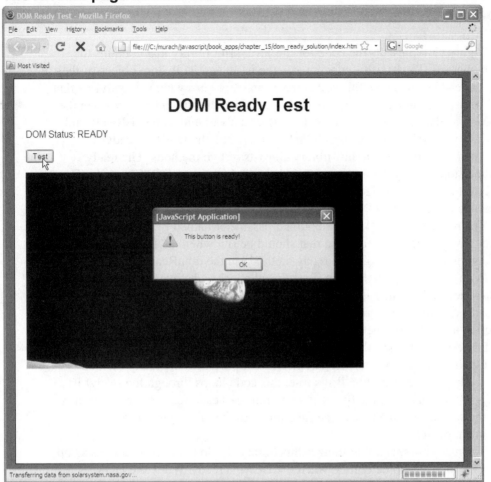

The XHTML that imports the library

```
<script type="text/javascript" src="jslib_dom_ready.js"></script>
```

A method of the jsLib.dom object

Method	Description
ready(function)	Runs the specified function as soon as the DOM is ready.

An except from the ready_test.js file

```
// A function to run when the DOM is ready
var domReady = function () {
    $("btnTest").onclick = testClick;           // Attach event handler
    $("status").firstChild.nodeValue = "READY"; // Update status
}

jsLib.dom.ready( domReady );  // The call to the library
```

Figure 15-3   How to use a ready method to detect when the DOM is ready

The JavaScript library that contains the ready method

Figure 15-4 presents the code for the JavaScript library that contains the ready method. To start, this code creates the jsLib and jsLib.dom objects if they don't already exist. Next, this code creates an empty array named readyList that will be used to store references to all the functions that should be run when the DOM is ready. Then, this code creates a Boolean variable named isReady and sets it to false. This variable will be set to true when the DOM is ready.

The rest of the code in this library consists of two methods. The ready method stores the functions that should be called when the DOM is ready. The readyInit method initializes the library and calls the ready function with no parameters when the DOM is ready.

The ready method takes one optional parameter named fn. This parameter stores a reference to the function that should be run when the DOM is ready. In the last figure, for example, the ready method ran the domReady function.

Within the ready method, an if statement checks whether the fn parameter is provided and whether it's a function. If so, the ready method checks the isReady variable. If it's true (meaning the DOM is ready), this code calls the function in the fn parameter with its this keyword set to the document object. If it's false, this code adds the function to the readyList array.

On the other hand, if the fn parameter isn't provided, the ready method checks the isReady variable. If it's true, this code loops through the readyList array. Within this loop, the first statement removes each function from the array, and the second statement calls the function with the this keyword set to the document object.

The readyInit method initializes this library. To do that, this method sets up the test conditions to determine when the DOM is ready. When the DOM is ready, this method sets the isReady variable to true and calls the ready method with no parameters. This executes any functions that have been stored in the readyList array before the DOM was ready.

The readyInit method begins by using the DOM event model to detect when the DOM is ready. To do that, an if statement checks whether the addEventListener method exists in the document object. If so, the DOMContentLoaded event is used to detect when the DOM is ready. This event is part of the HTML 5 specification, which is currently in development and subject to change before final release. However, this event is already supported by Firefox, Safari, and Opera.

If the DOM event model is supported, the readyInit method adds an event handler to the DOMContentLoaded event of the document. This event handler contains two statements that run when the DOM is ready. The first statement sets the isReady variable to true, and the second statement calls the ready method with no arguments. As a result, the ready method runs any functions that have been stored in the readyList array.

The jslib_dom_ready.js file

```
if ( ! jsLib ) { var jsLib = {}; }
if ( ! jsLib.dom ) { jsLib.dom = {}; }

// Define an array that stores the functions to call when the DOM is ready
jsLib.dom.readyList = [];

// Define a Boolean property that indicates if the DOM is ready
jsLib.dom.isReady = false;

// Define a function named ready that stores the functions to run
jsLib.dom.ready = function ( fn ) {
    if ( fn instanceof Function ) {
        if ( jsLib.dom.isReady ) {
            fn.call(document);
        } else {
            jsLib.dom.readyList.push( fn );
        }
    } else {
        if ( jsLib.dom.isReady ) {
            while ( jsLib.dom.readyList.length > 0 ) {
                fn = jsLib.dom.readyList.pop();
                fn.call(document);
            }
        }
    }
}

// Define a method that initializes this library
jsLib.dom.readyInit = function () {
    if ( document.addEventListener ) {   // DOM event model
        document.addEventListener(
            "DOMContentLoaded",
            function () {
                jsLib.dom.isReady = true;
                jsLib.dom.ready();
            },
            false
        );
```

Figure 15-4   The JavaScript library that contains the ready method (part 1 of 2)

If the DOM event model isn't supported, the readyInit method uses the IE event model. To do that, this code checks whether the attachEvent method exists in the document object. If so, the readyInit method checks whether the doScroll method exists in the documentElement object. In addition, it checks to make sure that the document isn't in an iframe.

If both conditions are true, this code uses the *doScroll polling technique* to determine when the DOM is ready. This technique was developed by Diego Perini and released under the GNU Public License at this web site:

`http://javascript.nwbox.com/IEContentLoaded/`

This code simulates the DOMContentLoaded event of the DOM event model for the Internet Explorer. To do that, this technique takes advantage of the fact that the doScroll method of the IE event model throws an error if the DOM isn't ready.

The doScroll polling technique begins by creating a function named doScrollPoll. Within this function, the first statement checks the isReady variable and exits the function if it's true. Next, the doScrollPoll function uses a try-catch statement to test if the doScroll method throws an error. If so, the function sets a timer to run the doScrollPoll function again and returns to the top of the function. If the doScroll method doesn't throw an error, the function sets the isReady variable to true and calls the ready method to run any functions in the readyList array.

If the document is in an iframe or the doScroll method isn't supported, this code uses the onreadystatechange event to detect when the DOM is ready. This event occurs some time after the DOM is actually ready, but before the load event of the window occurs. In other words, it's faster than using the load event, but not as fast as using the DOMContentLoaded event or the doScroll polling technique.

This code uses the attachEvent method to attach an anonymous event handler to the onreadystatechange event. This event handler begins by checking whether the readyState property of the document equals "complete". If so, the event handler sets the isReady variable to true and calls the ready method to run any functions in the readyList array.

As a last resort, this code uses the attachEvent method to attach an event handler to the load event of the window. This makes sure that this code detects that the DOM is ready even if there are problems with the other two IE techniques. In most cases, though, one of the first two techniques will detect that the DOM is ready and run the ready method. As a result, the readyList is usually empty by the time this event handler calls the ready method.

The last statement in this library calls the readyInit method that initializes this library.

The jslib_dom_ready.js file (continued)

```javascript
        } else if ( document.attachEvent ) { // IE event model
            // Are we in an iframe?
            if ( document.documentElement.doScroll && window == window.top ) {
                // No, we're not in an iframe. Use doScroll polling to
                // simulate DOMContentLoaded. By Diego Perini at
                // http://javascript.nwbox.com/IEContentLoaded/
                var doScrollPoll = function () {
                    if ( jsLib.dom.isReady ) return;
                    try {
                        document.documentElement.doScroll("left");
                    } catch( error ) {
                        setTimeout( doScrollPoll, 0 );
                        return;
                    }
                    jsLib.dom.isReady = true;
                    jsLib.dom.ready();
                }
                doScrollPoll();
            } else {
                // Yes, we are in an iframe or doScroll isn't supported.
                // Use the onreadystatechange event
                document.attachEvent(
                    "onreadystatechange",
                    function () {
                        if ( document.readyState === "complete" ) {
                            jsLib.dom.isReady = true;
                            jsLib.dom.ready();
                        }
                    }
                );
            }

            // Use the onload event as a last resort
            if ( window.attachEvent ) {
                window.attachEvent(
                    "onload",
                    function () {
                        jsLib.dom.isReady = true;
                        jsLib.dom.ready();
                    }
                );
            }
        }
    }
}

// Call the method that initializes this library
jsLib.dom.readyInit();
```

Figure 15-4   The JavaScript library that contains the ready method (part 2 of 2)

How to search the DOM

When coding JavaScript applications, you often need to search the DOM tree. That's why this topic shows you how to walk the DOM tree using a generic method named walk. Then, it shows you how to use a more specific method to search the DOM and return a particular type of element. Finally, it describes a JavaScript library that provides these methods.

How to use a walk method to walk the DOM tree

Figure 15-5 presents an application that walks the DOM tree, creates a string that represents the DOM tree, and displays that string in a dialog box. To start, this figure shows the dialog box that's displayed when this application runs. This dialog box contains the elements in the DOM tree and their attributes and values. Here, each element is listed on its own line and indented under its parent element. As a result, this string is a "sideways" representation of the DOM tree where the top level is on the left and deeper levels are shifted to the right.

Next, the figure shows the XHTML file for the application. Here, the <script> tags load three JavaScript files. The first loads the jslib_dom_ready.js file that's in the previous figure; the second loads the jslib_dom.js file that's in figure 15-7, and the third loads the show_dom_tree.js file that's in part 2 of this figure.

The DOM tree displayed in a dialog box

```
[JavaScript Application]                        [X]

   html (xmlns="http://www.w3.org/1999/xhtml")
      head
         title
         style (type="text/css")
         script (src="jslib_dom_ready.js" type="text/javascript")
         script (src="jslib_dom.js" type="text/javascript")
         script (src="show_dom_tree.js" type="text/javascript")
         script (src="show_centered_elements.js" type="text/javascript")
      body
         div (id="content")
            h1 (class="center")
            p (class="center")
            ul (id="imageList" class="center")
               li
                  a (title="Casting 1" href="casting1.jpg")
               li
                  a (title="Casting 2" href="casting2.jpg")
               li
                  a (title="Catch and Release" href="catchrelease.jpg")
               li
                  a (title="Fish" href="fish.jpg")
               li
                  a (title="Lures" href="lures.jpg")

                     [    OK    ]
```

The XHTML file

```
<!DOCTYPE html PUBLIC "-//W3C//DTD XHTML 1.0 Transitional//EN"
    "http://www.w3.org/TR/xhtml1/DTD/xhtml1-transitional.dtd">
<html xmlns="http://www.w3.org/1999/xhtml">
<head>
<title>Image Gallery</title>
<link rel="stylesheet" type="text/css" href="image_gallery.css"/>
<script type="text/javascript" src="jslib_dom_ready.js"></script>
<script type="text/javascript" src="jslib_dom.js"></script>
<script type="text/javascript" src="show_dom_tree.js"></script>
</head>

<body>
<div id="content">
    <h1 class="center">Fishing Image Gallery</h1>
    <p class="center">Click one of the links below to view the image.</p>
    <ul class="center" id="imageList">
        <li><a href="casting1.jpg" title="Casting 1">Casting 1</a></li>
        <li><a href="casting2.jpg" title="Casting 2">Casting 2</a></li>
        <li><a href="catchrelease.jpg" title="Catch and Release">Catch
            and Release</a></li>
        <li><a href="fish.jpg" title="Fish">Fish</a></li>
        <li><a href="lures.jpg" title="Lures">Lures</a></li>
    </ul>
</div>
</body>
</html>
```

Figure 15-5   How to use a walk method to walk the DOM tree (part 1 of 2)

Part 2 of this figure begins by describing the walk method of the jsLib.dom object. This method is stored in the jslib_dom.js file that's shown in figure 15-7.

The walk method walks through the nodes of a DOM tree, and it has four parameters. The first parameter is required, and it must specify a function that does the processing for each node. The next two parameters are optional, and they can provide functions that do processing before or after a node is processed. The fourth parameter is also optional, and it can specify the node that you want to start the walk at. If you don't specify a node for this parameter, the walk method begins walking at the document node.

The show_dom_tree.js file uses the walk method to build a string that represents the DOM tree. To start, this code creates two empty text strings named domTree and indent. The domTree variable stores the string representation of the DOM tree. The indent variable stores the amount of indentation to add at the front of each line in the string for the DOM tree, and the value of this variable changes as the DOM string is built.

The addNode function is the function that does the processing for each node of the tree that is being walked, and the walk method passes the current node to this function. Within this function, the first statement adds the indentation and the tag name of the node to the domTree variable. Then, this function checks whether the node has any attributes. If it does, it adds a left parenthesis to the node's line in the domTree variable. Next, it loops through each attribute. Within the loop, the code adds the attribute name, an equal sign, a quotation mark, the attribute value, and another quotation mark. It also adds a space as a separator for all the attributes except the last one. After it loops through all of the attributes, this code adds a right parenthesis. Finally, the addNode function adds a new line character to the domTree variable.

The moreIndent function is the function that does the processing before each child node of the tree is processed. This function adds four spaces to the indent variable. This adds extra indentation before the child nodes are processed.

Similarly, the lessIndent function does the processing after each child node of the tree is processed. This function removes four spaces from the indent variable. This removes the extra indentation after the child nodes are processed.

In this example, the showDomTree function calls the walk method of the jsLib.dom object with the addNode, moreIndent, and lessIndent functions as its parameters. Since this call doesn't include the fourth parameter, the walk method starts at the document node. This builds the string representation of the entire DOM tree and stores it in the domTree variable. Then, the domTree variable is displayed in a dialog box. Since this showDomTree function is called by the ready method, it runs as soon as the DOM is ready.

Incidentally, when you call the walk method, you can use the undefined keyword for any parameters that aren't needed. For example, to specify a postFn parameter, but not a preFn parameter, you can call the walk method like this:

```
jsLib.dom.walk (main, undefined, after);
```

Or, to specify a starting node but no preFn or postFn functions, you can use this call:

```
jsLib.dom.walk (main, undefined, undefined, node);
```

A method of the jsLib.dom object

Method	Description
walk (nodeFn, preFn, postFn, node)	This method walks some or all of the DOM tree and uses the specified functions to process each node. The nodeFn parameter specifies the function that processes each node. The optional preFn and postFn parameters specify the functions to run before and after each child node is processed. The optional node parameter specifies the starting node. If this parameter isn't specified, the walk method starts at the document node.

The show_dom_tree.js file

```
var domTree = "";
var indent = "";

// Define the main processing function
var addNode = function (node) {
    domTree += indent + node.tagName.toLowerCase();
    if (node.hasAttributes()) {
        domTree += " (";
        for ( var i = 0; i < node.attributes.length; i++) {
            domTree += node.attributes[i].name + "=\"";
            domTree += node.attributes[i].value + "\"";
            if ( i < node.attributes.length - 1) {
                domTree += " ";
            }
        }
        domTree += ")";
    }
    domTree += "\n";
}

// Define the preprocessing function
var moreIndent = function () {
    indent += "    ";
}

// Define the postprocessing function
var lessIndent = function () {
    if (indent.length >= 4) indent = indent.slice(0,-4);
}

// Define a function that calls the walk method
var showDomTree = function () {
    jsLib.dom.walk(addNode, moreIndent, lessIndent);
    alert(domTree);
}

// Call the showDomTree function
jsLib.dom.ready( showDomTree );
```

Figure 15-5   How to use a walk method to walk the DOM tree (part 2 of 2)

How to use a getElementsByClassname method to search the DOM

Figure 15-6 shows how you can search the DOM by using another method of the jsLib.dom object that's stored in the jslib_dom.js file. This figure begins by describing the method, which returns an array of Element objects that have the class name that's specified in the parameter.

Next, this figure presents the <script> tags for the three files that are needed for this example. The first two load library files. The third one loads the show_centered_elements.js file.

Last, this figure presents the JavaScript file that searches the DOM and displays a dialog box that shows the results of the search. To start, this file defines a function named showCenteredElementsCount. Within this function, the first statement uses the getElementsByClassName method of the jsLib.dom object to return an array of Element objects that have a class attribute of "center". Then, the second statement displays a dialog box that indicates the number of elements that were returned. Finally, this file uses the ready method of the jsLib.dom object to run the showCenteredElementsCount method.

A method of the jsLib.dom object

Method	Description
getElementsByClassName (className)	Returns an array of Element objects that have a class attribute that matches the specified className parameter.

The XHTML that imports the necessary JavaScript files

```
<script type="text/javascript" src="jslib_dom_ready.js"></script>
<script type="text/javascript" src="jslib_dom.js"></script>
<script type="text/javascript" src="show_centered_elements.js"></script>
```

The show_centered_elements.js file

```
var showCenteredElementCount = function () {
    var centeredElements = jsLib.dom.getElementsByClassName("center");
    alert("Centered elements: " + centeredElements.length);
}

jsLib.dom.ready( showCenteredElementCount );
```

The resulting dialog box

```
[JavaScript Application]                    X

    ⚠   Centered elements: 3

                    ┌──────────┐
                    │    OK    │
                    └──────────┘
```

Description

- The function in the show_centered_elements.js file uses the getElementsByClassname method to get an array of all the elements that have a class attribute with a value of "center".

Figure 15-6   How to use a getElementsByClassName method to search the DOM

A JavaScript library for walking and searching the DOM

Figure 15-7 shows the code for the jslib_dom.js file. This code defines the walk and getElementsByClassName methods of the jsLib.dom object. To start, this code creates the jsLib and jsLib.dom objects if they don't already exist.

This is followed by the walk method that defines the four parameters that you've already been introduced to. Within this walk method, the first statement checks whether the required nodeFn parameter is undefined. If so, the method returns to the calling program. Otherwise, if the optional node parameter is undefined, the node is set to the documentElement property of the document object.

Next, the walk method checks whether the node parameter is an element. If so, it calls the function stored in the nodeFn parameter with the node parameter as its argument. This performs the main processing for the node.

After performing the main processing for the node, the walk method checks whether the node has any child nodes. If so, it calls the preFn function if one exists. Then, it loops through each child node. Within this loop, a single statement makes a recursive call to the walk method. This call specifies the child node as the starting node for the walk method. Finally, the walk method calls the postFn function if one exists.

The walk method is followed by the getElementsByClassName method. This method uses the walk method to return an array of Element objects that have a class attribute that matches the className parameter. To start, this method defines an array that will be used to store references to the elements that are returned.

Next, this method defines a function named nodeTest. This function is the main processing function that will be passed to the walk method. Within this function, an if statement checks whether the className parameter matches the className property of the node parameter of the nodeTest function. If so, the nodeTest function adds the node to the elements array.

After defining the main processing function, this method calls the walk method and passes the nodeTest function to it. This adds any elements that match the specified className parameter to the array of elements.

The last statement in this method begins by checking whether the elements array contains any elements. If so, this method returns the elements array. Otherwise, this code returns an undefined value.

The jslib_dom.js file

```javascript
if ( ! jsLib ) { var jsLib = {}; }
if ( ! jsLib.dom ) { jsLib.dom = {}; }

jsLib.dom.walk = function ( nodeFn, preFn, postFn, node ) {
    if ( nodeFn == undefined ) return;
    if ( node == undefined ) node = document.documentElement;

    // If the node is an element
    if (node.nodeType == 1) {

        // Pass the node to the main function
        nodeFn(node);
        if ( node.hasChildNodes() ) {
            // If necessary, pass the node to the pre-child function
            if ( preFn !== undefined ) preFn(node);

            // Use a recursive call to process each child node
            for(var i = 0; i < node.childNodes.length; i++) {
                jsLib.dom.walk( nodeFn, preFn, postFn, node.childNodes[i]);
            }

            // If necessary, pass the node to the post-child function
            if ( postFn !== undefined ) postFn(node);
        }
    }
}

jsLib.dom.getElementsByClassName = function ( className ) {
    // Define a variable to store the elements
    var elements = [];

    // Define the main function
    var nodeTest = function (node) {
        if ( className == node.className ) {
            elements.push( node );
        }
    }

    // Call the walk method
    jsLib.dom.walk(nodeTest);

    return (elements.length > 0) ? elements : undefined;
}
```

Description

- The jsLib.dom.walk method recursively walks the DOM tree and processes each node using the functions referred to by the nodeFn, preFn and postFn parameters.
- The jsLib.dom.getElementsByClassName method uses the jsLib.dom.walk method to search the DOM tree and return a list of elements from the DOM tree that match the specified class name.

Figure 15-7   A JavaScript library for walking and searching the DOM tree

How to modify the DOM

If you need to modify the DOM, you can create new nodes, add nodes to the DOM, and remove nodes from the DOM. You can also use document fragments to work with a subtree of DOM nodes. The next topics show you how.

How to create new DOM nodes

Figure 15-8 shows three ways you can create a new DOM node. First, you can use the createTextNode method of the document object to create a Text node that contains the text for another node. For instance, the first example in this figure creates a textNode that contains some text for an <li> node.

Second, you can use the createElement method of the document object to create an Element node. When you use this method, you can specify the type of Element node by passing any valid XHTML tag name to the method. For instance, the second example creates an Element node for an <li> node.

Third, you can use the cloneNode method of a node to create a new node by cloning, or copying, the existing node. This works because every DOM node provides a method named cloneNode. This method returns a copy of the node including the attributes of the node. However, it doesn't copy any child elements of the node. This is known as a *shallow copy*.

However, the cloneNode method has an optional parameter that can be used to indicate that the child nodes of the node should also be copied. If this parameter is set to true, the returned node includes copies of its child nodes and their attributes. This is known as a *deep copy*.

Whether you perform a shallow or deep copy, the cloneNode method doesn't copy the event handlers for the node. As a result, if you want to attach an event handler to one of the events of the cloned node, you need to write code to do that.

The last example in this figure shows how to modify the attributes of a new node after it's created. This lets you set the attributes of the new node before you add it to the DOM tree. Here, the first statement creates an Element node for an <img> tag. Then, the second statement sets the src property for this element.

When you create new DOM nodes, they aren't displayed on the web page until they are added to the DOM tree. As a result, if you want to display a DOM node, you must add it to an existing node in the DOM tree as shown in the next figure.

Two methods of the document object for creating new nodes

Method	Description
createTextNode(text)	Creates a new Text node using the specified text as the nodeValue property for the new node.
createElement(tagName)	Creates a new Element node for the specified type of tag.

How to create new nodes

How to create a Text node

```
var textNode = document.createTextNode("Lightweight Neoprene Waders");
```

How to create an Element node

```
var liNode = document.createElement("li");
```

A method to create a copy of an element

Method	Description
cloneNode(deep)	Creates a copy of a node and its attributes, but not of its event handlers. If the optional parameter is set to true, this method does a deep copy that includes the child nodes of the node. Otherwise, this method does a shallow copy that doesn't include the child nodes of the node.

How to clone a node

How to copy an existing Element node

```
var list = document.getElementById("headlines");
var newList = list.cloneNode();
```

How to copy an existing Element node and its child nodes

```
var list = document.getElementById("headlines");
var newList = list.cloneNode(true);
```

How to modify the attributes of a new node

```
var imgNode = document.createElement("img");
imgNode.src = "lures.jpg";
```

Description

- A newly created node isn't displayed in the browser until it is added to the DOM tree. To add a node to the DOM tree, you can use one of the methods described in the next figure.
- A *shallow copy* of a node doesn't include its child nodes.
- A *deep copy* of a node includes its child nodes.

Figure 15-8   How to create new DOM nodes

How to add and remove DOM nodes

Figure 15-9 shows how to add nodes to and remove nodes from the DOM tree. When you modify the DOM tree, the browser displays the updated content in the web page.

You can use the appendChild method to add a newly created node as the last child of the specified node. In other words, this method appends the new node to the end of the childNode array for the specified node. For instance, the first example in this figure adds a Text node as the last child node of an Element node for an <li> tag. In this case, there can be only one Text node for the Element node, so it doesn't matter whether the Text node is added as the first or last child node.

You can use the insertBefore method to insert a new node before an existing child node in the childNode array. For instance, the second example inserts the <li> node that was created in the first example before the first child node for a <ul> node. To do that, this code uses the firstChild property of the <ul> node. As a result, the browser displays the newly created node as the first item in the unordered list. Conversely, if you want to add the <li> node as the last item in the unordered list, you can use the appendChild method to do that.

You can use the removeChild method to remove the specified child node from the DOM tree. This method returns a reference to the removed node so it can be used later. For instance, the example removes the last child node from the <ul> node, and it stores a reference to the removed node in the variable named removedNode.

You can use the replaceChild method to remove the specified child node and replace it with another node. Like the removeChild method, this method returns a reference to the removed node so it can be used later. For instance, the example replaces the first child node in a <ul> node with a newly created <li> node, and it stores a reference to the replaced node in the variable named replacedNode.

When you add a node to the DOM, you typically add a newly created node. In this figure, for example, all of the nodes that are added to the tree were created by the code in the previous figure.

However, you can also add a node that already exists in the DOM. Then, the node is removed from its old location in the DOM before it's added to its new location. When you use this technique, though, you can't add a node to one of its descendant nodes. To illustrate, consider this chain of nodes:

```
div > ul > li > img
```

In this case, you can't replace the <img> tag with the <div> tag because it would create a circular reference.

When you add or remove nodes, you must follow the rules for constructing valid XHTML documents. For example, an anchor element can't have another anchor element as a descendant element. Similarly, a form element can't have another form element as a descendant element.

Two methods to add a node as a child node

Method	Description
appendChild(newNode)	Adds the new node as the last child in the childNode array.
insertBefore(newNode, childNode)	Inserts the new node just before the child node in the childNode array. If childNode is the first child, the new node will be added at the beginning of the childNode array.

How to make one node a child of another node

Adding one node as the last child node

```
liNode.appendChild( textNode );
```

Adding one node as the first child node

```
var ulNode = document.getElementById("headline");  // A ul element
ulNode.insertBefore( liNode, ulNode.firstChild );
```

A method to remove a child node

Method	Description
removeChild(childNode)	Removes the child node and returns a reference to the removed node.

How to remove a child node

```
var removedNode = ulNode.removeChild( ulNode.lastChild );
```

A method to replace a child node with another node

Method	Description
replaceChild(newNode, childNode)	Replaces the child node with the new node and returns a reference to the replaced node.

How to replace a child node with another node

```
var replacedNode = ulNode.replaceChild( liNode, ulNode.firstChild );
```

Description

- When you add or remove nodes, you must follow the rules of the document type. For example, you can't add one <a> tag node as the child of another <a> tag node.

Figure 15-9   How to add and remove DOM nodes

How to use a document fragment

Figure 15-10 shows how to use a *document fragment* to create a group of DOM nodes. It also shows how to add a document fragment to the DOM tree with a single method call.

To start, you can use the createDocumentFragment method of the document object to create a document fragment. For instance, the first example in this figure creates a document fragment named docFrag.

Then, you can use the techniques of the last two figures to create nodes, append them to each other, and append them to the document fragment. To illustrate, the next set of examples shows how to use the createText and createElement methods to create five new nodes. Then, it uses the appendChild method to add these nodes to each other. This creates a <p> node and a <ul> node. Finally, it uses the appendChild method to add the <p> and <ul> nodes to the document fragment.

Once you've created a document fragment, you can use the appendChild, insertBefore, or replaceChild methods to add the document fragment to the DOM tree. To illustrate, the last example begins by getting a reference to a <div> node in the DOM tree. Then, it appends the document fragment to the childNode array of the <div> node. As a result, all nodes in the document fragment are appended to the <div> node in the same order as they are in the document fragment.

To understand how this ordering works, let's assume that there's a document fragment named docFrag with three nodes named X, Y, and Z. Let's also assume that there's an Element node named contentDiv with three child nodes named A, B, and C. In that case,

```
contentDiv.appendChild( docFrag );
```

stores A, B, C, X, Y, and Z as the child nodes of the Element node. On the other hand,

```
contentDiv.insertBefore ( docFrag , B );
```

stores A, X, Y, Z, B, and C as the child nodes of the Element node. Finally,

```
contentDiv.replaceChild( docFrag , B );
```

stores A, X, Y, Z, and C as the child nodes of the Element node.

A method of the document object for creating a document fragment

Method	Description
createDocumentFragment()	Creates a new document fragment.

How to create a document fragment

```
var docFrag = document.createDocumentFragment();
```

How to append nodes to a document fragment

How to create the nodes

```
var liText = document.createTextNode( "Lightweight Neoprene Waders" );
var liNode = document.createElement("li");
var ulNode = document.createElement("ul");

var pText = document.createTextNode("Mike's Bait and Tackle Shop");
var pNode = document.createElement("p");
```

How to append the nodes to each other

```
liNode.appendChild( liText );
ulNode.appendChild( liNode );

pNode.appendChild( pText );
```

How to append the nodes to a document fragment

```
docFrag.appendChild( ulNode );
docFrag.appendChild( pNode );
```

How to append a document fragment to the document

```
var contentDiv = document.getElementById("content");
contentDiv.appendChild( docFrag );
```

Description

- You can use the createDocumentFragment method of the document object to create a new document fragment.

- You can pass a document fragment to the appendChild, insertBefore, and replaceChild methods instead of passing a single node.

Figure 15-10   How to use a document fragment

The Headlines application

To show how some of the skills you've just learned can be used in an application, this chapter concludes by presenting the Headlines application. This application turns an unordered list of items into a rotating list of headlines. This allows a long list to fit in a smaller space.

The user interface

Figure 15-11 shows the Headlines application in the browser. When this application starts, it displays four headlines beneath the New Products heading, and it rotates these headlines. At this point, the user can stop the headlines from rotating by clicking on the pause image. Then, the user can resume rotating the headlines by clicking on the play image.

Similarly, when the headlines are rotating, the user can pause them by moving the mouse over the list of headlines. Then, the user can restart the headlines by moving the mouse out of the list of headlines.

The XHTML file

This figure also shows the XHTML file for the Headlines application. Here, the <script> tags for this file load the core event library described in chapter 14 and the DOM ready library described in this chapter. As a result, this application can use the objects and methods provided by these libraries to attach events as soon as the DOM is ready.

The <ul> tag in this file defines the list that displays the headlines. This tag has an id attribute of "headlines". Within the <ul> tag, this file contains eight <li> tags that define the headlines that rotate. When this application begins, it only displays the first four of these <li> tags. Then, it rotates through all eight of them. If you want to add more headlines to this application, you can just add more <li> tags to the <ul> list. This makes it easy for web designers who don't know JavaScript to update the application.

Each headline for this application is coded within an anchor tag that's coded within an <li> tag. To keep this application simple, the links for the href attributes of the anchor tags aren't set. In practice, though, they would be set so the user could click on one of them to open the web page for the related product.

The Headlines application in the browser

The XHTML file

```
<!DOCTYPE html PUBLIC "-//W3C//DTD XHTML 1.0 Transitional//EN"
    "http://www.w3.org/TR/xhtml1/DTD/xhtml1-transitional.dtd">
<html xmlns="http://www.w3.org/1999/xhtml">
<head>
<title>Mike's Bait and Tackle Shop</title>
<style type="text/css">
    @import "main.css";
</style>
<script type="text/javascript" src="jslib_event.js"></script>
<script type="text/javascript" src="jslib_dom_ready.js"></script>
<script type="text/javascript" src="headlines_library.js"></script>
<script type="text/javascript" src="headlines.js"></script>
</head>

<body>
<div id="content">
    <h1 class="center">Mike's Bait and Tackle Shop</h1>

    <div id="new_products">
    <p id="np_head">New Products <img src="pause.gif" id="toggle" /></p>
    <ul id="headlines">
        <li><a href="#">Aqua Cam Camera Case</a></li>
        <li><a href="#">Lightweight Boat Box for Saltwater Flies</a></li>
        <li><a href="#">Stretch Pants for Wet Wading</a></li>
        <li><a href="#">Microfleece Zip-Neck with 4-Way Stretch</a></li>
        <li><a href="#">Best Drift Inflatable Indicators</a></li>
        <li><a href="#">Pin-On Floating Fly Keeper Box</a></li>
        <li><a href="#">Lightweight Neoprene Waders</a></li>
        <li><a href="#">Compact High-Volume Air Pump</a></li>
        <li><a href="#">Hook Disgorger and Sharpener</a></li>
        <li><a href="#">Tailwaters XT Wading Jacket</a></li>
    </ul>
    </div>

    <p>Welcome to Mike's Bait and Tackle Shop. We have all the gear you'll
    need to make your next fishing trip a great success!</p>
    <p>Contact us by phone at 559-555-6624 to place your order today.</p>
    <p class="copyright">&copy; 2009 Mike's Bait and Tackle Shop</p>
</body>
</html>
```

Figure 15-11   The Headlines application (part 1 of 3)

The headlines_library.js file

The headlines_library.js file starts with the standard $ function. Then, it defines the constructor for a Headlines object that will control the list of headlines.

The Headlines constructor takes three parameters. The first parameter is the id of the <ul> tag that contains the headlines. The second parameter is the id of the <img> tag that displays the pause and play images. The third parameter is optional and sets the number of headlines to show. If it isn't provided, it defaults to 3 headlines.

Within this constructor, the first statement copies the this keyword into a variable named headlines. This will be used to make the Headlines object available to the event handlers that are defined later in this constructor.

After initializing the headlines variable, this constructor validates the number of arguments and throws an error if an invalid number of arguments has been passed to it. As a result, the user must pass two or three parameters to this constructor.

After validating the number of arguments, this code copies a reference to the <ul> node into the ulNode property. It also copies a reference to the <img> node into the imgNode property.

After setting up the ulNode and imgNode properties, this constructor validates the headlineCount argument. If the headlineCount argument wasn't passed to the constructor, this code sets this argument to a default value of 3. Otherwise, this code uses the parseInt method to convert this argument to an integer. If the resulting integer isn't a number or is less than one, this code throws an error.

After validating the headlineCount argument, this code sets three properties. Here, the headlineCount property stores the number of headlines to show. The items property stores an array of <li> nodes for the headlines. And the running property stores a Boolean value that indicates whether the headlines are currently rotating.

After setting these properties, this code removes all child nodes from the <ul> node. If a child node is an <li> node, it is added to the items array. But other nodes, such as comment nodes, are discarded. For the XHTML file presented in this chapter, this removes all eight <li> nodes from the DOM and adds them to the items array.

After removing the <li> nodes, this code adds some of the <li> nodes back to the <ul> node. The number of <li> nodes that this code adds depends on the value of the headlineCount property. If, for example, the headlineCount property is set to 4, this code adds four <li> nodes to the <ul> node. However, if the headlineCount property is greater than the number of <li> nodes in the XHTML file, this code adds all <li> nodes to the <ul> node.

In the loop that appends the <li> nodes to the <ul> node, the next property is the index for the items array. Then, when this loop finishes, this code decrements this property so it contains the correct index for accessing the next item in the array. Without this statement, the headlines application would skip over an item in the array.

The headlines_library.js file

```
var $ = function (id) { return document.getElementById(id); }

var Headlines = function ( ulId, imgId, headlineCount ) {
    var headlines = this;

    // Validate the number of arguments for the method
    if ( arguments.length < 2 || arguments.length > 3) {
        throw new Error("Headlines: wrong number of arguments.");
    }

    // Store references to the element nodes as properties
    this.ulNode = $(ulId);
    this.imgNode = $(imgId);

    // Convert the headlineCount argument to an integer value and validate it
    if (arguments.length == 2) {
        headlineCount = 3;
    } else {
        headlineCount = parseInt(headlineCount);
    }
    if ( isNaN(headlineCount) || headlineCount < 1 ) {
        throw new Error("Headlines: Headline count is not a valid number.");
    }

    // Define the application parameters
    this.headlineCount = headlineCount;
    this.items = [];
    this.running = false;

    // Remove the LI nodes from the UL node and store them in the items array
    var node;
    while ( this.ulNode.hasChildNodes() ) {
        node = this.ulNode.removeChild( this.ulNode.firstChild );
        if ( node.nodeType == 1 && node.tagName == "LI") {
            this.items.push(node);
        }
    }

    // Append the appropriate number of LI nodes to the UL node
    this.next = 0;
    while ( this.next < this.headlineCount && this.next < this.items.length) {
        this.ulNode.appendChild( this.items[this.next] );
        this.next++;
    }
    this.next--;

    // Define the event handlers
    this.imgClick = function () { headlines.toggle(); };
    this.ulOver   = function () { headlines.pause(); };
    this.ulOut    = function () { headlines.play(); };
```

Figure 15-11   The Headlines application (part 2 of 3)

After adding the appropriate number of <li> nodes to the <ul> node, this code defines three event handlers. The first event handler calls the toggle method to toggle the running state of the headlines when the image is clicked. The second event handler calls the pause method to pause the headlines when the mouse enters the headlines area. And the third event handler calls the play method to play the headlines when the mouse leaves the headlines area.

After defining the three event handlers, this code attaches these event handlers to the appropriate events of the <img> and <ul> nodes. To accomplish this task, these three statements use the add method of the jsLib.event object that's available from the JavaScript library that was presented in chapter 14.

The constructor finishes by calling the play method of the Headlines object. This begins rotating the headlines. The rest of the code in this file adds four methods to the Headlines object.

The showNext method increments the object's next property and sets it back to 0 if it goes past the length of the items array. Then, it removes the first <li> node from the <ul> node and appends the next <li> node in the items array to the end of the <ul> node. This rotates the items in the headlines list by one item.

The pause method of the Headlines object cancels the timer that updates the headlines list. It changes the play/pause image to the play image. And it sets the running property to false.

The play method of the Headlines object creates a variable named headline that stores a reference to the Headlines object that's returned by the this keyword. It uses this variable to set a timer to show the next headline every three seconds. It changes the play/pause image to the pause image. And it sets the running property to true.

The toggle method of the Headlines object begins by checking if the running property is set to true. If so, it calls the pause method. Otherwise, it calls the play method.

The headlines.js file

The headlines.js file creates the Headlines object when the DOM is ready. To start, this code creates a global variable named headlines that stores a reference to the Headlines object.

Then, this code defines a function named headlinesStart that creates a new Headlines object and stores it in the headlines variable. Here, the ids of the <ul> and <img> tags are sent to the constructor and the headlineCount parameter is set to a value of 4. As a result, the Headlines object displays four headlines at a time.

Finally, this code uses the ready method of the jsLib.dom method to run the headlinesStart function when the DOM is ready. This method is available from the JavaScript library described earlier in this chapter.

The headlines_library.js file (continued)

```javascript
        // Attach the event handlers to events
        jsLib.event.add( this.imgNode, "click", this.imgClick );
        jsLib.event.add( this.ulNode, "mouseover", this.ulOver );
        jsLib.event.add( this.ulNode, "mouseout", this.ulOut );

        // Call the play method
        this.play();
}

Headlines.prototype.showNext = function () {
    this.next++;
    this.next = this.next % this.items.length;
    this.ulNode.removeChild( this.ulNode.firstChild );
    this.ulNode.appendChild( this.items[this.next] );
}

Headlines.prototype.pause = function () {
    clearInterval( this.timer );
    this.imgNode.src = "play.gif";
    this.running = false;
}

Headlines.prototype.play = function () {
    var headlines = this;
    this.timer = setInterval( function() { headlines.showNext(); }, 3000 );
    this.imgNode.src = "pause.gif";
    this.running = true;
}

Headlines.prototype.toggle = function () {
    if ( this.running ) {
        this.pause();
    } else {
        this.play();
    }
}
```

The headlines.js file

```javascript
var headlines;

var headlinesStart = function () {
    headlines = new Headlines( "headlines", "toggle", 4);
}

jsLib.dom.ready( headlinesStart );
```

Figure 15-11   The Headlines application (part 3 of 3)

Perspective

The skills that you've learned in this chapter can be used to build complex JavaScript applications that rewrite the web page. In chapter 17, you'll learn how to use these skills to work with tables and forms. And in chapter 18, you'll learn how use these skills to do animations. But first, in the next chapter, you'll learn how to use these skills to change the CSS properties of DOM elements.

Terms

cache busting script	deep copy
doScroll polling technique	document fragment
shallow copy	

Exercise 15-1   Run the Ready Test application

1. Use the Firefox browser to view the index.html file in the dom_ready_problem folder that's in the chapter 15 folder for the book applications. Note how long it takes before the page is loaded and you can use the Test button. Now, do the same thing for the index.html file in the dom_ready_solution folder.

Exercise 15-2   Modify the Slide Show application

1. Use the Firefox browser to view the index.html file in the slide_show folder that's in the chapter 15 folder for exercises. Note that it includes a Hide Instructions button at the bottom of the page.

2. Use your text editor to open the index.html file and the JavaScript files for this application. Then, review this code. Note that the JavaScript files include the jslib_dom_ready library that's described in this chapter.

3. Modify the index.html file so it loads the jslib_dom.js library.

4. Modify the slide_show.js file so it uses jsLib.dom.ready method to create the SlideShow object as soon as the DOM is ready. Then, test this change. The application should work like it did before.

5. Modify the JavaScript files for this application so the user can click on the Hide Instructions button to hide the instructions for using the mouse and keyboard. To do that, you need to pass some additional ID attributes to the constructor for the SlideShow object. Then, you need to write the event handler for the click event of this button, and you need to attach this event handler to the event. If your event handler calls a method, you also need to write that method. Now, test these changes.

6. Modify the JavaScript files for this application so it toggles between a Hide Instructions button and a Show Instructions button and between hiding and showing the instructions. Then, test this change.

16

How to script CSS

In this chapter, you'll learn how to use JavaScript to control CSS. First, you'll learn how to work with entire style sheets. Then, you'll learn how to work with the styles for a specific element. At the end of this chapter, you'll review a Menu Bar application that shows how you can use these skills to add an interactive menu bar with drop-down menus to your applications.

How to work with style sheets **556**
Three types of external style sheets 556
How to enable and disable style sheets 558
How to add and remove style sheets 560

The Style Selector application **562**
The XHTML file 562
The JavaScript files 562

How to modify the style of an element **564**
How to set the style of an element 564
How to get the computed style of an element 566
How to change the appearance of an element 568
How to change the position of an element 570
How to get the current position of an element 572
A JavaScript library for working with styles 574

The Menu Bar application **576**
The XHTML file 576
The menubar.css file 578
The menubar_library.js file 580
The menubar.js file 586

Perspective **588**

How to work with style sheets

In chapter 5, you learned how to work with style sheets. Now, you'll learn more about external style sheets, and you'll learn how to use JavaScript to work with them.

Three types of external style sheets

Figure 16-1 shows two ways to include an *external style sheet* in a web page. First, you can use a <style> tag to import an external style sheet. Second, you can use a <link> tag to include an external style. In general, if your page only uses a single external style sheet, there's not much practical difference between using the <style> and <link> tags. However, if you have multiple external style sheets, a <link> tag is probably the better choice.

In the early days of the Internet, it was generally considered a best practice to use a <style> tag to import external style sheets because this technique hid the style sheet from older browsers that didn't support CSS. As a result, newer browsers would use the style sheet, and older browsers would ignore the style sheet. However, all modern web browsers support CSS. As a result, there is no longer a need to hide style sheets from older browsers.

Today, it is generally considered a best practice to use the <link> tag to import external style sheets. There are two reasons for this. First, using the <link> tag yields better performance since it allows the browser to download the CSS files in parallel and display the page more quickly. Second, using the <link> tag allows you to create three different types of style sheets within a page.

When you use a <style> or <link> tag as shown in the first two examples, you create a *persistent style sheet*. A persistent style sheet is always applied to the web page regardless of any user actions. So far in this book, all of the style sheets have been persistent style sheets.

However, when you use the <link> tag, you can also create a *preferred style sheet* or an *alternate style sheet*. If you include preferred and alternate style sheets, the browser uses the preferred style sheet in addition to any persistent style sheets when it loads the page. Then, if the user selects one of the alternate style sheets, the browser uses the alternate sheet instead of the preferred sheet.

This figure shows how to use the <link> tag to create preferred and alternate style sheets. To create a preferred style sheet, you can code a rel attribute of "stylesheet" and a title attribute such as "Default". To create an alternate style sheet, you can code a rel attribute of "alternate stylesheet" and a title attribute such as "Red". Whenever necessary, you can group these types of style sheets by coding the same title for all style sheets in the group.

When you create preferred and alternate style sheets, most modern web browsers provide a way to switch between these style sheets. In this figure, for instance, you can see how to use the View→Page Style menu that's available from Firefox to switch between preferred and alternate style sheets. In IE 8, you can use the Page→Style menu to switch between preferred and alternate style sheets.

Two ways to include external style sheets in a web page

A <style> tag that imports two external style sheets

```
<style type="text/css">
    @import "main.css";
    @import "menu_bar.css";
</style>
```

Two <link> tags that import two external style sheets

```
<link type="text/css" href="main.css" rel="stylesheet" />
<link type="text/css" href="menu_bar.css" rel="stylesheet" />
```

Three types of styles sheets that you can create with the <link> tag

How to create a persistent style sheet

```
<link type="text/css" href="main.css" rel="stylesheet" />
```

How to create a preferred style sheet

```
<link type="text/css" href="default.css" rel="stylesheet" title="Default" />
```

How to create an alternate style sheet

```
<link type="text/css" href="main.css"
    rel="alternate stylesheet" title="Red" />
```

How to use Firefox to switch between preferred and alternate style sheets

Description

- An *external style sheet* is stored in a CSS file.

- A *persistent style sheet* is a style sheet that's always applied. It has a rel attribute of "stylesheet" and no title attribute.

- A *preferred style sheet* is an optional style sheet that's enabled when the page is loaded. It has a rel attribute of "stylesheet" and a title attribute.

- An *alternate style sheet* is an optional style sheet that's not enabled when the page is loaded. It has a rel attribute of "alternate stylesheet" and a title attribute.

- To group multiple preferred or alternate style sheets, use the same title for all sheets in the group.

Figure 16-1   Three types of external style sheets

How to enable and disable style sheets

Figure 16-2 lists the properties of the link element in the DOM. Then, the examples in this figure show how to use these properties to work with the style sheets of a web page.

The first example shows how to get all the link elements that refer to a style sheet. To start, the first statement declares an array named sheets to store the link elements. Then, the second statement gets all the link elements from the document and stores them in the links array. Next, this code loops through the links array. Finally, if the rel property of the link contains the text "stylesheet", this code adds the link element to the sheets array. This test is necessary because <link> tags can be used for other elements besides style sheets.

The second example shows how to enable the persistent and preferred style sheets and to disable the alternate style sheets. By default, a browser sets the style sheets to this state when it loads a page. As a result, you can use this code to reset style sheets to their original state whenever that's necessary. To start, this code loops through each link element in the sheets array that was created in the first example. Then, if the rel property of the element contains the text "alternate", this code disables the element. Otherwise, it enables the element.

The third example shows how to enable all the style sheets with a specified title. To start, this code loops through each link element in the sheets array. Then, if the title property of the element is either empty or has the correct title, the style sheet is enabled. This enables all persistent style sheets and the correct preferred or alternate style sheets. All other style sheets are disabled.

Unfortunately, when you change style sheets, Internet Explorer might not update all parts of the page. For example, if changing the style sheet changes the background from gray to blue, Internet Explorer might display parts of the background in blue while other parts remain gray. In that case, you can use the code in the fourth example to force Internet Explorer to refresh the entire page. It does that by setting the display property of the top-level XHTML element in the page to "none" and then clearing this property.

Properties of the link element

Property	Description
href	The url of the external style sheet.
rel	The relationship of the external file to the document. Set to "stylesheet" for persistent and preferred style sheets. Set to "alternate stylesheet" for alternate style sheets.
title	The title of a preferred or alternate style sheet. Set to null for persistent style sheets.
disabled	The property that controls whether the link element is disabled or enabled. Set to true to disable the link element. Set to false to enable the link element.
media	The media types to use this style sheet with. The default is all types.

How to get the link elements that refer to style sheets

```
var sheets = [];
var links = document.getElementsByTagName("link");
var link;
for ( var i = 0; i < links.length; i++ ) {
    link = links[i];
    if ( /stylesheet/.test( link.rel ) {
        sheets.push(link);
    }
}
```

How to enable all persistent and preferred style sheets

```
var sheet;
for ( i = 0; i < sheets.length; i++ ) {
    sheet = sheets[i];
    if ( /alternate/.test(sheet.rel) ) {
        sheet.disabled = true;
    } else {
        sheet.disabled = false;
    }
}
```

How to enable all style sheets for a particular title

```
var title = "Default";
var sheet;
for ( i = 0; i < sheets.length; i++ ) {
    sheet = sheets[i];
    if ( sheet.title == "" || sheet.title == title ) {
        sheet.disabled = false;
    } else {
        sheet.disabled = true;
    }
}
```

How to force the Internet Explorer to redraw the entire screen

```
document.documentElement.style.display = "none";
document.documentElement.style.display = "";
```

Figure 16-2   How to enable and disable style sheets

How to add and remove style sheets

Figure 16-3 shows how to use JavaScript to add and remove style sheets from the current web page. To do that, you can use the techniques for working with the DOM that were presented in chapter 15.

The first example shows how to add a style sheet to the current page. To start, this code creates a new link element. Then, this code sets the properties of this new element. This creates a link for an alternate style sheet with a title of "Green" that's stored in a file named green.css. Alternately, you can set these properties so they're appropriate for any type of style sheet. Finally, this code appends the new link element to the head element.

The second example shows how to remove a style sheet. To start, this example uses the code shown in the previous figure to create an array named sheets that stores all the link elements that refer to a style sheet. Then, this code copies the link element for the last style sheet into the variable named sheet. Finally, it removes the link element from its parent element.

The third example shows how to remove all the style sheets from the document associated with a specific title. To start, this example uses the code shown in the previous figure to create an array named sheets that stores all the link elements that refer to a style sheet. Then, this code loops through the sheets array and copies a reference to the current link element into a variable named sheet. Finally, if the title of the style sheet matches the specified title, this code removes the link element from its parent element.

How to add a style sheet to a page

Create a link element and set its properties

```
var link = document.createElement("link");
link.href="green.css";
link.type="text/css";
link.rel="alternate stylesheet";
link.title="Green";
```

Add the link element to the document

```
var headNode = document.getElementsByTagName("head")[0];
headNode.appendChild(link);
```

How to remove a style sheet

```
// Use the code in figure 16-2 to create a sheets variable
// that stores the link nodes for the style sheets

var sheet = sheets[ sheets.length - 1 ];
sheet.parentNode.removeChild( sheet );
```

How to remove style sheets from the page by title

```
// Use the code in figure 16-2 to create a sheets variable
// that stores the link nodes for the style sheets

var title = "Blue";
var sheet;
for ( var i = 0; i < sheets.length; i++ ) {
    sheet = sheets[i];
    if ( sheet.title == title ) {
        sheet.parentNode.removeChild(sheet);
    }
}
```

Description

- To add a new style sheet to a document, create a new link element, set its properties, and add it to the head element.
- To remove a style sheet, call the removeChild method on the parent element of the style sheet.

Figure 16-3   How to add and remove style sheets

The Style Selector application

When you use preferred and alternate style sheets, most web browsers add the style sheet titles to a menu so the user can switch style sheets. In figure 16-1, for example, you can see how to use a menu provided by Firefox to switch between style sheets. However, prior to version 8, Internet Explorer didn't provide this type of menu. In addition, some users don't know that their browser provides this type of menu.

To provide for either case, you can add a style selection control to a web page to make it easy for all users to switch style sheets. In figure 16-4, for example, the Style Selector application provides a drop-down list that allows the user to switch between the preferred and alternate style sheets.

The XHTML file

The XHTML file for the Style Selector application uses four <link> tags to load four external style sheets. The first tag loads a persistent style sheet that contains the styles in the page that won't be changed. The second tag loads the preferred style sheet named Default. The last two tags load alternate style sheets named Red and Blue.

After the <link> tags, the XHTML uses four <script> tags to load the JavaScript files for the application. Of these files, you should be familiar with the first four from previous chapters. However, the last two <script> tags load the JavaScript files that are new for this application.

At the bottom of the XHTML, a <select> tag defines the drop-down list that lets the user change the style sheet for the page. When the page loads, the JavaScript code populates this tag with the titles from the <link> tags.

The JavaScript files

The code for the styleswitch_library.js and styleswitch.js files isn't shown in this chapter. However, you can review the JavaScript code for these files in the downloaded book application. If you understand the previous three figures, you shouldn't have any trouble understanding the code in these JavaScript files, which includes comments that describe what the code is doing.

The Style Selector application in the browser

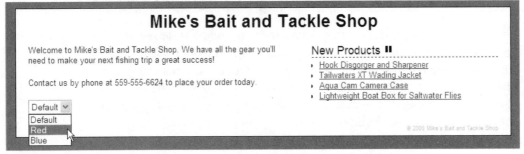

The XHTML file

```
<!DOCTYPE html PUBLIC "-//W3C//DTD XHTML 1.0 Transitional//EN"
    "http://www.w3.org/TR/xhtml1/DTD/xhtml1-transitional.dtd">
<html xmlns="http://www.w3.org/1999/xhtml">
<head>
<title>Mike's Bait and Tackle Shop</title>
<link rel="stylesheet" type="text/css" href="main.css" />
<link rel="stylesheet" type="text/css"
    href="default.css" title="Default" />
<link rel="alternate stylesheet" type="text/css"
    href="red.css" title="Red" />
<link rel="alternate stylesheet" type="text/css"
    href="blue.css" title="Blue" />

<script type="text/javascript" src="jslib_dom_ready.js"></script>
<script type="text/javascript" src="jslib_event.js"></script>
<script type="text/javascript" src="headlines_library.js"></script>
<script type="text/javascript" src="headlines.js"></script>
<script type="text/javascript" src="styleswitch_library.js"></script>
<script type="text/javascript" src="styleswitch.js"></script>
</head>
<body>
<div id="content">
    ...
    ...
    <p>Welcome to Mike's Bait and Tackle Shop. We have all the gear you'll
    need to make your next fishing trip a great success!</p>
    <p>Contact us by phone at 559-555-6624 to place your order today.</p>
    <p><select id="styleSelect" ></select></p>
    <p class="copyright">&copy; 2009 Mike's Bait and Tackle Shop</p>
</body>
</html>
```

Description

- The styleswitch_library.js and styleswitch.js files are included with the downloadable files for this application.

- You can review the JavaScript code for this application in the downloaded book application. If you understand the code in the last three figures, you should be able to follow this code without much trouble.

Figure 16-4   The Style Selector application

How to modify the style of an element

Now that you know how to use JavaScript to switch style sheets for a web page, you're ready to learn how to use JavaScript to modify the style for a specific element within a web page. Since this topic assumes that you are familiar with the CSS attributes presented in chapter 5, you may want to refer back to that chapter if you need to refresh your memory about any of the attributes that are used in this chapter.

How to set the style of an element

Most elements in the DOM can have a CSS style applied to them. For these elements, you can use the style property of the element to access the Style object for the element. This Style object contains a collection of properties that correspond to CSS style attributes as shown in figure 16-5. For example, the fontSize property corresponds to the font-size attribute.

There are two important points to take away from the list of Style object properties. First, this figure only shows a sampling of the properties that are available from the Style object. In fact, the Style object provides a property that corresponds with every CSS attribute. As a result, to work with any CSS attribute, you just need to use the naming convention in this figure to access the CSS attribute.

Second, the cssFloat property is the only property that doesn't follow this naming convention. That's because float is a JavaScript reserved word. As a result, if you want to work with the CSS float attribute, you must use the cssFloat property of the Style object.

Once you understand how the Style object properties correspond to the CSS attributes for an element, you can use them to change the style for an element. In this figure, for instance, the first statement in the example returns an element. Then, the second statement sets the fontSize property of the Style object for that element to a value of "12px". As a result, this code sets the font-size attribute for that element to a value of "12px". This has the same effect as setting an inline style attribute in the XHTML code since it overrides any conflicting attributes in any external or embedded style sheets.

The style property of the Element object

Property	Description
style	The Style object for the element.

Style object properties compared to CSS attributes

Property	CSS attribute	Notes
fontFamily	font-family	
fontSize	font-size	
color	color	
textAlign	text-align	
backgroundColor	background-color	
backgroundImage	background-image	
borderTop	border-top	
border	border	
borderStyle	border-style	
position	position	
cssFloat	float	This property doesn't follow the naming convention.
clear	clear	
top	top	
left	left	
width	width	
height	height	
margin	margin	
padding	padding	

How to set the style of an element

```
var headlines = document.getElementById("headlines");
headlines.style.fontSize = "12px";
```

Description

- The Style object properties correspond to the CSS attributes for an element.
- This figure only lists a sampling of the attributes and properties. To learn more about CSS attributes, refer to chapter 5. For a complete list of CSS attributes, you can search the Internet.

Figure 16-5   How to set the style of an element

How to get the computed style of an element

If you're using external style sheets as recommend by this book, the properties of the Style object are initialized to empty strings. In other words, the Style object properties don't provide access to the CSS attributes that are set by external style sheets.

As a result, if you want to check the final CSS attributes that the browser uses to display an element, you can use the techniques shown in figure 16-6 to get a read-only Style object that contains the computed styles for an element. These styles include the results of applying all external, embedded, and inline styles.

In the DOM model, you can use the getComputedStyle method of the global window object to get the computed styles for an element. This method accepts two parameters. The first parameter specifies the element, and the second parameter specifies the pseudo element. Most of the time, you don't want to get the computed style for the pseudo element. As a result, you pass a null value to the second parameter. In this figure, for instance, the example displays a dialog box that shows the computed style for the font-size attribute of an element.

In the IE model, you can use the currentStyle property of an element to get the computed styles for that element. In this figure, for example, the code for the IE model accomplishes the same task as the code for the DOM model.

If you want to provide a standard way to get the computed styles for an object, you can use the code in the last example to add a getComputedStyle method to the IE model. This code begins by testing for the presence of the getComputedStyle method in the window object. If this method isn't present, this code creates it. Then, the statement within the method uses the currentStyle property of the specified element to return the Style object for that element. As a result, when this code is included in an application, the application can use the getComputedStyle method in both the DOM and IE models.

The syntax of the getComputedStyle method in the DOM model

```
var currentStyle = window.getComputedStyle( element, pseudoElement );
```

Parameters of the getComputedStyle method

Parameter	Description
element	A reference to the element whose style you want to retrieve.
pseudoElement	The CSS pseudo-element of the element. To retrieve the computed style of the element, set this parameter to null. To retrieve the computed style for the pseudo-element, specify the name of the pseudo element.

How to get the computed style of an element in the DOM model

```
var menubar = document.getElementById("menubar");
var computedStyle = window.getComputedStyle(menubar, null );
alert("Menubar font-size: " + computedStyle.fontSize );
```

The currentStyle property of an element in the IE model

Property	Description
currentStyle	Returns a read-only Style object for the specified element.

How to get the computed style of an element in the IE model

```
var menubar = document.getElementById("menubar");
var computedStyle = menubar.currentStyle;
alert("Menubar font-size: " + computedStyle.fontSize );
```

Code that standardizes the getComputedStyle method

```
if ( !("getComputedStyle" in window) ) {
    window.getComputedStyle = function (element) {
        return element.currentStyle;
    }
}
```

Description

* The getComputedStyle method and the currentStyle property returns a read-only Style object that results from applying all external, embedded, and in-line styles to the element.

Figure 16-6   How to get the computed style of an element

How to change the appearance of an element

Figure 16-7 shows how to change the appearance of an element. To start, the first example shows two statements that return the two elements that are used in the rest of the examples. Then, the other examples set the properties of the Style object that control the appearance of these elements.

The second example shows how to set the properties of the Style object that correspond to the CSS font attributes. These statements change the font size and font style of the specified element. Note that the values used in these properties are the same as they are for CSS. For example, the first statement sets the fontSize property to a value of "12px", which sets the font-size attribute to a value of "12px".

The third example shows how to set the properties that correspond to the CSS text attributes. These statements change the color, text indentation, and line height of the specified element.

The fourth example shows how to set the properties that correspond to CSS background attributes. These statements set a background color and image. In addition, for the background image, these statements set the repeat, position, and attachment attributes.

The fifth and sixth examples show how to set the properties that correspond to the CSS border attributes. In the fifth example, the statements set the width, style, and color of the bottom border of an element. In the sixth example, the statements use shortcut properties to set the width, style, and color of a border with a single statement. Since the values for these shortcut properties work the same as they do with CSS, you should understand how they work. If you don't, you can review chapter 5.

The seventh example shows how to set the properties that correspond to CSS list attributes. The statement in this example sets the list style type of an ordered list. However, you can use other properties to change other aspects of the appearance of ordered and unordered lists.

The eighth example shows how to set the properties that correspond to the CSS table attributes. These statements set the caption side and border spacing of two elements.

The last example shows how to set the properties that correspond to the CSS display attributes. These statements set the display and visibility properties of an element.

Two statements that return elements

```
var menubar = document.getElementById("menubar");
var headlines = document.getElementById("headlines");
```

How to use the font properties

```
menubar.style.fontSize = "12px";
menubar.style.fontStyle = "italic";
```

How to use the text properties

```
menubar.style.color = "rgb(50%,25%,100%)";
menubar.style.textIndent = "3px";
menubar.style.lineHeight = "24px";
```

How to use the background properties

```
menubar.style.backgroundColor = "maroon";
menubar.style.backgroundImage = "url(logo.gif)";
menubar.style.backgroundRepeat = "no-repeat";
menubar.style.backgroundPosition = "bottom right";
menubar.style.backgroundAttachment = "fixed";
```

How to use the border properties

```
menubar.style.borderBottomWidth = "3px";
menubar.style.borderBottomStyle = "dashed";
menubar.style.borderBottomColor = "silver";
```

How to use the border shortcut properties

```
menubar.style.border = "1px dotted sliver";
menubar.style.borderWidth = "1px 3px 1px";
menubar.style.borderBottom = "1px dashed black";
```

How to use the list properties

```
headlines.style.listStyleType = "lower-roman";
```

How to use the table properties

```
document.getElementById("resultsCaption").style.captionSide = "bottom";
document.getElementById("resultsTable").style.borderSpacing = "5px";
```

How to use the display properties

```
headlines.style.display = "inline";
headlines.style.visibility = "hidden";
```

Description

- To change the appearance of an element, use any of the properties that are available from the Style object.

Figure 16-7   How to change the appearance of an element

How to change the position of an element

Figure 16-8 shows how to change the position of an element. Here, the first example shows a statement that returns the element that's used in the rest of the examples. Then, the other examples set the properties of the Style object that control the position of this element.

The second example shows how to use absolute positioning to position an element on the page. Here, the first statement sets the element's position property to a value of "absolute". Then, the second statement sets the width of the element to 200 pixels. Finally, the last two statements move the element to the top left corner of the page.

The third example shows how to float an element on the page. Here, the first statement sets the element's position property to a value of "static". Since this is the default value for the position property, you typically don't need to include a statement like this in your code. However, if your code has previously changed the default value of this property, you can include a statement like this to return to the default value. After setting the position property of the element, the second statement sets the element's width to 200 pixels. Finally, the third statement uses the cssFloat property to float the element to the right.

The fourth example shows how to set the properties of the Style object that correspond to the CSS margin attributes. These statements change the top and left margins of an element.

The fifth example shows how to set the properties that correspond to the CSS padding attributes. These statements change the left and right padding of an element.

The sixth example shows how to use the shortcut properties for margins and padding that correspond to the CSS shortcut attributes for margins and padding. Here, the first statement changes the top margin to 1em, the left and right margins to auto, and the bottom margin to 0. Then, the second statement sets the top and bottom padding to 0 and the left and right padding to 10 pixels.

A statement that returns an element

```
var headlines = document.getElementById("headlines");
```

How to position an element

```
headlines.style.position = "absolute";
headlines.style.width = "200px";
headlines.style.top = "0px";
headlines.style.left = "0px";
```

How to float an element

```
headlines.style.position = "static";
headlines.style.width = "200px";
headlines.style.cssFloat = "right";
```

How to use the margin properties

```
headlines.style.marginTop = "5px";
headlines.style.marginLeft = "0.25em";
```

How to use the padding properties

```
headlines.style.paddingLeft = "5px";
headlines.style.paddingRight = "10px";
```

How to use the margin and padding shortcut properties

```
headlines.style.margin = "1em auto 0";
headlines.style.padding = "0 10px";
```

Description

- To change the position of an element, use the properties shown in this figure or other similar properties that are available from the Style object.

- To uses relative or absolute positioning for an element, set its cssFloat property to a value of "none".

- To float an element, set its position property to a value of "static".

- When positioning or floating an element, it's common to specify its width property.

- To move an element horizontally, set its left or right property, but not both.

- To move an element vertically, set its top or bottom property, but not both.

- When using relative positioning, set the top, bottom, left, and right properties to "push" the element from the specified side. For example, setting the top property to "10px" moves the element down 10 pixels.

- When using absolute positioning, the top, bottom, left, and right properties specify the distance from the edge of the document.

Figure 16-8   How to change the position of an element

How to get the current position of an element

Figure 16-9 begins by showing five properties of the Element object that you can use to get the position of the current element. In all browsers, every element has an offsetTop and an offsetLeft property that you can use to determine an element's current position. However, in the DOM model, these properties measure the distance from the top and left edges of the web page. In the IE model, they measure the distance from the top and left edges of the parent element that's identified in the offsetParent property.

The first two examples in this figure show two methods named getOffsetTop and getOffsetLeft. These methods get the distance from the top and left edges of the web page for both the IE and DOM models. Both of these methods take an element as a parameter, and both declare a variable named offset with an initial value of 0.

Then, both of these methods contain a while loop that runs as long as the element isn't null. Within the loop, the value of the element's offset property is added to the offset variable, and the element parameter is reset to the element that's returned by the offsetParent property. For the DOM model, this means that the loop will run only once because the offsetParent element will be null. For the IE model, though, this loop may run multiple times as it loops through multiple parent elements and adds more offset to the offset variable each time through the loop.

The third example shows how to use the getOffsetTop and getOffsetLeft methods. Here, the first statement gets a reference to an element. Then, the second and third statements get the top and left offsets for the top left corner of that element. Next, this example shows how to use the offsetHeight and offsetWidth properties to calculate the bottom and right offsets for the element. Here, the fourth statement calculates the bottom offset by adding the height offset to the top offset, and the fifth statement calculates the right offset by adding the width offset to the left offset.

Positioning properties of the Element object

Property	Description
offsetTop	Returns the offset from the top edge of the offset parent element in pixels.
offsetLeft	Returns the offset from the left edge of the offset parent element in pixels.
offsetParent	Returns the element that's defined as the offset parent of the current element. In the DOM model, this returns the document element. For the IE model, this returns the parent element of the current element.
offsetHeight	Returns the offset height of the current element in pixels.
offsetWidth	Returns the offset width of the current element in pixels.

A method that returns the top offset for both the DOM and IE models

```
var getOffsetTop = function ( element ) {
    var offset = 0;
    while ( element !== null ) {
        offset += element.offsetTop;
        element = element.offsetParent;
    }
    return offset;
}
```

A method that returns the left offset for both the DOM and IE models

```
var getOffsetLeft = function ( element ) {
    var offset = 0;
    while ( element !== null ) {
        offset += element.offsetLeft;
        element = element.offsetParent;
    }
    return offset;
}
```

An example that uses these methods

```
var headlines = document.getElementById("headlines");
var offsetTop = getOffsetTop(headlines);
var offsetLeft = getOffsetLeft(headlines);

var offsetBottom = offsetTop + headlines.offsetHeight;
var offsetRight = offsetLeft + headlines.offsetWidth;
```

Description

- In the DOM model, the offsetTop and offsetLeft properties of the element are measured from the top and left edges of the document. In other words, the offsetParent property of the element returns the document element.

- In the IE model, the offsetTop and offsetLeft properties of the element are measured from the edge of the parent element. In other words, the offsetParent property of the element returns the parent element in the DOM tree.

Figure 16-9   How to get the current position of an element

A JavaScript library for working with styles

Figure 16-10 shows a JavaScript library that makes it easier to work with the styles for an element. To start, this code creates the jsLib object if it doesn't exist and the jsLib.css object if it doesn't exist.

Then, this library fixes the getComputedStyle method for the IE model. Since this code works the same as the code described in figure 16-6, you should already understand how it works. As a result, if you load this library, you can use the getComputedStyle method to get the computed styles for all web browsers.

Finally, this library defines the getOffsetTop and getOffsetLeft methods described in the previous figure. As a result, if you load this library, you can use these methods to get the distance from the top and left edges of the web page for all web browsers.

The jslib_css.js file

```javascript
if ( ! jsLib ) { var jsLib = new Object(); }
if ( ! jsLib.css ) { jsLib.css = new Object(); }

// Fix getComputedStyle method for IE model
if ( !("getComputedStyle" in window) ) {
    window.getComputedStyle = function (e) {
        return e.currentStyle;
    }
}

// Define the getOffsetTop method
jsLib.css.getOffsetTop = function ( element ) {
    var offset = 0;
    while ( element !== null ) {
        offset += element.offsetTop;
        element = element.offsetParent;
    }
    return offset;
}

// Define the getOffsetLeft method
jsLib.css.getOffsetLeft = function ( element ) {
    var offset = 0;
    while ( element !== null ) {
        offset += element.offsetLeft;
        element = element.offsetParent;
    }
    return offset;
}
```

Description

- This library adds the getComputedStyle method to the IE model.
- This library defines the getOffsetTop and getOffsetLeft methods of the jsLib.css object that you can use to return standard offset values for both the DOM and IE models.

Figure 16-10   A JavaScript library for working with styles

The Menu Bar application

Drop-down menus provide a convenient way to organize the navigation links for a web site. The Menu Bar application presented in figure 16-11 scripts the CSS to turn an unordered list into an interactive menu bar with drop-down menus.

As a result, when the user moves the mouse over one of the items in the menu bar, a drop-down menu appears. Conversely, when the user moves the mouse out of the menu, the drop-down menu disappears after a delay of a few tenths of a second. This delay prevents the drop-down menu from immediately disappearing if the user accidentally moves the mouse out of the menu while moving the mouse down the menu.

The XHTML file

The XHTML file for the Menu Bar application is similar to the Headlines application presented in chapter 15. However, there are a few differences that are highlighted. First, this XHTML includes the menubar.css file. This file contains the styles that turn the unordered list into a menu bar.

Second, this XHTML uses <script> tags to load three new JavaScript libraries. To start, this code loads the JavaScript library presented in the previous figure. Then, it loads the two JavaScript libraries presented in this figure.

Third, this XHTML adds a <div> tag for the menu bar. This <div> tag contains the unordered list that will display the top level of menu items. Within this list, this code uses the non-standard menu attribute to identify items that have a drop-down menu. This attribute identifies the id of the <div> tag to be used as the drop-down menu for this item. For example, the <div> tag with an id value of "productmenu" is the <div> tag for the Products drop-down menu.

The Menu Bar application in the web browser

The XHTML file

```
<!DOCTYPE html PUBLIC "-//W3C//DTD XHTML 1.0 Transitional//EN"
    "http://www.w3.org/TR/xhtml1/DTD/xhtml1-transitional.dtd">
<html xmlns="http://www.w3.org/1999/xhtml">
<head>
<title>Mike's Bait and Tackle Shop</title>
<link type="text/css" href="main.css" rel="stylesheet" />
<link type="text/css" href="menubar.css" rel="stylesheet" />
<script type="text/javascript" src="jslib_dom_ready.js"></script>
<script type="text/javascript" src="jslib_event.js"></script>
<script type="text/javascript" src="jslib_css.js"></script>
<script type="text/javascript" src="menubar_library.js"></script>
<script type="text/javascript" src="menubar.js"></script>
<script type="text/javascript" src="headlines_library.js"></script>
<script type="text/javascript" src="headlines.js"></script>
</head>

<body>
<div id="content">
    <h1 class="center">Mike's Bait and Tackle Shop</h1>
    <div class="menubar">
        <ul>
            <li><a href="#">Home</a></li>
            <li><a href="#" menu="productmenu">Products</a></li>
            <li><a href="#" menu="servicemenu">Services</a></li>
            <li><a href="#">About Us</a></li>
        </ul>
    </div>
    <div id="new_products">
        <p id="np_head">New Products <img src="pause.gif" id="toggle" /></p>
        <ul id="headlines">
        <li><a href="#">Aqua Cam Camera Case</a></li>
        <li><a href="#">Lightweight Boat Box for Saltwater Flies</a></li>
        <li><a href="#">Stretch Pants for Wet Wading</a></li>
        <li><a href="#">Microfleece Zip-Neck with 4-Way Stretch</a></li>
        <li><a href="#">Best Drift Inflatable Indicators</a></li>
        <li><a href="#">Pin-On Floating Fly Keeper Box</a></li>
        </ul>
    </div>
```

Figure 16-11   The Menu Bar application (part 1 of 6)

Fourth, this XHTML file adds two <div> tags to the end of the file for the drop-down menus. If JavaScript has been disabled in the browser, the browser displays these menus at the bottom of the page. As a result, the menu items are still available to the user. On the other hand, if JavaScript is enabled, the browser displays the drop-down menus as shown in this figure.

Please note in this XHTML code that the href attributes in the <a> tags in the list items are all set to "#". As a result, application won't go to a new page when the user selects a menu item. In practice, of course, these links would be set to the URLs for the appropriate pages.

The menubar.css file

The CSS code stored in the menubar.css file defines the styles for the menu bar and its drop-down menus.

The first style selects the <div> tag for the menu bar. Then, it uses the margin property to add space above and below the menu bar, and it uses the font-weight property to make all text inside the menu bold.

The second style selects the unordered list within the menu bar. Then, it sets its width to 85% of its containing element, sets a small amount of top and bottom padding, and applies a border to the menu bar. In addition, it centers the list within the <div> tag, and it centers the text within the list.

The third style selects the items within the menu bar. Then, it displays the list items as inline elements instead of as block elements. This causes this list to be displayed on the same line instead of having each item displayed on a separate line. In addition, this style sets a negative right margin to reduce the space between these items.

The fourth style selects the links within the menu bar. Then, this style sets some padding and a left border for these links, and it sets the margins to 0. Since links are usually blue and underlined, this style also sets the text color to black and removes the underlining by setting the text-decoration attribute to a value of "none".

The fifth style selects the links in the menu bar when the link has a class attribute with a value of "highlight". This style sets the background color of the link to red. Although this class isn't included in the XHTML file for the page, the Menu Bar application uses JavaScript code to add this class to the link when the user moves the mouse over the link.

The XHTML file (continued)

```
<p>Welcome to Mike's Bait and Tackle Shop. We have all the gear you'll
need to make your next fishing trip a great success!</p>
<p>Contact us by phone at 559-555-6624 to place your order today.</p>
<p class="copyright">&copy; 2009 Mike's Bait and Tackle Shop</p>

<div class="dropmenu" id="productmenu">
    <ul>
        <li><a href="#">Tackle</a></li>
        <li><a href="#">Bait</a></li>
        <li><a href="#">Clothing</a></li>
        <li><a href="#">Boating Gear</a></li>
    </ul>
</div>
<div class="dropmenu" id="servicemenu">
    <ul>
        <li><a href="#">Custom Flies</a></li>
        <li><a href="#">Repairs</a></li>
        <li><a href="#">Trip Planning</a></li>
    </ul>
</div>
</body>
</html>
```

The menubar.css file

```css
.menubar {
    margin: 1em auto;
    font-weight: bold;
}

.menubar ul {
    width: 85%;
    padding: 0.2em 0;
    border: 1px solid black;
    margin: 0 auto;
    text-align: center;
}

.menubar ul li {
    display: inline;
    margin-right: -0.25em;
}

.menubar ul li a {
    padding: 0.22em 0.5em;
    border-left: 1px solid black;
    margin: 0;
    color: black;
    text-decoration: none;
}

.menubar ul li a.highlight {
    background-color: red;
}
```

Figure 16-12   The Menu Bar application (part 2 of 6)

The sixth style selects the <div> tags for the drop-down menus. This style sets the width of these menus to 200 pixels. In addition, it sets the z-index for these menus to 1. As a result, these menus are displayed on top of other page elements. Finally, this style removes the margins and padding from these menus and sets their backgrounds to white so the text behind them won't show through.

The seventh style selects the unordered list for the drop-down menus. This style removes the margins and padding for these lists, and it gives them a 1 pixel solid black border.

The eighth style selects the list items for the drop-down menus. This style removes the bullets from these items by setting the list-style attribute to a value of "none". Then, it sets the margins to 0, it sets the top and bottom padding to 0, and it sets a small amount of left and right padding. Finally, this style sets a bottom border to the items in the list.

The ninth style selects the list items tag in the drop-down list when the list item tag has a class attribute with a value of "highlight". This style sets the background color of the item to red. Although this class isn't included in the XHMTL file for this application, the JavaScript code adds this class to the item when the user moves the mouse over the item.

The last style selects the links in the drop-down menus. This style sets the text color to black and removes the underlining by setting the text-decoration to none.

The menubar_library.js file

The menubar_library.js file defines the MenuBar object that controls the menu bar in the page. For the sake of brevity, the code in this figure doesn't include the statements in the downloadable files that do data validation and library checking. Instead, this listing focuses on the statements that are necessary for the application to run correctly, and on the statements that illustrate the techniques that are described in this chapter.

To start, the code in this file creates the standard $ function. Then, it defines a constructor for the MenuBar object. This constructor takes the id of the <div> tag for the menu bar as its only parameter.

Within the MenuBar constructor, the first statement copies the contents of the this keyword into the that variable. Then, the second statement stores a reference to the menu bar in the menuBar property. Next, the third statement uses the getElementsByTagName method to get an array of the links that are available from the menu bar, and it stores this array in the links property.

After defining the menuBar and links properties, the constructor adds a right border to the last link in the menu bar. This is necessary because the styles in the external style sheet only add a left border to the links. To add the right border, the first statement gets a reference to the last link. Then, the second statement gets the computed styles for the link. Finally, the last three statements copy the left border's width, style, and color properties to the right border.

The menubar.css file (continued)

```css
.dropmenu {
    width: 200px;
    z-index: 1;
    margin: 0;
    padding: 0;
    background-color: white;
}

.dropmenu ul {
    margin: 0;
    padding: 0;
    border: 1px solid black;
}

.dropmenu ul li {
    list-style: none;
    margin: 0;
    padding: 0 0.2em;
    border-bottom: 1px solid black;
}

.dropmenu ul li.highlight {
    background-color: red;
}

.dropmenu ul li a {
    color: black;
    text-decoration: none;
}
```

The menubar_library.js file

```javascript
var $ = function (id) { return document.getElementById(id); }

var MenuBar = function ( menuId ) {
    var that = this;

    // Store a reference to the menu bar as a property
    this.menuBar = $(menuId);

    // Store a reference to the menu bar links as a property
    this.links = this.menuBar.getElementsByTagName("a");

    // Add a right border to the last menu bar link
    var lastList = this.links[this.links.length - 1];
    var linkStyle = getComputedStyle(lastList, null);
    lastList.style.borderRightWidth = linkStyle.borderLeftWidth;
    lastList.style.borderRightColor = linkStyle.borderLeftColor;
    lastList.style.borderRightStyle = linkStyle.borderLeftStyle;
```

Figure 16-12   The Menu Bar application (part 3 of 6)

After adding the right border, the constructor loops through each of the links in the menu bar. Within the loop, the code attaches event handlers to the mouseover and mouseout events of each link. These event handlers highlight the link when the mouse moves over it and return the link to normal when the mouse moves out of the link. Note, however, that the highlight and normal methods are not the event handlers. Instead, they are "factory" functions that create and return a customized event handler through the use of closures.

After attaching the event handlers, the constructor checks whether the link has a menu attribute. If so, this code gets the name of the drop-down menu from the menu attribute, and stores a reference to that drop-down menu in a variable named dropMenu.

After creating the dropMenu variable, this code checks whether the dropMenu variable refers to a <div> tag. If so, this code gets the list item elements from the drop-down menu and stores them in a variable named listItems. This code also removes the bottom border from the last item in the listItems list so the drop-down menu doesn't display two bottom borders.

After removing the bottom border, this code loops through the items in the list. Within this loop, the second and third statements attach event handlers to the mouseover and mouseout events. These event handlers are created and returned by the hightlight and normal methods.

After attaching the event handlers, this code sets the drop-down menu's visibility to hidden and its position to absolute. This hides the menu until it is ready to be displayed.

After hiding the drop-down menu, this code attaches event handlers to mouseover and mouseout events of the link and menu items for the drop-down menu. These event handlers display the menu when the mouse moves into the link or drop-down menu. In addition, they hide the menu after a delay of a fraction of a second when the mouse moves out of the link or drop-down menu. These event handlers are returned by the displayMenu and hideMenuWithDelay methods. Like the highlight and normal methods, these methods use closures to create the event handlers.

The last two lines of the code in this constructor are the else clause that is executed if the link doesn't have a menu attribute. In that case, this code attaches an event handler to the link's mouseover event. This event handler is created and returned by the hideMenu method, and it immediately hides any visible drop-down menu, which is an appropriate action for a link that doesn't have a drop-down menu to display.

The menubar_library.js file (continued)

```
        // Loop through each menu bar link
        var dropMenu, linkIndex, link;
        var listItems, itemIndex, item;
        for ( linkIndex = 0; linkIndex < this.links.length; linkIndex++) {
            link = this.links[linkIndex];

            // Add an event handler to each menu bar link
            jsLib.event.add ( link, "mouseover", this.highlight(link) );
            jsLib.event.add ( link, "mouseout", this.normal(link) );

            // If a drop-down menu exists for the menu bar link...
            if ( link.getAttribute("menu") ) {

                // Store the menu in the array of drop-down menus
                dropMenuName = link.getAttribute("menu");
                dropMenu = $( dropMenuName );

                if ( dropMenu && dropMenu.tagName == "DIV" ) {
                    listItems = dropMenu.getElementsByTagName("li");

                    // Remove the extra bottom border from the last menu item
                    last = listItems.length - 1;
                    listItems[last].style.borderBottom = "none";

                    // Add the event handlers to the items
                    for (itemIndex=0; itemIndex < listItems.length; itemIndex++) {
                        item = listItems[itemIndex];
                        jsLib.event.add( item, "mouseover", this.highlight(item));
                        jsLib.event.add( item, "mouseout", this.normal(item));
                    }

                    // Hide the drop-down menus and specify absolute positioning
                    dropMenu.style.visibility = "hidden";
                    dropMenu.style.position = "absolute";

                    // Attach the event handlers that display the drop-down menu
                    jsLib.event.add( link, "mouseover",
                        this.displayMenu( dropMenu, link )
                    );
                    jsLib.event.add( dropMenu, "mouseover",
                        this.displayMenu( dropMenu, link )
                    );
                    jsLib.event.add( link, "mouseout",
                        this.hideMenuWithDelay()
                    );
                    jsLib.event.add( dropMenu, "mouseout",
                        this.hideMenuWithDelay()
                    );
                }
            // If no drop-down menu exists for the menu bar link...
            } else {
                jsLib.event.add( link, "mouseover", this.hideMenu() );
            }
        }
    }
}
```

Figure 16-12   The Menu Bar application (part 4 of 6)

The last two pages of this file present five methods that are added to the Menubar object.

The highlight method of the MenuBar object takes an element as its only parameter. This method returns a function that sets the className of the element to hightlight. In other words, this function sets the class attribute of the element to a value of "highlight". As a result, this code applies the highlight class that's defined in the menubar.css file to this element, which applies a background color of red to the element.

The normal method of the MenuBar object works like the highlight method. However, it sets the class attribute to an empty string, which removes the background color from the element.

The displayMenu method of the MenuBar object takes two parameters and returns a function. The first parameter refers to the drop-down menu to display. The second parameter refers to the link in the menu bar for the drop-down menu. The function that's returned by this method accomplishes five tasks.

First, this function checks whether a hide timer is running. If so, it clears the timer and deletes the hideTimer property.

Second, this function checks whether a menu is currently being displayed. If so, it hides that menu and deletes the visibleMenu property.

Third, this function calculates the position for the top left corner of the menu. To do that, this code uses the getOffsetTop and getOffsetLeft methods defined of the jsLib.css object to return the top and left offsets for the link. Then, it adds the offset height of the link to the top offset. As a result, this code displays the drop-down menu just below the link. In addition, this code checks whether the tag name of the offset parent is not equal to "BODY". If it isn't, it means that the browser uses the IE model, so the code makes a minor adjustment by adding one pixel to the top offset and two pixels to the left offset.

Fourth, this function sets the top and left position properties of the drop-down menu to the calculated values for the top and left offsets. To do that, this code adds the "px" unit of measurement to the calculated offset values.

Fifth, this function sets the visibleMenu property so it refers to this menu, and it uses the menu's visibility property to display the menu.

The menubar_library.js file (continued)

```javascript
MenuBar.prototype.highlight = function ( element ) {
    return function () {
        element.className = "highlight";
    }
}

MenuBar.prototype.normal = function ( element ) {
    return function () {
        element.className = "";
    }
}

MenuBar.prototype.displayMenu = function ( menu, link ) {
    var that = this;
    return function () {
        // If a timer exists, clear it and delete the hideTimer property
        if ( that.hideTimer ) {
            clearTimeout ( that.hideTimer );
            delete that.hideTimer;
        }
        // If a menu is visible, hide it
        if ( that.visibleMenu ) {
            that.visibleMenu.style.visibility = "hidden";
            delete that.visibleMenu;
        }

        // Calculate the position for the drop-down menu
        var offsetTop, offsetLeft;
        offsetTop  = jsLib.css.getOffsetTop(link);
        offsetTop += link.offsetHeight;
        offsetLeft = jsLib.css.getOffsetLeft(link);
        if ( link.offsetParent.tagName != "BODY" ) {
            offsetTop += 1;
            offsetLeft += 2;
        }

        // Set the Style object properties for the drop-down menu
        menu.style.top = offsetTop + "px";
        menu.style.left = offsetLeft + "px";

        // Store a reference to the drop-down menu and display it
        that.visibleMenu = menu;
        menu.style.visibility = "visible";
    }
}
```

Figure 16-12   The Menu Bar application (part 5 of 6)

The hideMenuWithDelay method of the MenuBar object returns a function that hides the current drop-down menu after a delay of three quarters of a second. To do that, this function creates a timer that calls the hideMenu method after 750 milliseconds. In addition, this function stores a reference to the timer in the hideTimer property. That way, the hideMenu and displayMenu methods can access a reference to this timer.

The hideMenu method of the MenuBar object type returns a function that hides the current drop-down menu. The function that's returned by this method accomplishes two tasks. First, it checks to see whether a hide timer is running. If so, it clears the timer and deletes the hideTimer property. Second, this function checks the visibleMenu property to see whether a menu is currently being displayed. If so, it hides that menu and deletes the visibleMenu property.

The menubar.js file

The menubar.js file creates a function that runs when the DOM is ready. This function creates a new MenuBar object and stores it in a global variable named menuBar. To do that, this code passes the id attribute of the <div> tag for the menu bar to the constructor of the MenuBar object.

The menubar_library.js file (continued)

```javascript
MenuBar.prototype.hideMenuWithDelay = function () {
    var that = this;
    return function () {
        // Hide the menu after 750 milliseconds
        that.hideTimer = setTimeout( that.hideMenu(), 750 );
    }
}

MenuBar.prototype.hideMenu = function () {
    var that = this;
    return function() {
        // If a timer exists, clear it and delete the hideTimer property
        if ( that.hideTimer ) {
            clearTimeout ( that.hideTimer );
            delete that.hideTimer;
        }
        // If a menu is visible, hide it
        if ( that.visibleMenu ) {
            that.visibleMenu.style.visibility = "hidden";
            delete that.visibleMenu;
        }
    }
}
```

The menubar.js file

```javascript
var menuBar;

jsLib.dom.ready( function () {
    menuBar = new MenuBar( "menubar" );
});
```

Figure 16-12   The Menu Bar application (part 6 of 6)

Perspective

In this chapter, you learned how to use JavaScript to work with CSS. More specifically, you learned how to use JavaScript to change the appearance and position of the elements on a web page. These skills let you build interactive applications like the Menu Bar application, and they provide the foundation for creating animations like the one in chapter 18.

Terms

external style sheet
persistent style sheet
preferred style sheet
alternate style sheet

Exercise 16-1   Run the Style Selector application

If you're interested in reviewing the code for the Style Selector application that was presented in this chapter, you can do this exercise.

1. Use the Firefox browser to view the index.html file in the style_selector folder that's in the chapter 16 folder for the book applications. Then, use the drop-down list to change the style sheet for the page.

2. Use your text editor to open and review the blue or red css file. There you can see that the style changes are minimal, although they could be far more extensive.

3. Use your text editor to open and review the code for the styleswitch.js and styleswitch_library.js files. There, you can see how the style sheet is changed when you select a style sheet from the drop-down list.

Exercise 16-2   Modify the Slide Show application

This exercise gives you a chance to script the styles for the Slide Show application. In addition, it gives you a chance to use the libraries for working with menus that are described in this chapter.

1. Use the Firefox browser to view the index.html file in the slide_show folder that's in the chapter 16 folder for exercises.

2. Use your text editor to open the index.html file and the JavaScript files for this application. Then, review this code.

3. Modify the code so it changes the background color of the <p> tag that contains the caption to green when the application is in Play mode and red when the application is in Pause mode. To do that, you can use the parentNode property of the caption to access the node for the <p> tag.

4. Modify the code so it changes the font color for the text in the <span> tag that contains the caption to yellow when the application is in Play mode and white when the application is in Pause mode.

5. Set the color of the caption text to the same color as the background for the <div> tag for the content. To do that, you need to get the computed styles for the content element.

6. Modify the index.html file so it uses the same three <div> tags to display the menu bar and drop-down menus as the Headlines application in the last chapter. Then, view this change.

7. Copy the CSS file for the menus from the Headlines application to the Slide Show application, and modify the index.html file so it uses this CSS file to format the menus. Then, view this change.

8. Copy the JavaScript files for the menus from the Headlines application to the Slide Show application, and modify the index.html file so it uses these files to display the menus. Then, view this change.

17

How to script tables and forms

In this chapter, you'll learn how to script tables and forms. To start, you'll learn how to add and remove rows and cells from a table, and you'll learn how to sort a table by any column in the table. Then, you'll learn some advanced skills for scripting forms that build on the skills that you learned in chapter 6.

How to script tables **592**
How to add rows and cells 592
How to remove rows and cells 594
How to reorder rows 596

The Table Sort application **598**
The XHTML file 598
The tablesort_library.js file 600
The product_list.js file 606

How to script forms **608**
How to handle form events 608
How to script radio buttons 610
How to script select lists 612
A JavaScript library for working with text selections 614
How to use the JavaScript library to work with text selections 616

The Product Configuration application **618**
The XHTML file 618
The config_library.js file 622
The config.js file 628

Perspective **630**

How to script tables

In chapter 15, you learned how to use the appendChild and removeChild methods to add and remove nodes from the DOM. Now, you'll learn how to apply these techniques to tables and how to use some new techniques that are specific to tables.

How to add rows and cells

Figure 17-1 shows how to add rows and cells to a table. Keep in mind, though, that you can't add a row directly to a table element. Instead, you must add the row to the tbody element, which is a child element of the table element. If the tbody element isn't included in the XHTML code, the browser automatically creates this element when it builds the DOM.

To access an array of the tbody nodes for a table, you can use the tBodies property of the table node. Normally, though, a table includes only one tbody node so you just need to refer to the first tbody node in the array.

The first group of examples in this figure shows two ways to add a row to a table node named tableNode. The first way is to use the appendChild method that you learned about in chapter 15. To do that, you can use the tBodies property of the table to check whether a tbody node exists. Then, if it doesn't exist, you can create a tbody node and append it to the table element. Otherwise, you can get the first tbody node in the tBodies array. Last, you can create a row and use the appendChild method to append the row to the tbody node.

The other way to add a row to a table is to use the insertRow method of a tbody node. When you use this method, the new row is automatically created, and the parameter specifies where you want to add the row starting with 0 for the first row. To add the row to the end of the table, you use the value -1. Finally, note that the insertRow method returns a reference to the newly created row node. This is useful because it provides a way to add cells to the row that's created by this method.

Incidentally, with a DOM-compliant browser like Firefox, the insertRow method automatically creates the tbody node when you call the method from the table node. For Internet Explorer, though, you need to call the method from the tbody node so you should always do that for browser compatibility.

The second group of examples in this figure shows two ways to add a cell to a row. Here again, the first way is to use the appendChild method. In this example, this method is used to add a text node named textNode to a cell node, and then to add the cell node to the row node.

The other way to add a cell to a row is to use the insertCell method, which works like the insertRow method. Specifically, this example uses the insertCell method to add a cell to the end of a row. Then, it uses the appendChild method to add the text node to the cell.

Although it's easy enough to use the appendChild and insertCell methods to add content to a table, these methods can become cumbersome if you need to

Two ways to add a row to a table

How to get a table element

```
var tableNode = document.getElementById("item_list");
```

How to use the appendChild method to add a row

```
var tbodyNode;
if ( tableNode.tBodies.length == 0 ) {
    tbodyNode = document.createElement("tbody");
    tableNode.appendChild(tbodyNode);
} else {
    tbodyNode = tableNode.tBodies[0];
}
var rowNode = document.createElement("tr");
tbodyNode.appendChild(rowNode);
```

How to use the insertRow method to add a row

```
var rowNode = tbodyNode.insertRow(-1);
```

Two ways to add a cell to a row

How to create a text node

```
var textNode = document.createTextNode("$9.95");
```

How to use the appendChild method to add a cell

```
var cellNode = document.createElement("td");
cellNode.appendChild( textNode );
rowNode.appendChild( cellNode );
```

How to use the insertCell method to add a cell

```
var cellNode = rowNode.insertCell(-1);
cellNode.appendChild(textNode);
```

How to use the innerHTML property

How to add text to a cell

```
cellNode.innerHTML = "<i>$10.95</i>";
```

How to add cells to a row

```
rowNode.innerHTML = "<td>MBT-2843</td><td>Aqua Case</td><td>$10.95</td>";
```

Description

- You can't add a row directly to a table element. Instead, you must add the row to the tbody element for the table, which the browser creates when it builds the DOM.

- You can use the tBodies property of a table element to return an array of the tbody elements for the table, but most tables only have one tbody element in the array.

- You can use the appendChild method to add rows and cells to a table, but you must add rows to a tbody element.

- You can use the insertRow and insertCell methods to add rows and cells to a table, but you must add rows to a tbody element. When you use these methods, the row and cell positions start at 0, and you can use -1 to insert the row or cell at the end of the list.

- You can use the innerHTML property to set the HTML content of any node.

Figure 17-1   How to add rows and cells to a table

add a subtree of nodes to a cell or if you need to add formatted text to a cell. In cases like those, you can use the innerHTML property of a node. Although this property isn't currently part of any standard, all modern browsers support it, and it is expected to be a part of the new HTML 5 standard. The third group of examples in this figure illustrates the use of this property.

In this group of examples, the first statement uses the innerHTML property to add content to a new cell that includes formatting. The second statement uses this property to add three cells to a new row. This code automatically generates all of the necessary cell and text nodes and adds them to the DOM.

How to remove rows and cells

Figure 17-2 shows how remove rows and cells from a table. Although you can use the removeChild method described in chapter 15 to do that, the deleteRow and deleteCell methods are easier to use. As a result, this figure doesn't show how to use the removeChild method.

The first set of examples in this figure shows how to remove a row from a table. Here, the first three statements call the deleteRow method from a tbody node to remove rows from the table. For instance, the first statement deletes the first row in the table, and the second statement removes the last row.

The third statement in this set of examples is a while statement that executes a loop once for each row in the tbody node. Within the loop, the deleteRow statement deletes the last row in the table. As a result, all of the rows in the table are eventually deleted.

Like the insertRow statement, Internet Explorer requires that you call the deleteRow method from a tbody node, not a table node. So for browser compatibility, you should always do that.

The next set of examples shows how to remove a cell from a row. Here, the first statement uses the rows property of the table element to get a reference to the last row in the table. Then, the next three statements use this reference to remove cells from that row. For instance, the second statement uses the deleteCell method to remove the first cell from the row. The third statement removes the last cell from the row. And the fourth statement is a while statement that uses the deleteCell method to delete each cell in a row.

Although the deleteRow and deleteCell methods are easier to use than the removeChild method described in chapter 15, these methods don't return a reference to the element that's being deleted. So if you need to get a reference, you need to use the removeChild method.

How to remove a row from a table

How to remove the first row

```
tbodyNode.deleteRow(0);
```

How to remove the last row

```
tbodyNode.deleteRow(-1);
```

How to remove all rows from a table

```
while ( tbodyNode.rows > 0 ) {
    tbodyNode.deleteRow(1);
}
```

How to remove a cell from a row

How to get the last row

```
var rowNode = tableNode.rows[ tableNode.rows.length - 1 ];
```

How to remove the first cell

```
rowNode.deleteCell(0);
```

How to remove the last cell

```
rowNode.deleteCell(-1);
```

How to remove all cells from a row

```
while ( rowNode.cells.length > 0 ) {
    rowNode.deleteCell(-1);
}
```

Description

- You can use the rows property of a table element to return an array of rows for the table.
- For DOM-compliant browsers, you can use the deleteRow method of a table node to delete the specified row from the table. But for Internet Explorer, the deleteRow method must be used on the tbody node, not the table node.
- When you use the deleteRow method, the rows are numbered starting at 0, and you can use -1 to delete the last row in the table.
- You can use the cells property of a row element to return an array of rows for the table.
- You can use the deleteCell method to delete a cell from a row. The cells are numbered starting at 0, and you can use -1 to delete the last cell in the row.

Compatibility with Internet Explorer

- For browser compatibility, you should always code the deleteRow method on the tbody node, not the table node, since that's what Internet Explorer requires.

Figure 17-2   How to remove rows and cells from a table

How to reorder rows

Figure 17-3 shows how to change the order of the rows in a table. Here, the first example shows how to reverse the order of the rows. To start, the first statement gets a reference to the table node, and the second statement gets a *node list* of all the rows in the table.

A node list is similar to an array in many ways, but it is also different. The primary difference is that a node list is a "live" list. In other words, when changes are made to the DOM, the node list is automatically updated. As a result, if you remove rows from a table, you also remove those rows from the node list, and you lose the references to those row nodes.

After getting a reference to the rows in the table, the first example creates a new array named rows. Then, it uses a loop to copy the references to the row nodes from the node list into the array. This preserves the references to the row nodes even when they are removed from the DOM.

After storing the rows in an array, this code gets a reference to the tbody node by using the parentNode property of the first row in the array. Then, it uses a loop to remove all the rows from the table. At this point, the rowNodes list is empty, and the rows have been removed from the DOM, but the rows array still contains references to the rows.

After removing the rows from the DOM, this code calls the reverse method of the rows array to reverse the order of the rows. This method is a built-in method that's available from any array. Finally, this code uses a loop to add the nodes stored in the rows array back to the tbody node.

You may have noticed that this example uses the removeChild and appendChild methods instead of the deleteRow and insertRow methods. That's because the removeChild and appendChild methods work fine for this task. For some tasks, though, the deleteRow and insertRow methods will clearly work better.

The second example in this figure shows how to add a new method named shuffle to the Array object. This method uses the Fisher-Yates algorithm to randomly shuffle the rows in an array. This algorithm loops through the elements from the end of the array to the beginning. Each time through the loop, it randomly selects an element from the first part of the array and moves it to the end of the array. When the loop is complete, the elements have all been randomly moved within the array.

If you add the shuffle method to the Array object as in this example, you can call it from any array. For instance, the third example shows how you can use the shuffle method to shuffle the order of the rows instead of reversing the order of the rows.

If you need to sort the rows in a table by specific columns, you need to create a custom comparison function, and you need to pass that custom function to the sort method of the Array object. The Table Sort application in the next figure shows how this works.

How to reverse the order of rows in a table

```
var tableNode = document.getElementById("item_list");
var rowNodes = tableNode.getElementsByTagName("tr");

// Store the rows in an array
var rows = [];
var i;
for ( i = 0; i < rowNodes.length; i++ ) {
    rows.push( rowNodes[i] );
}

// Remove the rows from the DOM
var tbodyNode = rows[0].parentNode;
for ( i = 0; i < rows.length; i++ ) {
    tbodyNode.removeChild(rows[i]);
}

// Reorder the array
rows.reverse();

// Add the rows to the DOM
for ( i = 0; i < rows.length; i++ ) {
    tbodyNode.appendChild(rows[i]);
}
```

How to add a shuffle method to the Array object

```
Array.prototype.shuffle = function () {
    var i, j, element;
    for ( i = this.length - 1; i >= 0; i— ) {
        j = Math.floor( Math.random() * (i+1) );
        element = this.splice(j,1);
        this.push(element[0]);
    }
}
```

How to call the shuffle method of the Array object

```
rows.shuffle();
```

Description

- You can't work directly with the rows returned by the getElementsByTagName method. Instead, to reorder the rows, you need to copy the rows into an array and remove them from the DOM. Then, you can reorder the array and add the rows back into the DOM.

- You can customize the sort method of the Array object by writing a custom comparison function and passing that function as an argument to the sort method. This technique is described in figure 9-5 of chapter 9, and it is used by the application in the next figure.

Figure 17-3   How to reorder rows in a table

The Table Sort application

Figure 17-4 presents the Table Sort application. When the user clicks on one of the up and down arrows to the right of each header column, the table is sorted by the values in that column. The first time the user clicks on the arrows for a column, this application sorts the table in ascending order. For subsequent clicks on the same column, the application toggles the sort order between ascending and descending order.

If you have trouble envisioning how this application works, you may want to run it before you continue. Then, you'll see how the arrow images change each time the table is sorted. You'll also see that the first two columns are sorted alphanumerically, but the third column is sorted by numeric value. As shown in this figure, the table is sorted by the Description column.

The XHTML file

The XHTML file for the Table Sort application begins by loading two style sheets. Here, the table.css file provides styles that are specific to the table. These styles left-align text columns and right-align numeric columns.

Then, this code imports four JavaScript files. Since the first two were presented in previous chapters, you should already be familiar with them. The second two are presented after the XHTML in this figure.

Finally, this code defines a table with an id of "product_list" that displays four rows. Here, the first row is a header row, and the next three rows contain the data for products. Note that each cell has a class attribute that describes the column. This value is used by the application when it sorts the rows.

The Table Sort application in the web browser

Product List

Code ⌃	Description ⌃		Price ⌃
MBT-2843	Aqua Cam Case		24.95
MBT-1348	Floating Fly Keeper Box		9.95
MBT-5201	Neoprene Waders		59.95

The XHTML file

```
<!DOCTYPE html PUBLIC "-//W3C//DTD XHTML 1.0 Transitional//EN"
    "http://www.w3.org/TR/xhtml1/DTD/xhtml1-transitional.dtd">
<html xmlns="http://www.w3.org/1999/xhtml">
<head>
<title>Product Manager</title>
<link rel="stylesheet" type="text/css" href="default.css" />
<link rel="stylesheet" type="text/css" href="table.css" />
<script type="text/javascript" src="jslib_event.js"></script>
<script type="text/javascript" src="jslib_dom_ready.js"></script>
<script type="text/javascript" src="jslib_tablesort.js"></script>
<script type="text/javascript" src="product_list.js"></script>
</head>

<body>
<div id="content">
    <h1>Product List</h1>
    <table id="product_list" border="0" cellspacing="0" cellpadding="3">
        <tr>
            <th class="product-code">Code</th>
            <th class="product-descr">Description</th>
            <th class="product-price">Price</th>
        </tr>
        <tr>
            <td class="product-code">MBT-2843</td>
            <td class="product-descr">Aqua Cam Case</td>
            <td class="product-price">24.95</td>
        </tr>
        <tr>
            <td class="product-code">MBT-1348</td>
            <td class="product-descr">Floating Fly Keeper Box</td>
            <td class="product-price">9.95</td>
        </tr>
        <tr>
            <td class="product-code">MBT-5201</td>
            <td class="product-descr">Neoprene Waders</td>
            <td class="product-price">59.95</td>
        </tr>
    </table>
</div>
</body>
</html>
```

Figure 17-4   The Table Sort application (part 1 of 5)

The tablesort_library.js file

The tablesort_library.js file defines the constructor for a TableSort object. This constructor prepares a table for sorting by adding an image to each header column and by attaching an event handler to each image. Then, when the user clicks on an image, the library sorts the table by the values for that column.

The TableSort constructor takes the id of the table that will be sorted as its only parameter. Within the constructor, the code stores a reference to the table node in the table property. Then, it validates this node by checking if it is a DOM table element and by throwing an error if it isn't.

After validating the table node, this code creates three more properties. The sortColumn property stores the current sort column for the table. The sortUp property stores a Boolean value that indicates whether the column is sorted in ascending order. And the imageNodes property is an array that stores references to each of the sort images that are added to the header row.

After declaring these properties, this constructor gets the header cell nodes from the table's header row, and it loops through each of the header cells. Within this loop, the code creates a node for the image. Then, it copies the node's class name into a variable named columnName. Next, if this node is the first column, the sortColumn variable is set to the column name and the image node's src property is set to the arrow_up.png image to indicate that the column is sorted in ascending order. Otherwise, the image node's src property is set to the arrow_off.png image to indicate that the column is not currently a sort column.

After adding the images to the header row, the code in this loop calls the imageClickHandler method that's defined later to get an event handler for the click event of each image node. Then, this loop attaches this event handler.

After attaching the event handler for the image, this loop adds the image node as a child of the header cell node. This causes the image to be displayed after the text for the header column. This code also adds the image node to the imageNodes array.

The last statement in this constructor calls the sort method that's defined later. This method sorts the table by the specified column in the specified order. At this point, this statement sorts the table by the first column in ascending order.

The tablesort_library.js file

```javascript
var TableSort = function ( tableId ) {
    var that = this;

    // Store a reference to the table node as a property
    this.table = document.getElementById(tableId);

    // Validate the table node
    if ( this.table && this.table.nodeType != 1 ) {
        throw new Error("TableSort: Table id is not a DOM element.");
    }
    if ( this.table.tagName != "TABLE" ) {
        throw new Error("TableSort: Table id is not a table element.");
    }

    // Set three global properties
    this.sortColumn = "";
    this.sortUp = true;
    this.imageNodes = [];

    // Get the header nodes
    var headers = this.table.getElementsByTagName("th");

    // Loop through the header nodes
    var header, columnName, imageNode, imageClick;
    for ( var i = 0; i < headers.length; i++) {
        header = headers[i];

        // Create a node for the image
        imageNode = document.createElement("img");

        // Add the "sort arrow" images to the header column
        // and set the first column as the default sort column
        columnName = header.className;
        if ( i == 0 ) {
            this.sortColumn = columnName;
            imageNode.src = "arrows_up.png";
        } else {
            imageNode.src = "arrows_off.png";
        }

        // Get the event handler for the image
        imageClick = this.imageClickHandler(columnName);

        // Add the event handler to the image
        jsLib.event.add(imageNode, "click", imageClick);

        // Add the image node to column header and to array of image nodes
        header.appendChild(imageNode);
        this.imageNodes[columnName] = imageNode;
    }

    // Sort the table
    this.sort();
}
```

Figure 17-4   The Table Sort application (part 2 of 5)

The imageClickHandler method of the TableSort object takes a column name as its only parameter, and it returns a function that the application uses as the event handler for the click event of an image node. This function sorts the table on that column name in ascending order. Or, if the table is already sorted on that column, this function changes the direction of the sort.

Within the imageClickHandler method, the first statement copies the contents of the this keyword into the that variable. Then, the second statement returns the function that will be used as the event handler for click event of the image.

The returned function begins by using an if statement to check the value of the sortColumn property. If the current column is already the sort column name, this code changes the direction of the sort. Otherwise, it turns off the sort arrows of the previous column, sets the sortColumn property to the current column name, and sets the sort direction to ascending. After the first if statement, a second if statement sets the arrow image for the current sort column so it matches the current sort direction. Finally, the returned function calls the sort method to sort the table.

The sort method of the TableSort object uses the sortColumn and sortUp properties to sort the table rows. To start, this method copies the contents of the this keyword into the that variable. Then, it stores the table rows in a variable named rowNodes. If there aren't at least three rows (the header row and two other rows), this method ends since it doesn't need to do any work. Next, this method copies the references to the table rows from the rowNodes node list to the rows array, gets the tbody node for later use, and removes the header row from the array.

After setting up the rows array, the sort method loops through each of the remaining rows in the array. For each row, it removes the row from the table. As a result, this loop removes all rows except the header row from the DOM.

The tablesort_library.js file (continued)

```
TableSort.prototype.imageClickHandler = function (columnName) {
    var that = this;

    // return an event handler
    return function () {
        // If current sort column, toggle the sort direction
        if ( that.sortColumn == columnName ) {
            that.sortUp = ! that.sortUp;
        // Otherwise...
        } else {
            // Set the image for the old sort column
            that.imageNodes[that.sortColumn].src = "arrows_off.png";

            // Switch the current sort column and sort ascending
            that.sortColumn = columnName;
            that.sortUp = true;
        }

        // Set the appropriate arrows for the current sort column
        if ( that.sortUp ) {
            that.imageNodes[that.sortColumn].src = "arrows_up.png";
        } else {
            that.imageNodes[that.sortColumn].src = "arrows_down.png";
        }

        that.sort();
    }
}

TableSort.prototype.sort = function () {
    var that = this;
    if ( this.sortColumn == "" ) return;

    // Get the rows from the table
    var rowNodes = this.table.getElementsByTagName("tr");
    if (rowNodes.length <= 1 ) return;

    // Store a reference to each row in the rows array
    var rows = [];
    for ( var i = 0; i < rowNodes.length; i++) {
        rows.push( rowNodes[i] );
    }

    // Get a reference to the tbody node
    var tbodyNode = rows[0].parentNode;

    // Remove the header row from the array (but not the DOM)
    rows.shift();

    // Remove all rows except the header row from the DOM
    var row;
    for ( i = 0; i < rows.length; i++ ) {
        row = rows[i];
        row.parentNode.removeChild(row);
    }
```

Figure 17-4   The Table Sort application (part 3 of 5)

After removing the rows from the DOM, this sort method defines a function named isDate that returns true if its parameter is a text string that can be converted to a date. It also defines a function named isMoney that returns true if its parameter is a text string that can be converted to a number after removing any dollar signs and commas.

After these functions, the sort method defines a variable named direction. If the sortUp property is true, this variable is set to a value of 1. Otherwise, it's set to a value -1. Later in this file, the compareColumnValues method uses this variable to sort the rows in the correct direction.

After defining the direction variable, the sort method defines a function named compareColumnValues that takes two items from the rows array as parameters. This function is the custom comparison function that's passed to the sort method of the rows array. As a result, it must return a value of 1, 0, or -1 to specify the sort order for the two array items that are being compared. More specifically, it returns a value of 1 if the first item should be before the second item, -1 if the first item should be after the second item, and 0 if they're the same.

That means that the compareColumnValues function compares the values in the current sort column and returns the appropriate number. To do that, this function gets the values that are stored in the current sort column, compares them, and returns the appropriate number.

To start, the compareColumnValues function gets the cells from the first row. Then, it loops through the cells and copies the text from the cell with the same class name as the sort column into the valueA variable. Next, this function uses the same technique to get a value for the valueB variable.

After getting the text for the appropriate values, the compareColumnValues function converts these text values to number, date, or time values if that's necessary. To do that, this code checks to see whether both values are numbers, dates, or money values. If so, this code converts these values to the appropriate data type. If not, this code leaves these values as text strings. This allows the function to accurately sort number, date, and money values.

The tablesort_library.js file (continued)

```
// Define two functions that check for data types
var isDate = function ( value ) {
    var d = new Date(value);
    return ! isNaN(d);
}
var isMoney = function ( value ) {
    var m = value.replace( /[$,]/g, "" );
    return ! isNaN(m);
}

// Define the direction variable
var direction = ( that.sortUp ) ? 1 : -1;

// Define the function that compares the rows
var compareColumnValues = function (rowA, rowB) {
    var valueA, valueB;
    var i, cell;

    // Get the cell value for row A
    var cellsA = rowA.getElementsByTagName("td");
    for ( i = 0; i < cellsA.length; i++ ) {
        cell = cellsA[i];
        if ( cell.className == that.sortColumn ) {
            valueA = cell.firstChild.nodeValue;
            break;
        }
    }

    // Get the cell value for row B
    var cellsB = rowB.getElementsByTagName("td");
    for ( i = 0; i < cellsB.length; i++ ) {
        cell = cellsB[i];
        if ( cell.className == that.sortColumn ) {
            valueB = cell.firstChild.nodeValue;
            break;
        }
    }

    // Convert the values to the appropriate data type
    if ( ! isNaN(valueA) && ! isNaN(valueB) ) {
        valueA = parseFloat(valueA);
        valueB = parseFloat(valueB);
    } else if ( isDate(valueA) && isDate(valueB) ) {
        valueA = new Date(valueA);
        valueB = new Date(valueB);
    } else if ( isMoney(valueA) && isMoney(valueB) ) {
        valueA = parseFloat(valueA.replace( /[$,]/g, "" ));
        valueB = parseFloat(valueB.replace( /[$,]/g, "" ));
    }
```

Figure 17-4   The Table Sort application (part 4 of 5)

After converting the column values to the appropriate data types, the compareColumnValues function returns 1, -1, or 0 based on the relationship between the two values. To understand this code, remember that the direction variable stores a value of -1 if the sortUp property is false. As a result, this code reverses the value that's returned for descending sort order. This ensures the rows are sorted in the appropriate order.

After defining the compareColumnValues function, the sort method passes the compareColumnValues function to the sort method of the rows array. As a result, that sort method sorts the rows the right way.

Then, after the rows are sorted by the sort method of the array object, the sort method of the TableSort object adds the rows back to the DOM. To do that, it loops through all rows in the rows array and appends each row to the tbody node. This displays the sorted rows on the web page.

The product_list.js file

To use the TableSort object to sort a table, you just need to create a new TableSort object for the table when the DOM is ready. This is illustrated by the code for the product_list.js file. Here, the id of the table is passed to the TableSort constructor as its only parameter. This adds the sort images to the column headers for the table and sorts it by the first column in ascending order.

The tablesort_library.js file (continued)

```
        // Compare the two values and return the appropriate comparison value
        if ( valueA < valueB ) {
            return -1 * direction;
        } else if ( valueB < valueA ) {
            return 1 * direction;
        } else {
            return 0;
        }
    }

    // Use the compareColumnValues function to sort the rows array
    rows.sort( compareColumnValues );

    // Append the sorted rows to the table body node
    for ( i = 0; i < rows.length; i++) {
        tbodyNode.appendChild( rows[i] );
    }
}
```

The product_list.js file

```
jsLib.dom.ready( function () {
    itemList = new TableSort("product_list");
});
```

Figure 17-4   The Table Sort application (part 5 of 5)

How to script forms

In chapter 6, you learned some basic skills for working with the controls on a form. Now, this topic builds on those skills.

How to handle form events

Figure 17-5 reviews some of the events that can occur with forms and controls. These events trigger whether the user uses the mouse or keyboard. For example, the submit event triggers if the user clicks a submit button or if the user uses the Tab key to move the focus to the submit button and then presses the Enter key. Similarly, the control events trigger whether the user uses the mouse or keyboard to trigger the event. As a result, the event handlers for these events work more reliably than the event handlers for click events.

The submit event is commonly used to validate the data in a form. To do that, the event handler for this event checks whether the data on the form is valid. If it is, the default action of the event submits the form to the server. Otherwise, the event handler cancels the default action of the event, which prevents the form from being submitted to the server.

The reset event can be used to customize the reset process. By default, when the user clicks on the reset button for a form, the browser resets all the controls on the form. However, it doesn't reset any other data such as tags that are used to display error messages. To reset such tags, you can code an event handler for the reset event.

The change event triggers when the state of a control has changed and the control loses the focus. You can use this event to update error messages for a control as the user fills out a form.

The select event triggers when the user selects text in a text box or a text area. You can use this event to get the selected text and to modify it.

The focus and blur events trigger when a control gains or loses focus. This can occur when the user uses the mouse or keyboard to move the focus. This can also occur when JavaScript code calls the focus or blur methods to move the focus to or from a control. You can use the focus and blur events to update the appearance of a control so it's highlighted when it has the focus. You can also clear an error message associated with a control when it gains the focus. This gives the user a chance to correct the error.

Form events

Event	Description
submit	Triggers when the form is submitted, which typically occurs when the user clicks on a submit button.
reset	Triggers when the form is reset, which typically occurs when the user clicks on a reset button.

Control events

Event	Description
change	Triggers when the control's state changes and the control loses focus.
select	Triggers when the user selects text in a text box or text area.
focus	Triggers when the control gains focus.
blur	Triggers when the control loses focus.

Description

- The submit event can be used to validate the data on a form before that data is submitted to the server. If the data is invalid, the submission can be canceled.

- The reset event can be used to customize the reset process. For example, you can reset error messages in the form when the form is reset.

- The change event can be used to validate a specific control as the user fills out the form. This allows you to display error messages as the user fills out the form.

- The select event can be used to determine when the user selects some text in a control. You can then access the text and modify it. For example, when the user selects text in a text area, you can enable a button that formats the selected text.

- The focus and blur events can be used to modify a control when it gains or loses focus. For example, you can clear an error message associated with a control when the user moves to the control to correct the error.

Figure 17-5   How to handle form events

How to script radio buttons

In chapter 4, you learned that you can create groups of radio buttons by using the same value for the name property of each button in the group. However, you typically specify different id attributes for each button.

In chapter 6, you learned how to script two radio buttons. To do that, you can use the button's id attribute. For several radio buttons, however, it becomes more convenient to retrieve an array of buttons rather than use the id attribute of each button.

Figure 17-6 shows how to work with a group of radio buttons. Here, the first set of examples shows how to retrieve the value of the selected button in the group. To start, it defines the getSelectedRadioButton function. This function takes the name of the radio button group as its one parameter. Within the function, the first statement uses the getElementsByName method to get all radio buttons with the specified name. Then, it loops through each of the buttons and returns the button that's selected.

The second part of this set of examples shows how you can use the getSelectedRadioButton function to get a reference to the selected button in the specified radio button group. Then, this code uses an if statement to check whether a button was returned. If so, it displays its value. Otherwise, it displays a message that no button was selected.

The second set of examples in this figure shows how to select the radio button that has a specified value. To start, it defines the setSelectedRadioButton function. This function takes two parameters: the name of the radio button group and the value of the button to select. Within the function, the first statement uses the getElementsByName method to get all radio buttons with the specified name. Then, it loops through these buttons and selects the radio button that has the specified value. Finally, this method returns a reference to the button.

The second part of this set of examples shows how to use the setSelectedRadioButton function to select the radio button in the "memory" group that has a value of "2GB". Note that this code doesn't store a reference to the radio button that's returned by the setSelectedRadioButton function.

How to determine which radio button is selected

A function that returns the selected radio button

```
var getSelectedRadioButton = function ( groupName ) {
    var buttons = document.getElementsByName(groupName);
    for ( var i = 0; i <= buttons.length; i++ ) {
        if ( buttons[i].checked ) {
            return buttons[i];
        }
    }
}
```

Code that uses the getSelectedRadioButton function

```
var selectedButton = getSelectedRadioButton("memory");
if ( selectedButton ) {
    alert ("Value: " + selectedButton.value);
} else {
    alert ("No radio button selected.");
}
```

How to select a radio button with a specific value

A function that selects the radio button with the specified value

```
var setSelectedRadioButton = function ( groupName, value ) {
    var buttons = document.getElementsByName(groupName);
    for ( var i = 0; i <= buttons.length; i++ ) {
        if ( buttons[i].value == value ) {
            buttons[i].checked = true;
            return buttons[i];
        }
    }
}
```

Code that uses the setSelectedRadioButton function

```
setSelectedRadioButton( "memory", "2GB" );
```

Description

- Within the XHTML for a page, you can create a group of radio buttons by specifying the same value for the name property of each radio button.

- You can use the getElementsByName method to return a list of elements with the specified name property. Then, you can loop through the list to find the radio button that's selected. Or, you can loop through the list to select a radio button with a specific value.

Figure 17-6   How to script radio buttons

How to script select lists

In chapter 6, you learned how to work with a select list that allows the user to select a single option. However, you can also create a select list that lets the user select multiple options. Then, you can use the techniques shown in figure 17-7 to work with the list.

The first example in this figure defines a function named getSelectedValues. This function takes the id of the select list as its only parameter, and it returns an array containing the values of the selected options. To do that, this function uses the options property of the select list node to return an array of options. Then, it loops through the options. Next, if the option is selected, it adds that option's value to the array of values. When the loop finishes, this function returns the array of values.

The second example defines a function named clearOptions. This function takes the id of the select list as its only parameter, and it clears all options in the specified select list. To do that, this function loops through the options in the select list and sets each option's selected property to false.

The third example defines a function named setSelectedValue that selects the option with the specified value in a select list. This function takes three parameters: the id of the select list, the value of the option to select, and an optional parameter that can be used to deselect the other options in the list. To start, this function loops through the options in the select list. If the option's value matches the value parameter, this code sets the option's selected property to true. Otherwise, if the clearOthers parameter is set to true, this code sets the option's selected to false. In other words, if the clearOthers parameter is set to true, this function selects the option with the specified value, and it deselects all other options.

The fourth example shows how to add an option to a select list. Here, the first statement creates an option node. The second statement gives that node a value of "linux". The third statement uses the innerHTML property of that node to set the display text for that node to "Ubuntu Linux". And the last two statements append that node to the select list.

How to get the values for the selected options

```
var getSelectedValues = function (id) {
    var select = document.getElementById(id);
    var values = [];
    for ( var i = 0; i < select.options.length; i++ ) {
        if ( select.options[i].selected ) {
            value.push(select.options[i].value);
        }
    }
    return values;
}
```

How to deselect all options

```
var clearOptions = function (id) {
    var select = document.getElementById(id);
    for ( var i = 0; i < select.options.length; i++ ) {
        select.options[i].selected = false;
    }
}
```

How to select an option

```
var setSelectedValue = function (id, value, clearOthers) {
    var select = document.getElementById(id);
    for ( var i = 0; i < select.options.length; i++ ) {
        if ( select.options[i].value == value ) {
            select.options[i].selected = true;
        } else if ( clearOthers ) {
            select.options[i].selected = false;
        }
    }
}
```

How to add an option

```
// create the option
var optNode = document.createElement("option");
optNode.value = "linux";
optNode.innerHTML = "Ubuntu Linux";

// add the option to the select list
var select = document.getElementById("os");
select.appendChild(optNode);
```

Description

- Within the XHTML for a page, you can code select lists that allow single or multiple items to be selected.

- You can use the options property of a select list node to return an array of option nodes. For each option node, you can use the selected property to determine if the option is selected, and you can use the value property to work with the option's value.

- You can use the innerHTML property to set the XHTML content of any node including a select list.

Figure 17-7   How to script select lists

A JavaScript library for working with text selections

To work with selections in text areas and text boxes, you need to accommodate both the DOM and Internet Explorer models for doing that. To make that easier, you can use a JavaScript library like the one shown figure 17-8. This library consists of a constructor and three methods that let you get a selection in a text box or text area as well as the starting index and ending index of the selection.

To start, this library defines a constructor for a TextSelection object. This constructor takes the id of the text box or text area as its only parameter. Then, it stores a reference to the specified node in the node property, and it validates that node.

The getSelectedText method returns the selected text for the specified element. To start, this method checks to see whether the selectionStart property exists. If so, that means that the browser is using the DOM model so this method can use the selectionStart and selectionEnd properties to return a substring that contains the selected text.

If the selectionStart property isn't present, that means that the browser is Internet Explorer. As a result, this getSelectedText method checks whether the selection object of the document object exists. If so, it uses the createRange method of the selection object to get a reference to the range object that contains the selected text. If the text in the range is within the text element, this code returns the selected text. Otherwise, it returns an empty string.

The getStartIndex method returns the index for the first character in the selection. Here again, this method starts by checking whether the selectionStart property exists. If so, this code returns that property's value. Otherwise, this method checks whether the selection property of the document object exists. If so, it returns the starting index by passing a value of "start" to the getIEIndex method that's in this library.

The getEndIndex method returns the index for the last character in the selection. This method works like the getStartIndex method, but when it calls the getIEIndex method it passes "end" as the parameter.

A JavaScript library for working with text selections

```
var TextSelection = function (id) {
    this.node = document.getElementById(id);

    // Validate the node
    if ( this.node && this.node.nodeType != 1 ) {
        throw new Error (
            "TextSelection: id does not specify an element.");
    }
    var isTextBox = (this.node.tagName == "INPUT" &&
                     this.node.type == "text");
    var isTextArea = ( this.node.tagName == "TEXTAREA" );
    if ( ! ( isTextBox || isTextArea ) ) {
        throw new Error (
            "TextSelection: Element is not a text box or text area.");
    }
}

TextSelection.prototype.getSelectedText = function () {
    if ( this.node.selectionStart !== undefined ) {        // DOM
        var start = this.node.selectionStart;
        var end = this.node.selectionEnd;
        return this.node.value.substring(start, end);
    } else if ( document.selection ) {                     // IE
        var range = document.selection.createRange();
        if ( this.node == range.parentElement() ) {
            return range.text;
        }
        return "";
    }
    return "";
}

TextSelection.prototype.getStartIndex = function () {
    if ( this.node.selectionStart !== undefined ) {        // DOM
        return this.node.selectionStart;
    } else if ( document.selection ) {                     // IE
        return this.getIEIndex("start");
    }
    return 0;
}

TextSelection.prototype.getEndIndex = function () {
    if ( this.node.selectionEnd !== undefined ) {          // DOM
        return this.node.selectionEnd;
    } else if ( document.selection ) {                     // IE
        return this.getIEIndex("end");
    }
    return 0;
}
```

Figure 17-8   A JavaScript library for working with text selections (part 1 of 2)

The getIEIndex method takes one parameter that determines which index to retrieve, and it returns that index. To do that, this method begins by moving the focus to the text element. Then, it retrieves a reference to the range object for the selection. Next, if the text range isn't from the text element, this method returns a value of 0.

After initializing the index variable to a value of 0, the getIEIndex method uses a loop to move either the start or end point of the text range back one character at a time. Each time it moves the text, it increments the index variable by 1. Then, when the text range is outside of the text element, the parentElement of the range is no longer the text element node. As a result, the code exits the loop, subtracts a value of 1 from the index variable, and returns that variable.

How to use the JavaScript library to work with text selections

To show you how you can use this JavaScript library, this figure ends with a simple example. To start, this example creates a TextSelection object from the text area with the id of "text_area", but you could also pass this constructor the id for a text box. Then, this example uses the three methods of the TextSelection object to return the selected text, the starting index of the selected text, and the ending index. Finally, it displays this data in a dialog box.

Although this example doesn't do anything useful, it shows how to get all the data that you need for doing something useful with a selection. If, for example, you wanted to add formatting before and after the selected text, you could use this code as a starting point. You could also add methods to this library for doing specific tasks with a selection.

If you would like to see a simple text editor application that uses an enhanced version of this library, you'll find one in the text_editor folder for this chapter's book applications. After you enter text into the text area, this application lets you apply XHTML tags to selected text by clicking on the Bold or Link button.

A library to work with text selections (continued)

```
TextSelection.prototype.getIEIndex = function (which) {
    this.node.focus();
    var range = document.selection.createRange();

    if ( this.node !== range.parentElement() ) return 0;

    var index = 0;
    while ( range.parentElement() == this.node ) {
        if (which == "start") {
            range.moveStart("character", -1);
        } else {
            range.moveEnd("character", -1);
        }
        index++;
    }
    return index - 1;
}
```

How to use the JavaScript library to work with a text selection

```
var ts = new TextSelection("text_area");

var selectedText = ts.getSelectedText();
var startIndex = ts.getStartIndex();
var endIndex = ts.getEndIndex();

alert("Selected text:  " + selectedText + "\n" +
      "Start index:    " + startIndex + "\n" +
      "End index:      " + endIndex + "\n");
```

Description

- This library consists of a constructor for a TextSelection object and three methods for getting the selection when the user selects text in a text box or a text area.

- The getSelectedText method gets the selected text. The getStartIndex method gets the starting index of the selection. And the getEndIndex method gets the ending index.

- Since these methods provide for both the DOM and the Internet Explorer models, they will work with all browsers.

Figure 17-8   A JavaScript library for working with text selections (part 2 of 2)

The Product Configuration application

Figure 17-9 presents a Product Configuration application that helps the user configure some of the components for a desktop computer. Specifically, the user can select a processor for the computer, and the user can select one or two optical drives. This illustrates the use of a group of radio buttons and two select lists.

When the user selects an option, this application updates the system cost that's displayed at the top of the page. This application also updates the text to the right of each option to reflect how that option changes the system cost. Finally, this application uses JavaScript to validate the data in the form as the user makes selections.

This validation prevents the user from configuring a system that doesn't make sense. For example, the first optical drive should be the same or better than the second optical drive. As a result, if the user selects a second optical drive that's better than the first optical drive, the application displays an error message as shown in this figure.

If you have any trouble envisioning how this application works, you may want to run it before you continue. Then, you can see how the prices in the parentheses for each option change when an option is selected, and you can see how the error message is displayed when the user selects an option that doesn't make sense.

In practice, of course, an application like this would provide for many other options. If you're interested in how that might work, you can check out the extended version of this application. It is in the product_config_extended folder for the chapter 17 book applications.

The XHTML file

The XHTML for this application begins by loading two CSS files. Here, the first CSS file provides general styles that apply to all elements, and the second CSS file is specific to the form for this application.

After the CSS files, the XHTML loads four JavaScript files. Since the first two are presented in previous chapters, you should already know how they work. The last two are presented after the XHTML.

The Product Configuration application in a web browser

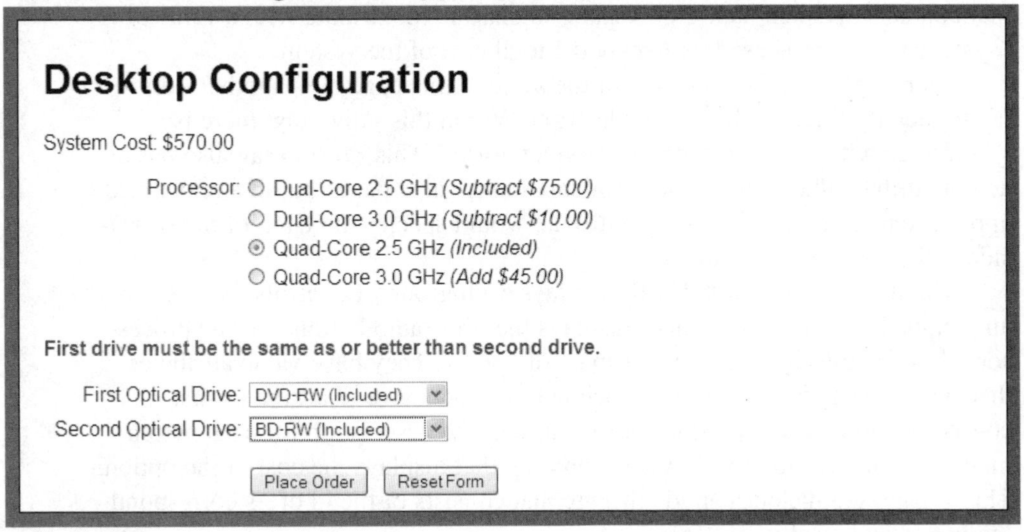

The XHTML code

```
<!DOCTYPE html PUBLIC "-//W3C//DTD XHTML 1.0 Transitional//EN"
    "http://www.w3.org/TR/xhtml1/DTD/xhtml1-transitional.dtd">
<html xmlns="http://www.w3.org/1999/xhtml">
<head>
<title>Desktop Configuration</title>
<link rel="stylesheet" type="text/css" href="default.css" />
<link rel="stylesheet" type="text/css" href="config.css" />
<script type="text/javascript" src="jslib_event.js"></script>
<script type="text/javascript" src="jslib_dom_ready.js"></script>
<script type="text/javascript" src="config_library.js"></script>
<script type="text/javascript" src="config.js"></script>
</head>
```

Description

- An extended version of this application that provides more options for configuring a system is provided with the downloadable files for this chapter in a directory named product_config_extended.

Figure 17-9   The Product Configuration application (part 1 of 6)

The body for the page begins with a <div> tag, an <h1> tag, and a <p> tag that contains a <span> tag. This <span> tag has an id attribute with a value of "system_cost" and is used to display the total cost of the system.

After displaying the total cost of the system, this page uses another <div> tag to identify the form for the application. Within this <div> tag, there is a <form> tag with an id attribute of "product_form". This <form> tag also has an action attribute that submits the form data to the same page. But in a real-world application, of course, this action attribute would specify the URL of the server-side script for processing the order.

Within the form, this XHTML displays each group of controls. For example, the first group of controls displays the four radio buttons for the processor. These buttons have a name attribute of "proc". They have value attributes that start at 0 and increment with each button. They have id attributes that consist of "proc" and the value for the button. The description for each button includes some text followed by a <span> tag that displays the cost of the option. This <span> tag includes an id attribute that consists of the id of its corresponding button and a suffix of "_cost".

After the controls for the processor, the XHTML displays a group of controls for configuring the optical disks. To start, this code displays a <p> tag that's used to display an error message. Then, this code displays two select lists. The first select list has three options for the primary optical disk. This list has a name and id of "optical0", and the options available from this list have values that start at 0 and increment with each option. The second list has four options for the secondary optical disk, including a first option of "None". This list has a name and id of "optical1", and the options available from this list have incremental values starting at 0.

Note that this code uses a naming convention to correlate the select lists with their error messages. Specifically, this code gives a prefix of "optical" to the optical drives group. Then, this code appends a suffix of "_err_p" to the paragraph for the error message, and it appends a suffix of "_err" for the <span> tag for the error message.

Note also that this code uses <br> tags to start new lines for the form controls. In addition, the final <br> tag in each group of controls has a class attribute of "double", which the CSS uses to provide additional vertical space between groups.

This XHTML ends by displaying two buttons. First, it displays a submit button that has an id of "config_submit". Then, it displays a regular button with an id of "config_reset". Although this button isn't an XHTML reset button, the JavaScript event handler for the click event of this button resets all controls to their default values, resets the pricing text for each option, and resets the error messages for the form.

The XHTML code (continued)

```
<body>
<div id="content">
    <h1>Desktop Configuration</h1>
    <p>System Cost: <span id="system_cost"> </span></p>
    <div class="formLayout">
        <form action="#" method="get" id="product_form">

        <label for="proc">Processor:</label>
        <input type="radio" name="proc" value="0" id="proc0"
            checked="checked" />
        Dual-Core 2.5 GHz <span class="cost" id="proc0_cost"> </span>
        <br />
        <label> </label>
        <input type="radio" name="proc" value="1" id="proc1" />
        Dual-Core 3.0 GHz <span class="cost" id="proc1_cost"> </span>
        <br />
        <label> </label>
        <input type="radio" name="proc" value="2" id="proc2" />
        Quad-Core 2.5 GHz <span class="cost" id="proc2_cost"> </span>
        <br />
        <label> </label>
        <input type="radio" name="proc" value="3" id="proc3" />
        Quad-Core 3.0 GHz <span class="cost" id="proc3_cost"> </span>
        <br class="double" />

        <p class="error" id="optical_err_p">
            <span id="optical_err"> </span></p>
        <label for="optical0">First Optical Drive:</label>
        <select name="optical0" id="optical0">
            <option value="0">DVD-RW</option>
            <option value="1">BD-ROM</option>
            <option value="2">BD-RW</option>
        </select>
        <br />
        <label for="optical1">Second Optical Drive:</label>
        <select name="optical1" id="optical1">
            <option value="0">None</option>
            <option value="1">DVD-RW</option>
            <option value="2">BD-ROM</option>
            <option value="3">BD-RW</option>
        </select>
        <br class="double" />

        <label> </label>
        <input type="submit" id="config_submit"
            value="Place Order" />
        <input type="button" id="config_reset"
            value="Reset Form" />
        <br />
        </form>
    </div>
</body>
</html>
```

Figure 17-9   The Product Configuration application (part 2 of 6)

The config_library.js file

The config_library.js file defines the constructor for a ConfigForm object and the methods for that object. This object controls the behavior of the Product Configuration application.

This file begins by defining two shortcut functions. First, it defines the standard $ function. Then, it defines a $setSpan function that sets the text in a <span> tag. Its parameters are the id of the <span> tag and the text for that tag.

After these shortcut functions, this file defines the getSelectedRadioButton method. This method returns a reference to the selected button in a radio button group, and it works like the function in figure 17-6. However, this method provides two enhancements. First, if this method can't find any radio buttons with the specified name, it throws an error. Second, if this method determines that no radio buttons in the group have been selected, it selects the first radio button and returns it.

After the getSelectedRadioButton method, this file defines the constructor for the ConfigForm object. This constructor begins by defining the baseCost property and storing the base cost of the system in this property. Then, this constructor defines two arrays that store the prices for the options. Here, the opticalCost array is a two dimensional array. Finally, this constructor calls the reset method that's defined in this file to reset the controls, the pricing text, and the error messages for the form.

After the constructor for the ConfigForm object, this code defines the priceText method of the ConfigForm object. This method takes two parameters: the price of the currently selected option and the price of another option. Then, this method returns the text that needs to be added to the description of an option to show how selecting that option will affect the price.

Within the priceText method, the first statement calculates the difference between the two price parameters. If the difference is positive, the second statement sets the variable named action to "Add". Otherwise, it sets this variable to "Subtract". Then, the third statement gets the absolute value of the difference between the prices. Finally, the fourth statement returns a text string with the difference between prices converted to a dollar value.

After the priceText method, the processorClick method defines the code that runs when the user selects one of the processor radio buttons. Within this method, the first statement uses the getSelectedRadioButton method to get the value of the selected button and the parseInt method to convert this value to an integer. Then, the second statement gets a node list of references to the radio buttons in the group. Next, this method loops through each of the buttons in the node list.

Within this loop, this code compares the value of the current button to the value of the selected button. If the current button is the selected button, this code sets the text for that button's description to "(Included)". Otherwise, this code uses the priceText method to return the appropriate text for the button's description. This text is used for the button's <span> tag. The id for the span tag is "proc" followed by the index for the button and "_cost". After the loop, the

The config_library.js file

```javascript
var $ = function (id) { return document.getElementById(id); }

var $setSpan = function (id, text) { $(id).firstChild.nodeValue = text; }

var getSelectedRadioButton = function ( radioName ) {
    var buttons = document.getElementsByName( radioName );
    if (buttons.length == 0) {
        throw new Error("No radio buttons found with name " + radioName);
    }
    for ( var i = 0; i <= buttons.length; i++ ) {
        if ( buttons[i].checked ) {
            return buttons[i];
        }
    }
    button[0].checked = true;
    return button[0];
}

var ConfigForm = function () {
    this.baseCost = 145;                            // Base cost
    this.processorCost = [ 125, 190, 200, 245 ];    // Processor costs

    this.opticalCost = [
        [ 25, 125, 200 ],        // First Optical Drive costs
        [ 0, 25, 125, 200 ]      // Second Optical Drive costs
    ];

    this.reset();
}

ConfigForm.prototype.priceText = function (currentPrice, newPrice) {
    var difference = newPrice - currentPrice;
    var action = ( difference > 0 ) ? "Add" : "Subtract";
    difference = Math.abs(difference);
    return " (" + action + " $" + difference.toFixed(2) + ")";
}

ConfigForm.prototype.processorClick = function () {
    var choice = parseInt(getSelectedRadioButton("proc").value);
    var buttons = document.getElementsByName("proc");
    var index, value, text;
    for ( index = 0; index < buttons.length; index++ ) {
        value = buttons[index].value;
        if ( value == choice ) {
            text = "(Included)";
        } else {
            text = this.priceText(this.processorCost[choice],
                                   this.processorCost[value]);
        }
        $setSpan( "proc" + value + "_cost", text );
    }
    this.updateForm();
}
```

Figure 17-9   The Product Configuration application (part 3 of 6)

processorClick method calls the updateForm method to validate the controls on the form and update the total price of the system.

After the processorClick method, the opticalChange method defines the code that runs when the user changes one of the select lists for the optical drives. This method updates the text that's displayed in the drop-down lists.

To start, this method gets the value of the selected option for the first optical drive, and it gets a node list of the options in the select list. Then, this method loops through each of the options in the select list. For each option, it gets the text from the option and removes all the text from a space and a parenthesis to the end of the string. This removes any previous price text from the option's text. Next, this method compares the value of that option to the value of the selected option. If the current option is the selected option, this code appends "(Included)" to the text for that option. Otherwise, this code uses the priceText method to append the appropriate price text for the option.

Within the opticalChange method, the first group of statements works like the second group of statements. The main difference is that the first group of statements use a value of 0 for the first index of the opticalCost array to select the first optical cost array. Then, they use another value for the second index to get the value for the option from the first optical cost array. In contrast, the second group of statements works with the second optical cost array. To do that, these statements use a value of 1 for the first index of the opticalCost array. Then, they use another value for the second index of the second optical cost array.

After the lists for both optical drives have been processed, the opticalChange method calls the updateForm method. This validates the controls on the form and updates the total price of the system.

After the opticalChange method, this file defines the showError method. This method takes two parameters: an error message and a group name. Then, it displays the error. To do that, this method begins by checking whether the error message exists. If so, this code sets the error in the group's <span> tag, displays the <p> tag that contains the <span> tag, and returns a value of true. Otherwise, this code clears the group's <span> tag, hides the <p> tag that contains the <span> tag, and returns a value of false.

The config_library.js file (continued)

```
ConfigForm.prototype.opticalChange = function () {
    var choice = parseInt($("optical0").value);
    var options = $("optical0").options;
    var index, option, value, text;
    for( index = 0; index < options.length; index++ ) {
        option = options[index];
        value = option.value;
        text = option.text.replace( / \(.*$/ , "" );
        if ( value == choice ) {
            text += " (Included)";
        } else {
            text += this.priceText(this.opticalCost[0][choice],
                                   this.opticalCost[0][value]);
        }
        option.text = text;
    }

    choice = parseInt($("optical1").value);
    options = $("optical1").options, option;
    for( index = 0; index < options.length; index++ ) {
        option = options[index];
        value = option.value;
        text = option.text.replace( / \(.*$/ , "" );
        if ( value == choice ) {
            text += " (Included)";
        } else {
            text += this.priceText(this.opticalCost[1][choice],
                                   this.opticalCost[1][value]);
        }
        option.text = text;
    }

    this.updateForm();
}

ConfigForm.prototype.showError = function ( error, groupName ) {
    if (error) {
        $setSpan(groupName + "_err", error);
        $(groupName + "_err_p").style.display = "block";
        return true;
    } else {
        $setSpan(groupName + "_err", "");
        $(groupName + "_err_p").style.display = "none";
        return false;
    }
}
```

Figure 17-9   The Product Configuration application (part 4 of 6)

On the last page of code for this file, the opticalValidate method validates the optical drive choices by checking to make sure that the first drive is the same as or better than the second drive. Then, if the second value is greater than 0 and the second drive is better than the first drive, this code assigns a message to the error variable. The condition in this if statement subtracts 1 from the value for the second drive because that drive has "None" as its first option. The last statement in this method calls the showError method and returns its result, which will be false if the error parameter that's passed to it doesn't contain a message.

After the opticalValidate method, the validateAll method calls all of the validation methods for the form. In this case, the opticalValidate method is the only validation method for the form, but this validateAll method could easily be extended for a form with more controls by adding more method calls. Then, if any of those methods returns a value of true, which indicates an invalid control, the validateAll method should return a value of true. As you will see, this method is called by the event handler for the Submit button of the form to determine whether or not the form should be submitted for processing.

The updatePrice method updates the cost of the total system and displays it on the page. To do that, it gets the selected options from the form. Then, it uses these choices as the indexes for the cost arrays. Next, it adds the cost of each option to the base cost of the system to get the total cost for the system. Finally, it displays the total in the <span> tag for the system cost.

The updateForm method calls the validateAll and updatePrice methods. This updates the error messages and system cost after an option in the form has been changed.

The reset method calls each of the event handlers for the controls to update the price text for each control. In addition, this method calls the updateForm method to update the error messages and total system cost.

The config_library.js file (continued)

```javascript
ConfigForm.prototype.opticalValidate = function () {
    var error;
    var groupName = "optical";
    var choice0 = parseInt($("optical0").value);
    var choice1 = parseInt($("optical1").value);
    if ( choice1 > 0 && (choice1 - 1) > choice0 ) {
        error =
            "First drive must be the same as or better than second drive.";
    }
    return this.showError( error, groupName );
}

ConfigForm.prototype.validateAll = function () {
    var error = false;
    error = this.opticalValidate();
    return error;
}

ConfigForm.prototype.updatePrice = function () {
    var proc = parseInt(getSelectedRadioButton("proc").value);
    var optical0 = parseInt($("optical0").value);
    var optical1 = parseInt($("optical1").value);

    var total = this.baseCost;
    total += this.processorCost[proc];
    total += this.opticalCost[0][optical0];
    total += this.opticalCost[1][optical1];

    $setSpan("system_cost", "$" + total.toFixed(2) );
}

ConfigForm.prototype.updateForm = function () {
    this.validateAll();
    this.updatePrice();
}

ConfigForm.prototype.reset = function () {
    this.processorClick();
    this.opticalChange();
    this.updateForm();
}
```

Figure 17-9   The Product Configuration application (part 5 of 6)

The config.js file

The config.js file initializes the Product Configuration application. To start, this file defines a global config variable that stores a reference to the ConfigForm object that controls the application. Then, this file defines an anonymous function that runs when the DOM is ready.

Within this anonymous function, the first statement defines a new ConfigForm object and stores it in the config variable. Then, this code defines four event handlers. The first two event handlers call one of the methods in the config object.

The third event handler is called when the user clicks on the reset button. To start, this function calls the reset method of the form element to reset the radio buttons and select lists to their initial values. Then, it calls the reset method of the config object to reset the pricing text for each option, the error messages for the form, and the system cost.

The fourth event handler is called when the user submits the form by activating the submit button. This event handler takes an event object as its parameter. Within this function, the first statement calls the validateAll method of the config object and stores the result in the error variable. Then, if the error variable is true, this code displays a dialog box that asks the user to fix the errors, and it calls the preventDefault method of the event object to prevent the form from being submitted.

After defining the four event handlers, the last eight statements in this function attach the event handlers to the events. Here, the first four statements attach the processorClick event handler to the click event of the four radio buttons for selecting a processor. The next two statements attach the opticalChange event handler to the change events of the select lists. And the last two statements attach the formReset and formSubmit event handlers to the click and submit events of the reset and submit buttons.

Note here that this application attaches the event handlers in the function that runs when the DOM is ready. In contrast, the other applications in this section attach the event handlers to their events with code that's in the object library. For example, the Table Sort application in this chapter attaches the event handlers within the library that creates the TableSort object.

Which approach is better? That depends on the application and your preferences. As always, your goals should be to use the approach that leads to the code that's easiest to read, debug, and maintain.

The config.js file

```
var config;

jsLib.dom.ready( function () {
    config = new ConfigForm();

    var processorClick = function () {
        config.processorClick();
    }
    var opticalChange = function () {
        config.opticalChange();
    }
    var formReset = function () {
        $("product_form").reset();
        config.reset();
    }
    var formSubmit = function (evt) {
        var error = config.validateAll();
        if (error) {
            alert("Please fix the errors before placing order.");
            evt.preventDefault();
        }
    }

    jsLib.event.add( $("proc0"), "click", processorClick );
    jsLib.event.add( $("proc1"), "click", processorClick );
    jsLib.event.add( $("proc2"), "click", processorClick );
    jsLib.event.add( $("proc3"), "click", processorClick );

    jsLib.event.add( $("optical0"), "change", opticalChange );
    jsLib.event.add( $("optical1"), "change", opticalChange );

    jsLib.event.add( $("config_reset"), "click", formReset );
    jsLib.event.add( $("product_form"), "submit", formSubmit );
});
```

Figure 17-9   The Product Configuration application (part 6 of 6)

Perspective

Now that you've learned how to script tables and forms, you have seen most of the common DOM scripting applications. You should also be able to apply the skills that you've learned in this section to other DOM scripting applications. And you should be able to use the applications that you've seen as models for your own code.

In the next chapter, though, you'll learn how to develop one other type of DOM scripting application. That is an application that provides animation.

Terms

node list

Exercise 17-1 Modify the Table Sort application

This exercise gives you a chance to script tables.

1. Use the Firefox browser to view the index.html file in the table_sort folder that's in the chapter 17 folder for exercises. Then, test this application to see how it works.

2. Use your text editor to open the index.html file and the JavaScript files for this application. Then, review this code. Note that the JavaScript files include the tablesort_library.js file described in this chapter.

3. Modify the tablesort_library.js file so it uses the deleteRow method instead of the removeChild method to remove the rows from the DOM in the sort method. Then, test this change with both Firefox and Internet Explorer. The application should work the same as it did before.

4. Modify the product_list.js file so it adds a fourth product to the table when the browser loads the application. For this product, use this data:

   ```
   MBT-6114        Fly Rod                 214.95
   ```

   To do that, you need to add the product to the table before you create the TableSort object. Then, test this change with both Firefox and Internet Explorer. *Hint:* You can use the className property of the cell node to specify the class attribute for the cell.

5. Modify the product_list.js file so it removes the first product from the table when the browser loads the application. Then, test this change with both Firefox and Internet Explorer.

Exercise 17-2 Modify the Product Configuration application

This exercise gives you a chance to script forms.

1. Use the Firefox browser to view the index.html file that's in the product_config_extended folder that's in the chapter 17 folder for exercises. Note that this application works like the shorter version of the Product Configuration application that was presented in this chapter.

2. Use your text editor to open the index.html file and the JavaScript files for this application. Then, review this code. Note how these files extend the Product Configuration application presented in this chapter.

3. Modify the config_library.js file so it includes the setSelectedRadioButton method described in figure 17-6.

4. Modify the config_library.js file so it automatically sets the Memory group to 4 MB if the user selects the Premium options from the Operating System group. Then, test this change. Make sure that this code updates the pricing text for the options in the Memory group.

18

Animation with DOM scripting

In this chapter, you'll learn how to use DOM scripting to animate elements on a web page. To start, you'll learn how to create 2-dimensional animations. Then, you'll learn how to create 3-dimensional animations like the Carousel application that's presented at the end of this chapter.

As you read this chapter, you'll soon realize that you're not learning new DOM scripting techniques. Instead, the focus is on the math and trigonometry that's required by applications that provide animation. As a result, this chapter will be easier for those who have a strong math and trigonometry background, and more difficult for those who don't. At the least, this chapter will give you a realistic view of the skills that are required for animation applications.

How to animate elements **634**
A review of the math used in animation 634
How to change the position of an element over time 636
How to detect boundaries 640
How to simulate depth 642

The Carousel application **644**
The image path in the carousel 644
The XHTML file 646
The CSS file 646
The carousel_library.js file 648
The carousel.js file 656

Perspective **658**

How to animate elements

This topic begins by showing how to update an XHTML element's position over time and how to detect when an image hits a boundary. These are the skills you need for 2-dimensional (2D) animations. Then, this topic shows how to simulate depth. This is the skill you need for 3-dimensional (3D) animations. But first, this topic reviews the mathematical concepts that you need for working with animations.

A review of the math used in animation

Figure 18-1 reviews some of the math that's required for animation. For instance, the first example shows how to calculate the distance traveled based on speed and time. Here, the first statement sets the speed to 90 pixels per second. Since most monitors use about 90 pixels per inch, this translates to about 1 inch per second. Then, the second statement sets the time to 0.1 seconds, and the third statement calculates the distance by multiplying the speed and time.

The second example shows how to calculate the distance between two points. To do that, it uses the formula for the sides of a right triangle ($a^2 + b^2 = c^2$) where c is the distance). As a result, this code gets the difference between the two x coordinates and the difference between the two y coordinates and uses the Math.pow function to square these differences. Then, this code adds these results together and uses the Math.sqrt function to get the square root of the result. Since the Math.sqrt function always returns the positive root, this calculation always returns a positive value regardless of which point is specified first.

The third example shows how to work with two directional systems: compass headings and radians. To start, the diagram shows the differences between the two systems. For compass headings, 0 points up, degrees increase clockwise, and there are 360 degrees in a full circle. For radians, 0 points right, radians increase counterclockwise, and there are 2pi radians in a full circle.

When working with animations, many programmers find it easier to think in the traditional degrees of a compass. However, the Math.sin and Math.cos methods are needed to work with animations, and these methods accept a parameter in radians. As a result, it's often necessary to convert between these two systems. To do that, you can use the compassToRadians and radiansToCompass methods presented in this figure.

The last example shows how to update a position based on a distance and a directional heading. To start, the first two statements specify a distance of 90 pixels and a heading of 145 degrees. Then, the next two statements specify a starting position with x and y coordinates of 100 and 150.

Next, this code calculates the amount of change to apply to the x and y coordinates. To do that, the fifth statement uses the Math.cos method to calculate the change in x (deltaX) as the distance times the cosine of the heading. Then, the sixth statement uses the Math.sin function to calculate the change in y

How to calculate distance over time

```
var speed = 90;              // pixels per second - about 1 in/s
var time  = 0.1;             // seconds
var distance = speed * time; // 9 pixels - about 0.1 inch
```

How to calculate the distance between two points

```
var x1 = 5;  // First point
var y1 = 7;
var x2 = 25; // Second point
var y2 = 36;
var distance = Math.sqrt(Math.pow(x2-x1, 2) + Math.pow(y2-y1, 2));
```

How to work with compass heading degrees and radians

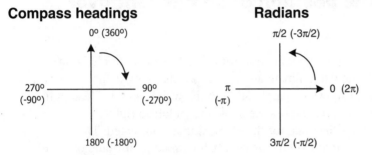

How to convert compass heading degrees to radians

```
var compassToRadians = function ( compass ) {
    var radians = ( 180 - compass - 90 ) * Math.PI / 180 % (2 * Math.PI);
    return ( radians < 0 ) ? radians + (2 * Math.PI) : radians;
}
alert( compassToRadians(0).toFixed(6) );      // 1.570796 or (π/2)
alert( compassToRadians(270).toFixed(6) );    // 3.141593 or (π)
alert( compassToRadians(-90).toFixed(6) );    // 3.141593 or (π)
```

How to convert radians to compass heading degrees

```
var radiansToCompass = function ( radians ) {
    var compass = ( 90 - ( radians * 180 / Math.PI ) ) % 360;
    return ( compass < 0 ) ? compass + 360 : compass;
}
alert( radiansToCompass(0) );                 //   90
alert( radiansToCompass( Math.PI ) );         //  270
alert( radiansToCompass( -3 * Math.PI / 2 ) ); //   0
```

How to update a position based on distance and heading

```
var distance = 90;            // 90 pixels
var heading  = 145;           // 145°
var x = 100;
var y = 150;
var deltaX = distance * Math.cos( compassToRadians(heading) );
var deltaY = distance * Math.sin( compassToRadians(heading) );
x = Math.round( x + deltaX );  // x is now 152
y = Math.round( y - deltaY );  // y is now 224
```

Figure 18-1   A review of the math used in animation

(deltaY) as the distance times the sine of the heading. For both of these statements, the compassToRadians method is used to convert compass degrees to radians.

Finally, this code updates the position by calculating the new position and updating the x and y variables. To start, the seventh statement updates the horizontal position by adding deltaX to x and rounding the result. Then, the eighth statement updates the vertical position by subtracting deltaY from y and rounding the result. Here, deltaY is subtracted instead of added because the y values for a computer screen increase downward instead of increasing upward as they do with traditional Cartesian coordinates.

How to change the position of an element over time

Figure 18-2 shows a simple application for a 2-dimensional application. This application shows how to animate an element by changing its position over time. To start, this figure shows the application in the web browser. This application moves an image of a fish across the screen from left to right.

The XHTML contains the code for the element that's animated. This element is an <img> tag for a PNG image of a fish with an id attribute of "fish". This application uses the PNG format, because this format lets you combine the 24-bit colors allowed in a JPEG image with the transparency normally found in a GIF image.

The CSS for the fish element sets the position property to absolute, the left property to 0, and the top property to 50. As a result, when the page is loaded, this image is positioned at the left edge of the page, 50 pixels from the top.

The JavaScript code in the animate.js file begins by including the compassToRadians function described in the previous figure.

The Animation application in the web browser

Mike's Bait and Tackle Shop

Welcome to Mike's Bait and Tackle Shop. We have all the gear you'll need to make your next fishing trip a great success!

Contact us by phone at 559-555-6624 to place your order today.

© 2009 Mike's Bait and Tackle Shop

The XHTML file (excerpt)

```
<link rel="stylesheet" type="text/css" href="main.css" />
<script type="text/javascript" src="jslib_css.js"></script>
<script type="text/javascript" src="jslib_event.js"></script>
<script type="text/javascript" src="jslib_event_mouse.js"></script>
<script type="text/javascript" src="jslib_event_keyboard.js"></script>
<script type="text/javascript" src="animate.js"></script>
...
<body>
    ...
    <img src="fish.png" id="fish" />
    ...
</body>
```

The CSS file (excerpt)

```
#fish {
    position: absolute;
    left: 0px;
    top: 50px;
}
```

The animate.js file

```
var compassToRadians = function ( compass ) {
    var radians = ( 180 - compass - 90 ) * Math.PI / 180 % (2 * Math.PI);
    return ( radians < 0 ) ? radians + (2 * Math.PI) : radians;
}

// continued on page 639
```

// continued on page 639

Figure 18-2   How to change the position of an element over time (part 1 of 2)

Next, this file defines the AnimationElement object. This object provides a method for getting the current position of the element that's being animated and a method for updating the position of that element.

The constructor for the AnimationElement object takes a reference to the element as its parameter. Then, it copies a reference to the element into a property named element.

The getPosition method returns the current position of the image. To do that, this method uses the getComputedStyle method that was described in chapter 16 to get the current position of the image. Then, it returns a simple object that has an x property that stores the image's horizontal position and a y property that stores the image's vertical position. For this method to work, the jslib_css.js library from chapter 16 must be loaded.

The updatePosition method takes two parameters: a distance parameter and a heading parameter. To start, this method gets the current position of the image. Then, it uses the techniques in figure 18-1 to calculate a new position for the image. Finally, it updates the position of the image by changing the left and top properties of the element's style.

After the AnimationElement object is defined, this file defines an ElementAnimator object that performs the animation. The constructor for this object takes two parameters: an AnimationElement object and a speed. Then, this constructor copies these parameters into the element and speed properties, and it sets the heading property to 90 degrees, which moves the element in a straight line to the right.

The onTimer method updates the position of the element. This method is used by the timer that's created by the play method that follows. To start, the onTimer method gets the current time in milliseconds and calculates the elapsed time since the last update. Then, the third statement updates the lastUpdate property to the current time. The fourth statement calculates the distance from the speed and the elapsed time. And the fifth statement updates the image's position by passing the distance and heading values to the updatePosition method of the AnimationElement object.

The play method starts the animation. Here, the second statement sets the initial value of the lastUpdate property. Then, the third statement uses the setInterval method to start a timer that calls the onTimer method every 50 milliseconds. In addition, this statement stores a reference to the timer in the timer property. Although this property isn't used by this application, this application could be enhanced so it uses this reference to stop the timer.

Last, this file contains code that uses the AnimationElement and ElementAnimator objects to start the animation. First, this code creates two global variables named fishElement and animator to hold the AnimationElement and ElementAnimator objects. Then, when the page is loaded, the first statement creates a new AnimationElement object for the fish element in the DOM, and the second statement creates a new ElementAnimator object to animate that element. The third statement starts the animation by calling the play method of the ElementAnimator object.

The animate.js file (continued)

```
/*********************************************
 * Define the AnimationElement object
 *********************************************/
var AnimationElement = function ( element ) {
    this.element = element;
}

AnimationElement.prototype.getPosition = function() {
    var style = getComputedStyle( this.element, null );
    return { x: parseInt( style.left ), y: parseInt( style.top ) };
}

AnimationElement.prototype.updatePosition = function ( distance, heading ) {
    var position = this.getPosition();
    var deltaX = distance * Math.cos( compassToRadians(heading) );
    var deltaY = distance * Math.sin( compassToRadians(heading) );
    var x = Math.round( position.x + deltaX );
    var y = Math.round( position.y - deltaY );
    this.element.style.left = x + "px";
    this.element.style.top  = y + "px";
}

/*********************************************
 * Define the ElementAnimator object
 *********************************************/
var ElementAnimator = function ( element, speed ) {
    this.element = element;
    this.speed = speed;
    this.heading = 90;
}

ElementAnimator.prototype.onTimer = function () {
    var now = new Date().getTime();
    var elapsedMS = now - this.lastUpdate;          // ms since last update
    this.lastUpdate = now;
    var distance = this.speed * elapsedMS / 1000;   // Convert ms to seconds
    this.element.updatePosition( distance, this.heading );
}

ElementAnimator.prototype.play = function() {
    var that = this;
    this.lastUpdate = new Date().getTime();
    this.timer = setInterval( function() { that.onTimer() }, 50 );
}

/*********************************************
 * Start the animation
 *********************************************/
var fishElement, animator;

jsLib.event.add( window, "load", function () {
    fishElement = new AnimationElement( document.getElementById("fish") );
    animator = new ElementAnimator( fishElement, 150 );
    animator.play();
});
```

Figure 18-2   How to change the position of an element over time (part 2 of 2)

How to detect boundaries

The application in the previous figure moves an element from the left side of the web page to the right. However, when the element reaches the right side of the page, the element moves off the screen. Now, figure 18-3 shows how to detect when an element reaches a boundary so you can the stop the element or change its direction so it doesn't move off screen.

The first example in this figure shows a function named getWindowSize that gets the width and height of the browser window. The code in this function adjusts for the differences in DOM and IE browsers by using the OR operator to use the right properties for each type of browser to get the height and width of the window. When the OR operator is used in this way, it doesn't just return true or false. Instead, if the value in the expression on its the left is "truthy," it returns that value. Otherwise, it returns the value of the expression on its right, which can be another logical expression.

As a result, this function uses the innerWidth and innerHeight properties of the window object to return the width and height for DOM browsers. But for IE browsers, it uses the clientWidth and clientHeight properties of either the document.documentElement object or the document.body object. If none of these properties are available, this function returns zeros.

The second example in this figure shows the isOutsideWindow method. This method can be added to the AnimationElement object in the previous figure to detect when the animation element attempts to move outside the browser window. To start, this method gets the size of the window and the position of the element. Then, it calculates the maximum values for the x and y coordinates as the width (or height) of the window minus the width (or height) of the element. Finally, if the element's x coordinate is less than zero or greater than the maximum value for the x coordinate, this method returns a true value. Or, if the image's y coordinate is less than zero or greater than the maximum value for the y coordinate, this method also returns a true value.

The third example shows the center method. This method can also be added to the AnimationElement object in the previous figure. It centers the animation element in the browser window. To start, this method gets the size of the window. Then, it calculates the new position of the image by subtracting half the image width (or height) from half the browser window width (or height). Finally, it moves the image to the new coordinates.

The fourth example shows the onTimer method. This method is a modified version of the onTimer method of the ElementAnimator object in the previous figure. The first five statements of this method are the same as before. After the fifth statement, though, this code uses the isOutsideWindow method to check whether the image is outside the browser window. If so, this code uses the center method to center the element. Then, this code uses the Math.random method to generate a random heading for the element. As a result, once the image moves out of the browser window, this code centers the element in the browser window and moves it in a randomly chosen direction.

A function that determines the size of the browser window

```
var getWindowSize = function () {
    var width =  window.innerWidth ||                      // DOM
                 document.documentElement.clientWidth ||   // IE
                 document.body.clientWidth || 0;           // IE or 0
    var height = window.innerHeight ||                     // DOM
                 document.documentElement.clientHeight ||  // IE
                 document.body.clientHeight || 0;          // IE or 0
    return { w: width, h: height };
}
```

Two methods for the modified AnimationElement object

A new method that checks if the element is outside the browser window

```
AnimationElement.prototype.isOutsideWindow = function () {
    var windowSize = getWindowSize();
    var position = this.getPosition();
    var maxX = windowSize.w - this.element.width;
    var maxY = windowSize.h - this.element.height;
    return position.x < 0 || position.x > maxX ||
           position.y < 0 || position.y > maxY;
}
```

A new method that centers the element in the browser window

```
AnimationElement.prototype.center = function () {
    var windowSize = getWindowSize();
    var x = Math.round( windowSize.w / 2 - this.element.width  / 2 );
    var y = Math.round( windowSize.h / 2 - this.element.height / 2 );

    this.element.style.left = x + "px";
    this.element.style.top  = y + "px";
}
```

A modified method of the ElementAnimator object

```
ElementAnimator.prototype.onTimer = function () {
    var now = new Date().getTime();
    var elapsedMS = now - this.lastUpdate;          // ms since last update
    this.lastUpdate = now;
    var distance = this.speed * elapsedMS / 1000;   // Convert ms to seconds
    this.element.updatePosition( distance, this.heading );

    if ( this.element.isOutsideWindow() ) {
        this.element.center();
        this.heading = Math.random() * 360;
    }
}
```

How the OR operator works in an assignment statement

* When you use the OR operator as in the getWindowSize function at the top of this figure, the expression doesn't return true or false. Instead, if the expression to the left of the OR operator is "truthy," the value of the expression is returned. Otherwise, the value of the expression on the right is returned.

Figure 18-3   How to detect boundaries

How to simulate depth

The skills presented in the previous two figures are useful for working with 2D animations. Now, figure 18-4 shows how to simulate depth, a skill that's needed for working with 3D animations.

To simulate depth, you need to consider two factors: size and layering. First, as an element moves away from the viewer, it should get smaller. To resize an element, you can set the height and width properties of the element's style.

Second, as an element moves towards the viewer, it should be displayed in front of other elements that are farther away. To control layering, you can set the zIndex property of an element's style. By default, an element that's displayed on a web page has a zIndex value of 1. However, you can give an element a higher or lower zIndex value to display it in front of or behind other elements. You can even give an element a negative zIndex value.

The first example in this figure shows how to update the constructor for the AnimationElement object of figure 18-2 so it provides for 3D animation. To do that, this constructor stores the width and height of the element that's passed to it in the properties named originalHeight and originalWidth.

The second example shows the setDepth method. You can add this method to the AnimationElement object of figure 18-2. Then, you can use it to set the depth of an element. To start, this method takes an integer parameter that specifies the depth of the object. Then, the first four statements set the maximum and minimum bounds for the depth value and for the scale variable that's used to calculate the size of the element.

The fifth statement stores the depth variable in the z variable. But first, it uses the Math.max and Math.min method to make sure the depth variable is within the maximum and minimum bounds. Then, the sixth statement calculates the scale and stores it in the scale variable. This works so the z variable and the scale variable are adjusted relative to one another. In this figure, for example, when the z variable is 100, the scale variable is 1. Conversely, when the z variable is 1, the scale variable is .05.

The last three statements set the style of the element. Here, the first statement sets the zIndex property. Then, the last two statements use the scale variable to calculate the width and height of the element, and they set the new width and height values in the width and height properties of the element's style.

The third example shows how to update the onTimer method of the ElementAnimator object so it works with depth. To start, this code decreases the depth property by 1. Then, it passes this property to the setDepth method. This decreases the zIndex property and the size of the element. Finally, when the element moves outside the browser window, this code sets the depth to a value of 100.

As a result, when this code runs, a centered element has a zIndex of 100 and is 100% of its original size. Then, as the element moves away from the center, the zIndex property and size of the element decrease. However, the element will always have a minimum zIndex property of 1 and a minimum size of 5% of its original size.

The AnimationElement constructor and its setDepth method

An updated constructor that stores the original height and width

```
var AnimationElement = function ( element ) {
    this.element = element;

    this.element.originalWidth = this.element.width;
    this.element.originalHeight = this.element.height;
}
```

A new method that sets the depth

```
AnimationElement.prototype.setDepth = function ( depth ) {
    var maxDepth = 100;
    var minDepth = 1;

    var maxScale = 1;
    var minScale = 0.05;

    var z = Math.max( minDepth, Math.min( maxDepth, depth ) );
    var scale = z / maxDepth * (maxScale - minScale ) + minScale;

    this.element.style.zIndex = z;
    this.element.width = parseInt( this.element.originalWidth * scale );
    this.element.height = parseInt( this.element.originalHeight * scale );
}
```

A modified onTimer method for the ElementAnimator object

```
ElementAnimator.prototype.onTimer = function () {
    var now = new Date().getTime();
    var elapsedMS = now - this.lastUpdate;              // ms since last update
    this.lastUpdate = now;
    var distance = this.speed * elapsedMS / 1000;  // Convert ms to seconds
    this.element.updatePosition( distance, this.heading );

    this.depth--;
    this.element.setDepth(this.depth);
    if ( this.element.isOutsideWindow() ) {
        this.element.center();
        this.heading = Math.random() * 360;
        this.depth = 100;
    }
}
```

Description

- To simulate depth in your animations, you need to consider both size and layering. As an element moves away from the viewer, it should get smaller. As an element moves toward the viewer, it should be displayed in front of elements that are farther away.

- To change the size of an element, you set the height and width properties of its style.

- To control the layering of an element, you set the zIndex property of its style. Then, elements with a higher zIndex value appear on top of other elements, elements with a lower zIndex value appear behind other other elements, and elements with zIndex value below 1 appear behind normal elements on the page. The default value is 1.

Figure 18-4   How to simulate depth

The Carousel application

This topic shows how to code a 3D Carousel application that takes a list of images and animates them along an elliptical path. Figure 18-5 shows this application in a browser as it displays five images. As these images approach the back of the ellipse, they become smaller and are displayed behind the other images. As they approach the front of the ellipse, they become larger and are displayed in front of the other images.

This application lets the user control the carousel with the mouse or the keyboard. For example, when the user moves the mouse over the carousel, the position of the mouse determines the speed and direction of the images. If the user positions the mouse in the "null zone" in the middle of the carousel, the carousel stops. Otherwise, the carousel spins to the left or right depending on the position of the mouse.

On the other hand, if the user wants to use the keyboard to control the carousel, the user can press the Ctrl-Left and Ctrl-Right keys to spin the carousel to the left or right. Or, the user can press Ctrl-Up and Ctrl-Down to tilt the ellipse that the images follow. Finally, the user can press the Escape key to pause the carousel.

Before you continue reading, it's a good idea to run the Carousel application. That way, you'll get a better idea of what the code is doing.

The image path in the carousel

The diagram in this figure shows the image path for the carousel. When the carousel starts, this application displays the first image at an angle of 0 degrees. Then, the application spaces the remaining images evenly around the ellipse.

Note that this path uses degrees that are similar to the compass heading degrees described in figure 18-1. However, for this image page, 0 degrees points to the right instead of pointing up. This makes it easier to convert from degrees to radians.

When the carousel starts, the images move counterclockwise around the ellipse. When an image reaches the back of the ellipse, it has an angle of 90 degrees. At this angle, the application gives the image a smaller zIndex property and size than the other images in the ellipse. Conversely, when an image reaches the front of the ellipse, the application gives the image a larger zIndex property and size.

To control the tilt of the ellipse, this application uses a parameter named aspect that can range from -0.75 to 0.75. This parameter adjusts the height of the ellipse. When the aspect is positive, the front of the ellipse is lower than the back. This creates the appearance of looking down at the images. When the aspect is negative, the front of the ellipse is higher than the back. This creates the appearance of looking up at the images. When the aspect is zero, the front and back of the ellipse are at the same height.

The 3D Carousel application in the web browser

The image path in the carousel

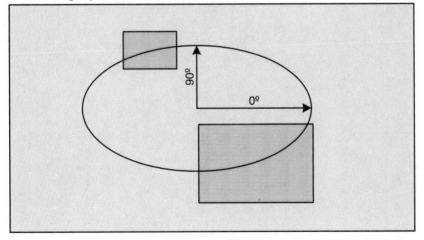

Figure 18-5   The user interface and image path for the Carousel application

The XHTML file

Figure 18-6 shows the XHTML file for the application. This file uses one CSS file and six JavaScript files. The first four JavaScript files were presented in the previous chapters so you should already understand how they work. The last two JavaScript files are in the next figure.

Within the body of this page, the <div> tag with the id attribute of "fishing_pics" contains the images that are displayed in the carousel. Here, the <img> tags are coded within <a> tags. Although these <a> tags don't have href attributes that go to new web pages, they could be coded that way. Then, when the user clicks on an image, a new page will be loaded.

The CSS file

This figure also shows the CSS code that's specific to the <div> tag for the carousel. To start, this code gives the element with the carousel class a black border and a light gray background. To do that, this code uses a color name of "lightGrey" with an "e" not an "a". That's because Internet Explorer only supports this color when it is spelled with an "e", even though both spellings are correct and are supported by other browsers. After setting the background color, this code removes the border from the <img> tags in the carousel. This removes the blue border that's often displayed around an image that's coded inside a link.

The XHTML file

```
<!DOCTYPE html PUBLIC "-//W3C//DTD XHTML 1.0 Transitional//EN"
    "http://www.w3.org/TR/xhtml1/DTD/xhtml1-transitional.dtd">
<html xmlns="http://www.w3.org/1999/xhtml">
<head>
<title>3D Carousel</title>
<link rel="stylesheet" type="text/css" href="carousel.css" />
<script type="text/javascript" src="jslib_css.js"></script>
<script type="text/javascript" src="jslib_event.js"></script>
<script type="text/javascript" src="jslib_event_mouse.js"></script>
<script type="text/javascript" src="jslib_event_keyboard.js"></script>
<script type="text/javascript" src="carousel_library.js"></script>
<script type="text/javascript" src="carousel.js"></script>
</head>

<body>
<div id="content">
    <h1 class="center">Mike's Bait and Tackle Shop</h1>
    <h2 class="center">Gallery of our Products in Use</h2>
    <div class="carousel" id="fishing_pics">
        <a href="#"><img src="images/casting1.jpg" alt="Casting 1" /></a>
        <a href="#"><img src="images/casting2.jpg" alt="Casting 2" /></a>
        <a href="#"><img src="images/catchrelease.jpg"
            alt="Catch and Release" /></a>
        <a href="#"><img src="images/fish.jpg" alt="Fish" /></a>
        <a href="#"><img src="images/lures.jpg" alt="Lures" /></a>
    </div>
    <ul class="instructions">
        <li>Use CTRL-Left and CTRL-Right or move the mouse over the
        carousel to spin the carousel.</li>
        <li>Use CTRL-Up and CTRL-Down to tilt the carousel view.</li>
        <li>Press ESC to pause/resume the carousel.</li>
    </ul>
</div>
</body>
</html>
```

The CSS file (excerpt)

```
.carousel {
    border: 1px solid black;
    background-color: lightGrey;
}

.carousel img {
    border: none;
}
```

Figure 18-6   The XHTML and CSS files for the Carousel application

The carousel_library.js file

The carousel_library.js file in figure 18-7 defines the ImageElement and Carousel objects that provide most of the functionality of this application.

To start, this code adds a method named sign to the Math object. This method returns a value of 1 if the value of the parameter is positive, -1 if the parameter is negative, and 0 if the parameter is zero. Later, this method is used by the updateImage method of the ImageElement object.

The ImageElement object controls the images in the carousel. Its constructor takes a reference to the carousel element and the image element as its two parameters. First, it stores references to these elements in the div and image properties of the object. Then, it stores the original height and width of the image as properties. Last, it sets the position of the image to absolute.

The getOriginalSize method of the ImageElement object returns a simple object with the width and height properties set to the original width and height of the image.

The updateImage method takes four parameters: a maximum image size, the image angle, the carousel aspect, and a minimum image size. Then, it updates the position of the image based on these values.

The first group of statements calculates the bounds for the image. Here, the maxWidth and maxHeight variables store the maximum size of the image. The centerX and centerY variables store the coordinates for the center of the carousel. The maxX and maxY variables store the farthest distances that the images are allowed to move from the center of the carousel. And the maxZ variable stores the maximum depth of the image.

Note that this group of statements defines the shape of the image path. To start, the maxHeight variable depends on the aspect parameter. More specifically, the maximum height of an image grows smaller as the absolute value of the aspect parameter grows larger. In turn, the maxY variable depends on the maxHeight variable. As a result, the vertical axis of the image path grows smaller as the absolute value of the aspect parameter grows larger.

The second group of statements calculates the 3D position of the image. Here, the angleRadians variable specifies the angle of the image after it has been converted from degrees to radians. Then, the deltaX and deltaY variables specify the change in the horizontal and vertical distance from the center of the carousel to the center of the image. And the deltaZ variable specifies the change in depth. This variable ranges from 1 to twice the maxZ variable.

The third group of statements calculates the image size based on its depth. The first statement calculates the scale variable based on the deltaZ variable and makes sure the calculated value is between the minSize parameter and 1. The next two statements calculate the width and height of the image by multiplying the maximum width and height values by the scale variable.

The fourth group of statements calculates the x and y coordinates for the image's position on the screen. And the fifth group of statements sets the position, zIndex, and size of the image to the values that were calculated earlier in this method.

The carousel_library.js file

```javascript
Math.sign = function (value) {
    if (value > 0) return 1;
    if (value < 0) return -1;
    return 0;
}

/***********************************************
 * Define the ImageElement object
 ***********************************************/
var ImageElement = function ( divNode, imageNode ) {
    this.div = divNode;
    this.image = imageNode;
    this.originalWidth = this.image.width;
    this.originalHeight = this.image.height;
    this.image.style.position = "absolute";
}

ImageElement.prototype.getOriginalSize = function () {
    return { width: this.originalWidth, height: this.originalHeight };
}

ImageElement.prototype.updateImage = function (
        maxSize, angle, aspect, minSize) {

    // 1. Calculate bounds for images
    var maxWidth = this.div.clientWidth / 2;
    var maxHeight = this.div.clientHeight * (1 - Math.abs(aspect));
    var centerX = jsLib.css.getOffsetLeft(this.div) + this.div.clientWidth/2;
    var centerY = jsLib.css.getOffsetTop(this.div) + this.div.clientHeight/2;
    var maxX = this.div.clientWidth / 2 - maxWidth / 2;
    var maxY = this.div.clientHeight / 2 - maxHeight / 2;
    var maxZ = 100;

    // 2. Calculate 3D position
    var angleRadians = angle * Math.PI / 180;
    var deltaX = Math.cos(angleRadians) * maxX;
    var deltaY = Math.sin(angleRadians) * maxY * Math.sign(aspect) * -1;
    var deltaZ = Math.sin(angleRadians) * maxZ * -1 + maxZ;

    // 3. Calculate image size
    var scale = (deltaZ / (maxZ * 2) ) * (1 - minSize) + minSize;
    var imageWidth = maxSize.width * scale;
    var imageHeight = maxSize.height * scale;

    // 4. Calculate image edge offset
    var x = centerX + deltaX - this.image.width / 2;
    var y = centerY + deltaY - this.image.height / 2;

    // 5. Apply size and position values
    this.image.style.left = Math.round(x) + "px";
    this.image.style.top  = Math.round(y) + "px";
    this.image.style.zIndex = Math.round(deltaZ);
    this.image.width = Math.round(imageWidth);
    this.image.height = Math.round(imageHeight);
}
```

Figure 18-7   The JavaScript files for the Carousel application (part 1 of 5)

The Carousel object controls the carousel. The constructor for this object takes two parameters. The first parameter is the id attribute of the div element for the carousel. The second is a simple object named options whose properties contain the optional parameters for the carousel.

The constructor for the Carousel object sets the properties for the carousel based on the properties that are stored in the options parameter. Here, the first group of statements creates an options object if necessary. This prevents unnecessary errors from occurring.

The second group of statements sets the height property for the carousel. To do that, this code checks whether the options parameter has a height property that stores a valid height. If it doesn't, this code sets the carousel's height to a default value of 400 pixels. Otherwise, this code sets the carousel's height to the height that's stored in the options variable with a minimum height of 50 pixels.

The next three groups of statements use similar techniques to set the maxAspect, minSize, and maxSpeed properties of the carousel. As a result, the maxAspect property has a default value of 0.5, a minimum value of 0, and a maximum value of 0.75. The minSize property has a default value of 0.15 (15%), a minimum value of 0.05 (5%), and a maximum value of 0.95 (95%). And the maxSpeed property has a default of 10, a minimum value of 1, and a maximum value of 45.

The sixth group of statements sets some internal properties and variables. Here, the first statement sets the initial value for the aspect property to 0.4 or to the maxAspect property depending on which value is smaller. The second statement sets the initial value for the speed property to the maxSpeed property. The third and fourth statements set the paused property to false and the angle property to 0. And the fifth statement stores a reference to the Carousel object in the variable named that.

The carousel_library.js file (continued)

```
/***********************************************
 * Define the Carousel object
 ***********************************************/
var Carousel = function(id, options) {
    // 1. If necessary, create the options object
    if (!options) options = {};

    // 2. Set default for height or get from options parameter
    if (isNaN(options.height)) {
        this.height = 400;
    } else {
        this.height = parseInt(options.height);
        this.height = Math.max(this.height, 50);
    }

    // 3. Set default for maxAspect or get from options parameter
    if (isNaN(options.maxAspect)) {
        this.maxAspect = 0.5;
    } else {
        this.maxAspect = parseFloat(options.maxAspect);
        this.maxAspect = Math.max(this.maxAspect, 0);
        this.maxAspect = Math.min(this.maxAspect, .75);
    }

    // 4. Set default for minSize or get from options parameter
    if (isNaN(options.minSize)) {
        this.minSize = 0.15;
    } else {
        this.minSize = parseFloat(options.minSize);
        this.minSize = Math.max(this.minSize, 0.05);
        this.minSize = Math.min(this.minSize, 0.95);
    }

    // 5. Set default for maxSpeed or get from options parameter
    if (isNaN(options.maxSpeed)) {
        this.maxSpeed = 10;
    } else {
        this.maxSpeed = parseFloat(options.maxSpeed);
        this.maxSpeed = Math.max(this.maxSpeed, 1);
        this.maxSpeed = Math.min(this.maxSpeed, 45);
    }

    // 6. Set internal properties and variables
    this.aspect = Math.min( this.maxAspect, 0.40 );
    this.speed = this.maxSpeed;
    this.paused = false;
    this.angle = 0;
    var that = this;
```

Figure 18-7   The JavaScript files for the Carousel application (part 2 of 5)

The seventh and eight groups of statements get the div element for the carousel and the image nodes from the div element.

The ninth group of statements creates a property named images that stores an array of ImageElement objects. Then, it loops through each image node. For each image node, this code creates an ImageElement object and adds that object to the array of ImageElement objects.

The tenth group of statements sets the height of the div element for the carousel.

The eleventh group of statements attaches two event handlers. First, it attaches the mousemoveHandler method that's defined later to the mousemove event of the carousel element. Then, it attaches the keydownHandler method that's defined later to the keydown event of the html element.

The last group of statements in the constructor starts the animation. Here, the first statement calls the onTimer method to move the images to their initial positions. Then, the second statement starts a timer that calls the onTimer method every 50 milliseconds, or 20 times per second.

The mousemoveHandler method updates the speed of the carousel when the user moves the mouse over the carousel. To start, the first group of statements calculates the size of a "null zone" in the middle of the carousel. When the user positions the mouse over this area, this application sets the speed to 0. The width of this zone depends on the maxSpeed property of the carousel. The nullMin and nullMax variables depend on the nullWidth variable and are used to center the null zone on the carousel element.

The second group of statements calculates the position of the mouse in percent distance across the carousel element. To start, the first statement gets the x coordinate for the carousel element. Then, the second statement sets the mousePct variable. For example, this code sets the mousePct variable to a value of 0 when the mouse is on the left edge of the carousel, 1 when the mouse is on the right edge, and 0.5 when the mouse is in the middle.

The carousel_library.js file (continued)

```
    // 7. Get div element from id param
    this.div = document.getElementById(id);

    // 8. Get image nodes
    var imgNodes = this.div.getElementsByTagName("img");

    // 9. Store image nodes in images property
    this.images = [];
    var imageNode, imageElement;
    for ( var i = 0; i < imgNodes.length; i++ ) {
        imageNode = imgNodes[i];
        imageElement = new ImageElement(this.div, imgNodes[i]);
        this.images.push( imageElement );
    }

    // 10. Set height of div element
    this.div.style.height = this.height + "px";

    // 11. Attach event handlers
    jsLib.event.add(this.div, "mousemove", function(evt) {
        that.mousemoveHandler(evt);
    });
    var htmlElement = document.getElementsByTagName("html")[0];
    jsLib.event.add(htmlElement, "keydown", function(evt) {
        that.keydownHandler(evt);
    });

    // 12. Start animation
    this.onTimer();
    setInterval( function() { that.onTimer(); }, 50 );
}

Carousel.prototype.mousemoveHandler = function (evt) {
    // 1. Set null zone width to stop carousel
    var nullWidth = 1 / (this.maxSpeed * 2 + 1);
    var nullMin = 0.5 - ( nullWidth / 2 );
    var nullMax = 0.5 + ( nullWidth / 2 );

    // 2. Determine mouse position in percent
    var baseX = jsLib.css.getOffsetLeft(this.div);
    var mousePct = (evt.clientX - baseX) /
        this.div.clientWidth;
```

Figure 18-7   The JavaScript files for the Carousel application (part 3 of 5)

The third group of statements set the speed of the carousel based on the mouse position. If the mouse is in the null zone, the speed is set to 0. If the mouse is to the left of the null zone, the speed is set to a negative value between 0 and the negative maximum speed. If the mouse is to the right of the null zone, the speed is set to a value between 0 and the maximum speed. Note that the speed for this application specifies the number of degrees per second. As a result, a faster speed causes the image to move faster around the image path.

The keydownHandler method updates the speed, aspect, or paused properties of the carousel depending on which key the user presses. If the user presses Ctrl-Up, this method adds 0.05 to the aspect property with a maximum value that's specified by the maxAspect property. If the user presses Ctrl-Down, this method subtracts 0.05 from the aspect property with a minimum value that's the negative maxAspect property.

If the user presses Ctrl-Right, this method sets the speed property to 70% of the maxSpeed variable and sets the paused property to false. If the user presses Ctrl-Left, this method sets the speed to 70% of the negative maxSpeed property and sets the paused property to false.

And if the user presses the Escape key, this method toggles the paused property. In other words, if the carousel is moving when the user presses the Escape key, this method stops the carousel. Or, if the carousel is stopped, this method starts the carousel.

The carousel_library.js file (continued)

```
    // 3. Set speed based on mouse position
    if ( mousePct > nullMin && mousePct < nullMax ) {
        this.speed = 0;
    } else if ( mousePct <= nullMin ) {
        this.speed = Math.floor(
            -this.maxSpeed * ((nullMin - mousePct) / nullMin)
        );
    } else {
        this.speed = Math.ceil(
            this.maxSpeed * ((mousePct - nullMax) / nullMin)
        );
    }
}

Carousel.prototype.keydownHandler = function (evt) {
    switch( evt.keyIdentifier ) {
        case "Up":      // CTRL-Up
            if ( evt.getModifierState("Ctrl") ) {
                this.aspect += 0.05;
                this.aspect = Math.min(this.aspect, this.maxAspect);
            }
            break;
        case "Down":    // CTRL-Down
            if ( evt.getModifierState("Ctrl") ) {
                this.aspect -= 0.05;
                this.aspect = Math.max(this.aspect, -this.maxAspect);
            }
            break;
        case "Right":   // CTRL-Right
            if ( evt.getModifierState("Ctrl") ) {
                this.speed = this.maxSpeed * 0.7;
                this.paused = false;
            }
            break;
        case "Left":    // CTRL-Left
            if ( evt.getModifierState("Ctrl") ) {
                this.speed = -this.maxSpeed * 0.7;
                this.paused = false;
            }
            break;
        case "U+001B":  // Escape key
            this.paused = !this.paused;
            break;
    }
}
```

Figure 18-7   The JavaScript files for the Carousel application (part 4 of 5)

The onTimer method updates the size and position of all the images in the carousel. The timer that's created by the constructor for the carousel calls the onTimer method every 50 milliseconds.

Within the onTimer method, the first group of statements checks to make sure the carousel isn't paused. If it isn't, the onTimer method updates the angle by adding the current speed.

The second group of statements finds the widest and tallest images. These values are used to calculate the image scale.

The third group of statements calculates the value for the scale variable. To do that, the first two statements calculate the maximum width and height available. Then, the third and fourth statements calculate the values for the scaleX and scaleY variables. These variables store the scale value needed to size the widest and tallest images so they fit within the maximum width and height. Next, the fifth statement gets the scale variable by getting the smallest value of the scaleX and scaleY values.

The fourth group of statements begins by looping through each image. Within the loop, these statements update the size and position of each image. To do that, this code gets the original image size and uses the scale variable to calculate a new size for the image. Then, this code calculates an angle offset and stores it in a variable named angleOffset. Next, this code adds the angle offset to the carousel angle and stores it in a variable named angle. The last statement calls the updateImage method of the ImageElement object to update the image's size and position.

The carousel.js file

The carousel.js file creates a Carousel object to control the images in the carousel. To start, this code defines a global variable named fishing_pics to store a reference to the Carousel object. Then, this code creates an anonymous function that runs when the page is loaded. For this application, the jsLib.dom.ready function isn't used because the images need to be loaded before the application runs. This will ensure that the application has access to the image sizes.

The anonymous function begins by creating an object named options and setting its height property to 500 and its maxSpeed property to 5. This causes the carousel to have a height of 500 pixels and a maximum speed of 5. Then, this anonymous function creates a new Carousel object by passing it two arguments. The first argument is a string that specifies the id attribute of the carousel element, and the second argument is an object that contains the optional parameters for the carousel. Once this code creates the Carousel object, the code in the constructor for this object causes the carousel to start automatically.

The carousel_library.js file (continued)

```javascript
Carousel.prototype.onTimer = function () {
    // 1. Update angle if not paused
    if ( ! this.paused ) {
        this.angle = (this.angle + this.speed) % 360;
        this.angle = (this.angle < 0 ) ? this.angle + 360 : this.angle;
    }

    // 2. Find tallest and widest image
    var largestWidth = -Infinity;
    var largestHeight = -Infinity;
    var i, imageSize;
    for (i in this.images ) {
        imageSize = this.images[i].getOriginalSize();
        largestWidth = Math.max( largestWidth, imageSize.width );
        largestHeight = Math.max( largestHeight,imageSize.height );
    }

    // 3. Calculate scale for images to fit in largest size
    var maxWidth = this.div.clientWidth / 2;
    var maxHeight = this.div.clientHeight * (1 - Math.abs(this.aspect));
    var scaleX = maxWidth / largestWidth;
    var scaleY = maxHeight / largestHeight;
    var scale = Math.min(scaleX, scaleY);

    // 4. Position and size images
    var angle, angleOffset;
    for (i in this.images) {
        // Calculate image size
        imageSize = this.images[i].getOriginalSize();
        imageSize.width *= scale;
        imageSize.height *= scale;

        // Calculate image angle
        angleOffset = 360 * ( i / this.images.length );
        angle = (this.angle + angleOffset) % 360;

        // Call updateImage method
        this.images[i].updateImage( imageSize, angle,
                                    this.aspect, this.minSize );
    }
}
```

The carousel.js file

```javascript
var fishing_pics;

jsLib.event.add( window, "load", function() {
    var options = {
        height: 500,
        maxSpeed: 5
    }
    fishing_pics = new Carousel("fishing_pics", options);
});
```

Figure 18-7   The JavaScript files for the Carousel application (part 5 of 5)

Perspective

In this chapter, you learned how to script the DOM to create 2D and 3D animations that can make your applications more engaging. But be careful not to overuse animation, because that's a common pitfall that applies to many web pages. In general, users quickly get tired of animations unless they serve a useful purpose.

If you had a hard time understanding the Carousel application, that's due to its math and trigonometric requirements. This illustrates that once you have learned all of the JavaScript and DOM scripting techniques of the first 17 chapters, the trick is applying them to applications like games and animations that have new levels of conceptual complexity.

Exercise 18-1   Modify the Animation application

This exercise gives you a chance to work with 2D and 3D animations as described in this chapter. Make sure to test your changes after each step.

1. Use your text editor to open the index.html and animate1.js files that are in the animate folder that's in the chapter 18 folder for exercises. Then, review this code and run the application. Note how the fish moves off the right side of the page.

2. Open the animate2.js file and review this code. Then, modify the index.html file so it uses this file instead of the animate1.js file and run the application. Note how the fish moves in a random direction and returns to the center of the page when it reaches the edge of the browser window.

3. Open the animate3.js file and review this code. Then, modify the index.html file so it uses this file and run the application. Note how the fish grows smaller as it moves away from the center of the page.

4. Modify the animate3.js file so the fish has a minimum size of 40% of its original size.

5. Modify the animate3.js file so the fish starts from halfway down the left edge of the screen. To do that, you can create a new method named left that positions the fish. Also, modify the code so that the fish moves directly to the right (a compass heading of 90 degrees) instead of moving in a random direction.

6. Modify this application so it creates a second fish that has a speed of 300 pixels per second. To do that, you'll need to modify the XHTML and CSS files for this application as well as the animate3.js file.

7. Modify this application so the first fish has a speed of 200 pixels per second. At this point, the larger fish should be displayed in front of the smaller fish when the two fish overlap, which creates the appearance of a third dimension.

Exercise 18-2   Modify the Carousel application

This exercise gives you a chance to modify the Carousel application described in this chapter.

1. View the index.html file in the carousel folder that's in the chapter 18 folder for exercises. Then, experiment with this application until you understand how to control it with both the mouse and the keyboard.

2. Use your text editor to open the index.html file, the carousel_library.js file, and the carousel.js file for this application. Then, review this code.

3. Modify the index.html file so it doesn't include <a> tags around the <img> tags. Then, test this change. The application should work the same as it did before.

4. Modify the carousel.js file so it doesn't pass an options object to the constructor for the Carousel object. Then, test this change. This carousel should use all of the default values for the optional parameters.

5. Modify the carousel.js file so it passes an options object to the constructor of the Carousel object that creates a carousel with these optional parameters:

```
height = 550
maxAspect = 0.3
minSize = 0.4
maxSpeed = 4
```

Then, test this change. If you want to experiment with these values, try other combinations until the carousel works the way you want it to.

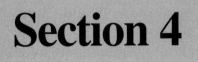

Section 4

Other JavaScript skills

To round out your JavaScript skills, this section presents two more chapters. Chapter 19 shows you how to control the browser by working with browser windows, browser objects, and cookies. Chapter 20 shows you how to use third-party libraries like jQuery and Dojo to add browser-compatible features to your applications with a minimum amount of code.

19

How to control the web browser

In this chapter, you'll learn how to use the browser objects to manipulate and print browser windows and to get information about the browser. You'll also learn how to use JavaScript to put cookies on a user's web browser and how to read and use those cookies.

How to script browser windows **664**
How to open and close windows 664
How to move and resize windows 666
How to scroll a window 668
How to print a window 670
How to use window events 672

How to script browser objects **674**
How to use the navigator object 674
How to use the location object 676
How to use the history object 678
How to use the screen object 680

How to use cookies **682**
An introduction to cookies 682
How to create cookies 684
How to read cookies 686
How to delete cookies 688

The Task List application **690**
The user interface 690
The XHTML file 690
The jslib_cookies.js file 692
The tasklist_library.js file 694
The tasklist.js file 694

Perspective **698**

How to script browser windows

In this topic, you'll learn how to use the methods and properties of the window object to control browser windows. Keep in mind, though, that if you overuse the window methods, you're likely to irritate some users. Also, most browsers provide options that let the user prevent the window methods from working so you can't be sure your methods are going to work.

How to open and close windows

Figure 19-1 shows how the open and close methods work. The open method loads a URL into a new or existing window. This is the method used to create pop-up ads. Because the use of these ads has been abused, most web browsers now include pop-up blockers. As a result, a window that is opened by the open method will most likely be blocked, unless you open the window in response to a user action such as clicking a button.

The open method takes one to four parameters and returns a reference to the window object of the new window. The first parameter specifies the URL to load in the new window. This works the same as the href attribute of an <a> tag.

The second parameter specifies the name of the target for the new window. If a window or frame with that name exists, the URL will be loaded into that window. If it doesn't exist, a new window will be created with that name.

When the predefined value _blank is used as the target parameter, the URL is opened in a new window or in a new tab of a tabbed browser. Whether a new window or new tab is used depends on the browser settings, and JavaScript can't be used to change them. Although there are three other predefined values that you can use for the target parameter (_self, _parent, and _top), they only apply to frames, and I recommend that you avoid the use of frames.

The third parameter of the open method is a comma-separated list of features for the new window, and the table in this figure describes several of these features. For features that control the presence or absence of browser controls (such as menubar and scrollbars), the feature can be enabled by specifying *feature*=yes or just including the feature name in the list. The feature can be disabled by specifying *feature*=no or not listing the feature name in the list. In the third example in this figure, the code first builds an array of features, then uses the join method of the array in the third parameter of the open method to create a comma-separated list of the features.

If a Firefox browser is set so new windows are loaded as tabs, you can force them to be new windows by providing one or more features in the third parameter. In Internet Explorer, however, if the user has new windows loaded as tabs, the features in the third parameter will be ignored and the new window will be opened in a new tab.

The close method closes a window. As the last example in this figure shows, the closed property of the window object can be used to detect whether a window has been closed. That way, you won't try to close a window that is already closed.

The syntax of the open and close methods of the window object

```
open( URL, target, features );
close();
```

Common window features

Feature	Description
resizable	Lets the user resize the window.
menubar	Displays the menu bar in the window.
location	Displays the location bar in the window.
toolbar	Displays the toolbar in the window.
status	Displays the status bar in the window.
scrollbars	Displays scrollbars in the window when needed.
height	Sets the height of the window in pixels.
width	Sets the width of the window in pixels.
top	Sets the distance in pixels from the top edge of the screen.
left	Sets the distance in pixels from the left edge of the screen.

One property of the window object

Property	Description
closed	Set to true when the window is closed.

Examples of the open and close methods

Open a URL in a new window or tab

```
open("http://www.murach.com", "_blank");
```

Open a URL in a new window or tab and store a reference to the window

```
var helpWin = open("/help/topic1.html", "_blank");
```

Open a new window and set its features

```
var features = [];
features.push("scrollbars", "menubar", "location", "toolbar");
features.push("status", "resizable", "height=400", "width=600");
var helpWin = open("/help/topic1.html ", "_blank", features.join(",") );
```

Close a window

```
if ( helpWin && !helpWin.closed ) { helpWin.close(); }
```

Description

- Pop-up blockers work by stopping the open method from working. To prevent that, you should only call the open method in response to a user event like a click event.

- The features parameter is a comma-separated list of features. If you use this parameter with Firefox, the URL will be opened in a new window, not a new tab. If you use this parameter with Internet Explorer and it's set for tabs, it will ignore this parameter.

- If you close a window that wasn't created by the open method, the users will have to confirm that they want the window closed.

Figure 19-1   How to open and close windows

How to move and resize windows

Figure 19-2 summarizes the methods that you can use to move or resize a window. These methods are illustrated by the examples in this figure.

The first set of examples shows how you can move a window. Here, the moveTo method moves a window to a specific position on the screen, and the moveBy method moves the window relative to its current position. If negative values are used for the right or down parameter of the MoveBy method, the window will move left and up.

The second set of examples shows how to resize a window. Here, the resizeTo method sets the window to a specific size, and the resizeBy method changes the size of the window relative to its current size. If negative values are used for the wider or taller parameter of the resizeBy method, the window will be made narrower or shorter.

To determine the left and top positions of the current window, you can use the window properties that are illustrated by the third set of examples. If the window.screenX property exists, its value is used for the left distance. If it doesn't exist, the window.screenLeft property is used. Likewise, either the window.screenY or window.screenRight property is used for the top distance. When you use both sets of properties, you avoid browser incompatibilities.

To determine the width and height of the current web page, you can use the clientWidth and clientHeight attributes of the body element in the web page. This is illustrated by the example. Here, the getElementsByTagName method of the document object is used to build an array of body elements. Then, the clientWidth and clientHeight attributes get the width and height for the first element in the array, which is the only body element.

Note that the width and height values are for the web page only so they don't include items like menu bars, status bars, or scroll bars. In Firefox, you can use the outerWidth and outerHeight properties of the window to get the same results, but since there is no equivalent in Internet Explorer that leads to browser incompatibilities.

Last, this figure shows a function that shakes the current window by moving it 10 times. To do that, the shakeWindow function uses closures (see figure 10-6 of chapter 10) to keep track of how many times the window has been moved. Within the shakeWindow function, the nested moveWindow function does the shaking.

In the nested moveWindow function, if the times variable is even, the distance variable is set to -5 pixels. If it's odd, the distance variable is set to 5 pixels. Then, the moveBy method moves the window left or right, and the times variable is reduced by one. If this variable is greater than zero, a timer is created to run the moveWindow method again 50 milliseconds later. After the moveWindow function is defined, it is called once by the outer function.

After the shakeWindow function, you can see a statement that calls this function. This statement creates a timer that calls the shakeWindow function after a three-second delay. In practice, of course, you wouldn't normally want to shake a user's window, but it might be okay for a special effect.

The syntax of the methods for moving and resizing a window

```
window.moveTo( left, top );
window.moveBy( right, down );
window.resizeTo( width, height );
window.resizeBy( wider, taller );
```

How to move a window

Move a window to the top, left corner of the screen

```
window.moveTo( 0, 0 );
```

Move a window left and down 10 pixels

```
window.moveBy( -10, 10 );
```

How to resize a window

Make a window 300 pixels wide and 200 pixels tall

```
window.resizeTo( 300, 200 );
```

Make a window 25 pixels wider and shorter

```
window.resizeBy( 25, -25 );
```

How to determine the position of the left and top window edges

```
var left = ( window.screenX ) ? window.screenX : window.screenLeft;
var top = ( window.screenY ) ? window.screenY : window.screenTop;
```

How to determine the visible width and height of a page

```
var width = document.getElementsByTagName("body")[0].clientWidth;
var height = document.getElementsByTagName("body")[0].clientHeight;
```

A shakeWindow function that shakes the current window

```
var shakeWindow = function () {
    var times = 10;
    var moveWindow = function () {
        var distance = ( times % 2 == 0 ) ? -5 : 5;
        window.moveBy ( distance, 0 );
        times-;
        if ( times > 0 ) {
            setTimeout( moveWindow, 50 );
        }
    }
    moveWindow();
}
```

A statement that calls the shakeWindow function

```
setTimeout( shakeWindow, 3000 );
```

Description

- Many web browsers let the user prevent a script from moving or resizing windows.
- Internet Explorer, Safari, and Opera support the screenLeft and ScreenTop properties that find the left and top edges of a window. Firefox and Safari support screenX and screenY.
- To determine the width and height of a page, you can use the clientWidth and clientHeight properties of the body tag.

Figure 19-2   How to move and resize windows

How to scroll a window

Figure 19-3 shows the two methods that JavaScript provides for scrolling a window. The scrollTo method lets you scroll a window to a specific point while the scrollBy method lest you scroll a window relative to its current position. If negative values are used for the right or down parameter of the scrollBy method, the window will scroll left or up.

To determine the overall height or width of a web page, you can use the scrollWidth and scrollHeight attributes of the body tag for a page as shown by the first set of examples. To determine the position of a specific element on the page, you can use the offsetTop and offsetLeft attributes of the element.

The next set of examples shows how to use the scrollTo and scrollBy methods. Here, the last example uses the offsetTop attribute to determine how far the footer element is from the top of the page. Then, it scrolls the window to that position.

The last example is a function named cyclePTags that highlights the paragraph tags in a page, one tag at a time. Here again, this function uses closures (see figure 10-6 in chapter 10) to keep track of the paragraph tags until they have all been highlighted. First, this function calls the getElementsByTagName method to get an array of all the tags in the page. Then, it initializes the counter named pIndex to 0.

Within the cyclePTags function, the nextPTag function performs three tasks. First, it returns the background color of the current paragraph to normal by storing an empty string in the backgroundColor attribute of the element's style. Second, it increments the pIndex counter so that counter points to the next paragraph tag. Third, if pIndex is less than the length of the pTags array, it sets the background color of the next paragraph to silver, uses the scrollTo method to scroll to that paragraph, and sets a timer to run the nextPTag function again after one second.

After the nextPTag function is defined, the cyclePTags function sets the background color of the first paragraph to silver and starts a timer to run the nextPTag function after a one second delay. Then, the nextPTag function runs until all of the other paragraph tags have been highlighted and scrolled to.

After the cyclePTags function, you can see the code that calls the function from the event handler for the onload event. This ensures that the page is loaded and the DOM is constructed before the first call to the getElementsByTagName function runs in the first line of the cyclePTags function.

The syntax of the scrollTo and scrollBy methods

```
window.scrollTo( left, top );
window.scrollBy( right, down );
```

How to determine the entire width and height of a page

```
var pageWidth = document.getElementsByTagName("body")[0].scrollWidth;
var pageHeight = document.getElementsByTagName("body")[0].scrollHeight;
```

How to determine the offset of an element in the page

```
var top = element.offsetTop;
var left = element.offsetLeft;
```

How to use the scrollTo and scrollBy methods

To scroll the window to the top of the page
```
window.scrollTo( 0, 0 );
```

To scroll the window to the middle of the page
```
window.scrollTo( 0, parseInt(pageHeight/2) );
```

To scroll the window to the bottom of the page
```
window.scrollTo( 0, pageHeight );
```

To scroll up 100 pixels
```
window.scrollBy( 0, -100 );
```

To scroll an element into view
```
var top = document.getElementById("footer").offsetTop;
window.scrollTo( 0, top );
```

A cyclePTags function that highlights all the p tags in a page

```
var cyclePTags = function () {
    var pTags = document.getElementsByTagName("p");
    var pIndex = 0;

    var nextPTag = function () {
        pTags[pIndex].style.backgroundColor = "";
        pIndex++;
        if ( pIndex < pTags.length ) {
            pTags[pIndex].style.backgroundColor = "silver";
            scrollTo( 0, pTags[pIndex].offsetTop );
            setTimeout( nextPTag, 1000 );
        }
    }

    pTags[pIndex].style.backgroundColor = "silver";
    setTimeout( nextPTag, 1000 );
}
```

A statement that calls the cyclePTags function from the onload event handler

```
window.onload = function() { cyclePTags(); }
```

Description

- Scrolling the window can be done to bring an element into view on the page.

Figure 19-3   How to scroll a window

How to print a window

To print a window, you use the print method of the window object. This method prints the current web page. This is typically done within an event handler for a print button in your application, and this is similar to printing a web page by using the File→Print command or clicking on the print button in the toolbar.

However, when you use JavaScript to print a window, you can control the way the page is printed by providing an alternate style sheet for printing. This is illustrated by the first example in figure 19-4. Here, the media attribute of the link tag is set to print so the style sheet named main_print will be used when the page is printed.

Within the style sheet, you can specify formatting for the XHTML elements that makes the content better for printing. You can also hide buttons and other elements that don't need to be printed.

Hiding a button is illustrated by the second set of examples in this figure. Here, in the XHTML for the page, the print button is defined with an id of btnPrint. Next, the CSS for the main_print style sheet sets the display property of the print button to none. This hides the button when the page is printed. Last, the JavaScript defines an event handler for the print button that calls the print method, and this event handler is attached to the button's onclick event by the onload event handler for the page.

The syntax of the print method

```
window.print();
```

How to specify a different style sheet for printing a web page

```
<link rel="stylesheet" type="text/css" href="tasklist.css" media="print" />
```

How to have a print button on the page disappear when printed

The XHTML for the button

```
<input type="button" value="Print" id="btnPrint" />
```

The CSS for the button in the main_print.css file

```
#btnPrint { display: none; }
```

The JavaScript for the button

```
var print_click = function () {
    window.print();
}
```

The code that sets the event handler for the print button

```
window.onload = function () {
    document.getElementById("btnPrint").onclick = print_click;
}
```

Description

- If you provide a print button in your application, you can use a separate style sheet for the printed version of the page. To do that, you set the media attribute of the style sheet to "print".

- The print style sheet can hide unnecessary elements, remove background images, and set a width for the document that is compatible with the width of the printer.

Figure 19-4   How to print a window

How to use window events

Besides the onload event that you're familiar with, you can use other window events. Five of these are summarized in figure 19-5. Each of these events represents an action that happens to the web page or to the web browser.

When the user leaves the web browser and switches to another application, the browser loses focus and the onblur event occurs. When the user returns to the web browser, the browser gains focus and the onfocus event occurs. In this figure, the first set of examples uses these events to set the background color to red when the user leaves the browser and to return the background color to normal when the user returns to the browser.

When the user leaves the current page, the onunload event occurs. In the second example in this figure, this event is used to display a "Thank you" message. Of course, you can also use this event for other actions.

When the user or JavaScript resizes the browser window, the onresize event occurs. This is illustrated by the third set of examples. Here, the update_size function is used to display the size of the window in a span tag whenever the size of the window changes. This function is called in the onload event handler so the size is displayed when the page is loaded. It's also called in the onresize event handler so the size is displayed whenever it is changed.

Last, this figure illustrates the use of the onerror event. This event is triggered whenever a JavaScript error occurs. In this example, the onerror event handler just displays a message. Then, the code retrieves the current date and tries to display it, but this causes an onerror event because the getFullYear method is spelled wrong.

Common window events

Event	Triggered when...
onfocus	...the browser window becomes the active window.
onblur	...the browser window loses focus.
onunload	...the user leaves the current web page.
onresize	...the browser window is resized.
onerror	...there is a JavaScript error.

Event handlers for the onblur and onfocus events

```
window.onblur = function () {
    document.documentElement.style.backgroundColor = "red";
}

window.onfocus = function () {
    document.documentElement.style.backgroundColor = "";
}
```

An event handler for the onunload event

```
window.onunload = function () {
    alert("Thank you for visiting.");
}
```

An event handler for the onresize event

An XHTML span tag that displays the window size

```
<p>Size: <span id="size"> </span></p>
```

A JavaScript function that updates the display

```
var update_size = function () {
    var width = document.getElementsByTagName("body")[0].clientWidth;
    var height = document.getElementsByTagName("body")[0].clientHeight;
    document.getElementById("size").firstChild.nodeValue =
        width + "x" + height;
}

window.onresize = update_size;
window.onload = function () { update_size(); }
```

An event handler for the onerror event

```
window.onerror = function () {
    alert("An unhandled error occurred.");
}

var today = new Date();
alert( today.getFullYeer() );  // Unhandled error triggers onerror event
```

Description

- The window events let you respond to common user actions and unhandled errors in your code.

Figure 19-5   How to use window events

How to script browser objects

There are four browser objects that comprise what is informally called the *Browser Object Model*, or *BOM*. Although there isn't any standard for the properties and methods of these objects, this topic presents a set of properties and methods that are common to all modern browsers.

How to use the navigator object

The navigator object provides information about the web browser as a program. It can also tell you if cookies (which you'll learn about in this chapter) and Java are enabled by the user. To do that, you use the properties and methods in figure 19-6.

One of the more interesting properties is the user agent string. This information is sent to every web server, and the third table in this figure presents some typical strings. In these strings, Internet Explorer 7 is identified as MSIE7.0, the Windows XP operating system is identified as Windows NT 5.1, and Windows Vista is identified at Windows NT 6.0. Also, Gecko is the render engine for Firefox, WebKit is the render engine for Safari, and Presto is the render engine for Opera.

For two reasons, though, I recommend that you shouldn't use the user agent string to detect which browser the user has. First, some browsers let the user change the user agent string. This was done because some web sites displayed an error message if you tried to view the site with something other than Internet Explorer.

Second, if you use the user agent string, you have to be constantly alert for new browsers and operating systems and new versions of existing ones. For example, the 64-bit version of Windows XP is identified as Windows NT 5.2 but can display any web page that the 32-bit version of Windows XP can. If you only detect versions 5.1 and 6.0 as valid, then you've excluded users of XP 64.

For these reasons, it's better to detect whether a browser has the features that you want to use, like JavaScript or cookies. This is a more reliable way to determine whether your code will work with the browser.

In the examples in this figure, you can see how you can use a function named $span to display browser information in a series of span tags. This can be useful if you're trying to figure out what the settings for a specific browser are.

Properties of the navigator object

Property	Description
appName	Name of the web browser.
appVersion	Version of the web browser.
platform	Identifies the user's operating system.
userAgent	Complex string that provides web browser details.
cookieEnabled	Boolean value set to true if cookies are enabled.

One method of the navigator object

Method	Description
javaEnabled()	Returns true if Java is available and enabled.

Typical user agent strings for browsers

Browser	User agent string
Internet Explorer 7	Mozilla/4.0 (compatible; MSIE 7.0; Windows NT 5.1)
Firefox 3.0.6 Firefox/3.0.6	Mozilla/5.0 (Windows; U; Windows NT 6.0; en-US; rv:1.9.0.6) Gecko/2009011913
Safari 3.1.1	Mozilla/5.0 (Windows; U; Windows NT 5.1; en-US) AppleWebKit/525.18 (KHTML, like Gecko) Version/3.1.1 Safari/525.17
Opera 9.60	Opera/9.60 (Windows NT 5.1; U; en) Presto/2.1.1

How to display the navigator information in span tags

```
var $span = function (span, text) {
    document.getElementById(span).firstChild.nodeValue = text;
}

window.onload = function () {
    $span("appname", navigator.appName);
    $span("codename", navigator.appCodeName);
    $span("version", navigator.appVersion);
    $span("platform", navigator.platform);
    $span("agent", navigator.userAgent);
    $span("java", ( navigator.javaEnabled() ) ? "Yes" : "No" );
    $span("cookies", ( navigator.cookieEnabled ) ? "Yes" : "No" );
}
```

Description

- The navigator object is one of the four objects of the *Browser Object Model* (*BOM*).

- The user agent string can't be trusted for many web browsers because it can be changed by the user. So it's better to check whether the feature that you want to use is present.

- The web site http://www.useragentstring.com will parse a user agent string and explain its components. This site also has a list of many of the user agent strings seen on the web.

- The web page http://msdn.microsoft.com/en-us/library/ms537503.aspx explains how a user agent string is generated in Internet Explorer.

Figure 19-6   How to use the navigator object

How to use the location object

The location object has properties and methods that parse the URL that's in the address bar of the browser. This is illustrated in figure 19-7, which starts with a URL that contains the six parts that can be parsed. This URL includes the parameters that are sent to the server along with the HTTP request. These parameters are taken from the fields within an XHTML form.

In the URL, these parameters start with the question mark after the URL address. These parameters consist of name/value pairs that are connected by equal signs. If more than one parameter is passed to the server, they are separated by ampersands. In this example, two parameters named first and last are sent to the server.

After the parameters, this URL contains an anchor name that starts with the # symbol. It represents an anchor (or bookmark) on the page that has been created by an <a> tag. Then, when the page is loaded, it is scrolled to the anchor.

With that as background, you can better understand what the eight location properties in the table in this figure represent. For example, the href property stores the entire URL. The host property stores a combination of the hostname and port properties. And the other six properties store parts of the URL.

Next, this figure summarizes two methods of the location object. The first method lets you reload the current page either from cache memory or from the server if the force parameter is set to true. The second method lets you load a new page while replacing the current page in the browser history.

The first example in this figure shows how to parse the parameters from the search property. After the question mark is removed from the search parameters, the query string is converted into an array of name/value pairs by splitting the search string on the ampersand. For instance, this would convert the search string in the URL at the top of this figure into an array of two elements with first=Ray as the first element and last=Harris as the second element.

Next, the code loops through the name/value pairs and separates each pair into an array that consists of the name and value by splitting the pair on the equal sign. Then, the name is used as the index for an associative array of parameters named params, and the value is stored in the array. However, before the value is stored, the decodeURIComponent function is used to convert any ASCII encoded characters to the actual characters. You'll learn more about this in figure 19-11.

At this point, the associative array can be used to retrieve a search parameter. To illustrate that, the last statement in this example retrieves and displays the value of the parameter named first.

The second example in this figure shows two ways to use the location object to load a new page in the browser. The third example shows you how to use the reload method to reload pages. And the fourth example shows how to use the replace method to load a new page.

When the replace method is used to load a new page, the current page in the URL history is overwritten. To illustrate, suppose the user first visits page1.html and then visits page2.html so page1 and page2 are in the browser's history list.

A URL with search parameters

```
http://www.murach.com:8181/javascript/location.html?first=Ray&last=Harris#result
```

Properties of the location object

Property	Description	Value in the URL above
href	The complete URL of the web page.	Complete URL
protocol	The protocol portion of the URL including the colon.	http:
hostname	The host name portion of the URL.	www.murach.com
port	The port number of the web server.	8181
host	The host name and port number.	www.murach.com:8181
path	The path to the web page.	/javascript/location.html
search	The query string from the URL.	?first=Ray&last=Harris
hash	The anchor name from the URL.	#result

Methods of the location object

Method	Description
reload(*force*)	Reloads the current webpage. If the parameter is set to true, the browser loads the page from the server rather than from cache memory.
replace(*url*)	Loads a new page in the browser and overwrites the current page in the history list.

How to parse the search parameters

```
var query = location.search.replace( "?", "" );
var params = [], nameValue;
query = query.split("&");
for ( i = 0; i <= query.length; i++ ) {
    nameValue = query[i].split("=");
    params[ nameValue[0] ] = decodeURIComponent(nameValue[1]);
}
alert( params["first"] );      // With the URL above, this displays "Ray"
```

How to load a new web page

```
location.href = "http://www.murach.com/javascript";
location = "http://www.murach.com/javascript";
```

How to reload a web page

```
location.reload();         // Reloads the current page from the cache or server
location.reload(true);     // Reloads the current page from the server only
```

How to load a new page and overwrite the current history page

```
location.replace("http://www.murach.com/catalog");
```

Description

- The properties of the location object let you examine different parts of the current URL, especially the search parameters.
- The methods of the location object give you greater control over how a new page is loaded into the browser.

Figure 19-7   How to use the location object

Then, if page2 uses the replace method to load page3.html, page3 will replace page2 in the history list. At that point, if the user clicks the browser's Back button, the user will go to page1.html instead of page2.html.

This is useful when a page checks to see whether a feature like cookies or Java is enabled and loads different pages depending on the result. To illustrate, suppose the index.html page uses the replace method to load main_cookies.html if cookies are enabled and main_nocookies.html if they aren't. Without the replace method, if the user clicks the Back button, the index.html page will be loaded again, and the user will end up back at one of the main pages. With the replace method, though, the index.html page won't be in the history list.

How to use the history object

The history object represents the user's history list of viewed web pages. However, because of privacy concerns, the amount of information you can get from the history object is limited. As a result, the properties and methods of the history object are limited as shown by figure 19-8.

For instance, the length property tells how many URLs there are in the history list. However, there's no way to find out at which position the current page is in the history list. As a result, you can't tell whether the current page is first, last, or somewhere in the middle of the history list.

Similarly, the methods shown in this figure are limited. Here, the back method is equivalent to clicking the Back button in the browser. The forward method is equivalent to clicking the Forward button. The go method with a numeric parameter lets you simulate multiple clicks of the Forward or Back button. And the go method with a substring parameter goes to the last URL in the history list that contains that substring.

One property of the history object

Property	Description
length	The number of URLs in the history object.

Methods of the history object

Method	Description
back()	Goes back one step in the URL history.
forward()	Goes forward one step in the URL history.
go(*position*)	Goes forward or back the specified number of steps in the URL history.
go(*substring*)	Goes to the most recent URL in the history that contains the substring.

How to use the back method

```
history.back();
```

How to use the forward method

```
history.forward();
```

How to use the go method

Go forward two URLs

```
history.go(2);
```

Go back three URLs

```
history.go(-3);
```

Go to the most recent URL that contains "google"

```
history.go("google");
```

Description

- The history object is an array that holds a history of the pages that have been loaded.
- There is no way to determine what the URLs in the history object are. You can only get the URL of the current page from the location object.
- Since there is no way to determine the position of the current URL in the history object, you can't find out if there are pages to go back or forward to.

Figure 19-8   How to use the history object

How to use the screen object

You can use the properties of screen object to get the dimensions of the user's screen. This can be useful when you're using the move or resize methods of the window object.

These properties are summarized in figure 19-9. Here, the availWidth and availHeight properties give the dimensions of the available space on the screen so it doesn't include the space used by features like toolbars or scrollbars.

For the colorDepth property, this figure shows some common values and the number of colors that can be displayed for each of those values. Today, most monitors have a color depth of 24 or 32, and only mobile web devices like cell phones and game consoles have a lower color depth.

The first example in the figure shows how to resize the window so it fills the screen. To that, it first calculates the location of the top and left edge of the available space on the screen and moves the window there. Then, it resizes the window to fill the available width and height.

Note here that the calculations for the top and left positions are approximations. They just subtract the available screen height and width from the full screen height and width and divide the differences by two. That will move the location of the window up and to the left, but it can't take into account where features like toolbars and scrollbars are located. This demonstrates the difficulties of adjusting the screen with JavaScript.

The second example shows how to resize the window to fill half the screen and center the window in the screen. To do that, it first retrieves the width and height of the screen. Then, it moves the browser to one-quarter the distance from the top and left edges, and it resizes the browser to one-half the height and width of the screen.

Properties of the screen object

Property	Description
width	The total width of the user's screen in pixels.
height	The total height of the user's screen in pixels.
availWidth	The available width of the user's screen in pixels.
availHeight	The available height of the user's screen in pixels.
colorDepth	The base-2 logarithm of the number of colors available.

Common values of the colorDepth property

colorDepth	Number of colors
8	256
16	65,536
24	16,777,216
32	16,777,216 with 256 levels of transparency

How to resize the window so it fills the screen

```
var top = parseInt( (screen.height - screen.availHeight) / 2 );
var left = parseInt( (screen.width - screen.availWidth) / 2 );
window.moveTo( left, top );
window.resizeTo( screen.availWidth, screen.availHeight );
```

How to resize the window so it fills half the screen

```
var w = screen.width;
var h = screen.height;
window.moveTo( parseInt(w/4), parseInt(h/4) );
window.resizeTo( parseInt(w/2), parseInt(h/2) );
```

Description

- The screen object gives you information about the user's screen.
- You can use the properties of the screen object with the resize and move methods to set the size and position of the browser window.
- Today, most screens have a color depth value of 24 or 32, but mobile devices have lower values.

Figure 19-9   How to use the screen object

How to use cookies

Cookies let a web server or web page store information in your browser and retrieve it when you request a new page. This concerns some web users because they've heard rumors that cookies can transmit viruses, steal passwords, and copy files from your hard drive. Although those rumors aren't true, it is true that the use cookies is often abused.

One of the common abuses is done by advertisers who use cookies to track the web sites you have visited. These cookies are called *third-party cookies* because they are sent from the advertisers, not the web sites you visit. To combat this abuse, modern web browsers let you block third-party cookies by changing browser options.

In this topic, you'll learn how to use cookies in a way that makes a web application work better for the user. In particular, you'll learn how to use cookies to save user data so the users won't have to re-enter that data the next time they use the application.

An introduction to cookies

A *cookie* is a short text string that is stored by the browser as a name/value pair. When you request a web page, the server can return a cookie as part of the HTTP response. If it does and the browser has cookies enabled, the web browser will store the cookie. Then, when you load another page from the server, the browser sends the cookie back to the server as part of the HTTP request. This process is illustrated in figure 19-10.

At the least, a cookie must start with a name and value pair that's connected by an equal sign. For instance, the first example in this figure pairs the cookie name email with the value joel@murach.com. This pair can then be followed by any of the attributes that are listed in the table. Note that these name/value pairs must be separated by semicolons and spaces.

If a cookie doesn't include a max-age attribute, it is called a *session cookie*. This type of cookie is deleted when the browser window is closed. But if a cookie includes a max-age attribute with a positive value, the cookie is a *persistent cookie* that will be stored by the web browser on the user's hard drive until the number of seconds in this attribute elapses. This is illustrated by the second example in this figure which sets the max-age attribute to 21 days (21 * 24 * 60 * 60 = 1,814,400 seconds).

Typically, the path attribute for a cookie is set to the root folder of the web site as shown in both examples. That way, every page in the web site will have access to the cookie.

Next, you're going to see how JavaScript can be used to create, read, and delete cookies. As far as the web browser is concerned, cookies created in JavaScript are treated the same as cookies received from the web server.

A browser usually gets a cookie as part of an HTTP response

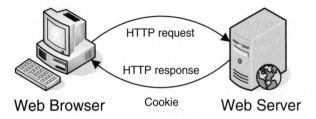

A browser sends the cookie back to the server with each HTTP request

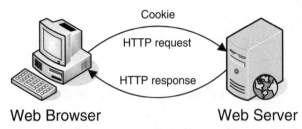

Attributes of a cookie

Attribute	Description
max-age	The lifetime of the cookie in seconds
path	The path on the web server that can see the cookie
domain	The domain names that can see the cookie
secure	If present, the cookie must be encrypted when it is transmitted, and it can only be transmitted when the browser and server are connected by HTTPS or another secure protocol.

Cookie examples

```
email=joel@murach.com; path=/
username=rharris; max-age=1814400; path=/
```

Description

- A *cookie* is a small text string that is stored by a web browser. A cookie consists of name/value pairs, and it must start with a name/value pair that names the cookie and provides a value for the cookie.

- The browser usually gets a cookie from a web server as part of an HTTP response. Then, the browser sends the cookie back to the server as part of each HTTP request.

- A *session cookie* is deleted when the web browser is closed.

- A *persistent cookie* is saved by the web browser after the browser is closed. This type of cookie has an expiration date that is after the current date.

- JavaScript can also be used to create, read, and delete cookies.

Figure 19-10   An introduction to cookies

How to create cookies

To work with cookies, JavaScript provides a special object called the document.cookie object, but it doesn't work like other JavaScript objects. Instead, to create a cookie, you first create a text string that represents the cookie. Then, you set the document.cookie object equal to the cookie's text string. This causes the browser to create and store the cookie.

This is illustrated by the examples in figure 19-11. To create a session cookie, the first example stores the name of the cookie (tasklist) and an equal sign in a variable named cookie. Then, it appends the value for the name/value pair to the cookie variable.

Note, however, that cookie values can't include semicolons, commas, or white space, but this value does. As a result, the encodeURIComponent function is used to encode the illegal characters so they can be used. For instance, the comma in this value will be converted to %2C. Later, when the cookie is retrieved, the decodeURIComponent function will be used to convert the data back to its original form.

The next statement in this example appends a path to the cookie string. This path is separated from the name and value by both a semicolon and a space. Then, the cookie string is assigned to the document.cookie object, which stores the cookie on the browser. Because this is a session cookie, though, it will be deleted when the browser is closed.

The second example in this figure creates a persistent cookie. This works like the first example, but it adds a max-age attribute to the cookie. This time, the cookie will be stored on the user's hard drive, but it will be deleted after 21 days.

The third example is a function named setCookie that can be used to add a cookie to the web page. This function takes up to three parameters with the first two required. The name is the name of the cookie, the value is the data for the cookie, and seconds is how many seconds should elapse until the cookie expires. If the seconds are omitted, a session cookie is created instead of a persistent cookie.

To start, the function checks to make sure that at least two arguments are passed to it. Next, it uses a regular expression to make sure that the cookie name doesn't contain any whitespace, commas, or semicolons. If the name is valid, a cookie string is created with the name/value pair that's retrieved from the name and value parameters. Then, if a valid seconds parameter is passed to the function, a max-age attribute is created and appended to the cookie string. Last, the path is added to the cookie, and the cookie is stored in the document.cookie object, which stores it on the user's browser.

After the code for the setCookie function, you can see two statements that use this function. The first one creates a session cookie with username=rharris as the name/value pair. The second creates a persistent cookie that lasts for 30 days (30 times the number of seconds in a day).

How to create a session cookie

```
var cookie = "tasklist" + "=";              // Create the cookie name
cookie +=                                    // Encode and add the data
    encodeURIComponent("Feed dog,Water plants");
cookie += "; path=/";                        // Add the path
document.cookie = cookie;                    // Store the cookie
```

How to create a persistent cookie

```
var cookie = "tasklist" + "=";              // Create the cookie name
cookie +=                                    // Encode and add the data
    encodeURIComponent("Feed dog,Water plants");

cookie += "; max-age=" + 21 * 24 * 60 * 60; // Add the max-age attribute

cookie += "; path=/";                        // Add the path for the cookie
document.cookie = cookie;                    // Store the cookie
```

A setCookie function that creates a cookie

```
jsLib.cookies.setCookie = function (name, value, seconds) {
    if ( arguments.length < 2 ) return;

    var name_pattern = /^[^\s,;]+$/;         // Exclude , ; and whitespace
    if ( !name_pattern.test(name) ) {
        alert("Invalid Name");
        return;
    }

    var cookie = name + "=" + encodeURIComponent(value);    // Add value
    if ( seconds !== undefined ) seconds = parseInt(seconds);
    if ( !isNaN(seconds) ) {
        cookie += "; max-age=" + seconds;                   // Add max-age
    }
    document.cookie = cookie + "; path=/";                  // Add path
}
```

Code that uses the setCookie function

```
// Setting a session cookie
jsLib.cookies.setCookie( "username", "rharris" );

// Setting a persistent cookie that expires in 30 days
jsLib.cookies.setCookie( "tasklist", "Feed dog,Water plants", 30 * 86400 );
```

Description

- Cookie values can't include semicolons, commas, or whitespace, but you can use the encodeURIComponent function to encode values that do include them.

- If you use the encodeURIComponent function to encode a value, you need to use the decodeURIComponent function to decode it when the cookie is retrieved.

Figure 19-11   How to create cookies

How to read cookies

Figure 19-12 shows how to read the cookies that have been stored on a browser. To start, note that more than one cookie can be stored in the document.cookie object. If so, the name/value pairs are separated by a semicolon and a space.

To parse the cookies in the document.cookie object, you can use a function like one in the first example. This parseCookies function extracts the cookies from the object and returns them as an associative array. To start, this function splits the cookie string into an array named raw_cookies using the semicolon and a space as the separator. Then, for each cookie in the raw_cookies array, the name/value pair is split at its equal sign into an array named cookie that contains two elements that store the name and value of the cookie.

Next, this function stores the cookie name in the name variable and the cookie value in the value variable. However, before the value is stored, the decodeURIComponent function is used to convert any encoded data to normal data. Then, this name/value pair is added to the cookies array using the name as the index of this associative array. When all of the name/value pairs in the raw_cookies array have been processed and the cookies have been added to the cookies array, the for loop ends and this function returns the cookies array.

The next example in this figure shows the code for a hasCookie function that tests whether a cookie exists. This function first uses the parseCookies function to retrieve the cookies. Then, it returns true if the cookies array has an element with the name that's passed to it as a parameter.

The third example in this figure shows the code for a getCookie function that returns the value of a cookie. This function first uses the parseCookies function to retrieve the cookies. Then, it returns the element from the cookies array that has the name that's passed to it as a parameter. If there isn't any cookie with that name, this function will return an undefined value.

Last, this figure presents an example that uses the hasCookie and getCookie functions. Here, an if statement tests whether a cookie named tasklist exists. If it does, the value of the cookie is displayed. If it doesn't exist, an error message is displayed.

Three cookies stored in the document.cookie object

```
username=rharris; status=active; tasklist=Feed dog%2CWater plants
```

A parseCookies function that extracts all cookies into an associative array

```javascript
jsLib.cookies.parseCookies = function () {
    var raw_cookies = document.cookie.split("; ");

    var cookies = [], cookie, name, value;

    for ( var i = 0; i < raw_cookies.length; i++ ) {
        cookie = raw_cookies[i].split("=");
        name = cookie[0];
        value = decodeURIComponent(cookie[1]);
        cookies[name] = value;
    }

    return cookies;
}
```

A hasCookie function that tests whether a cookie exists

```javascript
jsLib.cookies.hasCookie = function(name) {
    var cookies = jsLib.cookies.parseCookies();

    return cookies[name] !== undefined;
}
```

A getCookie function that gets a cookie from the browser

```javascript
jsLib.cookies.getCookie = function(name) {
    var cookies = jsLib.cookies.parseCookies();

    return cookies[name];
}
```

Code that gets a cookie by using the hasCookie and getCookie functions

```javascript
if ( jsLib.cookies.hasCookie("tasklist") ) {
    alert( jsLib.cookies.getCookie("tasklist") );
} else {
    alert( "No tasks in task list.");
}
```

Description

- The parseCookies function separates the data and values in the cookies and stores them in an associative array with the cookie name as the index for the array.

- The hasCookie function returns true if there is a cookie with the specified name.

- The getCookie function returns the data from the cookie with the specified name. If that cookie doesn't exist, it returns undefined as the value.

Figure 19-12   How to read cookies

How to delete cookies

To delete a cookie, you store the cookie a second time, but with a max-age attribute that has a value of zero. Although the value for the cookie can be empty, the other parts of the cookie such as the path and domain must be set the same as when the cookie was first created. If you try to change the path or domain of the cookie, your attempt to modify the cookie will be ignored.

Figure 19-13 shows how to delete a cookie. Here, the first example is the cookie to be deleted, and the second example is the code for deleting it. If you study the code for deleting a cookie, you'll see that the code is similar to the code for creating a persistent cookie, but with two differences. First, no data is supplied for the cookie. Second, the max-age attribute is set to zero. Then, when the updated cookie is stored in the document.cookies object, the cookie will be deleted.

The third example in this figure shows a deleteCookie function that deletes a cookie. It calls the setCookie function of figure 19-11 with the cookie name, an empty string for the data, and a zero value for the seconds parameter. This causes the cookie to be deleted. After this function, you can see a statement that calls it to delete the cookie named tasklist.

The cookie to delete

```
tasklist=Feed dog; max-age=1814400; path=/
```

How to delete a cookie

```
var cookie = "tasklist=";               // Set the name and data
cookie += "; max-age=" + 0;             // Set max-age to 0
cookie += "; path=/";                   // Set the path
document.cookie = cookie;               // Delete the cookie
```

A deleteCookie function that deletes a cookie

```
jsLib.cookies.deleteCookie = function (name) {
    jsLib.cookies.setCookie( name, "", 0 );
}
```

Code that deletes a cookie by using the deleteCookie function

```
jsLib.cookies.deleteCookie("tasklist");
```

Description

- To delete a cookie, you set its max-age attribute to 0.

- When you delete a cookie, the data must be empty, but the equal sign is still required. Also, the path and domain must match the path and domain that were used when the cookie was created.

- There is no way to determine the path and domain for a cookie once it has been created.

Figure 19-13   How to delete cookies

The Task List application

To show you how you can use cookies to make an application more useful, this chapter concludes by presenting a Task List application. This application saves the items in the task list in a persistent cookie. That way, the task list will be available to the user each time the user accesses the page.

The user interface

Figure 19-14 presents the user interface for this application, which is similar to applications that you've seen before. In short, the three buttons let the user add, edit, and delete tasks, and the task list is displayed in the text area.

The difference is that the task list is stored in a cookie. Then, if the cookie exists when the user starts the application, the contents of the cookie are used to display the task list. Note, however, that the task list items are stored on the user's computer, not in a database on the server. So, if the user switches to a different computer, the task list items won't be available.

The XHTML file

This figure also presents the XHTML file for the Task List application. This application uses one CSS file, which isn't shown, and three JavaScript files. The JavaScript files consist of a library file for handling cookies, a library file that consists of the objects, properties, and methods that are needed by this application, and a file that handles the user actions for this application.

The Task List application in the browser

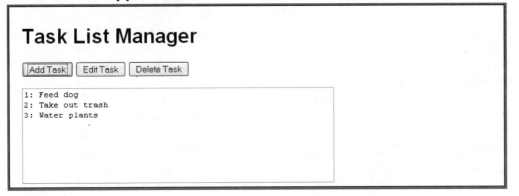

The XHTML file

```
<!DOCTYPE html PUBLIC "-//W3C//DTD XHTML 1.0 Transitional//EN"
    "http://www.w3.org/TR/xhtml1/DTD/xhtml1-transitional.dtd">
<html xmlns="http://www.w3.org/1999/xhtml">
<head>
<title>Task List Manager</title>
<link rel="stylesheet" type="text/css" href="tasklist.css" />
<script type="text/javascript" src="jslib_cookies.js"></script>
<script type="text/javascript" src="tasklist_library.js"></script>
<script type="text/javascript" src="tasklist.js"></script>
</head>

<body>
<div id="content">
    <h1>Task List Manager</h1>
    <p><input type="button" name="add_task" id="add_task"
        value="Add Task" />
    <input type="button" name="edit_task" id="edit_task"
        value="Edit Task" />
    <input type="button" name="delete_task" id="delete_task"
        value="Delete Task" />
    </p>
    <textarea rows="8" cols="60" id="task_list"></textarea>
</div>
</body>
</html>
```

Figure 19-14   The user interface and XHTML for the Task List application

The jslib_cookies.js file

Figure 19-15 presents the jslib_cookies.js file for this application. This file contains the library of the functions that work with cookies. Since all of these functions have been presented earlier in this chapter, I won't describe them now. But you should note how the first two statements in this file work.

The first statement creates a jsLib object if one doesn't already exist. The second statement creates a jsLib.cookies object if one doesn't already exist. Then, the statements that follow store the functions in the jsLib.cookies object. By storing the functions in this way, the functions are either stored in an existing object named jsLib or a new object named jsLib. This means that two different libraries can use an object named jsLib without any conflicts.

Incidentally, when you store the functions in the jsLib.cookies object, those functions become methods. In this chapter, though, we'll continue to refer to them as functions.

The jslib_cookies.js file

```javascript
if ( ! jsLib ) var jsLib = {};
if ( ! jsLib.cookies ) jsLib.cookies = {};

jsLib.cookies.setCookie = function (name, value, seconds) {
    if ( arguments.length < 2 ) return;
    var name_pattern = /^[^\s,;]+$/;
    if ( !name_pattern.test(name) ) {
        alert("Invalid Name");
        return;
    }
    var cookie = name + "=" + encodeURIComponent(value);
    if ( seconds !== undefined ) seconds = parseInt(seconds);
    if ( !isNaN(seconds) ) {
        cookie += "; max-age=" + seconds;
    }
    document.cookie = cookie + "; path=/";
}

jsLib.cookies.parseCookies = function () {
    var raw_cookies = document.cookie.split("; ");
    var cookies = [], cookie, name, value;
    for ( var i = 0; i < raw_cookies.length; i++ ) {
        cookie = raw_cookies[i].split("=");
        name = cookie[0];
        value = decodeURIComponent(cookie[1]);
        cookies[name] = value;
    }
    return cookies;
}

jsLib.cookies.hasCookie = function(name) {
    var cookies = jsLib.cookies.parseCookies();
    return cookies[name] !== undefined;
}

jsLib.cookies.getCookie = function(name) {
    var cookies = jsLib.cookies.parseCookies();
    return cookies[name];
}

jsLib.cookies.deleteCookie = function (name) {
    jsLib.cookies.setCookie( name, "", 0 );
}
```

Figure 19-15   The cookies library for the Task List application

The tasklist_library.js file

Figure 19-16 presents the rest of the JavaScript code for this application. Here, the tasklist_library.js file defines the TaskList object and its associated methods. This object will be used to store the tasks while the application is running. It also provides methods to retrieve the task list and add, edit, or delete tasks.

This file starts with the TaskList constructor function that's used to initialize the task list. It has one optional parameter that provides an array of tasks. If the tasks array is passed to the constructor, the elements of the array are converted to strings and stored in the internal task list. If this array isn't passed, the task list will start empty.

This constructor is followed by seven methods that you should be able to follow without much trouble. For instance, the hasTasks method determines whether the task list contains any tasks. The validIndex method determines whether the index that's passed to it is valid. The getList method returns the tasks in a formatted text string so it can be displayed in the text area. And the getCookieList method returns the tasks formatted as a comma-separated list that can be used with the setCookie method.

The tasklist.js file

The tasklist.js file provides the event handlers that control the user interface. It also provides the code that loads the task list from the tasklist cookie if it exists when the application starts.

To start, this file defines the standard $ function and an array named tasks. Then, if the tasklist cookie exists, the cookie is retrieved and split into an array of tasks named raw_tasks. Next, each of the tasks in that array is decoded and added to the array named tasks. Finally, the tasks variable is used to initialize a new TaskList object named list. If the tasks variable is undefined because no cookie exists, the list object will also be empty.

This initialization code is followed by a display_list function that updates the text area and the cookie. To do that, it first uses the getList method of the TaskList object named list to display the task list in the text area. Then, if the list has tasks, it uses the getCookieList method of the list object to get the comma-separated list of tasks, and it uses the setCookie method to create or update the tasklist cookie. If the list doesn't have any tasks, this method deletes the tasklist cookie.

This display_list method is followed by four event handlers that end with calls to the display_list method. Since you've seen methods like this several times before, you shouldn't have any trouble following them.

The tasklist_library.js file

```javascript
var TaskList = function (tasks) {
    this.list = [];
    if ( tasks instanceof Array ) {
        for ( var i in tasks ) {
            this.list[this.list.length] = tasks[i].toString();
        }
    }
}

TaskList.prototype.hasTasks = function () {
    return this.list.length > 0;
}

TaskList.prototype.validIndex = function (index) {
    index = parseInt(index);
    if ( isNaN(index) ) {
        alert("You did not enter a number.");
        return false;
    } else if ( index < 0 ) {
        alert("The task number is too low.");
        return false;
    } else if ( index >= this.list.length ) {
        alert("The task number is too high.");
        return false;
    } else {
        return true;
    }
}

TaskList.prototype.getList = function () {
    var tasks;
    if ( this.list.length == 0 ) {
        tasks = "There are no items in the task list.";
    } else {
        tasks = "";
        for ( var i in this.list ) {
            tasks += (parseInt(i)+1) + ": " + this.list[i] + "\n";
        }
    }
    return tasks;
}

TaskList.prototype.getCookieList = function () {
    var tasks = [];
    for ( var index in this.list ) {
        tasks.push( encodeURIComponent(this.list[index]) );
    }
    return tasks.join(",");
}

TaskList.prototype.addTask = function(task) {
    this.list.push( task );
}
```

Figure 19-16   The other JavaScript files for the Task List application (part 1 of 3)

The tasklist_library.js file

```javascript
TaskList.prototype.editTask = function(index, task) {
    if ( this.validIndex(index) ) {
        this.list[index] = task;
    }
}

TaskList.prototype.deleteTask = function(index) {
    if ( this.validIndex(index) ) {
        this.list.splice(index, 1);
    }
}
```

The tasklist.js file

```javascript
var $ = function (id) { return document.getElementById(id); }

var tasks;
if ( jsLib.cookies.hasCookie("tasklist") ) {
    var raw_tasks = jsLib.cookies.getCookie("tasklist").split(",");
    tasks = [];
    for ( var i in raw_tasks ) {
        tasks.push( decodeURIComponent(raw_tasks[i]) );
    }
}

var list = new TaskList(tasks);

var display_list = function () {
    $("task_list").value = list.getList();
    if ( list.hasTasks() ) {
        var tasks = list.getCookieList();
        jsLib.cookies.setCookie("tasklist", tasks, 365 * 86400);
    } else {
        jsLib.cookies.deleteCookie("tasklist");
    }
}

var add_task_click = function () {
    var task = prompt("Enter a task:");
    if ( task != "" ) {
        list.addTask(task);
    }
    display_list();
}

var delete_task_click = function () {
    if ( list.hasTasks() ) {
        var index = parseInt( prompt("Enter the task number to delete:") );
        index--;
        list.deleteTask(index);
        display_list();
    }
}
```

Figure 19-16   The other JavaScript files for the Task List application (part 2 of 3)

The tasklist.js file   **Page 2**

```javascript
var edit_task_click = function () {
    if ( list.hasTasks() ) {
        var index = parseInt( prompt("Enter the task number to edit:") );
        index--;
        if ( list.validIndex(index) ) {
            var task = prompt("Enter update for task " + (index+1) );
            if ( task != "" ) {
                list.editTask(index, task);
                display_list();
            }
        }
    }
}

window.onload = function() {
    $("add_task").onclick = add_task_click;
    $("edit_task").onclick = edit_task_click;
    $("delete_task").onclick = delete_task_click;
    display_list();
}
```

Figure 19-16   The other JavaScript files for the Task List application (part 3 of 3)

Perspective

Now that you've finished this chapter, you have all the skills that you need to work with browser windows and cookies. But please remember that the window methods may be disabled by the browser and can be an annoyance so they shouldn't be misused. Also, remember that cookies aren't secure so you shouldn't store personal information or passwords in them.

Terms

Browser Object Model (BOM)
cookie
session cookie
persistent cookie
third-party cookie

Exercise 19-1   Enhance the Task List application

In this exercise, you'll enhance the Task List application that was presented in this chapter. This will give you a chance to work with windows and cookies.

Open and test the Task List application

1. From your Firefox browser, open the index.html file in the task_list folder that's in the chapter 19 folder for exercises. Notice that this web page now provides Print List and Go To buttons.

2. Test this application, but ignore the Print and Go To buttons because they haven't been implemented. After you add a few tasks to the list, close the browser and reopen it to see that the task list has been retained.

3. Use your text editor to open all of the files for this application, and notice that there are six files: an HTML file, two CSS files, and three JavaScript files.

Work with windows

4. Implement the Go To button so a new window or tab is opened when the button is clicked. This window should display the page at www.murach.com. When you test this with Firefox, the URL will be opened in a new tab.

5. Modify the open method that you used for the Go To button so it provides for four features: a menubar, a toolbar, a height of 400, and a width of 800. Note that you don't have to use an array to set these features as in figure 19-1. When you test this with Firefox, the URL will be opened in a new window.

6. Enhance this application so it uses the code in figure 19-9 to resize the window so it fills the screen when the application is loaded. Test this by manually reducing the size of the window and then reloading the page. Note that this could be useful for some applications.

7. Enhance this application so it also resizes the window to fill the screen when the onresize event occurs. Then, test this and note how irritating this could be.

8. Implement the Print button so it prints the task list, but doesn't print the buttons. To do this, you need to change the XHTML file and the CSS file for printing as shown in figure 19-4. Then, you need to implement the event handler for the Print button.

9. When the application is loaded, display the browser settings for Java and cookies to see whether they're enabled.

Work with cookies

10. Create a cookie named timesused that keeps track of the number of times the user has loaded the page. Then, display a message like "Number of visits to our site: 6. Thanks!" when the application starts. To implement this, of course, you must increment the counter each time the user loads the application.

11. Create a new function in the cookies library named displayCookies that displays all of the cookies for this page with one line per cookie in this format:

    ```
    tasklist = Feed dog,Water plants
    ```

    Then, call this function from the onload event handler so it displays the cookies when the application starts. Be sure to use the decodeURIComponent function to convert the encoded values to normal characters.

12. Test this application with Internet Explorer to see if everything works the same. At the least, you'll see that the times used value starts at 1. This shows that each browser has its own cookies.

20

How to use JavaScript libraries

In prior chapters, you've learned how to create and use your own libraries. But now, you'll learn how to use JavaScript libraries that are available from other sources. Many of these are free libraries that provide features that can help you develop complex applications more efficiently.

In this chapter, you'll learn how to use two of these libraries: jQuery and Dojo. These libraries provide features that help you select and modify XHTML elements, apply special effects, and manipulate the DOM. In addition, Dojo has an extension called Dijits that provides enhanced controls that help you validate user entries.

How to use jQuery **702**
How to get started with jQuery 702
How to select elements with jQuery 704
How to use jQuery effects 706
How to handle events with jQuery 708
How to use jQuery to work with XHTML elements 710
How to use jQuery to work with the DOM 712

How to use Dojo **714**
How to get started with Dojo 714
How to select elements with Dojo 716
How to handle events with Dojo 718
How to use Dojo effects 720

How to use Dijits **722**
How to get started with Dijits 722
How to use the Form Dijit 724
How to use the Button Dijit 724
How to use the CheckBox Dijit 726
How to use the RadioButton Dijit 726
How to use the ValidationTextBox Dijit 728
How to validate a credit card with ValidationTextBox Dijits 730
How to use the FilteringSelect Dijit 732

The Register application **734**
The XHTML 734
The JavaScript 738

Perspective **742**

How to use jQuery

The jQuery library was developed by John Resig to make it easier to modify documents, handle events, and apply effects and animations. This library is designed to work with all modern web browsers, and it is free, open-source software. In the pages that follow, you'll learn some basic skills that will help you decide whether you would like to use it. Then, you can read more about it at http://www.jquery.com.

How to get started with jQuery

Figure 20-1 shows you how to get started with jQuery. First, you need to load jQuery in your application. To do that, you can download jQuery to your web server and then load it from the server. Or, you can load jQuery from the Google Code web site. Then, if a new version of jQuery is released, you just need to change the version number in the URL.

Once jQuery is loaded, you can use either of two global objects to refer to the library. The jQuery object is the primary reference to the library, and the $ object is a shortcut to the library. Unfortunately, the $ shortcut creates a problem if you use the $ variable in your own JavaScript files, but jQuery provides two solutions to this problem. These are shown next in this figure.

In both solutions, you must make sure that you load jQuery last. Then, in the first solution, you just call the jQuery.noConflict method. This restores your $ object to its original state. Then, you use only the jQuery object to access the jQuery functions. In the second solution, since the jQuery.noConflict method returns a reference to the jQuery object, you call it and store the reference in a new shortcut variable. In this example, $jq is used as the new variable that you can use to refer to jQuery.

In the rest of this chapter, though, I'll use $ as the shortcut for jQuery, as if there is no conflict with other JavaScript files. That will help make the examples easier to read.

Once you've loaded jQuery and resolved any $ conflict, you can use the ready method to run a function as soon as the DOM is ready. This is illustrated by the last example in this figure, and this is similar to using an event handler for the window.onload event. The difference is that the ready method doesn't wait for media elements such as images to be loaded before executing the function that's coded as a parameter. This lets the application become active as soon as the DOM is ready without having to wait for large images and graphics to be loaded.

One of the features that jQuery offers is called *implicit iteration*. This means that after you use jQuery to select two or more XHTML elements, you can call a jQuery method that applies to all of them. In other words, you don't have to use a for loop to apply the method to each element. You'll see this illustrated in the next two figures.

Where to get information about the jQuery library

```
http://www.jquery.com
```

Where to download the jQuery library

```
http://code.google.com/p/jqueryjs/downloads/list
```

How to include the jQuery library in an application

From a local file

```
<script type="text/javascript" src="jquery.js"></script>
```

From the Google Code web site

```
<script type="text/javascript"
    src="http://jqueryjs.googlecode.com/files/jquery-1.3.2.min.js"></script>
```

Two objects that refer to the jQuery library

Object	Description
jQuery	Main object for the jQuery library
$	Shortcut object for the jQuery library

How to avoid conflicts with other libraries that use the $ variable

Load jQuery last when you're using two or more libraries with $ variables

```
<script type="text/javascript" src="other_library.js"></script>
<script type="text/javascript" src="jquery.js"></script>
```

Then, return $ to its original object by using the noconflict method

```
jQuery.noConflict();
```

Or, assign a new shortcut object that you can use to refer to jQuery

```
var $jq = jQuery.noConflict();
```

How to use the ready method to run a function after the DOM is loaded

```
$().ready( function () {
    // Your code goes here
});
```

Description

- jQuery is a JavaScript library that lets you first select a set of elements and then work with them by changing their appearance or content or by applying effects and animations to them.
- jQuery works with all modern web browsers; it supports CSS selectors to retrieve elements from the page; and it uses implicit iteration and method chaining to let you write compact code.
- *Implicit iteration* allows one method call to work on multiple elements in a set without having to use a for loop.
- The ready method runs the function that's passed to it after the DOM has been loaded. This is similar to using a window.onload event handler.

Figure 20-1   How to get started with jQuery

How to select elements with jQuery

When you use jQuery, you start by selecting one or more elements. This is illustrated by the examples in figure 20-2. Then, you can use jQuery methods to work with those elements, which is illustrated by the next four figures.

The first group of examples in this figure shows that you can select the document object by calling the $ function with document as its parameter or with nothing as its parameter. Then, any jQuery methods that are applied to the result will affect either the html tag or the body tag, whichever is appropriate.

The second group of examples shows how to use CSS selectors to select elements from a page. With jQuery, all CSS 1, 2, and 3 selectors are supported, even if the browser doesn't support them.

The third group of examples shows how to find elements by attribute and attribute value. Here, the attribute name and value are placed inside brackets after the element name. If you omit the element name, though, all elements will be searched for the specified attribute and value.

If you specify just the attribute name, any value will be matched. If you use the equal sign, the value must match exactly. If you use ^=, the attribute must begin with the specified value. If you use $=, the attribute must end with the specified value. And if you use *=, the attribute must contain the specified value.

The fourth group of examples shows how to use custom selectors. Recall that in CSS the > selector means that the element on the right must be a direct child of the element on the left. As a result, #content > p selects all paragraphs that are children of the element with an id of content.

If a selection finds more than one match, you can use the eq selector to select a specific element. For instance, since the numbering starts at zero, p:eq(2) selects the third paragraph. You can also use the even and odd selectors to select alternating elements. Here again, the numbering starts at zero, so the first element is even, not odd.

Last, you can use the contains selector to select an element if its text contains the specified text, and you can use the not selector to select an element if it doesn't match the specified selector. The content of the not selector can be as simple as a single element or as complex as a full CSS selector. In the last example in this figure, the not operator is used to select img elements that don't have alt attributes.

How to select the document object

Method 1: Calling the $ function with the document object as the argument
```
$(document);
```

Method 2: Calling the $ function with no arguments
```
$();
```

How to select elements by tag name, class, or id

How to select all paragraph tags
```
$("p");
```

How to select all elements that have a class named error
```
$(".error");
```

How to select the element with btnSubmit as its id
```
$("#btnSubmit");
```

How to select elements by attributes

How to select all image tags that have an alt attribute
```
$("img[alt]");
```

How to select all image tags with a src attribute that begins with tn
```
$("img[src^='tn']");
```

How to select all image tags with a src attribute that ends with .gif
```
$("img[src$='.gif']");
```

How to select all anchor tags with an href attribute that contains "google.com"
```
$("a[href*='google.com']");
```

How to use custom selectors

How to select the third paragraph tag in the content div tag
```
$("#content > p:eq(2)");      // Numbering starts at 0
```

How to select even and odd paragraph tags in the content div tag
```
$("#content > p:even");       // First tag is even, not odd,
$("#content > p:odd");        // since numbering starts at 0
```

How to select paragraph tags in the content div tag that contain "Murach"
```
$("#content > p:contains('Murach')");
```

How to select all div tags that don't contain p tags
```
$("div:not(p)");
```

How to select all img tags that don't have alt attributes
```
$("img:not([alt])");
```

Description

- The jQuery $ function selects elements from a web page based on the criteria that you pass to it as a parameter. It returns a jQuery object that is a set of selected elements.
- See http://docs.jquery.com/selectors for a complete list of selectors.

Figure 20-2   How to select elements with jQuery

How to use jQuery effects

After you select one or more elements, you can use jQuery methods to apply interesting effects or animations to the selected elements. This is illustrated by the examples in figure 20-3. In all of these examples, h1 is used as the selector, which will select all of the h1 elements in the page. Then, thanks to implicit iteration, if more than one is selected, the effect is applied to all of them.

The first group of examples shows how to use the hide, show, and toggle methods. The hide and show methods take "fast", "slow", or a number as their first parameters to control the speed of the animation. If you use a number, it represents the number of milliseconds to use for the duration of the effect. The toggle method toggles the visibility of an element each time it's executed.

As an element is being animated, the hide and show methods adjust both the height and width of the element, which will sometimes affect the layout of a page. These methods can also accept a function as their second parameter. Then, the function is called when the effect is completed.

The second group of examples shows how to use the slideUp, slideDown, and slideToggle methods, which are similar to hide, show, and toggle. The difference is that they only animate an element's height. By keeping an element at its full width, width-based layout problems are avoided.

The third group of examples shows how to fade an element in or out. The fadeOut method fades an element to 0% opacity. The fadeIn method fades an element to 100% opacity. And both methods let you specify a speed and a function to run when the method is done. In contrast, the fadeTo method fades an element to a specified opacity that ranges from 0 to 1 in 0.01 steps. For instance, a 25% opacity is specified as 0.25.

Last, this figure presents a function named flash that uses an inner function and closure to flash an element by fading it in and fading it out. To start, the flash function takes a jQuery selector as its one parameter. Then, it defines a variable named keepFlashing that is set to true. It also defines an inner function named flashIt that flashes the selected element or elements as long as keepFlashing is true.

The flashIt function first fades the selection out and then fades it back in using the fadeOut and fadeIn methods. In this case, though, the second parameter of the fadeIn method is a function that calls the flashIt function again if the keepFlashing variable is still true. Note here that the if statement in this function would cause a recursion error if it were coded at the end of the flashIt function instead of within this parameter function.

The flash function then starts the selected elements flashing by calling the flashIt function. Last, the flash function returns a *callback function*. When this function is called from outside the flash function, it will set keepFlashing to false, which will cause the function in the fadeIn method to not call the flashIt function. And that will stop the flashing.

How to hide and show elements

How to hide an element immediately
```
$("h1").hide();
```

How to hide an element slowly
```
$("h1").hide("slow");
```

How to show an element over 3 seconds
```
$("h1").show(3000);
```

How to show an element quickly and then run a function
```
$("h1").show("fast", function() { alert("Welcome!"); });
```

How to toggle the visibility of an element
```
$("h1").toggle();
```

How to hide or show elements by animating their height

How to hide an element by sliding it up
```
$("h1").slideUp("fast");
```

How to hide an element by sliding it down
```
$("h1").slideDown(2000);
```

How to toggle the visibility of an element by sliding it
```
$("h1").slideToggle("slow");
```

How to hide or show elements by fading them in or out

How to hide an element by fading it out
```
$("h1").fadeOut("slow");
```

How to show an element by fading it in
```
$("h1").fadeIn(3000);
```

How to fade an element to a specifiy opacity
```
$("h1").fadeTo("fast", 0.25);  // Fades to 25%
```

A function that flashes an element
```
var flash = function (selector) {
    var keepFlashing = true;
    var flashIt = function () {
        $(selector).fadeOut("slow");
        $(selector).fadeIn("slow", function () {
            if ( keepFlashing ) flashIt();
        });
    }
    flashIt();
    return function () { keepFlashing = false; }
}
```

A ready method that calls the flash function
```
$().ready( function () {
    var flashStop = flash("h1");
    setTimeout( flashStop, 10000 );
});
```

Figure 20-3   How to use jQuery effects

After the flash method, you can see the code that calls it. When the document is ready, the flash function is called to flash all h1 headers, and the return function is stored in a variable named flashStop. Then, a timer is set that calls the flashStop function after 10 seconds.

Of course, you could code a simple loop that would flash the h1 headers without using closure and a callback function. By using closure and the callback function, though, you can turn the flash function off from outside the function. In this example, the flash function is stopped by the setTimout method. But it could also be stopped by an event handler for some other event.

How to handle events with jQuery

With jQuery, it's relatively easy to add more than one event handler to an event, remove event handlers, and trigger events. This is illustrated by the examples in figure 20-4.

In the first group of examples, you can see two ways to attach an event handler to an event. First, you can use the bind method with the name of the event as the first parameter and either a named or an anonymous function as the second parameter. Second, you can use the shortcut method that's shown.

In the second group of examples, you can see how to use the unbind method to remove a named event handler. Here, the first parameter is the name of the event and the second parameter is the name of the event handler. After the unbind method is executed, the event handler won't run when the event occurs.

The third group of examples shows two ways to trigger an event on an element. First, you select the element and call the trigger method with the name of the event as its parameter. Second, you select the element and call the shortcut method for the event with no parameters. Either way, this causes all the event handlers for the event to run.

The fourth group of examples shows how to prevent an event's default action from occurring. For instance, the default action of the click event on a link is to load that link in the browser. But in some web applications, you don't want that to happen.

To prevent the default action from happening, you first modify the event handler so it accepts an event object as its first parameter. In this example, this parameter is named evt. Then, to cancel the default action, you call the preventDefault method of the event object. In this example, this stops the browser from loading www.example.com.

Last, this figure shows how to automatically remove an event handler after it runs once. In this case, you use the one method instead of the bind method to add the event handler to an event. In this example, the event handler confirms the submission of a form when the user clicks on a submit button, and then it prevents the default action, which is the submission of the form. But since this event handler runs only once, it won't stop the submission the next time the user clicks the submit button.

How to add event handlers to elements

With the bind method

```
$("#btnSubmit").bind("click", function() { alert("Thank you!"); });
```

With a shortcut method

```
$("#btnSubmit").click(function() { alert("Thank you!"); });
```

How to remove an event handler

The event handler must be a named function

```
var submit_click = function () { alert("Thank you!"); }
```

How to attach the event handler

```
$("#btnSubmit").click(submit_click);
```

How to remove the event handler with the unbind method

```
$("#btnSubmit").unbind("click", submit_click);
```

How to trigger an event

With the trigger method

```
$("#btnSubmit").trigger("click");
```

With a shortcut method

```
$("#btnSubmit").click();
```

How to prevent an event's default action from happening

A link in a page

```
<a href="http://www.example.com" class="exampleLink">Example Link</a>
```

How to prevent the link's default action

```
$(".exampleLink").click( function (evt) {
    alert("Not a real link");
    evt.preventDefault();
});
```

How to remove an event handler after it runs once

An event handler

```
var confirm_click = function (evt) {
    alert("Are you sure? Click again to submit.");
    evt.preventDefault();
}
```

How to set the event handler so it runs only once

```
$("#btnSubmit").one("click", confirm_click);
```

Description

- The jQuery bind method and its shortcuts let you attach multiple event handlers to an element.

Figure 20-4   How to handle events with jQuery

How to use jQuery to work with XHTML elements

To make it easier for you to work with XHTML elements, the jQuery library provides a variety of methods. Some of the more useful ones are illustrated in figure 20-5.

In the first group of examples, you can see how jQuery can be used to work with classes. For instance, the addClass method is used to add a class named error to all span tags with an id that ends in _error. The hasClass method is used within an if statement to return true if the element with an id of register has a class named centered. And the removeClass method is used to remove the centered class from the element with a register id.

Similarly, the toggleClass method toggles the presence of a class on an element. When it's called with just the name of the class, it adds the class if it's missing and removes the class if it's present. When it's called with the name of the class and a Boolean variable, the method adds the class if the variable is true and removes the class if the variable is false. In the last example in this group, this method is used to toggle the error class on a set of span tags.

In the second group of examples, you can see how jQuery can be used to retrieve, set, or remove the attributes of an element. Here, the attr method with just the attribute name as its parameter retrieves the value of that parameter. But if the attribute isn't present on the element, the attr method returns undefined. And if the selector selects multiple elements, the attr method only works on the first element that's selected. For instance, the first statement in this group retrieves the value of the title attribute from the first img tag.

When you call the attr method with an attribute name and a value as its parameters, this method sets the attribute to that value on all of the selected elements. For instance, the second statement in this group sets the alt attribute to "No description available" for all img elements that don't have an alt attribute".

The third statement in this group shows how to use the removeAttr method to remove an attribute from an element. Here, the href attribute is removed from all links.

Finally, the third group of examples shows how jQuery can be used to manipulate the contents of an element. Here, the text method retrieves only the plain text content of an element; the html method retrieves all the content of an element including the XHTML; and the val method retrieves the value of a form field element, including the selected element of a select box. Conversely, to set text, XHTML, and form field values, you use the same methods, but with the values as the parameters.

How to add, remove, and toggle classes on elements

How to add a class to all elements with ids that end with "_error"
```
$("span[id$='_error']").addClass("error");
```

How to check if a class is present
```
if ($("#register").hasClass("centered")) $("#reset_form").show();
```

How to remove a class
```
$("#register").removeClass("centered");
```

How to toggle a class
```
$("span[id$='_error']").toggleClass("error");   // Adds or removes the class
```

How to toggle a class based on the Boolean value of the second parameter
```
$("span[id$='_error']").toggleClass("error", validForm); // Adds if true
                                                         // Removes if false
```

How to retrieve, set, and remove attributes

How to retrieve an attribute
```
alert( $("img:eq(0)").attr("title") );
```

How to set an attribute
```
$("img:not([alt])").attr("alt", "No description available.");
```

How to remove an attribute
```
$("a").removeAttr("href");
```

How to read and modify the contents of an element

How to read the text from an element
```
alert( $("h1:first").text() );
```

How to read the html from an element
```
alert( $("div.formLayout:last").html() );
```

How to read the value from a form element
```
alert( $("#exp_date").val() );   // Gets value from a text box
alert( $("#card_type").val() );  // Gets value from a select box
```

How to set the text in an element
```
$("#last_name_error").text("Last name is required");
```

How to set the XHTML in an element
```
$("p.notice").html("<b>All</b> fields are <i>required</i>.");
```

How to set the value in a form element
```
$("#first_name").val("");        // Sets value in a text box
$("#card_type").val("v");        // Sets option in a select box
```

Description

- jQuery provides many methods that simplify the process of working with XHTML elements, including form fields.

Figure 20-5   How to use jQuery to work with XHTML elements

How to use jQuery to work with the DOM

To make it easier for you to work with the DOM, the jQuery library provides a variety of methods. Some of the more useful ones are illustrated in figure 20-6.

The first group of examples shows how to create new content. Here, the $ function, when called with a string of XHTML, will create one or more DOM nodes as a document fragment and return a reference to the newly created nodes. This reference can then be used with other methods to add the new nodes into the page.

The second group of examples shows how to add XHTML content inside a node by using the prepend and append methods. Here, the first example prepends text to the beginning of all elements in the notice class. The second example appends an image to the end of all h1 elements.

The third group of examples shows how to add XHTML content before or after an element by using the before and after methods. In this case, the new XHTML becomes a sibling, not a child, of the selected element. Here, the first example adds the nodes referenced in the copyright variable after any element with the class notice. The second example adds an image in a div tag just before any h1 element.

The fourth group of examples shows how to delete nodes by using the remove and empty methods. The remove method removes any selected elements and their children, including their event handlers. The empty method removes the child nodes from the selected elements but leaves the elements.

The fifth group of examples shows how to copy nodes. Here, the clone method creates a copy of an element and all its child nodes. If you pass a true parameter to the clone method, it will also copy all of the event handlers for the element. The cloned nodes can then be inserted into a document by using the append, prepend, appendTo, or prependTo methods.

The appendTo method is similar to the append method, except that the order of nodes is switched. Specifically, the append method appends its parameter to the selected node, but the appendTo method appends the selected node to its parameter. This works the same for the prepend and prependTo methods.

In the examples in this group, the first two statements get the same result: they append a copy of the h1 node to the end of the #content node. However, I think the statement that uses the appendTo method is easier to understand and maintain. Similarly, the next two statements prepend a copy of the #register node and its events to the #content node.

Finally, the last group of examples shows how to replace a node. Here, the replaceWith method first removes the selected element. Then, if it's called with XHTML as its parameter, it creates the new nodes and inserts them in place of the removed element. But if it's called with a reference to another element, that element is moved to where the selected element was removed. And if it's called with a reference to a variable that contains nodes, those nodes are moved to where the selected element was removed.

How to create new content

How to create a single node
```
var newSpan = $("<span />");
```

How to create multiple nodes
```
var copyright = $("<p>&copy; " + (new Date()).getFullYear() + "</p>");
```

How to add XHTML to an element's content

How to prepend XHTML content
```
$(".notice").prepend("Notice: ");
```

How to append XHTML content
```
$("h1").append("<img src='logo.gif' />");
```

How to add XHTML before or after an element

How to add content after an element
```
$(".notice").after(copyright);
```

How to add content before an element
```
$("h1").before("<div><img src='logo.gif' /></div>");
```

How to remove nodes from a page

How to remove a node
```
$("h1").remove();
```

How to delete all of a node's child nodes
```
$("#card_type").empty();
```

How to copy nodes

How to copy and move a node
```
$("#content").append( $("h1").clone() );
$("h1").clone().appendTo("#content");
```

How to copy a node and its events
```
$("#content").prepend( $("#register").clone(true) );
$("#register").clone(true).prependTo("#content");
```

How to replace a node

How to replace a node with XHTML
```
$("h1").replaceWith("<p>Registration form</p>");
```

How to replace a node with another node
```
$("h1").replaceWith( $(".notice") );   // Moves existing node
$(".notice").replaceWith( copyright ); // Uses newly created nodes
```

Description

- jQuery lets you add, replace, remove, and copy nodes from the DOM. This lets you control the structure of a page while an application is running.

Figure 20-6   How to use jQuery to work with the DOM

How to use Dojo

The Dojo library was developed in 2004 to simplify the development of JavaScript applications. This library is designed to work with all modern web browsers, and it is free, open-source software. In the pages that follow, you'll learn some basic skills that will help you decide whether you would like to use it. Then, you can read more about it at http://www.dojotoolkit.org.

Dojo is a modular library that consists of modules that are divided into three categories: Core, Dijit, and Dojox. The base module is part of the Core and must be loaded first. Then, you can load other modules as needed. The Core modules provide functionality that is similar to that of the jQuery library, and you'll learn about them next.

In contrast, the Dijit modules provide JavaScript enhanced controls for page layout and forms, and the Dojox modules provide stable but experimental features that may be moved into the Core or Dijit modules in a later release. If you use the Dojox modules, be sure to check their documentation for any changes when you upgrade to a new version of Dojo.

How to get started with Dojo

Figure 20-7 shows three ways to include the base Dojo module in your application. First, you can load Dojo from a file on your web server. Second, you can load it from the Google APIs web site. Third, you can load it from the AOL Content Distribution Network. The last two methods let you use Dojo without hosting the JavaScript files on your web server. Then, if a new version of Dojo is released, you just need to change the version number in the URL when you're ready to use it.

Once the base module is loaded, you use the Dojo require method to load additional modules. This lets you load additional modules without having to use additional script tags in your XHTML document. If, for example, you want to load the module for special effects, you use dojo.fx as the parameter for the require method.

Once you've loaded all the Dojo modules that your application needs, you can use the addOnLoad method to run a function after the DOM has been loaded. This is similar to using the jQuery ready method. It allows the application to become active as soon as the DOM is ready without having to wait for large images and graphics to be loaded.

Where to download the Dojo library

```
http://www.dojotoolkit.org
```

Where to get the Dojo documentation

```
http://api.dojotoolkit.org
```

Dojo modules fall into three categories

Category	Description
Core	Provides modules that let you select elements, manipulate them, and apply affects. This is similar to the functionality of the jQuery library.
Dijit	Provides enhanced controls for page layout and forms.
Dojox	Provides experimental but stable features that may be moved into the Core or Dijit categories in a later release.

How to include the Dojo library in an application

A template for loading the Dojo library

```
<script src="URL" type="text/javascript"></script>
```

A URL for a local file

```
dojo-release-1.2.3/dojo/dojo.js
```

A URL for the Google APIs web site

```
http://ajax.googleapis.com/ajax/libs/dojo/1.2/dojo/dojo.xd.js
```

A URL for the AOL Content Distribution Network

```
http://o.aolcdn.com/dojo/1.2/dojo/dojo.xd.js
```

How to load additional modules

```
dojo.require("dojo.fx");                    // Loads the effects module
```

How to use the addOnLoad method to run a function when the DOM is loaded

```
dojo.addOnLoad( function () {
    alert("Ready");
});
```

Description

- The Dojo library provides many of the same features that jQuery provides, but it also provides features that go well beyond what jQuery provides.

- You can use the require method to load Dojo modules as they are needed. This helps keep the size of the Dojo library small.

- The addOnLoad method runs the function that's passed to it after the DOM has been loaded. This is like the jQuery ready method, and it is more efficient than using the window.onload event handler.

Figure 20-7   How to get started with Dojo

How to select elements with Dojo

When you use the Core modules of Dojo, you start by selecting the elements that you want to work with. To do that, you can use the dojo.query and dojo.byId methods along with CSS selectors. This is illustrated by the examples in figure 20-8. Then, you can use other methods to work with the elements that you've selected.

The first group of examples in this figure shows how to use CSS selectors to select elements from a page. Like jQuery, all CSS 1, 2, and 3 selectors are supported by Dojo, even if the browser doesn't support them. In addition, you can use the dojo.byId method to select just the element with the specified id.

The second group of examples shows how to select elements by attribute and attribute value. In this case, the attribute name and value are placed inside brackets after the element name. If you leave out the element name, all elements will be searched for the specified attribute and value.

If you just specify the attribute name, any value will be matched. If you use the equal sign, the value must match exactly. If you use ^=, the attribute must begin with the specified value. If you use $=, the attribute must end with the specified value. And if you use *=, the attribute must contain the specified value.

The third group of examples shows how to use CSS pseudo-class selectors. Recall that in CSS, the > selector means that the element on the right must be a direct child of the element on the left. That is, #content > p selects all paragraphs that are children of the element with an id of content.

Then, the first-child and last-child selectors select the first and last child nodes of an element, and the nth-child selector selects a specific child node. In this case, since the numbering starts at one, p:nth-child(3) selects the third paragraph. You can also use the even and odd keywords with the nth-child selector to select even and odd numbered elements. This time, the first element is odd, not even.

Last, you can use the not selector to select an element if it doesn't match the specified selector. The content of this not selector can be as simple as a single element or as complex as a full CSS selector. This is illustrated by the last two examples in the third group.

How to use select elements by tag name, class, or id

How to select all paragraph tags

```
dojo.query("p");
```

How to select all elements with a class named error

```
dojo.query(".error");
```

Two ways to select the element with btnSubmit as its id

```
dojo.query("#btnSubmit");
dojo.byId("btnSubmit");
```

How to select elements by attributes

How to select all image tags that have an alt attribute

```
dojo.query("img[alt]");
```

How to select all image tags with a src attribute that begins with tn

```
dojo.query("img[src^='tn']");
```

How to select all image tags with a src attribute that ends in .gif

```
dojo.query("img[src$='.gif']");
```

How to select all anchor tags with an href attribute that contains "google.com"

```
dojo.query("a[href*='google.com']");
```

How to select elements by using pseudo-class selectors

How to select the first and last paragraph tags in the content div tag

```
$("#content > p:first-child");
$("#content > p:last-child");
```

How to select the third paragraph tag in the content div tag

```
$("#content > p:nth-child(3)");          // Numbering starts at 1
```

How to select the odd and even paragraphs in the content div tag

```
$("#content > p:nth-child(odd)");        // First tag is odd
$("#content > p:nth-child(even)");       // since numbering starts at 1
```

How to select all div tags that don't contain p tags

```
$("div:not(p)");
```

How to select all img tags that don't have an alt attribute

```
$("img:not([alt])");
```

Description

- The dojo.query method selects elements from a web page based on the criteria you pass to it as a parameter. It returns a NodeList object, which is an array of selected elements.
- The dojo.byId method selects just the element with the specified id. It is a more efficient version of the document.getElementById method.

Figure 20-8   How to select elements with Dojo

How to handle events with Dojo

To attach and remove event handlers, the Dojo library provides the connect and disconnect methods. Like jQuery's methods, these methods let you attach more than one event handler to a single event. This is illustrated in figure 20-9.

The first example in this figure shows how to attach an event handler to an event using the dojo.connect method. Here, the first parameter is a reference to the element that's found by using the dojo.byId method. The second parameter is the name of the event. And the third parameter is the event handler. When you use this method, you can attach either a named or an anonymous function as the event handler.

When you call the connect method, it returns a reference to the connection it created. Then, you can store this reference in a variable and use it to disconnect the event handler. This works for both named and anonymous functions.

The second example in this figure shows how to remove an event handler. Here, you just call the disconnect method with the reference to the connection as its parameter. After that, the event handler won't run when the event occurs.

The third example in this figure shows how to cancel an event's default action, which is an important part of event handling. To do that, you modify the event handler so it accepts an event object as its first parameter. Then, to cancel the default action, you call the preventDefault method of the event object. In this example, this stops the browser from loading the link to www.example.com.

Unlike jQuery, Dojo doesn't provide a way to automatically remove an event handler after it runs once. However, this can easily be added to an event handler, as shown in the last example in this figure. Here, the last statement in the event handler disconnects itself. This will remove the event handler after it runs once.

How to add event handlers to elements with the connect method

```
var submit_click = dojo.connect(dojo.byId("btnSubmit"), "onclick",
    function() {
        alert("Thank you!");
    }
);
```

How to remove an event handler with the disconnect method

```
dojo.disconnect(submit_click);
```

How to prevent an event's default action from happening

A link in a page

```
<a href="http://www.example.com" id="exampleLink">Example Link</a>
```

How to prevent the link's default action

```
dojo.connect(dojo.byId("exampleLink"), "onclick",
    function (evt) {
        alert("Not a real link");
        evt.preventDefault();
    }
);
```

How to remove an event handler after it runs once

```
var submit_click = dojo.connect(dojo.byId("btnSubmit"), "onclick",
    function (evt) {
        alert("Are you sure? Click again to submit.");
        evt.preventDefault();
        dojo.disconnect(submit_click);
    }
);
```

Description

- The Dojo connect method lets you attach multiple event handlers to an element. The disconnect method lets you remove event handlers.

- Be sure to place the connect calls inside the function called by the dojo.addOnLoad method to ensure that the elements are loaded before the calls are made.

Figure 20-9   How to handle events with Dojo

How to use Dojo effects

After you select one or more elements, you can use some of the Dojo methods to apply effects or animations to the selected elements. This is illustrated by the examples in figure 20-10. Although the fade effect is in the base module, you need to load the dojo.fx module for the wipe effect.

The first group of examples in this figure shows how to use the wipeOut and wipeIn methods to hide and show elements. These methods accept an object as a parameter. Then, the node property of this object specifies the id of the element to animate, and the duration property specifies the number of milliseconds that the animation should take.

Note, however, that these methods don't start the animation. Instead, they create animation objects. Then, to start these animation objects, you call their play methods. In these examples, method chaining is used to call the play methods after the wipe methods create the animation objects.

The second group of examples shows how to use the fadeOut and fadeIn methods to hide and show elements. Here again, these methods accept objects as parameters, and the properties of the objects specify the elements and durations. Then, the play methods of the objects start the animations.

The third group of examples shows how to combine two or more animations. To play two or more animations in parallel, you use the dojo.fx.combine method. To play them in series, you use the dojo.fx.chain method. In either case, the animations to be played are first stored in an array. Then, the combine or chain method is called with the array as the parameter to create a combine or chain object. Last, the play method of the combine or chain object is called.

Finally, this figure shows a function named flash that flashes an element repeatedly. This is similar to the jQuery flash function in figure 20-3, but the nested flashIt function chains two animations in series so they fade the element out and in.

To make this work, the Dojo animation object has an event named onEnd that is triggered when the animation is complete. Then, you use the connect method to attach an event handler to the onEnd event that calls the flashIt method if the keepFlashing variable is still true. By placing this statement in the onEnd event handler, you prevent a recursion error from taking place. The last statement in the nested flashIt function calls the play method of the chain object. After the nested flashIt function, the flash function calls the flashIt function to start the flashing, and it returns a callback function that sets the keepFlashing variable to false.

Then, to run this function, you call the flash function. In this case, when the document is loaded, the flash function is called to flash the registration_form element, and the return function is stored in a variable named flashStop. Last, a timer is set up that calls flashStop after 10 seconds, which ends the flashing.

How to include the Dojo FX module

```
dojo.require("dojo.fx");
```

How to hide and show elements by wiping them out or in

How to hide an element by wiping it out

```
dojo.fx.wipeOut( {node: "registration_form", duration: 2000} ).play();
```

How to show an element by wiping it in

```
dojo.fx.wipeIn( {node: "registration_form", duration: 2000} ).play();
```

How to hide or show elements by fading them out or in

How to hide an element by fading it out

```
dojo.fadeOut( {node: "registration_form", duration: 2000} ).play();
```

How to show an element by fading it in

```
dojo.fadeIn( {node: "registration_form", duration: 2000} ).play();
```

How to combine two or more animations

How to combine two animations in parallel

```
var anim = [];
var args = { node: "registration_form", duration: 2000 };
anim.push( dojo.fx.wipeOut( args ) );
anim.push( dojo.fadeOut( args ) );
dojo.fx.combine( anim ).play();
```

How to combine two animations in series

```
var anim = [];
var args = { node: "registration_form", duration: 2000 };
anim.push( dojo.fadeOut( args ) );
anim.push( dojo.fadeIn( args ) );
dojo.fx.chain( anim ).play();
```

A method that flashes an element

```
var flash = function (id) {
    var keepFlashing = true;
    var args = { node: id, duration: 1000 };
    var flashIt = function () {
        var anim = [];
        anim.push( dojo.fadeOut(args) );
        anim.push( dojo.fadeIn(args) );
        var chain = dojo.fx.chain(anim);
        dojo.connect( chain, "onEnd", function () {
            if ( keepFlashing ) flashIt();   });
        chain.play();
    }
    flashIt();
    return function () { keepFlashing = false; };
}
```

An addOnLoad function that calls the flash function

```
dojo.addOnLoad( function () {
    var flashStop = flash("registration_form");
    setTimeout( flashStop, 10000 );   });
```

Figure 20-10   How to use Dojo effects

How to use Dijits

Dijit is one of the three categories of Dojo. It provides controls called Dijits that you can use to enhance your forms. These controls make it easier for you to validate the data in the controls.

How to get started with Dijits

Figure 20-11 shows what you need to do to get started with Dijits. First, you need to load a Dijit theme. To do that, you code a link tag with the right URL and theme. In the first group of examples in this figure, you can see the three URLs that you can use to get the Dojo toolkit that you need. And all three of these examples load the tundra theme.

The *theme* for Dijits is a standard CSS file that affects the way the controls look. Dojo provides three themes named Tundra, Soria, and Noir, but you can also build your own theme. In the examples in this figure, the Tundra theme is used, but you can change that by replacing both instances of tundra in the URLs with either soria or noir.

Because Dijits are defined in the body of a web page by adding attributes to standard XHTML elements, the XHTML must be parsed in order to create the Dijits. This parsing can be done automatically or manually. Either way, you have to load the parser module as shown in the second group of examples.

Then, to parse automatically, you just add the djConfig attribute to the script tag with its parseOnLoad parameter set to true. This causes Dojo to parse the document as soon as it is loaded and before any addOnLoad functions are executed.

However, if you need to define any objects that the Dijits will use as they're parsed, you need to manually parse the Dijits. To do that, you call the parse method of the parser module in the addOnLoad event handler. As you will see, you need to load the Dijits manually when you use the FilteringSelect Dijit.

Last, this figure shows how to return a reference to a Dijit. To do that, you use the dijit.byId method with the id of the XHTML element that the Dijit was created from. This works because a Dijit consists of DOM nodes that replace the original XHTML element, but the Dijit inherits the original id. Note, however, that the dojo.byId method won't work correctly with a Dijit. Also, as you would expect, the dijit.byId method can't be called until after the document is parsed.

How to include a Dijit theme

A template for loading the Tundra theme

```
<link rel="stylesheet" type="text/css" href="URL" />
```

A URL for a local file

```
dojo-release-1.2.3/dijit/themes/tundra/tundra.css
```

A URL for the Google APIs web site

```
http://ajax.googleapis.com/ajax/libs/dojo/1.2/dijit/themes/tundra/tundra.css
```

A URL for the AOL Content Distribution Network

```
http://o.aolcdn.com/dojo/1.2/dijit/themes/tundra/tundra.css
```

How to parse Dijits

Load the parser module

```
dojo.require("dojo.parser");
```

A template for loading and parsing the Dijits automatically

```
<script src="URL" type="text/javascript" djConfig="parseOnLoad:true">
</script>
```

A statement for parsing the Dijits manually

```
dojo.addOnLoad( function() {
    dojo.parser.parse();
});
```

How to access a Dijit after a document has been parsed

```
var first_name = dijit.byId("first_name");
```

Description

- Dijits (Dojo widgets) are Dojo-enhanced controls for web applications. Some of these controls provide automatic data validation.

- Dijits must be parsed by the Dojo parser before they can be used. They can be parsed either automatically or manually.

- Once the parsing is complete, Dijits can be accessed by calling the dijit.byId method.

- Dojo provides three *themes* for Dijits: Tundra, Soria, and Noir. If you use Dijits for some of the controls on a form, you should use them for all the controls so they will have the same style.

Figure 20-11   How to get started with Dijits

How to use the Form Dijit

The Form Dijit is used to enhance a form element so it interacts correctly with other Dijits. As you will see, these Dijits can be set up so they automatically test the validity of the data that they hold. Then, by default, a Form Dijit won't submit the data if any Dijits in the form are invalid.

Figure 20-12 shows how to create a Form Dijit. First, you load the dijit.form.Form module that defines the Form Dijit. Then, you modify the XHTML form tag to indicate that it should be converted to a Form Dijit. To do that, you set the dojoType attribute to dijit.form.Form. Once you create a Form Dijit, you can use the three methods in this figure to work with the data in the Dijits that are on the form.

Next, this figure shows to use the isValid method of a Form Dijit in an event handler named checkFormClick that handles the click event of a standard XHTML button. In this case, the checkFormClick function displays one message if the isValid function returns true and another message if it returns false. If it returns true, it means that all of the Dijits on the form are valid.

How to use the Button Dijit

This figure also shows how to use Button Dijits. That insures that the buttons will have a consistent appearance with the rest of the Dijits on the form. To start, you must load the dijit.form.Button module that defines the Button Dijits. Then, you set the dojoType attribute of an XHTML button to dijit.form.Button.

In these examples, you can see that you use the button tag rather than the input tag to create a Button Dijit. These examples also show that you can use the type attribute to create submit and reset buttons that automatically submit or reset a form, or you can omit the type attribute. If you omit this attribute, you need to use the isValid method of the form to check to see whether all of the Dijits on the form are valid, and you need to use the submit and reset methods to submit and reset the form.

Next, this figure shows how to create a button and attach an event handler for the click event of the button to the checkFormClick function that's defined earlier in this figure. Note here that the dijit.byId method, not the dojo.byId method, is used to refer to the button when the event handler is attached.

Last, this figure shows how to change the label on a button and disable it. To do that, you use the attr method of the Button Dijit to change its label and disabled attributes.

How to load the Form and Button modules

```
dojo.require("dijit.form.Form");
dojo.require("dijit.form.Button");
```

How to create a Form Dijit

```
<form action="register_account.html" method="get"
    id="register_form" dojoType="dijit.form.Form">
</form>
```

Methods of a Form Dijit

Method	Description
isValid()	Returns true if every Dijit in the form is valid.
submit()	Submits the form if every Dijit in the form is valid.
reset()	Resets the form to its original state.

A function named checkFormClick that uses the isValid method

```
var checkFormClick = function () {
    if ( dijit.byId("register_form").isValid() ) {
        alert("Form is ready to submit.");
    } else {
        alert("Please correct the errors in the form.");
    }
}
```

How to create a submit Button Dijit

```
<button type="submit" id="submit_form"
    dojoType="dijit.form.Button">Submit Form</button>
```

How to create a reset Button Dijit

```
<button type="reset" id="reset_form"
    dojoType="dijit.form.Button">Reset Form</button>
```

How to attach an event handler to the click event for a Button Dijit

The XHTML for the button

```
<button id="check_form" dojoType="dijit.form.Button">Check Form</button>
```

How to attach the event handler to the button

```
dojo.addOnLoad( function() {
    dojo.connect( dijit.byId("check_form"), "onclick", checkFormClick );
});
```

How to change the label on a button and disable it

```
dijit.byId("submit_form").attr("label","Please Wait").attr("disabled",true);
```

Description

- A Form Dijit is used to enhance a form so it will work properly with other Dijits.
- Button Dijits are commonly used to submit and reset the controls in a Form Dijit.
- By default, a Form Dijit won't submit the form to the server if any of the Dijits that provide data validation aren't valid.

Figure 20-12   How to use the Form and Button Dijits

How to use the CheckBox Dijit

The CheckBox Dijit provides enhanced checkboxes that have a consistent appearance with the rest of the Dijits in the form. To use this Dijit, you need to load the Checkbox module and set the dojoType attribute of an XHTML checkbox as shown in figure 20-13.

Next, this figure shows how to work with a CheckBox Dijit. To do that, you use the attr method of the CheckBox. If you call this method with the parameter "checked", this method returns true if the checkbox is checked. If you call it with the parameters "checked" and true, this method checks the box. If you call it with the parameters "checked" and false, this method unchecks the box. And if you call it with the parameters "checked" and the not operator followed by the name of a variable that reflects its current status, it toggles the value of the box.

How to use the RadioButton Dijit

The RadioButton Dijit provides enhanced radio buttons that have a consistent appearance with the rest of the Dijits in the form. To create a RadioButton Dijit, you load the same module as the CheckBox Dijit, and you set the dojoType attribute of an XHTML radio button as shown in this figure. Then, you use the name attribute to give the radio buttons a group name, and you use the value attribute to give each button a unique value, but you don't use the id attribute. Instead, the radio buttons will be assigned ids by the parser.

Next, this figure shows a function named getRadioValue that determines the value of the selected radio button. This function takes the name of the radio button group as its parameter, and it starts by defining a variable named value that will store the return value. Next, it selects all the elements in the page that have the name of the parameter. Then, for each element, it runs a function using Dojo's forEach method. This function gets a reference to each RadioButton Dijit by using the id that was set by the parser, and it sets the value variable to the button's value if the button is checked. If, for example, the second button is checked, value is set to "vi". When the forEach loop ends, this function returns the contents of the value variable. However, if the name that was passed to it was invalid or if no button in the group was turned on, this value is undefined.

Last, this figure shows a function named setRadioValue that checks a radio button in a group. This function takes the name of the radio button group and the value of the button to check as its parameters. To start, this function selects all the elements in the page that have the specified group name. Then, it uses Dojo's forEach method to run a function on each element that checks the button if it has the specified value.

How to load the module for CheckBox and RadioButton Dijits

```
dojo.require("dijit.form.CheckBox");
```

How to create a CheckBox Dijit

```
<input type="checkbox" id="accept_policy" value="yes"
    dojoType="dijit.form.CheckBox" />
```

How to detect and change the state of a CheckBox Dijit

How to detect the state of a CheckBox

```
var accepted = dijit.byId("accept_policy").attr("checked");
```

How to check a CheckBox Dijit

```
dijit.byId("accept_policy").attr("checked", true);
```

How to uncheck a CheckBox Dijit

```
dijit.byId("accept_policy").attr("checked", false);
```

How to toggle a CheckBox Dijit

```
var checked = dijit.byId("accept_policy").attr("checked");
dijit.byId("accept_policy").attr("checked", !checked);
```

How to create RadioButton Dijits

```
<input type="radio" name="card_type" value="mc" checked="checked"
    dojoType="dijit.form.RadioButton" /> MasterCard
<input type="radio" name="card_type" value="vi"
    dojoType="dijit.form.RadioButton" /> Visa
```

A function that reads the value of a RadioButton group

```
var getRadioValue = function ( name ) {
    var value;
    dojo.query("[name=" + name + "]").forEach(function(element) {
        var button = dijit.byId(element.id);
        if ( button.attr("checked") ) value = button.attr("value");
    });
    return value;
}
```

A statement that calls the function

```
alert( getRadioValue("card_type") );
```

A function that checks a button in a RadioButton group

```
var setRadioValue = function ( name, value ) {
    dojo.query("[name=" + name + "]").forEach(function(element) {
        var button = dijit.byId(element.id);
        if ( button.value == value ) button.attr("checked", true);
    });
}
```

A call to the function that checks the button that has a value of "vi"

```
setRadioValue("card_type", "vi");
```

Figure 20-13   How to use the CheckBox and RadioButton Dijits

How to use the ValidationTextBox Dijit

The ValidationTextBox Dijit lets you create an enhanced text box that can validate the data in it and display an error message if the contents aren't valid as soon as the focus leaves the text box. To use this type of Dijit, you need to load the ValidationTextBox module and set the dojoType attribute of an XHTML text box as shown in figure 20-14. Then, to validate an entry in the text box, you can use the attributes that are illustrated in this figure.

For instance, the first example in this figure shows how to use the required, trim, and invalidMessage attributes. If you set the required attribute to true, the user must enter something in the text box. If you set the trim attribute to true, leading and trailing spaces will be trimmed from the user's entry before it is submitted. If you set the invalidMessage attribute to a message string, the message will be displayed if the user's entry is invalid. In this case, that means the message will be displayed if the user doesn't enter anything in the text box.

The second example shows how to use the regExp attribute with a ValidationTextBox Dijit. When you use this attribute, you code a regular expression like the ones you learned about in chapter 12. Then, that expression is used to validate the contents of the text box. When you use this attribute, though, there is an implicit ^ at the beginning of the regular expression and an implicit $ at the end of your expression. So, in this example, the regular expression matches either a 5- or 9-digit zip code. Note, however, that you must still code the required attribute if you want to check for a missing entry.

The third example in this figure shows how to create a ValidationTextBox Dijit that uses a regular expression generator. The generator is a function that returns a regular expression for a specific type of entry, and Dojo provides predefined generators for some common types of entries.

To use the predefined generators, you must load the dojox.validate.regexp module as shown in this example. Then, you set the regExpGen attribute to indicate which function you want to use. In this example, the emailAddress generator is used, but some of the other common generators are also listed.

The last example in this figure shows how to use a ValidationTextBox Dijit with a custom validation function. This function is used to check whether the entry in the verify text box matches the entry in the password text box. To do that, the validator attribute of the verify text box is set to the name of the validation function. Then, the constraints attribute provides an object that will be sent to the validator function as a parameter. For this example, this object provides a property named matchId that contains the id of the password field.

In the code for the validator function, you provide for two parameters. The first is for the value of the field that calls the function, which will be passed automatically. The second is for the constraint object. Then, the function provides the validation code.

In this example, the function uses the matchId property of the constraints object to get a reference to the password field. Then, if the field is found, the function returns the result of comparing the value of the verify field with the value of the password field, which is true if they're equal, false if they aren't.

How to load the ValidationTextBox module

```
dojo.require("dijit.form.ValidationTextBox");
```

How to create a ValidationTextBox Dijit

```
<input type="text" name="first_name" id="first_name"
    dojoType="dijit.form.ValidationTextBox"
    required="true" trim="true"
    invalidMessage="First name is required." />
```

How to use a regular expression with a ValidationTextBox Dijit

```
<input type="text" name="zip" id="zip"
    dojoType="dijit.form.ValidationTextBox" required="true"
    regExp="[\d]{5}(-[\d]{4})?"
    invalidMessage="Required. Use 5 or 9 digit ZIP code." />
```

How to use regular expression generators with a ValidationTextBox Dijit

How to load the regular expression module

```
dojo.require("dojox.validate.regexp");
```

The XHTML for a ValidationTextBox Dijit

```
<input type="text" name="email" id="email"
    dojoType="dijit.form.ValidationTextBox" required="true"
    regExpGen="dojox.regexp.emailAddress"
    invalidMessage="E-mail is required." />
```

Common generators for regular expressions

```
regExpGen="dojox.regexp.emailAddress"    // Email address
regExpGen="dojox.regexp.ipAddress"       // IP address (e.g. 192.168.1.50 )
regExpGen="dojox.regexp.url"             // Web site URL
```

How to use a custom validation function with a ValidationTextBox Dijit

The XHTML for a ValidationTextBox Dijit

```
<input type="password" name="verify" id="verify"
    dojoType="dijit.form.ValidationTextBox"  required="true"
    validator="matchValues"
    constraints="{matchId: 'password'}"
    invalidMessage="Passwords do not match." />
```

The validator function

```
var matchValues = function ( value, constraints ) {
    var matchField = dijit.byId(constraints.matchId);
    if (matchField) {
        return value === matchField.attr("value");
    }
    return false;
}
```

Figure 20-14   How to use the ValidationTextBox Dijit

How to validate a credit card with ValidationTextBox Dijits

To validate credit cards, Dojo provides experimental validator functions in its dojox.validate.creditCard module. These functions go beyond just checking that a card number entry has the right number of digits. They also provide for other restrictions. For instance, one restriction is that certain card types must start with a set value like 6011 for Discover cards. Another restriction is that the digits must pass a mathematical test called a *checksum*. A *checksum function* ensures that a typo in a card number won't result in a valid card number.

For testing purposes, the credit card companies have issued test numbers that will pass their basic validation tests. For MasterCard, the test number is 5105-1051-0511-5100. For Visa, it's 4012-8888-8888-1881. For Discover, it's 6011-0009-9013-9424. And for American Express, it's 3714-496353-98431.

In figure 20-15, you can see how the Dojox validator functions work. Here, the first example uses the Dojox isValidCreditCard function to test the validity of the credit card number. The second example uses the Dojox isValidCvv function to check the validity of the CVV number for a card. And the last example shows how to set up event handlers so the card and CVV numbers are validated again if the card type is changed.

To validate a credit card number, the validation functions need to know what type of card the user has. To get the card type, you can use a select box or a radio button group. When you pass the card type to the Dijits validation functions, you must use "mc" for MasterCard, "vi" for Visa, "di" for Discover, and "ax" for American Express. In the examples in this figure, radio buttons are used to get the card type.

In the first example, the validator attribute of the ValidationTextBox Dijit for the credit card number sets the function name to checkCardNumber. Then, the constraints attribute sets the ccTypeName property of the object to card_type. In contrast, if the card type were stored in a select box, the code would set the ccTypeId property.

In the checkCardNumber function, the code first determines the card type. If the ccTypeId property is set, it gets the card type from the Dijit with that id. If the ccTypeName property is set, it gets the card type from the radio button group by using the getRadioValue function that's defined in figure 20-13. Then, if this function gets a card type, it passes it to the Dojox isValidCreditCard function, which validates the credit card number and returns true or false.

Similarly, in the second example, the validator attribute of the Dijit for the CVV number sets the function name to checkCardCVV, and the constraints attribute sets the ccTypeName property to card_type. Then, the checkCardCVV function gets the card type and uses the Dojox isValidCvv function to validate the CVV number.

Last, this figure shows how to validate the card and CVV numbers whenever the card type changes. It does that by using the connect method to set up event handlers that run the validate functions for the card_number and card_cvv Dijits whenever the selected radio button in the card_type group is changed. This is a form of the connect method that's designed for working with Dijits.

How to load the credit card validation module

```
dojo.require("dojox.validate.creditCard");
```

How to validate the Dijit for the credit card number

The XHTML for the Dijit

```
<input type="text" name="card_number" id="card_number"
    dojoType="dijit.form.ValidationTextBox" required="true"
    validator="checkCardNumber" constraints="{ ccTypeName: 'card_type' }"
    invalidMessage="Valid card number required." />
```

The custom validator function

```
var checkCardNumber = function ( value, constraints ) {
    var ccType;
    if ( constraints.ccTypeId ) {
        ccType = dijit.byId(constraints.ccTypeId).attr("value");
    } else if ( constraints.ccTypeName ) {
        ccType = getRadioValue( constraints.ccTypeName );
    } else { return false; }
    if (ccType) {
        return dojox.validate.isValidCreditCard(
            this.attr("value"), ccType );
    }
    return false;
}
```

How to validate the Dijit for the CVV number

The XHTML for the Dijit

```
<input type="text" name="card_cvv" id="card_cvv"
    dojoType="dijit.form.ValidationTextBox" required="true"
    validator="checkCardCVV" constraints="{ ccTypeName: 'card_type' }"
    invalidMessage="Valid card CVV number (on back) required." />
```

The custom validator function

```
var checkCardCVV = function ( value, constraints ) {
    var ccType;
    if ( constraints.ccTypeId ) {
        ccType = dijit.byId(constraints.ccTypeId).attr("value");
    } else if ( constraints.ccTypeName ) {
        ccType = getRadioValue( constraints.ccTypeName );
    } else { return false; }
    if (ccType) {
        return dojox.validate.isValidCvv(this.attr("value"), ccType);
    }
    return false;
}
```

How to set up event handlers for when the card type changes

```
dojo.query("[name=card_type]").forEach( function(element) {
    var button = dijit.byId( element.id );
    var card_number = dijit.byId("card_number");
    var card_cvv = dijit.byId("card_cvv");
    dojo.connect( button, "onChange", card_number, "validate" );
    dojo.connect( button, "onChange", card_cvv, "validate" );
});
```

Figure 20-15   How to validate a credit card with ValidationTextBox Dijits

How to use the FilteringSelect Dijit

A FilteringSelect Dijit is an enhanced text box that presents the user with a drop-down list of choices. Then, the user can either select an item from the list or type in the first characters of an item to filter out the items that don't start with those characters. If the user types in an item that isn't in the list, the entry is treated as invalid.

When you use a FilteringSelect Dijit, the list of items is often retrieved from a database. However, you can also use a *data store* on your web server to provide the list items. To do that, you (1) load the Dojo ItemFileReadStore module; (2) code the data store and save it in a text file; and (3) use XHTML or JavaScript to load the data store for your application. These tasks are illustrated in the first part of figure 20-16.

When you code the data store, you create a JavaScript object with two properties. The identifier property names the identifier that will hold the selected value of the FilteringSelect Dijit that is associated with the data store. The items property is an array of item objects, and each item object has multiple properties. The name property is the text that is displayed by the Dijit, and the value property is the value that will be submitted by the Dijit. The other properties are ignored. When you're through coding the data store, you save it in a text file.

To load the data store, you can use either of the two methods in this figure. The first method uses an empty XHTML div tag with a dojoType attribute set to dojo.data.ItemFileReadStore. Then, its jsId attribute specifies the name of the JavaScript variable that will be used to store the data store, and its url attribute specifies the name of the file that contains the data store.

The second method uses JavaScript to create a new ItemFileReadStore object and passes the URL for the item file as the constructor's parameter. Then, the data store is loaded and saved in a JavaScript variable. In both of these examples, the data store is stored in a variable named stateList.

Once a data store has been created, you can use it to populate a FilteringSelect Dijit. To do that, you (1) load the Dijit FilteringSelect module, and (2) create the FilteringSelect Dijit. This is illustrated in the second part of this figure. When you create the FilteringSelect Dijit, you use the store attribute to identify the JavaScript variable that contains the data store.

Finally, this figure shows how to reset a FilteringSelect Dijit when the form is reset. Code like this is necessary because there's a bug in the FilteringSelect Dijit's reset method so it doesn't work right. To get around this bug, you first code a simple function that resets the displayedValue attribute of the Dijit to an empty string. Then, you use the dojo.connect method to run that function whenever the Dijit's reset event is triggered.

How to load the ItemFileReadStore module

```
dojo.require("dojo.data.ItemFileReadStore");
```

An item data store that stored in the file named states.txt

```
{   identifier: "value",
    items: [
        {name: "Alabama", value: "AL" },
        {name: "Alaska",  value: "AK" },
        // 47 states omitted
        {name: "Wyoming", value: "WY" }
    ]
}
```

Two ways to create a data store

With XHTML

```
<div dojoType="dojo.data.ItemFileReadStore" jsId="stateList"
    url="states.txt"></div>
```

With JavaScript

```
stateList = new dojo.data.ItemFileReadStore( {url: "states.txt"} );
```

How to load the FilteringSelect module

```
dojo.require("dijit.form.FilteringSelect");
```

How to create a FilteringSelect Dijit

```
<input type="text" name="state" id="state"
    dojoType="dijit.form.FilteringSelect" store="stateList" />
```

How to reset a FilteringSelect Dijit

A function that resets the FilteringSelect Dijit

```
var stateReset = function () {
    dijit.byId("state").attr("displayedValue", "");
}
```

How to attach the function to the Dijit

```
dojo.connect( dijit.byId("state"), "reset", stateReset );
```

Description

- You can use the ItemFileReadStore module to retrieve a *data store* from a text file and store it in your web site. This is useful if you don't have access to a database or if you need to quickly create some test data for an application.

- If you use JavaScript to create a data store that will be used by a Dijit, the store must be created before the parser runs. This means that you will have to manually run the parser as shown in figure 20-11.

- A FilteringSelect Dijit is a text box with a drop-down list, and the items in the list can come from a data store.

- When a user types in the text box of a FilteringSelect Dijit, the drop-down list is filtered so it only displays entries that contain the entered text. If the user enters a value that isn't in the data store, the Dijit will be invalid.

Figure 20-16   How to use the FilteringSelect Dijit

The Register application

Now, to show you how the use of a JavaScript library can help you develop applications more efficiently, this chapter ends with a Register application that has the user interface shown in figure 20-17. As you can see, this application is similar to the one that you saw in chapter 12. However, this version uses Dijits from the Dojo toolkit to validate the form fields.

In the user interface in this figure, you can see that several fields are shaded (colored) and contain exclamation points within triangular symbols. These are fields that are invalid. For instance, the Verify Password field doesn't match the Password field; the Last Name field is required; and the ZIP Code field isn't a valid 9 digit number. If you click in one of these invalid fields, the invalid message for the Dijit is displayed as shown for the Verify Password field.

The XHTML

This figure also presents the XHTML code for this application over three pages. On page 1, the link tags load a local CSS style sheet and the style sheet for the Dijit Tundra theme from the Google APIs web site. Then, the first script tag loads a loads version 1.2 of the Dojo toolkit from the Google APIs web site, and it sets the parseOnLoad option to false even though that's the default.

On page 2, the body tag is given a class of tundra. That ensures that all Dijits in the document will use the Tundra theme. Then, the form tag is turned into a Form Dijit. That ensures that the form won't be submitted if any of the Dijit fields are invalid.

The rest of the XHTML code on pages 2 and 3 is the same as or similar to the code that you've already studied. As a result, you should be able to follow it without much trouble. For instance, the Dijit for the email field uses the Dojox regular expression generator for emailAddress. The Dijit for the password field uses a regular expression to ensure that the password is at least six characters long. The Dijit for the state field uses a data store named stateList. And the RadioButton Dijits that are used to get the credit card type, return the values that are required by the Dojox validation functions.

The last field on the form is for the expiration date of a credit card. It uses a regular expression to ensure that the date is in the correct format. Note, however, that this expression will accept a valid month followed by any four-digit year, which means that it doesn't check whether the expiration date has passed.

This XHTML file ends by defining the Register and Reset buttons for the form. Because the type of the Register button is "submit", the form will be submitted when the button is clicked, but only if all of the form fields are valid. Also, because the type of the Reset button is "reset", all of the form fields will be reset when the button is clicked. Remember, though, that there's a bug in the reset method of the FilteringSelect Dijit, so you have to reset the state field with JavaScript.

The Register Account application in the web browser

Register for an Account

Account Information

E-Mail:	ray@harris.net
Password:	••••••••
Verify Password:	•••••••• ⚠ ← Passwords do not match.

Contact Information

First Name:	Ray
Last Name:	⚠
Address:	4340 N. Knoll Road
City:	Fresno
State:	California ▾
ZIP Code:	93722-98 ⚠
Phone Number:	559-555-1234

Payment Information

Card Type:	○ MasterCard ● Visa ○ American Express ○ Discover
Card Number:	4012-8888-8888-1881
Card CVV:	1234 ⚠
Expiration Date:	10/2011

Submit Registration

Register   Reset

All fields are required.

The XHTML file   Page 1

```
<!DOCTYPE html PUBLIC "-//W3C//DTD XHTML 1.0 Transitional//EN"
    "http://www.w3.org/TR/xhtml1/DTD/xhtml1-transitional.dtd">
<html xmlns="http://www.w3.org/1999/xhtml">
<head>
<title>Account Registration</title>
<link rel="stylesheet" type="text/css" href="register.css" />
<link rel="stylesheet" type="text/css" href=
http://ajax.googleapis.com/ajax/libs/dojo/1.2/dijit/themes/tundra/tundra.css/>
<script src="http://ajax.googleapis.com/ajax/libs/dojo/1.2/dojo/dojo.xd.js"
    type="text/javascript" djConfig="parseOnLoad:false">
</script>
<script type="text/javascript" src="register.js"></script>
</head>
```

Figure 20-17   The user interface and XHTML for the Register application (part 1 of 3)

The XHTML file

```
<body class="tundra">
<div id="content">
    <h1>Register for an Account</h1>
    <form action="register_account.html" method="get" id="register_form"
        dojoType="dijit.form.Form" >
    <h2>Account Information</h2>
    <label for="email">E-Mail:</label>
        <input type="text" name="email" id="email"
            dojoType="dijit.form.ValidationTextBox" required="true"
            regExpGen="dojox.regexp.emailAddress"
            invalidMessage="E-mail is required."
        /><br />
    <label for="password">Password:</label>
        <input type="password" name="password" id="password"
            dojoType="dijit.form.ValidationTextBox" required="true"
            regExp=".{6,}"
            invalidMessage="Password must be at least six characters."
        /><br />
    <label for="verify">Verify Password:</label>
        <input type="password" name="verify" id="verify"
            dojoType="dijit.form.ValidationTextBox" required="true"
            validator="matchValues"
            constraints="{matchId: 'password'}"
            invalidMessage="Passwords do not match."
        /><br />
    <h2>Contact Information</h2>
    <label for="first_name">First Name:</label>
        <input type="text" name="first_name" id="first_name"
            dojoType="dijit.form.ValidationTextBox"
            required="true" trim="true"
            invalidMessage="First name is required."
        /><br />
    <label for="last_name">Last Name:</label>
        <input type="text" name="last_name" id="last_name"
            dojoType="dijit.form.ValidationTextBox"
            required="true" trim="true"
            invalidMessage="Last name is required."
        /><br />
    <label for="address">Address:</label>
        <input type="text" name="address" id="address"
            dojoType="dijit.form.ValidationTextBox"
            required="true" trim="true"
            invalidMessage="Address is required."
        /><br />
    <label for="city">City:</label>
        <input type="text" name="city" id="city"
            dojoType="dijit.form.ValidationTextBox"
            required="true" trim="true"
            invalidMessage="City is required."
        /><br />
    <label for="state">State:</label>
        <input type="text" name="state" id="state"
            dojoType="dijit.form.FilteringSelect" store="stateList" />
        <br />
```

Figure 20-17   The user interface and XHTML for the Register application (part 2 of 3)

The XHTML file   Page 3

```xhtml
    <label for="zip">ZIP Code:</label>
        <input type="text" name="zip" id="zip"
            dojoType="dijit.form.ValidationTextBox" required="true"
            regExp="[\d]{5}(-[\d]{4})?"
            invalidMessage="Required. Use 5 or 9 digit ZIP code."
        /><br />
    <label for="phone">Phone Number:</label>
        <input type="text" name="phone" id="phone"
            dojoType="dijit.form.ValidationTextBox" required="true"
            regExp="[\d]{3}-[\d]{3}-[\d]{4}"
            invalidMessage="Required. Use 999-999-9999 format."
        /><br />
    <h2>Payment Information</h2>
    <label for="card_type">Card Type:</label>
        <input type="radio" name="card_type" value="mc" checked="checked"
            dojoType="dijit.form.RadioButton" /> MasterCard
        <input type="radio" name="card_type" value="vi"
            dojoType="dijit.form.RadioButton" /> Visa
        <input type="radio" name="card_type" value="ax"
            dojoType="dijit.form.RadioButton" /> American Express
        <input type="radio" name="card_type" value="di"
            dojoType="dijit.form.RadioButton" /> Discover
        <br />
    <label for="card_number">Card Number:</label>
        <input type="text" name="card_number" id="card_number"
            dojoType="dijit.form.ValidationTextBox" required="true"
            validator="checkCardNumber"
            constraints="{ ccTypeName: 'card_type' }"
            invalidMessage="Valid card number required."
        /><br />
    <label for="card_number">Card CVV:</label>
        <input type="text" name="card_cvv" id="card_cvv"
            dojoType="dijit.form.ValidationTextBox" required="true"
            validator="checkCardCVV"
            constraints="{ ccTypeName: 'card_type' }"
            invalidMessage="Valid card CVV number required."
        /><br />
    <label for="exp_date">Expiration Date:</label>
        <input type="text" name="exp_date" id="exp_date"
            dojoType="dijit.form.ValidationTextBox" required="true"
            regExp="(0?[\d]|1[012])\/[\d]{4}"
            invalidMessage="Required. Use mm/yyyy format."
        /><br />
    <h2>Submit Registration</h2>
    <label> </label>
        <button type="submit" id="submit_button"
            dojoType="dijit.form.Button" >Register</button>
        <button type="reset" id="reset_button"
            dojoType="dijit.form.Button" >Reset</button>
        <br />
    </form>
    <p class="notice">All fields are required.</p>
</div>
</body>
</html>
```

Figure 20-17   The user interface and XHTML for the Register application (part 3 of 3)

The JavaScript

The JavaScript for this application is shown in figure 20-18. To start, it loads all the Dojo modules that are needed by this application. This includes modules from the Core, Dijit, and Dojox categories. Then, this file creates a variable named stateList that will hold the states data store.

This code is followed by six functions, and you've seen all but the last function before. For instance, the matchValues function is the custom validator that's used to compare the entries in the password and verify fields. The stateReset function is used to reset the FilteringSelect Dijit for the state field because its reset method doesn't work. And the getRadioValue function gets the value of the radio button in the named group and returns the value associated with that button like "mc" for MasterCard or "vi" for Visa.

Next, the checkCardNumber function gets two parameters: (1) the credit card number to be validated and (2) an object that provides the name of the radio button group or the id of the select box that holds the card type. Then, this function gets the value for the credit card type and passes the credit card number and card type to the Dojox isValidCreditCard method, which does the validation.

The register.js file

```javascript
dojo.require("dojo.parser");
dojo.require("dojo.data.ItemFileReadStore");
dojo.require("dijit.form.Form");
dojo.require("dijit.form.ValidationTextBox");
dojo.require("dojox.validate.regexp");
dojo.require("dojox.validate.creditCard");
dojo.require("dijit.form.FilteringSelect");
dojo.require("dijit.form.CheckBox");
dojo.require("dijit.form.Button");

var stateList;

var matchValues = function ( value, constraints ) {
    var matchField = dijit.byId(constraints.matchId);
    if (matchField) {
        return this.attr("value") === matchField.attr("value");
    }
    return false;
}

var stateReset = function () {
    dijit.byId("state").attr("displayedValue", "");
}

var getRadioValue = function ( name ) {
    var value;
    dojo.query("[name=" + name + "]").forEach(function(element) {
        var button = dijit.byId(element.id);
        if ( button.attr("checked") ) value = button.attr("value");
    });
    return value;
}

var checkCardNumber = function ( value, constraints ) {
    var ccType;
    if ( constraints.ccTypeId ) {
        ccType = dijit.byId(constraints.ccTypeId).attr("value");
    } else if ( constraints.ccTypeName ) {
        ccType = getRadioValue( constraints.ccTypeName );
    } else {
        return false;
    }
    if (ccType) {
        return dojox.validate.isValidCreditCard(this.attr("value"), ccType);
    }
    return false;
}
```

Figure 20-18   The JavaScript for the Register application (part 1 of 2)

As you have already seen, the checkCardCVV function works much like the checkCardNumber function. The difference is that it uses the Dojox isValidCvv method to do the validation.

This file ends with an anonymous function that's coded for the Dojo addOnLoad method, which means that it runs when the document is ready. First, this function creates a data store from the states.txt file and stores it in the stateList variable. This is the data store that's used by the FilteringSelect Dijit for the state field.

Second, this function runs the parser to create all the Dijits in the XHTML file. This has to be done manually instead of automatically because the stateList data store has to be created before the parser creates the Dijit that uses the store.

Third, this function connects the stateReset function to the reset event of the FilteringSelect Dijit in the State field. This gets around the reset bug for this Dijit and allows this Dijit to be properly reset when the form is reset.

Fourth, this function selects each radio button in the card_type group and sets up two event handlers for its onChange event. The first event handler is the validate function for the card_number text box; the second event handler is the validate function of the card_cvv text box. This ensures that the card number and card CVV numbers are validated again if the card type is changed.

Last, this function calls the focus method of the email field. This places the cursor in the first field on the form so the users don't have to click in that field before they start typing.

* * *

At this point, you may want to compare the code you've just reviewed with the code for the Register application in chapter 12. That will help you see how different the two approaches to the Register application are. With Dijits, you have more XHTML code, but a lot less JavaScript code. Whether or not that appeals to you, it should be clear that the use of JavaScript libraries has the potential to help you develop applications more quickly.

The register.js file   **Page 2**

```javascript
var checkCardCVV = function ( value, constraints ) {
    var ccType;
    if ( constraints.ccTypeId ) {
        ccType = dijit.byId(constraints.ccTypeId).attr("value");
    } else if ( constraints.ccTypeName ) {
        ccType = getRadioValue( constraints.ccTypeName );
    } else {
        return false;
    }
    if (ccType) {
        return dojox.validate.isValidCvv(this.attr("value"), ccType);
    }
    return false;
}

dojo.addOnLoad( function () {
    stateList = new dojo.data.ItemFileReadStore({url: "states.txt"});
    dojo.parser.parse();
    dojo.connect( dijit.byId("state"), "reset", stateReset );
    dojo.query("[name=card_type]").forEach( function(element) {
        var button = dijit.byId( element.id );
        var card_number = dijit.byId("card_number");
        var card_cvv = dijit.byId("card_cvv");
        dojo.connect( button, "onChange", card_number, "validate" );
        dojo.connect( button, "onChange", card_cvv, "validate" );
    });
    dijit.byId("email").focus();
});
```

Figure 20-18   The JavaScript for the Register application (part 2 of 2)

Perspective

This chapter has introduced two of the more popular JavaScript libraries: jQuery and Dojo. My goal in doing that was to show you how the use of JavaScript libraries can help you provide special effects and simplify your code. With that as background, you should be able to decide whether you like the idea of using JavaScript libraries and want to learn more about them.

If you want to learn more about JavaScript libraries, you may be interested in four of the other general-purpose libraries that have become popular. They are:

Yahoo User Interface
MooTools
Prototype
Script.aculo.us

If you're using Adobe Dreamweaver, you may also be interested in the Spry library that comes with it. And if you're using ASP.NET, you may also be interested in the Microsoft JavaScript Library, which is available as a separate download.

Terms

implicit iteration
callback function
theme
checksum function
data store

Exercise 20-1   Enhance the Register application

In this exercise, you'll enhance the Register application that was presented in this chapter. This will give you a chance to work with Dijits.

Open and test the Register application

1. From your Firefox browser, open the index.html file in the register folder that's in the chapter 20 folder for exercises.

2. Test this application by entering your own data in the Register form, but be sure to skip some required fields and enter some invalid data. After you've entered invalid data, click in the field to see the error message.

3. Enter valid data for all of the fields. For the credit card entries, you can use Visa, the credit card number in figure 20-17, and 123 for the CVV number. Then, click the Register button. This displays a new web page that shows the data that has been submitted. In the address bar for this page, you can see that the form data has been appended to the URL.

4. Use your text editor to open the register_account.html file for this application. This is the XHTML for the page that is displayed when the form is submitted. Note that it uses the location object that's presented in chapter 19 to get the data that has been submitted. Now, close this file.

5. Use your text editor to open the index.html and JavaScript file for this application. Note that they are the same as the ones shown in the text.

Enhance the validation for the Expiration Date Dijit

6. Enhance the validation for the Expiration Date entry so the entry will be treated as invalid if it doesn't match the regular expression or if the expiration date has passed. To do that, use a custom validation function with just one parameter that gets the value of the control. As a guide to coding this function, you may want to refer to the code for the Register application in chapter 12.

Use the isValid, submit, and reset methods of the Form Dijit

7. Delete the type attributes from the XHTML for the Register and Reset buttons for the form. Then, modify the JavaScript so it uses the isValid, submit, and reset methods of the form to make sure that all of the Dijits are valid, to submit the form if they are valid, and to reset the form when the Reset button is clicked. To do that, you need to set up event handlers for the Submit and Reset buttons.

Flash the form when it is loaded

8. Add a function with no parameters to the application that flashes the registration form three times after the document is loaded. To do that, you can use a for loop.

Appendix A

How to set up your computer for this book

This appendix shows how to install the software that we recommend for editing, testing, and debugging JavaScript applications. That includes either the Notepad++ or TextWranger text editor, the Firefox browser, and the Firebug extension to Firefox. This appendix also shows you how to download and install the source code for this book.

As you read these descriptions, please remember that most web sites are continually upgraded. As a result, some of the procedures in this appendix may have changed since this book was published. Nevertheless, the procedures in this appendix should still be good guides to installing the software.

How to install a text editor for JavaScript programming .. 746
How to install Notepad++ 746
How to install TextWrangler 746
How to install Firefox and Firebug 748
How to install Firefox 748
How to install Firebug 748
How to install the Rainbow extension for Firebug 748
How to install the source code for this book 750

How to install a text editor for JavaScript programming

If you're already comfortable with a text editor that works for editing XHTML, CSS, and JavaScript files, you can continue using it. But otherwise, we recommend that you use Notepad++ on a Windows system or TextWranger on a Mac OS system. Although you can get more powerful editors, both of these are free and they provide all of the capabilities that you need for developing JavaScript applications.

How to install Notepad++

Figure A-1 shows how to download and install Notepad++ on a Windows system. Since this is a typical text editor, you shouldn't have any trouble using it. In case it helps, though, the first figure in chapter 2 gives you a quick introduction to it.

How to install TextWrangler

Figure A-1 also shows how to download and install TextWrangler on a Mac OS system. Since this is a typical text editor, you shouldn't have any trouble using it.

The web site address for downloading Notepad++

```
http://notepad-plus.sourceforge.net
```

How to install Notepad++

1. Go to the web site address above.
2. Click on the Download link at the top of the page, and click on the "Download Notepad++ executable files" link.
3. Click on the latest version of the Installer file (e.g., npp.5.4.3.Installer.exe) and save it on your C drive.
4. Use Windows Explorer to find the Installer file on your C drive and double-click on it to run it. Then, follow the instructions.

The web site address for downloading TextWrangler

```
http://www.barebones.com/products/textwrangler
```

How to install TextWrangler

1. Go to the web site address above.
2. Click the Download Now button, click the Download link for the Disk Image file that's right for your release of Mac OS, and save the disk image on your desktop.
3. Double-click the disk image on your desktop. This will open the disk image, which places a TextWrangler disk icon on the desktop. This will also open the TextWrangler disk window.
4. If the TextWrangler disk window doesn't appear, double-click the TextWrangler disk icon on the desktop.
5. In the TextWrangler disk window, drag the TextWrangler icon on top of the Applications folder icon. Then, close the TextWrangler window.
6. Drag the TextWrangler disk icon to the trash can to eject the disk image.
7. Browse to the Applications folder in Finder or press Command+Shift+A, and double-click the TextWrangler icon to start TextWrangler.
8. To keep the TextWrangler icon in your dock, control-click the icon and select "Keep in Dock".

Discussion

- If you're using a Windows system, we recommend that you use Notepad++ for entering and editing XHTML, CSS, and JavaScript files.
- If you're using a Mac OS system, we recommend that you use TextWrangler for entering and editing XHTML, CSS, and JavaScript files.

Figure A-1   How to install Notepad++ or TextWrangler as your text editor

How to install Firefox and Firebug

When you develop JavaScript applications, you need to test them on all of the browsers that the users of the application are likely to use. For a commercial application, that usually includes Internet Explorer, Firefox, Safari for Macs, Opera, and Google's new Chrome browser. Then, if an application doesn't work on one of those browsers, you need to debug it.

As you do the exercises and work with the applications in this book, though, you can use just one browser, and the one we recommend is Mozilla Firefox. Then, if you need to debug an application, you can use the Firebug extension to Firefox, which is an excellent debugging tool. Both of these components are free, they don't take long to install, and chapter 3 shows you how to use them.

Last, if you want to add color to Firebug, you can install the free Rainbow extension to Firebug. Although this isn't necessary, it does enhance the Firebug display.

How to install Firefox

Figure A-2 shows how to download and install Firefox. As you respond to the dialog boxes for the installer, we recommend that you make Firefox your default browser.

How to install Firebug

Figure A-2 also shows how to install the Firebug extension to Firefox, and chapter 3 shows you how to use it.

How to install the Rainbow extension for Firebug

Figure A-2 also shows how to install the Rainbow extension to the Firebug extension. This extension adds color to the Firebug display, but that isn't necessary. If you do install it, please note the warning at the start of the procedure and make sure you have the latest releases of Firefox and Firebug.

The web site address for downloading Firefox

```
http://www.mozilla.com
```

How to install Firefox

1. Go to the web site address above.
2. Click on the Download Firefox - Free button.
3. Save the exe file to your C drive.
4. Run the exe file and respond to the resulting dialog boxes.

How to install the Firebug extension for Firefox

1. Click Tools➔Add-ons to open the Add-ons window.
2. Click on the "Get Add-ons" button at the top of the window, then click "Browse All Add-ons".
3. In the search text box, type "Firebug" and press enter.
4. In the search results, click the "Add to Firefox" button next to Firebug.
5. In the Software Installation window, click the Install Now button.
6. When the installation is complete, click the Restart Firefox button.
7. When Firefox has restarted, close the Add-ons window.

The web site address for installing the Rainbow extension

```
https://addons.mozilla.org/en-US/firefox/addon/7575
```

How to install the experimental Rainbow extension for Firebug

Warning: To use this extension, you must have FireFox 3.0 or higher and Firebug 1.3 or higher. If you add this extension to an earlier version of either Firefox or Firebug, Firebug will no longer work. Then, you will have to uninstall the Rainbow extension to get Firebug to work again.

1. Go to the web site address above to download the Rainbow extension.
2. Check the box labeled "Let me install this experimental add-on."
3. Click the Add to Firefox button.
4. In the Software Installation window, click the Install Now button.
5. When the installation is complete, click the Restart Firefox button.
6. When Firefox has restarted, close the Add-ons window.

Description

- We recommend that you use Firefox as your default browser and the Firebug extension as your primary debugging tool.
- If you want the code in the Script tab of Firebug to be highlighted with colors, you need to install the Rainbow extension for Firebug.

Figure A-2   How to install Firefox, Firebug, and the Rainbow extension

How to install the source code for this book

Figure A-3 shows how to install the source code for this book on either a Windows or a Mac OS system. This includes the source code for the applications in this book, and the source code for the exercise starts.

When you finish this procedure, the book applications and exercise starts will be in the folders that are shown in this figure. Then, you'll be ready to do the exercises in this book.

The Murach web site

www.murach.com

The default installation folder for the source code on a Windows system

c:\murach\javascript

The Windows folders for the book applications and exercises

c:\murach\javascript\book_apps
c:\murach\javascript\exercises

How to download and install the source code on a Windows system

1. Go to www.murach.com, and go to the page for *Murach's JavaScript and DOM Scripting*.
2. Click the link for "FREE download of the book applications." Then, click the "All book files" link for the self-extracting zip file. This will download a setup file named mdom_allfiles.exe onto your hard drive.
3. Use the Windows Explorer to find the exe file on your hard drive. Then, double-click this file. This installs the source code into the folders shown above.

The Mac OS folders for the book applications and exercises

documents\javascript\book_apps
documents\javascript\exercises

How to download and install the source code on a Mac OS system

1. Go to www.murach.com, and go to the page for *Murach's JavaScript and DOM Scripting*.
2. Click the link for "FREE download of the book applications." Then, click the "All book files" link for the regular zip file. This will download a setup file named mdom_allfiles.zip onto your hard drive.
3. Move this file into the Documents folder of your home directory.
4. Use Finder to go to your Documents folder.
5. Double-click the mdom_allfiles.zip file to extract the folders for the book applications and exercises. This will create a folder named javascript in your Documents folder that will contain the book_apps and exercises folders.
6. If you are going to download the files for more than one book, you may want to add a murach folder to your documents folder and then move the javascript folder into that folder. Then, the paths to the javascript files will be consistent with the Windows paths shown above.

Description

- All of the source code for this book is contained in two files that can be downloaded from www.murach.com. One file is for Windows users, the other file is for Mac users.

Figure A-3   How to install the source code for this book

Index

\ escape character, 260, 261
<a> tag, 142, 143
<button> tag, 152, 153
<fieldset> tag, 162, 163
<form> tag, 150, 151
<img> tag, 144, 145
<input> tag
   for buttons, 152, 153
   for fields, 154-157
<label> tag, 154, 155
<legend> tag, 162, 163
<link> tag, 130, 131, 180, 181
<meta> tag, 130, 131
<optgroup> tag, 158, 159
<option> tag, 158, 159
<script> tag, 130, 131
<select> tag, 158, 159
<span> tag, 238, 239
<style> tag, 180, 181
<table> tag, 146-149
<td> tag, 146-149
<textarea> tag, 160, 161
<th> tag, 146-149
<title> tag, 130, 131
<tr> tag, 146-149

A

abs method, 256, 257
Absolute positioning, 212, 213
Absolute unit, 182, 183
Absolute URL, 142, 143
Add style sheet, 560, 561
addEventListener method, 490, 491
addOnLoad method (Dojo), 714, 715
Agent string, 674, 675
AJAX, 28, 29
alert method, 64, 65
Alternate style sheet, 556, 557, 670, 671
Americans with Disabilities Act, 35
Anchor, 142, 143
AND operator, 280, 281
Animation, 633-658
   Dojo, 720, 721
   jQuery, 706, 707
Anonymous function, 328, 329, 358, 359
Apache web server, 10, 11
appendChild method, 544, 545, 592, 593

Application
   Carousel, 644-657
   DOM search, 534-537
   Future value, 80-83
   Headlines, 548-553
   Image gallery, 446-451
   Image rollover, 442, 443
   Invoice (functions), 342-351
   Invoice (objects), 374-383
   Menu bar, 576-587
   Product configuration, 618-629
   Register, 402-415
   Register (Dijits), 734-741
   Sales tax, 30-33
   Slide show, 456-465
   Slide show (event libraries), 480-485
   Style selector, 562-563
   Table sort, 598-607
   Task list, 320-323
   Task list (cookies), 690-697
Application mapping, 8, 9
Application server, 8, 9
apply method, 336, 337
Argument, 62, 63
   of a function, 328, 329
   of a method, 356, 357
Arguments property, 334, 335, 346, 347
Arithmetic expression, 58, 59
Arithmetic operator, 58, 59
Array, 301-324
   associative, 316, 317
   constructor, 302, 303
   element, 302, 303
   index, 302, 303
   length, 302-305
   methods, 310-313
   multi-dimensional, 318, 319
   object, 356, 357, 368, 369
Array of arrays, 318, 319
ASP.NET, 10, 11
Assignment operator, 60, 61
Assignment statement, 60, 61
Associative array, 316, 317
Attach event handler, 476, 477, 490-493
attachEvent method, 490, 491
Attr interface, 432, 433
Attr node, 424, 425
Attribute, 14, 15, 124-127

Attribute node, 18, 19
Attribute selector, 186, 187
Auto-completion, 44, 45

B

back method, 678, 679
Background (CSS), 206, 207
Berners-Lee, Tim, 10-11
Binary operator, 254, 255
Binary search, 340, 341
Block scope, 332, 333
Block tag, 134, 135
blur method, 236, 237, 438, 439
BOM (Browser Object Model), 674, 675
Boolean data type, 56, 57
Boolean object, 356, 357
Border (CSS), 198-201, 204, 205
Box model (CSS), 198-203
break statement, 296, 297
Breakpoint, 104, 105
Browser Object Model, 674, 675
Bubbling phase, 470, 471
Bug, 90, 91
Bullet (for list), 196, 197
Button, 152, 153
    Digit, 724, 725

C

Cache busting script, 526, 527
Call
    a method, 62, 63
    a function, 76, 77, 328, 329
call method, 336, 337
Callback function, 706, 707, 720, 721
Camel casing, 54
Capturing phase, 470, 471
Carousel application, 644-657
Cascade rules (CSS), 190, 191
Cascading method, 368, 369
Cascading Style Sheets (see also CSS), 16, 17
Case label, 286, 287
Case structure, 286, 287
Case-insensitive flag, 386, 387
Case-sensitive, 52, 53
catch block, 400, 401
CDATA tag, 128, 129
ceil method, 256, 257
Cell, 146-149, 592, 593
Chaining method calls, 368, 369

Character entity, 140, 141
CharacterData node, 424, 425
charAt method, 262-265
Check box, 156, 157
    Digit, 726, 727
    state, 230, 231, 242, 243
Checkbox field, 156, 157
Checkbox object, 230, 231
Checksum, 730, 731
Child selector, 186, 187
Chrome, 10, 11
    error messages, 116, 117
    keyboard events, 508-513
Class attribute, 132, 133
    jQuery, 710, 711
clearInterval method, 454, 455
clearTimeout method, 452, 453
Client, 4, 5
Client-server architecture, 4, 5
Client-side processing, 12, 13
cloneNode method, 542, 543
close method (window), 664, 665
Closing tag, 14, 15, 124-127
Closure, 338, 339, 706, 707
Coldfusion, 10, 11
Color, 206, 207
Column, 146-149
Command key, 158, 159
Comment
    CSS, 178, 179
    JavaScript, 52, 53
    XHTML, 124-127
Comment node, 18, 19, 424, 425
Complex conditional expression, 280, 281
Compound assignment operator, 60, 61
Compound conditional expression, 70, 71, 280, 281
Compressed code, 38, 39
Computed style, 566, 567
concat method
    array, 310-313
    string, 262, 263
Concatenate, 58, 59
Conditional breakpoint, 104, 105
Conditional expression, 70, 71, 276-281
Conditional operator, 254, 255
confirm method, 226, 227
Console object, 106, 107
    Firebug, 336, 337
Constructor, 378, 379
Constructor function, 62, 63, 362, 363
Continue statement, 296, 297

Control, 150, 151
 floating, 216, 217
 grouping, 162, 163
Control statement, 70, 275-298
Cookie, 682-697
 create, 684, 685
 delete, 688, 689
 read, 686, 687
Core module (Dojo), 714, 715
Core specification (DOM), 422, 434
cos method, 634, 635
Cosine, 634, 635
createDocumentFragment method, 546, 547
createElement method, 542, 543
createTextNode method, 542, 543
Credit card validation, 396, 397, 409
 Dijits, 730, 731
Cross-browser compatibility, 12, 34, 35
CSS, 16, 17, 169-219
 attributes, 564, 565
 box model, 198-203
 cascade rules, 190, 191
 comment, 178, 179
 print, 670, 671
 rule set, 178, 179
 scripting, 555-588
 selector, 178, 179, 184-191
 standards, 22, 23
 style sheet 174-177
Ctrl key, 158, 159

D

Data store (Digit), 732, 733
Data validation
 credit card, 396, 397, 409, 730, 731
 date, 396, 397, 410, 411
 Dijits, 728, 729
 email, 396, 397
 phone number, 396, 397, 409
 regular expressions, 396, 397
 state, 408, 409
 zip code, 396, 397, 409
Database server, 8, 9
Date constructor, 266, 267
Date methods, 66, 67, 268-271
Date object, 66, 67, 266-271, 356, 357, 366, 367
Date validation, 396, 397, 410, 411
Debug flag, 106, 107
Debugging, 90, 91
 Chrome, 116, 117

Firebug, 98-105
Firefox, 94, 95, 98-105
Internet Explorer, 110, 111
Opera, 114, 115
Safari, 112, 113
Decimal value, 56, 57
Declaration
 CSS, 16, 17, 178, 179
 of a variable, 60, 61
Decorating text, 194, 195
Deep copy (node), 542, 543
Default action (event), 440, 441
Definition list, 138, 139
delete operator
 array, 304, 305
 object, 360, 361
deleteCell method, 594, 595
deleteRow method, 594, 595
Deleting
 array element, 304, 305
 cookie, 688, 689
 object, 360, 361
Descendent selector, 186, 187
Detach event handler, 476, 477, 490-493
detachEvent method, 490, 491
DHTML, 18
Diego Perini, 532
Dijit module (Dojo), 714, 715
Dijits, 722-741
Disable style sheet, 558, 559
Displaying data
 span tag, 238, 239
 text area, 244, 245
do-while statement, 292, 293
DOCTYPE declaration, 14, 15
Document fragment, 546, 547
Document interface, 428, 429
Document methods, 64, 65
Document node, 424, 425
Document object, 64, 65
Document object model (see also DOM), 18, 19
Dojo, 714-741
Dojox module (Dojo), 714, 715
DOM (Document object model), 18, 19
 Core specification, 422, 434
 HTML node, 434-439
 HTML specification, 422, 434
 model, 614-617
 node, 422-433, 542-547
 standards, 22, 23

DOM scripting, 26, 27, 421-466
    animation, 633-658
    CSS, 555-588
    form, 608-629
    jQuery, 712, 713
    table, 592-607
DOM search application, 534-537
Domain name, 36, 37
doScroll polling technique, 532, 533
Dot operator, 62
Dreamweaver, 44
Drop-down list, 158, 159
Dynamic HTML (DHTML), 18
Dynamic web page, 8, 9

E

ECMAScript versions, 24, 25
Editor, 44, 45
Effects
    Dojo, 720, 721
    jQuery, 706, 707
Eich, Brenden, 20
Element,
    floating, 210, 211
    node, 18, 19, 422-425
    object, 564, 565
    of an array, 302, 303
    positioning, 208, 209, 570-573
Element interface, 430, 431
Else clause, 72, 73, 282, 283
Else if clause, 72, 73, 284, 285
Em, 174, 182, 183
Email validation, 396, 397, 408, 409
Embedded
    JavaScript, 50, 51
    style sheet, 16, 17, 180, 181
    style, 180, 181
Empty string, 56, 57
Enable style sheet, 558, 559
encodeURIComponent function, 684, 685
Enumerable, 370, 371
Equality operator, 276, 277
Error, 90, 91
Error console (Firefox), 48, 49
Error object, 398, 399
Escape character, 388, 389
Escape sequence, 56, 57, 260, 261
Ethernet, 4
Eval script, 102, 103
Event, 26, 27, 78, 79, 236, 237
    control, 608, 609

    default action, 440, 441
    form, 608, 609
    reset, 608, 609
    submit, 608, 609
    window, 672, 673
Event-driven programming, 26, 27
Event handler, 26, 27, 78, 79
Event handling, 236, 237, 469-520
    Dojo, 718, 719
    jQuery, 708, 709
    library, 476, 477, 504, 505, 514-519, 530-533
    load event, 524-527
    phases, 470, 471
Event object, 440, 441
    DOM standard, 486-489
    Internet Explorer, 486-489
    keyboard events, 506-513
    mouse events, 500-503
    standardized, 478, 479
Event script, 102, 103
Exception, 400, 401
Exception handling, 398-401
Exponent, 56, 57
Expression
    arithmetic, 58, 59
    conditional, 70, 71
Extensible hypertext markup language (see XHTML)
Extensible markup language (XML) 28, 29
External
    JavaScript, 50, 51
    style sheet, 16, 17, 180, 181, 556, 557

F

Factor, 294
Fall through, 286, 287
Field, 150-165
    floating, 216, 217
FIFO array, 310, 311
finally block, 400, 401
Firebug, 98, 99
    breakpoint, 104, 105
    console object, 106, 107
    Console tab, 100, 101
    profiler, 100, 101
    Script tab, 102, 103
Firefox, 10-11
    change style sheet, 562
    Error Console, 48, 49, 94, 95
    keyboard event, 508-513
First-in, first-out array, 310, 311

Flag, 288, 289, 392, 393
   debug, 106, 107
Flash element, 706, 707, 720, 721
Float
   control, 216, 217
   element, 210, 211
Floating-point value, 56, 57
Floor method, 256, 257
Focus method, 236, 237, 438, 439
Font, 192, 193
Font family, 192, 193
Font styling, 192, 193
For loop, 74, 75
   with array, 306, 307
for statement, 74, 75, 294, 295
   with array, 306, 307
For-in loop
   with array, 306, 307, 316, 317, 320, 321
   with objects, 370, 371
for-in statement, 306, 307, 316, 317, 370, 371
Form, 150, 151
   Digit, 724, 725
   scripting, 608-629
forward method, 678, 679
FTP access, 44
Function, 76, 77, 327-352
Function object, 334, 335, 356, 357
Future value application, 80-83
FX module (Dojo), 720, 721

G

Get method, 150, 151
get methods (Date), 268-271
getAttribute method, 430, 431
getComputedStyle method, 566, 567
getElementsByClassname method, 538, 539
getElementsById method, 428, 429
getElementsByName method, 428-431
getElementsByTagName method, 428-431
getModifierState method, 478, 479
getOffsetLeft method, 572, 573
getOffsetTop method, 572, 573
GIF (Graphic Interchange Format), 144, 145
Global flag, 392, 393
Global method, 54, 55
   alert, 64, 65
   confirm, 224, 225
   parseFloat, 64, 65
   parseInt, 64, 65
   prompt, 64, 65, 224, 225

Global object, 64, 65
Global property, 54, 55
Global scope, 332, 333
Global variable, 332, 333
GNU Public License, 532
go method, 678, 679
Google, 10, 11
Graphic Interchange Format (GIF), 144, 145
Grouping controls, 162, 163

H

Hard return, 234, 235
hasAttribute method, 430, 431
Head section tags, 130, 131
Headlines application, 548-553
Hexadecimal value, 182, 183
Hidden field, 154, 155
Hide button, 670, 671
Hide element (jQuery), 706, 707
History list, 676, 677
History object, 678, 679
Hot linking, 144, 145
Hover, 188, 189
HTML specification (DOM), 422, 434
HTML standards, 22, 23
HTMLAnchorElement interface, 436, 437
HTMLButtonElement interface, 438, 439
HTMLElement interface, 436, 437
HTMLElement node, 434, 435
HTMLImageElement interface, 436, 437
HTMLInputElement interface, 438, 439
HTTP (Hypertext transport protocol), 6, 7
HTTP method, 150, 151
HTTP request, 6, 7
HTTP response, 6, 7
Hyperlink, 142, 143
Hypertext Markup Language (HTML), 7

I

id attribute, 132, 133
Identifier, 54, 55
Identity operator, 276, 277
IEEE 754 specification, 250
If clause, 72, 73
If statement, 72, 73, 282-285, 288, 289
IIS (Internet Information Services), 10, 11
Image
   background, 206, 207
   formats, 144, 145
   preload, 444, 445

Image gallery application, 446-451
Image rollover, 442, 443
Implicit iteration, 702, 703
in operator, 372, 373
Index (array), 302, 303, 316, 317
indexOf method, 262-265
Infinity, 250, 251
Inheritance
    Error objects, 398, 399
    from an object type, 364-369
    HTMLElement nodes, 434, 435
    nodes 426, 427
    object, 356, 357
Inherited style, 174
Inline style, 180, 181
Inline tag, 134-137
Inner function, 338, 339
innerHTML property, 592, 593
insertBefore method, 544, 545
insertCell method, 592, 593
insertRow method, 592, 593
Instance, 62, 63
instanceof operator, 372, 373
Integer, 56, 57
Interface, 426, 427
Internet, 4, 5
Internet Exchange Point (IXP), 4, 5
Internet Explorer, 10-11
    currentStyle property, 566, 567
    deleteRow method, 594, 595
    element offsets, 572, 573
    error messages, 110, 111
    event attaching, 490, 491
    event detaching, 490, 491
    event handling, 470, 471
    Event object, 486-489
    getComputedStyle method, 574, 575
    insertRow method, 592, 593
    keyboard events, 508-513
    mouse events, 500, 501
    text selection, 614-617
    window
Internet Information Services (IIS), 10, 11
Internet Protocol (IP), 6, 7
Internet Service Provider (ISP), 4, 5
Intranet path, 36
Invoice application (functions), 342-351
Invoice application (objects), 374-383
isNan method, 70, 71, 250, 251
ISP (Internet Service Provider), 4, 5
Iteration structure, 290-297
IXP (Internet exchange point), 4, 5

J

JavaScript, 12, 13, 20, 21
    Boolean data type, 56, 57
    comment, 52, 53
    common errors, 92, 93
    embedded, 50, 51
    external, 50, 51
    global method, 54, 55
    global property, 54, 55
    identifier, 54, 55
    name origins, 24
    naming conventions, 54
    number data type, 56, 57
    primitive data type, 56, 57
    reserved word, 54, 55
    statement, 52, 53
    string data type, 56, 57
    syntax rules, 52, 53
    variable, 60, 61
    versions, 24, 25
JavaScript engine, 12, 13
JavaScript object, 62, 63
    Array, 356, 357, 368, 369
    Boolean, 356, 357
    Date, 66, 67, 266-271, 356, 357, 366, 367
    Error, 398, 399
    Function, 334, 335, 356, 357
    Math, 256, 257, 366, 367
    Number, 66, 67, 356, 357
    Object, 356-359
    Regular expression, 386, 387
    String, 66, 67, 262, 263, 356, 357, 366, 367
JavaScript object notation, 28, 29
JavaScript statement, 52, 53
    assignment, 60, 61
    break, 296, 297
    do-while, 292, 293
    for, 74, 75, 294, 295
    for-in, 308, 309, 370, 371
    if, 72, 73, 282-285, 288, 289
    return, 76, 77
    switch, 286, 287
    try-catch, 400, 401
    while, 74, 75, 290, 291
javaEnabled method, 674, 675
join method, 310-313
Joint Photographic Experts Group (JPEG), 144, 145
JPEG (Joint Photographic Experts Group), 144, 145
jQuery, 702-713
Jscript versions, 24, 25
JSON (JavaScript object notation), 28, 29
JSP, 10, 11

K

Key codes, 510-513
Keyboard event library, 514-519
Keyboard events, 474, 475, 508-513

L

Label, 154, 155
LAN (Local area network), 4, 5
Last-in, first-out array, 310, 311
Length (array), 302-305
Lexical scoping, 332, 333
Library, 346
    attaching events, 494-499
    Dijits, 722-741
    Dojo, 714-741
    event handling, 476, 477
    jQuery, 702-713
    keyboard events, 514-519
    mouse events, 504, 505
    ready method, 530-533
    styles, 574, 575
    text selection, 614-617
    walking and searching, 540, 541
LIFO array, 310, 311
Link, 142, 143, 188, 189
List, 138, 139
    select, 158, 159, 232, 233
List box, 158, 159
List bullet, 196, 197
List formatting, 196, 197
Literal
    numeric, 60, 61
    regular expression, 386, 387
    string, 60, 61
LiveScript, 24
Load event, 524-527
Load new web page, 676, 677
Local area network (LAN), 4, 5
Local scope, 332, 333
Local variable, 332, 333
Location object, 676, 677
log method (Console object), 336, 337
Logic error, 90, 91
Logical operator, 70, 71, 280, 281
Loop, 290-297

M

Margin (CSS), 198-203
match method, 394, 395
Math for animation, 634, 635

Math object, 256, 257, 366, 367
max method, 256, 257
Menu bar application, 576-587
Merge cells, 148, 149
Method, 62, 63
    cascading, 368, 369
    of an object, 356-361
Method call, 62, 63
Microsoft Expression Web Designer, 44
min method, 256, 257
Mocha, 24
Mono project, 10
Monospace font, 192, 193
Mouse event library, 504, 505
Mouse events, 474, 475, 500-503
moveBy method (window), 666, 667
moveTo method (window), 666, 667
Mozilla Firefox (see also Firefox), 10, 11
Multi-dimensional array, 318, 319
Multiline flag, 392, 393

N

Named function, 328, 329
NaN, 250, 251
Native object type, 356, 357
    adding methods to, 366, 367
Navigator object, 674, 675
Nested
    arrays, 318, 319
    if statements, 72, 73
    loops, 74, 75
    objects, 358, 359
    XHTML tags, 126, 127
Netscape, 20, 24
Netscape Navigator, 10, 11
Network, 4, 5
Network interface card, 4
NIC (Network interface card, 4
Node, 18, 19, 422-439
    interface, 426, 427
    methods, 542-547
    object, 426, 427
    types, 424, 425
    tbody, 592, 593
    text, 592, 593
Noscript tag (XHTML), 50, 51
NOT operator, 280, 281
Notepad++, 44, 45
Number, 250, 251
Number data type, 56, 57
Number methods, 66, 67, 252, 253

Number object, 66, 67, 356, 357
    methods, 66, 67, 252, 253
    properties, 250, 251
Numeric literal, 60, 61

O

Object, 62, 63
Object chaining, 62, 63, 68, 69
Object object, 356-359
Object type, 356, 357
    adding methods to, 366, 367
Object inheritance, 356, 357
Objects, 355-384
open method (window), 664, 665
Opening tag, 14, 15, 124-127
Opera, 10, 11
    error messages, 114, 115
    keyboard events, 508-513
Operator
    arithmetic, 58, 59
    assignment, 60, 61
    compound assignment, 60, 61
    conditional, 254, 255
    delete, 304, 305, 360, 361
    equality, 276, 277
    identity, 276, 277
    in, 372, 373
    instanceof, 372, 373
    logical, 70, 71, 280, 281
    relational, 70, 71, 278, 279
    typeof, 336, 337, 372, 373
OR operator, 280, 281
    in assignment statement, 640, 641
Order of precedence
    arithmetic expression, 58, 59
    conditional expression, 70, 71, 280, 281
Ordered list, 138, 139, 196, 197
Outer function, 338, 339

P

Padding (CSS), 198-203
Parameter, 62, 63
    of a function, 328, 329
parseFloat method, 64, 65
parseInt method, 64, 65
Passed by reference, 330, 331
Passed by value, 330, 331
Password field, 154, 155

Path
    URL, 36, 37
    intranet, 36
Pattern (regular expression), 386-391
Perl, 10, 11
Persistent cookie, 682, 683
Persistent style sheet, 556-559
Phone number validation, 396, 397, 409
PHP, 10, 11
Pixel, 182, 183
PNG (Portable Network Graphics), 144, 145
PNG format, 636, 637
Point (unit of measure), 182, 183
pop method, 310-313
Pop-up blocker, 664, 665
Portable Network Graphics (PNG), 144, 145, 636, 637
Positioning
    absolute, 212, 213
    element, 208, 209, 570-573
    relative, 214, 215
Post method, 150, 151
pow method, 256, 257
Preferred style sheet, 556-559
Preloading images, 444, 445
preventDefault method, 440, 441, 478-489, 628, 629
    Dojo, 718, 719
    jQuery, 708, 709
Prime number, 294
Primitive data type, 56, 57
Primitive type, 330, 331
Printing a window, 670, 671
Product configuration application, 618, 619
Profiler, 100, 101
Progressive enhancement, 26, 27
prompt method, 64, 65, 224, 225
Property, 62, 63
    CSS, 178, 179
    node, 426, 427
    object, 356-361
propertyIsEnumerable method, 370, 371
Protocol (URL), 36, 37
Prototype inheritance, 364-369
Prototype object, 362-369
Pseudo-class selector, 188, 189
push method, 310-313
Python, 10, 11

Q

Quantifier, 390, 391

R

Radian, 634, 635, 638, 639
Radio button, 156, 157, 610, 611
    Dijit, 726, 727
        state, 228, 229, 240, 241
Radio field (see Radio button), 156, 157
Radio object, 228, 229
Rainbow extension, 102, 103
random method, 258, 259
Random number, 258, 259
Random number generator, 258, 259
RangeError object, 398, 399
ready method, 528, 529
    jQuery, 702, 703
Recursive function, 340, 341
Reference to an object, 360, 361
ReferenceError object, 398, 399
Refresh button, 46, 47
RegExp constructor, 386, 387
RegExp object, 386, 387
Register application, 402-415
Register application (Dijits), 734-741
Regular expression, 386-397
Regular expression literal, 386, 387
Regular expression object, 386, 387
Regular expression pattern, 386, 387, 388-391
Relational operator, 70, 71, 278, 279
Relative positioning, 214, 215
Relative unit, 182, 183
Relative URL, 142, 143
Reload button, 46, 47
reload method, 676, 677
Reload web page, 676, 677
Remove style sheet, 560, 561
removeAttribute method, 430, 431
removeChild method, 544, 545
removeEventListener method, 490, 491
replace method, 394, 395, 676, 677
replaceChild method, 544, 545
Reserved word, 54, 55
Reset button, 152, 153, 440, 441, 620, 621
Reset event, 608, 609
reset method, 400, 401, 414, 415, 628, 629
Resizing a window, 680, 681
resizeBy method (window), 666, 667
resizeTo method (window), 666, 667
return statement, 76, 77
reverse method, 310-313, 596, 597
RGB value, 182, 183
RIA (Rich Internet application), 28, 29

Rollover application, 442, 443
round method, 256, 257
Round trip, 8, 9
Router, 4, 5
Row, 146, 147, 148, 149, 592, 593
Ruby, 10, 11
Rule (CSS), 16, 178, 179
Rule set, 16, 17, 178, 179
Runtime error, 90, 91

S

Safari, 10, 11
    error messages, 112, 113
    keyboard events, 508-513
Sales tax application, 30-33
Sans-serif font, 192, 193
Scope, 332, 333
Screen object, 680, 681
Script tag (XHTML), 50, 51
Scripting language, 10, 11
Scroll a window, 668, 669
scrollBy method (window), 668, 669
scrollTo method (window), 668, 669
Search an array, 340, 341
search method, 394, 395
Search parameters (URL), 676, 677
Select list, 158, 159, 232, 233, 612, 613
Selection structure, 282, 289
Selector (css), 16, 17, 178, 179, 184-191
    specificity, 190, 191
Self-closing tag, 126, 127
Serif font, 192, 193
Server, 4, 5
Server-side processing, 12
Session cookie, 682, 683
set methods (Date), 268-271
setAttribute method, 430, 431
setInterval method, 454, 455, 638, 639
setTimeout method, 452, 453
Shake window, 666, 667
Shallow copy of a node, 542, 543
shift method, 310-313
Shorthand property (CSS), 192, 193, 202, 203, 204, 205
Show element (jQuery), 706, 707
Shuffle rows, 596, 597
sin method, 634, 635
slice method, 310-313
Slide show application, 456-465
Slide show application (event libraries), 480-485
Soft return 234, 235

sort method, 310-313, 596, 597, 606, 607
  compare function, 604-607
Source code, 38, 39
Span tag output, 238, 239
Spanned column, 148, 149
Spanned row, 148, 149
Sparse array, 304, 305
Specificity (selector), 190, 191
splice method, 310-313
split method, 314, 315
sqrt method, 256, 257
Stack (array), 310, 311
Stack trace, 100, 101
Standards, 22-25
  target, 25, 34
State validation, 408, 409
Statement (see JavaScript statement), 52-53
Static web page, 6, 7
Step through application, 104, 105
stopPropagation method, 478-489
String, 56, 57
  comparison, 264, 265
  concatenation, 58, 59
  trimming, 264, 265
String data type, 56, 57
String literal, 60, 61
String methods, 66, 67, 314, 315, 394, 395
String object, 66, 67, 262, 263, 356, 357, 366, 367
Style, 16, 17, 178-181
Style library, 574, 575
Style object, 564, 565
Style object properties, 564, 565, 568-571
Style selector application, 562-563
Style sheet, 174-177, 180, 181, 556-561
  alternate, 670, 671
  print, 670, 671
  user, 190, 191
Styling fonts, 192, 193
Submit button, 152, 153, 440, 441, 620, 621, 718, 719
  Dijit, 724, 725
  preventDefault method, 628, 629
Submit event, 608, 609
submit method, 152, 153, 400, 401, 414, 415
Subpattern, 390, 391
substring method, 262-265
switch statement, 286, 287
Switch, 288, 289
Syntax, 52, 53
  error, 90, 91
  highlighting, 44, 45

JavaScript, 52, 53
XHTML, 126, 127
SyntaxError object, 398, 399

T

Tab key, 164, 165
Tab order, 164, 165
Table, 146-149
  scripting, 592-607
Table sort application, 598-607
Tag, 124, 125
  block, 134, 135
  CDATA, 128, 129
  inline, 134-137
Target phase, 470, 471
Task list application, 320-323
Task list application (cookies), 690-697
tbody node, 592-595
TCP/IP, 6, 7
Ternary operator, 254, 255
test method, 386, 387
Testing, 46, 47, 90, 91
  phases, 90, 91
Text area, 160, 161, 234, 235, 244, 245
Text box, 154, 155
Text decoration, 194, 195
Text editor, 44, 45
Text field, 154, 155
Text formatting, 194, 195
Text node, 18, 19, 422-425, 592, 593
Text-only web site, 34, 35
Text selection, 614-617
Text transform, 194, 195
Textarea field, 160, 161
Textarea object, 234, 235
Textbox methods, 68, 69
Textbox object, 68, 69
Textbox properties, 68, 69
TextMate, 44
TextWrangler, 44
Theme (Dijit), 722, 723
this keyword, 336, 337
  in constructor, 362, 363
this parameter, 336, 337
throw exception 398, 399
throw statement, 398, 399
Timer, 452-455
title attribute, 132, 133
toDateString method, 268, 269
toExponential method, 252, 253

toFixed method, 252, 253
toLocaleString method, 310, 311
toLowerCase method, 262-265
Tomcat web server, 10, 11
toPrecision method, 252, 253
toString method
   array, 310-313
   date, 268, 269
   number, 252, 253
toTimeString method, 268, 269
toUpperCase method, 262, 263
Trace stack, 100, 101
Tracing
   console.log method, 108, 109
   with alert statements, 96, 97
Transforming text, 194, 195
Transmission Control Protocol, 6, 7
try block, 400, 401
try-catch statement, 400, 401
Type coercion, 276, 277
TypeError object, 398, 399
typeof operator, 336, 337, 372, 373

U

Unary operator, 254, 255
Undefined, 77
Unicode character, 260, 261
Uniform resource locator (URL), 36, 37
Unit of measurement, 182, 183
Universal selector, 186, 187
Unordered list, 138, 139, 196, 197
unshift method, 310-313
URIError object, 398, 399
URL (Uniform resource locator), 36, 37, 142, 143
User accessibility, 34, 35
User agent string, 674, 675
User style sheet, 190, 191

V

Validation
   credit card, 396, 397, 409, 730, 731
   date, 396, 397, 410, 411
   Dijits, 728, 729
   email, 396, 397
   phone number, 396, 397, 409
   regular expressions, 396, 397
   state, 408, 409
   zip code, 396, 397, 409
Value (CSS), 178, 179
Variable, 60, 61

W

W3C Markup Validation Service, 128, 129
walk method, 534-537
WAN (Wide area network) 4, 5
Web application, 8, 9
Web page, 170, 171
Web server, 4, 5
Web standards, 22-25
While loop, 74, 75
while statement, 74, 75, 290, 291
Whitespace, 52, 53, 124, 125
Wi-Fi, 4
Wide area network (WAN), 4, 5
Window
   event, 672, 673
   methods, 64, 65, 664-671
   object, 64, 65, 664-673
   resizing, 680, 681
World Wide Web, 4
Wrapper function, 336, 337
Wrapping a method, 106-109

X

XHTML, 14, 15, 121-168
   attribute, 124-127
   block tag, 134, 135
   button, 152, 153
   character entity, 140, 141
   comment, 124-127
   control, 150-165
   core attributes, 132, 133
   description, 124, 125
   document, 14, 15, 124, 125
   element, 14, 15
   event, 472, 473
   field, 150-165
   form, 150, 151
   head section, 130, 131
   inline tag, 134, 135
   jQuery manipulation, 710, 711
   list, 138, 139
   nesting, 126, 127
   script tag, 50, 51
   standards, 22, 23
   syntax, 126, 127
   table, 146-149
   tag, 124-127
   validation, 128, 129
   with CSS, 122, 123
   with no CSS, 122, 123

XML, 28, 29
XMLHttpRequest object, 28, 29

Z

Zip code validation, 396, 397, 409

What software you need for this book

- To develop JavaScript applications, you can use any text editor, but we recommend Notepad++ for Windows users and TextWrangler for Mac OS users. Both are available for free, and both can be used for entering and editing XHTML, CSS, and JavaScript code.

- To test and debug a JavaScript application, you need a web browser with debugging capabilities. For that, we recommend Mozilla Firefox and its Firebug extension. Both of these are also free.

- To help you install these products, appendix A provides the web site addresses and procedures that you'll need.

- To help you use these products, the first figure in chapter 2 provides a quick guide to using Notepad++ and chapter 3 provides a tutorial on using Firebug.

The downloadable applications and files for this book

- All of the applications presented in this book.

- The starting files for the exercises in this book.

How to download the applications and files

- Go to www.murach.com, and go to the page for *Murach's JavaScript and DOM Scripting*.

- Click the link for "FREE download of the book applications."

- If you're using a Windows system, click the "All book files" link for the self-extracting zip file. That will download an exe file named mdom_allfiles.exe. Then, find this file in the Windows Explorer and double-click on it. That will install the files for this book in folders that start with c:\murach\javascript.

- If you're using a Mac, click the "All book files" link for the regular zip file. That will download a zip file named mdom_allfiles.zip onto your hard drive. Then, move this file into the Documents folder of your home directory, use Finder to go to your Documents folder, and double-click on the zip file. That will create a folder named javascript that contains all the files for this book.

- For more information, please see appendix A.

www.murach.com